THE PROFOUND TREASURY
OF THE OCEAN OF DHARMA

VOLUME ONE
The Path of Individual Liberation

VOLUME TWO
The Bodhisattva Path of Wisdom and Compassion

VOLUME THREE
The Tantric Path of Indestructible Wakefulness

Published in association with Vajradhatu Publications, a division of
Shambhala Media (www.shambhalamedia.org).

VOLUME ONE

THE PROFOUND TREASURY
OF THE OCEAN OF DHARMA

The Path of
Individual Liberation

CHÖGYAM TRUNGPA

COMPILED AND EDITED BY

Judith L. Lief

SHAMBHALA • BOSTON & LONDON • 2014

Shambhala Publications, Inc.
Horticultural Hall
300 Massachusetts Avenue
Boston, Massachusetts 02115
www.shambhala.com

© 2013 by Diana J. Mukpo
Frontispiece: Photograph of Chögyam Trungpa in Scotland, circa 1968, provided by
Tendzin Parsons. From the collection of the Shambhala Archives. Photographer unknown.

See page 615 for further credits and permissions.

9 8 7 6 5 4 3 2 1

First Paperback Edition
Printed in the United States of America

⊗ This edition is printed on acid-free paper that meets the
American National Standards Institute z39.48 Standard.
♻ Shambhala makes every attempt to print on recycled paper.
For more information please visit www.shambhala.com.

Distributed in the United States by Penguin Random House LLC
and in Canada by Random House of Canada Ltd

Designed by Dede Cummings Designs

THE LIBRARY OF CONGRESS CATALOGUES THE HARDCOVER EDITION OF THIS BOOK AS FOLLOWS:
Trungpa, Chögyam, 1939–1987.
The profound treasury of the ocean of dharma / Chögyam Trungpa;
compiled and edited by Judith L. Lief.—First Edition.
pages cm
Compilation of Chögyam Trungpa Rinpoche's
Vajradhatu Seminary teachings in three volumes.
Includes index.
ISBN 978-1-59030-708-3 (hardcover set)
ISBN 978-1-59030-802-8 (v. 1 hardcover)
ISBN 978-1-59030-803-5 (v. 2 hardcover)
ISBN 978-1-59030-804-2 (v. 3 hardcover)
ISBN 978-1-61180-104-0 (v. 1 paperback)
ISBN 978-1-61180-105-7 (v. 2 paperback)
1. Buddhism—Doctrines. I. Lief, Judith L., editor of compilation. II. Title.
BQ4165.T75 2013
294.3'w4—dc23
2012022795

CONTENTS

PART ONE Entering the Path

Encountering the Dharma

Taking Refuge

Reflecting on the Three Jewels

PART TWO   Discipline/Shila

Taming Neurosis

Cultivating Virtue

PART THREE   Meditation/Samadhi

Shamatha: The Practice of Mindfulness

Refining Your Shamatha Practice

Working with the Mind

The Four Foundations of Mindfulness

Vipashyana: The Practice of Awareness

PART FOUR   The Four Noble Truths

Suffering

CONTENTS

The Karmapa

Like any great Buddhist teacher, Chögyam Trungpa Rinpoche offered diverse teachings in diverse settings, adapting the Dharma each time to the capacities and needs of those listening. Rinpoche had a particular genius in presenting the Dharma to Western audiences, and he did so at a time when Tibetan Buddhism was new and unfamiliar to most in the West.

Many of the public Dharma talks that Trungpa Rinpoche offered to his Western students over the years have already been made available in various books. They benefited many readers at all levels of interest and spiritual experience. But the present volumes represent the teachings Rinpoche gave to his senior-most disciples, as part of the famous Vajradhatu Seminaries. At his request, these fortunate students have set about transcribing and organizing more than four hundred different Dharma teachings given by Rinpoche, in a massive project that has taken them three decades. In these extensive volumes, we can see the great care they are taking to offer to others what they themselves most valued receiving from their own lama. In this, these volumes are upholding Rinpoche's spirit as well as preserving his words.

The Vajradhatu Seminary teachings that Rinpoche gave are signs of his kindness and compassion for his disciples. Their efforts to preserve his teachings are signs of their devotion to him. As such, these volumes display the far-reaching goodness that can be created in the world when compassion and devotion come together.

OGYEN TRINLEY DORJE
June 8, 2011

FOREWORD
BY THE VERY VENERABLE
NINTH KHENCHEN THRANGU
RINPOCHE

The Vidyadhara Chögyam Trungpa Rinpoche made an enormous contribution to the spread of Buddhism to the West. This enlightened Vajra Master was able to make the teachings understandable through his insight, his compassion, and his extraordinary ability to connect with others, particularly the young during the sixties and seventies who were longing for spirituality and genuine teachings.

He was a rare teacher. One seldom has the opportunity to meet such a great master. At long last his teachings given during seminaries will be published in several volumes. They should be of great benefit in upholding his teaching lineage for both his older students and the younger generations on the Buddhist path.

THE VERY VENERABLE NINTH
KHENCHEN THRANGU RINPOCHE
February 28, 2011

FOREWORD
BY THE SEVENTH
SHECHEN RABJAM

I first met Chögyam Trungpa Rinpoche in 1976 when I was just seven years old. I had traveled to America with my grandfather, Dilgo Khyentse Rinpoche, at the invitation of Trungpa Rinpoche. He invited Khyentse Rinpoche again in 1982 around the time that Trungpa Rinpoche had begun to reveal his Shambhala Mind Treasures (*dgongs-gter*).

Khyentse Rinpoche asked to see the revealed treasures, or *terma*, and kept it with him overnight. The next day he asked Trungpa Rinpoche for the transmission and, along with Khyentse Rinpoche, I was one of the first to receive it. I was also present during Khyentse Rinpoche's third visit to the United States when he presided over the funeral arrangements for his longtime spiritual friend.

Trungpa Rinpoche and Dilgo Khyentse Rinpoche were very old and close friends. As far as we can tell, their friendship began in the far reaches of Kham in eastern Tibet, decades before I was born.

In his youth Khyentse Rinpoche traveled extensively, wandering from place to pilgrimage place to receive teachings, meet teachers, and engage in meditation retreats. During his travels he would often stay at Surmang Monastery. From the early years of Khyentse Rinpoche's life the lamas of Surmang held him in very high esteem. He gave many teachings in Surmang and also put into writing some of his own revealed treasures while staying there.

Even though Chögyam Trungpa was the head of Surmang Monastery, his principle teachers were all from Shechen Monastery. His main guru was Shechen Kongtrul Pema Drimed, and his tutor was Shechen Khenpo Gangshar. Khenpo Gangshar was quite an extraordinary and unconventional master. Before his "crazy wisdom" manifested he was a very pure monk. Later in his life he almost died and went into what can only be described as a sort of coma. When he awoke from his "coma" he was a completely different person and displayed many ways of interacting with people like the great siddhas of the past, activities that Trungpa Rinpoche called "crazy wisdom."

This term in Tibetan means "to enter in yogic conduct"—the action of behaving in unconventional ways as a means to enhance one's practice and convey the teachings in a very abrupt manner.

In this way, Khenpo Gangshar taught thousands of people in Kham, trying to prepare them to face the horrors of what was to come later during the Chinese occupation. There is no doubt that Khenpo Gangshar's style of teaching deeply inspired Trungpa Rinpoche, who himself adopted his own way of manifesting for the benefit of beings while teaching in the West.

Trungpa Rinpoche was, and remains, an authentic master of the Tibetan Buddhist practice tradition. While his style may have seemed eccentric, it was deeply rooted in the traditions he inherited from his teachers from within the lineages of the Nyingma and Kagyud schools of Tibetan Buddhism. He had mastered it to a degree that gave him the confidence that he could, like Khenpo Gangshar, teach in a very direct and beneficial style.

This style was based on his profound and unique insight into the Western psyche, which allowed him to present the true meaning of the tradition, but without the cultural trappings often attached to it.

This can clearly be seen in the level and depth of the teachings included in these three volumes. He was clearly a master who had completely overcome hope and fear, and I feel very happy to have met such a realized teacher.

Trungpa Rinpoche has kindly left us a huge spiritual legacy that will surely benefit generations to come. When the young reincarnation of Dilgo Khyentse, Yangsi Rinpoche, read some of his books, he became intrigued with Trungpa Rinpoche's life story and teachings, and was pleased to be able to visit his centers in the West in 2010.

Through these edited and compiled transcripts of Trungpa Rinpoche's many years of seminary teachings, even though he is not physically present with us, we still have a chance to meet and connect with him. They will be an invaluable resource for Buddhist practitioners now and in the future.

SEVENTH SHECHEN RABJAM
Bodhgaya, India
December 10, 2011

FOREWORD
BY TULKU THONDUP RINPOCHE

The Profound Treasury of the Ocean of Dharma is an extraordinary collection of common and uncommon teachings on buddhadharma taught by one of the greatest Tibetan Buddhist scholars and saints of our age—Chögyam Trungpa Rinpoche.

According to Buddhism, Buddhahood, the fully enlightened state, is the true nature of the universe. The Buddhist path leads to realizing that universal nature, regardless of one's individual abilities or cultural traditions. Through his thought-provoking teachings and groundbreaking writings based on the universal vision, logic, and language of Buddhism, Rinpoche became one of the first pioneering masters to cross the cultural and ideological boundaries to inspire great numbers of Westerners as awakened Buddhists.

Many of these ambrosia-like teachings that transpired between the wisdom of Rinpoche's mind and the devout hearts of his disciples—in their golden ages—have been enshrined intact in these three volumes. These volumes encompass the entire spectrum of Buddhist lore, ranging from the exoteric teachings for novices entering the path to the esoteric instructions for accomplished adepts soaring through the high trainings and realizations of sutra, tantra, mahamudra, and maha ati (dzogchen).

In these volumes, readers at every level will find teachings to guide them to paths and goals specific to their ability and culture. We must respect and follow these teachings as if they were Rinpoche in person, since they are the essence of his heart-wisdom. Urging students to respect the teachings of his Master, the great Paltrul Rinpoche writes:

> Fortunate beings, who will come in the future,—
> Please hold these teachings with devotion
> As you would to the enlightened Master in person;
> For I believe these are the unerring essence of his
> teachings.

Acharya Judy Lief has offered such a great service for many by preserving and sharing these invaluable treasures with great devotion and dedication.

TULKU THONDUP RINPOCHE
The Buddhayana Foundation

FOREWORD
BY DIANA JUDITH MUKPO

The Vidyadhara, Chögyam Trungpa Rinpoche, my late husband, has had a profound impact on Tibetan Buddhism and the Practicing Lineages coming to the West. The systematic way in which he presented the teachings from his ancient tradition and the way in which he mixed these teachings with current conditions and understandings made them all the more powerful. At the time that he gave these teachings, we could hardly have imagined the effect they would have. Through the power of who he was and how he taught, he has actually affected Western culture as a whole.

At the time he gave these teachings, the audience was limited to his closest students, and he wanted much of this material to remain private during his lifetime. However, later in his life, he also directed that these teachings be published, as he felt they would be very helpful to generations of future practitioners.

The world has changed, and now it is the right time for this material to be made available. In a sense *The Profound Treasury of the Ocean of Dharma* is a form of terma. Terma teachings appear when the situation and influences are correct and when the teachings are needed. I feel that this is such a time for the teachings from the Vajradhatu Seminaries contained in these three volumes.

Acharya Emeritus Judith Lief has done a great service in compiling and editing these teachings. Shambhala Publications has also done a service in their publication of this material, as well as so many of Rinpoche's books.

I believe that the Vidyadhara would be very pleased by the publication of these volumes—and surely, it is time! Twenty-five years have passed since his passing into nirvana. Yet the archive of his teachings continues to bring forth new and profound teachings for the current era.

Let us celebrate this profound treasury. May it benefit beings and may it be the vanguard for even further oceans of dharma to be published in years to come.

In the vision of the Great Eastern Sun,

DIANA JUDITH MUKPO
Druk Sakyong Wangmo
November 25, 2011

PUBLISHER'S FOREWORD

In the early spring of 1969, a London publisher, Mr. Vincent Stuart of Stuart & Watkins, placed a manuscript into my hands. I was inspired by both the profundity and direct language of this very short but pithy manuscript titled *Meditation in Action*. It was the best explanation I had read of the reasons for putting Buddhist philosophy into practice through meditation. It became the first book in the first season of publication of a fledgling American publishing house that some friends and I had just begun, Shambhala Publications of Berkeley, California. *Meditation in Action* immediately became a manifesto for open-minded young Western spiritual seekers to make a connection with a 2,500-year-long tradition of Buddhist thought and meditation practice.

Now, some forty-three years later, Shambhala Publications has published this three-volume set, *The Profound Treasury of the Ocean of Dharma*. These volumes are arguably the most important Buddhist books to be published in a Western language. They present a full overview of the Buddhist path with an encyclopedic thoroughness. These volumes are the crown jewel in the canon of books that have been created from the speech of the great master Chögyam Trungpa Rinpoche. To study these volumes is to have a real taste of the breadth of Buddhist thought. They will also serve as an invaluable reference work to students and teachers of almost all sects of Buddhism.

Although Trungpa Rinpoche came from the Kagyu and Nyingma traditions of Tibetan Buddhism, he is able to clearly articulate the basic teachings of the Buddha, and the big view of the Mahayana, as well as provide an excellent overview of the intricacies of the tantric or esoteric teachings of Buddhism. I dare say that his presentation is the most thorough and accessible presentation of the complete three-vehicle approach. To become familiar with this work is to become familiar with the whole of Buddhism, and it provides inspiration to explore further. What is presented also provides the right view that a practitioner can use to develop the practice for complete enlightenment. Yes, this is an Atlas of Complete Enlightenment.

About one year before his passing, Trungpa Rinpoche invited me into his office at Naropa University in Boulder, Colorado (it was called Naropa Institute at that time). During this meeting, we discussed the plans for the publication of his future works. Although we discussed many topics, the two items that were stressed as being of the utmost importance were the publication of his teachings on mind-training (published as *Training the Mind and Cultivating Loving-Kindness*) and the publication of his magnum opus, a three-volume set that was to be edited from the transcripts of the various seminaries that he had taught in North America. He made me solemnly promise that I would do everything within my "publishing power" to fulfill his request. It is with great joy and pride that these volumes now exist and that Shambhala Publications and I have been instrumental in bringing them into the world.

These volumes exist in their present form because one of Trungpa Rinpoche's most trained and trusted editors, Judith L. Lief, was willing to put her complete devotion and attention to the great task. She has spent thousands of hours weaving the talks given by Trungpa Rinpoche over several years into this unified format. It is an extraordinary achievement, and I sincerely pray that the merit of her selfless work is the basis for her enlightenment. Countless numbers of students and practitioners over the expanse of time and space will be forever grateful to her and to the understanding, discipline, and direct connection to Trungpa Rinpoche's mind that she brought to this project. It is more than monumental.

It is with utmost devotion to Chögyam Trungpa Rinpoche, the Eleventh of the Trungpa Tulkus of Surmang, the mahasiddha who sparked the dawn of buddhadharma through his speech and enlightened activity in the Western world, that I make this offering of the treasure that is these volumes. SARVAMANGALAM!

SAMUEL BERCHOLZ
Shambhala Publications
Chairman and Editor-in-Chief

PREFACE BY THE SAKYONG, JAMGÖN MIPHAM RINPOCHE

I am delighted that *The Profound Treasury of the Ocean of Dharma* has finally been completed. It feels especially timely since this year marks the twenty-fifth anniversary of the passing of the Vidyadhara.

This work was initially the idea of the Vidyadhara himself. He wanted to present a comprehensive book that clearly shows the depth and breadth of the buddhadharma. His teachings are a unique mixture of the traditional with the groundbreaking. When the Vidyadhara first began to teach, many of the traditional teachings were available only in Sanskrit, Pali, or Tibetan. However, not only did he speak directly in English, he also infused these teachings with his personal experience and adapted them to the cultural context.

I personally attended many of these teachings. The programs where he presented them became an annual event that I always looked forward to. His method of teaching was not simply scholastic, for the sessions of teaching and study were interspersed with periods of deep meditation. He always emphasized that he was mixing the relative and the absolute— practice and study.

These teachings were also being presented at a time in the West when there was not a great deal of literature available about Buddhism. Since then, much has been translated and published, but I believe that his teachings are still a unique presentation, because they came directly from the Vidyadhara. What he was attempting to do—and I believe he accomplished it—was to bring the dharma alive in the English language.

Therefore, his use of English challenged even native speakers, since he was using its full breadth.

One of his favorite examples was that the study and practice of the dharma should be like combing one's hair: one returns to the roots and begins again and again. Therefore in his presentation there was often a systematic approach to the three yanas—the hinayana, which emphasized personal discipline and renunciation; the mahayana, which expressed profound insight and vast conduct; and the vajrayana, which taught sacred outlook and great dedication. He also emphasized that these three were sequential and inseparable.

In this approach, he was paying heed to all the great traditions of the Buddha. Even though whenever he taught the dharma, every word seemed laden with meaning and profundity, certain key teachings began to change the spiritual landscape, such as his presentation of lojong, or mind training; his emphasis on mindfulness meditation; as well as certain words like *klesha* and *maitri*, which began to enter the vernacular.

Thus, one can look at this book not only as a source of knowledge, but as a part of our spiritual history. Whether or not we had the good fortune to meet the Vidyadhara, his presentation has had a major influence on the modern standing of Buddhism as a whole. Now, readers can see for themselves where such truth and richness came from.

I am especially appreciative and grateful to Acharya Emeritus Judy Lief for her dedication, tremendous heart, and for not giving up on this project. I am sure my father would be very proud of that. I sincerely hope that the teachings within this book may be a true source of inspiration for generations to come.

I am also especially gladdened that these words of profundity are being presented at this time, for more than ever the world needs compassion and wisdom. I hope that this treasury will be of benefit to all who read it—and to the world.

THE SAKYONG, JAMGÖN MIPHAM
RINPOCHE
Namgyal Potrang, The Kalapa Court
Halifax, Nova Scotia
January 15, 2012

ACKNOWLEDGMENTS

The three volumes of *The Profound Treasury* are based on talks given by Chögyam Trungpa Rinpoche in his thirteen Vajradhatu Seminaries. These seminaries took place annually over a period of thirteen years, from the first seminary in 1973 to the final one in 1986. Trungpa Rinpoche's spoken teachings were recorded, transcribed, and lightly edited into a collection of twenty-five volumes. This collection of tapes and transcripts provided the raw material for the three volumes of *The Profound Treasury*. The work of producing these volumes would not have been possible without the efforts of the many volunteers who originally recorded and archived these talks, the transcribers who diligently put these teachings down on paper, and the editorial and production staffs who generated the series of lightly edited Vajradhatu Seminary transcripts.

The project of editing and compiling Chögyam Trungpa Rinpoche's collected seminary teachings into three volumes began at his request in the 1970s. Sarah Coleman and I worked together and started organizing this material using literal cut-and-paste techniques, but it soon became apparent that embarking on such an undertaking was premature. Later, Jim and Ellen Green committed themselves to the project with great devotion, but it was still not the right time to proceed. After these initial efforts, the project was tabled for a number of years. These early compilers set an example of devotion and dedication that is worthy of emulation.

Eventually causes and conditions came together in a way that made it possible to complete this project and fulfill Chögyam Trungpa Rinpoche's request. In October 2006, during the auspicious occasion of a major conference on the literary legacy of Chögyam Trungpa being held at Naropa University, representatives of Vajradhatu Publications and Shambhala Publications met at The Kitchen, a restaurant in Boulder, Colorado. This meeting was attended by Shambhala Publications founder Samuel Bercholz and his daughter Sara Bercholz; Vajradhatu Publications director Ben Moore, executive editor Judy Lief, and managing editor Ellen Kearney; and Carolyn Gimian, the director of the Chögyam Trungpa Legacy Project.

In a cooperative venture, a new initiative was launched that night, and the commitment was made to finish the project that had been started so many years before. Through the combined support of Vajradhatu Publications, Shambhala Publications, Shambhala Media, Shambhala Archives, and Kalapa Recordings, this important work was resumed. Since the Vajradhatu Seminary transcripts contained Trungpa Rinpoche's innermost teachings to his closest students, we decided to call this venture "The Root Text Project."

Samuel Bercholz has been not only an instigator but a steady supporter throughout this project. His determination, persistence, and generosity have kept this work moving forward. Recognizing the importance of these teachings and their potential impact, Carolyn Gimian has also been unwavering in her commitment to help bring this project to fruition. She contributed her fine editing skills to crucial sections of volume 3, and gave both insightful feedback and heartfelt support.

Nalanda Translation Committee members Larry Mermelstein, Scott Wellenbach, Tingdzin Ötro, and Mark Nowakowski checked the accuracy of the many Tibetan and Sanskrit terms, and also gave invaluable advice on points of dharma. Tingdzin applied his meticulous attention to the thorny issue of ensuring consistent Tibetan spelling, and he also compiled glossaries for each volume. In addition, the Nalanda Translation Committee members provided background material for the translations, such as the original note cards Trungpa Rinpoche used for his talks.

The scholar-translator Derek Kolleeny was a rock. He was particularly insightful concerning the best way to structure each book so that the reader could enter into the logical flow of the teachings. Derek's knowledge of the vajrayana tradition and its classic texts proved to be extremely useful, and throughout the project he was both cheerful and generous with his support and knowledge.

Emily Sell and Terry Rudderham of Vajradhatu Publications, and Peter Turner and Nikko Odiseos of Shambhala Publications also provided exceptional trust and encouragement. Gordon Kidd of Kalapa Recordings provided audio files in a timely manner. Barbara Blouin showed tireless dedication as she took on the lengthy task of checking the accuracy of the original seminary transcripts, and she could always be relied on to point out errors that may have crept into the source material. The brilliant Liza Matthews cheerfully took time from her busy schedule to research images and to photograph the illustrations.

Ellen Kearney worked closely with me on this project from beginning to end. As we went over the manuscript together line by line, she applied her sharp intellect and spirit of inquiry, as well as her feel for language and wry humor. Ellen also was invaluable in gathering permissions, working with illustrations, and compiling the glossaries. Ellen's combination of devotion and skepticism was a delight, as was her deep appreciation for the Vidyadhara and his teachings.

The editing of *The Profound Treasury* would not have been possible without the financial support of the Mukpo family, the Shambhala Trust, the Khyentse Foundation, the backing of Vajradhatu Publications and Shambhala Publications, and many individual friends and donors. The generosity of such patrons is profoundly moving.

Liz Shaw, my editor at Shambhala Publications, went through these manuscripts multiple times, always finding ways to refine and improve upon the material. Her persistence helped keep this project moving forward. Florence Wetzel provided meticulous copyediting, and Ben Gleason also provided tremendous editorial support.

Diana J. Mukpo, Trungpa Rinpoche's widow, gave this initiative her blessings and her enthusiastic support and encouragement. Lady Diana has been instrumental in protecting her husband's legacy and helping to insure that his teachings are published and brought into the world. Her support and the support of the entire Mukpo family are unwavering.

Trungpa Rinpoche's son, Sakyong Mipham Rinpoche, who has elegantly taken his seat as the head of the Shambhala Buddhist lineage and dedicated himself to furthering the vision of his father, has also provided his blessings for this project. He has been consistent in his support for the task of editing and publishing this material, as well as other treasures from Trungpa Rinpoche's archives.

I would also like to acknowledge the students of Trungpa Rinpoche, who requested these teachings, who attended seminaries, and who through their devotion and open hearts created a receptive environment for such teachings to manifest.

In this listing I have pointed out many people who made this project possible, all of whom deserve to be acknowledged, but this list is by no means complete. To all those who have contributed to this project in whatever way, I offer my gratitude and respect.

I would like to thank my husband and best friend, Chuck Lief, for his love and support, his shared appreciation for the profound vision of the Vidyadhara, and his steady encouragement, not to mention patience. I would like to thank my family—my daughters Jessica and Deborah, my sons-in-law Jeremy and Frazier, and my delightful grandchildren Niamaya and Neruda—who I treasure.

Above all, I would like to thank my root teacher, the Vidyadhara Chögyam Trungpa Rinpoche, who set a personal example of wisdom, kindness, humor, discipline, and daring—qualities that are so lacking in this troubled world. May the rays of his compassion shine forth for generations to come. May his teachings be read, put into practice, and realized, and may doing so awaken us to our true nature. May we emulate his dedication to others, remembering his words, "Never give up!" May the power of the dharma transform war into peace, confusion into wisdom, complacency into engagement, and hate into love, for the benefit of all beings.

EDITOR'S INTRODUCTION

THE CONTEXT FOR THESE TEACHINGS

This volume is the first of three based on the teachings Venerable Chögyam Trungpa Rinpoche presented in a series of three-month meditation and study retreats called Vajradhatu Seminaries. From 1973 to 1986, Trungpa Rinpoche conducted thirteen seminaries and gave over three hundred talks. He structured these seminaries according to the three main stages of the Buddhist path laid out in the Tibetan Buddhist tradition: hinayana, mahayana, and vajrayana. (See below in this introduction for a brief overview of the *yanas*, or "vehicles.")

THE ORAL TRADITION

In reading this volume, it is good to keep in mind the nature of these talks and the context in which they were presented. Buddhism is primarily an oral tradition, and it is rooted in the direct transmission of the Buddhist teachings, or *buddhadharma*, from teacher to student. The early *sutras*, or discourses, maintain this quality and always mention the place, time, setting, and who was present when the Buddha taught a particular topic. In keeping with the oral tradition, sutras typically begin with the phrase, "Thus have I heard." Likewise, this book is based on the oral tradition. The talks at the root of this volume were spoken to particular students in a particular way, at particular times and places. Unlike the sutras of the Buddha, however, they were recorded, and the recordings were transcribed, providing the raw material for this book.

The speaker in this case was the Venerable Chögyam Trungpa Rinpoche. Since Trungpa Rinpoche was recognized at a young age as a *tülku,* or "incarnate lama," he was referred to as *rinpoche,* or "precious one." He could also be referred to by the titles *vajracharya,* "vajra master," or *vidyadhara,* "knowledge holder." Born in eastern Tibet in 1940, Trungpa Rinpoche was the eleventh holder of the Trungpa lineage of Tibetan Buddhism. This lineage is within the Kagyü school of Tibetan Buddhism, a school known as the "practice lineage" due to its emphasis on meditative training and direct personal experience. Trungpa Rinpoche trained at Surmang Monastery in eastern Tibet to take on the duties and responsibilities expected of a lineage holder, but at the time of the Chinese invasion in 1959, he left all that behind and became a refugee. Trungpa Rinpoche arrived in North America in 1970 at the age of thirty-one and continued to teach in the West for seventeen years, from 1970 until his death in 1987. He was one of the first Tibetan masters to teach Tibetan Buddhism in North America. He was also one of the few Tibetan teachers to present the dharma in the English language. (For more on Chögyam Trungpa's life, see the detailed biography at the end of this book.)

THE VAJRADHATU SEMINARIES

The students who received these oral teachings at the Vajradhatu Seminaries had stumbled upon Buddhism in various ways, found a teacher in Trungpa Rinpoche, and had been accepted to attend one of these programs. Most had been studying the dharma for a period of three years or more, had a personal connection to the Vidyadhara, and had begun to practice meditation. Seminaries were held just once a year at various locations in North America, and a student might not be accepted the first time he or she applied.

Trungpa Rinpoche considered the seminary programs to be of crucial importance for training his students and for the future propagation of the dharma. In talking about the role of such seminaries, he told his students:

> You could become a very powerful, important implement in propagating the true dharma. We are building this body of teachings so that everything does not become bottlenecked by my own particular existence alone. It could go beyond just me. You could continue to expand your vision after my death. What happens in the future

The Venerable Chögyam Trungpa Rinpoche, 1973 seminary, Jackson Hole, Wyoming.
Photograph provided by Tendzin Parsons.

completely depends on your intelligence and discipline and exertion, so you had better take more responsibility.

All of this is going to be handed over to you anyway, sooner or later, whether you would like to take it or not. You could reject it or throw it in the dust, but it is up to you to take responsibility for the presentation of the dharma. You need to help future students, not only in this country, but in the rest of the world, including Tibet and India. By then people there will have forgotten dharma, so a fresh first generation of American dharma practitioners could come to India or Tibet. That would help a lot.

Our vision is very extensive and large, and as far as the work that needs to be done, it is also highly demanding. Hopefully you have actually managed to understand something. If you haven't understood, we will have to put you through another examination process—again and again and again. I am not willing to give up on you. People may try to make sure that they are given up, but that won't be the case, as far as I am concerned.*

Although the three-yana structure formed the basis of all the seminaries, the settings varied and the times and culture shifted considerably from the first seminary in 1973 to the last in 1986, so each seminary was unique. Typically, the program would begin with a meditation intensive lasting one to two weeks, followed by a study period focusing on the hinayana. This would be followed by another meditation intensive, and the mahayana study period. Finally there would be a third practice intensive, followed by the vajrayana study period. During the practice periods students would spend the entire day in meditation, alternating between sitting and walking meditation practice. They would eat their meals in the meditation hall, as well, practicing a form of mindful eating adapted from Zen, known as *oryoki*. During the study periods, in addition to the main course, which was taught by Trungpa Rinpoche, students took a course taught by senior students focusing on the study of previous seminary transcripts. They also took classes on topics such as lineage and devotion, Buddhist psychology, and the teachings of the Shambhala tradition, which emphasizes basic goodness and the creation of an enlightened society. Both the

---

* Vajradhatu Seminary, 1975. *Talk 3: Yana.*

*The Venerable Chögyam Trungpa Rinpoche, 1980 seminary,
Lake Louise, Alberta. Photograph by Paula Breymeier.*

*The Venerable Chögyam Trungpa Rinpoche being served oryoki, 1980
seminary, Lake Louise, Alberta. Photograph by Paula Breymeier.*

teachers and students participated in oral examinations at the end of each study period.

Trungpa Rinpoche was quite proud of the seminary form with its alternation of deep practice and intense study. As he told his students:

> I would like to introduce learning and practicing at the same time. That has always been the Kagyü style. We always practice and we always study. It is not particularly complicated. So I would like to have all of you take part in the sitting practice of meditation and also to have your learning situation under control. In other words, I would like you to work hard, whether in hearing, contemplating, or meditating.
>
> This is a very rare moment for you, and it may only happen once in your life. So please think of that and try to practice as much as you can and learn as much as you can. Pay heed to how you spend your time, your very valuable time. You worked hard, and finally you got here. I am so glad and grateful that you are all here. So let us make use of this.
>
> What has been happening with the students here, as far as I can see, makes me extremely pleased. You are extremely sweet, wonderful, and hardworking. On the whole, I am so pleased to be your teacher. You are great students. So it is, as they say, "a gift of God," to be your teacher. Let us keep it that way. Please continue wholeheartedly.*

At each seminary, Trungpa Rinpoche taught the stages of the path of Tibetan Buddhism from beginning to end in great detail, and each year he was able to build on all that he had previously presented. After each seminary, transcripts of his talks were published, so as he was presenting new teachings, students were able to review the material from previous years. As the years went by, the body of teachings that he built upon grew larger and larger.

Trungpa Rinpoche created the seminary form as a vehicle that would allow his closest students to access the sophistication and depth of the training he had received in Tibet. In doing so, he was able to infuse the dharma with a quality of transmission. In keeping with the intimate nature

---

* Vajradhatu Seminary, 1981. *Talk 12: The Qualities of Dharma.*

The Venerable Chögyam Trungpa Rinpoche, 1981 seminary, Lake Louise, Alberta.
Photograph © 1981 by Marvin Moore.

Group oryoki, 1981, Lake Louise, Alberta. Photograph © 1981 by Marvin Moore.

of these teachings, access to the seminary transcripts was restricted, with a few exceptions, to students who had attended a Vajradhatu Seminary. In particular, Trungpa Rinpoche was concerned that the vajrayana teachings be presented properly, to the right students at the correct time.

Describing the three-yana path, Trungpa Rinpoche said:

> In your training, you start in a narrow gorge, then you get to the plains, and finally, you climb up a very steep hill, a mountain range, which is the preparation to understand and experience the vajrayana. In order to do that, you have to put a lot of effort and energy into your practice. If students are not ready, if they have not put any effort into their practice, the effort of the teacher becomes futile. It is like talking to a blank wall, without eyes, ears, or expressions. The teacher is talking to pure confusion alone.*

Trungpa Rinpoche was quite conservative in his offering of vajrayana teachings and was careful to protect the integrity of the transmission.

---

* Vajradhatu Seminary, 1979. *Talk 17: Guidelines of Mind Training.*

Students at seminary, 1981, Lake Louise, Alberta. Photograph © 1981 by Marvin Moore.

However, it was always his wish that ultimately even his highest teachings be made available to the world, to enable more people to come to know the dharma in a sophisticated way, with a more penetrating and profound understanding.

A BRIEF OVERVIEW OF THE THREE YANAS

Briefly, the hinayana refers to individual development and the path of the arhat ("worthy one"); the mahayana refers to the joining of wisdom and compassionate action and the path of the bodhisattva ("awake being"); and the vajrayana refers to fearless engagement and spiritual daring and the path of the *siddha* ("holder of spiritual power"). The three-yana approach presents a map of the path based on a student's natural, developmental progression.*

---

* In this context, the terms *hinayana, mahayana,* and *vajrayana* refer to stages of the path, not to the various schools of Buddhism. Although the term *hinayana* can be used in a deprecatory or sectarian way, Trungpa Rinpoche repeatedly stresses the role of hinayana as the foundation and essential starting point of a student's entire journey.

The Hinayana

The path begins with the hinayana. The term *hinayana* means "lesser or smaller vehicle." According to Trungpa Rinpoche, "The hinayana is called the smaller vehicle, not because it is simpleminded or lacking in vision, but because it is a pragmatic, deep-rooted approach." The hinayana introduces core Buddhist teachings on the nature of mind, the practice of meditation, the reality of suffering, and the possibility of liberation. It examines the nature of suffering, impermanence, and egolessness, with an emphasis on personal development through meditative discipline and study.

The formal entry into the hinayana and the Buddhist path altogether is the refuge vow, in which a student goes for refuge to the Buddha, or the teacher; the dharma, or the teachings; and the *sangha,* or the community. The hinayana path is based on training in mindfulness and awareness, cultivating virtue, and cutting grasping. Those who accomplish this path are called arhats, worthy ones who have completely severed their ties to this world of confusion and suffering, or samsara, and attained peace, or nirvana.

The Mahayana

The mahayana, or "great vehicle," rests on the foundation established by the hinayana. The meditative training and ethical insight of the hinayana is essential for the aspiring mahayana practitioner, and the value placed on mindfulness and awareness, gentleness and simplicity, continues. At this point, having trained and seen the benefits of looking within, the practitioner begins to shift their focus outward to the broader world.

Formal entry into the mahayana occurs with taking the bodhisattva vow. Mahayana practitioners dedicate themselves to the service of all sentient beings, aspiring to save them from sorrow and confusion, and vowing to bring them to perfect liberation. This yana emphasizes the cultivation of wisdom through the view and experience of emptiness, or *shunyata,* in which all phenomena are seen to be unbounded, completely open, ungraspable, and profound. From the ground of shunyata, compassionate activity is said to arise naturally and spontaneously.

In addition to mindfulness and awareness, the mahayanist practices *lojong,* or "mind training," based on the cultivation of the *paramitas,* or

The Venerable Chögyam Trungpa Rinpoche with students, 1983 seminary, Bedford Springs, Pennsylvania. Photograph by Ken Wallace.

"transcendent virtues": generosity, discipline, patience, exertion, meditation, and *prajna*, or "knowledge." As a component of lojong, *tonglen*, or "sending and taking," is practiced in order to increase *maitri*, or loving-kindness. Those who accomplish the mahayana, who join emptiness and compassion, or wisdom and skillful means, are called bodhisattvas, or "awake beings." Because of the courageous nature of such heroes and heroines, they are also referred to as "bodhisattva warriors."

The Vajrayana

The vajrayana, or "diamond vehicle," also referred to as tantra, draws upon and extends the teachings of the hinayana and mahayana. As with the hinayana and the mahayana, the formal acceptance into the vajrayana is marked by a vow, in this case the *samaya* vow. There is an emphasis in this yana on the student-teacher relationship and on the quality of devotion. Teachings are transmitted directly from teacher to student.

Generally, students must complete preliminary practices, called *ngön-dro*, to prepare themselves for initiation into the vajrayana path before going further. Having done so, they then receive the appropriate empowerments to begin tantric practices. There are empowerment ceremonies of many kinds, called *abhishekas*. The vajrayana includes both form practices, such as visualizations and *sadhanas* (ritual liturgies), and formless practices based on allowing the mind to rest naturally in its inherent clarity and emptiness. Although on the surface, there is much greater complexity in tantric practices, the principles of mindfulness and awareness and the cultivation of compassion and skillful action continue to be of central importance.

The tantric path requires complete engagement and fierce dedication. It is said to be a more rapid path, but it is also more dangerous. There is a quality of directness, abruptness, and wholeheartedness. *Tantrikas*, or vajrayana practitioners, recognize that the most challenging aspects of life, the energies and play of confused emotions and frightening obstacles, can be worked with as gateways to freedom and realization. Accomplished practitioners of vajrayana are called *siddhas*, which means "those who have power."

Trungpa Rinpoche repeatedly stresses that all three yanas are necessary and important, so it is not advisable to bypass any one of them. The grounding of the hinayana, the magnanimity of the mahayana, and the

*The Venerable Chögyam Trungpa Rinpoche with the Sakyong, Mipham Rinpoche
and Lady Könchok Paldrön, 1986 Seminary, Rocky Mountain Dharma Center.
Photograph by Diana Church.*

daring of the vajrayana make up one continuous journey. In that sense there is only one yana.

PRIMARY REFERENCES

In preparing his seminary teachings, Chögyam Trungpa referred over and over again to two primary sources: *The Treasury of Knowledge* by Jamgön Kongtrül Lodrö Thaye, and *The Jewel Ornament of Liberation* by Gampopa. According to Trungpa Rinpoche:

> In offering these teachings, I would like to present the buddha-dharma in its fullest sense, beginning with a vajrayana approach to hinayana. I have done my own study, my homework, so to speak, using the same book that I've used for years and years: *The Treasury of Knowledge* (Tib.: *Sheja Dzö*), Jamgön Kongtrül's work on the three-yana teachings.*

Renowned as an accomplished master, scholar, and writer, as well as the founder of *Ri-me,* or the nonsectarian movement, Jamgön Kongtrül Lodrö Thaye (1813–1899) authored more than one hundred volumes of scriptures, of which the most well-known is the *Five Treasuries,* a comprehensive work spanning the entire range of Tibetan Buddhism. Many Tibetan teachers carry a compact edition of this monumental work, and consult it again and again. *The Treasury of Knowledge* is one of these *Five Treasuries.* Trungpa Rinpoche's root teacher, Jamgön Kongtrül of Shechen (1901–1960), was one of at least five incarnations of the great Kongtrül, and is considered to be the most learned of his spiritual heirs.

Gampopa (1074–1153) was known as a great healer and physician as well as a foremost teacher and author. He was one of the two principal students of the great yogi-poet Milarepa. Of the many significant texts he wrote, *The Jewel Ornament of Liberation,* is considered by many to be the most well-known and important. In it he presents a classic overview of Buddhism and the essential teachings of the mahayana path.

Although Trungpa Rinpoche was deeply familiar with these two texts and the Buddhist canon, he was quite free in his interpretation of them and drew heavily from oral instructions he had received. He remarked:

---

* Vajradhatu Seminary, 1976. Talk 2: *Prajna and Dharma.*

I have adopted the approach of not just relying on notes, but on my upbringing and on what I have learned in my training. In general, I have been relying less and less on books. Instead, I have been working more with the education I have received, which you could call oral instruction or personal experience. That is the method I have been using. If you purely work with the texts, books, and commentaries, you may find some contradictions and inaccuracies. If you have actually practiced, you find more accuracy and the better reality of personal experience.*

THE STRUCTURE OF VOLUME ONE: HINAYANA

Entering the Path

Encountering the Dharma

The opening section of this book introduces the reader to basic Buddhist concepts such as meditation, dharma, path, individual salvation, the structure of ego, the nature of samsara, and relating with a teacher. Trungpa Rinpoche presents the hinayana path in the context of a three-yana journey—hinayana, mahayana, and vajrayana—and emphasizes the need to join intellectual study with meditative training and practice. He also discusses the contrast between theism and nontheism, and the notion of Buddhism as a nontheistic religion.

Taking Refuge

On the basis of study and practice, a student may be inspired to go further, or as Trungpa Rinpoche describes it, a student may catch "buddhadharma fever." At that point a person is ready to consider jumping in and making a commitment. This section of the book discusses the formal entry into the Buddhist path known as the refuge vow, the central commitment of the hinayana path. He introduces the idea of taking refuge in the three jewels: the Buddha, dharma, and sangha. According to Trungpa Rinpoche, committing yourself to the three jewels is a liberating step based on abandoning attachment to home ground and becoming stateless.

---

* Vajradhatu Seminary, 1984. *Talk 10: Tonglen.*

Reflecting on the Three Jewels

This section of the book contains a short text, the *Sutra of the Recollection of the Noble Three Jewels,* along with a detailed commentary. Following up on the discussion of refuge, Trungpa Rinpoche introduces the reader to the practice of deepening one's devotion and confidence in the qualities of the Buddha, the dharma, and the sangha by studying and chanting this traditional sutra.

Discipline / Shila

The hinayana can be looked at in terms of discipline, meditation, and knowledge, or *shila, samadhi,* and *prajna*. Discipline is of prime importance, for the path is a do-it-yourself project. In this section the importance of discipline—both in meditation practice and in daily life—is emphasized as a way of both taming the mind and living a dharmic lifestyle. Monastic discipline and the practice of the five precepts are also discussed. (A short daily practice that includes an homage to the Buddha, the refuge vow, and taking the five precepts can be found in appendix 1.)

Meditation / Samadhi

The fact that this is by far the longest section of the manuscript is an indication of the importance Trungpa Rinpoche placed on meditative training. It is divided into two main subsections: mindfulness and awareness (*shamatha* and *vipashyana*). These two terms are discussed in many ways, but in general Trungpa Rinpoche uses the term *mindfulness* to refer to the calming and settling of the mind, and the ability to hold the mind steady or to concentrate. He uses the term *awareness* to refer to the way that the mind naturally expands out once it is settled, and develops spaciousness and clarity. In his approach to meditation instruction, Trungpa Rinpoche points to a progression from mindfulness, to awareness, and then to the inseparable union of mindfulness and awareness.

Shamatha: The Practice of Mindfulness

Here the reader will find a discussion of basic principles of mindfulness practice. There are guidelines for working with the posture, breathing, and thought patterns. The technique of labeling thoughts is introduced, as is the technique of "touch and go." Trungpa Rinpoche points out common problems that arise in meditation practice and how they might be dealt with. He stresses the value of not restricting shamatha to formal meditation practice alone, but applying it in daily life through the practices of meticulousness and respect.

Refining Your Shamatha Practice

This section begins with a discussion of three classical descriptions of shamatha practice: the nine techniques of shamatha, the six obstacles to shamatha, and the eight antidotes. It proceeds to a discussion of the results of shamatha practice, primarily *pagyö*, or heedfulness, and *tren-she*, a form of intrinsic awareness. Trungpa Rinpoche goes on to talk about the power of shamatha to cut thoughts and overcome the six conflicting emotions, or *kleshas*. He concludes this section by reminding readers that shamatha practice is not simply a mental exercise, but is transformative and infused with magical power and energy.

Working with the Mind

The mind is the working basis for meditative practice, so it is important to explore the nature of mind and consciousness. In this section there is a discussion of different definitions of mind, such as *sem*, or minding; *rikpa*, or sharpness; and *yi*, or mental sensitivity. The eight types of consciousness—the six sense consciousnesses; *nyön-yi*, the conflicted consciousness; and the *alayavijnana*, or base consciousness—are introduced along with the power of meditation practice in rediscovering the depths of mind. Finally, Trungpa Rinpoche describes the traditional practice of mixing mind and space.

The Four Foundations of Mindfulness

The section on shamatha practice concludes with a discussion of the four foundations of mindfulness: mindfulness of body, mindfulness of life, mindfulness of effort, and mindfulness of mind. The presentation of this topic is unique, and differs significantly from traditional descriptions found in texts such as the *Satipatthana Sutra,* or *Discourse on the Foundations of Mindfulness.* Trungpa Rinpoche makes use of the teachings on the four foundations to "create a total picture of mindfulness." He emphasizes their value in freeing meditation practitioners from overly self-conscious involvement in their practice.

Vipashyana: The Practice of Awareness

The calming and settling of the mind in shamatha practice will naturally and effortlessly lead to the expansive awareness of vipashyana. Vipashyana is known as insight or clear seeing. It has a quality of inquisitiveness and positive doubt. In particular, vipashyana is the insight that leads to the realization of egolessness and glimpses of emptiness. Although vipashyana is often used to refer to intellectual analysis, here the emphasis is on vipashyana as a direct meditative experience of panoramic awareness. In daily life, vipashyana awareness leads to a heightened appreciation of the world and a quality of relaxed yet meticulous attention.

The Four Noble Truths

In his presentation of the four noble truths—the truths of suffering, the origin of suffering, the cessation of suffering, and the path—Trungpa Rinpoche skillfully interweaves a traditional analysis of the four truths with the kinds of experiential insights into them that arise in meditation and postmeditation practice. He describes the truth of suffering as a complex snowballing of deception. The truth of the origin of suffering is looked at in terms of ignorance and subtle shifts of thought leading to confused emotions and harmful actions. The truth of the cessation of suffering is described as a continual awakening and blossoming. The truth of the path is said to be a process of overcoming doubt and developing confidence. In the discussion of the fourth noble truth, there is also a brief introduction to the five paths: the paths of accumulation, unification, seeing, meditation, and no more learning.

The Hinayana Journey

In this section, the hinayana path is described in two ways: in terms of the nine-yana system and in terms of the five paths. In the nine-yana system, the two hinayana stages are called the *shravakayana,* the yana of hearing and proclaiming, and the *pratyekabuddhayana,* the yana of individual salvation. In terms of the five paths, the hinayana stages are the path of accumulation and the path of unification. In discussing shravakas and pratyekabuddhas, Trungpa Rinpoche makes the point that these two yanas do not refer to sequential stages of the path, but to practitioners' different styles of practicing and relating to the dharma, as well as their different limitations and accomplishments. In contrast, the five paths are a progression, beginning with accumulating merit and wisdom with the path of accumulation, and progressing toward the mahayana with the path of unification.

Knowledge / Prajna

The volume concludes with a discussion of knowledge, or prajna, completing the traditional triad of discipline, meditation, and knowledge. Here Trungpa Rinpoche returns to the fundamental misunderstanding called "ego" and the entrapment and suffering of ego fixation, and he describes how prajna penetrates the dullness of ego and catalyzes the realization of egolessness, which is a fundamental breakthrough of the hinayana. The three prajna principles of hearing, contemplating, and meditating provide a way of experiencing the hinayana path properly and fully. They provide a tool that is both sharp and gentle. Realizing prajna, the teachings of the Buddha can be taken to heart simply and naturally.

THE EDITING PROCESS

In editing and compiling this volume, I primarily drew from the one hundred and twelve talks given by Trungpa Rinpoche in the hinayana portions of the thirteen Vajradhatu Seminaries. These talks were available to me in the form of both audio recordings and lightly edited transcripts. Each individual seminary was unique, with a distinct tone and flavor. At the same time, taken as a whole, the seminary teachings can be seen to form a single coherent narrative. In compiling and editing this material, the goal throughout has been to bring out this rich and profound treasury of teachings in a form that is clear and accessible, that is true to the original voice, and that conveys the essential points. Any shortfalls are purely the fault of the editor.

NOTE ON FOREIGN TERMS AND DEFINITIONS

Tibetan, Sanskrit, and other foreign words and phrases are italicized on first appearance in these volumes. Tibetan terms are spelled phonetically in the body of the text. The glossary contains definitions of all terms, as well as transliterations of Tibetan terms. A special thank you to the Nalanda Translation Committee and to Ellen Kearney for preparing and editing the extensive glossary. Please see the credits page for a list of further acknowledgments for definitions and use of terms from other sources.

DEDICATION

May the teachings of Chögyam Trungpa Rinpoche continue to
  benefit countless beings.
May the practice of buddhadharma be uncorrupted and
  eternally liberating.
May the knots binding hearts and minds be untied,
And may all beings enjoy peace, prosperity, and true happiness.

PRONUNCIATION OF
SANSKRIT AND TIBETAN

SANSKRIT

Sanskrit words may seem intimidating at first sight because they are so long. However, once they are broken into syllables, they are easy to pronounce. Sanskrit follows very regular rules and contains no "silent letters" such as those in English.

Vowels

In general, vowels are pronounced as in Italian or Spanish. Sanskrit makes a distinction between long and short vowels in the case of *a, i,* and *u*. However, in this text they are not represented differently. Therefore, it is acceptable always to pronounce them as if they were long:

a as in c*a*r.
i as in f*ee*t.
u as in l*oo*t.

The following vowels are always considered long in Sanskrit:

e as in d*ay*
ai as in p*ie*
o as in g*o*
au as in h*ow*

Consonants

Most consonants are pronounced as in English. The aspirated consonants (*kh, gh, ch, jh, th, dh, th, dh, ph, bh*) are pronounced as the consonant plus a noticeable aspiration of breath. In particular, note that the consonants *th* and *ph* are not pronounced as in the words *th*ing and *ph*oto, but as in po*th*ole and she*ph*erd. The letter *g* is always pronounced hard as in *g*o, never as in gem. The letter *h* is pronounced as a breathing sound at the end of a word.

Accent

In classical Sanskrit, each syllable received approximately the same emphasis; vowels were lengthened rather than stressed. Although today we tend to stress syllables, it should not be so emphatic as in English. Accent is placed on the next-to-last syllable when this contains a long vowel or ends with more than one consonant (not including *h*). Otherwise, it is placed on the last previous syllable that contains a long vowel or ends in more than one consonant. If none exists, the stress is placed on the first syllable.

TIBETAN

In this text, Tibetan words have been spelled to reflect pronunciation as accurately as possible. As in Sanskrit, the consonants *th* and *ph* are not pronounced as in the words *th*ing and *ph*oto, but as in po*th*ole and she*ph*erd. The letters *ü* and *ö* are pronounced approximately as in the German words *über* and *möglich*, or as in the French words *connu* and *oeuvre*.

Note that the letter *e* is always pronounced at the end of a word. In some cases, words ending in *e* have been spelled with a hyphen in order to prevent mispronunciation: shi-ne, Ri-me.

Part One

ENTERING THE PATH

ENCOUNTERING THE DHARMA

I

Beginning at the Beginning

Hinayana is like building a castle on rock. It takes great vision as well as great discipline and practicality. Without this deep-rooted approach, it would be like building a castle on ice: when the ice melted, the castle would go down the drain.

I N O R D E R to understand the dharma, the teachings of the Buddha, we have to begin at the beginning. We have to work step by step, stitch by stitch—and the way to begin at the beginning is with the hinayana, the "path of individual salvation." In Tibetan, the term for hinayana is *thekpa chung. Thek* means "lifted up," and *pa* makes it a noun; so *thekpa* means "something that is lifted up," or "vehicle." *Chung* means "tiny," or "small," so *thekpa chung* (or in abbreviated form, *thekchung*) means "small vehicle." The hinayana is called the smaller vehicle, not because it is simpleminded or lacking in vision, but because it is a pragmatic, deep-rooted approach.

Hinayana is like building a castle on rock. It takes great vision as well as great discipline and practicality. Without this deep-rooted approach, it would be like building a castle on ice: when the ice melted, the castle would go down the drain. There is nothing frivolous in the hinayana approach. Everything is very direct and precise. It is the straight-and-narrow path. The hinayana notion of the absence of frivolity plays an extremely important part in the entire Buddhist path. Therefore, there is a need for reverence and respect for the understanding of the hinayana.

3

Buddhism says that confusion has to be dispelled and that there should be realization beyond confusion. It is based on the idea of transcending the highest ideals of the human mind completely, which is called enlightenment. Once you dissolve, once your particular expectations dissolve, that is liberation or enlightenment. Since enlightenment is based on dissolving the ego and its expectations, it has been said that you cannot watch your own burial, and you cannot congratulate yourself on becoming the first buddha of the age or the first buddha of New York.

The hinayana is important for our journey because we have our body, our neuroses,* our state of being, our mind, and our habitual patterns, and it is necessary to work with those things before we can go further on the path. We should not be too ambitious and reject what is around us. Moreover, the hinayana is important because with the hinayana we begin to see our experience as literal experience. If we put salt on our meal, when we taste the salt, we taste real salt. If we sprain our ankle, we really feel our sprained ankle. If we have a backache, we experience a real and direct backache.

In studying the dharma, we have to understand what we are doing. When a baker makes bread, he has to know the proper amount of yeast and water to use, as well as the right amount of flour. The best baker should also know how the wheat has been cultivated and manured. In a similar way, you have to know your mind: the neuroses, the positive possibilities, the obstacles, and the vicissitudes. You have to know realities as well as fantasies, hopes, and ideas. You need to know how certain situations produce either painful or wholesome possibilities for you. The teachings of the Buddha are quite realistic and pragmatic.

According to the hinayana, life is painful, with an occasional speck of pleasure. We are born, we get old, we experience sickness, and, last but not least, we die. We are each waiting to die. I'm afraid that is the bad news. Whether you are young or old doesn't make much difference—everybody will eventually die. So now is the time to do something with your life. We are not interested in developing eternity or immortality, or in preventing being sick or being born. We are interested in doing something

---

* Trungpa Rinpoche employs the psychological term *neurosis* not in the strictly Freudian sense, but to refer to the common human experience of conflicting emotions, or *kleshas*. He prefers to present the spiritual path as a journey from neurosis to sanity, rather than using more religious or philosophical terminology.

while we are alive, while we are breathing, while we can see the beauty of the snow, the flowers, the blue sky, the sunshine, and the many other things we can imagine.

Life is like a stew: everything is mixed together, which may or may not work. That mixture is what is called "samsara," or *khorwa* in Tibetan. *Khor* means "spinning around," and *wa* makes it a noun; so *khorwa* means "spinning around in our life." Samsara is not necessarily bad, but it makes us dizzy. We have no idea whether we are going to the east, south, west, or north. Samsara is like the epitome of a hallucinatory drug, a super-LSD—and here we are, in it. We are in samsara whether we like it or not.

The dharma shows us the possibility of getting out of samsara. So-called enlightenment is possible. You can do it. You can learn about it and you can do it. Enlightenment is like witnessing the brilliant sun for the first time in the morning. It is like seeing the beautiful flowers that grow in the woods, the frolicking deer, a bird flying proudly, or fish swimming. Life is not all that grim. In the morning when you brush your teeth, you can see how shiny they are. Reality has its own gallantry, spark, and arrogance. You can study life while you are alive. You can study how you can achieve the brilliance of life. However, the *desire* to be enlightened can be a problem. It is when it is not all that important to you that you will attain enlightenment.

Dharma is like the atmosphere: you cannot escape it. According to the dharma, delusion is not regarded as catastrophic, and bewilderment is not regarded as terrible. Nonetheless, we are stuck with them. The Buddha said that all human beings experience bewilderment. You need to hear that particular bad news, but please don't be startled, because you can do something about it. However, nobody is going to do it for you. You have to begin by yourself, so maybe you *should* be startled. You *should* be shocked when you realize that you have been trapped and imprisoned, because then you might do something about it. You have been too naive. You have enjoyed your samsaric life too much. You should have been shocked a long time ago! I'm sorry that I'm the one to bring you the bad news, although possibly, quite remotely, I might also be bringing the potential of good news. But to begin with, you have to experience that reality begins at home—in fact, in your own basement.

2

The Frozen Space of Ego

The skandhas present a complete picture of ego. According to Buddhist psychology, the ego is simply a collection of skandhas or heaps—but actually there is no such thing as ego. It is a brilliant work of art, a product of the intellect, which says, "Let's give all this a name. Let's call it 'I.'"

WITH ANY kind of spiritual practice, you need to have a basic understanding of where you are starting from, where you are going, and what you are working with. It is necessary to start with what you are and why you are searching. If you do not know that basic ground, there is no point, because your ideas become mere fantasy. Although you may hear about advanced ideas and experiences, your understanding will be based purely on your own expectations and desires. It is a weak aspect of human nature to always want to see and hear something colorful and extraordinary. But an emphasis on extraordinarily enlightening and delightful experiences only feeds your expectations and preconceptions, so your mind is preoccupied with what will be, rather than what is. That approach is rather destructive. It is not fair to people to perpetuate their weaknesses, their expectations, and their dreams. It is better to begin with the realistic starting point of what they are.

Before we speak of liberation or freedom, we need to discuss the basis of the path, which is confusion. It is important to begin by considering the development of what in the Buddhist tradition is called "ego." This may sound pejorative, but we do not have to be ashamed of what we are.

Although our background may not be particularly enlightened, peaceful, or intelligent, it is good enough. We can work with it. It is like plowing a furrow and planting seeds. So we are not trying to get rid of the ego, but simply acknowledge it and see it as it is.

OPEN SPACE

In the development of ego, at the beginning there is basic ground, basic consciousness, open space. There is openness, freedom, and spaciousness all the time. For example, in everyday life, at the first moment we see an object, there is a sudden recognition without logic or conceptualization. We just perceive openness. But immediately we panic, and we hurry to try to put something into that openness. We try to find a name or a pigeonhole so that we can locate and categorize that particular thing according to our own ideas and conceptualizations. As that process continues, the ego becomes more and more solid. However, the idea of ego as a solid ongoing entity is illusory; it is a mistaken belief. Although confused mind would like to view itself as solid, it is only a collection of tendencies and events. This collection is referred to as the five *skandhas,* or five "heaps": form, feeling, perception / impulse, concept / formation, and consciousness.

THE FIVE SKANDHAS

The First Skandha: Form

SOLIDIFYING SPACE In the beginning, there is open space belonging to no one, and within that space is primeval intelligence, or *vidya,* so there is both intelligence and space. It is like a completely open and spacious room in which you can dance about and not be afraid of knocking anything over. You are this space; you are one with it. But you become confused. Because it is so spacious, you begin to whirl and dance about. You become too active in the space.

As you dance, you want to experience the space more and more, to enjoy the dance and the openness. But at that point, space is no longer space, as such. It has become solid space because of your unnecessary urge to contact it. When you try to cling to space, to grasp it, the whole perspective is completely changed. You have solidified space and made it tangible. That sense of self-consciousness is the birth of duality. Spaciousness has become solid space, and you have begun to identify yourself with the "I." You are identified with the duality of "I" and space, rather than being completely one with space. You have become self-conscious, conscious that "you" are dancing in space. This is the birth of the first skandha, the skandha of form.

Having solidified space, you forget what you have done. Suddenly there is a blackout, a gap. Your intelligence suddenly collapses, and you are completely overwhelmed by ignorance in a kind of reverse enlightenment experience. When you wake up, you become fascinated with your own creation, acting as if you had nothing to do with it, as though you yourself were not the creator of all this solidity. You deliberately ignore the openness and intelligence, so the intelligent, sharp, precise, flowing, and luminous quality of space becomes static. There is still primeval intelligence, or vidya, but it has been captured and solidified. Therefore, it has become *avidya,* or ignorance. That blackout of intelligence is the source of the ego. From that sudden blackout, as you continue to explore, gradually things become more and more solid.

THREE STAGES OF IGNORANCE. The skandha of form has three stages. The first stage, the *birth of ignorance,* is a kind of chemical reaction in which you come to the conclusion of your own separateness. It is as if there were a desert, simple and basic, but strangely and suddenly one of the grains of sand popped up and began to look around.

The second stage is called the *ignorance born within.* Having noticed that you are separate, you feel that you have always been so. However, that instinct toward self-consciousness is awkward. You feel unbalanced, so you try to secure your ground and create a shelter for yourself. You take the attitude that you are a confused and separate individual, and that is all there is to it.

The third type of ignorance is *self-observing ignorance.* As you are watching yourself, you see yourself as an external object, which leads to the notion of "other." You are beginning to have a relationship with the so-called "external world." You are beginning to create the world of forms.

The Second Skandha: Feeling

Having managed to transform space into solidness, you would then like to possess it and grasp it. Having solidified the duality of self and other, you try to feel the qualities of that "other" in order to reassure yourself that you exist. You reach out to sense whether that "other" is seductive, threatening, or neutral. You think that if you can feel something "out there," then you must really be here. The mechanism of feeling you set up is extremely efficient.

The Third Skandha: Perception / Impulse

In the act of perception, having received information about the outside world from the skandha of feeling, you respond to that information in three ways: by drawing in, pushing away, or being indifferent. The skandha of feeling transmits its information, and you make judgments, you react. Whether you react for or against or indifferently is automatically determined by this bureaucracy of feeling and perception. If you find the situation threatening, you push it away; if you find it seductive, you draw it to you; if you find it neutral, you are indifferent. So perception / impulse is an automatic impulsive reaction to intuitive feeling.

The Fourth Skandha: Concept / Formation

The automatic reaction of the third skandha is not enough of a defense to protect your ignorance and guarantee your security. In order to protect and deceive yourself properly, you need intellect, the ability to name and categorize things. With intellect, you can label things "good," "bad," "beautiful," "ugly," and so on.

With each of the skandhas, the structure of ego is gradually becoming heavier and stronger. Up to this point, ego's development was purely based on action and reaction, but from this point on, the ego is becoming more sophisticated. You begin to experience intellectual speculation, to confirm and interpret yourself. The nature of intellect is quite logical, and your obvious tendency is to use that logic to create a positive condition for yourself. You use the intellect to confirm your experience, to interpret weakness as strength, to fabricate security, and to verify your ignorance. So although primordial intelligence is happening all the time, it is being employed by ignorance, by dualistic fixation.

The Fifth Skandha: Consciousness

The last stage of the development of ego is consciousness. Consciousness is an amalgamation of the intuitive intelligence of the skandha of feeling, the energy of the skandha of perception / impulse, and the intellectualization of the skandha of concept / formation. That combination produces thoughts and emotions. So at the level of the fifth skandha, we find emotional upheavals and the uncontrollable and illogical patterns of discursive thought. With the development of discursive thoughts and fantasies, the whole thing is completely secured.

The five skandhas present a complete picture of ego. According to Buddhist psychology, the ego is simply a collection of skandhas, or heaps—but actually there is no such thing as ego. It is a brilliant work of art, a product of the intellect, which says, "Let's give all this a name. Let's call it 'I.'" That "I" is the label that unifies that disorganized and scattered process into one entity. It is very clever.

The Path of Individual Salvation

The path of dharma is unlike the ordinary conception of religion as separate from secular life. Usually when you talk about business, you assume your business hat, and when you talk about religion, you assume your spiritual hat. But in this case, you don't wear two hats, you have only one hat—in fact, you have no hat.

T HE HINAYANA is referred to as the path of individual salvation, or *pratimoksha*. In Tibetan it is called *soso tharpa*. *Soso* means "individual," and *tharpa* means "salvation," or "liberation"; therefore, *soso tharpa* means "individual salvation." The hinayana path of individual salvation is based on the desire to develop peace or tranquillity within yourself and to prevent actions that are harmful, or possibly harmful, to others. On this basis you enter into various disciplines, such as taking the refuge vow.*

KEY HINAYANA TEACHINGS

A Nontheistic Path

In order to study the hinayana teachings and the *buddhadharma*, or the "teachings of the Buddha" altogether, you need to let go of theism.† You

---

* For a discussion of the *refuge vow*, see the section "The Refuge Vow" on page 82.

† The contrast between theism and nontheism is a recurring theme in Trungpa Rinpoche's teaching. He uses the term *theism* to refer to the belief in an external deity who might save or punish you, and in particular to deity-based religious traditions such as Christianity or Hinduism. More generally he uses *theism* to refer to the co-opting of any tradition, including Buddhism, as fuel for one's ego aggrandizement.

might think that nontheism amounts to a reaction against spirituality and that there is no hope in such an approach. However, people who have given up the theistic approach to religion and spirituality still feel a quality of magical power. They feel it is possible to practice and study very hard, and to develop strength or power over their situation. When you see that such nontheistic practitioners are becoming more sane, solid, and calm, you may begin to suspect that, in fact, something good is going on. As a reasonable person who is perturbed by your relationship with the so-called bread-and-butter world and uninspired by the prospects presented by this ordinary version of reality, you may begin to think of the possibility of getting into a different and higher realm of discipline and experience. If you do not want to do so within a theistic framework, you might decide to follow the nontheistic Buddhist path. The way to begin is with the hinayana, so it is important to understand how the hinayana teachings are structured.

Three Types of Learning

Hinayana understanding is structured according to three key principles: discipline, meditation, and knowledge, or in Sanskrit, *shila, samadhi,** and *prajna.*† Together, they govern the hinayana path.‡ Shila, samadhi, and prajna represent three types of learning: first, trusting in oneself; second, practicing one's trust in a meditative way; finally, expressing what one has trusted and learned. Discipline is the teacher as well as the teachings, the Buddha as well as the followers of the Buddha. Meditation is a way to relate your life to the spiritual path. And as for knowledge, if you want to learn the dharma, there's tons of it. There is so much to know that you can't cope with it all. But intellectual understanding alone cannot accomplish all that learning if it is without discipline and meditation. The three aspects of learning always work together.

---

* The term *samadhi,* translated here as "meditation," has the sense of meditative stabilization or absorption. The more general term for meditation in Sanskrit is *dhyana.*

† The term *prajna* has many levels of meaning, from ordinary intellectual understanding to direct intuitive insight into the nature of reality.

‡ For a more extended discussion of these three principles, see chapter 4, "Opening to the True Dharma."

Four Marks of View

Having developed the three aspects of learning, you can begin to realize how to view the world from the point of view of the path or the doctrine. In the hinayana, this is described in terms of the four marks of view: impermanence, suffering, egolessness, and peace.* The first two marks are based on looking at the samsaric environment, and the last two are the possibilities and potentialities you might discover out of that examination. In Tibetan, the four marks are known as *chaggya shi*. *Chaggya* means "mark," and *shi* means "four"; so *chaggya shi* means the "four marks," or four ways of viewing the phenomenal world.

IMPERMANENCE. The first mark of view is the impermanence of time and space. Time and space could not exist if there were no limitations put on them—and if there were no understanding of those limitations, time and space would be incomprehensible. Similarly, when you are speaking a language, you use words, but in order to make the language function, space is also necessary.

Impermanence is not particularly terrifying. It is a natural process that allows things to happen, a process connected with the gaps between situations, the gaps between space and subject matter. The Tibetan term for impermanence is *mitakpa*. *Takpa* means "permanent," and *mi* means "not"; so *mitakpa* means "not permanent." Whatever is collected is dispersed, and whatever comes into existence is subject to dissolution. The creation of something is at the same time the creation of its dissolution into something else or into nothingness. Very ordinarily, we could say that what goes up must come down.

All the happenings of the universe are subject to decay. No matter how glorious something may be in the beginning, it ends in decay and death. People are so naive: they think that they can construct something that will last forever. They fail to see that all composite things will dissolve in the

---

* Trungpa Rinpoche makes a subtle distinction between the term *four marks of view* and the more common *four marks of existence*. The former emphasizes one's attitude toward the phenomenal world, and the latter emphasizes the samsaric nature of phenomena. Later he discusses the same four topics as an aspect of the nontheistic view, using the term the *four norms of dharma*.

end and cease to exist. Nothing is permanent. Everything is formulated, gathered, and put together by our own conceptual mind—our own neat little ego-trip—and our attempt to put things together in that way is impermanent. We try to put things together or to figure things out, but that logic naturally dissolves. It's like building a house: if you build a house, since you built it yourself, it is also possible to dismantle it. That's the way it is.

SUFFERING. The second mark of view is that whatever you create could be regarded as a source of pain and suffering. Any comfort you might create is impermanent, and therefore liable to deteriorate sooner or later, and turn into discomfort. The Tibetan term for this is *sak-che tham-che dug-ngalwa*. *Sak-che* means "that which is collected or produced," *tham-che* means "all." *Dug* means "wretched," *ngal* means "continuing," and *wa* makes it a noun. *Dug-ngalwa* is like somebody continuously crying. So *sak-che tham-che dug-ngalwa* is the ongoing suffering resulting from the futility of creating anything permanent.

Pain cannot exist by itself. It exists if you have produced a comfortable situation with the idea that such perfection of comfort will continue. But then you begin to have second thoughts about that, or your comfort dissolves even before you have a second thought. So pain is based on the expectation that things will last continuously, although the truth is that the rug could be pulled out from under your feet at any moment. Therefore, anything that is produced is subject to pain.

Everything is suffering because the experience of our life becomes a nuisance. We are not just saying, "Our baby is a nuisance; therefore, we should send him or her to the babysitter." In this case, nuisance is not ordinary nuisance, but fundamental nuisance. Whenever you try to do something, it is always a nuisance. This makes things very inconvenient, but if you ask what else you can do, there is no answer.

Whatever we experience in our whole life takes effort and energy. We try to put something together and then we try to enjoy it. We try to make something out of our existence all the time, for the sake of goodness and happiness. This trying to put things together is painful, in varying degrees. For instance, you have a good cup of coffee in your hand. You put cream and sugar in it, and you stir it with satisfaction. You inhale the aroma, you drink, and you have a great sense of satisfaction. At last, a good cup of coffee! You have been looking forward to it for a long time—but now you have drunk it, it is gone, and your appreciation has become pain. You feel as if you never drank that cup of coffee at all. It is all gone, which is quite disheartening. You could fill the gap by drinking a second cup; but the second cup disappears as well, and you end up drinking so much coffee that you feel sick.

EGOLESSNESS. The third mark of view is that all dharmas, or experiences, are regarded as free from the fixation of ego. In Tibetan this is *chö tham-che dagmepa. Chö* means "dharmas," *thamche* means "all," *dag* means "self," or "ego," *me* means "without," and *pa* again makes it a noun; so *chö thamche dagmepa* means that all dharmas are free from ego in their true nature.

In the hinayana sense, "free from ego" means that there is nothing to hang on to from the point of view of the self. That makes an interesting nontheistic reference point: nobody can be saved because there's nobody home. Egolessness means that the situation is already clear. There could be a God, but who would worship God if there were no worshiper? The point is that you yourself do not exist, rather than that God does not exist and you are just sort of dangling. There could quite possibly be a house with furniture, but there is no one to occupy it. That is a far more important nontheistic reference point than believing that there is no God. From this point of view, *all* dharmas can be regarded as egoless.

By "all dharmas" we mean both the dharma of the projections and the dharma of the projector: the dharma of phenomena and the dharma of self or individuality. Basic, ordinary dharmas, or things as they are, like the dharmas of sky and earth, are referred to as projections. The projector is the person whose state of mind is deluded. The projector is the dharma of individuality, and the projection is the dharma of existence: me and my-ness. We keep holding on to things in order to make ourselves happy, but in fact we have no one to hang on and nothing to hang on to. It is futile. Nothing exists. Experiences that happen to us are no longer extraordinary, and things that exist within us are no longer serious. They are both equally bubbles, a futile mirage. I am taking a lighthearted approach, but actually it is very heavyhearted. Altogether, this mark qualifies the previous statement on suffering, in that there is no substance to suffering at all.

Saying that all dharmas are egoless means that everything we handle, feel, perceive—everything we do—has no receiver. You might find that somewhat outrageous, but it's true. When things happen they may look

could do it. It is true—anybody can do it. But that thought has never occurred to most people. So following the path of buddhadharma is quite extraordinary and unusual.

In order to become one with the dharma, to have the dharma as your path, you have to carry everything along as part of your journey. The path of dharma is unlike the ordinary conception of religion as separate from secular life. Usually when you talk about business, you assume your business hat, and when you talk about religion, you assume your spiritual hat. But in this case, you don't wear two hats, you have only one hat—in fact, you have no hat.

Whether you feel that things are difficult for you, like climbing uphill, or that things are easy for you, both are regarded as following the path of dharma. The path includes obstacles and difficulties of all kinds. It includes aggression, passion, and ignorance. It includes the temperature of the room, the taste of the food, the type of clothes you are wearing, bodily irritations such as aches in your knees and back, even whether or not your ballpoint pen is working. That is all part of the dharma. Anything that occurs, however small, is regarded as a part of the path. Nothing at all is separate from the path. Whatever you do is dharma.

The journey is delightful, from that point of view. You are totally in the dharma, rather than being a part-time dharma practitioner. That totality of being completely in the dharma provides tremendous joy, because you are not kidding yourself. That is how I personally feel. Whether I am sick or well, whether I am on a journey, flying in an airplane, or traveling in a car—in whatever I do, I feel that I am at the service of others. I feel that my function, the reason for my existence, is to serve the dharma and the *sangha*, the community of practitioners.

If you are a practitioner of buddhadharma, you do not take time off. You do not say, "Now I will take a break" or "After that heavy experience, I need a drink." You do not separate what is dharma from what is not dharma. Putting on your socks, washing your face, combing your hair, sending your clothes to the laundry, sitting on the toilet—whatever you do is dharma, the highest dharma, the buddhadharma. Because dharma is based on nonaggression and devotion, your perversion, hypocrisy, and egotism are all included. So whatever you are doing, the path of dharma goes along without a break, and everything you do is brought onto the path. In that way, you begin to be completely and thoroughly marinated in the dharma.

Through various techniques, you are being softened, rather than becoming a hardened individual or a hardened believer in a certain dogma. The main technique of marinating is by means of the discipline of mindfulness, or *shamatha*: the practice of sitting and walking meditation. The technique of sitting practice is both psychological and physical. Psychologically, you are simply trying to pay attention. It is like a mother trying to cut open an infected blister on a child's finger, that kind of simple care and consideration, that quality of being fully there. The physical aspect is your posture. You hold your head and shoulders properly. You are just like a rock—a sitting rock.

Possibilities of Freedom and Joy

The purpose of hinayana discipline is to attain cessation, in the sense of no longer struggling. When you feel completely at home when you meditate, it is a marvelous experience. Doubtlessness, harmony, tranquillity, and wholesomeness will take place once you are able to sit and meditate in that way. You will feel, personally, that you are there—you are absolutely there. Because you are able to liberate yourself from pettiness and wishful thinking, you will begin to enjoy greater possibilities of freedom.

Practice should carry along with it a sense of delight. It is completely secular and not at all religious or pious. When the gong strikes and you begin your meditation practice, notions of "ought" or "ought not," "should" or "shouldn't," notions of punishment or of being a good boy or good girl automatically begin to come up. You need to let go of such notions. You have to become completely ordinary and not associate what you are doing with religion. The problem with holding on to a religious attitude is that when you have bad posture or you miss a sitting session or think that you didn't meditate properly, you feel guilty. That builds up negativity, and in turn you are unable to hear the dharma—and because of that, there is no joy in being a buddhadharma practitioner.

As a practitioner, you could actually enjoy yourself. Enjoyment is not regarded as a sin. A good sitting-posture may seem very difficult and may be even painful to maintain; nonetheless, there still could be enjoyment and upliftedness. Sitting practice could be a festivity. You could enjoy being decent, being the best of human beings. Although that is what you always hope for, usually you substitute that with drinking and eating, wearing good clothes, going to parties, or swimming and lying in the dirt. But with sitting practice, you could develop real festivity. You could feel that you are a human being who is able to do wonderful things just by being able to be as you are. That seems to be a key point. It is why the Buddha is referred to as *sugata,* "he who has gone joyfully on the path." The Buddha is not referred to as "he who sat painfully," or "he who felt bad about himself," or "he who managed to get through his pain and has now attained buddhahood." He is referred to as joyful.

The path is joyful. Being a human being, being yourself, being a member of the sangha, is joyful. You should really enjoy yourself. Enjoyment comes from the sense of things being truly what they are. That brings great joy, and it brings the greater joy of uncovering buddha nature, your inherent capacity for awakening. Out of that, you begin to develop a sense of humor. You feel healthy and have fewer colds and less pain. You begin to feel wholesome because you are one piece rather than divided into different schizophrenic states of being. You are just one piece, one being. At the same time, you also begin to develop tremendous power and strength to help others, which is delightful and wonderful. That is a true miracle.

4

Opening to the True Dharma

Dharma is good at the beginning because it is fresh thought, inspired by the Buddha. . . .

The dharma is good in the middle because the process goes along in a very ordinary way. You have the sense that you are on a journey. . . .

The dharma is good at the end. . . . [Although] to say that the dharma is good in the end is deceptive, because there is no particular end. The notion of an end is purely a conceptual construct.

I N O R D E R to open yourself to the dharma, you need to drop any possible preoccupations of mind and simply try to listen and to understand. Sitting practice provides ground for that to happen, because in meditation all thoughts are regarded simply as discursive thoughts. None of them are regarded as at all valid or real. However, although such thought patterns are not that important, because they come and they go, you should regard them as part of your dharma practice. But there is something that is not purely a thought pattern, which is hearing the dharma.

The word *dharma* has many meanings. The first meaning is "way," "style," or "system." For instance, packages in Japan and China use the term to designate the directions for how to open the package and use its contents. Dharma can mean "basic norm," or "learning." It can mean the "cessation of pain." It can mean "what is perceived by the senses," or "what mind can conceive." It can mean what might happen in one's life: the possibilities, eventualities, expectations, and realities. It can mean fear as well as bliss. In Tibetan it is *chö,* and in Pali it is *dhamma.*

In the early Indian tradition, the word *dharma* did not mean anything heavy or special; it just meant the "thatness" or the "isness" of things. Ordinary dharma is the basic norm that exists in every individual situation, such as the dharma of food, the dharma of fire, or the dharma of water. For instance, the dharma of food is to fill the eater's belly; the dharma of fire is to make you warm and to cook your food; the dharma of water is to quench your thirst. That is, things take place in their own certain way. Ordinary dharma refers to how things work at the functional, pragmatic level.

Basic dharma is truth, but it is the lower level, bread-and-butter approach. Truth at that level is unimpressive and mundane. Although basic dharma has its own depth, it does not last beyond a few seconds, a few minutes, or a few hours. Even the biggest lower-level truth does not extend beyond that. It is like eating food: the time it takes to eat it, digest it, and finally flush it down the toilet is how long the mundane truth lasts. It does not last very long.

Ordinary dharma also includes the common norms of general morality, such as not telling a lie to your friend, not killing your friend, or not treating your enemy badly. A slightly higher level of ordinary dharma may include trying to develop a friendly attitude to your enemy as well as to your friend. So the original sense in which Buddha used the word *dharma* was quite basic, referring to things as they are. For the early Indians, dharma was a kind of jargon. If they could not figure something out exactly, they would say it was the "dharma of that" or the "dharma of this." The basic formula is: the dharma of *this* is that it is able to accomplish *that*. That is the first type of dharma, or ordinary dharma.

Along with that, we can then develop higher dharma. In order to distinguish lower dharma from higher dharma, we must distinguish purely functional dharma—like the dharma of food or the dharma of water— from the dharma of psychology, or one's state of mind. Reflecting on one's state of mind, whatever it is, is what distinguishes this higher level of dharma. We in the West do not seem to have an equivalent for the word *dharma*. People use words like *truth, norm,* or *doctrine,* but all those terms seem to have a hint of religion in them.

This is not purely an old-fashioned topic. Hinduism still uses the word *dharma,* as do other religions. Some teachers treat the word *dharma* as an expensive antique or work of art, implying that what they are presenting is much more expensive than mere teaching. By using the word *dharma,* they can push up the price another hundred or thousand. But according to Buddhist and Indian tradition, dharma simply means the straightforward truth. Dharma means truth, whether it is referring to the teachings of the Buddha or to more ordinary, mundane reality.

Dharma is not something to be abandoned or cultivated, but it is something you can work with. It is very simple and basic. Your entire life is filled with dharma. You are brought up with the dharma of your parents, who raise you in the dharma of bringing up children. You enter into the dharma of school, and after that you begin to take on the dharma of a certain profession or the dharma of dropping out of college and becoming a rebel, ascetic, or bandit. You get married, and have the dharma of marriage; fall in love, and have the dharma of love; start your own household, and have the dharma of raising children. The list of dharmas is very long. Basically it is just what happens in your life. Dharma involves facts, but those facts are not conceptual, mathematical, or analytical facts—they are realistic facts, personal experience, facts as they are. We seem to have a problem facing the facts of life straightforwardly, but dharma is both straightforward and ordinary.

Dharma is about more than simply using our resources. When we begin to realize the dharma of things, we see that it is about more than just feeding ourselves, going to sleep, or being entertained. We are educated human beings with a notion of things as they are, and we would like to explore them in-depth. At that point, the dharma becomes a path rather than a doctrine, and that path shows us that in order to understand the basic necessities of ordinary life, we need greater vision. Without such a reference point, we tend to make everything unnecessarily complicated, so that even cooking an egg sunny-side up is a philosophical and artistic issue. We might paint our eggs and sell them. We might fall in love with our eggs and be afraid to break them. We might feel that eggs are sacred and give birth to the world. However, we can go beyond that and handle the implications of our life very simply and directly. The dharmic lifestyle involves having a basic reference point of things as they are, precisely and clearly. It is not too philosophical, too humanistic, too poetic, too artistic, or too whatever.

SADDHARMA

Dharma is not regarded as a scheme, strategy, or trick, but as the real thing. It is known as the real thing because it has been practiced, worked out, tested, and proved to be effective for twenty-six hundred years of nonstop continuity, right up to the present. The one last legitimate thing is the dharma. When the Buddha talked about dharma, or truth, he meant something more than bread-and-butter language, something that lasts longer. To the term *dharma*, Buddha added the word *satya*, which means "truth," or "suchness," which combined with the word *dharma* becomes *saddharma*. Saddharma is slightly different than basic dharma. Saddharma is beginning to speak the truth, rather than simply referring to facts and figures. It is based on something deeper and more fundamental than the problems you have in your ordinary, everyday life.

Saddharma, or buddhadharma, has a particular definition: it is that which tames the mind. The meaning of *mind* in this case is somewhat negative, as mind is presumed to have passion, aggression, ignorance, hang-ups, and all kinds of conflicting emotions, or *kleshas,* that arise as mental contents. So saddharma is that which subjugates or tames the mind. That is the purpose of the teachings of the Buddha: to tame the mind.

Saddharma is said to cool off the mind. It is referred to as the medicine that cools off the heat of samsara or the heat of neurosis. It is that which cools off, or pacifies, any heated aggression, passion, or ignorance. We have an expression that says, "The sound of the dharma creates peace and utter coolness." That is, through dharma we are liberated from the turmoil of aggression, anxiety, paranoia, and confusion. We are purified completely by listening to dharma and by practicing the dharma. So dharma is cooling.

Saddharma is genuine because it begins to affect your state of mind thoroughly, much more than subconscious gossip. At the same time, saddharma does not fit into your thought patterns, because there is an element of foreignness in it—not because the dharma came from India, but because it does not fit into your scheme. It terrifies you a little, because it does not allow you any ground to indulge in your ego, and it tends not to cooperate with your basic desires.

Each of us comes to the dharma in our own particular way. We carry our own hang-ups, baggage, or garbage; and when we begin to click into the dharma, we click in a certain way. Because we want to hear things our own way, everything is interpreted in accordance with our own expectations, which gives us reassurance. Our expectations have been met and everything feels good, so we get turned on. Consequently we find that the dharma is suitable, that it makes sense, and that it seems to be right. Therefore, we begin to get into the buddhadharma.

As perceivers of the dharma, we are divided. In part we become emotionally attracted to our version of the teachings, and in part we have genuine insight into the teachings. A true presentation of the dharma is based on trying to wipe out the first part and keep the second. It is based on wiping out our habitual neurotic pattern of being inspired by the dharma purely insofar as it fulfills our expectations, and keeping the part of being inspired because dharma is related to our inherent insight. Generally, the sorting-out process takes place through sitting practice. Letting go of the first approach is an outcome of sitting practice and the feedback of the teacher and the sangha, who refuse to cooperate with your ego. It is a very living process by which people who have insight will study dharma, and people with ego trips will not.

No matter what aspect of the dharma we might be studying, there is always an element of picking and choosing. In regard to the teaching, the teacher, or our own experience, there is always a question of what needs to be given up and what needs to be taken along. On one hand, we could use the teachings to embellish our own ego and create a very secure situation. On the other hand, our attraction to the dharma could have nothing to do with ourselves personally, but be based on an intuitive connection and our ability to click into it. Those two options occur whenever the dharma is presented. Dharma in the fundamental sense is based on the second category, that of pure intuition. At that inherent level, a student is exposed to the true dharma. True dharma does not have to be excessively artistic, technological, political, humanistic, or anything of that nature. It can be dharma in a very ordinary sense.

The fundamental meaning of true dharma is passionlessness, peacefulness, and nonaggression. It has profound meaning and good words. If you are communicating the dharma to other people and you actually understand the dharma as it is, you will have no difficulty in relating it to others even though they may have confused notions of themselves and may never have heard the truth before, because you understand what you are speaking about and because of your conviction as to that particular truth. Communicating the truth of the dharma in this way has the quality of actually responding to people. Therefore, the dharma is well spoken. It is not mere verbosity.

Students who relate to dharma as a spiritual journey, rather than purely an ego embellishment, can actually hear and understand the meaning of dharma in its fullest sense. Such students begin to realize that there is something more true than the truth that is spoken on the spot. That is very impressive. The real truth is not actually spoken fully; rather, it is somewhat implied. This approach to truth makes things very powerful and thought provoking. It is an expression of the elegance of the Buddha.

The Buddha was able to make a great impression on people's minds when he spoke the dharma. To begin with, he taught the very hard-core students, his five friends who were extraordinarily critical of him. Later on, he extended his teaching, and according to the sutras, or discourses of the Buddha, eventually several thousand people at a time attended his talks. Everybody got something out of it—not because of the Buddha's flair, or his personality, or how articulate he was, but because it was the living truth, an example of true dharma. The dharma was no longer dead or being copied from anywhere else, but it actually was presented in its own right, with honesty, authenticity, and sincerity.

Saddharma has a quality of fathomlessness. You never know how far the saddharma is going to go, or how much truth it has to tell you. Fathomlessness is difficult for those who seek comfort, or self-snugness, in their own existence—those who seek to perpetuate their own ego. Saddharma is unworkable from that point of view, because you can't fit it into your particular scheme. You cannot promote your ego agenda and follow the dharma at the same time. Your personal inspiration to promote your own individuality, your so-called uniqueness, becomes questionable when you begin to study the dharma.

True dharma is at the same time both loving and threatening. In some ways, saddharma is a very complicated truth. There are a lot of descriptions of the various categories and levels of dharma and a lot of facts and figures. There are descriptions of the journey, including the mechanics of how we can do it, who is doing it, what is being done, what needs to be done, and what is the process.

Saddharma also has a quality of universality. When one person understands the dharma, that person's discovery is universal. Millions of others could do the same thing, in exactly the same way. What is this extraordinary saddharma all about? It is extremely simple; therefore, it is effective.

Saddharma transcends the three worlds and the kleshas.* Once you begin to recover from the kleshas, saddharma ceases to be a trick: it becomes real. Life is very simple. You are born, you get old, you get sick, you die, and that's it—you perish. It's very simple! That is saddharma, truth. Nothing can go wrong with that simplicity. Everything happens in that way.

CONTENTS OF ALL SADDHARMA

Basically, what the dharma is proclaiming is shila, samadhi, and prajna; or discipline, meditation, and knowledge. Shila, samadhi, and prajna are the contents of all the saddharma taught by the Buddha. In Tibetan this is referred to as *lappa,* which means "training." Lappa is largely based on the idea of taming your mind. According to the Buddhist approach, training is not a matter of being possessed by the Holy Ghost or of bringing any external agent into your system; instead, you are trying to awaken your own inherent capabilities.

Discipline / Shila

The first training is discipline. Discipline is controlling one's mind, or being, and bringing it into a state of tranquillity through shamatha practice. Its basic message is that you should be wholesome, free from fetters, free from wandering mind, and constantly on the dot. With shila, the basic faculties of mind can be fully used. The mind contains good and bad, wandering thoughts and precise thoughts; and ideally all these qualities should be used. Mindfulness, or being fully minded, plays a very important part in shila because before you can conduct yourself with decency, you have to be able to maintain a peaceful state of being. In other words, you have to calm yourself down, or train yourself, to be able to conduct your basic state of being in a proper manner and in accordance with common sense.

The attitude of shila is an upright one, a good one. Once you take that attitude, it is like deciding to take a shower: you are going to get rid of all

---

* The three worlds are the world of desire or passion, the world of form, and the formless world. The world of desire is the realm of humans and other living beings, and the form and formless worlds are god realms. For a discussion of worlds and realms, see chapter 9, "The Painful Reality of Samsara."

your dirt, including your smell, and you are going to wash and press your clothes as well. When you have taken a good shower and you are wearing fresh clothes, you feel dignity and wholesomeness. Morality, in the Buddhist sense, is strength. You are not subjugated by the flu, by fever, by attacks of malaria. You are free from all sorts of attacks, free from sleepiness, tiredness, and excitement.

There are many different levels of shila. The first level is somewhat manufactured and deliberate. From that artificial level of trying to emulate the possibility of shila, we then begin to experience real shila, or real discipline. It is like feeding meat to a young lion: because it has had the smell and taste of meat, when that young lion becomes an adult it automatically knows how to hunt. Similarly, we have the instinct to awaken. We are all would-be buddhas. We are all would-be bodhisattvas, or enlightened beings—we have that instinct. So whenever we try to mimic or to emulate the Buddha, we are actually practicing real shila.

The notion of discipline, or shila, is not quite the same as the Victorian ideal of good manners. In this case, you are organically tapping the source; and having organically tapped the source, true shila happens to you. This kind of discipline might hurt. If you sit for ten days in an upright posture, you might have a hell of a pain. But there is something beyond that. After that pain, you actually have learned how to sit fully and properly, and you find yourself learning to think like the Buddha, at least in small doses. So there is a lot of hope in this way of practicing.

Discipline may seem complicated, but it is actually very simple—it is what binds your life together. Without discipline, life is made up of successive indulgences and confusions based on aggression, passion, and ignorance. If you lack discipline, life becomes a joke and is not worth living. The accomplishment of discipline is based on renunciation, and renunciation is inspired by experience that is beyond samsara, beyond both the theistic and nontheistic worlds. In Tibetan this is called *ngelek*. *Nge* means "real," "complete," or "true," and *lek* means "good"; so *ngelek* means the "final good."

Discipline is not a dead end. It is not like trying to teach a tree to talk. It is like teaching human beings to talk. Even very young children can already say "Mommy" or "Daddy," and they soon begin to speak our language. Similarly, the shila principle is based on waking up a natural instinct. Basically, discipline always follows the same logic: whether it is at the hinayana, mahayana, or vajrayana level, it is never imposed. Sometimes it may *seem* to be imposed, but we are always dealing with what we intrinsically already have. Through shila, we are aspiring to wake up that intrinsic quality.

Meditation / Samadhi

The second training is samadhi, or absorption. In Tibetan it is *tingdzin*. *Ting* means "still," *dzin* means "holding"; so *tingdzin* means "holding yourself still." With tingdzin, you do not hang on to your particular preconceptions, but develop a state of mind that is clear, precise, and relaxed. Meditation is based on both mindfulness and awareness. Through shamatha (Tib.: *shi-ne*), or mindfulness practice, you develop concentration and one-pointedness, and with *vipashyana* (Tib.: *lhakthong*), or awareness practice, you develop expansiveness, relaxation, and a wider view.* Meditation, or samadhi, is connected with the idea of overcoming the constant search for entertainment. By overcoming that, you begin to cut through the sub-conscious mind, the mind that provides obstacles to meditation practice. Having done so, you begin to develop a state of absorption in the sense of complete presence. You develop a one-hundred-percent experience of being there.

In meditation, you are mixing your mind with the dharma. Once you attain that state of mind, you have no gaps in your mindfulness. You develop the potential of vipashyana as well, because, due to your training, you are so relaxed. You have already been thoroughly broken in, so to speak; therefore, you can hold yourself still, whether you are awake or asleep. You are seeing reality fully through the process of discipline. By means of training in the disciplines of shamatha and vipashyana, you have learned to control your mind. You learn how to evolve further, and not get stuck. You learn how you could be fully there, all the time.

Due to wandering mind, however, we would like to take a break. We would like to lie back, run into our room, and take a few puffs, whatever those puffs may be. A long time ago, I saw in *Time* magazine a photograph of the Dalai Lama holding a bottle of Coca-Cola, with the caption, "The

---

* *Vipashyana* means "clear seeing." Its usage varies considerably, from intellectual analysis, to direct perception, to an open and expansive meditative state. Trungpa Rinpoche also links vipashyana to postmeditation practice and to the cultivation of awareness in everyday life.

Dalai Lama is taking a break with Coca-Cola." I thought to myself, "Taking a break from what?" The notion of taking a break is very popular, actually. We think, "Give me a break!" But the idea of samadhi is meditation from which there is no break. A break is not needed because, in its essence, meditation is already a break from samsara.

Getting into the dharma is the greatest break you could ever think of. With samadhi, you have your break already. You don't need a break from a break; that would be going backward. It would be a pseudo-break, which is hard work. Samadhi does not need any break because it is already a release from pain. It is deliverance, freedom, liberation. It is the sense of fully being there constantly. You are utterly, thoroughly, accurately on the spot all the time, and at the same time you are rejoicing and appreciating the whole thing.

Of course, there is a battle at the beginning and a battle at the end. At the beginning there is resistance to sitting down to meditate; and at the end there is the excitement of getting up and going back to your wicked break. But the sitting practice itself is fine. It is as smooth as the ocean, vast and open. There are lots of waves; nevertheless, it is still. Although big things may be churning around, that is no problem, because there is a sense of being there utterly and fully and acknowledging what is happening.

With samadhi, the practice of absorption, you are entering into a particular world—a full world, a big world, a complete world of meditation. Many students have a problem with that, feeling they are only on the fringe of that world. But you have no reason to believe that you are on the fringe, as long as you carry your body, speech, and mind along with you, which everybody does. There is a feeling of poverty in hanging out on the fringe. Finding yourself on the edge of that big world is self-destructive. The destruction doesn't come from anybody else; it comes from putting yourself on the edge.

If you decide to sit on the wing of an airplane instead of getting inside the cabin, you know what will happen when you take off. You have a ticket that allows you to sit inside—you may even have a first-class seat waiting for you!—but once you are out on the wing, nobody can open the cabin door, because it would be too dangerous for the rest of the passengers. In the state of samadhi, you don't sit on the wing, and you don't have one foot on the inside and one foot on the outside—you have both feet inside, as well as your arms and your head!

When your whole being is inside, you experience totality. There is a feeling of being fully included, and an acknowledgment of your sense of being. The idea of absorption is that you are entering into a fully developed world of samadhi. When you are sitting, you begin to feel there is no other world than that of sitting on your cushion. You are fully there. That is conviction, that is absorption—being fully and utterly there.

If you seek confirmation, saying, "I'm not coming in unless you invite me in, otherwise I'll jump out," that approach is very poor. It is wicked and self-destructive. True confirmation only happens when you are inspired to become a real person, when you follow the teachings and do the work of the Buddha, the fully enlightened one. It can only happen when you see that you can transcend samsaric pain and work for the benefit of others.

Knowledge / Prajna

The third training is knowledge, or prajna. Prajna enables the hinayana practitioner to develop discriminating awareness. With higher prajna, you experience twofold egolessness: the egolessness of self or individuality and the egolessness of dharmas or phenomena.* You see the fruitlessness of carrying around that extra garbage, and you discover that the awareness of what is happening is preferable to always looking for entertainment.

With prajna, your understanding is not theoretical but much more practice oriented and related to your personal experience. Your state of being is an important point of reference, whatever facets of the world you might discover. The same evolutionary process takes place with prajna as with shila and samadhi. The world that you are getting involved in is not a cocoon. You cannot snuggle in and try to make the best of it. You see the entire world with sharpness and clarity. You understand the world's mind, systems, science, and functions completely. You are able to distinguish things as they are.

That kind of clearheadedness takes place all the time, from the time you get up in the morning and go about your business, to when you return to your home and fall asleep. All areas of your life are included in your wakefulness, which you have developed out of shila and samadhi.

---

* The Buddha taught that neither external phenomena nor the self, or ego, have independent inherent existence, and therefore both are empty. This is referred to as "twofold egolessness": the egolessness of self and the egolessness of dharmas.

You are able to look at and experience your life fully, so nothing is missed. Everything has a quality of sharpness and humor, which is a delightful aspect of prajna. With humor, you are awake and interested in everything that goes on, and you are gentle as well.

Since your discriminating awareness covers your entire life, you know exactly what to do. You know how to handle your existence with tremendous humor and precision. So you do not confuse cats with dogs. You do not accept or reject; you simply separate things. When you part your hair, you don't regard one side as bad and the other side as good: you see both sides as your hair. You see everything that way, with precision and accuracy. You know where to draw the line.

The contents of all saddharma are shila, samadhi, and prajna; even single words like *awake, discipline,* or *think* contain shila, samadhi, and prajna. All the dharma that has been taught in the universe has the qualities of these three trainings.

GOOD IN THE BEGINNING, MIDDLE, AND END

Dharma is said to be good at the beginning, good in the middle, and good at the end.

Good in the Beginning

Dharma is good at the beginning because it is fresh thought, inspired by the Buddha. When we first hear the truth, it is fresh. We have never heard it before, and it throws us back a little. We begin to realize that somebody has an entirely different way of looking at the journey, a different way of looking at things as they are. This realization makes us somewhat nervous and concerned, but that is not a big problem. In the process of realizing that there is a different way of looking at things, we may become confused. It is like the old analogy of a parent pointing out the moon to their child, and the child thinking the parent's finger is the moon. That kind of misunderstanding often takes place—in fact, always. We cannot avoid it.

In clarifying misunderstanding, the teacher does not try to explain too much. To avoid misunderstanding, the presentation of the dharma would have to become too complicated. They would have to use too many categories, so that when people had *that* kind of misunderstanding, the teacher could say *this,* and when people had *this* kind of misunderstanding, the teacher could say *that.* It would become completely complicated. Instead, the teacher just gives a hint. It is like showing someone a little corner of a square, which turns out to be a triangle. In studying this triangle, you may say, "I think this came out of a square, but it only has three points, and I have been told that a square has four corners. What about that?" You are completely occupied and at the same time confused. But that confusion is okay—it has some kind of root—so you have to keep tracing back to the original truth. However, in trying to get back to the original truth (the square), you find that since the corners were cut off, it now has more than four corners. So "good at the beginning" is thought provoking.

The dharma is good at the beginning because when you begin to listen to the dharma—the saddharma, rather than any old dharma—it is joyful to listen to. The presentation of dharma does not have to be gloomy or critical. In some theistic traditions, the teachings are meant to inspire guilt and pain. With saddharma, since we are completely free from someone upstairs, since nobody is watching us with a long face, we feel joyful hearing the dharma, because the dharma is truth. It is the people's truth, if I may go so far as to say, rather than hierarchical truth. It is the ultimate democracy. The dharma is joyful to hear because it is humorous and delightful. It makes sense, and it is very, very nice.

Good in the Middle

"Good in the middle" is much more sober and subdued. The dharma is good in the middle because the process goes along in a very ordinary way. You have the sense that you are on a journey. That is your frame of reference. "Good at the beginning" provided inspiration and ground, whereas "good in the middle" is a description of the path itself. The path is straightforward. It is straight and narrow—*very* narrow and *very* straight. The more you realize it, the more straight and narrow it is. It is monotone, somewhat gray. There is not even a yellow line down the middle to entertain you, as on a highway. There are no little garden arrangements on the side or any cities passing by. It is extraordinarily dull and uninviting.

Only people who by unusual circumstances would like to surrender their ego can take part in this particular path. People who do not want to surrender their ego would regard taking part in this path as ludicrous. They would think that you had gone outright mad, which could be true.

That kind of questioning leads you to understand the grayness of the path even more. You realize that dharma is very good, very basic, and very definite. And once you are in that format, so to speak, there is nothing you can do to put a little color into it or little personal touches. If you are bored with mailing your letters, you could occasionally put your stamps on upside down, but on this path such gestures are not allowed.

The dharma is "good in the middle" because it is presented without too much effort. It is presented without the extremes of eternalism or nihilism,* the idea that either everything is eternally good or the idea that everything is fatally bad. Neither of those extremes is included in the presentation of the dharma. Therefore, it is quite reasonable and quite effortless to present.

Good at the End

The dharma is good at the end because it is passionless. It leads us out of our bargaining mentality. We are always making deals, asking, "What am I going to get out of this?" From that point of view, the dharma is very aloof, because there is no deal and you are not going to get anything out of it. Actually, you might get a lot out of it that you don't particularly like. Therefore, the dharma is known as passionless. You are not going to come out like Superman or Wonder Woman—you are going to come out transcending passion.

But passionlessness does not mean that you will have difficulties with your lovers. Passionlessness is the equivalent of a sense of humor. When you have passion, desire, or lust, you don't smile. You make faces and you try to get something, whatever it may be. You are so serious and well meaning. You want to get out of this and into that. But with passionlessness, there is a quality of delight, in which you see everything clearly and face reality with a smile, without kvetching or complaining.

To say that the dharma is good at the end is deceptive, because there is no particular end. The notion of an end is purely a conceptual construct. We think that we are in a present situation, and that when the present situation is over, that will be the end of the present situation and we will be in the future. But it does not work that way—the sense of end contin-

---

* For a discussion on eternalism and nihilism, see chapter 54, "The Development of Set Patterns."

ues. Another way to understand it is that the middle has an aspect of the end at the same time. In particular, nobody is supposed to give a pitch, to publicize, or to advertise, the enormous and dramatic possibility of your becoming enlightened on the spot—or even later on. It has been suggested that doing so is not a good idea, and we are following that tradition. We have been receiving that instruction for over twenty-six hundred years of Buddhist tradition, and it is a very tall order. One could say that dharma is the realization of one's nature, but that sounds extraordinarily corny, so let me rephrase it: dharma is the realization that ending is not possible. You cannot just give up and find salvation: there is no end, and nobody is going to be saved. You still have to sit on your depression and your little pain or bigger pain. And usually when pain is smaller, it seems much bigger. So good at the end is somewhat fuzzy, but that seems to be okay.

Profundity and Vastness

The dharma is both profound and vast. It is profound because it penetrates your system, your whole being. It is vast because when you think that you have experienced the truth, you realize that this truth means much more to you than you had expected. Something might be profound but not necessarily vast, so the sense of vastness is important to understand, although you sometimes lose that point. You might not have achieved one-pointedness and profundity, and you might lose the implication behind the whole thing—so you have to stay awake, open, humorous, and committed.

To run through all this once again: the dharma itself is true. Saddharma, or true dharma, consists of three trainings: shila, samadhi, and prajna. By the practice of discipline, or shila, you learn to hold yourself together; on that basis, you can attain a state of meditation, or samadhi; and out of that, through the development of knowledge, or prajna, you can analyze the situation as it should be. The presentation of the saddharma is well said; it is free from the kleshas of the three worlds. The dharma is experienced by the threefold logic of personal experience, theory, and confirmation. Therefore, it is heard fully and properly. When you hear the dharma, in the beginning it is joyful; in the middle it is simple and true; in the end it transcends passion. Finally, the dharma is both profound and vast. These definitions apply to all three *yanas*, or vehicles—the hinayana, mahayana, and vajrayana—all the way through.

Ten Definitions of Dharma

If you understand what dharma means and what dharma does, that will help solve a lot of problems later on, so you do not have to go backward again and again. There are ten traditional definitions of dharma: dharma is what is knowable; dharma is the path; dharma is freedom from pain; dharma is the perception of mind; dharma is a sense of reward; dharma is a sense of time; dharma is doctrine; dharma is a complete true message; dharma is prediction or prophesying; and lastly, dharma is particular religious beliefs.

You could use the word *dharma* for all of those meanings. Nine of those ten definitions refer to the common meanings of the term *dharma*. They are very personally oriented, based on things like finding salvation, extending the life span, or telling the future. The only definition that refers to the buddhadharma, or saddharma, is the tenth one, which refers to doctrine in the sense of a religious sect. That notion of doctrine could be said to be the true dharma.

Sutras and Shastras

Saddharma, or buddhadharma, usually appears in two types of literature: *sutras* and *shastras*. The first type, sutras, refers to what the Buddha himself taught. The Sanskrit word *sutra* means "thread," as in a thread that holds things together. The Tibetan word for sutra is *do* (pronounced like the first syllable of *donut*), which means "junction," or "confluence." It is where things meet, like the confluence of rivers. So a sutra is where teacher and student meet. Sutras are the place where the teachings of the Buddha and the minds of common people meet and begin to make sense. When two big rivers emerge from two big valleys and meet, the two big rivers become an even bigger river. That sense of things reaching a greater scale is sutra. Sutras are considered to be one of the three components of the Buddha's teachings, called the *Tripitaka*, or "three baskets." Altogether, the Tripitaka is comprised of the *vinaya*, or teachings on monastic discipline; the sutras, or dialogues of the Buddha; and the *abhidharma*, or teachings on Buddhist psychology.

The second type of literature is known as shastras, which are the work of the students of the Buddha, the scholars and practitioners of Buddhism.

*The Jewel Ornament of Liberation** and the *Bodhicharyavatara*[†] are regarded as shastras because they were written by disciples, whereas the *Heart Sutra,*[‡] or *Prajnaparamita Hridaya Sutra* in Sanskrit, is regarded as a sutra because the event is said to have taken place at the very moment of time as the Buddha himself. Sutras and shastras are the two major categories of Buddhist literature that have been presented and are available to us.

There are various ways of describing the qualities of sutras and shastras. We could focus on how the dharma is presented. First, since neither the Buddha nor his disciples are neurotic, since they are free of kleshas, the dharma is presented properly, fully, and completely. Secondly, the dharma is always said for the benefit of sentient beings; teachers wouldn't just say it to themselves. Thirdly, teachers don't just say it occasionally; they say it always. Because teachers have a sense of duty and of mindfulness, their teachings are continuous. Fourthly, there is no way that the instructors would hide anything they have taught. Nothing is hidden or kept secret from their students; everything is kept open. Finally, the dharma is always workable; it is presented in accord with the students' mental capabilities. That is the kind of dharma taught in the sutras and shastras, and we are manifesting it in that way ourselves.

Information and Understanding

INFORMATION / LUNG. The dharma leads to both information and understanding. What has been told to you or presented in books and scriptures is referred to as "information," or lung. It has four subcategories.

- *The subject is meaningful.* Dharmic conversation or literature is meaningful in that it applies to your personal journey on the path.
- *The language is clear.* The dharma is presented in good clear language that is perfectly understandable. There are no side effects or impurities.

---

* Gampopa, *The Jewel Ornament of Liberation,* ed. Ani K. Trinlau Chödron, trans. Khenpo Konchog Gyaltsen Rinpoche (Ithaca, N.Y.: Snow Lion Publications, 1998).

† Shantideva, *The Way of the Bodhisattva,* trans. Padmakara Translation Group (Boston: Shambhala Publications, 1997).

‡ Nalanda Translation Committee, *The Sutra of the Heart of Transcendent Knowledge* (Halifax: Nalanda Translation Committee, 1978).

- *It transcends confusion.* Reading dharmic literature helps you to transcend any distortions or confusions in your understanding of dharma. It helps you transcend the three worlds: the world of desire, the world of the form gods, and the world of the formless gods. The world of desire is the world you exist in, which includes your physical hang-ups and domestic problems. The world of form gods is the world that exists in you: it is your spiritual, ethereal understanding about things. The world of formless gods is your greater expectations of how things should be fulfilled; it is your personally highest level of spiritual practice. All three worlds can be transcended by means of dharmic literature.
- *It leads to gentleness.* Reading such literature, you gradually develop understanding and gentleness. There is a change in your personality, in that you have less aggression, less complaining, less dog fighting, and less exuberance for making yourself into a guru or a hero.

UNDERSTANDING / TOKPA. What you actually understand is called *tokpa*. *Tokpa* means "realization," "understanding," or "experience." Tokpa is what all the literature is supposed to bring about: it is the effect. Tokpa is the result of reading books in which the contents are good, the presentation is spotless, and the reading helps you transcend the three worlds and gives you peace. Reading such literature begins to bring about discipline, meditation, and knowledge. Lung and tokpa always work together.

The Five Songs of Dharma

The dharma is also referred to in terms of five songs or melodies: it is like thunder, it is like a flute, it is soothing, it is clarifying, and it is never contradictory. The first melody is deep as thunder because when dharma is proclaimed, it shakes the basic ego-structure. The second melody is like a flute because the dharma takes your discursive thoughts and perverted views, which are usually rather ugly, and changes them into a more romantic, melodic, and melancholy tune. The third melody is soothing to your mind because the dharma speaks to the different levels of your mind. The fourth melody is clarifying because the dharma clears your mind and provides insight. The fifth melody is never contradictory because the logic of the dharma is not contradictory, no matter who listens to it. Those are the five melodies of dharma.

In the Buddhist tradition, listening to and understanding the dharma is not considered to be particularly jarring to a student's understanding or personal behavior; nonetheless, it is cutting. Dharma is cutting if you think you can contradict it. For example, you might believe that there should be ego, and in Buddhism we say that there is no ego, so there is a big battle and you are in conflict. Such conflict is not particularly melodic or accommodating. The message of egolessness would come under the category of thunder: when thunder resounds, the earth shakes. The message of nontheism would be at the level of thunder as well, because theism is the same as egohood, at least to some people's way of thinking.

When students present complaints or resistance to the dharma, that means they already have a faint suspicion that the dharma might go against their wishes. They feel there might be a presentation of dharma that does not agree with what they would like to see presented as dharma. The presentation of dharma has gone along with what those students expected; nonetheless, it is jarring, because the students do not want to hear what they are hearing.

The presentation of dharma should be very simple and workable. It should be somewhat elementary, not out of disrespect for the audience, but out of respect for the simplicity of the dharma. You could appreciate the simplicity of dharma in the same way you might appreciate a Ming vase or jade cup. A Ming vase is so well made and so simple, and you appreciate that simplicity. It doesn't need to have any complications. Dharma is like that: it is so good and precious and lovely.

In studying the dharma, we are studying our complexity and simplicity put together. We are studying dark and light, speed and slowness, thoroughness and sloppiness put together. Dharma is like going through a traffic jam with red and yellow stoplights. We have to sort out all the possibilities. We have to understand pain and pleasure. We have to understand the meaning of anger, joy, and jealousy. We have to understand who we are. We have to learn to read the alphabet of our life. I am sorry to be like a schoolteacher, but we have to know how to add and subtract, how to wash our dishes, and how to sit on our potties. We have to learn how to walk and how to talk. We have to see the difference between green, yellow, black, white, and red. We have to learn how to protect ourselves so that we don't hurt ourselves crossing the street. That is dharma: basic reality. It is very elementary, Watson. We are just being. We are learning how to live our life. We are protecting our being so that we can help others and build an enlightened world.

5

Joining Study and Practice

Intellect and intuition both play an important role, so you cannot negate either of them. You cannot purely rely on meditation practice alone, without experiencing a sharpening of your basic intelligence, and in order to understand the sense behind the words, you have to have personal meditative experience. So those two approaches are complementary.

B UDDHIST TRAINING combines meditation and study. Throughout the path, learning and comprehending basic Buddhist teachings is as important as meditation practice. Since you are not going to spend all your time alone, all by yourself, you should be thinking in terms of helping others sooner or later. In fact, you should expect it. And in order to help others, study is important. For some practitioners, intellect is regarded as secondary and rather worldly. Such practitioners just sit and practice meditation in a purely intuitive style. But intellect and intuition both play an important role, so you cannot negate either of them. You cannot purely rely on meditation practice alone; you also need to sharpen your basic intelligence, and in order to understand the sense behind the words, you have to have personal meditative experience. So those two approaches are complementary.

Learning and practice are the essence of the Buddhist way. The mark of practice is a lessening of the kleshas, or neurotic thought-patterns. In mindfulness practice, your concentration is a very thin, sturdy wire going through all your clouds of thoughts. The practice of going back to the breath, back to reality, is taking place all the time. So it is very necessary for you to practice mindfulness utterly and completely.

The mark of learning is gentleness. It is being tame and peaceful. So learning is not purely academic. Proper learning requires an attitude in which you are not intimidated by the presentation of Buddhism. You are neither too enthusiastic about understanding Buddhism nor are you too disinterested. You might think, "I couldn't care less about scholarship. I just want to sit and make myself a good Buddhist." But that's not quite possible. You cannot become a real, good, enlightened person if you do not understand what your life is all about. With gentleness, what you study becomes part of your psychological geography. You can understand topics fully and thoroughly without having to push. You can know what Buddhism is all about, and you can have some understanding of where things fit within this big soup of Buddhist intellect.

How to be in your life is meditation practice; how to understand your life is scholarship. That combination comes up in ordinary life as well. For instance, eating food is meditation practice, and talking about how to cook that food is scholarship. So those two factors work together. If you rely on sitting practice alone, quite possibly you could become just a stupid meditator. But if you study too much and don't meditate enough, you could become busy-stupid, without any essence or purpose to your life. So both sides are important, both the heart and the brain.

The great Buddhist educational institutions of the past like Nalanda University, Vikramashila University, and Samye Monastery* developed the educational approach called turning the three wheels: the wheel of meditation, the wheel of study, and the wheel of activity. Those three principles are constantly interlinked—they are the wheels that carry you on the path of enlightenment. Buddhist teaching deals with your own basic being. Nothing is regarded as a foreign element or non-Buddhist. Whatever the subject matter, the object of learning is to develop a higher, more sophisticated way of thinking and of viewing the world. The object is to produce scholars who are at the same time great yogis. By studying and practicing properly, you could influence yourself and your fellow sentient beings. That seems to be much more compassionate than simply

---

* Nalanda and Vikramashila Universities were centers of Buddhist and worldly studies in North India. Samye Monastery is said to be Tibet's first monastery and university.

snatching up knowledge or running into the mountains and finding yourself enlightened.

The Buddha had a basic Indian secular education and he had knowledge of Hinduism, but that was simply his cultural heritage. In essence, Buddha's mind is enlightened mind. When such a mind speaks, it is almost inconceivable for ordinary people. It cannot be compared with even the greatest wisdom of Western psychologists or scholars. The mind of the Buddha is sophisticated, spontaneous, and vast.

The Buddha's learning is inconceivable. The Buddha knows the best way to boil an egg, as well as how to develop enlightenment on the spot. His mind encompasses everything. Such a mind is not divided into intuition and intellect. However, what Buddha taught has been categorized. His disciples wrote down everything he said, so the Buddha's teachings have been passed on. At one of the early sangha conferences, his disciples decided to categorize the Buddha's teachings into vinaya, sutras, and abhidharma: monastic vows and discipline, discourses and dialogues, and philosophy and psychology. However, those categories are simply different aspects of the mind of the Enlightened One.

Proper training consists of practice and study put together. When you practice properly, you also begin to develop a state of mind that allows you to study properly. This twofold system of study and practice is very, very old. We used this system in Tibet, and it was also used quite a lot in India. Traditional monastic discipline consisted of alternating periods of practice and study. Nalanda University and Vikramashila University, among others, used this twofold system to train people's minds and at the same time develop their intellects. In turn, those ancient centers of learning produced great teachers and scholars like Padmasambhava, Atisha, and Naropa. Maybe you could be one of those people!

Usually when you go to a college or university, you cannot study properly because you are always being interrupted by your own subconscious gossip, your own background noise, and the feedback of your own neurosis. You have problems learning because so much interference and so many interruptions are taking place. An ideal educational system allows for a period of time in which you can simply work with your state of mind. Then when you are ready for it—and even if you think you are not—you have a period of time in which to launch into study. In that way, you can actually grasp what you have been studying and practicing. You can learn about yourself and your mind, and you can learn about how things work in your life and in your world. Elucidating those things is what the study of the Buddhist path is all about. Learnedness is not enough. You should practice what you preach, take your own medicine.

Buddhist education is based on what is known as threefold logic, the threefold thought process of ground, path, and fruition. Threefold logic is very simple and straightforward; however, as you get into more difficult subjects, it becomes more subtle and complex. An example of threefold logic is:

Since I saw a completely blue sky this morning (ground),
It is going to be a sunny day (path);
It is definitely going to be a hot one (fruition).

In this example, the ground is blue sky, the path is sunny day, and the fruition is a hot day. So threefold logic is very simple: it is the process of coming to a conclusion.*

THE ROLE OF PRACTICE

The discipline of mindfulness, or shamatha, should combine practice and study in the fullest sense. Shamatha is not related with sitting practice alone; it is also connected with how we learn and absorb the teachings of the Buddha intellectually. Shamatha practitioners are able to understand the technical information taught by the Buddha; they are able to hear the dharma. So shamatha is an intellectual tool as well as a practice tool. Shamatha is an intellectual tool because it allows us to hear the dharma very clearly; it is a practice tool because it allows us to quell mental disorder. When we have no mental disorder, we are able to learn. Therefore, dwelling in the peace of shamatha discipline is necessary for both study and practice. However, by peace we do not necessarily mean tranquillity or bliss. In shamatha, peace is orderly comfortableness. It is orderly because the environment is right; it is comfortable because you are using the right technique to control your body, speech, and mind. Therefore, fundamental decency takes place. In short, shamatha could be referred to as that which cools off intellectual obscurations and psychological disorders.

---

* For further discussion of threefold logic, see appendix 2.

Shamatha is the beginning of the beginning of how to become a practicing Buddhist.* Shamatha practice is essential. Unfortunately, many Tibetan teachers teaching in the West do not emphasize shamatha practice. Perhaps this is because in Tibetan culture, when people requested training, they had already been raised in a Buddhist nation by Buddhist parents, so they were familiar with mind training as a natural process. But according to everything in the Buddha's hinayana, mahayana, and vajrayana teachings, there are no other options. The only possibility is to begin at the beginning, and the one and only way to do so is through shamatha discipline. Therefore, we have to get a grasp on the teaching of shamatha, and understand that discipline as much as we can.

Thinking Dharmically

Dharma is not once removed. You start from the immediate situation, your mind and body, and you work with what you have. You start with sitting practice and with your pain and anxiety. That's good! That's the best! It is like the fuse of a cannon, which first hisses, then goes *boom!* You can't make a fuse out of crude gunpowder. It has to be ground into refined gunpowder in order to coat the fuse and ignite the cannon. In the case of shamatha practice, basic anxiety becomes the refined gunpowder that allows you to set a torch to ego-clinging so that your cannon can go *boom!*

There is no medicine, no surgery that will make it easy for you to study and practice the dharma. It is hard. However, once you realize it is hard, it becomes easy. Practice instructions do not come along with suggestions such as "Take two aspirins, and then you can do it" or "Have a few shots of Johnnie Walker Black so that you can jump in." Advice like that doesn't help. You just have to do it. There is no service that helps you to get into dharma practice easily—if there were, it would be terrible. That would not be true dharma, because you would not have to sacrifice even one inch, one discursive thought. You would be blissed-out on the dharma, or on enlightenment, which is impossible. In true dharma, hard work and really diving into it bring further cheerfulness. You realize that

---

* Although in this case Trungpa Rinpoche emphasizes shamatha as the starting point on the path of meditation, in later discussions he points out that shamatha remains an essential practice from the beginning of the path to the very end.

you have dived in and you have no other choice—but it feels so good to do that.

We practice meditation so that our mind may be one with the dharma. Becoming one with the dharma means that whatever you think, any flicker of thought that occurs, becomes a dharmic thought. That is why we practice meditation, so that our mind could become like that. When your mind is one with the dharma, you don't have to say, "Now I'm being bad and now I'm being good" or "Now I can switch into being either wicked or good." If your mind has become one with the dharma, you naturally begin to think dharmically.

Thinking dharmically does not mean you always think religious thoughts or that you become a holy man or a holy woman, a monk or a nun. It means that you become a mindful person. You watch every step that happens to you. You are trying to be a decent lady or gentleman of the world. Being one with the dharma is based on natural ethics. You don't do things at the wrong time or in the wrong way, and you don't mix good and bad together. You have respect for the world as well as for your own mind and body and their synchronization. You have respect for your family, for your husband or wife, and your children, if you have any. One of the fundamental obstacles to becoming one with the dharma is the delusion, anxiety, and ignorance that result from samsaric neurosis. In order to overcome that obstacle, it is necessary to practice shamatha, and in order to practice shamatha, you need to reorganize your life.

Buddha said that the dharma should be an antidote for desire, that dharma means taming the mind and being free from desire. Where did desire come from and what has to be tamed? Desire is anything that causes us to look for something other than what we normally perceive. In contrast, normal perception is just a simple business affair. We are simply seeing red, simply seeing green, simply seeing white. We are simply drinking a hot cup of tea, as opposed to looking for something to help us cure our pain, ease our loneliness, or fulfill our passion or aggression. Desire is the excess baggage of mind. So in order to tame desire, the mind has to be tamed. Therefore, sitting practice is known as the practice of taming: we are taming ourselves.

6

Achieving Sanity Here on Earth

With discriminating awareness, comforts of all kinds, including the religious experiences of spiritual materialism, begin to turn into something else. We begin to feel that we are engaged in a much more profound project—a project that has depth and brilliance. When we realize that, we are no longer spiritual materialists.

THE IMPORTANCE OF INTELLECT

In order to understand dharma, we need to develop intellect, or prajna. It is the starting point of the hinayana path. Prajna enables us to discriminate dharmas. By doing so, we can also see the true dharma in its own purest sense. There are two types of prajna: lower prajna and higher prajna. With lower prajna, we see ordinary reality. When you say, "I'm thirsty, I need water to drink" or "I feel cold, I have to turn up the heat," lower dharma is being perceived by lower prajna. It is very basic and ordinary. With higher prajna and higher dharma, you might say, "I need water because I'm thirsty. But why am I thirsty?" or "Why am I nervous, and why do I need relief from my nervousness?" or "I'm here, sitting on my meditation cushion, but why am I doing that? What makes me do such a thing at all?" That is a slightly higher level of prajna, a more psychologically oriented prajna.

In the hinayana tradition, what we are trying to do is to cultivate the higher level of dharma by means of the higher level of prajna, known as the prajna of discriminating awareness. You might wonder what is so high about that. It seems to be just slightly better than ordinary. But if you think about it, it is very high when you begin to tune your mind in to a psychological approach to reality. The Tibetan for discriminating-awareness knowledge is *chö raptu nampar jepa sherap. Chö* means "dharma," *raptu* means "very," or "profoundly," *nampar* means "completely," *jepa* means "separating," or "qualifying," *sherap* means "prajna," or knowledge; so *chö raptu nampar jepa sherap* means "prajna that enables you actually to separate dharmas one from the other." That is to say, you are able to distinguish the dharmas, or norms, that exist in your ordinary, everyday life.

Because you are able to separate one factor from another, completely and fully, you have an understanding as to how to work with ordinary problems, such as washing up your dishes. You also realize that certain problems are not workable without studying Buddhism properly under an appropriate teacher and within a sangha. That may sound impressive, but it is still only higher-level babyhood. Instead of just jumping at the mother's nipple, the baby has enough intelligence and physical coordination to be spoon-fed solid food.

The psychological approach has much more profundity than the impulsive, or animal-level approach. There is no religion and no spirituality in the purely functional approach. The notion of spirituality comes into the picture when we begin to relate to more than just our needs, more than just the problems at hand. That is precisely why Western psychology is turning to Buddhism. With discriminating awareness, comforts of all kinds, including the religious experiences of spiritual materialism, begin to turn into something else. We begin to feel that we are engaged in a much more profound project—a project that has depth and brilliance. When we realize that, we are no longer spiritual materialists, using spirituality only as a means of comfort or self-confirmation.

You can't be a Buddhist if you think in a naive way that the height of living is if your vacuum cleaner is working or if you are rich enough to pay off your bills. Moreover, you can't be a Buddhist if you keep looking for different means of comfort. Spiritual comforts, such as twenty minutes of soothing meditation, may make you feel happy, carefree, gleamy, or euphoric, but that's it. That's the end of it. It is naive to approach spirituality as another way of looking for comfort in one's life.

The psychological approach of actually being able to see what you are doing and what you are up to is very important. It is the foundation. You need to be able to extend your intelligence further in order to reveal the higher dharma that exists in our ordinary, everyday life. With the higher prajna of discriminating-awareness knowledge, you are able to distinguish which part of your being is purely seeking various subtle levels of comfort and pleasure and warding off hassles, and which part is not able to, and is not particularly interested in, warding off hassles, but wants to get into the depth of the depth of your profundity. At that point, Buddhism begins to happen.

What Buddha said at the very beginning was that it is very necessary for you to be intelligent about what you are doing. Lack of intelligence is one of the most significant problems in spirituality or religion. Buddha's statement that you have to be intelligent about what you are doing and about your commitment to spirituality automatically brings up the notion of nontheism. If you are getting into the true dharma, you have to check out your own psychological setup, first of all. You cannot simply trust somebody's blessing or magical power. You have to understand that your wretched setup is not so great, not so fantastic. That approach automatically eliminates the possibility of worshiping God, Brahma, or any other deity. All of that must go. You no longer worship your own emotionalized anything-at-all. You simply relate to your immediate psychological surroundings. You have to make that the important point. You no longer worship anybody or try to gain magical powers, so you are stuck with what you are—your existence, your livelihood, your everything.

In the theistic approach to dharma, the object is to achieve eternity and avoid the possibility of death. The basis for doing so is the belief in your own existence. But you then need someone else to confirm your existence—and conveniently, you find a friend. As Christopher Robin says in *Now We Are Six*,* "Binker's always Binker, and is certain to be there." Unlike Christopher Robin's imaginary friend Binker, however, this friend does not actually babysit you—rather, you babysit him, her, or it. The idea of such a babysitter appears in different traditions and cultures under different names, such as Amaterasu Omi Kami,† Jehovah, or Brahma. The names of the babysitter cannot all be spoken, there are too many of them. The discovery of a being who constantly cares for us, loves us, and creates things for us, including our own plastic toys, is a convenient trick of theism. The problem with that approach is that we are constantly preoc-

---

* A. A. Milne, *Now We Are Six* (New York: E. P. Dutton, 1961).

† "The one who makes the heavens shine." The Shinto goddess of the sun.

cupied with *that,* so we begin to forget *this,* meaning ourselves. We feel that we do not have to look into ourselves.

In the nontheistic approach, sacredness does not have to descend upon us or be exported from Mount Sinai or Mount Kailash. We are not dependent on local deities; we depend only on ourselves. That is why individual salvation is such a key idea. If you wonder why you go about things the wrong way, you need to ask yourself. When you do, you find that fundamentally, you don't want to wake up. You prefer to sleep, which seems much more enjoyable and less painful. But trying to maintain that sleep becomes a terrible burden, and trying to act according to social norms becomes a burden, as well. Truth is what actually happens—so avoiding the truth, or approaching the truth philosophically as a way to detour around it, takes a lot of work. It is quite ludicrous.

There is a traditional four-line chant attributed to the great Kagyü teacher Gampopa, called the Four Dharmas of Gampopa, that goes:

Grant your blessing so that my mind may be one with the dharma.
Grant your blessing so that dharma may progress along the path.
Grant your blessing so that the path may clarify confusion.
Grant your blessing so that confusion may dawn as wisdom.

In this chant, it is said that your mind should be one with the dharma. You individually are trying to mix your stream of being, your mind, with the dharma. You find dharma in yourself, in what you are, so your understanding of the dharma and your experience of it become a part of you. True dharma is found within your lifestyle, within your pain and within your pleasure. Rather than being something external, truth is within you constantly. You do not have to bring somebody else's style into your being—your style is the style of a buddha. If you work fully and thoroughly, if you look into yourself completely, you find individual salvation within you—you become buddha. The nontheistic approach is very simple and compassionate: you take a stand on giving up your trip and you do it. It's as simple as peanut butter.

NONTHEISTIC DHARMA

Nontheistic dharma can be divided into four aspects: view, practice, action, and result.

View: The Four Norms of Dharma

The first aspect of nontheistic dharma, view, includes the four norms of dharma: impermanence, suffering, egolessness, and peace.*

IMPERMANENCE. The first norm of nontheistic dharma is that all things are subject to impermanence. The theistic approach is to see the universe and oneself as creations that are everlasting and eternal. You look for ways to avoid death. The death of Christ is not accepted, and the doctrine of resurrection gives you the hope that you could sneak out of your coffin and exist eternally. The reality of decaying and dying is not acknowledged and causes tremendous fear, but in fact, nothing lasts. At the cosmological level things don't exist. They just disappear. So there is nothing to hang onto and nothing to fight. There is no Kingdom of God or Eternal Jerusalem. Things just begin to lift. And when they go, they are gone completely.

SUFFERING. The second norm of nontheistic dharma is that everything is suffering. The theistic approach is based on the possibility of enjoyment. You keep trying to get a rush of goodness or a zap of pleasure, so you chant more and more or inhale more and more. But you do not see that such a merchandise approach to spiritual practice only brings suffering. Even while you are enjoying a seemingly pleasurable experience, there is always an edge. When that happens you tend to blame yourself, saying, "I'm not relaxed enough. If I were relaxed and knew how to enjoy myself, I would have a good time. I'll try again next time." But somehow that next time never comes to anybody. Nobody in history has ever had any real satisfaction out of anything. You could write books about how fantastic a certain situation was, but if you examine your state of mind on the spot, although you are having a great time and enjoying yourself, you find that there is a tremendous edge to it. You discover that you are cheating yourself rather than actually enjoying anything. In the samsaric world there is no such thing as enjoyment at all. There is no enjoyment whatsoever.

EGOLESSNESS. The third norm of nontheistic dharma is that all dharmas are egoless. That experience of egolessness is something the theistic

---

* This list of four was discussed in chapter 3 as well, in the context of the general hinayana view of the world, referred to as the four marks of view.

approach rejects altogether. You do not want to supersede your practice with egolessness. Instead, you pursue your spiritual discipline in accordance with your ego ambition to reach the highest level of samsara—the realm of the gods.* By means of meditative absorptions, or jhanas, you hope to reach the highest levels of the god realm. But in the nontheistic approach, samadhi, or meditation, is simply clear thinking. In samadhi, you can be absorbed in clarity and ordinariness.

PEACE. The fourth norm of nontheistic dharma is peace, or relief. On the nontheistic path, step-by-step, every minute, you are giving up pain and developing peace. The theistic approach to peace is to cultivate tranquillity or euphoria. But for nontheists, peace is the absence of pain and grasping—it is the absence of everything. The process of things dropping away is peace. When you begin to draw away from ego hang-ups, there is peace. You discover that at the beginning there is blue sky.

The four norms of nontheistic dharma have to do with how to view reality. According to these four norms: reality is impermanence; reality is suffering; reality is egolessness; and reality is peace. This kind of reality is very basic reality. When you pick up your spoon before you eat food, the meeting together of the spoon, your food, and your hand speaks of that very truth of impermanence, suffering, egolessness, and peace, all happening at the same time. When you are sitting on your toilet seat, that process contains impermanence, suffering, egolessness, and peace. Very ordinary, simple things like opening a door—touching the door handle, turning it, pulling the door open, opening it wider, and walking through—contain impermanence, suffering, egolessness, and peace. Everything we do in our everyday life—snap our fingers, hiccup, sneeze, fart, or burp—contains these four norms of dharma.

In working with the four norms, we are not looking at them only from the point of view of following what we have been taught. We have been given the suggestion to think twice. At first, the whole idea of egolessness and peace may be absurd, but if you think twice, it becomes a reality. That is called renunciation. The idea is not to manipulate you into seeing things

---

* The *realm of the gods* is said to be the highest of the six samsaric realms: the realms of hell, hungry ghosts, animals, human beings, jealous gods, and gods. For more on the realms, see chapter 9.

in this way, and seeing in this way is not based on the confirmation of traditional theistic scriptures or teachers. Instead, strangely enough, these suggestions are designed to keep you away from such teachers or from any kind of authority. Although the first and the second norms could be taught by a theistic teacher, the third and fourth norms could not, because if you want to achieve egolessness and peace, you have to think for yourself, without any help. That's where the double twist comes in.

To review, at the level of higher prajna, dharmas are seen in four ways: as impermanence, suffering, egolessness, and peace. They are seen as both possibilities and problems. Looking at the first two, impermanence and suffering, you begin to realize that everything altogether is marked by overwhelming suffering. With the third, you realize that there is no one to suffer, because of egolessness. That takes care of having a grudge or being angry at anybody. And in the end, with the fourth norm, you realize that nothing exists but peace, which is vacant. You see that peace does not simply mean having a peaceful state of mind—it means that everything is wiped out altogether. It is quite a clever thought. Those are the four norms in a nutshell.

Practice: Meditation Transcending Spirituality

The second aspect of nontheistic dharma is *gompa,* which means "meditation practice." Any meditation practice we might be doing, such as shamatha-vipashyana practice, should transcend even the highest concept of spirituality. Both the ordinary lower-level world and the so-called "spiritual," or higher-level, world, are very materialistic—and meditation practice should be able to go beyond that. In meditation we are not trying to overcome or to defeat anything, and we are not trying to gain any level of high spiritual achievement for the sake of pleasure. Since the practice of meditation is not at all geared to pleasure, its achievement should also be beyond pleasure—and since it transcends pleasure, it also transcends pain. But transcending pain and developing peace are by-products of meditation practice rather than an immediate aim.

The spiritual goal of theism is to reach the highest possibility of the world's best idea. It is based on ideals such as becoming godly or reuniting with Brahma. The problem with such ideals is that there is no surrendering involved. You simply think that God is going to tuck you under his arm, saying, "My children, come along and join us at the top of the mountain. The kingdom of God is all around you. Let me present it to you. Take it, please." Actually, nontheists would like that as well. We all wish to be taken care of. We wish we could have practices, prayers, mantras, and chants that simply say, "Please accept me. Take me under your wing." But somehow that seems to go against the grain. There is no personal sacrifice in that kind of practice.

In the nontheistic tradition, the fundamental sacrifice is that your particular desires, your particular style, and your particular wishes are not being bought or accepted. However, at the same time, beyond that there is something that can be accommodated. You begin to discover your hollowness, your nonexistence, which could be the key. That discovery is free from ignorance. It is genuine and worthwhile. With that key, you are able to avoid the absorption of the realm of the gods. The practices of the Buddhist nontheistic tradition, such as shamatha-vipashyana, are deliberately designed to continually boycott any such conspiracy.

Theistic traditions also encourage you to go against your worldly desires, and the means to that end can be very orthodox and harsh. But that approach—and even the alternative, the yearning for the ultimate possibility of opening up—is still samsaric. It is the best and highest of the samsaric approaches, the most mannerly, the most refined, even kingly. The problem with that approach is that it has been corrupted by the good news that you can hold and cherish your particular ego, that you can possess your worldly and spiritual desires. So although becoming part of such a kingdom seems to require a lot of sacrifice, you inevitably find yourself agreeing with the corruption.

Action: Beyond the Extremes of Austerity or Indulgence

The third aspect of nontheistic dharma is action. Jamgön Kongtrül, the great master of the *Ri-me*, or nonsectarian tradition, said that your actions should transcend the extremes of austerity and indulgence. Examples of extreme austerity practices include eating no food, traditional Indian practices such as scorching yourself by surrounding yourself with bonfires, or simply giving yourself pain. The other extreme, that of extreme indulgence, involves completely immersing yourself in the highest levels of pleasure and euphoria spiritually, physically, or otherwise. The Buddhist path transcends those two extremes. There is a quality of moderation and celebration.

The nontheistic approach to action is based on Buddha's words to his close disciple and personal attendant Ananda: "If there is no food, there is no body. If there is no body, there is no livelihood. If there is no livelihood, there is no dharma. If there is no dharma, there is no enlightenment." We take care of our whole being. We are not trying to punish ourselves or indulge ourselves. We keep our discipline quite tight, but at the same time we eat good food, we wear good clothes, we sleep well, we breathe well, and we act decently. We are encouraged to be sane.

Result: Having Nothing to Give Up

The fourth aspect of nontheistic dharma is the result—having nothing to give up. Actually, everything just goes away rather than having to be given up, so the idea of giving up does not really apply. You begin to realize that the neurosis you are still trying to ward off is not happening anymore; it has just gone away. This happens naturally because of the very fact that you have practiced beyond any theistic or spiritually materialistic fashion. Therefore, you have found the best of the best of spiritual disciplines. Because of that, you find that all the so-called nuisances you used to have, have just gone away, rather than being given up.

Giving up things can become simply another way of feeding the ego. People survive on that all the time, by warding off some things and latching onto others. You might latch onto God to help you give up your problems, and when you give up alcoholism, smoking cigarettes, nymphomania, or whatever, you feel purified. It feels great! But *you* gave them up; they didn't just go. Because of that, they are going to come back. According to theism, you are threatened by the "forces of evil," by temptations of all kinds. But according to nontheism, evil does not exist and temptation does not exist. According to Buddhism, you yourself are the tempter. The situation does nothing but lift you up. So you don't particularly have to engage in warfare within a divine hierarchy. Things go up and things come down, but basically things lift themselves up. It's like the end of the rainy season: you still see dark clouds, but there's a little brightness in the sky. The clouds begin to lift, rather than you pushing them up.

The result of nontheism is liberation. But that liberation is not based on trying to race to heaven after your death—it is based on achieving fundamental sanity here on earth. Some traditions talk about the reward that comes when you get to know him or her. When you have been saved, it is said that you are given red-carpet service and invited to hang out in heaven eternally, which could be extremely boring. However, because you do not understand or believe in egolessness, this kind of earthly or heavenly VIP treatment eventually breaks down and bounces back on you.

There are two ways of relating to the notion of attainment: we could enter into reality, or we could enter into a dream world. If we think that the dharma comes from outside, from God or Brahma, we cannot let our whole being enter into the dharma. We can't get thoroughly soaked in it, because it feels like we are trying to relate with foreigners. But in the case of nontheism, we are simply trying to relate with ourselves, so there is very little distance. Nontheism is based on personal experience. We feel that we have actually experienced reality, that we have experienced the truth. We have learned how to go about opening ourselves fully and completely. That makes the whole thing very real and full.

To review, having developed the nontheistic view, you develop a meditation practice that transcends the highest euphoria of spirituality as well as ordinary worldly materialism. Then you develop action that transcends the extremes of asceticism and indulgence. You practice the middle way. Having done all that, the result is that you have nothing to give up—everything just goes. Without your having to give them up or push them out, obstacles begin to lift. We could repeat again and again—at the hinayana level, the mahayana level, and the vajrayana level—the view of the four norms of dharma, the practice that transcends worldly concepts, the action that is beyond extremes, and the result that the obstacles remove themselves.

7

The Path, the Vehicle, and the Traveler

In the midst of this samsaric countryside, a path has been cut,
which we might call the spiritual path. Once the path has been pre-
pared for us, once it has been cut and laid out, with an occasional
bridge or tunnel, we need to have some form of vehicle by which to
travel along that path. That vehicle is the body of the teachings. . . .
The sophistication of a particular vehicle depends on our situation
and our state of mind. . . . So we have the path as life experience,
the vehicle as the teachings, and the traveler as the student.

OUR RELATIONSHIP to the dharma could be problematic if we had
no understanding of the path, the vehicle, and the traveler. We have
the teachings, we have our life situation, and we have practitioners who
are going along the path, so we need to clarify the whole thing. The idea
of yana, or vehicle, is that we are making a journey from somewhere to
somewhere else. The notion of yana includes modes of transportation,
attitudes toward transportation, and attitudes toward the road itself. That
combination makes up the process of the journey.

The three basic yanas of hinayana, mahayana, and vajrayana can be
further divided into nine yanas.* As practitioners of one yana carry on
their journey, they are preparing the road for the next yana. In turn, in
order to travel on that particular road, practitioners of the next yana build

---

* The nine yanas include the two hinayana yanas of shravakayana and pratyekabuddhayana; the mahayana; and the six tantric or vajrayana yanas of kriyayogayana, upayogayana,
yogayana, mahayogayana, anuyogayana, and atiyoga.

more sophisticated chariots, so the standard of living begins to go up. So practitioners of one yana are not only journeyers, but they are also road builders for the next yana. The Buddha very cleverly instituted such traditions as a way to make students understand and to create some kind of breakthrough.

The idea of yana, or vehicle, is that of an ideal vehicle that is extremely accommodating. Its speed is based on the natural rhythm and evolution of the passengers. According to the sutras, whoever rides such a vehicle is going to reach a state beyond suffering. Although one of the sutras says that yana is like space and like a palace, the image is of a palace on wheels or flying in space, so the concept of vehicle still seems to fit. Ideally, the passengers themselves should have some bearing on the speed of the vehicle while the journey is still taking place. If you have powerful horses or very speedy sports cars pulling your carriage, before you can think twice you are already at your destination and you have no idea how to proceed. Therefore, the Buddhist masters presented the teachings according to the concept of yana and the idea of people making their own journey at their own speed.

If you are really good at traveling, you first have to think about the condition of the road and what kind of road you are going to take: a dirt road, a state road, or an interstate. Then you have to think about feeding your vehicle with some energy or fuel. You also have to think about your own state of being as the driver, or journey maker, and make sure to have a certain amount of sleep and rest. You also have to have some understanding of the mechanics of your particular vehicle, and take care that your wheels and engine are in good order. Maintaining the vehicle is part of the student's role. You have to keep up with the particular techniques and disciplines that have been presented to you.

The idea of yana is that we are on a path; we have not just parked our trailer in somebody's backyard. We are in a particular carriage moving along a particular road. Of course, that road could take different forms, but we are still moving along the road. According to this analysis, the logic of our life is being shaped by the path. We are on a certain type of journey. Sometimes it is a good journey, a smooth straightforward road, and occasionally it is rough and obstacles come up. Basically, the path is life experience.

Within the samsaric world, a road is being created, a highway is being introduced. In the midst of this samsaric countryside, a path has been cut, which we might call the spiritual path. Once the path has been prepared for us, once it has been cut and laid out, with an occasional bridge or tunnel, we need to have some form of vehicle by which to travel along that path. That vehicle is the body of the teachings. The teachings are connected with our basic state of existence, and the sophistication of a particular vehicle depends on our situation and our state of mind. At the hinayana level the mode of transportation may be fairly slow and functional. At the mahayana level it may be somewhat more accommodating and easier to get into. At the vajrayana level the vehicle is highly accommodating, but it may be too efficient for the riders. So we have the path as life experience, the vehicle as the teachings, and the traveler as the student. It says in the *Lankavatara Sutra** that the various yanas are presented in order to lead all sentient beings to nirvana. Yanas include the techniques, methods, and formats that we practice, like the various styles of sitting meditation or modes of living. But it is difficult to say which yana you are on.

Once you are on the path, you may seem to be going nowhere. However, you are still following a schedule, taking on a particular lifestyle, and involving yourself in a certain psychological development. You may seem to be going somewhere. You may feel that you are beginning to have a different perspective toward the world and your experience of your husband or wife, your friends, your job, or what you are going to do next. In either case, once you are in a particular mode of transportation, you carry that form of transportation along with you.

On the journey, you are not going anywhere; at the same time, you are going completely. You take a journey in order to realize that you are not going anywhere. On the way, you are shedding your ego, trying to surrender it completely. But when you reach the final destination, you realize that you have returned back home. You have gone in circles and come back to square one. You started from your home ground, samsara, and your journey has taken you back to that home ground. But that home has suddenly changed its name to enlightenment. That is the journey we are trying to make. It is the journey itself that is important.

There is a traditional story about some children who want to meet their father, whom they have never seen. Their father is supposed to be an extraordinarily famous and powerful person, but their mother keeps

---

* Daisitz Teitaro Suzuki, trans., *The Lankavatara Sutra: A Mahayana Text* (London: Routledge and Kegan Paul Ltd., 1932).

telling them that they cannot meet him just now. Finally she tells the children, "Okay, now I'm going to take you to meet your father." So they begin their journey. They climb up and down mountains and they ford rivers, and they go around and around. Finally they go through a valley into a house and open the door, and there they finally meet their father. They are so appreciative and happy, and they settle down and begin to relate with their father, to relax and socialize. Then they begin to run around the room and to explore the whole place, all the rooms in the house, and they suddenly discover that the house is the same place they were living in before. It is their mother's place! Like the children, we are at our destination already, but we have to be convinced. We have to be shed completely of our struggles and distrustfulness. That is the journey.

The *Lankavatara Sutra* says that as long as there is the existence of conceptual mind, there is no end to the yanas. When we need a mode of transportation, yanas are always provided for us. If you finally decide to settle down in one place instead of commuting here and there, you will no longer need such transportation. When you have definitely settled in a place that has all the resources you need, you do not need to buy a car. You can settle down in one spot, and you no longer have to make a journey. You are able to conquer the whole journey.

Yanas are referred to as vehicles that you drive along a road on the earth rather than ships you sail in the ocean, because there is nothing romantic about this type of journey. It is important to realize that this particular journey is very realistic. The nature of the journey depends partly on the journeyer, partly on the driving teacher, partly on the map maker, and partly on the guide who gave you a description of the road. You cannot expect that the guide will tell you about every exit, but such a guide can give you some rough guidelines and basic reference points.

The Buddhist tradition is personally oriented and journey oriented. People make a journey in their own way, particularly in the pragmatic West. Even when people are committed to an old-age home, they are on a journey—the journey of phasing out from this world. The Buddhist approach to the spiritual journey is nontheistic in the sense that you are not suddenly given some kind of reward from above. The nontheistic journey is not based on rewards but on moment-by-moment feedback, which may be painful or punishing, gray, black, or white. The journey is not achievement oriented but living oriented. You have some kind of exchange taking place all the time, so you do not have to wait for your carrot—you get a carrot every minute. You get a carrot with each step, not so much as a reward, but as an expression of feedback for what you are doing with your life. If you see clearly, you get visions back that enable you to go further all the time. So the journey is very pragmatic and very present-oriented.

The nontheistic journey is quite powerful and unedited. It is not based on a belief in any divine hierarchy or in messages coming from upstairs through thunderstorms, rainfalls, or snowfalls. We are talking about the ground-floor level. You cannot expect anything much to happen. The only thing happening is your own mind, which you have with you all the time. You may try to get rid of it, but somehow you never manage to do so, so you just keep carrying your mind along with you. Basically, mind is the journeyer; the particular style of working with yourself is the vehicle; and the situations you get into are the path. However, although you are on a journey, there is no point in talking about it. You don't need to talk about your journey—you just do your practice.

8

Relating with a Teacher

The teacher is made heavy by his or her own learning, wisdom, and discipline. On top of that, they are able to carry other people's neuroses, or burdens, on their back. If people have to be ferried across the river of samsara, the teacher will carry them all in one bundle. It is like carrying a sack of ten thousand little sentient beings across the border.

IN THE hinayana, the immediate vehicle, we work with our basic anxiety. When you are sick, you try to find a medicine that will cure your sickness. In order to find that medicine, you look for a physician who can prescribe something for you. Likewise, to find a cure for your anxiety, you need to find a teacher. You may never have thought of anything like the dharma at all. You may never have thought of the possibility of such a journey or discipline. You may be wrapped up in all sorts of ordinary things. But then maybe a teacher tells you there is such a thing as a path— and you begin to wonder. You begin to work on yourself, to look further. In doing so, quite possibly the discoveries you make will be your own discoveries completely.

At the early, crude level of dharma, what you discover is that there is pain, misery, neurosis, and anxiety. But having discovered all that, you need to talk to somebody. You need some kind of reference point. If you go to your parents, they say, "You're crazy. Go back to school." If you talk to your friends, they say, "Come and have a drink with me" or "Let's go to Acapulco and forget the whole thing." Therefore, you need to find someone else, an honest teacher who can keep you on track. Finding such a teacher seems to be absolutely necessary. You need someone who sees through you completely, but still loves you. That kind of balance is very difficult to find. You can't find it in your parents, your relatives, or your cronies, so you have to find a teacher who has those qualities. A teacher is different from other people in that he or she is removed from the passions that seduce you. The point of the teacher is that you need somebody who will say no or yes.

Terms for Teacher

Sthavira / Elder / Neten

In the hinayana, the teacher is known as the elder, or learned one. "Elder" in Sanskrit is *sthavira,* and in Pali it is *thera,* which means "older." The Tibetan word *neten* also has the sense of elder. *Ne* means "those who dwell," or "settled," and *ten* means "having established the settlement properly." The Zen term *roshi* also means elder. Whether we say sthavira, roshi, thera, or neten, we mean elder: old in wisdom, old in discipline, old in terms of familiarity with the dharma.

Acharya / Foremost Teacher / Loppön

Another term for the teacher is *acharya. Acharya* means the "foremost teacher." The Tibetan word for acharya is *loppön. Lop* means "learning" and *pön* means "chief."

Uttara / Person Who Is Above / Lama

We also have another term for teacher, which is *lama,* as in Dalai Lama. *La* means "above," and *ma* makes it the "person who is above." The Sanskrit word for lama is not *guru,* although people often think so. The Sanskrit word for lama is *uttara,* which means "upper," as well as "laborer." Strangely enough, both the Sanskrit and the Tibetan terms for "upper" also mean "carrier," "laborer," or "porter." It is an interesting idea: the teacher is the best porter of all, a super-porter who can carry the heaviest load. So although there is no immediate linguistic connection between *lama* and *llamas,* maybe there is a connection. The teacher is made heavy by their own learning, wisdom, and discipline. On top of that, he or she is able to carry other people's neuroses, or burdens, on their back. If people have to be ferried across the river of samsara, the teacher will carry them all in one bundle. It is like carrying a sack of ten thousand little sentient beings across the border.

Upadhyaya / Preceptor / Khenpo

Then we have what is known as *upadhyaya*. The Tibetan word for upadhyaya is *khenpo*, which means "preceptor." It refers to the person with whom you take the refuge vow, the person who enters you into the path of individual salvation. The preceptor is like a doctor who makes you take your medicine and promises you that you will be cured.

CONDUCTING YOURSELF WITH ELEGANCE AND DELIGHT

When we have a relationship with a teacher, we are connecting with the attitude and concepts that the teacher represents, with their learning and their care for self and others. All of that allows us to become meticulous and inspired. If there were no teachers to speak to us, we would be like dogs with an itch who scratch so much that the itch gets worse. It is said that scratching your itch seems to be pleasurable, but if there were no itch at all, it would be better. With that same logic, trying to explore your own neuroses could be quite pleasant—but if there were no neuroses at all, it would be better. Teachers represent the absence of neurosis by manifesting as one-hundred-percent persons who are basically on top of their situation. They are healthy and precise, and inspired by the dharma and the delight of teaching.

Inspired by the teacher, we begin to develop meticulousness. We find that the simple process of drinking a cup of tea—we lift the teacup, we bring it toward our mouth, we tilt it, we touch our lips to it, and we begin to sip—can express the absence of neurosis. That quality of meticulousness does not mean that you are completely blissed-out. It means that you are conducting yourself precisely with elegance and delight. Precision is the key to how human beings can be raised to a higher level of potential.

The basic principle of elegance from the Buddhist point of view is quite different than the Victorian notion of good manners, or knowing how to eat with a knife and fork. A chimpanzee could eat with a gold fork on the best bone china and sit on a brocade *zafu,* or meditation cushion, but eating chimpanzee-style is not the mark of the best human being or the best anything. A chimpanzee has never known the possibility of having a teacher.

As the best of human beings, you are not quite chimpanzees. You have the decency to relate with your teacher, and you are decent in terms of your behavior patterns. That basic decency, at a very ordinary and simple level, will bring enlightenment, individual salvation. If the Buddha were here right now, he would probably say that conducting yourself properly in accordance with your local culture could be considered twentieth-century vinaya, or monastic discipline.

9

The Painful Reality of Samsara

Samsara starts from one tiny little thing and then becomes exagger-
ated into all kinds of conditions. By thinking, "Because this is this,
therefore that should be that," and so on and so on, we are continu-
ously escalating our world of samsara, the karmic world.

TEACHERS REPRESENT the possibility of nirvana, or peace. But to
realize that possibility, we first need to realize the nature of samsara.
We need to study it and understand it. Samsara is a complex situation
based on passion, aggression, and ignorance.* Its essence is turmoil. But
unless you relate to passion, aggression, and ignorance as the path—
understanding them, working with them, and treading on them—you
will not discover the goal. Seeing the truth as it is, is the goal as well as
the path. By discovering the truth of samsara you are discovering nirvana.
In fact, the reality of samsara is equally the reality of nirvana. Truth does
not depend on formulas or alternative answers, but truth is seen to be one
truth without relativity.

THE WHEEL OF LIFE

In Tibetan iconography the activity of samsara is depicted as a wheel of
life, or *bhavachakra*. The wheel of life is a portrait of samsara. Therefore,
it is also a portrait of nirvana, or the undoing of the samsaric coil. The

---

* The Sanskrit term *moha*, here translated as "ignorance," is frequently translated as
"delusion."

wheel of life represents the compulsive nowness in which the universe recurs, as the death of one experience gives birth to the next within the realm of time. In this continual cycle of birth and death, each new experience contains the quality of the previous one. Within this realm of possibility, a pattern of chain reactions known as the twelve *nidanas* develops.

Yama Holds the Wheel

The image of the wheel of life is always shown as being held by Yama, the personification of death, who provides the space and time for birth, death, and survival. Yama provides the basic medium in which the different nidanas, or chain reactions, can be born and die. The image of a wheel held in the jaws of Yama is based on the teachings of the four noble truths. The outer ring portrays the nidanas as the evolution of suffering; the inner ring portrays the six realms as the perpetuation of suffering; and the center of the wheel portrays the three poisons of passion, aggression, and ignorance as the origin of suffering.*

The Outer Ring: The Twelve Nidanas

The outer ring of the wheel presents the evolutionary stages of suffering in terms of the twelve nidanas. The nidanas represent how chance occurrences can evolve to a crescendo of ignorance and death. The ring of nidanas may be seen in terms of causality, or as accidents that lead from one situation to the next. They represent an inescapable chain of coincidence that brings imprisonment and pain. You have been processed through this gigantic factory as raw material, and although you do not usually look forward to the outcome, there is no alternative.

---

* The four noble truths were the very first teachings the Buddha gave after his attainment of enlightenment. As such they are considered the very essence of his message. There is a detailed discussion of this teaching in part 4, "The Four Noble Truths." The remaining two truths, the cessation of suffering and the path, are also represented. Each of the six realms is portrayed with a buddha figure, signifying the possibility of liberation and the cessation of suffering. The path is depicted on the central hub of the wheel by figures walking upwards to freedom, in contrast to figures being dragged down into further suffering and confusion.

The Wheel of Life. In this version, the sixth nidana (contact) is illustrated by a couple embracing, and the tenth nidana (becoming) is illustrated by a person rising up or reflecting. Drawing provided by Liza Matthews; used by permission.

1. IGNORANCE / BLIND GRANDMOTHER. The first nidana is avidya, or ignorance. It is represented by a blind grandmother, who symbolizes the older generation giving birth to further generations, but remaining fundamentally blind. A blind grandmother has no chance to see her grandchildren. She has her own concepts and ideas about how the world should be, and she struggles constantly, trying to communicate with her grandchildren. But she is unable to see their own struggle properly and completely. She is highly inquisitive and extremely interested in any kind of gossip involving her grandchildren. But such gossip is endless: one gossip leads to another gossip and to yet another gossip.

The grandmother represents the basic intelligence that is the impetus for stirring up endless clusters of solidified thought and crowded energy. This creates such claustrophobia that the energy begins to see itself, and the intelligence is undermined. The overcrowded, clumsy discrimination of the blind grandmother, with its quality of thingness, or solidified space, is in the way. So nothing is left but deception and loneliness.

The first nidana is experienced as subtle irritation combined with subtle absorption, and this experience continues throughout the nidanas, from the grandmother to the grandchildren. The absorption of the first nidana is a form of bewilderment. It is the samsaric equivalent of samadhi. Indulgence in something intangible and trying to confirm what is intangible leads to a sense of solidified space. It is the beginning of self-consciousness, which is based on clinging to intangible qualities as if they were solid. You feel desolation in the background, and you have an urge to create habitual patterns. You have a feeling of discovery, for you have found a way to occupy yourself. It is as if you have broken away from something—but at the same time, you sense the possibility of losing ground forever.

2. FORMATION / POTTER'S WHEEL. The next nidana is called samskara, or "conceptual mind." It can also be translated as "formations."* Samskara is represented by the image of a potter's wheel. This nidana is based on impulsive accumulation: we turn the potter's wheel constantly. That wheel keeps turning, again and again, and with that wheel we could produce a pot, a sculpture, a cup, a teapot, a vase—all kinds of nice shapes. That

---

* Trungpa Rinpoche uses many different terms to refer to samskara, including concept, formation, and impulsive accumulation.

shaping process represents conceptual mind forming itself into certain patterns. It is the point at which karmic creation begins.

The Sanskrit word *karma* means "creation," or "activity." The Tibetan word *le* could be equated with labor, or with the idea of constantly doing things. Like a potter, we throw one aspect of our chaotic life, one piece of dirt, onto the potter's wheel, and then we work with that clay and form ourselves into a pot or a cup. That activity takes place constantly. Basically, karma is created by two situations: the sense of I-ness and the sense of other. They are like the water and clay that are mixed together to form the mud thrown onto the potter's wheel. The potter's wheel is the sense of obligation that we should make our life into something, that we should become a poet, professor, engineer, or social worker. Whenever we say, "I should become . . ." the potter's wheel is spinning. By means of the speed of the potter's wheel, we make ourselves into something—and as the revolution of the wheel goes on and on, it produces further speed.

3. CONSCIOUSNESS / MONKEY. Now that we are in charge of this individual and quite private game, an inkling of power begins to develop, because we have been able to set the wheel in motion. But there is a need to further this ambition, which leads to the third nidana, vijnana, or "consciousness." The symbol for consciousness is a monkey—a very busy monkey—who says, "I am a monkey!" Then that monkey defines itself further: "I am a monkey; therefore, I should climb trees and eat bananas and fruit." So another factor is involved. The monkey not only says, "I am a monkey," but "I am a monkey; therefore, I should be doing this and that." Things slowly escalate in that way. Samsara starts from one tiny little thing and then becomes exaggerated into all kinds of conditions. By thinking, "Because this is this, therefore that should be that," and so on and so on, we are continuously escalating our world of samsara, the karmic world.

4. NAME AND FORM / PERSON IN A BOAT. Having become a professional monkey, you then develop the fourth nidana, nama-rupa, or "name and form," which is symbolized by a person in a boat. You give yourself a name and function: "I am what I am. I have a physical form and I deserve a name as well. I should be called 'Jack' or 'Jill.'" This nidana is a gesture of hope and of a dream coming true. When an object has a conceptualized

name, it becomes significant. When you name a person, you are providing a home for that person. You create an image of the person in accordance with the house that you have created. If you think of a castle, you might call that person Princess So-and-So or King Such-and-Such. So name and form—the verbal concept and the visual concept—are the same. Names and forms serve as political or philosophical reinforcement. For instance, when you think of a king occupying a castle, you automatically expect that he ought to have an accompanying sense of dignity. You think that the title should fit the person.

5. Six Sense Faculties / Six-Windowed House. Once you have set up your patterns of existence in that way, the process continues. At this point, you can no longer simply exist alone without relating with the rest of the world, which leads to the next nidana, shadayatana, the "six sense faculties." You develop the six senses and you build a dwelling place for those senses. This nidana is represented by a monkey in a six-windowed house.* The six windows represent the five senses of sight, sound, smell, taste, and touch, as well as the sixth sense of mental faculty. The six sense faculties are connected with the corresponding sense organs of eye, ear, nose, tongue, body, and mind.

The six senses provide a relatively secure home for the monkey. But there is still a sense of the absence of somebody sophisticated and capable enough to run the place you have created. The whole situation is tentative and embryonic. The monkey is relatively awake, but there is a quality of paranoia, in that you suspect that the occupant of the house is very undignified. However, this monkey has to function both as guardian and as director, and that dual role naturally leads to some degree of sophistication and diplomacy.

6. Contact / Married Couple. The need to maintain this project leads us to the next nidana, sparsha, or "contact," represented by a married couple. Having already made your situation very solid and clear, you would like to test whether it is functioning properly or not, so you need to make some kind of contact with the situation. Sparsha is symbolized by the contact between the masculine and feminine principles, which complement each

---

* This nidana is often depicted as an empty house; Trungpa Rinpoche inhabits it with a monkey.

other. By trying to capture this fascination and make it into a solid thing, you develop personality. You develop self-respect that is not based upon domestic affairs alone, but also upon foreign relationships.

7. FEELING / ARROW THROUGH THE EYE. At this point, the next nidana, vedana, or "feeling," presents itself. Feeling is symbolized by an arrow through the eye. Having made contact, you get a rebound or echo from the world. The world outside reacts to you, depending on your style of functioning. Sometimes the world reacts ideally, such as when you manage to fulfill your business properly; sometimes you feel inferior and wretched, and you get hurt. So all kinds of feelings are involved with this nidana.

Feeling is a very penetrating and painful experience, as if someone had shot an arrow into your eye. The arrow doesn't go so far in as to burst your brain, which might have been good, but just pierces your eye. You cannot quite pull it out because it is too painful, but at the same time, you cannot just leave it in. So it is very tricky and touchy. The inquisitive mind pretends to accept this as a delightful surprise, even as a convenience, because it has no choice. There is sharp dramatic feeling, but there is no chance to indulge in it.

The arrow in the eye is the first real perception of this and that, the world outside. That arrow is not particularly regarded as a message of death, but as a message of life. It is like feeling alive, feeling that you are really living in this world. When you wake up on a spring morning, draw your curtains, hear the birds chirping, feel the cool breeze, and sense the freshness of the air, you say, "Ah. It's fantastic to be alive!" But there is still an arrow in your eye.

8. CRAVING / DRINKING MILK AND HONEY. This brings us to the next nidana, trishna, or "craving." Although craving is traditionally symbolized by drinking milk and honey,* it is more like eating ice cream or rice pudding—it is like food that you do not have to chew or even lick. It just comes into your mouth, you taste it, and it goes right through your body. You do not even bother to swallow; it is more as if it had swallowed you. It is very simple, no effort is involved. It is fantastic pleasure.

Having already made contact with your world properly and thoroughly, this nidana is accepting what has happened to you as further

---

* Tibetan classical sources say "liquor" in lieu of "milk and honey."

reinforcement of your pleasure and your life. With craving, you don't know what happened; you just did it. Milk and honey just go into you without even inviting them. It is instant, rather than deliberate. There is no intellectualization at all. Craving just happens to you—and it happens to you constantly.

You may be embarrassed because your wholehearted and eager reception of the arrow was too impulsive, and you may have a tendency to tone down. However, in spite of that tendency, you try your best to relate to the arrow (feeling). At the same time, you experience a natural self-indulgence—a craving for more milk and honey. You would like to just sip and taste, and to resist swallowing, but impulse takes over and leads you to the next nidana.

9. GRASPING / GATHERING FRUIT. The next nidana is upadana, or "grasping," symbolized by gathering fruit. You have a courtship with the world. You are demonstrating youthful exuberance—demonstrating how far you can jump, how sharp your youthful teeth are, and how good your muscles are. The analogy of gathering fruit is that you could just jump into a tree in an orchard simply because you feel so good and fresh in the autumn wind. You could just jump up and pluck an apple. You could bite into it and chew it while you are looking for another apple, with which you might do the same thing. You can jump and dance, you can pluck fruit and eat it. You can hand the apple to your colleagues, who also know the exuberant feeling of youth, or you can throw the apple up and see its redness against the blue of the sky. You are playing a game, like when kittens let a mouse go, then jump on it, then let it go, and then jump on it. You begin to regard life as a big joke. At the same time, it is enormously fun. Your life is so good, so absolutely good, that you are falling in love with it.

With this nidana, there is a tendency to do whatever you feel like doing. As you gather fruit, you are not concerned with who owns the orchard. You run out of your stuffy house and roam around the grounds trying to be outrageous. Apples are very definite, lumpy, and satisfying. It is very reassuring to hold them, even more so to bite into them without peeling them.

10. BECOMING / COPULATION. At this point, there is an inevitable tendency to feel that someone else could possibly share this experience, that at least

there might be someone to relate to. That loneliness and longing for companionship leads you to the next nidana, bhava, or "becoming."

The traditional picture for "becoming" is copulation. In this nidana, you have finally been caught. Instead of dancing around, listening to sweet music and enjoying everything, you have been captured by this life. Instead of continually roaming around in the orchard, you have found one apple, and you sit down and begin eating it. You are taking life more seriously, adopting a somewhat more defined form. You are actually getting into your life, into the nitty-gritty of things. Traditionally, we call this making love.

Making love means you are stuck with one apple—there is no choice—and you begin to feel that there is an obligation to finish your one apple, which is fantastically good and crunchy. It is bitable, because your teeth are sharp and youthful, and you feel the energy of holding the apple, but a tinge of self-consciousness begins to crop up. This is somewhat alarming! You were expressing so much freedom, but now you have ended up with one apple. You have a relationship with it, and at the same time you are stuck with it. So there is a faint quality of discomfort, although it is being suppressed because of your excitement. The memory of how you used to roam in the orchard somewhat helps, but at the same time your situation is uncomfortable. As you finish your one apple, you begin to look for a place to throw away the apple core. You sense that you might be littering the beautiful orchard, but you want to get rid of it. At that point, the discomfort begins to become much more serious and real.

The nidana of becoming celebrates the achievement of relating with another mind / body. Experiencing the shapes and sculptural qualities of the world is extremely satisfying. You develop a tremendous awareness of things, a heightened quality of vision and other sense perceptions.

11. BIRTH / WOMAN IN CHILDBIRTH. It seems that copulating is the only way of appreciating the organic natural world—but at the same time such sensual overindulgence invites valid proof. You want the evidence of being a father or mother to provide legitimacy, which leads to the next nidana, jati, or "birth."

With the nidana of birth, becoming has gone into action and produced karmic results. Birth is a fact of life. It is the truth. Cause and effect are actually happening; truth is taking place. Having given birth to something, a feeling of power begins to develop. The simplicity of being creator of the universe is not far away.

The symbol for birth is a woman giving birth.* In the process of making love and having enormous fun, you get pregnant. You are actually having a baby. At that point, all the fun and love that went on are reduced into the one-pointedness of producing another life—which is also your life. You are producing out of yourself another person. You are responsible for the whole thing; you are stuck with it, you cannot deny it.

The vitality of giving birth does not last. The discovery of change becomes irritating and the achievement of self-indulgence becomes questionable. There is nothing to relate with as continual entertainment—it becomes empty. You have to face the possibility of decay, feebleness, and imminent death. It is inescapable. The exuberance of youth automatically leads to the crescendo of old age. Extremely cunning intelligence leads to extreme clumsiness. Your demanding no longer fulfills its function, and you see that your game of efficiency is not that efficient after all. You have not realized that this derelict situation contains another outrageous discovery, which is the nidana of old age and death.

12. OLD AGE AND DEATH / FUNERAL PROCESSION. The twelfth nidana is jara marana, or "old age and death." This is symbolized by a funeral procession, with a corpse wrapped up in a coffin being carried to the funeral. You experience decay, sickness, and dying. It is an enormous thing, which is both possible and obvious. Having had so much fun playing with phenomena, finally birth and death become very close to one another. You think, "I feel that it was just yesterday that I was born, and now I am dying. My life went by so fast! Is it true, or is it just a joke? Maybe it is some misunderstanding in the cosmic language. Something has gone wrong." But it is no misunderstanding; it is the truth of life. It is death. Death includes the physically overpowering situation of having too many things to manage. Once upon a time that was exhilarating, but that excitement has become questionable. The many objects and relationships you have created become the inspiration for the charnel ground.

---

* The traditional citation for this nidana is a "baby being born," which would place more emphasis on the baby than the mother. Trungpa Rinpoche focuses on the mother instead.

The Inner Ring: The Six Realms

The inner ring shows how the confused mind finds different styles of occupation, which are called realms. Such realms can be said to refer to psychological states, rather than external situations such as a heaven above and hell below. Traditionally, six realms are described. These realms are known as the whirlpool of illusion, or samsara. There is no starting point and no definite order to the realms—you can take birth in any realm at any given time. According to abhidharma, or Buddhist psychology, we can take birth into any of these psychological realms in a matter of a sixtieth of a second. Furthermore, the concept of time itself is also dependent on our involvement in ignorance.

HUMAN REALM. The human realm is said to be the land of karma, because human beings can perceive and work with the karmic force. Suffering in this realm has the nature of dissatisfaction. The intelligence of human nature becomes a source of endless pain. Deliberate self-inflicted struggles lead to the pain of birth, old age, sickness, and death. The constant search for pleasure and its failure pushes the inquisitive intelligence into neurosis. But certain karmic coincidences bring the possibility of realizing the use-lessness of struggling, and these coincidences are the particular attribute of the human realm. The human realm presents the rare opportunity of hearing the dharma and practicing it. The seemingly solid body and seemingly real situations act as a vessel to preserve the Buddha's teaching, whereas the other realms are so exclusively involved with their own extreme situations that the dharma cannot be heard, and changes happen only as the karmic force of the hallucination wears out.

JEALOUS GOD REALM. In the realm of the asuras, or jealous gods, the ambition of gaining a victory and the fear of losing a battle cause you to feel alive, as well as cause you irritation. You lose the point of an ultimate goal, but in order to keep the driving force, you have to maintain the ambition. There is the constant desire to be the best, but the possibility of losing your game is too real. There is an occasional tendency to punish yourself. You strive to get away from the pain, but whenever you see any pleasurable, appealing situations, they seem to be too distant. The desire to bring them close to you is overwhelming. The whole world seems to be built out of golden promises, but it is irritating even to venture to fulfill them. You tend to condemn yourself for not striving, for not keeping strict discipline, and for not achieving the satisfaction of these promises.

GOD REALM. The realm of the gods, also known as heaven, is the product of self-indulgence in ideal pleasure. This realm has different degrees, and each degree of intensity of pleasure is based on a corresponding degree of maintenance of the pleasure and fear of losing it. The joy of meditative absorption saturates your seemingly solid body so that the basic energy is completely undermined. There are occasional flashes of thought, which irritate and threaten the meditative intoxication. The reason the realm of the gods is regarded as an impermanent state is that it is based on ego's game of maintenance, in which meditation is seen as separate from your own being. When the karmic situation of being in heaven wears out, there are suddenly violent thoughts accompanied by suspicion, and the whole blissful state collapses, including the self-conscious concepts of love and the security of being in love. Another hallucination takes control, and you are in another realm.

ANIMAL REALM. The stupidity of the animal realm is more one of laziness than of dullness. It is the refusal to venture onto new ground. There is a tendency to cling to the familiar and to fight your way from one familiar situation to another. This approach does not have a quality of openness or dance. In the animal realm, whenever there is an overpowering force that might lead you to explore new territory, the immediate reaction is to play dead or to camouflage yourself as though you were not there. This realm is marked by stubbornness and by intoxication with yourself.

HUNGRY GHOST REALM. The hungry ghost realm is one of an intense state of grasping in the midst of continual, overwhelming psychological poverty. The definition of hunger in this case is the fear of letting go. The hungry ghost realm has three veils: the external veil, the internal veil, and the individualistic veil.* The external veil is a result of too much accumula-

---

* The usual description of these three veils or obscurations is that those suffering from the outer veil cannot get any food or drink due to external factors; those suffering from the inner veil can't eat or drink due to internal factors; and for those suffering from the individualistic veil, food turns to fire in their belly, or they end up eating feces, urine, or their own flesh.

tion, but you long to become even hungrier so you can accumulate even more. With the internal veil, having been able to accumulate whatever you want, the end product is the reverse of what you expected—the satisfaction turns into dissatisfaction. The individualistic veil is trying any possible way of satisfying your hang-ups, but unexpectedly having the disappointment of being attacked from every direction from both wanting and not wanting, which is the state of conflicting emotions. On the whole, the pain of this realm is not so much that of not finding what you want; rather, it is the frustration of the wanting itself that causes excruciating pain.

HELL REALM. The realm of hell is not only the extreme of aggression and its passionate expression, but it extends beyond that. It backlashes and creates not only a force of energy, but an all-pervasive environment of aggression that is so intense it is unbearable. Even the wildness of the anger itself finds it unbearable to exist in such an environment. There is a tendency to try to escape, but the attempt to escape intensifies the imprisonment. Two images have been used to describe this realm. One is intense heat, which creates helplessness. You realize that you are radiating this heat yourself, but trying to find a way to turn off the heat becomes too claustrophobic. The other image is intense cold. Any movement toward trying to solve the problem is irritatingly painful, so you try to internalize the intense aggression, to freeze it. However, although it no longer cuts with a sharp edge, its blunt edge still hurts.

In the hell realm, there is a tendency to commit suicide for the relief of a change of scene, but each moment of change and each repetitive birth seems to take millions of years in this realm of hallucinations. There is not a moment to spare for anything other than your own existence in hell. There is such paranoia that the pain increases greatly. The level of anger does not allow you a moment for preparation, or a way to get involved in each instant. There is no pulsation to the pain—it is constant.

The Center of the Wheel

This brings us to the center of the wheel of life, which represents the origin of suffering and the path.* You have experienced the monotonous and

---

* Although the center of the wheel is traditionally represented by the poisonous emotions of passion, aggression, and ignorance, Trungpa Rinpoche points out that these are precisely the energies we must deal with if we are to progress along the path of awakening.

familiar games of the six realms of the world, and you have heard the buddhadharma, the truth of pain and the reality of suffering. That experience brings the primordial mind into a state of doubt. The conclusion arises that possibly, after all, things may be just as they are. At that moment, the subtler message of the first noble truth, the truth of suffering, begins to click. You are about to sense the meaning of all those useless ventures as the false occupation of ego.

IGNORANCE / PIG. The first response to that is bewilderment. The teaching is too potent and too true—it seems impossible to be so precise and accurate. It almost feels like a personal insult that there are awakened minds and that their teaching can communicate to your basic nature. There is a sense that you have been careless and not able to keep your secrets. The first hearing of the teaching is a shock. Your sense of inhibition is broken through, and your personal preservation through ignorance no longer applies. Traditionally, that deliberate ignoring is symbolized by a pig. The pig represents nondiscriminating perception. You relate purely to the sense of survival, consuming whatever comes up to be consumed. With ignorance, you are always grasping for what is comfortable and snug.

PASSION / ROOSTER. Confused passion is depicted in the symbol of the rooster. Passion feels inadequate, so it presents its spiky, sharp points in order to draw in objects of desire. It consumes and attracts attention at the same time. The rooster's display of its colorful feathers and beak can draw in the object of passion. Passion is seen as eliminating the beauty of the phenomenal world as it draws in such beauty by a succession of games.

AGGRESSION / SNAKE. When there is a threat to the success of drawing in, it appears that the only possible way of accomplishing the process is to subjugate the object of passion, either by putting out poison to paralyze it or by overpowering it. This is much the way a snake would proceed, either projecting poison through its fangs or coiling around the object of desire until it has been completely subdued. Thus the snake is the symbol of aggression. The pattern of aggression and passion is seen as capturing that which is close and destroying that which is beyond your control.

The Deadly Seriousness of Samsara

Throughout the whole process depicted in the wheel of life, the problem seems to be that we have been taking our life too seriously. We might think we are having enormous fun, but each step is actually an expression of death. Death could be fun, but usually nobody likes to look at it in that way. In the cycle of samsara, we end up dead. We end up on our deathbed, and not only that, but we end up in the coffin. Taking everything so seriously is not just about being solemn and unhumorous. It is that in every aspect of our life, we have been taking in so much and not giving out anything.

When we do not give out, automatically the input is heavy, heavy, heavy. We end up with old age and death. And when we try to ignore that particular fact, to ignore the truth of life, we become solid like a rock. By ignoring the reality of death, we go back and start the process all over again. So first there is the blind grandmother. From there, we go on to the potter's wheel, the monkey, the person in the boat, the house with six windows, the married couple, the arrow through the eye, drinking milk and honey, gathering fruit, copulating, giving birth, and the funeral procession. We do it all over, again and again, just to shield off our embarrassment of death.

The wheel of life seems to be a complete portrait of the karmic situation, of how we end up here. It has nothing to do with transmigration of the soul. For that matter, the notion that we continue with our life has nothing to do with the idea that we ourselves exist. The continuity is simply all the changes that take place. It is like spring and autumn changing to summer and winter. We put so much effort and energy into our life, and each time we do so, that results in something—and when we work on that result, that produces a further result, which makes us do something else. So we are constantly going on and on. Action, or karma, is continuous. As long as we live that way, we die that way, and we are born that way. The truth of death is the truth of life. So death is not regarded as an escape from or an ending to our life, but death is the beginning of another birth—and that process takes place constantly.

TAKING REFUGE

10

Buddhadharma Fever

We take refuge in order to effect our freedom. We are willing to admit to buddhadharma fever. Understanding that we have a choice, we want to take that step properly and formally. We know that when we take refuge, we are no longer just making a promise to ourselves, but there is some kind of magic involved. In taking the refuge vow, we can request that magic to enter into our system so that we could become worthy Buddha-like, dharma-like, sangha-like people.

WHEN WE know how best to listen to the teachings, we begin to grow up and develop as capable dharmic people. We simultaneously realize the illness of samsara and the healthiness of nirvana. We also see that we can develop the discipline to go against our habitual patterns and overcome them by means of shamatha and vipashyana. Therefore, the dharma can be understood properly and thoroughly, without any interruption or anti-logic. Because we have practiced and studied, the dharma makes sense to us, and the logic of the dharma is quite clear and precise in our mind. We realize that shopping for other kinds of spirituality is over. At that point, we look for further skillful means, or *upaya*. We are inspired to enter the world of buddhadharma by taking the refuge vow.

The Refuge Vow

The refuge vow is one of the most powerful and important aspects of hinayana discipline. With this vow, you are taking refuge in the Buddha, the dharma, and the sangha. The refuge ceremony takes many forms, but the vow itself is quite simple.* The person taking the vow repeats:

I take refuge in the Buddha.
I take refuge in the dharma.
I take refuge in the sangha.

Taking refuge means that you are committing yourself to the dharma; however, it does not mean that you are asking somebody to save you in the theistic sense. The inspiration to take refuge is based on the foundation of shamatha, the practice of naively resting your mind. With that foundation, you can take the refuge vow and enter properly and fully into the dharmic world. You are a complete person, at one with the dharma.

We take refuge in order to effect our freedom. We are willing to admit to buddhadharma fever. Understanding that we have a choice, we want to take that step properly and formally. We know that when we take refuge, we are no longer just making a promise to ourselves, but there is some kind of magic involved. In taking the refuge vow, we can request that magic to enter into our system so that we could become worthy Buddha-like, dharma-like, sangha-like people.

By taking refuge, you are trying to liberate yourself from basic anxiety, from samsara. Now that you have found an alternative, you yearn to get away from that anxiety and negativity—you yearn for individual salvation. You realize that without individual salvation you are trapped, but you also recognize that you could free yourself and practice delightfully. You find dharmic messages quite fitting, and you begin to feel very fortunate. But that goodness has to be shared. It is good to have a jar of marmalade, but it would be better to spread it on a slice of bread and offer it to your friends to eat. So first you share the goodness with yourself, then you share it with others, but in doing so you maintain your own sense of satisfaction. In that way, you become a true refugee.

---

* For an example of a daily refuge practice, see appendix 1, "A Hinayana Morning Liturgy."

CLEANING UP AFTER YOURSELF

When you are in a dharmic environment, you feel contained, free from suffering, uplifted. But when you step out of that environment even a little bit, you find yourself right back in that old familiar prison. You keep receiving the same message: your world is manufacturing its own samsara all the time. When you practice shamatha, you develop your strength and your connection with dharma; and when you practice vipashyana and extend your awareness, you see how samsara works and how ugly it is. There is so much deception, hypocrisy, and complete unpleasantness.

The idea of dealing with such confused people and such a confused world is so unpleasant that at first glance, you don't want to have anything to do with it. But at the same time that is where you came from, and you have to do something about it. Although you realize the disgusting quality of the world, you also take an interest in it. You begin to appreciate the world and what could happen with it. Instead of rejecting and accepting, you see the potential of insanity and sanity in every situation. So even though it is rather unpleasant, you still want to work with the world. The question is: What can you do about it? What is the next step?

Obviously, you should not immediately try to liberate others without first making your own commitment to the dharma. To begin with, your own intentions need to be pure and clean. If you yourself become less of a nuisance and produce less garbage, you then can begin to help clear out somebody else's garbage. That is why you take the refuge vow. You vow that you will always clean up after yourself. You vow that you will not distort the world you are living in with your own contribution of pollution. Your own pollution might seem quite small, considering the largeness of the world—but your contribution of *not* polluting the world could be quite powerful. If all of us cleaned up after ourselves, we could create a completely immaculate world!

You take the refuge vow in order to realize your own sanity and in order to make sure that you do not create chaos or harm others. By exemplifying your own sanity and commitment, you can clean up the potential garbage of the people around you. You can apply your sanity by means of example, rather than by talking too much or trying to convince people. Having developed some experience of shamatha and vipashyana, you begin to step out much more—and as you step out more, you also need to constrict yourself more. You need to hold your discipline properly and commit yourself to the vow you are taking.

LETTING GO OF THEISM

The initial experience of a student of Buddhism is one of dissatisfaction, pain, and suffering. When pain and dissatisfaction take place in your ordinary life, you usually look for some way to avoid the problem. However, if you try to achieve that avoidance through Buddhism, it is confusing because you find that there is no way to secure yourself. Instead, there is a sense of nonexistence along with a quality of drama and personal heroism.

When you first encounter the sangha, you see that sangha members who are already practicing and committed seem to be confident and happy. Because of that, you feel that you too want to commit yourself, but you still have a lot of resistance, uncertainty, and confusion. You label what you dislike and like about the sangha, in a sort of love-hate relationship. On one hand, you would like to follow the discipline and become part of the flock. But on the other hand, you are afraid of losing your individual intelligence and critical judgment. The problem is that either you want to become part of the flock or you want to become a revolutionary.

Taking the refuge vow means that you have a complete commitment to the practice. Most important of all, taking the refuge vow means you are declaring that you have become a nontheistic person. Taking refuge in the three jewels—the Buddha, dharma, and sangha—is a direct act: it is an acknowledgment that you do not commit yourself to any manufactured external authority. You do not commit yourself to conventional gods or to any god established on a sacred rock or a sacred mountain. In the nontheistic tradition, you are not trying to build yourself up by using such logic. You just have the experience of mind being completely twisted around from samsara to nirvana. To do that, you do not need a rock and you do not need to have a vision—you just sit and practice meditation.

As you practice, you realize that your psychology and your physical situation are interconnected. It feels so painful to have to sit still, which goes against the fickleness of mind and body, but you continue to practice. You keep going further, and finally something gives. It happens on the spot. Nobody has to talk you into anything or out of anything. It is like waking up. It's even better than waking up! You don't need your alarm clock—you simply sit and sit. As you sit, you begin to develop strength and a sense of reality that is perfect, and at the same time very ordinary. The magical power of wakefulness can be reflected into you. That is why taking the refuge vow is important to the student of Buddhism. If you do not take up the notion of wakefulness, you do not get it; if you do, you get a hint of being awake already.

With both theism and nontheism, it is possible to fall into extremes. In the extreme of theism, although you desire salvation, you think it can only be achieved by some greater power that exists outside you. In the extreme of nontheism, you think you can achieve salvation by hard work alone, purely by yourself. Instead of falling into such extremes, you should join together your effort and energy to try to be awake. When you do so, you realize that there is no problem of this and that, of which camp you belong to. You exert yourself so much just by sitting. You sit so long, practice so much, that you disband this and that, and that and this, altogether. Finally, you completely flop—and out of that comes the greatest joy! Something happens that is not earthbound. It happens not because there is a mountaintop, not because a gust of wind comes through, not because the ceiling drops on your head or the floor gives way, but simply it is *there*. That is why Buddhist practice is called nontheistic, because you don't have to rely on any aids. Nobody is going to jolt you, except for your own mind.

It is important to realize that when we take refuge in the Buddha, we are not viewing Buddha as God. Many writers of nineteenth-century English travelogues, and even modern writers, have misunderstood this. They thought that Asians worshiped idols like the Buddha, that they wanted to become like Buddha and that Buddha would give them happiness. However, as Buddhists we do not buy into anything like that, at all. It is important to realize the nontheistic basis of Buddhist practice, particularly if you go on to study the vajrayana, with its iconography of deities such as *yidams, herukas, dakinis, dharmapalas,* and all the rest.* We do not consider that such deities have any external manifestation; they are purely within, as nonmanifested manifestations.

---

* Vajrayana practice includes the visualization of deities or *yidams*—both male deities, or *herukas,* and female deities, or *dakinis*—as well as the visualization of protector figures, or *dharmapalas.*

Taking the refuge vow is the mark of nontheism. From this starting point we are able to develop individual salvation. We can afford to speculate. We can look at the flickering of our mind as it is happening and regard it as thinking. As we look at our mind, a thought comes up. For instance, we might think of the sharpness and greenness of a blade of grass in the summertime, the fresh smell, and the nice feeling of being outdoors in the sunshine. A blade of grass feels so nice; it would be nice to stroke our lips and our tongue with it. However, coming back from our speculation, we see that it is merely a blade of grass. This does not mean we are mocking that blade of grass, cutting our connection to it, or arrogantly throwing it into the garbage pail. We can simply appreciate that blade of grass, which is so fresh, as a total message of the phenomenal world. It is fine. It is good and precise. It is ideal shamatha on the spot, without any embellishment. It is so nice to hold that blade of grass in our hand. That is nontheism.

Everything has its own quality. A blade of grass is nobody's gift, nobody's virtue—it has its own virtue. Therefore, we do not reject its qualities. It is not that somebody worked for six days producing this nice blade of grass and rested on the seventh day. This same approach could apply to anything that goes on in your life—blades of grass you pluck from the earth when you are in love, or the lint you pick up from the carpet. Throughout your life, little incidental things are always happening—a fly lands on your nose or a flea jumps on your toe—and usually you regard such things as insignificant. If there is a black dot in your soup, you think, "Yuck!" However, although you might not like it, you could appreciate it as a message of the teacher, which could be very cheerful or very insulting. You could appreciate your life altogether, with or without little black dots in your clear soup.

DEVOTION AND HUMBLENESS

In order to take the refuge vow and become a refugee, it is first necessary to understand the importance of humbleness. Our lineage is based on humbleness.* In the Kagyü literature it is said: "Humbleness is the dwelling place of the ancestors." But who are the ancestors and how do we follow their example? The ancestors studied under certain teachers; practiced

---

* The Kagyü, or practice lineage, one of the lineages of Trungpa Rinpoche, is one of the four major lineages of Tibetan Buddhism: Nyingma, Kagyü, Sakya, and Geluk.

discipline; renounced their kleshas; discovered the enlightened world; and accomplished what they started out to do. Finally, they became enlightened, part of our lineage. Every one of them began with humbleness.

In the study and practice of hinayana, you could follow the tradition and go through the same process that the ancestors went through. In doing so, you too must maintain an attitude of humbleness. Humbleness rouses you to give birth to realization, because it allows you to hear and experience the teachings properly. With humbleness, your whole being is completely empty, waiting for the teachings to enter into you. If you are arrogant, you couldn't care less about what you hear or see. You may distort and edit the teachings. Arrogance makes things dry, sharp, and thorny, like cactuses. Arrogance does not allow you to be joyous; instead, you are always gloomy. Arrogance is like a big growth on your back: it is burdensome and embarrassing, but you keep carrying it around, saying, "This is the best wealth I've ever had. It is the best collection of logic, knowledge, and wisdom. I am carrying so much wisdom that I have a hunched back!" In order to remove such an accumulated growth of arrogance, more sitting practice and more discipline is needed. Basically, you need more mindfulness and more awareness. It's as simple as that.

Humbleness does not mean that you cannot take pride in the lineage and in the practice. That kind of arrogance is fine. Having good head and shoulders, holding yourself upright, and having a quality of presence is positive arrogance.* It is good decorum. It is not like saying, "I'm better than you are." Positive arrogance is not spoken, but manifested.

With humbleness, you could develop prajna, joy, and renunciation. In order for dharma to enter into your system, you have to bring along less baggage. To hear the dharma properly, you need to develop genuine devotion; and in order to develop genuine devotion, you need to become humble and willing to listen. Humbleness is not about being subservient—it is about being a simple and direct person without any preconceptions due to arrogance or pride. With humbleness, you do not look for the possibility of bringing your arrogance into the dharma; instead you look quite hard for the possibility of bringing *yourself* into the dharma.

Taking refuge means that you are giving up your own territory, your own arrogance, and becoming altogether stateless and groundless. Both

---

* Trungpa Rinpoche uses the term "head and shoulders" to refer to a posture that is upright, dignified, and radiating basic goodness and wholesomeness.

teachers and students give up a lot. We are educated, processed, trained, beaten down, and punished—we practice so thoroughly that we leave everything behind, including our fingernails. We have to leave everything behind in order to be accepted into the buddhadharma world.

Taking refuge in the Buddha as an example, we realize that we do not need any external deity. We realize that we have buddha nature, and fundamental excellence is within us already. Taking refuge in the dharma, we realize that we do not need to listen to any doctrines taught in the name of ego-clinging, ego fixation, or ego improvement. Taking refuge in the sangha, we realize that the companionship of brothers and sisters in the dharma sitting and practicing together is the best companionship. We do not need to look for better friends.

In taking refuge and becoming known as refugees, we are liberating ourselves independently, on our own. Because we have humbleness and an absence of pride, we begin to experience delight in what we have done. Because of the commitment we have made, our awareness begins to expand. We have discovered something worthy of taking refuge in, worthy of bowing to. With our palms joined at the level of our heart, we bow to those who have gone before us and experienced enlightenment. Such ancestors include anyone who has transmitted sanity to us, whatever the lineage or tradition. That is what it means to discover the dwelling place of the ancestors.

Taking Refuge in the Three Jewels

First, we take refuge in the Buddha as an example. The Buddha alone realized that neither spiritual trappings nor materialistic, worldly trappings are ultimate salvation; and having realized that, he abandoned all such trappings. . . .

Secondly, we take refuge in the dharma as path. . . . What the Buddha taught becomes the path we journey on, and we find tremendous truth in it. . . .

Finally, we take refuge in the sangha as companionship, . . . accepting our dharma brothers and sisters, those with whom we practice, as true friends.

BECOMING A REFUGEE

Taking refuge is a leap. It is not so much leaping out, as leaping in. You are letting yourself be as decent a person as possible. You are renouncing the samsaric ugliness that surrounds us, and the pain that goes with it. Through shamatha discipline, you have had a glimpse of how an ordinary Buddha-like person can achieve a perfect life. You have seen the contrast between the pain and pleasure of samsara and the orderliness of shamatha. You begin to realize that things could be orderly, peaceful, and right on the dot; and at the same time, you see how sloppy and confused the world is. Therefore, you take refuge. You vow to yourself that you will never give in to that sloppiness. You vow that you will try to maintain the purity and exactness of the shamatha-vipashyana experience, so that eventually you can relay what you have experienced to the rest of the world. That is the logic of the refuge vow. By taking refuge you are bound together with the Buddha, dharma, and sangha.

In ordinary language, taking refuge means seeking shelter; but in this case it means something slightly different. The Sanskrit refuge phrase, *sharanam gacchami*, "I go for refuge," does not imply that you are helpless and must seek support on somebody else's arm—it means leaving your home country and becoming a refugee. As a refugee, you are leaving your personal world, or your personal state of mind, which is your home ground. Although it is questionable whether anybody will accept you as a refugee, you must step out of your country and become stateless. In fact, you have become a refugee already, in that you are relating to the Buddhist world, which is no country. But this stateless country extends to the rest of the universe! When you take refuge, you are opening yourself up and jumping into new territory, which isn't actually a territory, but a wasteland—completely open ground.

To take refuge requires strength and willingness. It means you must give up your individual preoccupations and obsessions—the personal favoritisms that maintain your existence. If a would-be student of Buddhism has a particular talent that is not pure talent, but an ego-oriented talent that has helped that person maintain his or her existence all along, that has to be given up. You have to become an ordinary citizen. That is the true definition of humility.

Taking refuge is very direct and very simple. You need to take refuge; and not only that, but you *should* take refuge. You should take refuge with body, speech, and mind in the Buddha as example, the dharma as journey, and the sangha as companionship. When you take refuge in the Buddha as example, your mind is concentrated on, and given over to, the bravery of the Buddha. When you take refuge in the dharma as path, your speech—the intellectual, logical, reasoning mind of the modern world, or even the whole world—is none other than dharmic rational mind, which is good in the beginning, good in the middle, and good in the end. When you take refuge in the sangha as companionship, your body is included, because in accepting fellowship in the sangha, you are committed to the behavior patterns of the sangha. Therefore, your body is in complete accord with those who follow the Buddha and the dharma. You move slowly, you eat methodically, and you speak softly. You behave on the whole as a decent, dharmic person.

When you take refuge, there definitely has to be a connection with the preceptor, but your connection can be somewhat loose. Your teacher can be anybody who brings you into the buddhadharma. The relationship is not as severe, strong, and direct as when you take the bodhisattva vow or the vajrayana precepts. You simply appreciate the upadhyaya—the preceptor, leader, or elder—and you emulate him or her. Traditionally, the upadhyaya is the teacher who ordains you in the hinayana precepts. Your loyalty to the preceptor is like the kind of trust you might have in your schoolteacher. Your relationship to the preceptor is based on the fact that he or she is the first teacher who shows you how to become a nontheist.

TAKING REFUGE IN THE BUDDHA

First, we take refuge in the Buddha as an example. The Buddha alone realized that neither spiritual trappings nor materialistic, worldly trappings are ultimate salvation; and having realized that, he abandoned all those trappings. He decided to work on himself through the practice of meditation in the same way that you can work on yourself by practicing shamatha and vipashyana. After six years of intense meditation practice, the Buddha attained enlightenment at Bodhgaya, under the bodhi tree.

You might say that as ordinary human beings, we are not as well favored as the Buddha, so we might have difficulty manifesting such direct liberation and practice. But we can still follow what he did, what he said, and what he practiced. Therefore, we are worthy. We are not trying to become individualistic buddhas, but we are simply trying to follow his example, to practice sitting meditation as he did. Because of his techniques, his wisdom, and his infinite kindness to all of us, we can develop ourselves. We can mimic him and become like him.

The Buddha is an example of someone who has achieved what should be achieved and refrained from what should be avoided. He is an example of a perfectly disciplined person. By taking refuge in the Buddha, we are giving up any gods that might have been a part of our life. We are freeing ourselves from the idea of trying to please an external agent. There is no need for worship. Instead we are working on our own individual salvation, and we realize that any karmic consequences we experience are our own doing.

To take refuge in the Buddha, you should have some understanding of what a buddha is. The word *buddha* means "awake." A buddha is a person who has already woken up, with no egohood, no sleepiness, no confusion. It is like waking up in the morning and feeling fresh. The Buddha has gone beyond ignorance of any kind. He is awake, awake, awake.

The idea of taking refuge in the Buddha is to emulate all of his qualities, to actually become like him. We are capable of conquering, attaining, and going beyond.* We are capable of becoming pure and absolutely awake. In our case, this may not last more than a minute, or more than a second, but we are still trying. We are competing with him! We are trying to attain buddhahood and to understand that state of mind, which is very open, fantastic, and utterly powerful. With that state of mind, we could be "gone beyond," and "beyond beyond," but still keep up with our daily life, still cook our little pot of tea.

Taking Refuge in the Dharma

Secondly, we take refuge in the dharma as path. Taking refuge in the dharma allows you to understand and trust the true dharma, the expression of one's life. What the Buddha taught becomes the path we journey on, and we find tremendous truth in it. The teachings tell us that there are problems with life—there is anxiety, pain, and neurosis—but there is also the possibility of reversing the course of samsara altogether and gaining liberation. The dharma makes sense. Even at the beginner's level, you can understand it at least partially. By practicing meditation, you can overcome the crudest level of misery and anxiety, and become somewhat tamed, somewhat matured, and somewhat weathered. You can have a taste of liberation, and you can exaggerate that taste. Judging by that taste of liberation, you realize that if you go further, you are perfectly certain of overcoming the whole perpetually vicious cycle of samsara altogether, and gaining some kind of rest.

The dharma is known as passionlessness. Passion is based on struggle, aggression, and longing. It is based on hunger and thirst, on poverty mentality. We wish we could be better; we wish we could get something greater. That quality of wanting—wanting more, wanting to get something greater—is passion. Once the message of dharma has been trans-

---

* A reference to one of the traditional epithets of the Buddha: *bhagavat*, or *chom-den-de* in Tibetan, referring to the qualities of conquering, possessing, and transcending. See chapter 13, "The Buddha."

planted in us, we are no longer so very hungry. We see that pushing too hard does not help. However, not pushing at all does not help either, so a medium level of aspiration is preferable. You could be highly interested and open and somewhat hungry, but not just looking for the pleasure of one day becoming a happy person.

Taking refuge in the dharma means giving up your individual intellectual and metaphysical speculation. In terms of your shamatha practice, such occupations are problematic, so you should give them up. By taking refuge in the dharma, you are giving up your intellectual stronghold. You are giving up your intellectual point of view and even your experiential point of view. Although in the refuge formula, you first take refuge in the Buddha and then take refuge in the dharma, dharma comes first. For example, when you set up a shrine, you never put a statue on top of a book; you always place a book higher than a statue.

TAKING REFUGE IN THE SANGHA

Finally, we take refuge in the sangha as companionship. The sangha means those who have entered the path. Traditionally, it refers to the monastic community, those who are fully ordained and observe the rules of monastic discipline of a *bhikshu* or *bhikshuni*, a monk or a nun. The notion of *mahasangha*, or great sangha, is a more mahayana approach to the idea of sangha: it includes both fully ordained monks and nuns and laypeople. The mahasangha includes laypeople who have just taken the refuge vow and entered the path, as well as those lay practitioners who have also taken three or more of the first precepts, called *upasaka* (for men) or *upasika* (for women) or *genyen* in Tibetan. *Genyen* means "those who practice virtue." Having already accepted Buddha, dharma, and sangha as their working basis, the genyen have accepted the precept that renounces taking life; the precept that renounces taking advantage of others by not giving to them or by stealing; and the precept that renounces telling lies in order to deceive others for one's own benefit.

We should approach sangha as a continuation of our understanding of Buddha and dharma. Buddha is the teacher, dharma is the teaching, and sangha is the practitioners. When we understand the Buddha as an example, and the dharma as path, our understanding of sangha as companionship will happen naturally. Taking refuge in the sangha means accepting your dharma brothers and sisters, those with whom you practice, as true friends. When you feel that your dharma brothers and sisters are not true friends, you begin to shy away from them, and your practice begins to deteriorate into monkey business of all kinds. You are thrown back to your old wretchedness. It might be better if you jumped into the dishwasher and got yourself washed.

You take refuge in the sangha as a community of practitioners who stand on their own two feet. Since nobody is leaning on you, if you fall down, only you will fall down, so you do not create chaos. If someone else falls down, you could save that person. So although there is a mutual journey taking place, you are not dependent on the group. The comradeship of the sangha is based on individual dignity. Taking refuge in the sangha allows for an appreciation of sane companionship, sane community interaction. The community reminds you of your shortcomings, and gives you feedback as to how your journey is taking place.

There are lots of ordinary sanghas—flocks of people put together in a group, club, army, citizenry, or whatever. There are many collections of people who share the same goals or have the same ideas: factory workers, unions, men's clubs, women's groups, and all sorts of "isms." But even though we may call those groups all sorts of names, such as "The Brotherhood of the White Owl" or "The Order of the Best Hat," none of those groups are regarded as sangha. There is a particular term for the fellowship, or sangha, of buddhadharma: it is *aryasangha*, which means "noble sangha." There is a self-existing quality of nobility. The noble sangha could include different levels of sangha, such as baby sanghas, adult sanghas, and highly developed sanghas. The different levels of sangha are like the development of a duck: in its infancy, a baby duck has just learned to float, and only its neck sticks out of the water, whereas an adult duck can float with its whole body on top of the water and can even dive, and wiser and more skillful ducks can scoop in and out of the water to catch fish.

The noble sangha is free from theism. Being free from theistic conceptual mind, they are able to rest their minds in the saddharma, or perfect dharma. Saddharma is not regarded as precious, but as sharp and real, perfect and definite, steady and solid. It is sometimes fluid and sometimes static, depending on the condition of the perceiver. Nevertheless, the dharma itself remains saddharma.

Sangha members who do not understand saddharma may abuse the sangha for personal gain. Such sangha members are only superficially noble sangha. They do not want to give up their particular trips and anxieties, but hope that instead their anxiety will simply be lifted up by the magic of the dharma. That is not quite the case. The saddharma is like a frying pan heating over a fire: whatever you put into it is worthy of either being cooked or being burnt up and destroyed. As students of saddharma, you may experience certain challenges, such as criticisms of your individual behavior patterns and ego-clinging. However, simply indulging in a little pleasure does not necessarily make you a bad member of the sangha. To be a good member of the sangha, the fundamental requirement is that you have a quality of softness and genuineness.

When you take refuge, there should be some change taking place in you. Fundamentally, the idea of refuge is to reshape individuals into a noble sangha so that they could understand the true dharma. The goodness or decency of the sangha is based on learning how to behave, how to talk, and how to handle oneself. Those who have taken the refuge vow are connecting with a kind of dharmic elegance. Such elegance is not a matter of display or exhibitionism. You have good health and a good appearance because you manifest yourself in an elegant way. To manifest elegance, you do not have to move into a luxurious mansion. You might live in a cave or in a grass dome, like the yogis in India, but it is an elegant grass dome. You might camp on a patch of bare ground, but you still present yourself at your best, with uplifted human dignity.

The word *elegance* is somewhat analogous to the term *rinpoche,* which means "precious one" and is a synonym for "jewel." That idea of elegance is connected with the principle of the "three jewels": the Buddha, the dharma, and the sangha. In Sanskrit, we call the three jewels *triratna: tri* means "three," *ratna* is "jewel." Gold manifests itself as gold, not because of its audience, but simply because it is gold. A diamond is a diamond, not because of its audience, but simply because it happens to be a diamond. Not needing an audience is an expression of egolessness. Nonetheless, authentic brilliance and goodness exist within you always. So when you take refuge in the three jewels, you become a part of the noble sangha, not because you have an audience, not because you are trying to impress anybody, but because of what you are—and what you are is brilliance and richness. That is the basic point of taking the refuge vow.

12

The Sutra of the Recollection of the Noble Three Jewels

Trungpa Rinpoche expanded his discussion of the three jewels in the form of a commentary on the traditional sutra entitled the Sutra of the Recollection of the Noble Three Jewels, *or in Sanskrit the* Arya-ratnatraya-anusmriti-sutra. *This short sutra is traditionally chanted as a way of increasing a student's devotion to the Buddha, trust in the dharma, and respect for the sangha. Trungpa Rinpoche included this chant in the meal liturgy he created for extended group meditation retreats, such as Vajradhatu Seminaries.—Ed.*

THE BUDDHA

I prostrate to the omniscient one.

Thus, the Buddha, bhagavat, tathagata, arhat, samyaksambuddha, the learned and virtuous one, the sugata, the knower of the world, the charioteer and tamer of beings, the unsurpassable one, the teacher of devas and humans, is the Buddha bhagavat. The tathagata is in accord with all merit. He does not waste the roots of virtue. He is completely ornamented with all patience. He is the basis of the treasures of merit. He is adorned with the excellent minor marks. He blossoms with the flowers of the major marks. His activity is timely and appropriate. Seeing him, he is without disharmony. He brings true joy to those who long with faith. His knowledge cannot be overpowered. His strengths cannot be challenged. He is the teacher of all sentient beings. He is the father of bodhisattvas. He is the king of noble ones. He is the guide of those who journey to the city of nirvana. He possesses immeasurable wisdom. He possesses inconceivable confidence. His speech is completely pure. His melody is pleasing. One never has enough of seeing him. His form is incomparable. He is not stained by the realm of desire. He is not stained by the realm of form. He is not affected by the formless realm. He is completely liberated from suffering. He is completely and utterly liberated from the skandhas. The dhatus have no hold on him. His ayatanas are controlled. He has completely cut the knots. He is completely liberated from extreme torment. He is liberated from craving. He has crossed over the river. He is perfected in all the wisdoms. He abides in the wisdom of the buddha bhagavats who arise in the past, present, and future. He does not abide in nirvana. He abides in the ultimate perfection. He dwells on the bhumi where he sees all sentient beings. All these are the perfect virtues of the greatness of the Buddha bhagavat.

The Dharma

The holy dharma is good at the beginning, good in the middle, and good at the end. Its meaning is excellent. Its words are excellent. It is uncorrupted. It is completely perfect and completely pure. It completely purifies. The bhagavat teaches the dharma well. It brings complete vision. It is free from sickness. It is always timely. It directs one further. Seeing it fulfills one's purpose. It brings discriminating insight for the wise. The dharma spoken by the bhagavat thoroughly teaches training. It is renunciation. It causes one to arrive at perfect enlightenment. It is without contradiction. It is pithy. It is trustworthy and puts an end to the journey.

The Sangha

As for the sangha of the great yana, they enter completely. They enter insightfully. They enter straightforwardly. They enter harmoniously. They are worthy of veneration with joined palms. They are worthy of receiving prostration. They are a field of glorious merit. They are completely capable of receiving all gifts. They are an object of generosity. They are always a great object of generosity.

This concludes the Noble Sutra of the Recollection of the Noble Three Jewels.

—*Translated by the Nalanda Translation Committee under the direction of Vidyadhara the Venerable Chögyam Trungpa Rinpoche*

13

The Buddha

When we study the Buddha, we realize that the Buddha is quite different from us, that we are not the Buddha. We have the potential, but not the realization or the proclamation to make. At the same time, buddha is what we are. That is why we sit upright and breathe as Buddha breathed, very simply. We too do not have to imitate anything, for buddha is in us already.

I N T H E *Sutra of the Recollection of the Noble Three Jewels,* the Buddha is described as having many qualities. The point of learning all of these qualities is that we could emulate the Buddha, rather than seeing him as possessing qualities that are beyond our reach. *Buddha* basically means the "awakened one," somebody who has woken up from being asleep in samsaric sense perceptions, stuck in the hassles of samsara. Although we live in different circumstances, a different age, a different civilization, psychologically there is no difference at all.

To understand the meaning of the Buddha, it is important to remember that the Buddha was not a Buddhist. He had his own realization. Because he had buddhahood within him, he did not need to imitate anybody else's buddhahood. The Buddha sat beneath the bodhi tree to enlighten himself. This is how Buddha became Buddha. If he didn't enlighten himself, he could not enlighten others.

When we study the Buddha, we realize that the Buddha is quite different from us, that we are not the Buddha. We have the potential, but not the realization or the proclamation to make. At the same time, Buddha is what we are. That is why we sit upright and breathe as Buddha breathed,

Shakyamuni Buddha in earth-witness mudra and disciples Shariputra with Mahamaudgalyayana. Illustration by Glen Eddy. © 1973 Shambhala Publications.

very simply. We too do not have to imitate anything, for buddha is in us already. So on one hand, Buddha was a somewhat ordinary person; but on the other hand, only rarely—once in more than twenty-six hundred years—does somebody appear who has the courage to say what is right with the world and what is wrong with the world.

The Buddha was already a bodhisattva when he was inspired to run away from his home and abandon his servants and his court to become Buddha. When he sat beneath the bodhi tree to attain enlightenment, he already had the desire to liberate sentient beings. He wasn't doing it purely for himself, to get some kick out of it—he was doing it for others. Buddha is said to be the only refuge, because he is the one person in the universe who is not confused, who *is* the Buddha.

When you study the three jewels, you should try to understand everything, every word. You should try to understand the logic behind the logic. At some point, you may be able to enter into a dharmic environment where your buddha nature will blossom and your enlightenment will flourish and begin to bloom. In the meantime, you could put effort into sitting practice. You should realize that there is tremendous love and affection for practitioners coming from the lineage. The adoration and love of a teacher for a practicing student is limitless and always tender. It is the Buddhist equivalent of what Christians call "bleeding heart."

Sang-Gye:
The Tibetan Term for Buddha

The term for Buddha in Tibetan is *sang-gye. Sang* means "clarified," or "purified." If you had a stuffy room, *sang* would be like opening all the doors and windows and letting out the stuffiness. *Sang* means overcoming the heedlessness stemming from habitual patterns. Due to habitual patterns, you would like to dwell in your neurosis. *Sang* means overcoming those patterns; it means overcoming "I" or "self."

Gye means "expansion," or "blossoming." It has the sense of "splendidness," or "extension." Having overcome the problem of the domestication of ego, you are actually free from that. It is like a positive divorce. If you are having a terribly hard time being married and feel imprisoned in your marriage, when you break up, there is *gye*, freedom. Gye is connected with the vipashyana principle of perceiving things as they are, properly and fully. As an aspect of buddha, gye means being continuously loving and supportive of your endeavor to be free from this world.

Altogether, Buddha, or sang-gye, means being awakened and then expanding. Sang-gye means that you are expanding your own vision, and at the same time you are helping others. You are becoming cleared of any neurosis; therefore, you are expanding. Sang corresponds to shamatha, and gye to vipashyana. Sang is awake, and gye is the fruition of that wakefulness. This awakening comes automatically from sitting practice. When you sit, you have discriminations, thoughts, and mind pictures of all kinds arising from your habitual patterns. With sang, or sitting practice, you overcome these and experience gye, or openness. You are no longer trapped, but you are opening up. That is the spirit of the Buddha, or sang-gye, which applies to ourselves as well as being the buddha principle altogether.

Gye is connected with the *ayatanas,* or senses. You are relating with the ayatanas—with seeing, hearing, smelling, tasting, touching, and thinking—with awareness and mindfulness. You are no longer subject to the senses; instead, you develop awareness of them. You are free from the ayatanas, and at the same time you are very acutely perceptive of them, much more so than otherwise. You use the ayatanas as they are, as sensing machines, as vehicles for mindfulness, but you are not caught by them.

In the process of sitting meditation and awareness practice, when you hear a sound, that sound is not produced by preconceptions—it is simply sound. There is emptiness to that sound as well as fullness. It is there, but it is not there. It is a struggle to understand this at the beginning. You cannot simply hear sound alone, but it speaks, as if you had acquired a new parakeet. In perceiving sound as both there and not there, it is *there* because you heard it, and it is *not there* because you are absentminded. Due to absentmindedness, when you look up at the blue sky, you probably see pink. However, if you are in communication with reality as it is, hot is hot, cold is cold, black is black, white is white, and reality is reality. Your thought is thought, your breath is breath, your posture is posture, and the aches and pains in your spinal cord or your buttocks are real aches and pains. That kind of perception comes from sitting practice.

The *Sutra of the Recollection of the Noble Three Jewels* introduces several traditional Sanskrit terms for the Buddha. Since these terms qualify what a buddha should be, it might be helpful to look into them in some detail.

SANSKRIT TERMS FOR BUDDHA

The Sanskrit terms used in the sutra that qualify what a buddha should be are *bhagavat, tathagata, arhat,* and *samyaksambuddha.*

Bhagavat

Bhagavat has three categories: conquering, possessing, and transcending. In Tibetan, bhagavat is *chom-den-de. Chom* means "conquer," and refers to conquering the four *maras,* which are evil seductive forces, demons, or devils. At the hinayana level, the four maras are simply obstacles or enemies to the path. *Chom* means that one is conquering any such negative possibilities; one has power over those who prevent the practice of dharma. *Den* means "possessing." In this case, it means possessing the powers of wakefulness, kindness, and profundity. *De* means "gone beyond"; it can also mean "dead." *De* is related with the idea of transcending. One cannot call a buddha back to samsara; no regression is possible. It is not possible that a buddha could de-nirvanacize or de-enlighten. A buddha has gone beyond both worldly virtues and unworldly virtues, both at the same time. So altogether, chom-den-de means one who has conquered the four maras, is wakeful, and has gone beyond.

THE FOUR MARAS. The four obstacles, or maras, are devaputra-mara, klesha-mara, skandha-mara, and yama-mara.

Devaputra-mara. The Sanskrit term *devaputra* literally means "son of the gods." Because of the seduction of devaputra, we appreciate taking time off from true learning with pleasure, or as a saving grace. Devaputra refers to personal gratification, to love-and-light trips. This obstacle encourages us to make our experience pleasurable all the time, whether by attaining enlightenment or by whatever other means.

Klesha-mara. Kleshas are thought patterns and daydreams, which can become evil demons. Any state of mind contains its own possibility for entertaining you through passion, aggression, arrogance, jealousy, ignorance, and so forth. With klesha-mara, every thought pattern that might lead you to wake up, instead makes you fall more asleep. Kleshas make you deaf and dumb, more confused. From the point of view that it is actually possible to realize enlightenment, or to wake up, all such kleshas are counterproductive.

Skandha-mara. The skandhas refer to the five components of our state of being—form, feeling, perception / impulse, concept / formation, and consciousness. They are connected with individualism and with personal experience. The obstacle of skandha-mara encourages you to solidify the skandhas—you solidify the physical process of existence and all the rest of the skandhas. You solidify how you feel and how you experience your life. In doing so, you become dependent on what we are not supposed to depend on—the skandhas—which does not allow you to be happy or cheerful. Your dependence on the skandhas is monotonous. It is based on monolithic passion, aggression, and ignorance. According to Buddhist principles, those monoliths do not exist—but according to one's own wishes, they do exist.

*Yama-mara.** The last obstacle is *yama-mara,* the mara of Yama, the Lord of Death. We have a problem relating with death. We are unable to relate properly with ourselves, our death, or the corrosion of our body as we get older. We have a fear of death and the possibility of death. At the same time, death can be a temptation. Due to our speediness, we may want the death of the present moment, or present situation, so we can go on to the next one. Like busy executives, while we are seeing one group of people, we would like to get that over with so we can go on to the next group. With yama-mara, you are not given a chance to wake up or to be in a wakeful state. Rather, you are allowed to indulge completely, all the time, in your own personal fantasy.

Tathagata

The Buddha is also known as tathagata. In the term *tathagata, gata* means "gone," and *tatha* is "like that," or "thus." In Tibetan it is *teshin shekpa, teshin* meaning "like that," and *shekpa* meaning "gone." Like tathagata, teshin shekpa means "thus gone." Both terms imply that the Buddha has gone beyond, just like the previous buddhas. Referring to the Buddha as tathagata, or teshin-shekpa, links the Buddha with those who traveled on the path in the past and achieved the result, those who have gone beyond. Buddha has gone beyond with them, so there is a lineage connection.

---

* Trungpa Rinpoche prefers the term *yama-mara* to the more usual Sanskrit term *mrityu-mara.*

There were a lot of buddhas before Shakyamuni Buddha, who was the one person in our era who became the Buddha. Buddhahood is not a unique situation. Buddhas are quite common—there are hundreds and thousands of them. At the same time, although there are many buddhas, they appear only rarely. This world is a very rare one, too—at least, uncooked! It is a fresh world, and in this world you get all sorts of feedback. When the electricity fails, the room is cold; when the electricity is on, the room is warm. It is a basic world. In this world, fire is hot, snow is cold, and so forth. For another buddha to appear, the world has to die and be reborn again. It is very simple. The world exhausts itself; then there is a period of gap; then the world begins again in the same way as before. Dead or not, the world is a trick.

Arhat

The term *arhat* means "one who is worthy." In Tibetan it is *drachompa*. *Dra* means "enemy," *chom,* as before, means "conquering," and *pa* makes it a noun; so altogether *drachompa* is "one who conquers the enemy." When one is an arhat, the attack of the four maras and whatever other obstacles there may be have been completely conquered.

For an arhat, the attainment of enlightenment is not a threat to anybody's existence. Enlightened people may experience a kind of hangover or rebound, in that having attained enlightenment, they wonder what they are doing. But here there is none of that. When somebody becomes very, very successful, that person often has the experience of needing to live up to that success, and therefore feels threatened all the time. Such a person becomes more and more stiff and nervous trying to maintain their credentials. In contrast, in the case of an arhat, conquering one's enemies means being free from credentials, even the credential of enlightenment.

Samyaksambuddha

Samyak in Tibetan is *yang-dak-pe. Yang* means "utterly" or "completely," *dak-pe* means "pure"; so *yang-dak-pe* is "a person who has purified themselves completely." In other words, samyak means one who has achieved buddhahood completely, thoroughly, fully, without any trace of doubt. In particular, samyak refers to being free of hangovers of any kind from previous lives or previous experiences.

Sambuddha is the "perfect Buddha," or in Tibetan, *dzok-pe sang-gye*. *Dzokpa* (the undeclined form of dzok-pe) means "fully completed," and *sang-gye* is Buddha; so altogether *samyaksambuddha* means the "completely pure, perfect Buddha." Sambuddha means that one has attained real buddhahood, genuine buddhahood, the best of the best of all. Such a buddha's attainment is beyond both samsaric buddhahood and nirvanic buddhahood. It is beyond any hassles that reality might present. He or she has already conquered them, completely so.

The attainment of Buddha is completely pure, completely real. Buddha has gone beyond the two levels of ego: the ego of self and the ego of phenomena. Furthermore, he also has gone beyond any fixation on the two realms of egolessness. If there is any stain at all, Buddha has gone beyond it. So we could say that Buddha has gone beyond the two egolessnesses, and he has gone beyond beyond-egolessness, so nothing is problematic for him. He did the whole thing completely, utterly, one hundred percent. We could call it five-hundred-percent purity!

Dzok means that everything is gone beyond and that everything that needs to be achieved is achieved. It is found in the vajrayana term *dzokchen*, or *maha ati*, which also means "gone beyond." In vajrayana language, we use the word *crazy*, as in "crazy wisdom." Crazy refers to utterly overleaping any possible mental games. Such obstacles are completely scooped out and thrown away. Simultaneously, there is a quality of tremendous outsmarting. You might outsmart yourself once, but if you outsmart yourself a hundred times, there is no room left for anybody to play tricks on you, at all. The whole thing is completely scooped out, scooped in, transcended.

Epithets for the Buddha

The Learned and Virtuous One

The Buddha is referred to in the sutra as the learned and virtuous one. In this epithet, *learned* refers to those who have insight—in particular, the insight of shamatha-vipashyana. In Tibetan it is *rikpa denpa*. The learned are those who have the insight to see the falsity of samsara, the world of pain and pleasure. Learned ones possess the eye of prajna, the eye of insight that can look at reality from an enlightened point of view. This view is not a metaphysical view; it is the ability to see how the world functions, which develops with the insight of shamatha and vipashyana.

In Tibetan, this insight is called *rikpa,* which refers to the intelligence of the Buddha. The Buddha is learned; he possesses the eye of wisdom. So the first point is that the Buddha is learned in the way the world operates.

The second part of the epithet, after learned, is *virtuous.* By realizing discriminating-awareness wisdom, by being learned, the Buddha knows how to walk on the path. Therefore, he is virtuous. The *Sutra of the Recollection of the Noble Three Jewels* refers to the Buddha as "one who possesses feet," or *shapsu denpa,* meaning one who is able to walk on the path. The Buddha is the virtuous one because he knows how to walk on the path. He knows various and quite substantial ways to walk or to work. In Tibetan, this quality of walking on the path is known as *shap.*

THE EIGHT SUPERIOR WAYS OF SEEING. The Buddha's quality of being learned and virtuous is connected with eight superior ways of seeing— also known as the eight limbs of vipashyana.* In Tibetan, this is called lhakthong yenlak gye. Lhakthong, or vipashyana, means "superior way of seeing," or "insight," yenlak means "limbs," or "possibilities," and gye means "eight"†; so lhaktong yenlak gye means the "eight superior ways of seeing the world." The eight limbs, or eight ways of seeing, can be divided into two categories: looking and walking. Looking is connected with "learned," the first part of the Buddha's epithet, and the first limb falls into this category. Walking is connected with "virtuous," the second part of the Buddha's epithet, and the remaining seven limbs fall under this category. So working with these eight ways or limbs is like looking where you are walking: when you look where you are walking, you get to a better destination. We could actually change the translation of the Buddha's epithet to "looking and walking" instead of "learned and virtuous."

1. *View.* The first of the eight ways of seeing is connected with the quality of learnedness. It is called view, meaning that the Buddha thoroughly and fully experienced insight and clear perception. He saw how the world works, and he saw how practitioners should work. He saw that the path is subdivided into three parts, consisting of shila, samadhi, and prajna,

---

* The categories of the eight superior ways of seeing are the same as the eight categories of the noble eightfold path. For a further discussion of the noble eightfold path, see chapter 60, "The Five Paths."

† Literally this is translated as the "eight limbs of vipashyana," although some commentators link right view to "learned" and vipashyana, and the other seven to "virtuous" and shamatha.

or discipline, meditation, and knowledge. View means seeing things as they are and realizing things as they are. In Tibetan, this completely clear seeing is called *yang-dak-pe tawa*. *Yang* means "utterly," or "completely," *dak-pe* means "pure," and *tawa* means "seeing," or "view"; so *yang-dak-pe tawa* means the "utterly pure view."

From this first stage grows the rest of the journey of the Buddha. So first you realize the view, and then, after you see the path, you have to walk on the path. Walking comes later and includes the remaining seven stages. As you walk on the noble path of shila, samadhi, and prajna, you realize the discipline that comes from shamatha and vipashyana practice.

2. *Understanding.* The second of the eight ways of seeing of the Buddha is complete understanding. The first aspect (view) was connected with the thorough realization of shamatha-vipashyana experience. Here, having fully experienced shamatha-vipashyana, you begin to develop an understanding of that experience, which is called *yang-dak-pe tokpa*. *Tokpa* means "understanding," and *yang-dak-pe,* as before, means "utterly pure"; so *yang-dak-pe tokpa* is "utterly pure understanding."

3. *Speech.* The third way of seeing is *yang-dak-pe ngak*. *Ngak* means "speech," or "utterance"; so *yang-dak-pe ngak* is "utterly pure speech." This stage is connected with proclaiming or uttering properly and thoroughly, according to the dharmic principles of peace and nonaggression.

4. *End of karma.* The fourth way is *yang-dak-pe lekyi tha.* *Le* means "karma," *kyi* means "of," and *tha* means "ending"; so *yang-dak-pe lekyi tha* means the utterly pure ending of karmic debts. Once you become Buddha, there is a pure and complete ending of karmic debts.

5. *Livelihood.* Number five is *yang-dak-pe tsowa.* *Tso* means "live," and *tsowa* makes it a noun, so *yang-dak-pe tsowa* means utterly pure living. Pure living means not harming others and not causing chaos to others, but just simply being. You are living a life of purity, as the Buddha did.

6. *Effort.* Number six is *yang-dak-pe tsölwa.* *Tsölwa* means "effort," so *yang-dak-pe tsölwa* means utterly pure effort. For the Buddha, both effort and work are purified.

7. *Recollection.* Number seven is *yang-dak-pe trenpa.* *Trenpa* means "recognition," or "recollection," so *yang-dak-pe trenpa* means utterly pure recollection. It refers to the recollection of one's state of mind, or of one's practice of dharma altogether. It is the recollection of shamatha-vipashyana.

8. *Meditation.* The last one, number eight, is *yang-dak-pe tingdzin,* "completely pure meditation." *Tingdzin* is the perfect meditation that comes

from shamatha-vipashyana experience, so *yang-dak-pe tingdzin* is utterly pure meditation.

The basic point of all this is that the Buddha was not a con man. The Buddha actually experienced all eight ways of seeing. When he attained enlightenment, he never relied on other people's neurosis, pain, blood, or negativity. He just worked with himself, as he should, by himself. Simply realizing that the Buddha existed in that way is a part of our discipline—it is why we call ourselves nontheists. Nobody washed in the Buddha's blood, and nobody felt sorry for the Buddha because he had to practice so much. This is a very important point. We could say that nontheism depends on the prophets and that the Buddha was a prophet, but he was a prophet who did not gain any profit from others—their pain, pleasure, or otherwise. He was a simple man of the aristocracy, a prince, Siddhartha. He worked on himself and he worked for others very simply.

To understand why the Buddha was great and wonderful, we need to understand the teachings of the Buddha and his experience of shamatha-vipashyana, which is what made him special. The Buddha was the discoverer of shamatha-vipashyana practice and of many other mind-training practices. Therefore, the Buddha is known as the "learned and virtuous one."

Sugata

The Buddha has gone beyond with joy; therefore, he is known as sugata. *Dewar,* the Tibetan translation of the Sanskrit word *su,* means "joyfully," and *gata,* again, means "gone," in the sense of gone beyond, so sugata means "gone joyfully." He has experienced both pure joy and ordinary joy. Perfect joy is not clumsy or confused by conventional concepts of pleasure. The ordinary concept of pleasure is to please oneself and abandon others, but the sugata's concept of pleasure includes others' pleasure, as well. The Buddha experiences compassion, joy, and bliss, in which others are included.

There are many further epithets of the Buddha, as described in the *Sutra of the Recollection of the Noble Three Jewels,* such as the *charioteer* who leads you in the direction of enlightenment, the *knower of the world,* or the *king of noble ones.*

QUALITIES OF THE BUDDHA

The *Sutra of the Recollection of the Noble Three Jewels* also describes many qualities of the Buddha, as well as describing the Buddha's effect on those he encounters.

The tathagata is in accord with all merit. Merit is richness. It is not something you work hard to get—it is like digging in the earth and finding gold dust in your hand. *He does not waste the roots of virtue.* In shamatha-vipashyana, the virtues of the Buddha are always present. *He is completely ornamented with all patience.* If you are a teacher, when a student raises a question impatiently, you have to be patient and work with that student. *One never has enough of seeing him. His form is incomparable.* The Buddha's body is so beautiful and so tranquil that his very being is enough to bear witness to his awareness—so one never has enough of seeing him. It is unrequited love. *He is not stained by the realm of desire. He is not stained by the realm of form. He is not affected by the formless realm.* The Buddha is not stained by the realms of passion or form, and he is not living with Jehovah in his heaven. He is simply being himself at his best.

He is completely liberated from suffering. The Buddha is free from all pain. This also means he is free from passion, aggression, ignorance, jealousy, and pride. *He is completely and utterly liberated from the skandhas.* The Buddha is free from form, feeling, perception / impulse, formation / concept, and consciousness. *The dhatus have no hold on him. His ayatanas are controlled.* The Buddha sees things as they are, so he is not bound by the senses.* *He has completely cut the knots.* Thus, he is free from bondage; he is not tied up. *He is completely liberated from extreme torment.* The Buddha is free from torment of any kind. The notion of extreme torment is open to interpretation, but the idea is that once you attain a basic understanding and experience of shamatha-vipashyana, you are free from tormenting yourself. On one hand, since you experience further subtleties, you experience more acute and direct pain. On the other hand, you also experience that acute pain as workable, because you are able to single out individual perceptions one at a time. So when the Buddha experiences suffering,

---

* Dhatus refer to the components of perception as: the sense faculties, or sense organs; their corresponding sense objects; and the sense consciousnesses. Ayatanas refer to the components of perception as: the sense faculties, or sense organs; and their corresponding sense objects.

he does not dwell on it. *He is liberated from craving. He has crossed over the river.* The Buddha is free from attachment of any kind. Therefore, he has crossed over the river of samsara, which is very turbulent and confused. *He does not abide in nirvana. He abides in the ultimate perfection. He dwells on the bhumi where he sees all sentient beings.* The Buddha dwells at the very best extreme. He dwells on a level or *bhumi* that is free from all bondage, pain, and hang-ups. But he does not dwell in peace for his own benefit alone—he is working with all sentient beings. In fact, he is still with us.

All these are the perfect virtues of the greatness of the Buddha bhagavat. Gold and diamonds never say, "I am a diamond; I am gold." People value diamonds and gold because of what they see in them. Likewise, the Buddha never said, "I am the best. I am the one who exhausts samsaric pain," but people began to see him in that way. That does not mean they were enlightened. When you see expensive objects, you do not become rich right away, and when you see the sun, you don't become a sun.

Altogether, these descriptions of Lord Buddha show his greatness and give a rough outline of his existence.

14

The Dharma

We could say quite simply that the first thought of human beings is dharma, the second thought is dharma, and the third thought is also dharma. Without that kind of dharmic depth, nobody could think comprehensibly at all. It is very simple. Before neurosis, there is just that first, simple, innocent thought.

HAVING DISCUSSED the qualities of the Buddha, the *Sutra of the Recollection of the Noble Three Jewels* goes on to present the qualities of the holy dharma. *Dharma* means the "teachings." It means "truth," "law," or "path." The related term, *dharmachakra*, means the "constant revolving, or constant motion, of the dharma." It means that the dharma is ceaselessly turning. If you had dharma without dharmachakra, it would be like a weapon not employed by a warrior. The practitioner and the dharma should be walking together side by side—that is the idea of dharmachakra. Dharmachakra is the driving force that inspires us and makes us spiritually ambitious. It is that which destroys anti-dharma, or *adharma*, the psychological approach of sheer indulgence and entertainment without any sense of journey or accomplishment.

Often, we would like to perpetuate our indulgence: our aggression, passion, and intellectual speculation. For instance, although it is painful when we are in the state of hatred, at the same time we get some kind of pleasure out of it. We feel that we are not just lying idle, but we are busy and occupied, making use of our faculties. It is the same for passion and for philosophical speculation. The dharma should inspire us and protect us from useless indulgence that has nothing to do with the path.

The meaning of dharmachakra is that the dharma is used properly, with a good state of mind. Even if our state of mind is distorted by emotional eruptions and philosophical speculations, there is still the *intention* of using those materials on the path. That is the dharmachakra approach.

The holy dharma is spoken by the Buddha. It is well said and leads to painlessness. The dharma refers to that which mind conceives, as well as what might arise in the future. The Buddha is like a charioteer who knows the way, the path is the dharma, the rider is your companionship with the Buddha, and the chariot is your meditation cushion.

In order to realize the true meaning of dharma, we have to understand our mind, our state of being. Understanding the dharma is connected with shamatha-vipashyana. In shamatha-vipashyana, when a thought or a breath occurs, we pay attention to that one thought or breath. We take care, step by step, to be there, right on the spot. Whenever we have any experience of dharma, it is true, it is reality. We have no second thoughts about it. The dharma is always there. It is very simple and direct. Sometimes we forget, but we always come back.

The dharma is based on honesty, on not having self-deception of any kind. When the dharma says blue, it is blue; when it says red, it is red. Dharma is like saying fire is hot, or the sky is blue: it is speaking the truth. The difference is that dharma is the truth of the reality of the journey toward freedom. Saying that red is red does not particularly liberate you from seeing green or yellow. But when dharma speaks about reality, we see that it is worth stepping out of our little world of habitual patterns, our little nest. In that way, the dharma brings greater vision. Even though we may think we cannot understand the dharma, it still brings greater vision.

The holy dharma is good in the beginning if you join with it properly; it is *good in the middle* because you are on the path; and it is *good in the end* because it frees you from pain and torment. The meaning of the dharma is clear and definite, and *its words are excellent* and well spoken. It is not mixed up with other ideas or borrowed concepts, so it is *pure*, like good water. It is straight, direct, and completely able to liberate. By bringing an understanding of relief and freedom from pain, the dharma *directs one further* and *fulfills one's purpose*. The dharma shows you the path of renunciation from samsaric involvement, and allows you to go all the way to complete enlightenment.

The dharma *puts an end to the journey* between oneself and other, which is samsaric. It puts an end to ego fixation and to both eternalism and nihilism. In terms of ego, attainment could give rise to eternalism, and working with others could give rise to nihilism. The dharma cuts both those extremes. The interesting twist is that those extremes are reversed. If you are a nihilist, by studying the dharma you realize that you can attain everything eternally; and if you are an eternalist, you realize that you can cut the journey altogether. Those are the qualities of dharma according to the text of this sutra.

The brilliance and magnificence of the dharma is so great, it can seem to be too much, but I myself gave in at the age of thirteen. I continuously gave in until I experienced the other side of the situation, where the giver begins to realize what "giving in" means. If you are very thirsty and you want to drink water, you might wonder how to drink water, before you actually do it. You may be so thirsty that you are almost used to being thirsty. But you don't have to ask how—you could just drink the water. The sense of poverty has to be given up. Once you do that, your thirst is quenched, and the way to proceed further becomes very natural and ordinary.

We could say quite simply that the first thought of human beings is dharma, the second thought is dharma, and the third thought is also dharma. Without that kind of dharmic depth, nobody could think comprehensibly at all. It is very simple. Before neurosis, there is just that first, simple, innocent thought. Later we begin to jazz it up by means of neuroses of all kinds, but the first flicker of thought is very definitely innocent and unneurotic. The moment you wake up, the moment you open your eyes and see a ray of sunshine or hear your parents talking—those first perceptions are direct, innocent, and pure. They are the working basis that happens over and over up to this very point. That quality of first thought is happening here and now. It is happening all over the place.

15

The Sangha

The sangha usually is very gentle and genuine; therefore, the sangha is a great field of merit. By giving in to, respecting, and following the Buddha, the sangha has developed merit. . . . Merit is simply a field of openness, which allows individuals to realize that when the proper intentions are put into the proper situations, those intentions rebound and are automatically resolved.

HAVING DISCUSSED the Buddha and the dharma, the *Sutra of the Recollection of the Noble Three Jewels* goes on to discuss the sangha. If you have taken refuge vows, you are regarded as a member of the sangha. As a sangha member, you should practice simplicity. You should be free from the complications of life, and simply spend your life practicing and teaching others, if you can. In terms of sitting practice, you should sit properly on your meditation cushion or chair. In terms of eating, you should eat simple food with mindfulness and awareness.

SHAPING A NOBLE SANGHA

According to the sutra, there are ten conditions for shaping a noble sangha. These conditions are based on solidity and sanity in relating to yourself, together with diplomacy in relating with others. They are based on samadhi and prajna, on meditation and knowledge. All ten conditions are shaped by two factors: contentment and a lessening of emotionalism. The ten conditions are related with the hinayana level of sangha alone. They are not all that profound, but they are very perky and realistic.

The sutra arranges the ten conditions into three categories: entering properly, being worthy of veneration, and receiving generosity.

Entering Properly

The first four conditions—entering completely, entering insightfully, entering straightforwardly, and entering harmoniously—fall under the category of entering properly and are connected with relating to oneself.

As for the sangha of the great yana, they enter completely. Entering completely means that you enter the sangha without reservation. You are not holding back. You cannot enter completely into the sangha if you are holding on to your self or your ego, and you cannot enter completely if you are holding on to theistic philosophy. If you are nontheistic, you do not enter into anything other than sangha; therefore, you enter completely. Any theistic way of saving yourself is completely out of the question.

In Tibetan, this condition is called *lekpar shukpa: lekpar* in this context means "completely," and *shukpa* means "entering"; so *lekpar shukpa* means "entering completely." It also has the sense of entering gracefully, or entering beautifully. Although students may still play their particular tricks, it is recommended that a person enter into the dharma gracefully—there are more possibilities that way. As a member of the sangha, you should enter into shila, samadhi, and prajna properly. There is no hesitation; in fact, it is needless to speak of hesitation, at all.

Entering gracefully means that when you enter into the dharma, you don't claim that you were pushed into it by somebody else. Although you like the dharma and you want to get into it, you may try to fight back, as if you wanted to get out. That approach is not just current, it is classical. In fact, it even happened with Shariputra, whom we chant about in the *Heart Sutra.* That is not a bad record! There is no delicacy in such an approach, but the aftereffect is that you do get into the sangha, so it may not be so bad, after all. But the idea of entering gracefully is that *first* you make up your mind completely and perfectly, and *then* you get in.

They enter insightfully. Number two is *rikpar shukpa. Rikpar,* or *vidya* in Sanskrit, means "insight," or "wakefulness," and *shukpa* means "entering," so *rikpar shukpa* means "entering with insight" or "entering with wakefulness." Insightfulness in this case is based on a genuine appreciation for the teachings—and more particularly, for the contemplative practice of becoming like Buddha through meditation. You begin to feel that your sitting practice and your approach to the rest of your life are in accordance with the Buddha, the dharma, and the message of the four noble truths. At this level, your practice becomes much more workable and genuine, completely so. The pain of samsara is diminished, and you enter into the possibility of nirvana.

They enter straightforwardly. Number three is *trangpor shukpa. Trangpor* means "straightforwardly," or "directly," and *shukpa* means "entering," so *trangpor shukpa* means "entering straightforwardly." In other words, not telling any lies. You enter into the true dharma with straightforwardness and genuineness. It is important not to misunderstand the idea of genuineness. In the West, when you try to be genuine you begin to attack people with your genuineness, which is twisted logic. It is a psychologically argumentative approach. In the nontheistic tradition, when we talk straightforwardly and honestly with somebody, we are neither trying to include that person nor to attack them. In the theistic tradition, people may argue about whether God manufactured this world or not. But in the nontheistic tradition, we have no such problem, because nobody claims that anybody built any world anywhere at all! The world is built by people themselves with their own problems.

Genuineness or straightforwardness is not analytical. It is not playing at being genuine or trying to act genuine. Straightforwardness means not swaying to the right or left, just staying on the road. So the sangha is free from both nihilism and eternalism. You are free from complete negativity about life, and free from complete exuberance and positivity, as well. So you enter into the path of sangha-hood in a balanced way.

They enter harmoniously. Number four is *thünpar shukpa. Thün* means "agreement," or "accord," and *shukpa* means "entering," so *thünpar shukpa* means "entering harmoniously." In this context, it has the sense of friendship. Simply being straightforward and pure could be a problem, so along with that you need to develop friendship and kindness. You are willing to join together with other people, willing to understand them. Friendship and kindness means being in accord with others. You do not just want to go your own way, but you want to join your fellow humankind. In particular, you want to become a member of the sangha. You can enter harmoniously because you have been completely and thoroughly well-trained in the discipline of shamatha-vipashyana practice, so your body and mind are harmonious and synchronized.

Being Worthy of Veneration

The next two conditions are connected with the nature of relationships between sangha members. When a sangha has evolved, a charismatic situation occurs. Because individual sangha members have become elegant, insightful, straightforward, and friendly, it becomes possible for them to relate in that way to others. They respect one another. As a sangha member, you are not on an ego trip, and you are not trying to become a great hero or great leader before you even understand the dharma. Instead, you see that your fellow sangha members are worthy of being bowed to and shown respect.

They are worthy of veneration with joined palms. The Tibetan phrase *thalmo jar-we ösu kyurpa* means "being worthy of joining the hands together." *Thalmo* means "palms," *jar-we* means "join together," and *ösu kyurpa* means "worthy of"; so *thalmo jar-we ösu kyurpa* means that you are worthy of both offering and receiving the traditional Indian gesture of respect, or *namaste.* You are worthy of joining your hands together and bowing because you are part of the sangha. You think the situation is worthy of respect, so you bow properly. Your bowing is an expression of mindfulness, devotion, genuine longing, and respect. You are also worthy to receive somebody else's bow. You are not necessarily a saint, but you are truly sane. You are willing to work for the benefit of others. You are willing to work with your grandmother or grandfather; you are willing to work with your disturbed child; you are willing to work with the world around you. That is how much willingness is involved and how much worthiness is taking place.

They are worthy of receiving prostration. The second condition of relating to the sangha is that sangha members are worthy of giving and receiving prostrations, because they are so upright and virtuous. The Tibetan phrase *chak cha-we ösu kyurpa* means "worthy of prostrating." *Chak* means "prostration," *cha-we* means "doing, or acting"; so *chak cha-we* means "doing prostrations." *Ösu kyurpa* means "worthy of"; so *chak cha-we ösu kyurpa* means "worthy of prostrating." The sangha is worthy of giving and receiving prostrations if the sangha has lived up to the five previous categories.

Bowing and Prostrating. The practices of bowing and prostrating are quite subtle. When you bow, psychologically you open yourself completely, but physically you do not. Bowing is communication, and prostrating is completely giving—that is the difference between a bow and a prostration.

Just as the Western notion of shaking hands could be a form of favoritism, prostrating to a teacher or standing when the teacher walks into the hall could also be a form of favoritism, as if you were making a deal with that teacher.* But when you bow or prostrate properly, you are not trying to win someone over. You do not prostrate *for* somebody, and you do not bow *for* somebody. If a student is trying to win a teacher over to their side by putting on a great show, the teacher may view such a student as full of it. In a proper prostration or bow, instead of conning anyone, you are expressing your psychological beauty. If you are genuinely interested, you cannot help but bow. It is not possible to train someone how to bow, but when a person does it properly, it is very genuine and beautiful. It can be a very moving experience when such a person bows—or offers a handshake, for that matter.

When sangha members are bowed to or prostrated to, they do not get puffed up, but they cut their own trips each time. Through their mutual appreciation of the dharma, just purely that, those who bow and those who are bowed to are both cutting their own trips.

Receiving Generosity

The next four conditions of sangha-ship have to do with the traditional relationship of members of the sangha with laypeople and donors—those who feed the sangha, give them shelter, and so forth.

They are a field of glorious merit. The sangha is usually very gentle and genuine; therefore, the sangha is a great field of merit. By giving in to, respecting, and following the Buddha, the sangha has developed merit. In Tibetan, "glorious field of merit" is *sönam kyi palgyi shing. Sönam* means "merit," *kyi* means "of," *pal* means "glorious," *gyi* means "of," and *shing* means "field," so *sönam kyi palgyi shing* means "glorious field of merit." It is the greatest of merit.

Merit is simply a field of openness, which allows individuals to realize that when the proper intentions are put into the proper situations, those intentions rebound and are automatically resolved. It is very simple. If

---

* In the Tibetan tradition, it is customary to stand when a teacher enters the room, and in formal teaching situations it is customary to offer prostrations.

energy and sanity are put into a situation, that is what comes back. It is cause and effect. If you are kind and friendly with somebody, in turn they will be kind and friendly to you. There will be more friendliness surrounding them as well. That person will feel that you are a good person, friendly and trustworthy, and he will tell that to his parents, relatives, and friends. So a field of genuine friendliness can be created if people are happy, relaxed, and nonaggressive.

The sangha is an open world; it is not closed in. The Buddhist world is like a railroad station: anybody can come in and anybody can climb onboard. Hindus might say that you invite in a lot of impurities in this way, but the Buddhist world is much more open.

They are completely capable of receiving all gifts. The second condition in the category of receiving generosity is *yön yongsu jongwa chenpo. Yön* means "gift," *yongsu* means "completely," *jongwa* is "doing," or "paying," and *chenpo* means "great," so *yön yongsu jongwa chenpo* means "completely capable of receiving all gifts." Here *yön* implies that there is a profit. In other words, when people donate their money, time, and genuine effort to the sangha, they get their money's worth. Money donated to the sangha is never wasted. The sangha is definitely worthy of being supported. They are sane and their conduct is pure, so they are thoroughly worthy of receiving respect and gifts. Because the sangha has practiced generosity, that sangha is worthy to receive generosity.

They are an object of generosity. The next condition is *jin-pe nesu kyurpa,* which means very simply that the sangha is perfectly worthy of generosity, that it is an abode of generosity. *Jinpa* means "generosity," and *jin-pe* makes it "of generosity"; *ne* means "place" and *su* is "in," so *nesu* means "abode," and *kyurpa* means "become," so *jin-pe nesu kyurpa* means they "become an abode of generosity." This is so because when a gift has been given to the sangha, the sangha does not expect anything more from that person. As an interesting example of this, there is a tradition among Buddhist bhikshus regarding begging. According to this tradition, if somebody has been giving you a lot, you should beg elsewhere and ignore him or her. Also, the sangha does not use people in the political sense by offering them anything in return. Members of the sangha are a perfectly worthy object of generosity because they express the most basic sanity. So giving to the sangha is an attempt to shift the world toward sanity.

They are always a great object of generosity. The tenth condition of sangha, the fourth category of receiving generosity, is *küntu yang jin-pe nesu kyurpa chenpo,* which means that the sangha is completely worthy of receiving offerings. The addition of *küntu yang* or "always," and *chenpo* or "great" to *jin-pe nesu kyurpa* enhances the meaning to become, they are "always a great object of generosity." This category has a quality of expansion or completeness, whereas the previous category was just the possibility of that. The reason the sangha is completely worthy is that the sangha has no passion and no particular desire. They don't want to make allies of people if they are given something, and they don't cultivate relationships, as traditional fundraising people do.

Usually in fundraising, if people give you money, you correspond with them and are really diplomatic, inviting them for tea and coffee, sending them little knickknacks and little gifts of holy objects or relics. You include them in your particular gossip and your particular world. The approach of doing little things for donors is often based on your own desire to get yourself into cultural, psychological, economic, and social circles—into realities of all kinds. From the point of view of the sutra, there is something terrible about that approach. In contrast, the sangha has one intention: if people want to give, they should give, and if they don't want to give, they shouldn't give.

If you are fundraising in a dharmic way, you do not con people. You do not overkill them or underkill them, but you try to ignite their intelligence and relate with them very genuinely and faithfully. The guideline for donations is that you spend them on the particular cause the donor had in mind. It's very basic and simple.

To review, the first four conditions are connected with relating to oneself. They have to do with how to enter properly into sangha-ship. The next two are connected with relationships within the sangha. They have to do with how the members of the sangha behave themselves in order to be worthy of giving and receiving respect. The last four conditions are connected with the relationship between the sangha and people outside the sangha. They are about how the sangha becomes worthy of receiving generosity. Altogether, the sangha has to be worthwhile and disciplined. It has to be worthy of respect and generosity. Such worthiness is reflected in peoples' attitude toward the sangha and how it relates with bigger vision.

Tying the Buddha, dharma, and sangha principles together: Buddha is the example that you follow, dharma is the path that you tread on, and sangha is the community of practitioners who are making the same journey. The Buddha principle is like learning how to drive a car, the dharma is like the fuel needed in order to travel on the path, and the sangha is the driving. You may drive fast or slow, but if you drive too fast, you might get a ticket and be out of the sangha.

The teaching of the *Sutra of the Recollection of the Noble Three Jewels* is very simple and straightforward, but it is also very, very fundamental. It is fundamental to how you are and how you act. It is fundamental to how you conceive of yourself within, and how you relate with the rest of the world. It says pretty much everything about the qualities and capabilities of Buddha, dharma, and sangha in the hinayana—in fact, in all three yanas.

Part Two

DISCIPLINE / SHILA

16

The Loneliness and Joy of Discipline

You cannot develop yourself properly unless you give up your need for companionship. Once you give up your search for companionship, you can make friends with your loneliness. At that point, you become a genuine practitioner.

TAMING YOUR MIND AND DEVELOPING DECORUM

In order to understand the basis of the hinayana, we first need to consider the ground for being a Buddhist at all. In the Christian tradition, the way to be closer to Christ is to understand the crucifixion and to receive Communion. But in Buddhism, we do not have anything like that—we simply follow the Buddha's example so that our state of mind becomes workable. Buddhism is based on taming the mind.

"Taming" in Tibetan is *dülwa*, and in Sanskrit it is *vinaya*. The wildness of your discursive thoughts, subconscious gossip, and scheming about the future could be tamed with dülwa and made into a part of the path. An environment of dülwa is like a glass of sake: A glass is willing to accommodate whatever you put into it, so the glass represents you and the environment of dülwa around you. The sake inside the glass is your thoughts about what you might do, your clever ideas of all kinds, which have been captured in this glass so that they could be tamed. According to traditional Buddhist teachings, the sutras and commentaries, the process of taming begins by making yourself available to be tamed, available to stop re-creating your ego-centered notions.

Out of dülwa arises what is known as *pagyö* in Tibetan. *Pag* means "a sense of good or bad," *yö* means "possessing"; so *pagyö* means "possessing a sense of good or bad." It can be translated as "conscientiousness," or "attentiveness." Pagyö is completely the opposite of nonmindfulness or unmindfulness. It is often referred to as decorum. The idea of decorum originated with the aristocracy, but decorum applies to everybody: in terms of decorum, everybody is an aristocrat. Decorum is the way to keep your precision, to keep your sense of dignity, your sense of head and shoulders—to maintain your being altogether. Decorum is how to be and how to relate to the world. Even while you are eating steak tartare or vichyssoise, through decorum your basic being could be transformed. You could be a genuine person rather than a fake. With hinayana decorum, whatever you do should be done simply. By means of meditation practice, you make your being and your mind one-pointed. Whatever you do should be done with mindfulness and awareness.

When you have developed renunciation and become willing to restrain yourself from unwholesome actions, you begin to develop discipline. *Discipline* here is defined as "that which cools off neurotic heat." When the heat of neurosis is cooled, body, speech, and mind are at their best. Discipline is not quite ethics. It does not have to do with common law, but with individual salvation. Buddhist ethics are not a matter of good and evil; they are more a matter of tidiness and sloppiness. The Buddhist approach is not necessarily to make the world a good world, but to make the world a decent world. If you are tidy, then you are not creating any chaos for others.

Discipline is based on basic accommodation and fundamental sanity. Anybody could be accommodated—you could care less whether they are Sufis or Hasidics or whoever. As discipline becomes a reality, it actually abides as an entity in your state of mind. The various Buddhist schools all agree that discipline is an entity of its own. Discipline develops because you are willing to be good in the sense of being pragmatic, precise, and realistic. On the hinayana path, the unnecessary complications and confusions that occur in your state of mind can be overcome by the practice of meditation. In turn, proper discipline could develop. Therefore, you are able to develop individual salvation.

The essence of hinayana discipline is that one's mind is in the right place. The idea of one's mind being in the right place does not have anything to do with morality. It refers to mind being in its *own* place, the place where it is now, this very moment. Mind being in the right place has two categories: one-pointedness, or concentration, and discriminating awareness. One-pointedness is continual. It does not simply take place while you meditate; it happens constantly. Discriminating awareness is the intelligence that enables you to relate with the activities of life. It is the awareness of what is happening, with no blind spots.

THE POWER OF LONELINESS

If you look at hinayana discipline from another angle, it has to do with loneliness, or solitude, and the idea of retreat. You realize that there are no other resources than yourself, so you have to handle your life properly. You see that your husband or wife does not provide final protection, comfort, or refuge, so you are stuck with yourself. In society generally, we try to avoid that. Having married somebody, you would like to spend lots of time with that person. You would like to stay with that person so they can comfort you, treat you well, and reassure you of your existence. However, although you may be married to someone, you are separate people. In fact, marriage is the epitome of loneliness.

There are six categories of aloneness: less desire, contentment, avoiding unnecessary activities, morality, not wandering in the world of desire, and working with discursive thoughts. *Less desire* means that you have less need for security. *Contentment* means you are not always looking for something more. *Avoiding unnecessary activities* means not trying to occupy yourself or look for companionship. *Morality* means that you keep being brought back to your practice of meditation. *Not wandering in the world of desire* means that you do not constantly search for relationships. *Working with discursive thoughts* means that you are overcoming your thoughts. Instead of regarding them as entertainment, you are relating to them very simply.

Unless you have a sense of aloneness, you cannot develop wakefulness. So it is absolutely and utterly important and necessary to feel lonely—to the extreme, if you like. You are conceived alone, and you come out of your mother's womb alone. After you are born, your umbilical cord is cut:

you are alone in the world. Somebody feeds you, sends you to school, and helps you grow up. And if something goes wrong with your economy, you can get food stamps or public assistance. So people do help, obviously, but such help is not fundamental help; it is just temporary. Basically, you have no help. You are alone, absolutely alone. You are born that way and you die that way: you come in alone and you go out alone. You are nothing but yourself. You are without any other help but your own resources. Because you cannot borrow somebody else's flashlight, you have to dig one out of your own pocket and use it. If you really understood loneliness, you could become a tantric student. Loneliness is a link between hinayana and vajrayana.

Because people feel so lonely and so desperate, they look for God. Due to loneliness, people compose music, write songs and poetry, do all kinds of things. But no matter what you accomplish, no matter how many friends you have collected, whether or not you feel good, there is still a quality of loneliness. In Buddhism, the poets Bashō and Milarepa wrote about loneliness. But in the West, some Buddhists become overly involved with their own discoveries, and the experience of loneliness is discarded. So we definitely need the doctrine of loneliness. Fundamentally, you are not you, at all, but you have lost yourself. That is the Buddhist notion of loneliness or egolessness.

True loneliness is very definite, but halfhearted loneliness is feeble. With halfhearted loneliness, you are still trying to replace your fifty-percent loneliness with something else. You are still looking for entertainment. When you mix loneliness with the entertainment, the whole thing becomes hollow and fruitless. Nothing is really being entertained. In the beginning, you have expectations, but then nothing happens. That's how the world functions. Because of that, people feel like killing themselves. They jump off a cliff, or they jump off the Empire State Building, or they take an overdose of poison. They do all those things because they are lonely and feel that there is no way out—and no way in, either. But in this case, loneliness is the way. With loneliness there is a path.

Loneliness and aloneness are not two different words. You could be both alone and lonely. It is absolutely necessary to relate to aloneness and loneliness, because for a long time we have ignored them. Hinayana discipline is the discipline of loneliness and aloneness, particularly monastic discipline. The Catholics also have monasticism, but their loneliness is somewhat incomplete because they have an obstacle, which is known as God.

A lonely person could still relate with other people. You could be lonely, alone, and living in the midst of society at the same time. Aloneness does not mean that you have to be a mountain hermit. A lion in the zoo is still a lion. Loneliness is not the same as renunciation. Renunciation means that you reject something, but loneliness means that you have been rejected. With renunciation, you would like to give something up deliberately by choice, but loneliness doesn't give you any choice—it comes to you automatically. That is why the path of loneliness is so helpful.

The experience of aloneness in sitting practice, in your married life, in your professional life, and in your scholarly life brings greater mindfulness and awareness because you have no reference point. You are by yourself, alone. From that quality of aloneness, you begin to realize that not only are you alone, but you have very little to complain about. Who is there to complain to? What is there to complain about?

Aloneness seems to be the heart of discipline. According to the Buddhist tradition, seeing the helplessness of one's own experience is the only way to look at things helpfully. You may think that a golden chariot is going to descend in front of you full of food and companionship, but it will never happen. That is the basic philosophy of the Kagyü tradition, or the practice lineage.*

Loneliness is connected to the idea of being a hermit, or in Tibetan, ritröpa. Ri means "mountain," and trö means "among," so ritrö means "among mountains"; and if you add pa, you have ritröpa, which makes "hermit." The point is that you cannot develop yourself properly unless you give up your need for companionship. Once you give up your search for companionship, you can make friends with your loneliness. At that point, you become a genuine practitioner.

You do not have to seek out loneliness—it is always there. Egolessness is a concept, a philosophy, but loneliness is a reality that you experience. A feeling of loneliness is part of the journey. As for me, I feel that way constantly, and I think it's a very healthy feeling, a very real feeling. When you sense that you are not you anymore and that nothing can replace

---

* Due to its emphasis on meditative training, the Kagyü tradition is referred to as the "practice lineage."

that state, you begin to make discoveries. You discover devotion, and you discover a quality of richness and artistic expression that is very special. Being you, but not being you, is very resourceful. You become a complete mountain man: you know how to make fire and cook food. But it doesn't mean anything. You are still nobody. That is the inspiration.

17

Taming the Neurotic Mind

A basic point of hinayana training is the conviction that you can practice along with your problems. It is not because you can solve your problems that you can do it, and it is also not because somebody else suddenly became enlightened. The point is that you can do it because somebody else did not become enlightened and still was a follower of the path.

T HE HINAYANA begins with taming the mind. Taming the mind is very straightforward: you just relate with things as they are. You don't try to stock up. You don't collect more weapons in case you might need to defend yourself, or more food so that if you run out, you would have something to live on. You are not making sure that if you are kicked out of one organization, you have another organization to join. Trying to stock up and to make sure that there is some kind of security is the opposite of taming: it is aggression.

In sitting practice, you experience the mind, the body, and the breath working together. Anything except the breath itself, the body itself, and the awareness of the body and breath has to be somewhat excluded as extra paraphernalia. One has to regard anything else that comes up during meditation as simply concepts. Taming the mind is at the heart of the hinayana practice of discipline. Taming the mind is the definition of dharma; there is no other dharma than taming one's mind. So the question is, what is meant by *mind*?

The Four Mental Obstacles

According to the hinayana tradition, the ordinary neurotic mind consists of four basic obstacles: stupidity, mindlessness, emotional upheavals, and lack of faith. These four obstacles that come up in your mind are slightly different than the five skandhas, which are developmental mental states. In terms of the skandhas, the four mental obstacles all take place at the level of the fifth skandha, or consciousness.

Stupidity

The first obstacle is stupidity. Stupidity is a state of mind that is not open or informed. It is a state of mind that is uneducated. You might say that if you are uneducated, it is not your fault but the fault of the educator. Someone should have put you in a good school so that you could get a good education. You might make up excuses, saying that if you didn't know about something, you cannot call it a mistake. You think that, if you are in a foreign country and you drive on the wrong side of the road, it's not your fault. That is quite different from our approach. What we mean by being educated, informed, or learned, is being inquisitive enough to learn the rules and regulations for driving in that country.

In general, you should have inquisitiveness about what you are doing, rather than just sitting back and being lazy. If you are uneducated, it is your own fault, because you were not interested enough to find things out. Inquisitiveness does not need a further faculty. It just needs openness and the willingness to look into situations and understand them. The obstacle of stupidity means that you have not been inquisitive enough to learn.

Mindlessness

The second obstacle is mindlessness; it is the absence of awareness. You are unaware of yourself. It is quite simple. The potential of awareness is always there, but you are mindless. Things come up and things go away, but you just ignore them. You couldn't be bothered. In contrast, awareness is based on curiosity and inquisitiveness. Awareness is a natural instinct. Fundamentally, we are always aware, always inquisitive. However, human beings manage to push irritating things away. In doing so, we lose that natural awareness and go lower than the animals. Cultivating awareness means regaining that instinct of inquisitiveness and sharpness, regaining our antennae. In the modern world, we have all sorts of gadgets that allow us to avoid developing our awareness. If we forget something, we can always look it up in an encyclopedia or a book. That doesn't mean books are a problem; they could be a form of encouragement. But because we have produced all kinds of things that allow us not to have to work hard, our awareness has diminished, so we need to get that awareness back.

Emotional Upheavals

The third obstacle is emotional upheavals, or kleshas. In relationship to emotional upheavals, the other three obstacles are a kind of fringe, a way of copping out of the emotions. People have different emotional temperaments. One person may be short-tempered and get angry very quickly, another person may be jealous and get uptight very fast, and so forth. People usually want to be somebody or something important. They want to achieve something. Therefore, they express themselves in terms of the three basic poisons of passion, aggression, and ignorance, or in terms of jealousy, envy, or some other emotion. Emotional uptightness comes from wanting to stick to your own identity and to your own importance. However, trying to hold on to your identity by means of emotional uptightness is unnecessary and just creates further pain. The point is not necessarily to control your emotions or to try to be good. At the same time, there is the possibility that you could be watchful of yourself and your state of mind.

Lack of Faith

The fourth aggregate is not having enough faith. In this case, we mean not having faith in yourself, not having faith that you actually can achieve what you want to achieve. You give up altogether, feeling that you are dumb, so there is no point trying to find out what the teachings are all about. If you have faith in yourself, you will look into the teachings and learn the details. You will be interested in exploring the whole thing. Theistic religions may tell you not to question, but just have faith. The Buddhist view of faith is the opposite of that: you should think for yourself.

Faith means that you can do it. You don't need too much help. You can do it yourself. If necessary, you could remember that in the past a succession of people in the lineage actually achieved what they wanted to achieve. Faith needs a kind of surrendering to oneself. It is not so much thinking that you are going to be a great success or that you are going to become a millionaire one day. It is not based on any kind of reward. Instead, faith is knowing that this is the right path. It is based on actual experience.

THE ROLE OF MEDITATION

In relating to the four mental obstacles, we cannot isolate the practice of discipline from the practice of meditation. You need basic meditative training, or shamatha practice, the development of peace. In shamatha, you witness your stupidity, your unawareness, your emotional upheavals, and your faithlessness. By doing so, you are taming your mind. The term *taming* does not mean that you are trying to work with your mind so that everything is smooth and good. Taming means that you feel that there is a relationship taking place between you and your mind. When you sit and meditate, you do not necessarily become a great meditator, sitting for an hour or a day without any thoughts. You don't necessarily find yourself completely smooth. That is almost impossible—and that is not the point!

Taming the mind means that some kind of friendship is taking place between those four obstacles and you. You discover that your mind is workable, that meditation is actually happening. You realize that you are not just the wild, hopeless person you thought you were. So a very powerful sense of conviction begins to grow. A basic point of hinayana training is the conviction that you can practice along with your problems. It is not because you can solve your problems that you can do it, and it is also not because somebody else suddenly became enlightened. The point is that you can do it because somebody else did *not* become enlightened and still was a follower of the path.

Meditation is very important. You cannot keep basic discipline without the practice of meditation. The process of meditation brings out the details of the four mental obstacles, and it brings out their positive counterparts as well. The Kagyü lineage is known for its tough people, great meditators like Milarepa and Marpa. At the same time, if you put Milarepa and Marpa in the middle of New York City, they might be very soft and vulnerable. So maybe they were not such tough people, but they had faith and they knew how to handle themselves. Because of that, something actually happened in their systems, their states of being, so that they could walk on a spiritual path.

18

Cutting the Root of Samsara

The minute you wake up in the morning, when you have to strug-
gle to swallow a big piece of meat, or when you have a gigantic
sneeze—there are always occasions when a gap occurs in your mind
and you think, "What's next?" Those are the occasions when you
can plant something positive in your mind, when you can plant
shamatha in your mind in the form of mindfulness-awareness.

DISCIPLINE IS said to cool off the heat of neurosis and bring about the best behavior of body, speech, and mind. It is what delivers us to individual salvation. The logic of the Buddhist approach is to cut karma altogether at its root, and the way to do so is by means of mindfulness, discipline, and renunciation. It is by refraining from mindlessness and the desire to occupy ourselves with neurosis.

Discipline, or *tsültrim*, is planted in your state of mind with the understanding that you are going to stay with it for the rest of your life. So it is as much a real entity in your mind as a marriage, or even more so. You do not think of it as temporary, like a haircut. When you leave the barbershop, you know that you have had a haircut, but then you forget about it. When your hair grows longer, that haircut is no longer in effect. In contrast, discipline does not grow longer or shorter. Discipline is always supposed to stay the same.

Soso tharpa, or individual liberation, is based on individual discipline, rather than general discipline. For example, when you go to school, you have to learn to read and write on your own. The fact that everybody else is learning to do it wouldn't help you very much with your own reading and writing. With soso tharpa, you are making sure that you personally can properly read, write, spell, and do mathematics. As a result of individual discipline, your behavior of body, speech, and mind becomes admirable and good. You begin to develop a natural sense of not harming yourself or others. You begin to plant mindfulness in your basic consciousness, or *alaya*. You become a natural adept.

When you begin to practice, you need to have some understanding of the logic of the path. How are you going to eliminate your problems, and who knows how to do that? As far as the logic of the path is concerned, the one who knows is you: it is you who will find out for yourself. It has been said that samsara is generated from a very simple and minute beginning. That is, whenever a simple little desire, a simple little aggression takes form, we hang on to it. We begin to capitalize on it and to exaggerate it. As we exaggerate the whole thing, the end product becomes gigantic. We have created a mile out of an inch.

In the abhidharma teachings on Buddhist psychology, there are discussions about this key point of how what is minute tends to expand. Some scholars have found this logic difficult to understand, but frankly I don't see why they have any difficulty. Whenever there is a flickering of desire for even one moment, it becomes exaggerated, and it goes on for miles and miles. It is like an echo chamber. You take a look at a person for only a few seconds, and you are attracted to him or her. Then you want to get hold of and possess that person. Fifteen minutes later, you send out all the retinues of your desire. You send out rays to envelop that person completely and make them a part of you. Likewise, you may have a slight dislike for someone. Although you may have only had dealings with them for five seconds, you still begin to develop immense aggression toward them, and twenty-five minutes later, you have developed a gigantic fortress to defend yourself from them and whole armies to attack that person. Not only are you ready to destroy that person, but you are ready to uproot them altogether. Those are examples of what is known in Buddhist psychology as the expansion of what is minute. That is how things work in our samsaric world. In that way, we begin to create a gigantic world of samsara. We have been doing that for a long time.

Another pattern that comes up in samsara is having a perverted notion of what is going on. That is, when you encounter a situation that is not all that desirable from a common-sense point of view, somehow you manage to think that it is extraordinary. You begin to reinterpret it and change the logic of whatever is happening. For instance, you might regard somebody who is a nice person as a terrible person. Quite unnecessarily, you begin to develop the arbitrary logic of passion and aggression. That kind of change in logic evolves from neurotic tendencies at the level of what are called "mental contents" in abhidharma.* That is, the mind begins to change the message of reality by imposing its preconceptions on things.

Once our preconceptions have developed, once we have already made up our mind, we begin to create our own world out of our own desire or aggression. At that point, our aggression or desire has already produced its result, and by the law of cause and effect, or karma, that result determines future possibilities and results. Therefore, we are helpless. We are trapped in our own doing. Intense aggression in the present will result in our being unable to escape from undesirable situations in the future. So the only way to prevent the results of karma is to cut the present situation. And the way to do so is through mindfulness practice. Because you are being mindful, you do not follow desires when they come up. Each time there is a desire, you are mindful of it, but you don't follow it. In that way you cut the minute desires. Those desires might seem meaningless at the time; nevertheless, you don't follow them. Although they seem to be very small in proportion, if you cut an inch of small desires, in the long run you are cutting a mile of larger desires. So cutting desires an inch at a time goes a long way.

As realistic people who feel real pain and real pleasure, we are concerned with one main point: to cut the chain of karmic debt. We may experience the possibility of getting out of such a nuisance altogether, but to do so we need to understand how karma begins. Knowing how karma begins, right at the beginning, seems to be the key point.

We begin by planting seeds of memory in our alaya consciousness.† At the level of our alaya consciousness, the faculty of cognitive mind already exists, and rejecting and accepting begin to take place in our state of mind. Before we think, we already have the potential to think. We have the faculty of thinking, for making up our mind, for liking or not liking. That

---

* A reference to the fourth skandha, concept / formation or *samskara* (Skt.). According to Trungpa Rinpoche, this skandha refers to the tendency to accumulate mental states as territory. See chapter 2, "The Frozen Space of Ego."

† The alaya consciousness (*alayavijnana*) is the base or storehouse consciousness, also referred to as the eighth consciousness. For more on alaya and the other seven consciousnesses, see the section "Working with the Mind," on page 187.

is the point at which shamatha practice begins to become very effective. What we are trying to do in shamatha is to tackle that level of alaya consciousness. We are trying to plant a seed of mindfulness-awareness—a less habitual, less animal-like instinct—in the alaya consciousness. Rats always go for cheese, and rabbits always go for carrots, but we could do better than that. We do not always have to think immediately for our own sake and for our own comfort alone. Instead, right from the moment cognitive mind begins to function, we could think in terms of something more than that. As human beings, we could always go for sanity.

Mindfulness is not based on looking for danger, or saying, "Be careful! There might be trouble!" With mindfulness there is a quality of openness, or gap. The minute you wake up in the morning, or when you have to struggle to swallow a big piece of meat, or when you have a gigantic sneeze—there are always occasions when a gap occurs in your mind, and you think, "What's next?" People used to think that sneezing was an attack of the devil—not only that, but sneezing was the first hint that someone was sick with the plague. But as far as we are concerned, sneezing is usually good news! When such gaps occur, you might as well try to be more wakeful. Gaps are opportunities for you to plant something positive in your mind. You can plant shamatha in your mind in the form of mindfulness-awareness.

Whenever there is a gap, you see that you don't have to run your machine all the time. At that moment, the point is to be fully mindful. Look at yourself! You don't need a technique. Just be present, be mindful, just *be* there. If you cannot just be there, you can follow your breath in order to be there, which is the gentle way of doing so.

In ordinary situations, you can catch yourself, and just be awake. Just look! Don't reconnect with your stitchery all over again. Occasional gaps are nice and fresh. Each moment of openness is an opportunity. If you sneeze, try to be awake after you sneeze. Don't just grab a tissue right away, but allow yourself a little gap, a little space, which has a kind of spark and delight in it. It is the starting point of mindfulness.

According to the Buddha, when you are being mindful, walking is mindful, talking is mindful, breathing is mindful, feeling is mindful, hearing is mindful, sensation is mindful. Mindfulness is not regarded as a tax on your sense perceptions. You don't need to work harder to feel more than you usually feel, or to hear more than you usually hear. Rather, mindfulness is extra bliss. I am not trying to make a sales pitch for mindfulness, but it is somewhat joyful. You realize that you could be so uplifted by being mindful. You begin to feel very good that you could rise beyond your regular, ordinary struggles, which don't require awareness, but give you tremendous pain, misery, and mindlessness.

When renunciation is planted as a habitual pattern in your alaya consciousness, as part of the fundamental mindfulness process, your experience becomes fundamentally good. You begin to feel very soothed. You might be terribly sick, you might have a fever, you might have diarrhea, but you could still feel good. This is because you have something else going on beyond the immediate hassle of the moment—you have mindfulness. You could be mindful of the way you extend your arm, the way your arm comes back to your body, the way you move your fingers, the way you speak, the way you smell, the way you look around, the way you see bright green, blue, yellow, white, or gray. All those things you experience in your life do not have to be regarded as hassles.

Sometimes people think that everything they see, everything they experience, costs them money; and having to spend money implies expending effort as well. But that's not quite the case. We can always experience the joy of being alive as human beings. Tigers might have a different story, dragons might have a different story, snakes might have a different story—but let them speak for themselves! The way to appreciate life is to be mindful; otherwise, you cannot really appreciate your life. With no mindfulness, you have missed lots of things already, and you will miss a lot more. You are stuck with all those things that you have missed. You become like somebody who has been running a projector in a movie theater for sixty years and has never actually seen a movie. You keep on running the projector quite beautifully, but you get tired of yourself. So in order to cut the root of samsara, it is very important to have mindfulness-awareness.

Cutting the root of samsara does not mean you are cutting the root of your enjoyment. However, your style of enjoyment will certainly be different: it will be unconditional enjoyment rather than conditional enjoyment. In order to appreciate the world properly, in order to enjoy renunciation, you need to start at the beginning, by cleaning up. Cleaning up is best. Although it may have a ring of austerity, there is nothing better than cleaning up.

You have to learn to clean up after yourself. In order to be good to yourself, to develop *maitri*, or "loving-kindness," you first have to learn how to be good. It is very literal. You have to learn to eat properly and to clean up after yourself nicely. You don't give your dirty dishes to somebody else to clean for you; you do everything yourself. In turn, the world is beautified. The world begins to admire you, and you begin to beautify the world. You are not creating any nuisance. Beyond that, you begin to inspire the world because you are so industrious.

You might think that your mindfulness practice is not working, that you are still the same cranky person. But that doesn't really matter, as long as you continue to cut karmic roots through sitting practice. You can cut a lot of roots in one hour of meditation. And after years of practice, eventually you no longer have a samsaric occupation to uphold. If the karmic roots are not completely cleared out, the karmic debts will remain, as a banker would say. But once you have cut the karmic roots completely, to the extent that there are no roots left, you begin to cut karmic debts as well. That seems to be the logic. Therefore, sitting practice is regarded as very precious and important.

19

Continually Gnawing Rock

Discipline is not based on feeling guilty or trying to avoid painful situations and cultivate pleasurable ones. It is a natural process that binds together body, speech, and mind. When your mind is together, your body and speech will also be together. Your entire state of being will be in harmony, which makes a wholesome human being.

EGOLESSNESS AND DISCIPLINE

Ego's approach to reality is based on constantly reinforcing its own existence. When you see through that, you begin to experience twofold egolessness, the egolessness of self and the egolessness of phenomena, as a process of simultaneous loss and gain. You develop detachment from outer, or "am," and inner, or "I." Freedom from attachment to outer and inner naturally begins to bring about a sense of desolation. You can't be here and you can't be there, so you feel desolate. When that occurs, there is a feeling of perfect unity. There is a complete world that does not feed you and does not starve or reject you.

Desolation is very important and powerful. It becomes a reality in its own right, a very clean, pure, and absolute world. There is no here, no there; therefore, you cannot attach yourself anywhere. That makes it a spacious desolation. Desolation is very simple and direct: it is simply practicing. Your meditation cushion, yourself, and your sitting practice are neither here nor there. There is a sense of basic nonexistence. At the same time, of course, a kind of existence continues, since you still have such reference points as knowing which is your cushion and which is somebody else's.

Sitting practice should not build too much righteousness, as a lot of pseudo-meditators' practice does. Meditation practice is quite simple and direct: it is evenness and totality. The nonexistence of *this* and *that,* twofold egolessness, is experienced, or at least attempted to be experienced, but nothing extraordinary is taking place. There is no one to project anything extraordinary either. However, "I" and "am" in the heavy-handed sense do not exist.

Discipline is not based on pressure or on making a lot of demands on yourself. It is a different kind of demand: you are just invited to take part in a genuine, heartfelt way. But it is impossible to develop discipline if you don't have a taste of the nonexistence of both "I" and "that." Discipline begins to evolve and develop because you are not trying to fight any enemy and you are not trying to conquer anything. You are here. For what? That's it—for what. That is the question as well as the answer.

Once we understand the samsaric world we are in, and the anxiety it produces, we are inspired to go beyond it. We would like to overcome our anxiety, but we first have to realize that there is no technique and no trick for doing so. The only way to deal with it is by means of discipline. When we are in a state of anxiety, we usually look for preoccupations that might let us forget our anxiousness. We look for all kinds of alternatives, any form of entertainment. We might even use vajrayana religious practices to overcome our anxiety in a samsaric manner. In the vajrayana, we have things to say, known as mantra, and things to do, known as mudra, or a symbolic gesture. We could use those as a way of being fully babysat by the dharma. But from the vajrayana point of view, it is almost illegal to entertain our anxiety in that way.

Any religious practice other than the hinayana practice of straightforwardness could be used as a form of entertainment. For instance, you might be given a mantra to say whenever you have a backache, or you might be given a mantra which, if you say it just once, will liberate you on the spot. But such mantras do not work, because you have not even begun on your path or gone through the three-yana journey. You have to become a dharmic person in order to receive the effect of vajrayana magic. There are no tricks.

Discipline is about giving up the search for entertainment. You have to start right at the beginning, without religious fascinations of any kind. With the hinayana, you realize that you have to do things for yourself first; and with the mahayana, you understand that you are not doing things for yourself alone. You start with self-discipline and with shamatha practice. Shamatha is essential. You need to be willing to bend down to hinayana discipline. You have to relate with yourself and acknowledge your shortcomings before you can go beyond them. You need to sit and meditate more. Unfortunately, doing that is not very appealing or imaginative. You could blame that lack of imagination on the Buddha, but you still need to sit and practice. You just need to do it.

PROPER CONDUCT / TSÜLTRIM

The Tibetan word for discipline is *tsültrim*. *Tsül* means "proper," "in accordance with tradition," or "appropriate," *trim* means "law," "regulation," or "justice"; so *tsültrim* means "proper regulation," or "proper conduct." The Sanskrit term for discipline is *shila*. Shila is the cause of our being good. Shila is how to manifest or express our existence; it is how to behave properly, with good manners. By behaving properly, we cool off the heat of the kleshas. We practice according to the Buddha's example.

Although we translate *tsültrim* into English as "discipline," we could question the use of the English word *discipline* as a Buddhist term. In the Buddhist sense, being disciplined is not based on self-justification or personal enrichment. You are simply trying to practice good old-fashioned techniques in the style of the Victorians. That is, you just do it. In Victorian England, if you were a would-be statesman, you would go to public school where you had to make your own bed—and if you didn't get up early enough, ice-cold water was poured on your head. That's the spirit of discipline, or tsültrim.

Proper discipline is without any personal agenda. You could be involved for many years in a discipline such as macrobiotics and torture yourself infinitely, but because you get so excited about it, in the end it becomes entertainment rather than real discipline. In real discipline you are not entertained. You are simply presented with things—rock, jaw, chew. You are continually gnawing rock. Without even having the ambition to eat the whole mountain, you still keep chewing that rock.

Tsültrim brings about the possibility, or hint, of egolessness. The practice of any beginning student is not all that perfect. However, with discipline, there is a built-in possibility of beginning to see everybody around you as strange. Although you feel something is happening, you do not know what you are doing. You realize that, in fact, nobody knows what they are doing, but everybody feels they are doing something. At that point, there is the possibility of egolessness. Once that message of egolessness is heard, you begin to discipline yourself. The empty-heartedness of egolessness begins to take place.

With real discipline, even if you are squeezed into a corner by the sangha, you stick with the sangha rather than separating yourself from it. If you regard yourself as separate from the sangha, you are going to be squeezed even more. However, if you regard yourself as part of the sangha, you are not squeezed, but you are the squeezer—and as the squeezer, you put a lot of pressure on yourself as well. It is like hitting a gong: if you regard yourself as part of the stick that hits the gong, you make a sound; but if you are a little fly between the gong and the stick, you are killed. With tsültrim, you can be the beater of the gong as well as the gong itself. You have already lost your reference point of "this" and "that," or sense that you are about to, or at least take the attitude that it is possible. Discipline comes from egolessness. So trying to understand egolessness is not only a metaphysical issue, it is a reality in your life. It has to do with how you can survive and how you can develop the real meaning of practice. You could enjoy practice and celebrate within the vision of buddhadharma.

THE THREE CATEGORIES OF TSÜLTRIM

There are three categories of tsültrim. Number one is that *tsültrim is good,* because it allows us to manifest of body, speech, and mind in the best way. In Tibetan this is *lek-che: lek* means "good," *che* means "viewed," or "regarded as"; therefore *lek-che* means "regarded as good," or "well–thought of." Number two is that *tsültrim is action,* or *le* in Tibetan. Tsültrim is regarded as action because it is our complete occupation when we practice dharma. Finally, *tsültrim is a binding factor,* or *dompa.* Tsültrim is that which binds us together, so that body and mind are in harmony.

In spite of our anxiety, we discover that we can become good. In fact, it is because of our anxiety that we look for an alternative. With proper tsültrim, we can liberate ourselves individually. We can actually wake up and be fully ourselves.

Taming and Subjugating / Tülshuk

Another term for discipline is *tülshuk*. *Tül* means "to tame," or "to subjugate." It also means "to grind to dust," or "to conquer," like conquering Mount Everest. Tül is connected with egolessness and also with peace. It joins gentleness, or peace, with the notion of subjugating the "I" part of the ego. The "I" part of ego needs to be completely tamed, but it cannot be tamed by anything other than the sitting practice of meditation, or shamatha discipline. *Shuk* means "entering." Having tamed already, you can then enter. What are you entering into? You are entering into vipashyana. Having subjugated the "I," the "am" follows. If "I" does not have any room to accommodate itself, then the "am" automatically falls apart as well. If you do not have a light, then you will not have the rays from that light.

Tül and shuk put together make up the hinayana truth of gentleness and genuineness. The term *tülshuk* implies that you have an experience of journey as well as of discipline. This sense of journey is more spicy than a vocation, like the vocation of being a monk—it is vocation with a lot of chili in it. *Tülshuk* could be translated as "practitioner." The word *practitioner* has a ring of delight, as well as being highly in accord with discipline. Hinayana discipline is very genuine. If you cannot practice that discipline fully and properly, you cannot enter onto the path. But you can practice genuinely to tame yourself completely. To have a meditation cushion is no "I"; to have a sitter on the cushion is no "am"; so sitting on a cushion is a no "I am" situation.

It is possible to experience the profundity of egolessness, but that can't happen if you don't give up your various preoccupations. If you have a stronghold of any kind, it is impossible to experience no "am." Therefore, it is impossible to experience no "I," and impossible to experience full egolessness, or no "I am."

You cannot understand the real teachings of hinayana completely if you have no full and proper understanding and experience of discipline. Discipline means sitting diligently, practicing properly. Your everyday life should be included as well. Discipline is definitely a twenty-four-hour-a-day job. You can't take a day off to forget the whole thing. You can't take an hour off, or a week off, or even a minute off. To tell you the truth, I feel that way myself. Genuine discipline is a full experience. It is about being awake. I am haunted all the time, both when I am asleep and when I am awake. And if you decide to practice the dharma, you should be haunted, too.

In the hinayana, we use what we have. What do we have? We have our world, we have our body, and we have our life. So we just work with what we have in its best form, by means of the practice of meditation and postmeditation discipline. That is how we can begin at the beginning. We realize that engaging ourselves in the dharma is not once removed or many times removed from us, and it is not a myth. Because of that, we begin to have a very personal feeling toward the Buddha himself. We find that he is much closer to us than we had expected. He no longer seems like a figure from twenty-six hundred years ago who once lived and died. We feel that he is still with us, and we appreciate his existence. We begin to feel haunted by him, in the best sense, and we begin to feel good about being haunted.

THE THREE GATES OF DISCIPLINE

Tsültrim can only be developed by practicing certain techniques. There is not much to it. You do not have to jump up and down or stand on your head. Tsültrim boils down to beginning with what is immediately available to you: your body, speech, and mind. In Buddhist terminology, body, speech, and mind are described as the "three gates." They are known as the three gates because with body, speech, and mind, it is possible to enter into discipline. You are not a solid block, like a lump of iron, but there are three little gates in your existence called body, speech, and mind, through which you can approach yourself. There is hope, a beacon, a light at the end of the tunnel. In fact, there are three lights at the end of three tunnels. Those three lights are body, speech, and mind. We can use those three as the best and the most immediate way to practice the dharma, which is delightful. We should appreciate being human beings who possess the capability of listening, hearing, thinking, and talking. We should appreciate that we can practice the dharma.

Body

You discipline your body by going against its usual habitual tendencies. For instance, sitting on a meditation cushion on the floor is unusual for us. Even early in our infancy, we were propped up in a baby chair with a little tray in front of us and a knife and fork to bang with. Later on, in order to reach the table we were given a booster chair. But you are not following that particular habitual pattern—you physically lower yourself and sit down on the earth. Your posture used to be one of longing. You always wanted to get something out of your parents or your friends, so you hunched your head and shoulders and extended your arms, and said, "I want this and I want that." You wanted something all the time. But now you are sitting on the ground without that expression of longing and wanting. You have assumed your royal seat on your meditation cushion.

Speech

The discipline of speech is connected with postmeditation practice. Our constant chatter and lack of attention to what we say or how to say it can be controlled by speaking with proper formality. What we say should be somewhat free from the gibberish of American slang. We should try to speak good English or good German or good Dutch or good French or good Japanese—whatever language we speak. In any case, we do not just blurt out our sentences. Sometimes words are entirely the expression of the vomit of our state of mind. They are badly phrased, aggressive, and ugly. Our sentences are ungrammatical. We often just spew things out as the product of our irritation and lack of sophistication. At least as children we may have been told to say "thank you" and "please," although some of us may never have had that training.

Your words have a lot of power. When you open your mouth and say something, it represents your existence. Words are very important. In working on translation projects, we have realized more and more how important words are. You might have a word that you want to say, and it is a good word, but if you say it at the wrong time, its meaning gets lost. So what you say, when you say it, how you say it, and where you say it, are important.

We should pay attention to our language. Our language should not be purely the end product of struggle, so that our final resource is just to say

"I love it" or "I hate it." We shouldn't just burp out our language. As Buddhists, we should learn how to speak. Like the Buddha, we should present the dharma properly so that it is good and well said. We have to have some kind of self-respect for the way we speak. That doesn't mean that we have to whisper or that we have to shout. But having some understanding of a word as we utter it is good discipline, and paying attention to our state of mind as we talk goes along with that.

Mind

Finally we have discipline of mind, which comes naturally. In both meditation and postmeditation practice, we try to develop our intrinsic awareness. We pay attention to our body and its behavior patterns; we pay attention to our speech; and we pay attention to our state of mind. Since we do not talk during the sitting practice of meditation, we end up with just our mind and body, which work together. If we have bad posture, we can correct that with mental upliftedness. Our awareness should be acute and precise, and it should function with great goodness.

Your mind can function precisely because your body is already working toward that kind of precision. The traditional analogy is that of the rider of wakefulness riding the horse of the mind. When you ride your horse properly, it picks up every detail of your posture, whether it is good or bad. That is the way you ride your body with your mind. There is a feeling of wholesomeness, almost arrogance. You feel so healthy, so good to be what you are, expressing yourself at your best. With discipline, you are expressing the greatest potential of a human being.

In the hinayana, the only way to conduct yourself is according to the message of discipline. Discipline always comes first. When you have basic discipline, you can practice any further disciplines naturally, slowly and surely. Without discipline, you are useless. You have not made a connection with yourself because you have not actually experienced your body, speech, and mind properly and personally. If you never related with those three principles, you would be a hopeless case.

You need to begin at the beginning, by developing veneration. You need to recognize how very fortunate it is that you can actually follow the instructions given by the Buddha. You are worthy of doing that, and you have no problem connecting with the Buddha's instructions as long as you have a body. Sometimes you have too much body, and your body aches and hurts; sometimes you have too much speech, and you chatter; sometimes you have too much mind, and you think too much. But as long as you have those three heavy things called body, speech, and mind, you should actually make use of them.

Natural Discipline

Discipline can either become a natural part of your personal existence, or it can cause the deterioration of your personal existence. If you impose such a tremendous sense of discipline upon yourself that you begin to deteriorate, it is like punishing yourself in order to survive, which is a contradiction in terms. The more you punish yourself, the more your faculties and your state of being will deteriorate. It is a deadly thing to do. However, you could regard discipline as your personal adornment, as the glorification of your natural existence. Having gone through basic training, you are no longer punishing yourself. Instead, discipline has become food for your whole being. It is food that you like to eat, not like food you have to eat or medicine you have to take.

Discipline is like a chain reaction in the sense that the lineage holders of the past also went through this training and bound themselves to the teachings. That discipline is transmitted to you almost in the form of some abstract influence coming into your state of being. That is why you take the refuge vow. You require that same sense of discipline, and you are opening yourself up to it. You need to bind yourself just as past lineage-holders bound themselves with their state of being. At the same time, you should be self-sufficient.

When you take a vow, you enter into a real situation. It is not purely theoretical. That sort of commitment has the quality of making you stronger and more pleasant. You are willing to conduct yourself properly out of joy and appreciation, rather than regarding your commitment as a kind of punishment. Genuine commitment arises out of taking delight in practice. When practice is no hassle, you begin to feel openness and confidence. It is like children who have no hesitation opening a box when they know that there is a toy inside.

By means of discipline, you are developing the potential of knowing what to accept and what to reject. You do not accept something because it seems friendly, and reject something else because it seems hostile. You simply develop a sense of natural hierarchy and common sense.* Calling something "good" doesn't mean everything is for you, and calling something "bad" doesn't mean everything is against you. You are simply looking at black objects and distinguishing them from white ones. Accepting or rejecting does not have to be all that heavy-handed. You are simply seeing things as they are. It is as sensible as not stepping in dog shit.

Dharmic training is based on having a natural sense of what is good for you and what is not good for you. It is not based on following particular rules, but on fulfilling your natural potential to know what you should cultivate and what you should avoid. The extent to which you can fulfill that possibility depends on how open you are and how unforced your actions are. Discipline is not based on feeling guilty, or trying to avoid painful situations and cultivate pleasurable ones. It is a natural process that binds together body, speech, and mind. When your mind is together, your body and speech will also be together. Your entire state of being will be in harmony, which makes a wholesome human being.

---

* The term *natural hierarchy* refers to there being a natural sense of high, middle, and low, an appreciation of natural order. It is as simple as knowing that a hat goes on the head, clothes go on the body, and shoes go on the feet. See Chögyam Trungpa's book *Shambhala: The Sacred Path of the Warrior* (Boston: Shambhala, 2007).

20

Becoming a Dharmic Person

You can automatically recognize somebody who is tamed by the dharma. He or she is a different kind of person from those who are not tamed. Becoming a dharmic person means that in your everyday life from morning to morning, around the clock, you are not trying to kid anybody.

O N   T H E   Buddhist path, the hinayana is like the ground, or the earth. Without that foundation, you cannot develop an understanding of the dharma or establish basic sanity, but on that ground you can build the wisdom of the Buddha. As a beginning student of the buddhadharma, you have to start with the basics. As an example, if you are going to meet the president, when you wake up in the morning, you say to yourself, "Today I have an appointment with the president. I am going to meet this important person." You take a shower, shave, brush your teeth, and find clean underpants. You put on your shirt and trousers, tighten your belt, and check to see if the zipper on your trousers is fastened. Such details are important: if your belt is loose, when you shake hands with the president, your trousers might fall down and your dirty socks might show.

The attainment of enlightenment is very much like visiting the president: if you don't pay attention to the utmost details of how you are conducting yourself, you will have a big problem later on. So in the hinayana, the yana of details, you make sure that every aspect of your being is thoroughly and fully examined, understood, and trained so that you will be worthy later on to hear the teachings of the mahayana and the vajrayana. The whole point of the three-yana approach of Tibetan Buddhism is that the three yanas work together. Because the mahayana and vajrayana teachings are very alive, the hinayana teachings are also very alive. So a fully vajrayana person is also a fully hinayana person and a fully mahayana person.

One of the main characteristics of the hinayana is mixing your mind with the dharma. In the hinayana, your wildness, obnoxiousness, and mindlessness are being changed into a mindful, decent, good state of being. If this does not happen, you will have a great deal of difficulty understanding, or even glimpsing, the truth of the teachings. So to begin with, you have to learn to become a dharmic person, to the point where you are always a dharmic person—when you sleep, when you awaken, when you walk, when you eat, when you dream—in any activity in your life. In that way, your activities are not a way of taking a vacation from the dharma or from practice; instead, you always maintain a dharmic attitude or a dharmic beingness in yourself.

At the hinayana level, the dharma boils down to your own sitting practice. Through sitting practice you are being tamed, so that your ego neurosis and individual attachment do not play as big a part in your life. You are trying to become a decent person, like the Buddha himself. You are trying to become very civilized, with tremendous self-control and tremendous gentleness and warmth to yourself and others. At first, however, although you may have respect for the teachings and be quite reasonable, you are not yet fully decent. In order to transform reasonability into decency, your whole nature has to be completely tamed and conquered. The discipline of sitting practice has to enter much further into your being. You also need to study the dharma so that you can apply it to yourself.

Being civil often has an element of acting. However, in the hinayana, you are behaving rather than acting. Acting is trying to manifest yourself for the sake of display, whereas behaving is how you feel. Acting is the way you dance, and behaving is the way you sneeze or hiccup. You know if you are being genuine. You are the first person who knows. When you are acting, you are concerned with other people's possible reactions; but when you are behaving, you are just behaving. It's like sitting on the toilet seat and doing your duty: nobody is watching. It's your private concern, so there is a quality of genuineness. In the hinayana, you behave decently because the dharma is actually a part of you. That is the meaning of taming yourself.

When someone's mind is mixed with dharma properly and fully, when someone becomes a dharmic person, you can see the difference. Dharmic people behave differently: they walk differently, they eat differently, and they talk differently. You can automatically recognize somebody who is tamed by the dharma. He or she is a different kind of person from those who are not tamed. Becoming a dharmic person means that in your everyday life from morning to morning, around the clock, you are not trying to kid anybody.

The Seven Characteristics of a Dharmic Person

According to hinayana logic, being genuine is fundamental. We are trying to do everything properly, precisely the way the Buddha taught. How we can actually relate with ourselves in that vein is through the seven characteristics of a dharmic person: passionlessness, contentment, fewer activities, good conduct, awareness of the teacher, propagating prajna, and an attitude of goodness.* This traditional list of seven characteristics represents a long-standing tradition of discipline. It is how our forefathers in the Kagyü lineage fully practiced their discipline. Such lists were taught by the Buddha himself to his own monks and nuns. The seven characteristics of a dharmic person give us guidelines as to how to begin. They have to do with how we can train ourselves, how we can organize our livelihood, and how we can create a decent society. If you are going on a scout trip, you need to know how to gather wood and how to light a fire. If you are going out, you first need to shower and put on your clothes. Likewise, if you are studying Buddhism, you first have to be clean-cut and learn how to conduct yourself. That is absolutely basic.

---

* This discussion combines two slightly varying approaches to the characteristics of a dharmic person. The traditional list of seven is sandwiched within two more items—creating a proper physical environment, and remembering to follow all of these guidelines—to make a list of nine in all, which Trungpa Rinpoche describes as nine ways of organizing one's mind according to shamatha.

General Guidelines: Creating a Proper Physical Environment

As a general overall guideline, it is recommended that you begin by creating a proper physical environment for meditation practice. A good way to develop meditative discipline is to be in the right physical circumstances. Your location, where you take your seat, should be reasonable. It should not be too hot or too cold, and it should be somewhat isolated from the hustle and bustle of the city. You should be neither too full of food nor too hungry. Making sure that your environmental situation is right is just common sense. Having set up a proper environment for meditation, you can then begin to organize your life as a whole according to shamatha discipline.

1. Passionlessness

The first characteristic of a dharmic person is passionlessness. Having established the basic environment, you begin to pick up on all the little details of how you try to create your own local comfort zone. You see all the ways that you try to make yourself comfortable in the practice. Passionlessness means that instead of trying to create an overly comfortable situation for yourself, you reduce that desire.

Passionlessness is an interesting theme for Westerners. In the West, you have all kinds of ways to occupy yourself, from chewing gum to taking trips to the Bahamas. You are always looking for ways to solve your boredom—your boredom *problem*. In contrast, passionlessness means experiencing boredom properly and fully. In Western society, when any little irritation comes up, there is always something to cure it. They even sell little pads to stick on your spectacles to keep them from sliding down your nose. If you have chewing gum in your pocket, you develop an itch on your hip: you want to take some out and put it in your mouth right away. You are in such a hurry that you can't even open the package properly; you just dump the gum into your mouth and chew it. When the weather is cold, you can't stand even a few seconds of chill; you must rush into your bedroom to get a sweater. If your tea is slightly bitter, you automatically reach for the sugar pot and put in several more spoonfuls of sugar.

From little things like pads for your spectacles to the biggest of the biggest, as long as you can afford it, you try to cure any kind of boredom or irritation. That approach is a problem. You have not been taught how to deal with boredom, or the levelness in your life, and you are not able to withstand more extreme hardships, such as starving or freezing to death. With passion, you always need some kind of sustaining power, whereas with passionlessness, you are able to maintain yourself. You can relate with boredom, and you don't immediately fill every gap.

2. Contentment

The second characteristic of a dharmic person is contentment. You don't have to expand yourself; instead, you are contained in your own existence. You appreciate what you have and rejoice in it. Enough is enough! When you are constantly changing from one thing to another, you cannot celebrate your own life. You cannot celebrate what you have or what you are. You are unable to celebrate the simplicity of practice or the simplicity of life.

Contentment is related to passionlessness. With contentment, if you feel an itch to chew gum, but you don't have any chewing gum in your pocket on that particular day, you feel relieved: "For heaven's sake, I don't have any chewing gum! That's fine! It gives me a chance to appreciate simplicity." Instead of thinking in terms of obstacles like not having any chewing gum in your pocket or having a bad day, you switch gears altogether. If you lose your toes in an accident, you appreciate that you lost your toes. You might even organize a party to celebrate the loss of your ego hang-up. When you have lost something and it is gone, that gives you more space to breathe, so you could celebrate with no regrets. You have an appreciation of obstacles becoming simplicity. Contentment is unconditional. It is free and personal. You are free to sit and practice and develop your awareness.

3. Fewer Activities

The third characteristic of a dharmic person is not engaging in too many activities. You are reducing unnecessary activities, reducing nonfunctional talking and entertainment mentality.

This is important, because normally we tend to get involved in all kinds of projects and have all kinds of engagements. Instead of holding your discipline or your mindfulness, you can just jump from A to B to Z.

You have all sorts of choices. If you don't like tea, you can have coffee; if you don't like coffee, you can switch to Coca-Cola; if you don't like Coca-Cola, you can drink scotch or tequila. You can involve yourself in constant activity.

Sometimes you don't even know what you want to do. You come up with the idea that you need to be occupied with *something*, but you can't put your finger on anything in particular. And when you are sitting and meditating, you have that same problem. You make choices all the time. If you are sitting on a rug, for instance, you begin to choose which color to look at: the white or the black, the purple or the green. You decide which fantasy to dwell on: your future, your past, your desire for food, the eccentricities of your friends and relatives, or various creative activities like sex, cooking, or buying clothes. So even in sitting practice, you are involved in lots of activities. Engaging in fewer activities means that you are giving that up. You are giving up business deals, and such things as consulting your astrology chart or tarot cards or throwing dice, and you do not waste a lot of time retelling stories or developing frivolous jokes.

When you are too chummy with your world, it becomes endless. There are always new things to do, and you keep discovering things you had never even heard of before. There are infinite possibilities. However, when you finally have everything, it will drive you mad because the whole thing is too much and you can't possibly do it all. In the end, you feel that you are not capable of doing even one thing properly. That is the problem with materialism. According to the hinayana, you have to cut that down.

4. Good Conduct

The fourth characteristic of a dharmic person is good conduct. Good conduct is quite straightforward. It is based on being willing to work on yourself, which is the logic of individual salvation, and dedicating your deeds to the benefit of all sentient beings.* Good conduct is based on mindfulness and awareness in which you see whatever you are doing as an extension of your sitting practice. Awareness is not self-consciousness; it is simply looking at what you are doing. You respect yourself and the sacredness of your being. When you have self-respect, you don't spill your

---

* A reference to the basic intentions of the two main Buddhist vows, the refuge vow and the bodhisattva vow: making friends with oneself and developing compassion for others.

tea in your saucer and you don't put your shoes on the wrong feet. When you are aware, you appreciate your whole existence and the world around you. You appreciate the weather, your coffee, your tea, your clothes, your shower. There is a tremendous sense that for the first time, you have become a real human being.

Ordinarily when people talk about developing awareness, they mean being cautious or careful. In this case, awareness is simply a question of waking up. The opposite of waking up is falling asleep, which is unpleasant, sweaty, energy consuming, and degrading. It is like putting your head in the sand and trying to hide, ostrich-style. By falling asleep you are avoiding any possibility of realization. Instead, you just feel bad about yourself and the consequences of your existence, which is not as glamorous as you would like it to be. But you should not be embarrassed about yourself. It is possible to celebrate. You could be so sharp. You could be so smart that you could look at yourself and smile. You could be awake and aware at the same time, on the spot. When you reflect that sense of constant sunrise, when you are always awake and aware of what you are doing, that is good conduct.

5. Awareness of the Teacher

The fifth characteristic of a dharmic person is awareness of the teacher. You are aware of the teacher and of other realized people. As you are studying with such people, the idea is to be without shyness. Because you are without shyness, you could relate with the teacher as somebody who has already accomplished the path. In the hinayana, the teacher is an example, an elder who is behaving in a way that you should behave. You could emulate that teacher properly and fully. You have a sense of sacredness in studying and listening to the teacher. At the same time, you appreciate that you too are part of that same tradition and discipline.

Studying and receiving teachings from an authentic teacher will affect your state of mind, including your subconscious gossip. Therefore, it is important to take advantage of meeting a good teacher by studying and contemplating the dharma. If you study hard enough, when you have subconscious gossip during your shamatha practice, the chances are that your subconscious gossip will be dharmic, instead of reruns of past memories, such as hitting your grandmother on the head. However, although dharmic subconscious-gossip can be very helpful and good, you should not capitalize on dharmic thoughts, but regard them as thinking and come back to your breath.

6. Propagating Prajna

The sixth characteristic of a dharmic person is propagating prajna, or intellect. That is to say, you should understand who you are and what you are made of. You should find out what your mind is made out of, what your mind's projections are made out of, and what your relationship with your world is made out of. In doing so, the abhidharma teachings on Buddhist psychology will be very helpful. As you study and practice, you take pride in how much you have learned, and you begin to become more and more confident. It's like being a good horse in a good stable: you are well groomed and you are well fed. You feel that you are growing up and becoming a prideworthy dharmic person. You take pride in the dharma.

Taking pride in learning is a postmeditation discipline, rather than something you only do during your time on the cushion. It means that daily conversations and other postmeditation experiences could be changed into dharmic situations. You do not have to be pious and refuse to talk about anything but the dharma, but your conversations could take place within the context of the dharma. Whatever you do, you remain in the context of dharma, and you understand that your life is soaked in the dharma. You are free to crack jokes and sing songs in the shower, but you are not taking time off from anything. Your life is infested with dharma.

7. Attitude of Goodness

The seventh and last characteristic of a dharmic person is an attitude of goodness, which comes from studying the dharma. Properly considering the dharma will help you to realize and appreciate basic goodness. In your study of the dharma, you are given long lists to learn, and the way things work is explained very mechanistically and intellectually, but that approach is very helpful. By understanding the teachings logically, you understand why you are here and what you are—which is good.

According to some theistic traditions, you inherit a big sin right at the beginning, called "original sin." Therefore, that sin has to be purified. But according to the nontheistic Buddhist tradition, original sin is a myth. By studying how your mind can be unwound and by undoing what you are doing, you discover basic goodness. You recognize that fundamental quality in everybody.

The sense of goodness comes from your own shamatha practice and from the postmeditation discipline of considering properly. Considering properly means that the dharma is put through your mental process. When you study the dharma and work through the logic, you develop a sense of having a great command of dharma. It is no longer just foreign information coming at you, or something that you have never heard of before. Instead, there is a feeling of immediacy, and the dharma is available to you. You can comprehend the dharma so well, so purely, that you don't take in dharmic information naively. You don't feel that you are supposed to agree with everything, but you apply critical intelligence to the logic you are presented with. You can churn through the dharma quite thoroughly. It is like processing dough through a spaghetti machine to make good spaghetti, or beating and hammering raw gold to refine it and make it into jewelry. Good gold or good spaghetti—take your choice. The dharma is always true and reasonable; nonetheless, you do not feel belittled by the dharma. Instead you process it through your own intellectual and personal understanding, and also in the context of sitting meditation. Your objections and your inspirations are all included in your dharmic understanding.

8. Remembering to Be Dharmic

To the seven characteristics of a dharmic person we could add an extra step: remembering to do all of these! If we include this point and the first point, creating a proper physical environment, that makes nine altogether. That is a sort of baker's dozen approach, a way to make sure that everything happens properly. Altogether, becoming a dharmic person means that dharma is no longer regarded as a separate entity but as part of your basic existence. You are making friends with the dharma so that whether you are practicing or not, away or at home, you still have a sense of the immediacy, directness, rightness, truthfulness, and realness of the dharma. The conclusion, when dharma has soaked through everything in your existence, is known as mixing your mind with the dharma.

Becoming a dharmic person is based on both meditation and postmeditation practice. The practice of sitting meditation is included, in that when you sit, there is a sense that you are in the dharma already; and outside of sitting practice, in postmeditation, you are also in the dharma. You are in the dharma and with the dharma. In short, you become a dharmic person altogether. The hinayana approach has nothing to do with big explosions of enlightenment on the spot. It is about paying attention to details: you are paying attention to your mind and your behavior patterns. If you keep sitting, you will find out that both sanity and insanity exist in you. But insanity is not regarded as an obstacle; it is regarded as kindling wood. It is because of your insanity that you are here. But you don't stop there; you go beyond insanity. You brighten up greater sanity by sitting and by perfectly watching your activities.

When you first wake up and before you fall asleep, just look and be genuine. You can't fool yourself. If you have been attempting to fool yourself, don't—it won't work. If you try to fool yourself, you will experience constant torture. So you need to develop appreciation. You need to reduce your demands and stick to the point. In the hinayana, you begin to realize the need for very good toilet training. I hope I am not insulting you by saying you are not toilet trained. In fact, it could be seen as a compliment that you need a higher level of toilet training. It could be something to look forward to! The possibility that you could be toilet trained is a tremendous cause for celebration. Our lineage fathers, including my own teacher, were fully toilet trained. The basic hinayana approach is a kind of higher-level toilet training, very much so. With such training, you could actually relate with yourself fully and properly. You could be fully toilet trained with a smile on your face.

21

Refraining from Harm

It is good to take the precepts. The practice of taking the five precepts is not just a liturgy or purely ceremonial. You should pay heed to what you are doing. This is definitely the starting point of hinayana, and you should do it properly. You could become sane, spread the dharma, and work for others.

T HE IDEA of a pure life has often been based on monasticism, particularly in India. In the Buddhist monastic tradition, there are over two hundred rules of monastic discipline. These rules were developed by the Buddha for a reason—not just because he thought he should introduce rules, but as a result of the Buddha's own experience with his monks and disciples. Buddha was often invited, along with his bhikshus, or monks, to the homes of various devotees. He also would go out with groups of as many as forty bhikshus to receive food offerings from householders and disciples. When the Buddha taught, there might be three hundred disciples hosting him and listening to the teachings; and those disciples would scrutinize the behavior of the monks, including the Buddha himself. The disciples hoped to learn something from the monks about how to lead their lives and how to be mindful.

Consequently, however, some of those disciples witnessed a lack of mindfulness, and a certain heedlessness and wrong behavior on the part of the Buddha's monks. They saw that although the Buddha himself wasn't sloppy, individual monks were sloppy and needed more training. So the disciples reported what they had witnessed to the Buddha. For instance, when an elder disciple of the Buddha was offered a meal of rice and

DISCIPLINE / SHILA

condiments and a bowl full of water, he knocked over his water container, which spilled and made a mess in the middle of the assembly. When this was reported to the Buddha, he replied that in the future, monks should not be served water with their meals. Another time, the monks were eating curry—with their hands, of course—and one monk splashed his food around so much that it fell on his neighboring monks. When it was reported to the Buddha that one of his monks was not eating properly, the Buddha replied that in the future, monks should eat slowly and mindfully.

Buddhist monastic rules were not based on the concept of punishment or guilt; they were based on proper conduct and an ideal state of decorum. Proper decorum had to be established for the monks so that when they ate, they ate properly. Rules were also developed regarding how to stand up, sit down, and dress mindfully. The monks were not just to pull their clothes on quickly—they had to learn how to wear their monk's robes properly. Every three weeks the monks shaved their heads, and particular rules were developed for how they should do so. In that way, eventually over two hundred rules were developed for monks, and for nuns there were even more.

Hinayana discipline, or vinaya, refers to the monastic rules of conduct established by the Buddha. Dompa, or *samvara* in Sanskrit, refers to being bound to the discipline and to practices of all kinds. It relates to the actual practice of taking vows, such as the refuge vow. Binding yourself with the discipline is also referred to as *brahmayana*. *Brahma* is the Sanskrit word for "supreme," "pure," or "clean," and *yana* means "vehicle"; so *brahmayana* is the yana of entering into a supreme or pure state of being. The Tibetan term for brahmayana is *tsang-pe thekpa*. *Tsang-pe* means "complete," and *thekpa* means "vehicle," so *tsang-pe thekpa* means "complete vehicle." It is complete because it is wholesome and full, like having your arms and legs in place. Therefore, you can communicate life in its perfection to the rest of the world.

THE FIVE PRECEPTS

The discipline of pratimoksha, or individual salvation, actually enters your system or your state of existence when you take the five precepts, or *pancha-shila*. In Sanskrit, *pancha* means "five," and *shila* means "discipline," so *pancha-shila* means "five disciplines." These first precepts laid down by the Buddha are on the level of common sense, and many people take these precepts as part of the refuge vow. At the time of your commitment to the precepts, an abstract force enters into your being.* From that, you begin to act according to the norm, or law, of discipline. This leads to individual salvation because you are applying it to yourself with a basic appreciation of things as they are.

Refraining from Killing

The first of the five precepts is not to kill. In Sanskrit it is recited as *pranati-pata-viratih shikshapadam samadiyami. Prana* is "life force," or "strength," so *pranati* means "life," that which survives and breathes, that which can maintain itself. *Pata* means "to cut," or "to destroy," *viratih* means "to refrain" or "to abstain from" and *shikshapadam* means "vow" or "precept." *Sam* means "full," as in *samyak,* "fully," or "completely," and *adiyami* means "taking," or "to undertake"; so *samadiyami* means "completely taking" or "fully taking." Altogether, it means "I fully take on the precept of abstaining from the destruction of life."

Refraining from Stealing

The second precept is not to steal. It is recited as *adattadana-viratih shiksha-padam samadiyami,* which is exactly the same as the first precept except for the first word, *adattadanam,* which means "I fully take on the precept of abstaining from stealing." *Datta* means "something given," a "gift," and *a* is a negation, as in asexual or acultural, so *adatta* means "not given." In the next word, *adana, dana* is related to the word *donation,* so it too is the idea of a gift, and *a,* once again, is a negation. Since *da,* the root of both words, means "give," or "let go," *datta* and *dana* are both connected with the idea of "gift." So the second precept refers to refraining from taking that which is not given, which basically means "I will not steal."

Refraining from Lying

The third precept is not to tell lies, or *mrishavada-viratih shikshapadam samadiyami. Mrisha* means "falsehood," or "untruth," and *vada* means

---

* A reference to the transmission that occurs during the refuge ceremony, at the point when the preceptor snaps his or her fingers.

"proclaiming," or "talking." This precept means: "I completely and fully take on the precept of abstaining from speaking falsely, or lying."

Refraining from Sexual Misconduct

The fourth precept is not to engage in sexual misconduct, recited as *abrahmacharya-viratih shikshapadam samadiyami*, which means "I fully take on the precept of abstaining from sexual misconduct." *Brahma* is the name of the Hindu god, and *charya* means "action," so *brahmacharya* means the "action of Brahma," or pure action. *Abrahmacharya* means "going against the action of Brahma," or acting impurely. In this context, abrahmacharya is connected with the idea of sexual misconduct. The notion of abrahmacharya is that by behaving in a sexual manner you are taking life, so you are not acting fully or fulfilling your being. This largely refers to the problem of letting go of semen, and the idea that by having sexual intercourse you are destroying those small lives. Of course, sexual intercourse itself is not the only problem; it tends to bring about lots of other problems as well. It can bring up lots of aggression or passion, which make one not wholesome, not full, not a completely dignified person.

Refraining from Intoxicants

The fifth precept is not to drink alcohol. It is a long one: *sura-maireya-madyapana-viratih-shikshapadam samadiyami*. *Sura* refers to alcoholic beverages made out of grains, and *maireya* usually refers to spirits made through distillation, such as whiskey or vodka or arrack. *Madya* means "that which is intoxicating,"* and *pana,* which is still used in modern Hindi, means "to drink." So *surya maireya-madyapana* means "drinking that which intoxicates," whether it is spirits, or beverages made out of grain. And, once again, the lines of the precept say, "I fully take on the precept of abstaining from drinking intoxicating liquor."

Those are the five primary principles developed by the Buddha as a basic starting point.

---

* "That which is intoxicating" has been interpreted in a broader sense to include not only alcohol, but other intoxicating drugs, as well.

THE LITERAL QUALITY OF HINAYANA PRECEPTS

In the hinayana, in order for a precept to be considered broken, the intention, the application, and the fruition of that intention and application all have to be fulfilled. For instance, in order to break the precept of not taking life, you have to scheme in such a way that you actually manage to kill something. Only at that point is your vow broken. In order to break the precept of not stealing, you have to take control of the whole item. To break the rule of not lying, somebody actually has to believe you. You have to convince them that what you have told them sounds feasible or more than feasible. To break the precept of not indulging in sexuality, you have to actually engage in some form of sexual intercourse,* and to break the precept of not using alcoholic beverages, you have to actually get drunk.

The whole point is that in order to break a precept, the intention, the application, and the fruition of that intention and application all have to be fulfilled. From the hinayana point of view, if you don't achieve what you intend, although you may be trying very hard, you don't quite break the precept. Only if you manage to achieve things properly and fully is the precept broken. There has to be a somewhat professional level of breaking the rules, not just doing something or other on a whim. Only if you really do something fully, in a calculated way, have you broken the rules. At the hinayana level, we do not psychologize the precepts. They are based on definite actions. Whether you are violating the precepts or fulfilling the refuge vow depends upon how thorough you are in either activity. Half-breaking a precept is not that thorough, and only half-fulfilling the refuge vow is also not all that thorough. When you only do things halfway, you are not being thorough enough either to break the precepts or to achieve individual liberation.

Until the *tantrikas,* or tantric practitioners, came along, there was no respectability or virtue in drinking or sexuality. Celibacy and not drinking served to keep life absolutely simple. Sexuality obviously brings too many relationship issues, and drinking alcohol also leads to problems. In fact, drinking alcohol is the most harmful, because once individuals get drunk, they might turn either passionate or aggressive; one never knows. They

---

* In traditional sources, this precept is broken at the point when you penetrate someone's body.

become unpredictable. So the idea of not drinking seems to be based on the approach that one mustn't do anything chancy. One's life must be kept very simple and absolutely ordinary.

There is a story of a guy who was received by a maiden with a goat and a jar of liquor. She gave him three choices—would he rather drink, make love to her, or kill the goat? He thought the lesser evil would be to drink, which is harmless. But having done that, he did both the others.

PRECEPTS AS A DAILY PRACTICE

The five precepts are taken each morning for a period of twenty-four hours. At the end of that period of time, they are no longer in effect, so at that point you could take them again or you could take a day off. Although the precepts are taken for twenty-four hours at a time, other vows have longer time spans. For instance, the refuge vow is for one lifetime, the bodhisattva vow is for many lifetimes, and the vajrayana *samaya,* Sanskrit for "binding commitment," vow is for the rest of your existence.

Although the five precepts are only taken for a period of one day, there are two schools of thought on this. One says that the precepts are in effect until the following sunrise, and the other simply says that they are taken for twenty-four hours. In both cases, you are taking them for a cycle of one day and one night, not for longer periods of time. Since you are taking the vows for a limited time, you should feel that you are doing it intensely and properly in that particular time and situation.

You might feel that you have taken these precepts already, and that you are not going to kill anybody or steal from anybody or tell a lie. With the refuge vow as well, you might feel that you are a good Buddhist in any case: "I believe in the Buddha, I believe in the dharma, I believe in the sangha, and I believe in the guru, so why should I necessarily have to take the refuge vow?" But the concept of taking a vow is very important. You take a particular vow to maintain a particular commitment and discipline. So it is still important to take the refuge vow, saying that you will follow the Buddha as example, the dharma as path, and the sangha as companionship. And in the same way, it is good to take the precepts. The practice of taking the five precepts is not just a liturgy or purely ceremonial. You should pay heed to what you are doing. This is definitely the starting point of hinayana, and you should do it properly. You could become sane, spread the dharma, and work for others.

Part Three

MEDITATION / SAMADHI

SHAMATHA:
THE PRACTICE OF MINDFULNESS

22

Simplicity

Shamatha is both simple and workable. We are not just retelling myths about what somebody did in the past. Just being here without preconceptions is possible. In fact, it is much simpler than having all kinds of adornments and paraphernalia. Mindfulness practice is not particularly religious; it is not even a practice. It is a natural behavior that one begins to develop in a very simple manner.

SHAMATHA PRACTICE is designed for the mendicant and for the simple life. Vipashyana is the basis for scholarly learning and the communicating of knowledge. Our greatest task in bringing Buddhism to the West is to try to make shamatha simplicity the basis of sophisticated prajna-activity. That could be our contribution to the teachings and to Buddha. If we could do that, we would not have dry professors or bleeding-heart yogis. Instead, precision, mindfulness, and simplicity would become the source of learning. The world may seem complicated, but it could not be complicated unless it had a pattern, and that pattern is simplicity.

I prefer to discuss shamatha practice from the point of view of the contemplative tradition, using instructions given by craftspeople rather than by theologians—instructions you can use on the spot. My conviction is that there is a need to go back to the great contemplative traditions and to the personal experiences they describe. I hope to follow the contemplative tradition of Jamgön Kongtrül, so that shamatha practice becomes workable, or "practice-able," so to speak. I would like to make the discussion of shamatha as experiential as I can. Practice is a very personal experience.

The point of shamatha is to free ourselves from ill-birth or distortion. We carry ourselves in the so-called ordinary world in a very distorted manner. These distortions range from large-scale emotional upheavals, the crimes we commit, and the pain that we cause other people, to simply being unaware of what is happening in our everyday life. We have become masters of distortion, we have become unaware personalities, but that doesn't mean we are stuck with that approach. As long as we can understand that, and as long as there is room for discipline, the practice of shamatha can change our state of being.

Shamatha is geared to the idea of freeing ourselves physically and psychologically from the three lower realms—the hell realm, the hungry ghost realm, and the animal realm*—by paying attention to what is happening with us both psychologically and physically. Meditation practice at the shamatha level is very definite: we go step-by-step, from the microscopic level to the cosmic level. Shamatha is important so that as we go further on the path into mahayana and vajrayana, we do not collect mahayana neuroses and distortions and vajrayana neuroses and distortions. Shamatha is necessary in order to make the starting point clear and clean.

Unless we are willing to commit ourselves to shamatha practice, there is no way out of ill-birth or distortion. So shamatha is very important. It is purification. Shamatha does not make metaphysical or philosophical demands on our intelligence; it is just being here in the present. In general, unless we are *here*—actually, fully, and truly here—we cannot do anything properly. We are bound to make mistakes. Not only are we bound to make mistakes, but we are bound to mess up our life.

Shamatha practice is based on the three principles of body, speech, and mind. We are developing mindfulness of physical experience; mindfulness of emotions, or speech; and mindfulness of discursive thoughts, or mind. By doing so, we are freeing ourselves from the lower realms.

---

* This is a reference to the six realms of the cycle of rebirth, which are discussed in chapter 9, "The Painful Reality of Samsara": the higher realms of gods, jealous gods, and humans, and the lower realms of animals, hungry ghosts, and hell beings. The immediate goal is freedom from the lower realms; ultimately, the goal is to be free from rebirth in the higher realms as well.

Body is the most obvious and direct. It is related to the hell realm and anger. In the hell realm, physically you experience hot and cold temperatures, and psychologically you feel separateness between you and the other.

Speech is related to the hungry ghost realm and desire. Speech is like a wind that communicates between the phenomenal world and yourself. In the hungry ghost realm, speech is connected with hunger and the emotion of wanting something. It is related with ego's need for entertainment and continual occupation.

Mind is related to the animal realm and discursive thoughts. In the animal realm, mind is chattering and discursive. This realm is marked by stupidity: the mind is not open and you are in the dark. The three lower realms are bound by their own neuroses, and by our not wanting to relate with them but instead to get away.

At this stage, your understanding of the three lower realms does not have to be precise and clear, and you do not need to spend time sorting them out. The question is, how are you going to free yourself from those realms? The way to do that, always, is to sit and meditate, and through that to develop a state of awareness whether you are meditating or not. That is the only way to free yourself from those realms. You may have fanciful ideas about the transmutation of energies and making use of the manure of experience, but such ideas are premature. They are still concepts, rather than what you can do this very day, this very afternoon, right this moment.

Mindfulness is sometimes referred to as restful or relaxing, but this does not refer to the conventional concept of relaxation. It is not relaxing as in relaxing before you get hypnotized, or the relaxation you feel after intensive hatha yoga. In shamatha, relaxation means being without defense mechanisms, or if defense mechanisms arise, letting them go. Whenever you feel that you should be doing something to get yourself together, there is at the same time a defense mechanism, a quality of uneasiness. In shamatha, the idea is to go along with the uneasiness instead of trying to make everything smooth and ideal. You could use the uneasiness and irritation as part of the practice. But you don't sit on it too long; you just look at it and then let it go, look and let go. If you take the whole thing personally, it is not a problem, but if you take it as a larger threat, an impersonal cosmic plot, it becomes very complicated, and you cannot develop mindfulness of the here and now. However, if you let the defense mechanisms defend themselves rather than defend you, the defense mechanisms fall apart. If you are tense, for instance, let the tenseness be tense. Then tenseness has no substance. It becomes relaxation.

In Tibetan, the word for relaxation is *bakpheppa*. *Bak* means a kind of "sensory awareness feeling," a "twinkling in the nervous system," *phep* means "relaxed," and *pa* makes it a noun; so *bakpheppa* means the "relaxation of your quivering nervous system." That can only be done by relating with the tension itself. There is no other way. If you are trying to relax, you end up with so many reference points of relaxation that you cannot actually relax. It's like being on a vacation when you've got a television, a sauna, a swimming pool, a tennis court, and a restaurant: you have so many places to relax that you are too busy to really relax. In shamatha, relaxation is one-pointed. It is just to *be*, in a very simple manner.

In pure shamatha you are just being there constantly, haunted by your mindfulness. Mindfulness comes up as the constant sense that you are actually there. It could start in the context of the teachings, in connection with your own pain, or in connection with recollection. Mindfulness should be taking place all the time. On the whole, in order to understand buddhadharma, you have to *be* there; otherwise, buddhadharma cannot be grasped. Being there does not mean holding back or sitting still. You could go along with what's happening and still be there. As an example, His Holiness the sixteenth Gyalwa Karmapa,* the supreme head of the Kagyü lineage, could be there with the audience—with businesspeople, politicians, scholars, and all kinds of people. He was always there, always present. When he blessed three thousand people lined up in San Francisco, it took almost two hours for everybody to go through. But as he blessed them individually, he was there for each person. You could do the same thing. It is possible. It's a question of attitude. With shamatha, you are there; you are *always* there.

Being there requires loosening up, but as you loosen up, you discipline yourself more. So looseness and discipline operate simultaneously. Sometimes when you loosen up, you become silly or absurd, and when you hold back, you become spaced-out, noncommunicative, and statuelike. That is a problem. The idea of shamatha is that you can loosen up and be aware

---

* Chögyam Trungpa Rinpoche was instrumental in inviting the sixteenth Gyalwa Karmapa (1924–1981) to teach in the West. The current Kagyü lineage holder, the seventeenth Karmapa (b. 1985), has also begun to teach in the West.

at the same time. That is what is called *samyakshamatha*: "complete," or "perfect," mindfulness. It is not one-sided.

In shamatha, you are present. At the same time, your mind becomes so transparent, so penetrating and loose, that it becomes like a sieve. You think you are pouring teachings into it, but end up with nothing at all. If the buddhadharma were a theistic religion, based on the worship of a deity or savior, and if you thought you knew perfectly what you were doing, your mind would cease to be a sieve and instead become a cast-iron cauldron. That model seems very sympathetic, because one would like to have something very solid and definite to hold on to as opposed to becoming a sieve. But in the nontheistic tradition, your state of being becomes a sieve with which it is difficult to catch or to hold on to anything. Therefore, in order to understand the essence of the teachings, it is necessary to develop constant awareness.

The development of awareness is based on simple mindfulness-practice. Whether you are sitting on your meditation cushion or not, awareness should take place constantly. In Tibetan contemplative traditions, I don't think anybody feels that they can take time off. There's no room for that. It is a blanket approach, full-time work, twenty-four hours a day. Postmeditation practice in Tibetan is *jethop*. *Je* means "after," and *thop* means "receiving"; so *jethop* means "receiving after." In fact, a lot of teachers have said that it is much more important to experience jethop than to be too concentrated on formal sitting practice. Sitting practice provides a kind of anchor to start with, and in postmeditation that experience becomes real. So you don't just sit and then think you are finished. When you are done with your sitting practice, there is still the postmeditation experience.

On the whole, there are a lot of demands on students, as well as on the teacher, to be here, to be present. We should be present, not with a certain concept in mind, but simply being. We are simply being here. It is much easier in theistic traditions, because you always have something to do. For instance, with the Prayer of the Heart in the Greek Orthodox tradition,* you say the Jesus Prayer constantly until it begins to repeat itself, so you are not lost. In the nontheistic tradition, it is much looser and

---

* Repetition of the Prayer of the Heart, also known as the Jesus Prayer, was the central practice of the thirteenth-century mystical movement known as Hesychasm. The most frequently used form is "Lord Jesus, Son of God, have mercy on me, a sinner."

more complicated, so in a sense it is more difficult. It is difficult to be here, but at the same time, *not* to be here is very difficult!

It is very important to try to develop your shamatha and to understand it. Shamatha is the point where you begin to behave like a buddha—a real one, not a fake one. Once this kind of unconditioned mindfulness happens, you are here and you are automatically sane. You do not need to try to do anything in particular. You are here, ready for anything the other yanas might suggest or demand. It is very important to be Buddha-like and to understand that to be so is very simple and easy.

Shamatha is both simple and workable. We are not just retelling myths about what somebody did in the past. Just being here without preconceptions is possible. In fact, it is much simpler than having all kinds of adornments and paraphernalia. Mindfulness is not particularly religious; it is not even a practice. It is a natural behavior that one begins to develop in a very simple manner. At the beginning, you may feel it is somewhat false or that you are making it up. However, as you go on, mindfulness becomes natural and real, and at the same time very personal.

23

Following the Example of the Buddha

The sitting practice of meditation is regarded as one of the most profound and fundamental disciplines you could ever achieve. By doing this practice, you find that you become less crazy. You begin to develop more humor, more relaxation, and ultimately, more mindfulness.

M EDITATION IS about experiencing reality, and being as real as possible in your own existence. In order to experience reality, you have to tame your mind. In meditation practice you use yourself as a fundamental point of reference. You use subconscious thoughts, such as a desire for water or food, as a starting point for working on yourself. So meditation practice is very ordinary. We are not referring to psychic or outlandish experiences, and we don't expect any flying saucers to land on our heads. The practices of sitting meditation and walking meditation were developed by the Buddha. By practicing meditation, we are following his example: we are going through what the Buddha himself went through.

The key point of meditation practice is to develop sympathy for yourself. You could enjoy being yourself. You don't have to borrow anything or bring any foreign influences into your life. You are self-sufficient; therefore, you can make yourself comfortable. In meditation, you create a very natural situation for yourself. Although mindfulness practice may be a primitive technique, you have to begin at that level. You may want to start by trying to match the sophistication of confused mind with sophisticated intellectual methods, such as analyzing yourself to rediscover that you do not have an ego. But that does not seem to work. You have to start at the beginning, with sitting practice.

Meditation practice is based on the idea of being yourself, as you are—something you have rarely done. All along you have had problems with that. Even at an early age, you tried to please your world. You tried to please your mommy and daddy or your nanny, if you had one. Sometimes you got angry with your parents, but you never made a relationship with yourself. Instead, you created a kind of emotional insulation, which became more prominent as you grew from a teenager to an adult. Now you are continuously insulated. You carry that insulation with you in your timid smile and timid aggression. Such timidity, shyness, and uncertainty represent what is known in Buddhist psychology as passion, aggression, and ignorance. Because of that insulation, you have never experienced real life. You have not really learned to be with yourself, although you might have experienced a glimpse of such a possibility in a practice retreat. However, having recognized that fact, you also discover that your existence is workable. Your timidity, uncertainty, and fear can be worked with by means of sitting practice.

THREE ASPECTS OF SITTING PRACTICE

The purpose of meditation is to teach you how to be. It has three aspects: posture, technique, and joy.

Posture

Posture organizes your being and makes you a true human being with good head and shoulders, as opposed to an ape or a banana. Posture is one difference between animals and human beings. In *tüdro,* the Tibetan word for animal, *tu* means "bent over," and *dro* means "to go," or "to walk" so an animal is a sentient being that walks or moves bent over. Unlike animals, human beings are capable of sitting upright and having good head and shoulders.

Technique

The second aspect of sitting practice is technique. Basically speaking, the technique is to be spacious and not wait for anything. If something is about to happen, it will happen; if it is not going to happen, it won't. Don't expect anything from your practice. Sitting practice is not a punishment or a reward. Don't expect it will bring you sudden bliss or a new relationship with reality. You have to sever yourself completely from any such view! Nobody is going to help you; you are on your own. John Doe or Jane Doe. Be alone, be lonely. Loneliness has the quality of somebody playing a bamboo flute; it has the quality of somebody strumming a guitar at the foot of a waterfall. Occasionally you sneeze, which might shock you. Loneliness will make you resentful and horny. Loneliness will make you cry and laugh at the same time.

Joy

The third aspect of sitting is joy, or appreciation. Sitting practice is joyful, but not in the usual sense. It is hard joy, tough joy, but you will achieve something in the end. Joy is connected with hard work and exertion: you appreciate working hard and you are not trying to escape from pain. If you stay with the pain of practice, it is like carving a rock: it is not necessarily pleasurable, but you are achieving something. It is like sawing a tree or trying to swim across a big river: you keep going and appreciate keeping going.

Practice is like medicine: it is bitter, but good for you. Although it is a bittersweet experience, it is worth it. When you sit on your cushion, it is tearful and joyful put together. Pain and pleasure are one when you sit on your meditation cushion with a sense of humor. Sitting practice is remarkable, fantastic, extraordinary! It is like watching a traffic light: stop, wait, go. It is like an orgasm, which could be both painful and pleasurable. That is life.

THE INSPIRATION TO PRACTICE

Understanding how you came to be practicing and why is very important. You need to know why you are practicing or not practicing, what actually motivates you. Meditation is not like suddenly being fixed, which is impossible. So why do you stick with your practice? Why don't you go do something else and forget the whole thing? The motivation to practice arises because each time you practice, there is a sense of joy and well-being. From that feeling of well-being, conviction, or faith, arises.

The Tibetan word for motivation is *künlong*. *Kün* means "all," and *long* means "to rouse"; so *künlong* means "to rouse whatever is available." There are many levels of motivation. You may be inspired that what you are doing has a purpose. You may want to learn more about yourself and about meditation, so you put as much effort and energy into the practice as you can. Your motivation may be more long-range; it may be to have your entire life coincide with practice. But the ultimate motivation is to develop your meditation in order to learn how to work with other people.

Having developed motivation, you then develop *shinjang*, the sense of relaxation and joy that comes from sitting practice. People tend to complain to a greater or lesser extent. Sometimes people with complaints voice them, and sometimes they swallow them. There are all sorts of relative complaints, but the ultimate complaint is having utterly no joy. Without joy you feel like you are being crushed between two pieces of hot metal. It is like being put into a waffle iron and compressed, so you don't even get a chance to complain. Shinjang is precisely the opposite of that complaint mentality, for with shinjang, joy takes place.

Motivation also has to do with faith. The Tibetan word *tepa* means "faith," or "conviction." Tepa is basic faith in what you are doing, so it is similar to künlong. Because of faith, you have a sense of being, of existing. You are here and you are following a definite path, so it is not blind faith. If you do not happen to have faith, however, you could start simply. You could have faith in not having faith. If you are penniless and have faith that you are penniless, you could become a millionaire.

On the whole, the practice of meditation is about being here precisely, with joy and humor. You may be motivated to practice by your conviction and faith, but meditation is not at all goal oriented. You may be somewhat goal oriented, but your concept and understanding of the goal is uncertain. The fact that you have no idea what is going to happen, no real idea about the goal, seems to be the saving grace. When a lot of big promises are made—such as that you are going to be happy forever, or that you are going to perform miracles—when you have such solid goals, nothing happens. But you cannot begin perfectly. So if you are goal oriented, fine; just let it be that way. It might turn out to be a big joke. If you are not goal oriented, it might turn out to be a big promise. Who knows? It depends on the practice itself.

Over time, you may develop expectations based on having done a good job and wanting to do it again, or you may have the sense that nothing is happening. However, your practice does not have to match the level described in the scriptures. Your motivation could be that you are willing to be strenuous whether it turns out that way or not. Basically, motivation is the willingness to give in. It is the willingness to be open and to work hard. The question is whether you are willing to commit yourself or whether you are going to cop out. Your attitude or motivation is extremely important.

CHEERING UP

Traditionally, it is said that we are like drunken elephants. Whether we are drinking alcoholic beverages or not, we are still drunk in our basic being. In order to work with this drunken elephant, we have to make the elephant stay very still, so that the elephant can become sober. In the same way, we have to work with ourselves.

We are crazy. Everybody is crazy, I'm sorry to say. Even the psychologists are crazy! We are all crazy, including the animals, worms, and fleas. We are crazy and we have created this crazy world, which we think is fabulous and terrific. Nonetheless, we are all crazy. How do we get out of that? Purely by sitting. You could try it right now. You could hold up your posture this very moment! You could imitate Buddha.

The sitting practice of meditation is regarded as one of the most profound and fundamental disciplines you could ever achieve. By doing this practice, you find that you become less crazy. You begin to develop more humor, more relaxation, and ultimately more mindfulness.

Mindfulness practice depends on your cheerfulness. You should not regard yourself as being punished for your crazy outlook, or feel that you have to cleanse yourself. You do not have to regard sitting practice as a punishment, like going to church and sitting on a hard bench to purify the sins you have committed. It is not like going to confession and saying, "Bless me Father, for I have sinned." Instead, the idea of mindfulness and sitting practice is joyfulness. If you regard sitting practice as a joyful experience, even the pains in your back and in your legs will diminish.

If you regard spiritual discipline as a punishment for having done something bad, you are in trouble. You are still in the theistic framework. If you do not regard meditation practice as punishment, your speech becomes natural, and as a result there is less gossip. The more you suppress, the more reactions you get; therefore, you become less controllable. In contrast, the more relaxation and humor there is, the more you begin to understand. There is less chatter, due to the very fact that you don't suppress yourself. That seems to be the basic point: less suppression. In order to attain nirvana, or freedom, you have to suppress yourself less. You do this by means of sitting practice. In the beginning, it might be painful, but the end product is more enjoyable.

When the Buddha sat under the bodhi tree, he wasn't tormenting himself; he was enjoying himself. For six years he had a great time. The only time he had any second thoughts was when he spent forty days wondering how he could communicate the joy that he had experienced. He was not sure how people could be made to understand such joy and wakefulness. After he had spent forty days in that way, he began to speak. He began to present the teaching of the four noble truths to others. It is a very joyful occasion when someone presents the dharma. Once you are fully here, with mindfulness and awareness, it is known as holding buddha in the palm of your hand. Buddha is right here.

THE IMPORTANCE OF PRACTICE

There is no way one can attain freedom without sitting practice. To work with egolessness, we need training in letting go of our ground. There is a need for the rug to be pulled out from under our feet. Meditation is the only way to do that. In the early stages of the hinayana journey in particular, the sitting practice of meditation is regarded as the one and only way to attain peace.

Your approach to mindfulness practice and to life should be very precise and direct. There is no room for confusion or chaos. When you sit, you sit; when you do not sit, you do not sit. You may be doing activities around the environment of sitting, but that is not sitting. We cannot say that when you do not sit, you are still sitting, because you are *not* sitting. Even though what you are doing may be compassionate activity for a good cause, even though you may be working to bring the buddhadharma to the West, we still would not regard you as a good sitter. We could regard you as a good missionary or a good householder. But when you do not sit, you do not sit.

It requires selfless service to provide situations for other people to sit. For instance, when we were building Karmê Chöling, our retreat center in Vermont, the work crew had no time to sit. However, in that case, even though they themselves were not sitting, they were providing space for others to practice. When you don't sit for your own sake because you want to have a good time lounging around in your bedroom or kicking around ideas, it is a different situation. At Karmê Chöling our buildings and our meditation cushions were all made by meditators, so there is no way you can get away from meditation practice. It is in everything above, below, and in between. Your cushion could eat you from below.

Sitting practice has immense importance. If there is no sitting practice, there is no way at all of getting beyond the problem of ego. We need to recognize, realize, and manifest our ego problems properly, fully, and thoroughly; without sitting, we have no way of doing that. We could join primal-scream therapy, or go to an encounter group, or take a heavy dose of LSD, or smoke a gigantic joint, or drink a whole bottle of tequila. Although we may do all that in the name of spirituality, nothing really happens. The problem is that those are sudden measures; they only last for a short time. In order to be able to work with yourself properly, you have to sit. Meditation practice has to be considered the highlight of all your activities, the most important and best thing you do.

There is a lot of corruption taking place in the Buddhist world. One of the most critical is that Tibetans do not meditate. Even the highest people, who are reputed to be good sources of inspiration, do not sit. If communist China had not invaded Tibet, quite possibly we would have had no way of presenting the buddhadharma in the West. Tibetan Buddhism would be dead, having perished in its own graveyard. Our responsibility is to practice the real buddhadharma as the Buddha taught it and as the lineage has described it, which is that without the practice of meditation, nothing can happen.

Without sitting, there is no hope. Although you may have heard about Buddhism and studied the dharma, if you have not learned to sit properly, it is like producing a baby that cannot cry, piss, or shit. The dharma would be like a thousand-year-old egg, which has not been eaten, but is still sitting in somebody's Chinatown shop. It is a grim picture. Sitting practice is not always going to be smooth, pleasant, comfy, and nice—it is also going to be very painful. However, whether you are experiencing pain or pleasure, what really is needed is the subtle humor of somebody standing behind your back willing to kick you off the cliff. You may think you are drowning, but you have to drown more! It cannot be helped. You have to do it. The Buddhist motto is: "Actions speak louder than words."

You have to sit if you want to hatch eggs; you have to sit if you want to cook food; you have to sit if you want to perk up. Sitting is very dull. It does not say very much. There is no encounter group, no sensory awareness or touchy-feely. Sitting is very ordinary and very simple. Because of that, it is highly precious. It seems to be the best idea that humankind ever came up with, and the first person to have that idea was Buddha himself. We feel very grateful to the Buddha that he came up with such an idea. It is a fantastic thought! Not only was the Buddha enlightened, he was more than enlightened—he was an enlightened practical person. He knew how to handle us, even in the twentieth century. His logic never dies.

24

The Basic Minimum

In sitting meditation, you are dealing with body, speech, and mind simultaneously. You are developing a sense of precision and accuracy. There is no room, none whatsoever, for imagination or improvisation.

IN MEDITATION practice, discipline is not how many hours you sit; it is your total involvement in the practice. In shamatha, body, speech, and mind are completely and totally involved in the sitting practice. In vipashyana, there is also total involvement of body, speech, and mind; in addition, you are also completely aware of the environment around you. When you are involved so much that there is no longer an individual entity left to watch itself, that is the *shunyata,* or "emptiness," level of practice.* I encourage you to have that approach of total involvement in your sitting practice and in meditation in action, or everyday life. Commitment to the practice of meditation is a way of committing yourself to the teachings. Teachers are purely spokespeople for the teachings; the teachings themselves are based on your own involvement.

WORKING WITH THE MIND

In meditation practice, what we are working on, working with, working at, is the mind. Mind is what we use, apply, and manipulate. In Tibetan,

---

* Shunyata, or emptiness, is a central realization of mahayana Buddhism in particular. It is also sometimes described as complete openness, and is considered to be devoid of any limitations or falsity.

mind is known as *sem*. In Sanskrit, mind is known as *chitta*. *Chitta* means "mind," or "heart"; it is that which thinks, that which perceives thoughts. Mind and thoughts are inseparable, like a king and his retinue, or the hand and its fingers. Chitta, or sem, perpetually thinks, perpetually schemes. Mind perpetuates thoughts around us and in us, such as love or hate. Mind causes us to be fascinated by the world or, for that matter, turned off by the world. We are perpetually being turned off and turned on by this particular thing called mind. It makes us happy or sad, inspired or uninspired. Artists are turned-on by this; musicians are turned on by this; revolutionaries are turned on by this. Culture was created by this; the very room you are in was created by this. It is neither masculine nor feminine. We call it mind, or "it." This mind is what we have to work with. Although it is difficult, we cannot give up. We are stuck with this mind, like having chewing gum stuck on our fingers, and the way we are going to free ourselves, or free "it," is with dharma. It is the dharma that is going to liberate us. Therefore, we are practicing meditation.

Why will meditation free us, and how is it going to work? It works by picking up our end of the stick. Rather than by tackling mind as an enemy or a friend, you work gently, using the system developed by the Buddha, which is to let go and to tighten up. You loosen, or let go, by means of the out-breath; you tighten up, or concentrate, by using the body. Working with posture is the means to release the tension and frustration that exist in the mind. Straightening your posture will satisfy it, just like giving milk to a crying baby, or opening the doors and windows in a stuffy room. By using those two techniques of loosening and tightening, you will be able to free the mind. Within confused mind, or bewilderment, there is the possibility of awakening. Confused mind is like the night: although it is dark, there is still light because you can see the moon and the stars.

The sitting practice of meditation developed into different styles in different countries, and there are many levels of practice. The approach of my lineage, the Kagyü lineage of Buddhism, is surprisingly close to the Theravada school of Buddhism and to the Soto Zen tradition of Japan. The Zen tradition practices hinayana Buddhism in the light of mahayana inspiration; in Tibetan Buddhism, we practice hinayana discipline in the light of vajrayana. Nevertheless, we still have to practice at an ordinary, simple, strict, direct, clear level.

When I began teaching Westerns to meditate, I noticed that some students were able to tune in to openness directly. So I did not give them a technique, but encouraged direct opening, a sudden flash. However, in intensive meditation programs, that approach became a problem. Those students began to question whether that open experience was genuine or a hallucination. Although they had nothing to do but sit and let that openness happen, all kinds of thoughts began to churn up in the mind. Auditory, visual, and physical sensations began to take them over. So although such instructions are valid on their own merit, during intensive practice I feel that students should practice the more conservative approach of mindfulness of breathing. Also, there are different styles of breathing belonging to different levels of meditation practice, such as shamatha, vipashyana, *mahavipashyana,* or "great vipashyana," and shunyata. However, instead of classifying the different styles of practice, I prefer to present very simply and directly what it is necessary to do to begin sitting.

GOING OUT WITH THE
BREATH AND DISSOLVING

In sitting meditation, you are dealing with body, speech, and mind simultaneously. You are developing a sense of precision and accuracy. There is no room, none whatsoever, for imagination or improvisation in sitting practice or in walking practice. In mindfulness of breathing, you have a sense of the breath. You are being with the breath and the subtleties of the breath. You do not have to be too scientific concerning your lungs, your nostrils, hot and cold temperatures, or the impression the breath creates on your lips as you breathe out. Instead you should have a sense of the breathing as the ongoing survival mechanism that governs you. You are becoming mindful of the natural breathing. Mindfulness is not looking at, thinking about, or imagining something better or higher than your natural breathing. You have a sense of breathing out. You experience the breath going out and dissolving, and on the in-breath there is a gap. You do not have to follow the in-breath as you draw it in; you can let it drop. So the in-breath is an insignificant space, a gap; then you breathe out again.

In mindfulness practice, you are simply identifying with the breath. In particular, you are trying to follow the out-breath. The in-breathing is just a gap or space. You wait. Then, when you have breathed out, you dissolve, and—gap. You breathe out, dissolve, and—gap. In that way, openness and expansion take place constantly. By creating a gap area, there is less strain. Once you breathe out, you are sure to breathe in, so there's room for relief. It is a question of openness. Out-breathing is an expression of step-ping out of your system. It has nothing to do with centralizing in your body. Usually everything is bottled up, but here you are sharing, you are giving something out. All that is associated with the out-breath.

The out-breathing is an expression of being. In-breathing is a confirma-tion of being, because we need oxygen to live. Psychologically, however, it helps to put less emphasis on the thisness, and more on the ongoing process of going out. Also, strangely enough, you find that the attention on physical being, the awareness of body, becomes more precise if you begin to feel that sense of going out. Relating with yourself in terms of going out is automatic confirmation that you are breathing without any difficulties. Your breathing is no problem; you don't need an iron lung. The in-breathing is a sign of struggle. If you are short of breath, you breathe in. Out-breathing has a feeling of relaxation and well-being, a feeling of existing.

SIMPLIFYING

The shamatha approach is to simplify everything to the basic minimum. You should not try to improvise or do anything other than follow your breath very simply. You should walk in and sit down properly on your meditation cushion. You should arrange yourself fully; you don't just plop. You should feel your cushion and make yourself as comfortable as you can. Don't rush into the technique; first settle down and adjust your-self. After that, feel your breath, your ordinary breath. If you are alive, you are always breathing; unless you are dead, breathing is constant. Feel your breath, identify completely with the breath, *be* the breath. Become one with the breath. As your breathing goes out, you go out with the breath; and as the breathing dissolves, you dissolve. As you dissolve and the breathing dissolves, there is a momentary gap. Breathing in follows as the natural process of preparing for the next out-breath. You pick up on the breath again when you breathe out. So in the practice of meditation, you go out and dissolve: out-dissolve, out-dissolve. There is a gap; there is openness. It is a process of expanding.

Some traditions feel that you should be cranking up all the time. They think that you should be kept occupied, be a busybody, otherwise you are wasting your money. However, in our approach to shamatha, there is a contrast between doing something and doing nothing. That is the secret, actually! The gap is just a gap: you do nothing. So there is a slight tinge of vajrayana in our approach to shamatha practice; it is not exclusively hinayana. You should not be afraid of that gap. According to traditional historical accounts, when the Buddha first began to talk about emptiness, several of the arhats, or senior disciples, had heart attacks and died. That sense of gap is precisely where their heart attacks began! You might think, "What am I going to do if I don't have anything to do?" Precisely! That is a very beautiful illustration of this.

TAKE YOUR TIME

In group practice, when the leader rings the gong to begin, don't mentally start to practice right away. When the gong strikes, prepare yourself and pay attention to your body. Correct your posture. Feel your breath, your lungs, your legs, and your posture. Just feel them. The gong is the signal to feel your body, your head and shoulders, and your cushion. Just feel. Having felt everything, as the sound of the gong fades, you can start working on mindfulness of your breath.

The reason you should take your time is to make everything very genuine and honest. When the gong is rung, you don't just go *bam!* into samadhi. When you sit, you have to work with your mind and body and with everything that happens, so prepare yourself. This might take as much time as counting from one to twenty-five. When you first sit down on your cushion, be kind and gentle to yourself. Be natural. Don't tell yourself, "Now I'm going to give it a go, and I'm going to do it the hard way. I'm going to give myself pain." That doesn't work. When you sit down, first settle nicely on your cushion and treat yourself well. Give yourself a good time.

As the sound of the gong fades, having settled yourself on the cushion, raise your posture. Don't straighten up right at the beginning when you first sit down. You could even hunch down. Then as the sound of the gong fades away, raise yourself up so that you achieve good posture. Having done so, you can exert yourself further. Ideally, you should not have to reshuffle yourself too much as you are sitting. If you made a mistake when you first started to sit, you can correct that, but if possible don't reshuffle at all. If you take this approach, you can have a nice sitting.

When the sound of the gong has faded completely, having taken your posture, you are ready to start working with your breath. It is as if somebody were leading you on a mountain trail on horseback and finally gave you the reins: "You have to ride your own horse. It's all yours." So first you give yourself a good time, and then you become well disciplined.

To review, first you hear the gong, then you settle, then you go out with the out-breath—*tshoo!*—then you come back to your posture. So you have the mind together with the breath, with the body as an overall reference point.

25

Taking Your Seat

The meditation posture is quite universal. It is not particularly Buddhist. You can see this posture, this royal pose, in Egyptian sculptures and in South American pottery. It is not mystical or magical. The idea is to be a complete human being. In order to imitate the Buddha, you start with posture.

UPRIGHT POSTURE

In sitting practice, it is important to hold your posture. To begin with, hold your head and shoulders erect as if you were a great warrior. Have a quality of upliftedness. Then as your posture develops, think of your back. First feel your posture being supported by your head and shoulders; then you can begin to experience your lower torso. You should never slouch, siesta-style. Keep your posture clear and fresh. You should have a sense of who you actually are, without needing to ask. When you sit up, you can breathe. You can feel your head and shoulders. That becomes very powerful. It is fantastic.

Being upright brings a sense of clear perception. The ayatanas, or senses, are clarified, because most of the ayatanas are located on the upper part of your body: your eyes, nose, ears, and mouth. Upright posture also helps the spine. It clarifies depression, which is said to come from the heart and from the seventh, eighth, and ninth vertebrae, as well as the shoulder sockets. With good posture, you naturally develop your inner strength. In addition to that, with good posture, you feel uplifted and overcome

A lohan, or early accomplished student of the Buddha, in meditation. An example of proper meditation posture as a balance of both strength and ease. This lohan ceramic, housed in the British Museum, London, is reproduced with permission from Cool Grove Press, publisher of Disciples of the Buddha: Living Images of Meditation *by Robert Newman.*

drowsiness. Posture is connected with overcoming laziness, aggression, and the desire to take time off or to escape from the dharma.

When you meditate, you should straighten your body, but not to the extent of being military in style. You can use a simple cross-legged position, a half-lotus posture. You can also kneel, using a meditation bench for support. This posture comes from the Japanese tradition. Any of those postures seem to be accurate and good. You do not need to sit in the full-lotus posture, which may create problems for your feet, such as pins and needles. You can just sit cross-legged, letting your knees drop down, with your hands resting on your thighs, not too far to the front or back. If you have long legs, you may need to use a support cushion. Sometimes your hands might begin to feel as if each finger is monolithic, or you may feel that your tongue, your head, or another part of your body is extremely heavy and is pulling you down. Don't pay too much attention to any of those sensations; they will change.

You could adjust your posture if your body feels strained. However, you should not just take any old posture, because bad posture distracts you. It destroys your natural flow of breath and it interrupts your sense of ongoing spaciousness. In turn, if your breathing becomes self-conscious, that is reflected in your posture. With bad posture, you are involved with all kinds of one-sided feelings, as opposed to having a sense of balance. So posture is important.

It is not necessary to sit on a meditation cushion. It is also possible to meditate sitting on a chair. If you have a physical problem such as a strained knee or back, or you have been injured in an accident, there is no point in straining yourself. If your body is aged and it is difficult for you to position yourself on the cushion, I would also recommend that you sit on a chair. Sitting on a chair, known as the *Maitreya* asana, is an accepted meditation posture. However, when you sit on a chair for a long time, you automatically tend to lean back. Relying on the security of the chair back is unhealthy; it leads to a strained body and a weak circulation. So it is recommended that you sit upright, without anything to lean on. In that way, your posture is both upright and self-contained. You are relating with the floor, with the earth, and you can also feel the space around your body.

An upright back is extremely good and necessary. Having an upright back is natural to the human body; slouching is unnatural. Slouching is giving in to neurosis, which we call "setting sun." By sitting upright, you are proclaiming to yourself and to the rest of the world that you are going to become buddha, or awake, one day. Uprightness comes from sitting properly on the cushion or chair. Sitting in the middle of the meditation cushion provides the possibility of holding your seat. Then, because your back is upright, your head and neck are also in the proper position. You are not shy. You do not hang your head. You are not bending to anything. Because of that, your shoulders become straight automatically. You do not need to strain yourself by pulling up with your shoulders. When your back is upright, your energy goes up, and your head and shoulders are automatically good.

Your meditation cushion should not be regarded as a diving board. If you sit perched, as if you were about to launch yourself from a diving board, then all your weight will be on your knees. You will have difficulty holding your back properly, and your spine will be strained by an unnecessary bend, which will lead to pain and soreness in your shoulder blades and neck. Consequently, you cannot breathe properly. So it will be helpful if you do not perch on your cushion. Putting your cushion between your legs and riding on it is also not acceptable. Riding on your cushion, like riding a toy horse on the merry-go-round, has an infantile quality. You should assume some kind of dignity, rather than always trying to accommodate yourself.

Your posture is the saving grace in synchronizing your mind and body. If you don't have good posture, you can never do anything. You become like a lame horse trying to pull a cart. You should sit like the Buddha sits. The Buddha does not sit on the edge of his seat; he sits in the middle. When you begin to do that, you feel better. A square cushion, or *gomden*, is much better designed for sitting in this way than a round cushion, or zafu. With a gomden, you have your own seat, just as the Buddha had his seat under the bodhi tree. You are like the Buddha.

Sitting in the middle of the cushion is comparable to riding a horse. In dressage, you sit in the center of your saddle. Your legs are slightly bent so that your shoulders are aligned with your legs, and you are in a perfect, perpendicular, upright posture. The idea is that you should hold your seat, just like the Buddha on his lotus cushion. I have often noticed that instead of holding their seat, students follow a kind of orthotics approach. If you have a defect in your feet, you can go to a special shoemaker who takes a cast of your feet and makes special shoes for you. If your foot is tilted or you have a bad heel, the shoemaker can adjust your shoes so that you will be able to walk naturally. However, a meditation cushion is not at all like such a shoe. It is designed for people who can hold their seat and sit properly.*

The point of good posture is to enable you to feel your whole system together at once: your body, your head, your neck, your mouth, your belly. All your systems are there fully. You are sitting on the cushion or chair as one unit, one piece, as if you were a well-carved statue of the Buddha. Even on the ordinary physical level, you feel that you are doing the practice fully and properly. You are right there, with your spine in its proper place. The tip of your tongue is lifted to rest behind the upper front teeth. Your eyes are cast slightly down but not closed; and because

---

* Trungpa Rinpoche himself needed to wear orthotic shoes, which he called "space shoes," due to injuries he had suffered in an automobile accident.

of your posture, your breathing is regulated. You are paying attention to your shoulders, and your abdomen is in the right place, not bulged out or sucked in. There is a sense of straightforwardness, which stems from your backbone, your general posture, and your hips being in the proper place on your cushion.

Although posture is important, the Theravada and Tibetan traditions put less emphasis on the posture than the Japanese tradition, which takes it very literally. As Westerners, you could develop a middle way. The merit of being Westerners is that you have access to all the traditions and disciplines. However, if you get carried away, you could get caught up in spiritual materialism, the fascination with spiritual attainment and the exotic cultural trappings of the East. So you have to pay attention and remind yourself that you are meditating in your own society and culture, not somewhere else.

The meditation posture is quite universal. It is not particularly Buddhist. You can see this posture, this royal pose, in Egyptian sculptures and in South American pottery. It is not mystical or magical. The idea is to be a complete human being. In order to imitate the Buddha, you start with posture

General Guidelines for Meditation Practice

It is important to begin by taking a proper upright posture. Having done so, you can establish a firm foundation for meditation practice by following a few simple guidelines.

HAVING A SENSE OF SPACE. When you sit, having some room above your head is very helpful. You shouldn't feel cramped, but that you have room to expand. If you have hallucinations, you could come back to your body. You do not have to develop visionary samsaric recreation; instead, you can refer back to the body and to your posture. Having done so, you can let go and breathe out. And as you do so, you could try to relax—not by slouching, but by being on the dot.

RELAXING THE GAZE. In the meditation posture, you are being there properly, fully present. Therefore, your eyes are open and your gaze is down. Traditionally, the Buddhist scriptures say that your gaze should rest on the floor in front of you at a distance the length of an ox's yoke, which would be two to three yards. Often it has been taught that you should gaze down the line of your nose, but I suppose that depends on how big your nose is. The point is just to gaze down. At the same time, you try to keep your posture and gently go out with your breath.

PLACING THE HANDS. You can hold the hands in the "cosmic mudra" or rest them on your knees in the "relaxing-the-mind mudra." Both are acceptable. For the cosmic mudra, you rest your arms on your thighs, and place your hands one on top of the other, palms facing up. You relax your thumbs and fingers, and raise your thumbs to form a circle, but with your thumb tips slightly apart. You do not need to hold your hands above your thighs, which puts a strain on your arms and shoulders. You also should not hold your hands together tightly, but rest your hands on one another, with your thumbs just about to meet. In that way, your thumbs can remain quite steady. The idea is that if you have a good seat, you could relax your hands.

Cosmic or meditation mudra.

The hand position I usually suggest is the relaxing-the-mind mudra, in which you rest your hands on your knees. It is a much more royal posture, and a somewhat tantric position. This mudra is also called the "double earth-witnessing mudra." It is a good one. When the Buddha was asked who had witnessed his attainment of enlightenment, he said, "The earth is my witness. I sat on this earth; I practiced on this earth." Then with one hand he touched the earth as his witness, using the "earth-touching mudra." Here, since both hands are resting on the knees, it is the double earth-witnessing mudra. You could use either the cosmic mudra or the double earth-witnessing mudra.

Overall, the particular mudra or posture is not as important as the totality, or sense of unity. In meditation, you don't do just any old thing, but there is a sense of balance.

BREATHING THROUGH BOTH NOSE AND MOUTH. When you sit, you should keep your mouth open a little, as if you were saying "Ah." You should not restrict your breathing to your nostrils, but provide a space so that the

Relaxing-the-mind mudra.

out-breath comes from both your nostrils and your mouth. In particular, people with sinus problems would have difficulty meditating if they had to close their mouths.

TAKING YOUR SEAT AND PROJECTING OUT. When you are meditating, you are trying to mimic, or emulate, the Buddha. You should have a sense of openness and uprightness. You should feel that you are projecting out, as if you were a universal monarch or the Enlightened One. You should also learn to listen to dharma talks in this way. You don't have to stick your neck out and strain to look at the teacher, but you can hold your posture and keep your neck flexible. Every time you sit, you could project out in that way; not only in the formal meditation practice of relating with yourself and your mind, but also in everyday life.

When you sit, you do not have to become ego-centered, thinking that you are going to attain enlightenment in a couple of months or at least at some time in your life. You do not have to be that corny. However, you could develop ambition and real discipline. In doing so, posture plays an extremely important part. So before you begin any session of sitting practice, you should check your shoulders, your head, your neck, and your back; you should feel your hands on your knees. The minute you sit down, you could check through all that very quickly. This is not a trip, it is not body building; it is very simple. Each session of sitting should begin in that same way, by checking your posture, and after walking meditation, you create your posture again.

26

Breathing Out

[In meditation practice,] the body becomes insignificant, and space and breathing become more important. In fact, the breath is the most important part of the practice. Thoughts come up with the sense of body, the sense of "me" being here. However, if there is no central authority, if your practice is purely activity in space, thoughts become transparent.

A s you meditate, your breath is going in and out. You may have ideas about your breath or think there is some problem with the way you are breathing, but you should just try to go along with the breath you have. It is important to breathe normally. Your breath will be affected by your posture, by exercise, or by whether you had a heavy meal or a light meal. Your breathing is also affected by your vision. If your vision is too focused, for instance, your breathing will begin to pick up. Along with that will come sudden discursive thoughts: sexual fantasies, aggressive fantasies, all sorts of fantasies. So it is better not to focus your vision, but to let your vision rest. Even if your breathing is affected by such things, you still should not force yourself to breathe in a certain way, but let your breath flow naturally. And if your breathing happens to be fast, you should give it time to settle.

In meditation practice, you place your attention on the out-breath. As you are breathing, you just go out with the breath and the breath dissolves. As you breathe in, you wait, and then go out again. It is very natural and very slow. When thoughts come up, you label them "thinking," and return to the breath. You have to be very precise about the whole thing;

you can't miss an inch. You should not think twice, thinking that you are thinking "thinking." It has to be right on the dot. When you breathe, you are utterly there, properly there; as you breathe out, you dissolve or diffuse. Then you come back to your posture, and you are ready for another out-breath. Over and over you come back to your posture, breathe out, and come back again. It is quite hard work. As the breath dissolves, it is becoming less important. As your breath goes out and begins to reach beyond you, there is space. You just keep breathing out and dissolving; breathing in just happens. So it is out . . . rest . . . out . . . rest. You don't use any tricks; you just put an emphasis on *out*. And while you are practicing, you should not think about what you're going to get out of meditation. You just do it.

Learning How to Let Go

As you practice, you should keep it very simple. After each breath goes out, there is a gap—not a big drop, just a gap. That gap could be felt. You might feel it as a moment of waiting, or expectation, or being ready for the next out-breath. As you breathe out, ideally about twenty-five percent of your awareness is on the out-breath. Beyond that, you don't need to be aware of anything—there is simply a gap—then you breathe out again. If you do not scheme, but just sit and follow your breath, that makes life very simple.

The sitting practice of meditation is basically: out-breath . . . dissolve . . . gap; out-breath . . . dissolve . . . gap; out-breath . . . dissolve . . . gap. Keep it at that level. If any jolt takes place, it is usually due to your posture, so your posture has to be extremely good. If your out-breath doesn't quite dissolve, it isn't quite out-breath; so each time you breathe, your practice has to be precise—very simple, very direct, and very accurate.

When you breathe out, you do so with some tension or tautness. You look at your breath, but you do not use it as a means of achieving absorption. Sounds, temperature, the feeling of your clothes, the food you might or might not have in your stomach, all sorts of pains in your joints, your back, your neck, and your arms—you could regard all those as thoughts. It is all thinking.

The out-breath is connected with the idea of letting go. You are always breathing out. When you talk, you breathe out; when you eat, you breathe out. Breathing out is not gymnastics, but simply learning how to let go. You develop mindfulness as you let go. Mindfulness is in jeopardy when you are busy projecting toward something, or when your mind is distracted because you are trying to make sense of something as you are breathing out.

In meditation practice, you are in the process of developing action along with nonaction as you begin to touch the world. When you meditate, you have mindfulness of the breathing going out, then you cut that; then you have another mindfulness of the breathing going out, and you cut that. In other words, you go out with the transport—and suddenly you have no transport! Then you start again. In that way, the gap of the in-breath becomes extremely spacious. By focusing on the out-breath, your practice is not based on the ongoing speed of out-and-in, out-and-in, all the time. Instead, a leap is involved, a miniature leap. It takes a little effort, but you could feel very refreshed.

If you follow both the in-breath and the out-breath, you are being too faithful. The whole thing becomes very linear: you go out and you come in; you go out and you come in. If you go out and come in again and again, in the end that makes you very heady. You have no rest, and everything is extremely hard work. In contrast, when you go out, then nothing happens; then you go out again, and nothing happens—it is very clean-cut. The out-breath is threatening in a sense, but focusing on the out-breath is a much freer approach. If you allow yourself a rest as you breathe in, the out-breathing becomes more of a journey, however short that journey may be. You simply go out with the breath. When you do so, the body becomes insignificant, and space and breathing become more important. In fact, the breath is the most important part of the practice. Thoughts come up with the sense of body, the sense of "me" being here. However, if there is no central authority, if your practice is purely activity in space, thoughts become transparent.

LIGHT TOUCH

As you breathe, you should not try to reach perfect breathing; you just breathe. Even animals can do that. Breathing obviously comes from your lungs and your nose, but if you are just feeling the breathing coming out of your nostrils, you are not feeling where it actually begins and how it flows. At first, your sense of the breathing may be very general and vague, but as your mindfulness of breathing continues, you experience the whole process very specifically. There is a pattern as your breathing goes out, a sense of it really happening, so you do not have to focus on your nostrils. It is like hearing a noise: when you hear a noise, a sound traveling through space, you can relate with the sound rather than having to relate with your ears.

The practice of shamatha is environmental as well as technique oriented. In shamatha practice, a twenty-five-percent touch of awareness on the breath seems to be about right. In any case, you can't do more than that. Because you keep your eyes open, you see things; your ears are not clogged, so you hear things. You are aware of the way your clothes feel and of the temperature in the room. You are aware of your stomach being full or empty. If you took a shower before sitting, you feel clean. You feel your hairdo and the spectacles you are wearing. You feel whether your mouth is dry or wet. There are all sorts of little sensations like that, which leaves only about twenty-five percent of your awareness left for working with your breath.

That is a natural situation. You exist as a human being, and your sense perceptions are operating everywhere all the time. The idea of shamatha is to narrow all that down into twenty-five-percent awareness of the breath as a way of training yourself. You are internalizing a little, as opposed to trying to cast off the sights you see, the sounds you hear, the smells you smell, and the tastes you taste, and the physical sensations you experience. During your sitting practice, you reduce all that into the breath, which will be about twenty-five percent of your attention, if you calculate scientifically how much is going on in your body. You might as well come back to the breath. It is more joyful, more wholesome, and you don't have to be startled by anything. In shamatha, you are bringing the rest of the things going on in your existence back to one particular thing: the breath. It is very simple.

RELYING ON GUESSWORK

You may find that as you are keeping your heedfulness on the breathing, the thinking process continues to freely function at the same time. That is quite common; it happens with a lot of practitioners. Once you develop a feeling of the rhythm of the breath, you can be aware of the breathing and at the same time entertain yourself with all kinds of thoughts. The problem with that approach—by the way, it is not regarded as a problem at the beginning—is that it is a sign that you are not properly in contact with the breathing. The monotonousness of the breathing leads you to rely on guesswork. You are just guessing that when you breathe in, you automatically breathe out. You are not in contact with the well-being of the breathing at all.

COUNTING THE BREATHS

Counting the breaths is very popular, even in the Kagyü tradition. You count every out-breath up to ten, and then you count back down to one. That seems to be the starting point of learning how to be able to relate with space and the outgoing breath. The counting makes special note that breathing is going out, even if your breathing is shallow or rough. The outgoing breathing has a label, it is named by numbers, but the incoming breath has no label: it is just preparing to count one, two, three, and so forth. So each time you count, one part of the breathing is more emphasized than the other. That is the counting technique.

However, I don't think counting the breaths is necessary, and in fact your concentration may be weakened by using the counting technique. If you are having difficulty meditating, the problem is that you do not sufficiently experience *being there*. Therefore, Jamgön Kongtrül recommended that if you really experience that quality of being, even if you have difficulty handling the awareness of breathing, you have no problem, so it is not necessary to count. I have been trying to follow his direction in emphasizing a sense of being.

COOL BOREDOM

Mindfulness of breathing is a way of creating obstacles to subconscious dreams and mental activities. The technique of mindfulness of breathing *should* provide obstacles. It is a nuisance that you have to keep hassling back to the breath. However, unless you are able to do that efficiently, you will not get properly bored, and if you do not get properly bored, you will not be in tune with the power of the practice. Everything may be happening very smoothly on the surface level, but you are not in tune with the magic of meditation practice or the spiritual energy of the lineage.

Boredom is important because boredom is anti-credential, anti-entertainment—and as we develop greater psychological sophistication, we begin to appreciate such boredom. It becomes cool and refreshing, like a mountain river. That very real and genuine boredom, or "cool boredom," plays an extremely important role. In fact, we could quite simply say that the barometer of our accomplishment in meditation practice is how much boredom we create for ourselves. Cool boredom is rather light boredom: it has its uneasy quality, but at the same time it is not a big deal. Cool boredom is simply another expression of the experience of well-being. Cool boredom is like what mountains experience. With cool boredom, thought processes become less entertaining—they become transparent. Cool boredom is hopelessness at its most absolute level.

27

Labeling Thoughts

*Don't regard yourself as good or bad. You are just you, thinking
and coming back to the breath. You are not trying to push thoughts
away, nor are you trying to cultivate them. You are just labeling
them "thinking." No matter what thought comes up, don't panic;
just label it "thinking"—stop—and come back to your breath.*

T HE THINKING process takes place all the time. That is everybody's
problem. In order to solve that particular problem, you have to discover what goes on in your mind. It is very direct and personal. In sitting
practice, you spend at least eighty percent of your practice dealing with
thoughts, but that does not mean you are being extraordinarily naughty
or terrible. Even if you are so completely occupied with your thoughts
that you do not have much time left to work with the technique, don't
think you are being bad. You should feel grateful that your sitting practice
is not one-hundred-percent thoughts! Eighty-percent thoughts is pretty
good, so don't punish yourself. You are not doing anything wrong and you
are not committing any sin.

In meditation practice, you regard everything that takes place in your
mind—every little detail, every little explosion—as thinking. You are not
trying to separate thoughts from emotions. If you feel angry at somebody;
if you have a sudden burst of passion, your own private porn show; if you
are going through cookbooks and visualizing beautiful food or drink; if
you are on the coast swimming in the ocean or walking barefoot along
the seashore—all those little outbursts of anger or passion are regarded
as just thinking. Metaphysical dialogues or debates, evaluations of art and

music, questions of reality and enlightenment, ideas of mathematics and science, ideas of love and friendship—all those philosophical questions that come into your head are regarded as just thinking. Even if you have very dedicated thoughts or dharmic thoughts, they are still regarded as just thinking.

Regarding emotions as thoughts may seem dry, but when you have a strong thought it involves your whole being. For example, if you are in a battlefield, you can be shot to death by an enemy sniper at any time. That is a thought, but a very real thought. You think that to your right and to your left, your friends are turning into corpses instantaneously, and since you are standing in the middle you too could be a corpse pretty soon. Those are really strong thoughts. However, although such thoughts have some reference point of reality, they are still thoughts. Even when you take action, it is your thoughts that drive you into action. For instance, driving manuals talk about having a thinking distance, a braking distance, and a stopping distance. When a car in front of you stops, first you think about stopping, then you step on the brake, and finally you actually stop. It always works like that.

You might think you are making a breakthrough this very moment and that you are just about to dissolve into space. You might think you are going to kill your mother or father on the spot because you are so upset with them. You might think you are going to make love to somebody who is extraordinarily lovable. You might think you are about to have such a fantastic affair that it could exhaust the whole universe. You might have a thought of assassinating your guru, or you might want to make lemon juice and eat cookies. A large range of thinking goes on, but in terms of sitting practice, it does not matter whether you have monstrous thoughts or benevolent thoughts, sinful or virtuous thoughts—any thought is just thinking. So please don't be shocked by your thoughts, and don't think that any thought deserves a gold medal.

You do not need pigeonholes for all the concepts that arise. It doesn't make any difference whether you have good thoughts or bad thoughts, whether you think that you are the Buddha himself or you think you are in the realm of hell. It is all just thinking. Thoughts arise all the time. If you have a hierarchical bureaucracy in which every thought pattern that occurs in the mind is labeled as good or bad, all kinds of problems develop. When you feel hurt, you think about that; when you feel good, you think about that.

In the Buddhist approach, doubt is just a thought. Doubt could be said to be a powerful thought, but it is still a thought. You may have doubt as to whether doubt is a thought or not, but that doubt itself is a thought. Guilt is also just a thought. You do not try to get rid of guilt, and you do not try to feel that you are doing something worthwhile. If you have a guilty thought, so what? It is a thought. It is your mind.

In shamatha, you have to look at such thoughts, but not because they have a case history. It is like seeing rain, snow, a hailstorm, or a cloudy day—it's all just weather. This might seem too easy, but it is very useful to look at things in this way. We usually do not do so, however. If you are extremely angry with somebody and your wife comes along and tells you, "Darling, this is just your thought," then you get angry with her as well! You scream, "It's *not* just my thought! He did something wrong to me, and I am extremely angry. I want to kill him!" But we have to give up that idea. It seems to be a big thing to give up, but your wife is right—it is a thought.

We have to accept that all experiences are just thought patterns. Buddha said that when a musician plays a stringed instrument, both the strings and his fingers are his mind. According to Buddhist psychology, there are fifty-two different types of thought processes. Some are pious, some are political, some are domestic, some are sensible. But all of them are just thoughts. As far as meditators are concerned, that is the key. With that key, you begin to find that you can handle life as it happens around you. With so many pigeonholes, you cannot handle the whole thing. But once you begin to realize that everything is thought process, you can handle your life because nothing is complicated. Everything is thought.

The traditional technique for dealing with all those mental activities is mentally to note them and label them "thinking." Inevitably, once you are settled into your practice—*bing!*—there will be a thought. At that point you say "thinking," not out loud but mentally. Labeling thoughts in that way will give you tremendous leverage to come back to your breath. When a thought takes you over completely, so that you are not even on the cushion but somewhere else—in San Francisco or New York City—as soon as you notice, you say "thinking" and bring yourself back to the breath. You don't regard yourself as good or bad. You are just you, thinking and coming back to the breath. You are not trying to push thoughts away, nor are you trying to cultivate them. You are just labeling them "thinking." No matter what thought comes up, don't panic; just label it "thinking"—stop—and go back to your breath.

By labeling thoughts "thinking," you are simply seeing them and acknowledging them as they are. You acknowledge everything as thoughts, as the thinking process, and come back to the technique. Labeling practice has to become instinctual. You can talk to yourself, but that is a second-rate experience, arising out of extreme boredom. It is not necessary to verbalize. Rather than saying, "Now I should get back to the breath," just come back! There has to be some abruptness. Introductory remarks as to what you are going to do are a waste of time.

Coming back to your breath is not regarded as suppression; it is returning to where you began. Your work has been interrupted, so you are coming back to it. It is as if you were chopping wood, then your friend came along and you got involved in a conversation. You tell your friend, "I must get back to work," rather than "I must suppress our conversation." You don't come back to the breath because things are becoming unpleasant, or use coming back to the breath as a protection or shield. At the shamatha level, whether a thought is unpleasant or pleasant doesn't really matter. You just label it "thinking," and come back to the breath.

If you seem to be working with the breathing and having thoughts at the same time, that means you are unable to identify completely with your breath. There is some deception in thinking that you can work with the thoughts and the breath at the same time. If a thought occurs along with the breathing, you are thinking; if a sense perception such as hearing occurs, you are thinking. You cannot hear without thinking. If you hear a sound, you know which kind of sound it is, whether it is music or a gunshot. You cannot hear without categorizing, so you are still thinking. Everything is thinking. It goes on everywhere continually. We have not yet come to any conclusion as to whose fault that is. Instead, we just label everything "thinking," as in "I think I have a mosquito on my face."

Meditation practice is very simple and straightforward. Don't try to make a big game out of it. If you keep it simple, there is no confusion. While you are practicing, you should not think about what you are going to get out of it. You just do it. Also, unless it is practically necessary, it is very important not to think about what you are going to do after meditating. You should just settle down into the practice.

Everything that comes up in your mind is just thought process. It is thinking. Thinking might bring something else—nonthinking—but we are a long way from experiencing that. As far as the hinayana is concerned, no mahayana exists. Everything is hinayana, the narrow path. In shamatha practice, you regard everything as thought. When you sit, you should think, "There are no nonthoughts." Even techniques are thoughts. That is straight shamatha, without soda and ice.

28

Touch and Go

Touch is the sense of existence, that you are who you are. You have a certain name and you feel a certain way when you sit on the cushion. You feel that you actually exist. . . . That is the touch part. The go part is that you do not hang on to that. You do not sustain your sense of being, but you let go of it.

T HE ATTITUDE that brings about the possibility of mindfulness is mind's awareness of itself. Your mind is aware of itself, which means that you are *aware* that you are aware. Mindfulness is based on a sense of being and individuality. It is not mechanical. As an individual person, you relate with what is happening around you. We could use the phrase "touch and go." You touch or contact the experience of actually being there, then you let go. That touch-and-go process applies to your awareness of your breath and also to your awareness of day-to-day living. Touch is the sense of existence, that you are who you are. You have a certain name and you feel a certain way when you sit on the cushion. You feel that you actually exist. It doesn't take too much encouragement to develop that kind of attitude. You have a sense that you are there and you are sitting. That is the touch part. The go part is that you do not hang on to that. You do not sustain your sense of being, but you let go of it.

When you touch, you should experience that thoroughly, two hundred percent rather than one hundred percent. If you are committed two hundred percent, which is more than normal, you have a chance to let go, and you might end up experiencing one hundred percent. However, if you hang on to that awareness, touch becomes grasping. So you touch and go. You do not try to experience the whole thing, but you just let go of yourself completely, halfway through the experience. The approach of touch and go is not so much trying to *experience*, but trying to *be*.

Experience is not particularly important. Experience always comes up as long as you touch. But you don't hang on to your experience; you let it go. You intentionally disown it. That seems to be the basic point of touch and go. Clinging to experience reminds me of the pain of having a tick on the neck: if the tick gets too fat, it will die on your body, so you have to pull it out in order to save its life. Our state of mind is like a tick that doesn't have an outlet and always bottles things up. If we cling to experience constantly and don't let go, we are going to be gigantic, enormous. If we bottle up everything within ourselves, we cannot even move! We cannot play with life anymore because we are so fat.

A Sense of Being

In mindfulness practice, in touch and go, there is a sensation of individuality, of personhood. You are actually here: you exist. You might question that approach and think, "What about the Buddhist doctrine of nonexistence or egolessness? What about the issue of spiritual materialism? What's going to happen to me if I practice this? Isn't this some kind of pitfall?" Maybe it is, maybe it is not. There is no guarantee since there is no guarantor. I would recommend that you do not worry about future security. Just do touch and go directly and simply. Traditionally, such problems are taken care of by the sangha and the guru, somebody unshakable who minds your business. When you commit yourself to the dharma, you are asking somebody to mind your business, which could happen very heavy-handedly. So you do not need to feel too much concern about future security.

Acknowledging States of Mind

A further touch is necessary. Touch is not simply the general awareness of being. It also applies to mindfulness of your individual states of mind. That is, your mental state of aggression or lust also has to be touched. Such states have to be acknowledged. However, you do not just acknowledge them and push them off. You need to look at them without suppression or shying away. In that way, you actually have the experience of being utterly aggressive or utterly lustful. You don't just politely say, "Hi, good-bye. It's nice seeing you again, but I want to get back to my breath." That would be like meeting an old friend and saying, "Excuse me, I have to catch the train and make my next appointment." Such an approach is somewhat deceptive. In shamatha, you don't just sign off. You acknowledge what is happening and you look at it.

The basic point of shamatha is not to give yourself an easy time so you can escape the embarrassing, unpleasant, or self-conscious moments of your life, whether they arise as painful memories of the past, painful experiences of the present, or painful future prospects. When such thoughts arise, you could experience them, look at them, and *then* come back to your breath. This is extremely important.

It is possible to twist the logic, and relate to meditating and coming back to the breath as a way of avoiding problems, but such avoidance is itself a problem. You might feel good that you are sanctioned by the Buddha and you have the technique of mindfulness, which is extremely kosher, good, sensible, and real. You might think that you don't have to pay attention to all those little embarrassments that happen in your life; instead, you could regard them as unimportant and come back to the breath. However, in doing so, you are patching over your problems. You are bottling them up and keeping them as your family heirloom. Since this kind of attitude can develop, it is very important to look at those embarrassments and *then* come back to the breath. However, in doing so, there is no implication that if you do look at them, that is going to be freedom or the end of the game.

Your greatest problem is not that you are an aggressive or lusty person. The problem is that you would like to bottle those things up and put them aside. You have become an expert in deception. Meditation practice is supposed to uncover any attempts to develop a more subtle, sophisticated form of deception. It is important to realize that basic point and to work with it. So you should experience your aggressive thoughts; you should look at them. This does not mean that you are going to execute those thoughts. In fact, we do not execute more than five or ten percent of our thoughts, including our dreams, so there is a big gap. When you do act, unless you have looked at such thoughts, you will not act properly. However, if you look at your aggressive thoughts, you do not usually put them into practice, but they dwindle.

29

Encountering Problems

By meditating, you are doing something very honest, something that was done in the past by the Buddha himself. You could do it very literally, absolutely literally. There are no tricks and no magic. Everything can be very smooth, simple, and ordinary. You are just being. It is like floating in the Dead Sea.

I N MEDITATION practice it is common for obstacles to arise. So it is helpful to learn about the types of problems meditators have encountered in the past, and that are likely to arise for you as well.

COMMON OBSTACLES

Lack of Commitment

A lot of the problems students have with sitting practice are due to a lack of commitment. In sitting meditation, you need to have both ambition and commitment. The need for commitment does not mean that you have to join the party politics of Buddhism; it means you need to make a commitment to yourself. We all feel somewhat inadequate in one area or another. You may feel uninformed, that you are not quite making it, that you are not doing what you should be doing. Such doubts come out of a lack of commitment to making a good job of yourself. You may feel self-conscious and trapped in your particular situation, but unable to make the heroic leap of quitting it altogether. You are unable to handle your situation, which is awkward, but that awkwardness leads you to meditation practice, which is beautiful.

If there is no ambition, no real commitment, all kinds of entertainment come up in your mind, and you are hardly sitting at all. Your mind is miles away in your own private movie show, and you encourage that because it is entertaining. You could imagine endless things, like hitchhiking or flying in an airplane. However, although you could entertain yourself constantly in that way, the fact is that you haven't actually done anything. Your mind is taking a trip, but your body is still here. Your mind is tethered by the leash of karma, so you have to stay put, and you cannot achieve your wishful thinking. You are bound here, whether you like it or not. Both physically and psychologically, you are indebted. Your physical body is here because you are psychologically bound to solid ground by the expression of all kinds of neuroses. So it is hopeless, but that sense of hopelessness plays an extremely important role.

Lack of Synchronization

In meditation practice, you are working not only with your mind; you are working with your breath and your mind, your body and your mind. You never leave reality. That is the idea of shinjang, the ideal state of tranquillity in shamatha. You experience shinjang because you feel comfortable with your body. If you are untrained in synchronizing mind, breath, and body, you find lots of problems. Your body wants to slump and your mind is somewhere else. There is always that distortion. It is like a badly made drum: the skin doesn't want to go along with the frame and there's no consistent tautness, so either the frame breaks or the skin breaks. The idea of synchronization is that your mind goes out with the breath. Because of your posture, your breathing happens naturally. In turn, each breath serves as a way to correct your posture. The combination of your breathing and posture provides your mind with a reference point. By checking back to that reference point, it can correct each situation properly.

Beckoning of the Sense Perceptions

When you begin to get tired of your sitting practice, you entertain yourself by using the last exit you have: visual and auditory sensations. Overusing the sense organs in that way is problematic. It makes you completely cranky. The speed involved with seeing or listening gives you insomnia. You are so hyped up that you become like a little child who is put to bed too late and becomes neurotic and cries a lot and destroys things.

If you have good head and shoulders, your visual field should be somewhat dissolved. As you look out, relax your eye muscles and don't try to make visual perception sharp and clear. Open your eyes and diffuse your vision. Diffusing your vision relaxes you, so there is less neurosis in your back, neck, head, and shoulder muscles. With good posture, you should be less distracted by visual input or by sounds. When you slouch, sights are more vivid and sounds are louder, whereas if you are in an upright posture, sights and sounds are less distracting. If you hold yourself together properly with good head and shoulders, you do not pant after sights or sounds.

When you have proper posture, you are not fascinated by sights, sounds, or feelings, because you are somewhat self-contained. You have basic one-pointedness. It is like one of the stories of the Buddha attaining enlightenment. According to this story, while the Buddha was practicing meditation under the bodhi tree, his friends experimented on him by putting straws into his ears and up his nose, trying to figure out whether he was a statue or a human being. When they got no reaction from him, they thought he was mad. That is the idea, except not as extreme. I don't think it's likely that anybody is going to stick straws in your nose!

Meditation practice is a question of having some kind of trust, rather than trying to achieve an ideal state of mind that will make you okay. Your awareness of your clothing, whether it is heavy or light, your sensations of hot or cold, your awareness of your feet, your socks, your collar, your gomden, and the joints in your body can all be worked with. When your perceptions begin to relax, you can learn how to just be. You could regard visual and auditory tension as thoughts, as the thinking process. When you work with all those perceptions and accept them, rather than constantly looking for new gadgets to entertain yourself, your senses become simple. This is quite the opposite of the idea one of my students in Scotland thought up. He wanted to build an electronically rotating seat with a meditation cushion on it, so as he meditated the world would be constantly changing. I told him he was completely nuts.

Pain

In meditation practice, there are two levels of pain: psychological physical pain and actual physical pain. In the first level, psychological pain has been translated into physical pain: it feels physically unbearable because it is psychologically unbearable. The second level is actual physical pain. In terms of physical pain, people who are used to sitting for a long time, three hours a day or more, have less pain because they are used to not moving. People who haven't done so much practice have more problems with pain because they are not used to sitting that long. I find that some practitioners have developed a psychological clock within their physical system such that after forty-five minutes they become restless; before that, they have perfect posture and everything is fine.

When you are sitting, it is up to you to assess which type of pain you are experiencing. If you have real pain, or if you physically cannot handle the pain, you can rearrange your body. There is no point in trying to say that it is purely mind. Taking care of one's body is important, so don't strain yourself. If your back is not straight, if your front and back are not in balance, you might experience chest tension. You might get itches or tingling sensations, or some area of your back might become numb. The idea is not to exhaust your body and make it subject to the chiropractor. However, usually there is a first attack, which is just thinking or imagining pain. The mind says, "I have a terrible ache in my body, and I would like to get some entertainment out of that." Then it replies, "That's true, that's true. It is still going on." That mental dialogue may go on for ten or fifteen minutes, and eventually the actual physical body begins to feel that way as well. Your body begins to agree with your mind. When that happens, there is no point pushing yourself. Simply rearrange your body. Be generous with yourself—but not too generous.

You have to take care of your body, so you should not go to extremes. It is a delicate question how much heroism and sacrifice you make out of your practice, and how much genuine contact you have with the totality of your practice. If you relate to any pain in your body as purely psychosomatic, your attitude toward your body is too heavy-handed. At the same time, if you don't experience the totality of your body, speech, and mind—speech in this case being the ongoing energy, or pulsation, of your system—you could waste a great deal of time. You start thinking, "Should I shift positions or shouldn't I shift positions? Is this pain psychosomatic or is it in the body?" If you feel that a pain is an actual pain rather than dreamed up, it is important that you shift your posture immediately.

Drowsiness

Too much visual fascination while you sit creates eyestrain. Consequently, the visual perceptions become somewhat dull and gray, which brings drowsiness. If your activity level has been hectic, and suddenly you bring yourself down to a simple activity such as sitting, which gives you a temporary rest, that can also lead to drowsiness. If you have been practicing wholeheartedly and intensively, then come back to daily practice that is not as vigorous, you may take on a more casual attitude to practice and begin to look for entertainment, which also brings drowsiness.

As your breathing goes out, you experience the space behind you as well as in front, so as you breathe you are surrounded with space. When space is all around you, rather than being one-dimensional, there is a quality of lightness. Within that experience, the problem of falling asleep can come from holding back, from trying to make things too methodical and regular. Drowsiness can also come from too much bodily sensation, or from being too careful that the meditation should go smoothly. Drowsiness is not particularly a problem; it is just an energy level. If you regard it as a problem, that will create further drowsiness.

Tightness

The feeling of tightness may come from your practice being too formalized and deliberate. It happens because there is not enough identification with the technique. The technique is purely a hint. It is not like a wall that you dwell inside, which creates separation. Trying to hold still, to hold very tight, can become a problem. You need more openness. You need to let go and simply follow the technique.

Eyestrain

If you try not to blink, that will cause eyestrain; if you close your eyes, that could also cause eyestrain. Often, it is the psychological state behind your eyes that is the problem. When you look, you don't purely look, but you always try to bring what you see back to your brain. That is, when you look at objects, you always demand a visual reference-point. In that case, transporting visual objects into your brain is the hassle, rather than simply looking. The idea in meditation practice is just to look, without bringing anything back to your system. You are almost visually careless, in that you are just looking and not trying to pick anything up. Usually, whether you close or open your eyes, you are still expecting some kind of visual perception. If you close your eyes when you sit, it becomes like switching on to meditation when you shut your eyes, then switching it off when you open them again. There is too much contrast between meditating and not meditating, which is not particularly recommended.

Trance

If you feel very high or heady, that is often the result of too much body orientation. You should relate with any trancelike state as another thinking process, just a thought. Then it is just another sensation, no big deal.

Ringing in the Ears

If you have ringing or roaring in your ears, you are trying too hard. You have too introverted an approach, and you are not in contact with the space outside you. This is not such a big problem. However, if you try to quiet these noises, they begin to roar more. In fact, they begin to play all kinds of music!

SUGGESTIONS FOR RESPONDING TO OBSTACLES

Taking a Fresh Start

When you have difficulty with the constant interruptions that occur in following your breath, you could mentally take a break. That doesn't mean loosening your posture; you just mentally take a break and start again. You could do that over and over. It has been said in the scriptures that you can do that a hundred times an hour, if you like. Start again and start again and start again. Keep coming back. Take a break and come back.

Taking a break is not regarded as a failure. It doesn't mean that you cannot sit properly or that you are not an ideal meditator. So please don't blame yourself. Please don't think you are bad or unable to sit. Instead, whenever things get too tangled up, just cut it right there. Give the whole thing up and start fresh. Starting fresh means coming back to your posture, to your awareness of your head and shoulders, and then going back to the breath.

Practice is very simple as long as you keep your posture, but it is hard to do. It's quite different from what happens in a Pentecostal church, where people speak in tongues and cry and laugh. Shamatha practice is very hard-nosed. When you cry, you should keep your posture; when you laugh, you should sit with your laughter. Although tears might be coming down your cheeks, crying is just a thought, a mental burp; it is fine. Meditation has to be simple, otherwise we are creating another world. When we do so, we then need to create something else to resolve that other world, so we are perpetuating a huge snowball. Why can't we handle the world very simply, as human beings sitting down and meditating, breathing, and trying to pass the time?

Awareness takes hard work. You need a careful, ambitious approach to trying to work with yourself, to the point that you are becoming aware every moment. There is no other way. If you are not careful, it is neither the body's problem nor the breathing's problem. You have not sufficiently registered the idea of awareness in your head, so you drifted away. The idea of awareness has to become almost dogmatic. In a one-hour sitting practice, you have to pull yourself back at least sixty times. That takes programming, almost computerizing yourself.

You have got to come back. When you come back, you have your body and your breath. You cannot escape from that. Sometimes discipline becomes embarrassing; you are too self-conscious, too formal. However, you need *more* discipline of coming back to the breathing. You don't have to count down in order to let go, and you don't have to prepare to come back—you are right there. As soon as you begin to question that, you are already back.

Once you come back, everything becomes spacious. You have lots of room to sit. So don't feel pressured that you have to accomplish anything. You are not sitting to *accomplish* something, you are sitting to *understand* something. So you need to take a more passive attitude. You are trying to understand the meaning and the wisdom of the enlightened ones, the direct transmission of the Buddha's message to you, handed down from lineage holder to lineage holder. Accomplishing is different from understanding. To accomplish something, you have to push, to crank up your machine: you drive fast, talk fast, accomplish fast. However, if you are trying to understand something, pushing doesn't help.

By meditating, you are doing something very honest, something that was done in the past by the Buddha himself. You could do it very literally, absolutely literally. There are no tricks and no magic. Everything can be very smooth, simple, and ordinary. You are just being. It is like floating in the Dead Sea.

Exertion and Humor

In sitting practice, exertion is very important. It is important to follow the dharmic system of Buddhism and the disciplines it has developed, such as the five precepts. You can cook up lots of conspiracies and tricks when you don't want to go through with the discipline. Everybody knows that. In fact, when I was little I did that constantly. Once I pretended that I was constipated and couldn't do my memorizing, reading, and studying. I sat on the potty for about three months. The monks acknowledged my sickness and let me sit on the pot, and I didn't have to do any memorizing or studying for a long time. Finally, somebody did moxibustion on me, and when the herbs burned down to my skin, it hurt. After that, my sickness was cured! So I know all the tricks people can come up with.

I believe that most of students' complaints are not real. Your little complaints do not have to keep you from sitting practice. It is crucial to have a sense of humor. If you have humor, you do not take your practice as painful, and if you disobey a precept, you do not take it as a sin. Instead, you could develop discipline with pride, discipline with joy. Practice is bittersweet. We appreciate our life and have a good time—and at the same time, we need to have tremendous exertion.

30

Leading a Spotless Life

The practice of meditation is not so much concerned with the hypo-
thetical attainment of enlightenment, but with leading a good life.
In order to learn how to lead a good life, a spotless life, you need
continual awareness that relates with life constantly, directly, and
very simply.

P OSTMEDITATION PRACTICE, or meditation in action, is an intrinsic
discipline and an integral part of meditation practice. When you finish a session of sitting practice, you cannot say that you have finished your
Buddhist practice. In fact, the actual practice begins *after* you have finished
sitting on your gomden. So practice is constant. It is a question of heedfulness, looking at what you are doing. You could practice that anytime.

Postmeditation is the basis of tremendous sanity. Without postmeditation discipline, we would regard sitting practice the same way some
Christians regard going to church on Sunday. Sitting practice is like field
training: whether you are a good soldier or a bad soldier depends on how
much field training you have had. It is like cooking school: being a good
cook depends on how much you have learned about food. Sitting practice
is basic training, and postmeditation is developing openness and communication with the world at large.

WALKING MEDITATION

Walking meditation is a bridge between sitting and postmeditation. In
walking meditation your whole body has to be acknowledged. You notice

that now you are picking up your right heel, then your sole, and then your toe. You notice that as you are about to step down with the right foot, you are ready to lift your left heel, sole, and toe. It is very precise. That same precision applies at mealtime when you reach for your bowl, pick up your food, put that food in your mouth, chew it, and swallow it. The sense of sacredness is expanded so that whatever you might do—or whatever you might not do—is included.

In walking practice, when the gong rings and you stand up, the mindfulness of breathing is switched into mindfulness of the legs and the movement of walking. You don't just sit and then take off. Your walking should be spacious and relaxed, with neither extraordinary articulation nor sloppiness, which both require effort. You can follow the Zen tradition of holding the hands together in front of the stomach as part of the aesthetic of the practice, but that doesn't seem to be absolutely necessary, as long as your arms are in good balance and you are not self-conscious. As in sitting practice, during walking meditation you should continue to hold your posture.

Walking practice has a very interesting effect on your psychology. You may feel that you are walking naked and you have no pockets to put your hands into. You may feel that you do not know what to do with your hands or how to handle your body. However, your walking practice should be straightforward. You are simply moving through the air, walking at a reasonable pace, not too slow and not too fast. As you are walking, you may find it interesting that you do not actually walk, you just think. You take off like a helicopter. Physically you are walking, but your mind is miles away. When that happens, as in sitting meditation, you label whatever comes up as "thinking" and return to the technique. You simplify everything into right . . . left . . . right . . . left . . . dissolve . . . "thinking" . . . right . . . left . . . "thinking" . . . , and so forth.

MINDFUL SPEECH

In postmeditation, it is important to maintain discipline in speech. This might sound stern and dull, but you will find that you begin to enjoy speaking more mindfully. You begin to look good and to feel extraordinarily healthy. In fact, a lot of neurosis comes from babbling. Colds, influenza, back pains—all of those come from not paying attention to reality. So mindful speech has an almost medicinal quality. When you relate to

LEADING A SPOTLESS LIFE

speech in this way, you don't just bark each time your thoughts are ready to announce something; instead, you hold back. Before you bark, you respect what or whom you are barking at. This is helpful since we live in such a verbal world. You could also practice silence. Refraining from communicating is not regarded as a protest; it is a way to give yourself a rest.

CONTINUAL WAKEFULNESS

The idea of postmeditation, or jethop, is to develop something out of your sitting practice that continues. You are developing meditation in action. You could regard jethop as continuing your sitting practice in day-to-day situations such as sitting on a toilet seat, eating, coughing, yawning, or sneezing. In the postmeditation experience, whatever you are doing involves meditative discipline. You are doing postmeditation right now, in fact, as you are reading. You are experiencing a sense of here and now, so there is no particular separation from the practice of sitting meditation itself.

The point is that you should be wakeful every minute, in every situation, and not just slide or lose your awareness. Mindfulness literally means being fully minded. That is, no activity permits you to take time off. Every activity that you perform during the day, such as eating a meal, is part of that mindfulness. So you are right on the dot. The phrase "being right on the dot" in its Western linguistic connotation means "Be careful! Somebody hiding in the bushes might shoot at you!" But in term of postmeditation practice, being right on the dot means to be present every waking moment. Whatever you are doing, you should be in contact with reality as much as you can. You could be right on the dot while taking a shower. You could communicate with the sights, sounds, feelings, and temperatures around you. Mindfulness practice is not just about what is happening to you individually and personally—it is about how much you are going to transmit your sanity and your insanity to the rest of the world.

Postmeditation, as well as sitting meditation, is symbolized by the syllable AH. AH represents openness and humor—it represents dharma. In postmeditation, we experience AH based on our mindfulness and awareness. When we become aware of something, we say, "AH!" That "AH!" is what we are trying to experience. It is quite shocking! People tend to think of meditation practice as a way of calming down and soothing yourself, but in nontheistic traditions like Buddhism, there is sense of "AH!" You are not trying to calm yourself down—you are trying to be awake as opposed to asleep.

As you go about your everyday life, you should drop the technique of labeling, but keep some kind of watchfulness. You are going to have very little time for techniques, in any case. Instead, when there is a direct spark of awareness, just be there. Some meditation teachers say that in daily life, students should regard everything as thinking and come back to the breath, but that approach is too restrictive. It is possible to breed zombies out of intelligent people in that way, which is not so good. Creating intelligent people out of zombies is an entirely different matter! In postmeditation, you should check your head and shoulders. You should check how you walk and how you look at people. Try to transcend embarrassment. Take pride in being a human being and a practitioner. That kind of positive arrogance is completely acceptable and good. Maintain that proud state of existence.

In daily life, practice is a question of being present. You are picking up your glass, you are drinking, and you are putting it down. In doing so there is some kind of watchfulness, which is very intelligent, sharp, and precise. Such watchfulness is split-second. It has nothing to do with being careful. It is unconditional watchfulness, a quick awakening. During the day, you are awake already, not asleep. Nevertheless, that is not enough, because you are wandering around in your wakefulness. So some kind of spark has to take place. Just be there! Be there very precisely! And after such flashes of wakefulness occur, just forget them, disown them. Don't try to retain those flashes. When something else comes up, forget that as well! Be on the spot, but not on your tiptoes.

Indulgence is very much the challenge of meditation in action. You should worry about indulgence, because indulgence is destructive to yourself as well as to other people. In terms of effort, in postmeditation practice there has to be moderation. Your attitude should not be that you have gotten through another day, so you have one less day to practice. That is an extremely bizarre approach. You should also not be self-righteous. What I recommend instead is a sense of totality. Once you are involved with practice, that involvement begins to remind you. There is nothing particularly formal about it. Instead, it is as if you were haunted all the time—positively haunted. A total environment of practice is important. Once you experience that environment of totality, that environment echoes back on you.

You need strict discipline in your sitting practice, and when you are not sitting and practicing, you also need discipline. Otherwise, your approach to practice would be like working in a factory putting on bolts and nuts. When you finish your job, you sign out, come back home, take off your clothes, take a shower, and watch television. You feel a sense of relief: "Thank heaven today's over. Now it's time to be floppy." However, you could transcend that factory worker's attitude and approach things very directly and precisely.

Often, there is a big dichotomy, a shockingly big gap, between practice and the rest of our activities. If you develop such a gap, your sitting practice is going to feel like imprisonment. If you feel that the meditation cushion is where serious things take place, and then everything is back to normal when you get up, you are creating your own jail. You will develop hatred toward the time you spend sitting, while the times you are not sitting represent freedom, improvisation, and having a good time. My suggestion is that you even things out so that sitting is not so much a jail, and not sitting is not so much a vacation, and instead you have a good time all over the place.

When your basic attitude is evened out in that way, whether you sit or you stand, you eat or you squat, it is the same process. It is the good old world. You are carrying your world with you in any case. You cannot cut your world into slices and put it into different pigeonholes. You do not need to regard something like eating as completely outside of your practice. For the sake of good practice—and for the sake of good eating—I would like to recommend this to you very strongly. In fact, if you relate to eating as practice, your food will taste better. So openness and continuity are extremely important. The purpose of discipline is to develop a fuzzy edge between sitting and nonsitting—between eating and sitting, or sleeping and sitting.

It is a cultural habit, particularly in the Western world, to look for a change of mood so that every event in your life is a surprise. In England, even though you know that you are going to have four o'clock tea, when the maid actually comes with the tea, everybody says, "Ah, there comes the maid with the tea! Let's have tea! Please help yourselves to the cake!" When dinner comes, "It's dinnertime!" It is as if the unfinished or badly handled part of your late-afternoon life has been cheered up by having dinner, so life is worth living once more. Then it's bedtime. "You should get some sleep! You could have cocoa or hot milk, if you like! Have pleasant dreams!" And in the morning, when you wake up, they say, "Did you have a good night? Here is breakfast! Have some fruit juice!" There is always another shift of gear, a constant attempt to please, the pathetic gesture of trying to cheer oneself up each moment. It is like climbing a staircase: when you come down the staircase, you have to climb back up, then you come down again and climb back up and come back down. In this approach, you never face life. Not only is it pathetic, it drives people mad.

As far as we are concerned, life is a big blanket. It covers everything, and although there may be occasional bumps, it is still a blanket. Awareness is a big blanket, too. It is good and healthy all the way, so we do not have to scale down and then cheer ourselves up, back and forth. In our approach, drinking a cup of tea in the late afternoon is not a lifesaver, it's just drinking a cup of tea in the afternoon. Having dinner is a slightly bigger deal, I must admit, but it is still just eating dinner, not a particularly extraordinary event. We have lost the meaning of celebration and ceremony by holding those little ceremonies, which are not real ceremonies, but simply attempts to cheer ourselves up.

The practice of meditation is not so much concerned with the hypothetical attainment of enlightenment, but with leading a good life. In order to learn how to lead a good life, a spotless life, you need continual awareness that relates with life constantly, directly, and very simply. You do not have to be so poverty-stricken about your life. You don't have to try to get a little chip of chocolate from your life. If you try to hold on to that little chip of pleasure, all the rest will be sour. However, if you understand the meaning of pleasure as a totality, you see that such an approach is punishment, an unnecessary trick you play on yourself. With a view of totality, sitting meditation, postmeditation practice, and studying are a blanket approach, a gigantic pancake stretched over your life. If your body is hot and you dip your finger in ice water, it feels so good and so painful at the same time.

Without postmeditation experience, your practice is like beads without a thread: if there is no thread, you can't wear the beads on your neck. It is like a picture without a nail: you cannot hang a picture on the wall without a nail. It is like taking a bath without soap. It is like wearing shoes without tying your shoelaces. Sitting meditation without postmeditation discipline is like the sun without its brilliance. It is like a king without a court. Postmeditation is an integral part of meditation practice. That is why we do walking meditation; that is why we practice mindful eating; that is why we sit on a toilet; that is why we comb our hair; that is why we smile with our teeth. Postmeditation practice is regarded as absolutely important, particularly when we are in the midst of our own so-called world.

31

Resting in Shamatha

Shamatha discipline is the best way for you to work with your mind so that your mind and your body can be properly coordinated, and you can eventually attain enlightenment. That idea is the greatest idea ever thought of, thanks to Lord Buddha. He did it himself. We could thank the Buddha, our teachers, our lineage, and everybody who has done that. They all achieved enlightenment, and personally, I feel there is no problem—we could do it too!

THE POINT of shamatha is to achieve an even and completely balanced state of being by means of the nine techniques for resting the mind in shamatha discipline. Shamatha practice is one of tightness and looseness put together. That combination produces the best balance for the mind. When we are too tight, we are so enthusiastic that we apply the discipline too vigorously and burn ourselves out. When we are too loose, we couldn't care less about trying, and we avoid the whole issue. These are the two main problems that people face in sitting practice.

Shamatha is the ideal way to train yourself. In shamatha practice you are developing a good personal relationship with your own mind. An ongoing problem is that there is a quarrel between yourself and your mind. Sometimes your mind becomes you, and sometimes you become your mind. One moment you would like to be disciplined, and the next moment you couldn't care less. There seem to be schizophrenic possibilities of all kinds, and you have tremendous arguments with yourself.

However, through shamatha, you begin to develop a good relationship with yourself, which is the root of individual salvation and the foundation of Buddhist practice.

If you don't have a good relationship with yourself, you cannot understand the dharma, and your body and mind will not be properly coordinated. The practice of meditation helps you to coordinate your body and your mind. You realize that your mind can be directed to a particular effort, that your mind works. Through shamatha you are able to raise your mind to an adult level. Your mind does not jump all over the place whenever you try to do something. In this samsaric world, most of you have grown up physically, but psychologically you are very young. You can't concentrate. You can't eat even one good meal properly because your mind is constantly jumping all over the place. The basic message of shamatha practice is that your mind could be as adult as your body.

When a teacher teaches dharma, he or she would like to talk to adults, not become a babysitter, although sometimes it ends up that way. If your mind is so adolescent that you have no control over it, what you are taught is completely wasted, because you have not heard it—not because you are stupid, but because you are so distracted. You are sitting there physically and you appear to be listening, but your mind is miles away, jumping all over the place. Shamatha discipline is the best way for you to work with your mind so that your mind and your body can be properly coordinated, and you can eventually attain enlightenment. That idea is the greatest idea ever thought of, thanks to Lord Buddha. He did it himself. We could thank the Buddha, our teachers, our lineage, and everybody who has done that. They all achieved enlightenment, and personally, I feel there is no problem—we could do it too!

As a student of shamatha, you go to your meditation cushion, sit down on it, and take your posture. In doing so, you have an expectation that you are going to practice shamatha, an expectation that something will happen. It is as if you were sitting on your chair, about to dine, or as if you were taking off your clothes before going to sleep, or as if you were turning on the tap before taking a shower. That natural expectation and preparation is a good beginning.

THE NINE TECHNIQUES OF SHAMATHA

The actual technique for practicing shamatha discipline is known in Tibetan as *jokpa,* which means "placing," or "resting." The idea is to place your being, or to rest yourself, in the state of shamatha discipline. Jokpa is how you can begin to rest in shamatha. There are nine traditional techniques for resting in shamatha, common to all Buddhist traditions. These nine techniques are interconnected rather than sharply divided one from another. They are not necessarily linear; their sequence could be random. However, since they are famous, since they have been taught for centuries and centuries, and since they work, I will share them with you.

Each of the nine techniques has a corresponding power. Since there are only six powers, some of the powers go with more than one technique. The powers connect you to the discipline. They are both the effects you get out of the nine techniques of shamatha, and the inspiration for practicing them. The powers are a result of putting together the teachings and your state of mind.

THE NINE TECHNIQUES OR STAGES OF SHAMATHA

NINE STAGES	SIX POWERS
1. Resting the mind	1. Learning
2. Continuously resting	2. Experiencing
3. Literally resting	3. Recollection *(stages 3–4)*
4. Closely resting	
5. Taming	4. General recognition of decency *(stages 5–6)*
6. Pacifying	
7. Thoroughly pacifying	5. Exertion *(stages 7–8)*
8. One-pointedness	
9. Evenly resting	6. Familiarity *(stage 9)*

Resting the Mind

The first technique of resting in shamatha is known simply as "resting the mind." In Tibetan it is *sem jokpa: sem* means "mind," and *jokpa* means "resting," so *sem jokpa* is "resting the mind." In this technique, you sit down on your meditation cushion and draw yourself in, closing out all external feedback. You close yourself in, and place your mind on the sensations of your breathing and your thought patterns. Ideally, you reduce your mind thoroughly into your breath.

THE POWER OF LEARNING. Resting the mind is inspired by the first power, the power of learning, or the power of suggestion. You have been taught that it is possible to rest your mind and that you will achieve proper shamatha discipline by doing so, and you have developed a trust and respect for the heritage of generations of practitioners who have already done so.

Continuously Resting

The second technique is known as "continuously resting." In Tibetan it is *gyündu jokpa: gyündu* means "continuously," or "constantly," and *jokpa*, again, means "resting"; so *gyündu jokpa* means "continuously resting." Once you are on your cushion and you have started sitting, you elongate or extend the spirit of your sitting practice as much as you can. You do not have to give in right away to your discursive thoughts, or to sounds, sights, or other distractions; instead, you extend your practice. You should apply this technique at the start of each practice session. For instance, if you are going to sit for an hour, you should apply this technique by the third second of sitting practice so that you do not immediately give in to distractions.

THE POWER OF EXPERIENCING. The power that goes with the technique of continuously resting is known as the second power, the power of experiencing. You experience that you can be a good meditator this very year, this very month, this very day, this very hour, this very minute. You have both confidence and continuity. You are willing to stretch out the inspiration of the very first minute you sat on your meditation cushion as much as you can. You give yourself tremendous encouragement. You are not like a naughty child sitting at your desk in school, whose very first thought is what kind of pranks you could play on your teacher. You are much more decent than that. You sit and do your job properly.

Literally Resting

The third technique is "literally resting." In Tibetan, it is *len-te jokpa: len* means "naively," or "literally," and *jokpa* means "resting"; so *len-te jokpa* means "literally resting," or "naively resting." If the continuity of your sitting practice is interrupted by thought patterns or by subconscious gossip, you simply bring your mind back. Those of you who are parents know about this because it is like feeding a child. When you are trying to feed your child, you keep having to draw your child's attention back to the food: "Now you are going to have a second spoonful. Oops! There it goes into your mouth!" You try to give your child at least one good meal, but to do so you have to go step-by-step, spoonful by spoonful. Your child would rather throw things around or play with her food, but in spite of that, you say, "Take another spoonful. Here's a bird flying into your mouth!"

In the same way that parents draw their children's attention back to their food, you need to keep bringing yourself back to your breath. That is why this technique is called naive or literal. As much as you can, you bring yourself back. You could be millions of miles away, thinking about the solar system or about your hometown and your parents—but you bring yourself back to the cushion, right here, back to the breath.

THE POWER OF RECOLLECTION. The power that goes with literally resting is called the third power, the power of recollection. You remember that you are supposed to sit on your cushion and practice mindfulness, and just by remembering that, you bring yourself back. You might wonder, "What am I doing here?" But then you remember: "Oh, I am practicing shamatha. That's why I'm supposed to bring myself back." It is a very literal, simpleminded approach.

Closely Resting

The fourth technique of shamatha is "closely resting." In Tibetan, it is called *nyewar jokpa: nyewar* means "closely," as in "close shaven," or "dealing closely with situations," and *jokpa*, again, means "resting," so *nyewar jokpa* means "closely resting." In this technique, you are supposed to deal with the most minute, tiniest possibilities of little flickers of thought. Thoughts do not necessarily have to be dramatic or emotional; they could simply be little flickerings. Traditionally, big-deal thoughts are regarded as thinking, and smaller ones are just seen and dealt with right away. When thoughts become a big deal, you label them "thinking," but when they are little flickers, you just see them. It's like the difference between being walked on by an elephant and feeling a little flea on your nose.

At this stage, you become aware of refinement after refinement of thought. You become aware of the most subtle, tiny, discursive thoughts, and you try to overcome them and go back to your breath. Whether thoughts are very intense or whether they are little flickers, they are all just thoughts. Thoughts are just ripples—big ripples and small ripples— they don't stir up the ocean. The point of closely resting is not just to finger paint your shamatha, but to do the whole thing as completely and thoroughly as you can. You are doing a completely thorough job. Closely resting, like naively resting, is connected with the third power, the power of recollection.

Taming

The fifth technique of shamatha is "taming." In Tibetan it is *dülwar chepa: dülwar* means "taming," *chepa* means "doing," or "acting," so *dülwar chepa* means "the act of taming." Taming is connected with nonaggression. Aggression and gruffness are the opposite of tameness. When you practice taming, you no longer experience yourself as a nuisance or an obstacle. People often blame themselves, thinking, "This 'me' is impossible. How can I deal with myself? I'm wretched and hopeless." In contrast, you take the attitude that you can actually tame yourself, and that it is a very positive thing to do. You tell yourself, "You can do it. Keep doing it. You can do it. Keep going." You give yourself mental advice. When you talk to yourself or use such slogans, you are gentle, rather than getting completely pissed off at yourself. You practice nonaggression.

THE POWER OF THE GENERAL RECOGNITION OF DECENCY. The power that goes with taming is the fourth power, called the power of the general recognition of decency. This power, also called the power of awareness, is the power of being aware of the results of practice, and the benefits of practice for oneself and others.

Pacifying

The sixth technique is "pacifying." In Tibetan it is *shiwar chepa: shiwar* means "pacifying," and *chepa* means "doing" or "acting," so *shiwar chepa* means "the act of pacifying." Whenever you feel any resistance to the idea of shamatha or to sitting practice altogether, you apply shiwar chepa. Sometimes you are put off by practice, and you begin to feel that you have been given a bad deal. You don't want to touch your practice with a ten-foot pole. The thought of sitting practice makes you sick and tired; it really puts you off. When such a situation comes up, you pacify yourself. You acknowledge the joy and relief of being able to sit and deal with yourself so thoroughly. Usually such a possibility is unheard of, but you have a chance to do it. You have been told about it and you also know that others have done it. You have begun to make friends with your practice, and you have the general idea that you can do it, so you are not completely pissed off and put off. Instead, if you feel funny, you see that as purely a temporary nausea, which you can overcome.

Pacifying is like training a horse with a *longe* line. When you begin to longe your horse, you use a long rope, or longe line.* As you draw in the line and get closer to the horse, he may panic; but when you get very close, he begins to give in. Likewise, when you are distant from your practice—for example, half an hour before sitting—it is as if you are on a long longe-line. You don't want to sit at all. You don't even want to hear about it. But as the time gets shorter, and you are only a few inches away from your cushion, you begin to feel positive about what you are about to do. Pacifying, like taming, is connected with the power of the general recognition of decency. In the case of taming, this power has to do with the realization of choicelessness.

---

* A longe line is a leash held by the horse trainer as the horse circles the trainer at various paces.

Thoroughly Pacifying

The seventh technique of shamatha is "thoroughly pacifying." In Tibetan it is *nampar shiwar chepa*: *nampar* means "thoroughly," and *shiwar chepa* means "pacifying," so *nampar shiwar chepa* means "thoroughly pacifying." There are the three techniques for thoroughly pacifying yourself. Whenever the heat of aggression comes up, you put more emphasis on the outgoing breath, on the simplicity and windy, airy quality of your breath. Whenever you are distracted by passion or lust, you put more emphasis on the solidity of your posture, on your head and shoulders. Whenever you feel the drowsiness and dullness of stupidity or ignorance, you try to bring together the feeling of the space of the hall you are sitting in, your companions around you, your breath, and your head and shoulders. You broaden things out.

THE POWER OF EXERTION. Nampar shiwar chepa is connected with the fifth power, the power of exertion. It takes effort to overcome strong obstacles such as unhappiness, hatred, or regret.

One-Pointedness

The eighth technique of shamatha is "one-pointedness." In Tibetan it is called *tsechik tu chepa*: *tse* means "point," *chik* means "oneness," and *chepa* means "doing"; so *tsechik tu chepa* means "practicing one-pointedness." One-pointedness is similar to number four, thoroughly resting, in that even the tiniest discursive thoughts can be overcome, but at this stage you can rest your mind in the postmeditation experience as well as during sitting meditation. You are extending your shamatha practice to other activities.

One-pointedness, like thoroughly pacifying, is connected with the power of exertion. With one-pointedness, you can discipline yourself, but at the same time you begin to feel that your discipline is not too effortful. You can allow yourself a certain relaxation and freedom in bringing your mind back to your breath. If you push yourself too hard, you only produce further subconscious gossip and daydreams. At some point you have to let go of that—you need to give up trying to follow your breath and start over again. You do not literally walk away from your meditation cushion, but mentally you allow yourself a break and start fresh. In fact, you can do that every single minute of your sitting practice. When you start one-pointedly, you go right to your breath. Then if you feel harassed by your mind, by promises or by nagging, you could give yourself a break for a few seconds and regroup your being. In that way, as you work with your breath, you always start fresh, in good condition.

Resting Evenly

The ninth technique of resting in shamatha is "resting evenly." In Tibetan it is *nyampar jokpa: nyampar* means "evenly," and *jokpa*, once again, means "resting"; so *nyampar jokpa* is "resting evenly." In resting evenly, there is a quality of absorption and of making friends with your practice. It is said that in the same way that swans naturally swim and vultures naturally roam in the charnel ground, you should let your mind be as it is. The notion of resting evenly is to be kind to yourself, not torturing yourself or blaming yourself. You could take pride in being the greatest of shamatha students.

At this stage, mind is completely and thoroughly trained so that it can hang out in its own form. This doesn't mean that you are blissed out; it simply means that your mind can be your mind. In other words, you can be you in the purest sense. Up to this point, you have never really been yourself at all, because you have always been too involved with your own little tricks. Finally, you could be yourself. When you sit down on your meditation cushion, take your posture, and begin to follow your breath, you could be right there. That is the idea of resting evenly, or absorption. You are thoroughly and completely trained.

In this context, absorption does not refer to the attainment of samadhi, but simply to being decent. It is not very extraordinary. You are simply there, rather than being absorbed or absorbing. The purpose of hinayana discipline is to make you into a decent human being whose mind and body could be completely coordinated. You can give your attention to everything; you have less aggression and less passion; therefore, you are somewhat inclined toward enlightenment. Those same qualities are implied in the original meaning of the words *lady* and *gentleman*.

THE POWER OF FAMILIARITY. Resting evenly is connected with the sixth power, the power of familiarity. With the power of familiarity with practice, the mind can settle easily and naturally.

This drawing is a modern rendering of the traditional Tibetan image of the nine stages of resting the mind in shamatha practice. In this visual teaching, the mind is depicted as an elephant. As the elephant walks steadily along the path of mindfulness, it develops greater stability and power and overcomes the obstacles of wildness and dullness, represented by a monkey and a rabbit.

Starting at bottom:

The six bends in the path: the six powers. The first is the power of learning. In dependence upon this power, the first stage of resting the mind is accomplished.

The first stage, resting the mind, or placement: the placement of the mind through mindfulness (a rope) and awareness/introspection (a hook).

Flames: from here up to the seventh stage of resting the mind, the existence or nonexistence of the flames, and the differences in their size, represent the differences in the amount of exertion that must be aroused.

Elephant: the elephant is the mind, and its black color symbolizes mental dullness.

Monkey: the monkey is distraction, and its black color symbolizes mental wildness.

The second power, experiencing or contemplation: the second stage, continuously resting the mind, is accomplished by means of this power.

Mirror (sight), cymbals (sound), conch with saffron water (smell), cloth (touch), and fruit (taste): the five sense objects, the objects of wildness.

Whiteness: beginning here, the amount of white increases, starting from the head, which represents that the clarity and stability of the meditation is increasing.

The power of recollection or mindfulness: the third and fourth stages of resting the mind are accomplished by means of this power.

The third stage, literally or naively resting: the elephant caught with the hook of mindfulness turns around, as do the monkey and the rabbit. The monkey is no longer leading with the rope! The rabbit represents subtle mental dullness. From here on, one is able to distinguish both subtle and gross mental dullness. The elephant, monkey, and rabbit looking backward represent that the mind recognizes distraction and then directs itself to the meditation object again.

The fourth stage, closely resting: the elephant is stopped, caught by the rope of mindfulness.

The power of the general recognition of decency or awareness: the fifth and sixth stages of resting the mind are accomplished by means of this power. The monkey following behind: the previous ability of wildness to arise diminishes. The monkey picking fruit: When practicing shamatha, one must cut off and halt being distracted even by what is virtuous in the mind. However, one does not have to halt that at other times; one can pick the fruits of what is beneficial to oneself and to others. Awareness does not let the mind disperse, and inspiration leads the mind to samadhi.

The fifth stage, taming: the elephant is led by the meditator with the rope of mindfulness and hook of awareness.

The sixth stage, pacifying: the monk or nun looks forward with the hook of awareness and the rabbit of subtle mental dullness disappears.

The power of exertion: the seventh and eighth stages of resting the mind are accomplished by means of this power.

The seventh stage: thoroughly pacifying. At this point, even subtle mental dullness and wildness have difficulty in arising, and when they occur, one is able to abandon them as soon as they arise with little effort. No more rope, hook, or flames: the elephant goes forward on its own. The monk or nun is standing still, and the monkey sits in submission, but still has a trace of black.

The eighth stage, one-pointedness: here, the black part of the elephant is finished, and the monkey is gone. By applying just a little mindfulness and awareness at the start of meditation, one is able to enter into

one-pointed samadhi, which dullness, wildness, and distraction are not able to interrupt. The elephant is completely white with the monk or nun walking in front.

The power of familiarity: the ninth stage of resting the mind, evenly resting or resting in equanimity, is accomplished by this power. The monk or nun and elephant are completely resting. The path from here is one of rainbow light rays emerging from meditator's heart.

Meditator flying through the air: physical bliss. The body is completely processed (shinjang).

Meditator riding the elephant: the attainment of shamatha.

Meditator riding on the rainbow: mental bliss. The mind is completely processed.

Meditator holding sword: one cuts the root of samsaric existence by means of the union of shamatha and vipashyana, by meditation on emptiness. One examines the view with powerful mindfulness and awareness.

Strong flames: strong flames again arise. Great effort.

The nine categories of resting the mind in shamatha and their corresponding six powers are not necessarily linear. For instance, you could have absorption anytime, even in the first stage, resting your mind. For the mind and the body to hang together properly, you do not necessarily need these exercises, but you need the willingness to do them. It's like sneezing: first you feel that you are about to sneeze, you are psychologically prepared to sneeze—then you go, "Achoo!" At that point, your mind and body are together: you are in a state of absorption at the same time as you are in a state of sneeze. The whole sneezing process is not aiming toward anything; you just do it. It is the same with the nine stages of shamatha: you cannot actually cultivate any one of these states, but if you do the practice according to the tradition, you will arrive at these points quite spontaneously.

32

Identifying Obstacles to Shamatha

The six obstacles to shamatha are all temporary, like clouds cover-
ing the sun: they can be removed to let your basic goodness shine
through. . . . You commit yourself to the dharma because you feel
that you have something basically good within you. So dharma is
available to everyone. It is reasonable, workable, and true. It does
you good, and it makes you feel wholesome.

THERE ARE six main obstacles to shamatha practice. In discussing
these obstacles, I am not just bringing you bad news. Instead, the
point is to look at your dirt and face it, so that you will know how to
clean it up.

LAZINESS

The first obstacle to shamatha is laziness. In the West, it is thought that
you should run around and do a hundred things at once. By doing so,
it is felt that you will achieve a lot, and if you are not doing that, you
are considered to be lazy. Conventionally, laziness is also seen as a reaction against authority. For instance, if someone says, "Wash your socks
and your underpants," instead of doing so, you deliberately throw your
clothes on the floor.

In terms of shamatha practice, laziness is a feeling of heaviness in
which you have no appreciation of your existence. It is not seen as rebel-
liousness or a lack of speed. Instead, it is that you have no appreciation of

being a human being on this earth who is able to listen to the teachings and to practice.

When you are lazy, you have difficulty getting to your meditation cushion. If you check your psychological state on the way to sitting practice, you find that you feel very heavy, as if your legs were filled with lead. You have fickle thoughts, such as, "Must I do this? Is there any way out? Is it too late?" You do not want to cooperate with the discipline of shamatha practice. Your exertion has been undermined.

In contrast to such laziness, exertion has a quality of enthusiasm or joy. With exertion, you do not see meditation as a struggle, an ordeal, or an endurance test, and you don't see it as a competition. Instead, your meditation cushion is seen as an invitation, and shamatha practice is regarded as a way to wake yourself up.

FORGETFULNESS

Laziness is the difficulty in getting to your meditation cushion, whereas forgetfulness happens once you are already sitting on your cushion. Forgetfulness means feasting your mind on discursive thoughts, daydreams, and fantasies—all kinds of wandering mind—and forgetting to practice the technique. Laziness and forgetfulness can be controlled very easily. If you study the seven characteristics of a dharmic person properly and fully, I am sure you will have no problem in correcting these two obstacles.*

DROWSINESS AND DEPRESSION

The third obstacle to shamatha, drowsiness and depression, is connected with the three lower realms: the hell realm, the hungry ghost realm, and the animal realm. The lower realms are seen as savage realms. In the hell realm you are tremendously tortured; in the hungry ghost realm you are poverty-stricken and hungry; in the animal realm you are stupid and unwilling to relate with anything. The lower realms are accompanied by the physical sensation of drowsiness. Because your mind is so active, you begin to feel drowsy, although you are not necessarily tired. Actually, sit-

---

* See chapter 20, "Becoming a Dharmic Person."

ting practice energizes you if you do it fully and directly, but in this lower-realm approach, you are tired and drowsy.

Instead of building up your dignity as a human being and experiencing goodness in yourself, you associate yourself with the mentality of the animal realm, which feels much easier and more convenient. You would prefer to coil like a snake, snuffle like a pig, or lay eggs like a chicken, rather than sit on your cushion and perk up. So you begin to nod and you fall asleep. I have heard stories of people actually tipping over and falling off their cushions.

WILDNESS AND CRAZINESS

The fourth obstacle to shamatha is wildness and craziness. Your fantasies become absolutely too much, and you develop elaborate schemes. You might begin by visualizing yourself as an ant—and eventually you become the president of a powerful corporation! You build things up in that way. You think, "If only I could develop my talent, I could work my way up in the world and make trillions of dollars by the time I am done." Lots of people have that kind of fantasy. It could be called the "Rockefeller syndrome."

There are three types of wildness: lust, aggression, and regret. In the first type of wildness, based on lust and passion, you create an individual, private, discursive pornography show. In the second type of wildness, based on hatred, dislike, resentfulness, and aggression, you dig up old friends who have turned into enemies. The third type of wildness is based on regret. You regret that you have committed yourself to the path of dharma; you regret that you have decided to sit and practice. Feeling tremendous regret and remorse, you think, "Maybe it is too late, but if I hadn't done this, I could have done something fantastic!"

CARELESSNESS

The fifth obstacle to shamatha is carelessness. You know what should be overcome and what should be cultivated, and you have had some experience of that, but you couldn't be bothered.

LACK OF COORDINATION

The sixth obstacle to shamatha is lack of coordination. As you practice sitting meditation, you become so tender, so soft, and so vulnerable that you are willing to give in to any distraction. Whenever drowsiness comes up, you just give in to it; whenever there is wildness, you just give in; whenever there is any flicker of a possibility of entertaining yourself, you give in right away. You become like a baby. Maybe the primal-scream people would like to become babies again, but we are trying to grow up, which is an altogether different concept.

SAVING YOURSELF FROM YOURSELF

The six obstacles to shamatha practice are not particularly demanding, but they need to be overcome. To overcome them, you need to touch in with reality, and you need to connect properly and fully with your practice. It is very ordinary and quite simple. In fact, you could use the overcoming of these six obstacles to shamatha as the definition of individual salvation. Overcoming these obstacles saves you from the individual imprisonment you feel when you begin to practice meditation or any other discipline.

The obstacles to shamatha are not difficult to overcome—you'd be surprised. Overcoming them goes a very long way and makes a tremendous difference. They may seem to be quite petty and ordinary, but once you actually begin to work with them, your shamatha practice becomes so much better. Your practice becomes much more real, and you begin to appreciate things a lot more.

Laziness, forgetfulness, drowsiness, wildness, and so on all arise because you have enslaved yourself. So to begin with, you have to save yourself from yourself. That is the only way you could begin to see the possibility of enlightenment. You have not been very good to yourself for a long time, but you have the possibility of treating yourself well. You cannot do anything at all unless you save yourself from basic ego. Individual salvation means that you are free to save yourself from yourself.

In presenting these obstacles, I am not so much teaching Buddhism as simply teaching the dharma of how to behave and conduct yourself as a good dharmic person. I would like you to take your medicine, swallow it, and digest it. I prefer that to having you learn medical histories or theories. That is the basic hinayana approach. If you need any proof, I have done this myself. Over many generations, many centuries, countless other people have also practiced this. It worked for me, and it worked for them as well.

The six obstacles to shamatha are all temporary, like clouds covering the sun: they can be removed to let your basic goodness shine through. Even at the most primitive level of practice, they can be removed. People are willing to study and practice the dharma because they have had at least a hint of their basic goodness. Without such a glimpse of basic goodness, you wouldn't touch the dharma. You would take off, and you wouldn't want to have anything to do with it. You commit yourself to the dharma because you feel that you have something basically good within you. So dharma is available to everyone. It is reasonable, workable, and true. It does you good, and it makes you feel wholesome. The dharma is real, but you actually have to take it seriously and practice it. Since everything in the dharma comes from experience, you do not find any holes in it. The dharma is truth, and real truth comes from experience.

33

Antidotes to the Obstacles to Shamatha

You should always bring yourself back to awareness and to mind-fulness with the attitude that you are workable. However crazy you may be, you are still workable. In applying the antidotes, you can experience cheerfulness because you are not stuck with your own little stuff, but you can be reshaped. You are not giving up on your mind, but reshaping it.

EIGHT ANTIDOTES

The six obstacles to shamatha practice have eight antidotes, which may be more than you expected. These eight antidotes are based on coordinating mind and body and on developing a cheerful attitude. Ordinarily, cheerfulness is conditional. That is, you do not become cheerful without some reason for being cheerful. You think you are going to get something, or your friends have been helpful, or you feel well-fed and physically comfortable, or your day has gone well. But in this case, cheerfulness is unconditional.

Developing a cheerful attitude means appreciating the dharma. It means that the atmosphere of the dharma has entered into your whole being. You feel fundamentally worthy and fortunate. You have respect for your dharmic surroundings; therefore, in spite of chaos or the type of day it might be, you feel wholesome and good. Your existence is solid, steady, and balanced. Cheerfulness is one of the best "dharma fevers." It is almost as if the dharmic attitude and environment have possessed you. You feel unconditionally positive. Your whole being, your entire existence, is connected with the dharma; therefore, you feel tremendous rightness. You do not feel any threats at all, none whatsoever. The six obstacles to shamatha practice are the opposite of that unconditional cheerfulness.

Antidotes to Laziness

The first obstacle, laziness, has four antidotes: faith, respect, effort, and shinjang.

FAITH. Faith is based on rightness and healthiness. You feel that the dharma fits, that it works, that it is the right thing for you to do. Faith means that you have real trust in the dharma and forward vision.

RESPECT. With respect, you see that everything is sacred. When you are a dharmic person, the very cushion you sit on is sacred, every breath you take is sacred. The definition of sacredness is that your actions are not based on trying to embellish your own ego. Instead, you are willing to let go of your ego. You develop meekness. You have given up "mine," "my territory," "my world," "my privacy." Therefore, you experience sacredness and you are surrounded by gentleness.

OBSTACLES AND ANTIDOTES IN SHAMATHA PRACTICE

OBSTACLE	ANTIDOTE
1. Laziness	Faith Respect Effort Shinjang / Thoroughly Processed or Supple
2. Forgetfulness	Developing a Folksy Attitude
3. Drowsiness and Depression	Light-Handed Warning System
4. Wildness and Craziness	Light-Handed Warning System
5. Carelessness	Bringing Yourself Back to Mindfulness
6. Lack of Coordination	Equilibrium

EFFORT. You cannot just bliss out on faith and sacredness; you have to go beyond that, you have to exert yourself. You cannot just plop down and expect something to happen. Shamatha practice is not like hanging out on a frozen lake, expecting snowflakes to land on your eyelashes and nose. You might expect that things will work out and that you don't have to do anything, but that never happens in life—you always have to make some kind of effort. If you want to ski, you have to expose yourself to cold weather. You may put on warm clothes, but you still have to go out in the cold. You have to be willing to experience the cold and you have to be willing to go downhill.

Effort is necessary with any discipline. Any discipline of freedom that has ever been presented to human beings requires that you expose yourself to discomfort. You have to be willing to put up with some discomfort, whether it is the discomfort of the higher realms or the lower realms. You are expected to go out into the open air, whether it is terribly hot or extremely cold. Through that experience, you begin to become a decent person. You know how to relate with the whole of experience. If you don't do that, you are like a spoiled baby who has never experienced any inconvenience, a five-year-old who has never been toilet trained.

It takes effort to appreciate the dharma. The dharma actually mocks your ego. In fact, according to the dharma, you have to do something quite painful: you have to let go of the fundamental hang-up called ego. You have to go that far. Once you go that far, things become less problematic. If you make an effort, based on joy and upliftedness, things begin to happen. You have no more nightmares. Instead, everything becomes an invitation.

SHINJANG. The fourth antidote to laziness is shinjang. Shin means "thoroughly," and jang means "processed," or "purified"; so shinjang means "thoroughly processed," or "supple." In this case, shinjang means experiencing virtue, the absence of ego, and the feeling of freedom that goes along with that. Such virtue frees you from a depressed state of mind, from the depression of the lower realms.

With shinjang, you know how to ride your own mind. At first, you learn how to tame your mind. Then, having tamed your mind, you learn how to make friends with it. Having made friends with it, you learn how to make use of it. That is what is meant by riding your mind. It is like the

Zen Oxherding Pictures, in which the person who has finally made friends with his mind sits on an ox playing a little flute as his ox takes him for a nice walk in the countryside.*

Shinjang is a very important term. It often refers to the fruition, or the complete accomplishment, of shamatha discipline, when your mind is soothed and your body is completely relaxed. That level of shinjang could be called "big shinjang," or "final shinjang."

Shinjang as an antidote to laziness is early shinjang, not final shinjang. You are simply learning to make friends with yourself. You have a sense of relaxation. You are beginning to trust in yourself, and you are less paranoid about your own mind. You realize that your mind is workable and that there is an end to its suffering. In Tibetan, the trust that your mind is becoming workable is called *lesu rungwa: le* means "action," *su* means "as," and *rungwa* means "suitable"; so *lesu rungwa* means that your mind's "action has become suitable." You are playing a flute, riding on the ox of your mind.

Antidote to Forgetfulness

The antidote to the second obstacle, forgetfulness, is developing a folksy attitude toward your mind and your practice.

DEVELOPING A FOLKSY ATTITUDE. When you have put toothpaste on your toothbrush, you don't forget what you do next; you automatically brush your teeth. You naturally develop such folksy and ordinary behavior patterns. Likewise, during sitting practice, when you forget to work with the technique or the posture, your mind is brought back as an act of natural coordination. Whether you are sitting on your cushion or talking with someone afterward, you naturally and automatically maintain mindfulness. Mindfulness has become a natural process, almost a habitual pattern.

The dharma has to become fully domesticated, a part of your world, so that it is not a foreign word. You can lead your life decently: you pay

---

* The Oxherding Pictures of the Zen tradition portray the stages of meditative development. Trungpa Rinpoche was fond of these drawings, and wrote his own commentary on them. See *The Teacup and the Skullcup* (Halifax: Vajradhatu Publications, 2007).

your income tax, pay your bills, write your checks, wash your clothes, and take care of your babies and your children. That's the idea of folksiness. Dharma can be accommodated so well into your whole being, your whole system, that you don't have to say, "Now I'm a dharmic person. Do you see me?" and then, "Now I'm going to become Joe Schmidt in the street." Instead, there is a way for everything to hang together based on wakefulness, on watching the mood of every day and every hour of your life. It is very simple: your whole being can be worked with altogether.

Developing a folksy attitude means that you have made friends with your practice. You do not regard it as foreign or unusual, or something that someone has made you do, as if you were an animal in a circus. As a human being, you are fit to sit. You are equipped to sit on a gomden; and once you sit down, your posture is automatically right, and your mindfulness of breath is automatic. It all follows very ordinarily and simply.

Dharma is sometimes referred to as the most sacred thing of all. But if you make too much of it and put it on a pedestal, it becomes unworkable. The dharma is ourselves and we are dharma. That is what is meant by taking a folksy attitude. It is very direct.

The Antidote to Both Drowsiness and Wildness

Drowsiness and wildness, the third and fourth obstacles, have a mutual antidote: a light-handed warning system.

LIGHT-HANDED WARNING SYSTEM. This warning system is similar to a fire alarm, but it is warning you of your drowsiness or your wildness. That alertness or warning system comes up naturally, whenever you recognize that you are drowsy or wild. Therefore, when those obstacles occur, they are no longer regarded as obstacles, but as reminders of their opposites. You are not a victim of those obstacles; instead, whenever they occur, you are automatically warned and reminded of them right away. This early-warning system is based on wakefulness and cheerfulness, which come automatically from good posture on your meditation cushion. Such wakefulness and cheerfulness also occur during postmeditation. Whenever there is either drowsiness and dullness or tremendous speed, your own alarm system brings you back on the spot and wakes you up.

The Antidote to Carelessness

Obstacle number five, carelessness, is connected with both wildness and drowsiness. The antidote for carelessness is bringing yourself back into mindfulness.

BRINGING YOURSELF BACK INTO MINDFULNESS. The idea is that you are actually drawing yourself back to the point. When you do walking meditation practice, if your mind is wandering around, you bring your attention back to your feet: the way the heel, the sole, and the toe feel touching the ground. In sitting practice you follow your breath going out. Whenever you feel bored in your sitting practice or in the postmeditation practice of mindfulness, you bring to it a quality of cheerfulness and an appreciation of your tremendous freedom. That sense of freedom and cheerfulness sparks an intense awareness, which brings you back.

You can actually shape your mind with shamatha discipline. Your mind can be shaped like Play-Doh: you can make it into any shape you like. If you want to make your mind into a horse, an elephant, a giraffe, a square, a triangle, or just a round ball, you are free to do so. You can bring yourself back and you can reshape your mind according to the discipline of mindfulness. It has been done, and it is workable. Your situation is not all that bad. You have not been given an impossible task. You have been given a very possible task, and you can do it.

The Antidote to Lack of Coordination

The antidote to obstacle number six, lack of coordination, is equilibrium.

EQUILIBRIUM. Coordination comes from proper discipline. It is often said that discipline is like tuning the strings on an instrument: if you tune the strings too tightly, they break; if you tune the strings too loosely, nothing happens. That is, if you push yourself too hard, it doesn't work; and if you are too loose, there is no discipline at all. So proper tuning, or proper discipline, has balance or equilibrium.

In terms of balance, it is traditionally recommended that you put twenty-five percent of your awareness on your breath and the rest on the environment. Proper discipline is like being dressed up in a costume and holding a spoonful of water: the spoonful of water is awareness of the breath, and the costume is general awareness. You have a costume, or sense of the overall situation; at the same time, you don't want to drip your spoonful of water on your costume. When you are wearing a costume and holding a spoonful of water, it is taut and loose at the same time.

The point is to have a basic ground of awareness, so that when you walk into a room, there is nothing but open mind, sharp and soothing. You begin with a fullness, with complete awareness, but when you begin to pay attention to what you are doing, you discover that this fullness is divided into levels. Fullness is not continuous; otherwise, it would become very stubborn and stuffy. There is always some kind of gap. There is always room for humor.

On the whole, equilibrium makes things workable. If you push too hard in your practice, trying to achieve perfect posture or complete awareness, that effort might work for the first few seconds, but after a while it will cause an overreaction of wildness in your mind. However, if you don't make enough effort, you could become drowsy and fall asleep. You might begin to wake up your neighboring meditators with your snores.

Shamatha practice is considered to be the first step in the mahayana tradition of developing maitri, or gentleness to yourself. Shamatha practice is based on treating yourself gently and being critical of yourself at the same time. In the West, we have never treated ourselves that way. We have either been completely involved with our little ego-schemes and self-indulgence, or we have been trying to punish ourselves, cut everything out, and starve ourselves to death.

The point of equilibrium is that there is a way to train yourself very thoroughly. By working with the technique of suddenly bringing yourself back, combined with the practice of awareness, your mind becomes like a well-trained horse that is suitable to ride. Such a horse is both punished and treated very well, so it begins to trust its trainer. The horse doesn't mind having a saddle on its back, and it doesn't care whether it is whipped or fed with sugar cubes. Likewise, in bringing together tight and loose, you achieve balance and friendliness toward yourself. You treat yourself well and you are able to relax. But if you find that you are sidetracking, doing all sorts of naughty little things, you bring yourself back very sharply. Equilibrium is quite straightforward. You hold up your posture whether you are sitting or walking. You have a Buddhist look, a shamatha look, a head-and-shoulders look; and from there, you begin to unwind whatever goes on in your world. So there is both effort and relaxation.

The traditional idea of effort is a sudden flash of mindfulness. Some people even count their flashes. They might count as many as three hundred flashes a day—three hundred flashes of being there on the spot. At the same time, along with that effort, there is relaxation. You do not have to be hung up on your flash; instead, you feel appreciation. You realize that your existence is fine and you don't have to prove anything. That removes most of the demands based on ego's point of view. You have a tremendous sense of humor as you flash, so relaxation and tension hang together. It's not too tight; but at the same time, it is quite tight. It's not too loose; but at the same time, it is quite flamboyant.

With equilibrium, you begin to appreciate life, including your cup of coffee and your bite of doughnut. You actually begin to appreciate such things much more. If you wear good clothes, you feel good; if you eat good food, you feel good. You could open your window and enjoy the fresh air coming into your room. Life is beginning to become wholesome and good. Appreciation is not based on a mercenary philosophy. You do not need to cheat or to buy anything from anybody. It's very simple. You have your life, and you appreciate what you smell, what you hear, and what you see.

Working with the Antidotes

Altogether there are eight antidotes to the six obstacles to shamatha, and they are all applicable to you today. There is no myth about them, no philosophy, no guesswork. The practice of applying these antidotes has been done for centuries and centuries by many people, and it has worked. It has taken effect in the past and it is still very powerful today. Working with the antidotes is a way of getting into the dharma altogether. It is how you become a dharmic person. You begin to realize that your whole being can be steeped in dharma, that there are no longer any little corners left for you to be a non-dharmic person. You are ripe for dharma; dharma is possible, and you could actually experience a glimpse of it.

Even if you are a mahayana or vajrayana practitioner, you still have to begin at the beginning; there is no other way. That is why the hinayana comes first. It is how you begin on the path, and it is quite a cheerful entrance. You might have the idea that the hinayana is very grim and severe, but in fact it is quite delightful. Once you realize that, working with the antidotes can cheer you up.

Depression is a fundamental problem. Because of that, all the antidotes as well as your posture are connected with the cheering-up process. You do not panic because you think that your mind is unworkable. You don't need to say, "I have a bad mind. I have a strange mind. I'm completely stubborn and I can't be worked on." You should not give up working with your discipline of mindfulness and awareness. The obstacles or neuroses that come along are not regarded as signs of impossibility, but as signs of possibility. You should always bring yourself back to awareness and to mindfulness with the attitude that you are workable. However crazy you may be, you are still workable. In applying the antidotes, you can experience cheerfulness because you are not stuck with your own little stuff, but you can be reshaped. You are not giving up on your mind, but reshaping it.

Dharma is not a stranger that you are going to invite into your world; it is *always* there, and you can just dip into it. The dharma is workable. It is much less effort than taking a shower. It's a piece of cake! The dharma is like medicine, but if you don't make friends with your medicine it doesn't quite work, and it could even turn into poison. Nowadays, taking aspirin is a casual thing to do; likewise, dharma is a very natural and casual process.

In working with the antidotes, the point is not to make some sort of monumental statement. It is very individual. How you sit and how you practice depends on every mood of every hour. You have learned how to deal with yourself so you are not too tight and not too loose. It is not that you have been prescribed a particular system or tradition to impose on yourself. Rather, if you treat yourself gently, according to the vision of the dharma, you discover a middle way in which you do not condemn yourself or build yourself up. Within that, you have a decent relationship with yourself and a decent relationship with your world. In turn, you will also have a decent experience of the dharma.

34

Cutting Thoughts and Short-Circuiting the Kleshas

A sense of knowing, or seeing, always happens. If you are will-
ing to acknowledge its existence, there is the potential of being
wakeful, open, and precisely there constantly. This is not based
on being a sharp person, a smart person, or a very careful person.
Rather, it is about being a person who can actually be—by yourself,
very simply.

PAGYÖ: A RESIDUE OF MINDFULNESS

The result of shamatha practice is pagyö, a residue of mindfulness. *Pag*
means "residue," and *yö* means "possessing"; so *pagyö* means "possessing
residue." Pagyö is also translated as "conscientiousness" or "being heed-
ful." *Pag* refers to deposits of little fungi found on rocks. In Tibet, we used
these fungi, which are sometimes orange or red, and sometimes yellow or
jade green, to color our *tormas,* or ritual cakes.

Residues are produced when what you experience on the spot is
confirmed by your previous experience. Residues are partly a matter of
memory, and partly a matter of what you are presently experiencing. Having such residues gives you something to connect with. Based on your
experience of this world, you always have a residue of something or other.
When you look at red, you have a residue of red, and when you look at
white, you have a residue of white. Such residues enter into your system,

and those inputs should be acknowledged. Then you can begin to see things as they are. It's very basic.

The point of mindfulness is not to be aware of possible dangers, or to watch out in case something might go wrong. Mindfulness means being there on the spot, along with your residue. If somebody attracts your attention by saying, "Look out!" or "Look at this!" you do not have to be cautious; you could just look. You could raise your eyebrows and say, "What's going on?" You could be mildly attentive and inquisitive.

Sometimes pagyö is described as the gaze of an elephant. An elephant is not usually easy to startle. If you make a loud noise or if you throw a firecracker in front of an elephant, it just looks around. It has that "So what?" kind of approach. An elephant doesn't get excited. Likewise, pagyö is tentative but highly keen. You cannot be startled and you do not panic—you just have a residue of mindfulness. Pagyö is also referred to as decorum. Since you have developed perspective, sophistication, and subtlety, you are aware of what is going on. Pagyö is a very positive idea.

Tren-she: Recollection and Knowing

From mindfulness also stems *trenpa*, or "recollection," and *sheshin*, or "knowing." *Trenpa* can also mean "wakefulness." With trenpa, you are fully there, but you are not particularly overwhelmed by anything. Trenpa is a process of discovery in which you are touched precisely, rather than being overwhelmed by emotions or excitement. In the process of trenpa, you make very precise discoveries about yourself constantly.

With trenpa you have some kind of memory or recollection, and sheshin is a check on those recollections. *She* means "knowing," and *shin* means "as it is"; so *sheshin* means "knowing as it is." Sheshin is the kind of knowledge that makes you feel at home in the world, rather than regarding the world as a strange place and not knowing how to handle it. Sheshin functions within the environment of trenpa. Once you have a memory, you check it with what is happening in the present. It's like renting a car: if you rent a new car, you automatically refresh your memory of how to drive; you check out the gearshift, the brakes, the lights, and the steering wheel. Trenpa is the possibility of working with what is happening, and sheshin is actually dealing with what is happening.

The main point of trenpa and sheshin is that a sense of knowing, or seeing, always happens. If you are willing to acknowledge its existence, there is the potential of being wakeful, open, and precisely there constantly. This is not based on being a sharp person, a smart person, or a very careful person. Rather, it is about being a person who can actually *be*—by yourself, very simply. In our lineage, one example of such a person was His Holiness the sixteenth Gyalwa Karmapa. It may be rare, but it is possible that one could *be,* and at the same time act.

The combination of trenpa and sheshin, of recollection and knowing, is called *tren-she.* Tren-she is the kind of recollection that connects the past and the present together. For instance, you may remember that if you step in a puddle with your shoes on, it is likely that the water will run into your shoes, and your socks will get wet and dirty. It is something you have done before; therefore, you know what's going to happen if you do it again. The traditional analogy for tren-she is that of a warning, but I would like to correct that analogy. Tren-she does not simply mean being warned about something bad—it is realizing that you should be on the dot.

Tren-she is not concentrated awareness; it is a more general sense of awareness. For instance, if you are wearing a bright red coat, you are aware of the redness and brightness around you, and whether your coat is made of wool or cotton. Likewise, you are aware of your posture, your head and shoulders, and whether you are wearing your glasses or not, a watch or not, stockings or no stockings. That intrinsic awareness we always generate is like antennae. We know that "I have a beard" or "I have earrings on" or "I have a safety pin in my trousers to hold them up." We are aware of things of that nature, beyond simply being aware of the in-breath and out-breath.

With tren-she, you know what you know and what you have without being told. It is almost at the level of clairvoyance. For example, you may get a sudden flash that your father is in trouble, and it turns out to be true. That sense of tren-she is the very early stage of the development of superconsciousness or clairvoyance. However, you should be very careful about such things. You might have an image of your father falling down and find out that he is perfectly well and happy in Miami Beach! So things could be other than you think. Nonetheless, when tren-she takes place on the spot in your existence, you simply know. Tren-she allows you to be very sensitive and very precise.

Overcoming the Six Root Kleshas

The result of pagyö and tren-she is that you are able to use your awareness to overcome the six root kleshas: ignorance, aggression, passion, pride, jealousy, and avarice.* Kleshas intensify your claustrophobia and pain. They are the density of your mind, which brings further denseness, like a sponge soaked in oil. They are blockage. You are so thoroughly absorbed in the kleshas that there is no room to breathe. It is quite detrimental. Kleshas are connected with the naive desire to get what's best, without knowing how to get hold of it.

Ignorance

The klesha process begins with ignorance. The klesha of ignorance is not original ignorance, or avidya, but just naiveté, or delusion. It is basic, ordinary simpleton-mentality. In Tibetan, ignorance is *timuk*. *Ti* means "just so," and *muk* means "falling asleep" or "covered up"; so *timuk* means "just so, you are covered up." It is like being cross-eyed and becoming even more cross-eyed. *Muk* also means "dust." It is the thick fog that surrounds you while you are sitting there being cross-eyed.

Aggression

The second klesha is aggression, or *shedang* in Tibetan. You want to feel good, and if you can't, you get angry. In the English language, the word *aggression* can mean speediness, or a fast-moving and heavy-handed quality; but *shedang* very specifically means "hatred." In this case, *she* means "intention," and *dang* means "to expel," or "to pierce out"; so *shedang* means "wholeheartedly wanting to pierce out," which amounts to wanting to hurt somebody. You want to puncture somebody with your weapon. Once you are in an aggressive communication with somebody, you are in cahoots with him. You have a connection, otherwise you couldn't become

---

* The six root kleshas are an expansion of the three poisons as depicted in the wheel of life in the form of a rooster, a snake, and a pig, symbolizing passion, aggression, and ignorance. In different contexts, Trungpa Rinpoche uses variant forms of the primary six kleshas, most commonly: (1) passion, aggression, ignorance, greed, envy, and pride, and (2) desire, anger, pride, ignorance, doubt, and opinion.

angry with him. And when you hate someone, you want to tear him from the inside out.

Passion

Wanting comfort, wanting to feel good, brings passion, or *döchak* in Tibetan, the third root klesha. Because you hate yourself, because you are bored with yourself, you want something to occupy you, something to make you feel better. You want to entertain yourself. *Dö* means "wanting," or "longing," and *chak* means "glued to"; so *döchak* is "wanting to be glued to somebody or something." It's sort of like the end product of chewing gum. The word *chakpa* also means "lust."

Pride

Out of passion comes arrogance, or pride. You not only want to be entertained; you feel that you really *deserve* something good. You don't want to be scolded by your environment or your world. Arrogance, or pride, is *nga-gyal* in Tibetan. *Nga* is the word for "I," or "myself," and *gyal* means "victory"; so *nga-gyal* is "my victory," or "I-victory." With arrogance, you want to be on top, to have the upper hand. It is one-upmanship—me-upmanship.

Jealousy

The fifth klesha is jealousy, or *tragdok* in Tibetan. You become very hungry, and you begin to think that other people are getting better treatment than you. It may be purely your imagination, but other people seem to be doing better than you, so you become jealous. *Trag* means "shoulders," and *dok* means "claustrophobia," "not enough space," or "tight," so *tragdok* means "tight shoulders." The idea is that you do not have enough room to be macho. You feel so claustrophobic that you can't even extend your shoulders.

Avarice

Last, but not least, is avarice, or *serna* in Tibetan. You don't want to give anything away, you don't want to share anything. You don't want to spend your money, but you would like to hold on to whatever you have. You become filled with avarice. *Serna* literally means "yellow nose": *ser* means "yellow," and *na* means "nose." Each time you have to spend money, each time you have to extend your hospitality, you touch your nose, thinking, "Should I do this or not?" As a result, your nose becomes yellow, at least from the Tibetan point of view—maybe we should say "pink nose" for Westerners.

This list of six root kleshas is several thousand years old, if not even older. Our beloved teacher, the Lord Buddha, pointed out to us that we have these six problems. In fact, our whole samsaric existence—all our misery and all our problems—can be summed up by these six defilements. They govern our life. However, the kleshas can be overcome.

As you become more involved in the dharma, you develop greater certainty. You begin to realize that your own neurosis is no longer unreachable or incurable. By means of the sitting practice of shamatha and the awareness training of vipashyana, you have the possibility of actually getting in touch with your fundamental neurosis.

When you have committed yourself to the path and received directions for journeying on the path, you automatically experience a sense of reality. When the kleshas arise, you join your kleshas with the practice of mindfulness and awareness. You rub your awareness and your kleshas together, like rubbing two sticks together to start a fire. When you rub hard enough, you produce fire, and that flame burns both sticks at once—the awareness as well as the kleshas. So awareness is a temporary tool. Since one part does not give an inch, the other part does not receive an inch, so it is a mutual suicide. That is the basic idea of liberation, or nirvana, which comes from sitting practice. Sitting practice gives you no feedback of any kind; therefore, your kleshas don't get any nourishment.

Even at the level of profound hinayana-wisdom, both the technique and what the technique is applied to could be used up. Because of that, you can attain shinjang. When you attain shinjang, you are not supposed to have your technique hanging out, or the result of your technique hanging out. That would be like having cotton batting with a thorn inside it. Complete shinjang is like an eiderdown quilt: everything is thorough, comfortable, and straight. Shinjang is not a fairy tale, but a real possibility.

Ideally, we actually can cut our thoughts and short-circuit our kleshas. We can begin to go beyond the kleshas and realize the possibility of egolessness. At that point, the tool and what that tool is applied to destroy each other simultaneously, leaving us with nothing to hang on to. We realize that we do not need a savior or a "savee" or salvation. We can actually do without that extra baggage altogether. We see that individual salvation is like eating *momos,* or Tibetan dumplings: there is dough wrapped around meat, a container and what is contained, and we are supposed to eat the whole thing.

Such an inspiration can only come from the relaxation of having taken the refuge vow. As many teachers have said, if you do not take refuge, there is still the possibility of becoming sidetracked. When you take the refuge vow, you begin to find freedom. It makes you feel healthy and good. You realize that from now onward, there is only one journey. The journeyer and the journey become one single situation. You finally understand that individual salvation is indeed individual—and at the same time, it is universal.

35

An Element of Magic

Magic is the cause, and it is what we are creating in the simple practice of meditation. Through meditation we are putting that particular miracle into effect. So let us not regard meditation as a purely mechanical process that leads one to enlightenment. Instead, the essence of meditation is tuning oneself into higher truth or magic.

THE UNCONDITIONED truth, or dharma, has extraordinary power. In the mahayana sutras, such as the *Heart Sutra,* that power is referred to as a spell, or mantra. At the hinayana level, that power is referred to as merit. Practicing dharma is considered to be a meritorious deed, but the hinayana idea of merit is quite different from the ordinary idea of bargaining tit for tat, or the idea that if you do good, you're going to get a goody. It is more than a mere exchange in which you accumulate good karma so that you can have the reward of that good karmic action. Even at the hinayana level, the dharma has tremendous energy and power. Throughout the dharma there is hidden power and magic. According to the popular view of dharma, the idea that there is magic involved is, to say the least, corny, or even bizarre. But there *is* some kind of magic.

In meditation practice, we are tuning ourselves into an entirely different way of thinking, as opposed to our ordinary, samsaric way of thinking. We have decided to relate with the truth, to tune in to the dharma. Tuning ourselves in to the dharma, committing ourselves in to that stream or flow, means that we are automatically entered into a kind of spiritual power. It is not particularly exciting or extraordinary, but there is power and mystical energy. The reason dharma is regarded as sacred is because its contents are outrageous. It is in touch with the energy or cosmic flow of the world.

Magic is the cause, and it is what we are creating in the simple practice of meditation. Through meditation we are putting that particular miracle into effect. So let us not regard meditation as a purely mechanical process that leads one to enlightenment. Instead, the essence of meditation is tuning oneself in to higher truth or magic. The practice of meditation as a way of tuning oneself in to higher truth can only be taught by a competent teacher who has the message and the personal experience handed down through the lineage. Otherwise, if meditation could be approached from a purely scientific level, we could quite possibly read a book on how to meditate and attain enlightenment. The reason that this is not possible is because of the abstract magical quality of the dharma, handed down from generation to generation. That magical quality accompanies the experienced teacher, who has tremendous common sense and wisdom, and is the holder of the *vajra*,* or the mystical power.

It is very important to know about the magical quality of meditation. While it is true that Buddhism is very scientific, ordinary, and extremely straightforward, nevertheless it has magical power. At this point, that mystical power may involve nothing more than employing a simple meditative technique—but in doing so, something happens to you. It is quite different from a mere imitation of the lineage. It is not that you are converted to Buddhism or become a true believer, and it is not that you happen to zap yourself, or that you convince yourself through the power of suggestion. It is that even the simplest teaching has power. Introducing this power or truth is called "turning the wheel of the dharma," or dharmachakra.

When a person sits and meditates, it is a special situation, a sacred act. Patrül Rinpoche (1808–1887), a prominent Nyingma teacher and author of *The Words of My Perfect Teacher,* said that even if you have impure thoughts in the meditation hall, those thoughts are still regarded as sacred thoughts.† So in meditation, even the most impure, crude, or confused

---

* A vajra, or *dorje* in Tibetan, is a ritual scepter, used in tantric practice. The term *vajra* means "indestructible," or "adamantine." An empowered teacher is said to be a holder of the vajra and is called *vajracharya.*

† Patrul Rinpoche, *The Words of My Perfect Teacher,* trans. Padmakara Translation Group (San Francisco: Harper Collins, 1994).

thoughts are regarded as sacred. Discipline is important, whether you have accomplished that discipline or not. You may fall asleep on your cushion, or feel that you have not actually meditated at all. You may feel that as soon as you sat down on your cushion, you began to venture out all over the world, and the only thing that reminded you that you were meditating was that the gong rang and you realized you were supposedly meditating, at least physically. But even such daydreams are important. Viewing meditation as a sacred activity does not mean that the sitting practice of meditation has to be absolutely solemn and rigid. However, you should have the attitude that you are involved with a system and a tradition that is valid and has its roots in solid thinking. Meditation is a definite approach. It is an extremely valid thing to do.

36

Transcending Dualistic Mind

This world is mind's world, the product of mind. Although you may already know that, you might remind yourself. It is important to realize that meditation is not so exclusive, not something other than this world. In meditation, you are dealing with the very mind that built your glasses and put your specific lenses in the rims.

T HE WORKING basis of meditative practice is the mind. Without mind, without a state of consciousness, one cannot embark on the spiritual path. As far as meditation practice is concerned, the mind is what we are working on. Instead of trying to sort out our usual, daily problems, we are turning inward to the fundamental problem of "this" and "that." We begin mindfulness practice at the primeval level.

WHAT IS MIND?

Since mind is the working basis for the practice of meditation and awareness, mind has to be understood. What is mind? As sentient beings, as opposed to rocks, trees, or water, we possess mind. We are capable of discriminating awareness. We experience duality, both grasping and rejecting. The Tibetan word for mind is *sem*, which means "that which can associate with other." In the Tibetan phrase *yul la sem pena sem, yul* means the "other," or the "projection"; so *yul la sem pena sem* means "mind is that which can think of the other, or the projection." That is the definition of mind. So mind is not just something creepy inside our head or heart; and it is not something that just happens, like the wind blowing and grass growing. Mind, or sem, is a very specific, concrete term.

Mind is also referred to as "ego." Like mind, ego can only survive on reference points, not by itself. In order to wake up in the morning, you have to know it is morning. You need to see that there's light outside. Such simple experiences are examples of ego. Ego requires, survives, and thrives on reference points. We could refer to mind as ego, but practicing meditation due to a concern about our ego sounds like a very big deal. Talking about meditation as just working with the mind is more simple and real.

Mind contains a quality of perception that is very minute and precise: mind perceives objects. The objects it perceives are considered to be external, whether those objects are physical objects or thoughts that exist only in your imagination. In the process of perception, the mind begins to linger on something other than itself in order to prove that it itself exists, which is an erroneous belief. Since the opposite approach of first seeing that it exists and thereby proving that the other exists did not work, the mind somewhat hypocritically developed this mental trick to confirm its own existence.

Mind is not only the process of dualistic perception and ego confirmation; it also includes emotions, or mental highlights. Dualistic mind cannot exist without emotions. Daydreaming and discursive thinking alone are not enough. So out of boredom, we create waves of emotions, which go up and down. Passion, aggression, ignorance, pride, and all kinds of other emotions begin to be created as a deliberate process. Emotions are regarded as the center, or heart; the intellect and other sense perceptions are regarded as the fringe, or head. Emotions are the hot spots. They are personal and real, rather than accurate. They are total experience.

This process begins as a game to try to prove to yourself that you do exist, but eventually the game becomes a hassle. The more you play, the more you have to challenge yourself. It is as if you were a hunter trying to practice your accuracy by seeing if you can shoot all four legs of a deer, but the deer runs away so fast that you end up rushing after it and shooting the deer through the heart. You challenged yourself unnecessarily and you feel defeated. Likewise, the emotions are not a requirement for survival but a game we have developed, which has gone sour. Like the deer hunter, we begin to get terribly frustrated and feel absolutely helpless.

We have created a rather neat world, but it is bittersweet. Things seem to be amusing, but at the same time they are not so amusing; things seem to be terribly funny, but at the same time they are terribly sad. That whole setup is based on the mind. Mind created the whole thing. We might complain about the presidency, the economy, or the rate of exchange, but those are secondary concerns. They are the automatic reflections of the original process of primeval competitiveness, which has already been set up. All of this is our own production, our own neat work, called mind.

This understanding of mind is not something you should believe in because of what you have been told; it is an experience that can actually be felt personally. It could be worked on and related to. In order to understand mindfulness-awareness practice, it is very important for you to realize the complexities of your mind. When we feel hassled and we cannot sit and meditate, we tend to blame it on this thing. We get frustrated and feel completely wretched and sorry for ourselves, or we look for alternatives like going to the movies or buying chewing gum. But as far as the world of mind is concerned, somehow life is not as simple as that.

THE THREE ASPECTS OF MIND

There are several definitions of mind in Tibetan terminology. Mind has been described as *sem*, as *rikpa*, and as *yi*. However, this does not mean that there are three types of mind, but that one mind has three aspects. There are numerous other aspects of mind, but these three principles are the most important to be aware of, because you are going to deal with them as you practice.

Sem

Sem is the equivalent of mind as we generally think about mind. However, instead of using the word *mind* as a noun, we could use it as a verb, as in "minding" and "minding your own business." Minding is an active process. In other words, you can't have mind without an object of mind; they work together. Mind only functions with a relative reference point.

Rikpa

Rikpa literally means "intelligence," or "brightness." If somebody has rikpa, or what we call *rikpa trungpo,* that means he or she has a clever and sharp mind. Rikpa is kind of a sidekick that develops from the basic mind, or sem. It is almost like a lawyer's mentality. You do not have to be a lawyer as such, but if a problem is presented to you from one point of view, you look at it from different angles. You approach it on one hand and on the other hand, looking from that angle and from this angle. You analyze it and look at it from inside out and outside in.

Rikpa is the research worker, so to speak, in the administration of mind. Rikpa oversees sem and yi, and tries to find all the possibilities of where things could go wrong and where things could be put right. It is like a research worker in that, although it has some insight into such processes, it doesn't have enough energy or power to communicate with the outside or the inside. It just reviews the whole process. Rikpa doesn't have the actual power to execute foreign relationships, but is more like an adviser to the State Department.

Rikpa has the ability to see how things work, how things function. It is judgment. In order to judge something, you don't have to have energy particularly; you just judge. Energy comes after you have judged, so rikpa is not energy, but intelligence. Having been advised by your judgmental state of being, or rikpa, you then take a step. You have viewed the merchandise already, then you decide to make a move and buy it or not buy it.

At this point, rikpa is on the level of first glimpse. It is primitive rikpa, bread-and-butter rikpa. There are many different levels of rikpa and all kinds of definitions for rikpa—from logical insight, to the level of discriminating-awareness wisdom, and up to the ultimate crazy-wisdom level. If you make a big deal about all these levels of rikpa, the whole thing becomes very confusing. At this point, we are talking about the first level of rikpa we come across as we relate with ourselves in terms of meditation practice. We see that there is a kind of intelligence that acts as a spokesperson for us and the rest of the world in a very simple way.

Yi

The third aspect of mind is called *yi*. Traditionally yi is known as the sixth consciousness, or mental consciousness. The five sense consciousnesses are sight, smell, taste, hearing, and touch, and the sixth is mind, or yi. Yi is mental sensitivity, and is largely connected with the heart. It is a kind of balancing force, acting as a switchboard for the other five senses. When you see a sight and you hear a sound at the same time, the sight and sound are synchronized by yi. It acts as a kind of automatic editor. Because of yi, you can smell, see, hear, feel, and taste all at the same time. The sense perceptions are coherent and they make sense to you because of that central headquarters or switchboard, which makes all that into a total experience.

Yi is not as intelligent at manipulation as sem. In relationship with the world, sem is more political, whereas yi is more domestic. Yi is just trying to coordinate this and that, so that information filters through constantly and you have no problem of miscommunication. One's basic intelligence is based on sem. Sem maintains the reference point of split between subject and object, while at the same time trying to hold them together.

An Open Secret

We are continually exposed to the existence of the gigantic world of mind. This whole world, including the very pair of glasses you may be wearing, is made by your mind, by everybody's mind. Every bolt and nut was put together by somebody or other's mind. So this world is mind's world, the product of mind. Although you may already know that, you might remind yourself. It is important to realize that meditation is not so exclusive, not something other than this world. In meditation, you are dealing with the very mind that built your glasses and put your specific lenses in the rims.

Each of us has a different mental manifestation. Therefore, we could be identified by name, as individuals. Our different mental approaches also shape our physical features. So this world of mind is a living world. Working with mind is not a fiction and it is not mysterious. We are not working with something that is hidden, which we have to uncover. We are working with what is already hanging out in the world as an open secret. It seems to be a very open situation.

In meditation, the mind is quite harmonious. Meditation practice is a way to try to save yourself from psychosis. However, that is not so easy. It requires clarity. You are uncovering an alternative mind, one that does not need either the neurotic mentality or the neurotic world. That particular mind can go further and further. It does not have to continue to sharpen this neurotic world. Instead, it uncovers another world called nonduality. Such a world still has reference points, but much clearer reference points. So there is the possibility of developing a higher level of duality without using a dualistic approach. That is where the idea of enlightenment comes in.

Nonduality does not mean that you dissolve into the world or that the world becomes you. It is not a question of oneness, but of zero-ness. No synchronization of the sense perceptions is necessary. Everything is reduced into zero, and the whole thing becomes one-pointedness—or zero-pointedness. That is *moksha,* or "freedom." You do not have any hassles and no synchronization is necessary. Things just unfold by themselves.

37

Rediscovering Your Own Mind

Through meditation, you begin to understand the eight conscious-
nesses and to know their functions inside out and outside in. You
begin to understand the five skandhas as well. . . . Relating intelli-
gently with the technique of meditation does not have to be a project
of sticking out your neck and looking beyond what you are. You are
not trying to avoid or to transcend anything.

ACCORDING TO the Buddhist tradition, there are eight types of
consciousness: the alayavijnana, or the "storehouse consciousness";
the *nyön-yi*, or "instigator of the kleshas"; the yi, or "mind consciousness";
and the five sense consciousnesses of hearing, seeing, smelling, tasting,
and touching.* In the traditional way of counting, first you have the six
types of sense consciousness (which includes yi, or mind consciousness);
the seventh, or nyön-yi, is the subconscious; and the eighth, or alayavijnana, is the unconscious.

The eight consciousnesses are usually said to be components of the
fifth skandha, or consciousness, but are present as potentials within the
first skandha, or form. All eight should be used as the materials for meditation practice.

---

* Nyön-yi (or *nyönmong yikyi nampar shepa*), the seventh consciousness, is the equivalent
of the Sanskrit term *klista-manovijnana*, while yi (*yikyi nampar shepa*), or the sixth consciousness, is *manovijnana* in Sanskrit. In Sanskrit and Tibetan, the addition of the prefixes
klista or *nyön* implies the tainting of the mind by conflicted emotions.

ALAYAVIJNANA:
THE EIGHTH CONSCIOUSNESS

There are several types of alaya in the Buddhist tradition. In particular, there is the alayavijnana, the basis of consciousness, and there is also the more fundamental or higher form of alaya, on the level of *dharmadhatu*,* which gives rise to both samsara and nirvana, or the "basic split." Sometimes there are misunderstandings about these two types of alaya, so it is important not to confuse them.

As one of the eight types of consciousness, the alayavijnana is at a much lower level than fundamental alaya; it is at the level of subtle thoughts rather than a basic state of being, and has within it paranoia and stupidity, or ignorance. Alayavijnana, or basic unconsciousness, acts as a quiet but powerful reinforcement of the sense consciousnesses. At this point, we are simply trying to understand the mind; we are not yet touching the level of basic ignorance. We are working with the alayavijnana, rather than going further back and dealing with the greater ego, or fundamental alaya, which seems to be something that only tantric techniques rouse or are able to deal with.

Alayavijnana is the basis and the instigator of all the mental activities. However, it is important to understand that the alayavijnana is not the originator of karma. The alayavijnana is like a battery charger or transformer that you carry with you. The main current is the fundamental dharmadhatu-level alaya. That is where the basic split of fundamental ignorance occurs.

You cannot have alayavijnana without the other consciousnesses. The alayavijnana is like the payroll that sustains the workers: at the end of the week, you get your money, which keeps you going. Alayavijnana is the payroll, and the workers are the sense consciousnesses. The alayavijnana and the other consciousnesses happen almost simultaneously. The mechanism of our mind is extremely efficient. Whenever there is a gap between perceptions, we refer back to the alayavijnana. It keeps us going all the time. The alayavijnana is active at the same time that the other sense perceptions are active. Alayavijnana instigates the restlessness, the drowsiness, and the subconscious picturing, or subconscious gossip.

---

* Dharmadhatu or *chökyi ying* in Tibetan means "sphere of dharma" or "sphere of reality." It is the all-encompassing space in which all phenomena arise, dwell, and dissolve.

The experience of the eighth consciousness is the general sense of being in contact with what's happening, but without reference point. According to traditional texts, there is a quality of clarity and the spark of being alive. You are continually reassuring yourself that you are alive. When your mind is blank, you check that your mental faculties are still working. It is very basic. For example, if none of the other consciousnesses are functioning, or if there is some blockage, you always check whether you can actually think—and you realize that you can. The spark is still there.

You may be highly secure since you have your body, and your body is in relatively the right shape—but within that basically secure situation, there is always the sense that you are trying to maintain something. Since you began with a body, you continue to exist in that way, but the alaya has nothing to do with the body. Even though you may not have a body to relate with or sense organs or sense consciousnesses, you still have an ongoing situation because of your memories. The memories act as a body when you no longer have a body. Of course, the alayavijnana has a moment of birth and death like anything else, which follows the basic Buddhist logic that everything is born and dies simultaneously. Apart from that, there is no big gap of cessation and rebirth of the eighth consciousness. The alayavijnana is ongoing.

NYÖN-YI:
THE SEVENTH CONSCIOUSNESS

The seventh consciousness is called nyön-yi, which means "instigator of the kleshas." The seventh consciousness is rather heavily loaded; it is the state of mind that produces pain. In the term *nyön-yi*, the word *yi* is more a verb than a noun. *Yi la chepa* means "to occupy your mind," "to pay attention," or "to mind something." So in mindfulness practice, you use *yi*. When you get to tantra, there are different levels of yi related to the body, speech, and mind, but nyön-yi in terms of the eight levels of consciousness is definitely much lower than those. Nyön-yi is what I have decided to call the subconscious mind.

From the unconscious level, the subconscious begins to arise in the form of suggestions of all kinds of emotions and the sense of separateness, or duality. Nyön-yi is always referred to as duality. It is in the subconscious that the perception of "I" and "other" begins to arise. The unconscious is basic being, the basic existence of ego. It is like a mountain: a mountain exists apart from its shape and apart from its location—a mountain just exists. The unconscious, or alayavijnana, has the role of managing and maintaining everything. It acts as the instigator rather than the action itself. It also provides security to the other consciousnesses. The alayavijnana validates the other seven consciousnesses. It okays the whole thing.

From the unconscious, an embryonic consciousness begins to arise, which gives us materials for questioning reality, for questioning our basic ground, whether it be ego or otherwise, objects of love or hate. Nyön-yi is active involvement. Although it is subconscious, it is active, as if you were about to perceive something. In this case you have not yet perceived anything. You have the dream of it, so it is still forward-going energy.

The subconscious mind brings its faculties out into all the other consciousnesses and clarifies them, so that you are able to deal with sight, smell, sound, taste, and touch simultaneously. It is a tremendous mechanism, set up as a way of maintaining yourself and making sure that the dualistic world is valid and comfortable. Nyön-yi speaks for itself and reassures itself for you. That seems to be one of the basic purposes of clarity of perception in the conventional sense: that you should always be in touch and in control of things. You should not miss anything or let yourself be hampered by situations; instead, you should always be on top of things. How far we can manage that is another question! But we try to do that in any case, although it is quite beyond our level of mental sophistication.

YI: THE SIXTH CONSCIOUSNESS

The sixth sense, yi, the mind or mental sense consciousness, is connected with the heart and brain. Yi is a sense consciousness in that it simply reflects each situation; it is mental sensitivity and acts as the central headquarters or switchboard for the sense perceptions. Traditionally, it is said that if you put a ball of crystal on a five-colored cloth, it expresses itself through the five colors. In this image, the five colors represent the five sense consciousnesses, and the crystal ball the mental faculty. The sixth consciousness is rather mechanical and based purely on perception, without any further depth, subtlety, or sophistication. It is an instinct that animals also possess; it does not only happen on the human level. Yi is the faculty that is capable of holding contents. The term *yi la shak* means "able to rest the mind on whatever the subject matter may be."*

THE SIX SENSE CONSCIOUSNESSES

Altogether there are eight consciousnesses. In addition to alayavijnana, nyön-yi, and yi, we have the sense consciousnesses of vision, hearing, smell, taste, and touch. Since yi, or mental consciousness, is also considered to be a sense consciousness, that makes six sense consciousnesses in all. Each sense consciousness is connected with a particular sense-organ, such as the eyes, ears, or nose, and a particular sense-object, which makes six groups of three.† Then there is the memory of a sense consciousness, which comes from possessing a sense organ, using a sense, having a reference point to it, and thinking about it. The alayavijnana, or the eighth level, generates consciousness; nyön-yi, or the seventh level, brings the potential of sense consciousnesses and sense perceptions; and when you reach the sixth, or yi, you are really there.

Semiactive thoughts begin to come up in the seventh level, and active thoughts such as anger start in the sixth level, which then gets permission from the seventh and eighth levels. Dreams seem to take place at the seventh level, as the embryonic potential of going out into the world, using oneself as the audience as well as the performer. Memory also takes place at the seventh, or subconscious, level, but when you begin to relate with a memory, that is at the level of the sixth consciousness, or the mental faculty. The sixth, or mind consciousness, connects the subconscious mind and the particular sense consciousness.

But all of that comes from a sense organ to begin with. If you did not have sense organs, you would not perceive anything. If you mentally picture an orange, for instance, that picture comes from a sense organ. That

---

* Cognitive mind in general, from the first through the seventh consciousnesses, can be referred to as sem (Skt.: chitta). Sem is very conditioned, domesticated. It includes the sense of being, of central focus, of ego and the capacity for duality. Yi is more intelligent than sem in its capacity to pay attention and be mindful. A third mental component, rikpa, refers to mental sharpness and overview. See discussion in chapter 36, "Transcending Dualistic Mind."

† The six triads of sense organ, sense object, and sense consciousness are called the eighteen dhatus in Sanskrit, or *kham cho-gye* in Tibetan; the six pairs of sense organs and sense objects are called the twelve ayatanas in Sanskrit, or *kye-che* in Tibetan.

sense image is stored in the alayavijnana, the eighth consciousness, and from the alaya, it comes to the seventh, which in turn sends its message to the sixth. The sixth consciousness acts as an information service. That is, the mind consciousness distributes that information to the sight, smell, touch, taste, or hearing consciousness.

Models of Sense Perception

The Twelve Ayatanas:
The Meeting of Sense Organ and Sense Object

Our sense faculties are dependent on our particular sense organs and their objects.

SENSE ORGAN	SENSE OBJECT
Eyes	Sight
Ears	Sound
Nose	Smell
Tongue	Taste
Body	Touch
Mind	Thought

The Eighteen Dhatus:
The Meeting of Sense Organ, Sense Object, and Sense Consciousness

A conscious sense perception arises when the meeting of a sense organ and sense object is joined with a corresponding sense consciousness.

SENSE ORGAN	SENSE OBJECT	SENSE CONSCIOUSNESS
Eyes	Sight	Sight Consciousness
Ears	Sound	Sound Consciousness
Nose	Smell	Smell Consciousness
Tongue	Taste	Taste Consciousness
Body	Touch	Touch Consciousness
Mind	Thought	Mind Consciousness

Rediscovering Yourself

In meditation practice the meditator uses any and all of these eight types of consciousness, so you need to learn how to work with them. The popular idea of meditation is that of trying to attain a higher state of consciousness. You try to clean up the eight consciousnesses into an absolute consciousness or into a higher, superior form of eight types of consciousness. But that approach seems to be a problem. Relating intelligently with the technique of meditation does not have to be a project of sticking out your neck and looking beyond what you are. You are not trying to avoid or to transcend anything. Instead you could remain in the state of what you are.

In meditation practice, using the eight types of consciousness as material, you find to your surprise that you have not made a real and complete relationship with them. You simply exist as you were born, with eight types of consciousness, but you haven't actually looked at those happenings in your being. In that way, you are much more akin to an ape than to an intelligent being. Therefore the first project, so to speak, of meditation practice is to realize and rediscover these eight types of consciousness. In working with them, you are not trying to overcome them or do anything funny with them or manipulate them in some cunning way. You do not have to race with yourself. Instead you are rediscovering them and becoming a more refined animal by developing perfect and complete understanding of your own mind.

Through meditation, you begin to understand the eight consciousnesses and to know their functions inside out and outside in. You begin to understand the five skandhas as well. Realizing the subtleties of consciousness in this way is by no means reinforcing ego. It is like examining your body: you think your body is beautiful and active and powerful, but once you begin to study the muscles, bones, and interior organs, and once you see an X-ray, you begin to feel slightly insecure. At the same time, it is very interesting. You get a new perspective of your body and how your body functions.

Usually the eight consciousnesses are all lumped together; but meditation practice begins to sort them out. You begin to see the functions of mind completely and clearly. You know which part is which. In the meditative state, there could be an experiencer of the unconscious. That is the whole point. So far, the whole thing has been so lumped together that you have forgotten your being, your existence. But once you have time to slow down, think, and pay attention to the various little details, like breathing, you begin to realize yourself. It is as if you had been lying on a bed for a long time, not allowed to move around, and you began to rediscover your limbs, your fingers, and your toes—in meditation, you begin to rediscover yourself.

You might say, "What is the virtue of meditation, if we are just rediscovering ourselves? If we are already what we are, then what is the point of rediscovering ourselves?" But even if you develop a state of subtlety and sophistication, you are still rediscovering yourself. You can't change yourself from an ape to a divine being—that's impossible. The problem in not being able to see the real state of the eight types of consciousness is that you feel you are being condemned, punished, deprived, belittled. That sense of deprivation and condemnation comes from being unable to relate with yourself completely, let alone bring foreign information into your system. That is out of the question altogether, if there is any such thing. However, there does not seem to be anything transcendental or enlightened outside the eight types of consciousness. So the first step is to rest with what you have and not look ahead too far.

As you meditate, your experience of duality becomes sharpened, and you become more perky. Your deprivation becomes sharpened, but at the same time you begin to feel that your situation is workable. Before you were just stuck in the slums and you had no way of getting out, but now you begin to feel there are ways out. So the starting point is not to get out completely. Instead, you are given a kind of teaser: you get out partially. At that point, your original primitive pain is somewhat lessened—but then you have the ambition to get beyond that, to get completely better! You become very competitive. That kind of ambition grows and grows, and as ambition grows, confusion grows as well—but at a certain point, that confusion becomes encouragement rather than an obstacle. You feel much sturdier and more secure if you carry a heavy walking stick. Although it is heavy, it feels good.

It is exciting and it is good! You can practice the dharma by making use of the eight types of consciousness as vehicle, ground, food, shelter, inspiration, and information. You can become a dharma practitioner and turn the wheel of the dharma. To your surprise, turning the wheel of the dharma is not all that complicated. Anyone can do it.

38

Mixing Mind with Space

One of the problems meditators experience is that there is a slight, almost subconscious, guilty feeling that they ought to be doing something rather than just experiencing what goes on. When you begin to feel that you ought to be doing something, you automatically present millions of obstacles to yourself. Meditation is not a project; it is a way of being. You could experience that you are what you are. Fundamentally, sitting there and breathing is a very valid thing to do.

I N THE Kagyü tradition, we employ a special practice technique, which is the experiencing of *chung ne dro sum*. *Chung* is where the thoughts arise, *ne* is where they dwell, and *dro* is where they go, so *chung ne dro sum* is where the thoughts arise, dwell, and go. Those three are accompanied by the practice of *ying rik sewa*. *Ying* means "space," *rik* means "conscious mind," and *sewa* means "mixing"; so *ying rik sewa* means "mixing the conscious mind with space." Sometimes it is called *lung sem sewa*: "mixing the mind and breathing." *Lung* means "wind" or "air," *sem* is "mind," and *sewa* again means "mixing." In either case, the idea is to experience space. You do not need to deliberately try to mix the mind with the breathing with a solemn effort. Instead, you are simply in contact with the breathing. It is similar to the way that you feel the well-being of your body.

In being mindful of where the thoughts come from, where the thoughts dwell, and where the thoughts vanish, it is not that you are supposed to manufacture a thought and then let it come, let it dwell, and let it go. You have thoughts in any case, and you can be with them. As one thought vanishes, the next thought begins to arise; and by the time the next thought has arisen, the previous thought has already disappeared. You cannot usually experience the vanishing of a thought purely by itself, because to be aware of that thought you sustain it, so you do not really see the vanishing. The vanishing of a thought is seen in terms of the contrast of another idea coming up, at which point the previous thought has already subsided. The arising and dissolving of a thought is not exactly simultaneous, but the beginning, middle, and end happen very fast. When you acknowledge thoughts, they arise; in the process of acknowledging them, they dwell; after you acknowledge them, they drop. Acknowledging the dwelling of a thought does not mean staying with it for a long time, but just experiencing it as your thought. It is very simple.

Thoughts are generally connected with one or another of the eight types of consciousness, which are the working base for the practice of meditation. In meditation practice, you do not exaggerate the different levels of consciousness or disrespect them, but you have balance and respect. Generally, you begin with your physical well-being. You begin with your posture and your sense of discomfort or comfort. Your sense perceptions—the visions, sounds, sensations, tastes, smells, and thoughts that you experience—act as the fuse for your practice. Then, when those sense consciousnesses begin to wear themselves out a little bit, you become slightly bored with them and turn to the subconscious mind. Conversations are replayed, or particular events in your life are projected back to you in the form of a cinema show. Then there is a gap—a little gap where things don't happen and nothing occurs in the mind.

Physically, you may be comfortable and at rest with the sounds you hear and the visions that you see around you. You may be somewhat settled down. But then you dig up further excitement by looking into your personal relationships and emotional involvements with people. Are people being nice or nasty to you? Maybe you remember a particular scene, and experience the jealousy and passion you felt in that context, or maybe you plan your future. All kinds of thoughts begin to come up—and all of them should be experienced. If I say that you should be aware of the thoughts, then you will get into the area of being watchful, which is a project, and you will find that you are becoming a slave of your own awareness. That approach to practice does not work—it is too self-conscious—so I prefer the word *experience* to *awareness*.

The meditation technique universally used in all Buddhist traditions is mindfulness of the breathing, because breathing is an expression of being. For instance, you check whether a person is dead or just completely passed out by feeling whether the person is breathing or not. There is nothing particularly mystical about breathing. For instance, I do not think the early Buddhists thought about breathing in terms of prana, or life force; they were just breathing.

Traditionally, just being there is the outcome of the breathing technique. However, in the Tibetan tradition of formless meditation, you can also meditate without focusing on the breathing. The *shikantaza* practice of "just sitting," from the Japanese Zen tradition, is similar. Some people find it easy to do formless meditation without focusing on the breathing. If they are provided with a short session of sitting practice, it is easy for them to just be there because they do not have to hassle with any technique. However, for long-term sitting practice, it would be advisable to start with the mindfulness of breathing. Later, the awareness of breathing falls away, and at that point you just go along without it. That seems to be the best, most systematic approach.

In terms of both breathing and formless meditation, one of the problems meditators experience is that there is a slight, almost subconscious, guilty feeling that they ought to be doing something rather than just experiencing what goes on. When you begin to feel that you ought to be doing something, you automatically present millions of obstacles to yourself. Meditation is not a project; it is a way of being. You could experience that you are what you are. Fundamentally, sitting there and breathing is a very valid thing to do.

39

Mindfulness of Body

In mindfulness of body, you are simply trying to remain as an ordinary human being. When you sit, you actually sit. Even your floating thoughts begin to sit on their own bottoms. At that point, there is no problem: you have a base, solidity, and a sense of being, all at the same time.

THE FOUR FOUNDATIONS
OF MINDFULNESS

In order to free ourselves from too much self-conscious involvement in the practice—in thoughts, sense perceptions, and emotional play-back—a technique has been introduced called the "four foundations of mindfulness." The four foundations of mindfulness are mentioned in texts such as the *Satipatthana Sutra,** or the *Discourse on the Foundations of Mindfulness;* and the *Visuddhimagga,* or *The Path of Purification,*† which

---

* A translation and discussion of the *Satipatthana Sutra* can be found in Thich Nhat Hanh's book *Transformation and Healing: Sutras on the Four Establishments of Mindfulness* (Berkeley, Calif.: Parallax Press, 1990).

† Bhadantacariya Buddhagosha's *Path of Purification,* trans. from the Pali by Bhikkhu Nanamoli, is available from Pariyatti Publishing (Onalaska, Wash., 2003).

talk about the functions of your mind and how it can be worked with.*

The four foundations are usually presented as "mindfulness of body," "mindfulness of feeling," "mindfulness of mind," and "mindfulness of mental contents." That presentation has a slightly philosophical orientation, but in this discussion of the four foundations the emphasis is on meditation practice. Therefore, I have translated the four foundations as "mindfulness of body," "mindfulness of life,"† "mindfulness of effort," and "mindfulness of mind." The first foundation includes the body and other solid things, so I have called it "mindfulness of body." The second foundation is about relating with life as a whole, rather than simply with the skandha of feelings, so I have called it "mindfulness of life."‡ The third foundation is based on the idea of mental concentration, so I have called it "mindfulness of effort." The fourth foundation is based on "mindfulness of mental contents," and since the abhidharma definition of mind is "that which can perceive its own contents," I have called this foundation "mindfulness of mind."

In some traditions, the four foundations are used to separate very precisely what you are experiencing in your meditation practice. Teachers may use the four foundations in that way, dividing up the different categories of awareness and attention, but mindfulness practice does not need to be that scientific.

The four foundations of mindfulness are not four different practices, but four stages of shamatha practice. Although all four foundations are

---

* In his presentation of the four foundations, Trungpa Rinpoche deliberately departs from the more standard discussions of this topic, which is in keeping with his approach of infusing hinayana topics with a more tantric perspective.

† Trungpa Rinpoche originally used the phrase "mindfulness of livelihood" for this foundation. The term *livelihood* usually refers to one's means of support or subsistence. The way he uses it is closer to its archaic meaning of the quality of being lively, or quality of being alive. His usage of *livelihood* seems to be an intentional expansion of the idea of working for a living, to the broader sense of a natural and continual working for survival. Since the term *livelihood* usually refers simply to the workplace, and since Trungpa Rinpoche also speaks of this foundation as "mindfulness of life," we have chosen to use "mindfulness of life."

‡ Note that Trungpa Rinpoche has deliberately expanded his treatment of the second foundation beyond the traditional description found in the *Satipatthana Sutra*. In that sutra, the second foundation is mindfulness of "feeling," which in Tibetan is *tsor wa*. Trungpa Rinpoche is commenting on the similar term *tsowa*, which means "livelihood" or "life."

considered to be shamatha, they could also be considered to extend to vipashyana practice. The first foundation, mindfulness of body, is pure shamatha, because it only involves your own body and mind. You do not make an attempt to go out beyond that.

PENETRATING BEING

In the first foundation, mindfulness of body, you relate with the bodily sensations, the sense perceptions, and the eight types of consciousness. You don't have to build anything up; you just pay attention to what is happening. The meditation technique is identification with the breathing, which is a very real experience. There is no suggestion of anything other than paying attention to your breathing or your walking. That simplifies things a lot. There is no security other than sitting and breathing.

Mindfulness of the body is based on being right there on your cushion. It is partly influenced by bodily sensation, and partly influenced by audio-visual sensations and sense consciousnesses. You are not meditating on anything in particular, but just being with your body fully and completely. As much as you can, you stay right there—just sitting there. That sense of being is a very penetrating experience. It transcends the ordinary level of self-consciousness. Although occasionally you might experience that you are being there, that you are watching yourself being there, and that the watcher is watching itself, this is just a phase. It is another little project that wears out quickly and comes back into simply experiencing being.

BODY-BODY AND PSYCHOSOMATIC BODY

In referring to mindfulness of body, we mean not only this particular body, but any form or body-ness. We mean all body-ness: the body-ness of grass and water and sun and moon and everything else. However, mindfulness of body does not mean that you should be aware of each and every body—there would be so many bodies to be aware of at the same time—it means being aware of the totality. It is a general understanding of where things are, rather than being aware of each hair growing on your head. We are not talking about multiple-awareness systems. Instead, the whole approach is simple and direct: just sit and meditate. You sit and meditate, and you relate with your breath—there's no further promise. That is all we are talking about. It doesn't matter if you are a beginner, or old and accomplished. Since everybody is a professional samsara-dweller, in terms of samsara nobody is a beginner—everybody is a professional.

In the mindfulness of body, there is a need for solidness, presence, and groundedness. However, we might have difficulty with that. Although we possess a body—we sit on the ground, we eat, we sleep, we wear clothes—there are a lot of questions about the particular body we think we have. We are uncertain as to whether it is an unconditional body or a body of conceptualization. An ordinary person's experience of the body, known as the psychosomatic body, is largely based on concepts or ideas of body, whereas an enlightened person's attitude toward the body, known as body-body, is a simple, direct, and straightforward relationship with the earth. In our case, we don't have much of a relationship with the earth. We may have some relationship with our body, but we are uncertain. We flicker back and forth between the body and something else. Different levels are going on at the same time: the undercurrent is enlightened, and the superficial aspect is confused, or samsaric.

The experience of psychosomatic body could be quite solid in terms of conceptualization and expectations. You think, "My body exists; therefore, I have to refuel it, entertain it, wash it." It may include a feeling of being. For instance, when you are meditating, you may feel your body resting on your cushion. You may feel somewhat settled, not particularly nervous or self-conscious. If you are tense, however, you may begin to perch on the ground like a bird on a branch. When there are demands being made on you, you feel less of your body and more of your tension and nervousness. Even if you feel your body sitting on the ground and relaxed, it is not actually the body per se sitting on the ground, but your psychosomatic body.

It is your psychosomatic body sitting on the ground, because somehow sitting on the ground gives you ideas. You are doing the sitting down, but at the same time you are not doing it. Your mind is shaping itself in accordance with your body, so your mind is sitting on the ground, your mind is wearing a pair of glasses, your mind is having a certain hairdo, or wearing certain clothes. It is all mental activity. From that point of view, everybody is a self-portrait. That is known as the psychosomatic body. Since that psychosomatic body exists, activity takes place according to that body.

Whatever we do in our life, we are affected by the mind. Our true body is being pressured by the speed of the mind. Consequently, although you have the possibility of sitting properly, on this very spot, in a non-psychosomatic way, the whole situation has been brought together by that same driving force. It has been set up by that psychosomatic system. So fundamentally, the whole thing is psychosomatic. This is not regarded as a short-term sickness, but sickness in the long run, in terms of samsara.

A hang-up of some kind has brought you to sitting practice. The desire to study the teachings arises because you begin to be aware of your hang-ups; therefore, you would like to create a further hang-up to clear the existing hang-ups. That is the process. You never relate directly until the level at which you have flashes of the essential nature of mind. Until that point, anything you do is always by innuendo. So not only is the disease or hang-up psychosomatic, but even when you are healthy, it is psychosomatic. That is, you are infected by psychosomatic problems already, and disease is something extra, like yeast growing on your back. Therefore, in order to relate to the experience of body directly, the practice of mindfulness of body is suggested.

In meditation practice, we are trying to include this psychosomatic, mind-imitating body; we are going along with that bodylike attitude. Sitting practice has been suggested, practiced, and proven to be the best way to work with that. In sitting practice, the basic technique is working with the breath. Your breath is your physical body from the point of view of mindfulness of body. Sensations of all kinds go along with the breath, including pain, aches, and itches, as well as pleasurable feelings. Since all that goes along with the breath, the breath is the leading point. The idea of mindfulness is simply being precise as to what you are experiencing. However, those experiences are not regarded as your actual body's experiences. At this point, you are in no position to experience your body at all—that is impossible. Your bodily experiences are just thoughts: the thought of pain, the thought of itch, and so forth.

NOT SOLIDIFYING BODY MINDFULNESS

The special approach of the Kagyü tradition teaching on the mindfulness of body is the suggestion that deliberately focusing your attention on your body is unnecessary. In fact, there was a big controversy in Tibet about the Kagyü meditation technique. It was said that the Kagyüpas meditate like pigs: they just sit and breathe. According to the intellectual approach to the mindfulness of body, you are supposed to explore the inside of your body, the rising and falling of the abdomen, and so forth. People get a lot of reinforcement by observing their lungs, watching the air going through their nostrils, and feeling the rising and falling of the abdomen. It becomes a self-existing occupation. However, in the Kagyü approach, we generally do not do any of that when we meditate. We just sit and breathe.

There have been all kinds of attacks on the Kagyü technique of just sitting and breathing. The stubbornness of the Kagyü approach is regarded as too faithful, too believing, too solid, too unadventurous. As a result, the Kagyü approach is constantly challenged by other schools of Tibetan Buddhism. Nevertheless, the stuffiness of the self-sturdy feeling of being in the body is reinforced more in the intellectual approach than in what we do. So the idea of mixing mind and breathing, mixing mind and space, is highly recommended in our tradition.

At the same time, with that true-believer quality, you could become too solid and solemn, too believing. Seeing yourself sitting on the cushion and meditating in that way is hilarious. You are so gullible—somebody told you to meditate, so you just sit on the cushion and breathe. Therefore, you need to take the step of knowing what you are doing.

Using Literal Attention to the Body

If people have no span of concentration and can only hold themselves for one minute, then it is highly recommended that they start at the extremely elementary level of literally watching their body. If such people work only with the breathing, their concentration will drift away from them. The Buddha taught this method to extreme cases. For example, it is said that the Buddha had a disciple who was a stupid and forgetful person. When the Buddha began to teach him, first the Buddha taught him breathing meditation practice, but the disciple couldn't do it—he would forget what he was doing. So the Buddha gave him a broom and asked him to be the sweeper in the monastery, and taught him to repeat the words "Sweep and clean, sweep and clean" along with the motion of the broom as he was sweeping. The disciple was able to sweep, but he would forget the words, so he would come to the Buddha and ask, "What's after 'sweep'?" When his disciple had memorized "Sweep and clean" properly, the idea of the rising and falling of the abdomen was introduced to him. He was told, "Now go sit and feel your abdomen. It will go up and it will go down. Just go along with it." He didn't have to *remember* up and down—he *felt* it.

Body Mindfulness through Walking Meditation

Walking meditation helps one to develop mindfulness of body. In walking meditation, the movement of your legs becomes the focus, just as breathing is the focus in sitting meditation. Walking meditation practice is based on bodily sensations. As you walk, you have a natural sense of the movement of your legs and of relating with open space. You are using your legs to stir space as you would use an oar to stir water. If people are unable to relate with their legs, they begin to be self-conscious about their arms, head, and back, including the hair on their head. That is a sign of being unable to relate completely with the movement of their legs. Ideal walking practice is a slow motion of ordinary walking. If you feel perfectly comfortable with your body when you are walking, you do not have to introduce anything else—you simply walk.

Including Sensations as Reminders

Any bodily sensations you may have—an ache in the back, itches, sensations of hot and cold—are included in the mindfulness practice of breathing or walking. Rather than trying to sort out those problems, you include them as reminders that come up as bodily awareness. The meditation technique is a kind of shock absorber. That is, awareness of breathing or of walking is accentuated if there is an itch in your back, or if there is self-consciousness of your foot, or if there is a hole in your sock. All of those little self-consciousnesses are reminders of the general rhythm of the body. The point of mindfulness of body is to cooperate with one's whole being by concentrating on the technique of awareness of breathing or the technique of awareness of walking.

Solidity

There are several levels of mindfulness one can achieve, similar to those depicted in the Oxherding Pictures of the Zen tradition. At first, you are watching yourself. Then you do not have to watch yourself, because you can feel your own footprint, which reflects how confident you are. As you go along, you begin to feel that you are very much in control of everything, and the sense of being is always present. You could ride on yourself and complete the accomplishment of experiencing proper, total being. Then as you go beyond that, you can play a flute as you ride. Your well-being is so solid and so definite that you can extend greater awareness beyond the well-being of the body to include the well-being of life, and so forth.

Altogether, the idea of meditation is not to create states of ecstasy or absorption, but to experience being. In meditation, there is a quality of both being and rest. Our problem is that up to now we never fully experienced such a sense of being. Meditation practices are meant to arouse your trust. You could afford to treat yourself well, rather than being punished or tortured. The sense of well-being is a mishmash of a lot of things. It is an experience of egolessness along with some pinches of eightfold consciousness, and a little touch of deception as well. If we tried to define it, it would be too complicated—but it happens that we could afford to indulge ourselves in it, which is much safer.

Mindfulness means that when you sit and meditate, you actually *do* sit. As far as the psychosomatic body is concerned, you feel the ground, body, breath, and temperature, but you don't *watch* what's happening. You don't watch what's going on, and you don't try to formalize the sitting practice as special—you just sit. In doing so, you begin to experience solidity, which is not a product of deliberateness, but incidental. So you sit—and you breathe—and you sit—and you breathe. Sometimes you think, but you are thinking sitting-thoughts. Because the psychosomatic body is sitting, your thoughts are being produced from sitting, so your thoughts have flat bottoms.

You go on in that way constantly, and somehow there's a feeling that you have done something. That feeling is important; it is the most important experience in the mindfulness of body. You feel that you are actually doing something, that you have done something, that you are taking part in an experience and a project that has a flat bottom. Rather than being ball-shaped or having wings, your experience has a flat bottom. That is the mindfulness of body: solidity and connection with the earth. It is openness with a base, a flat bottom.

The mindfulness of body requires a great deal of trust. At this level a student might feel the need for change. Once a retreatant told me that when she sat, she felt her body and she felt grounded—but then she thought she should be doing something else, and the right book jumped into her lap and she happened to read it. At that point she did not have a solid base anymore. Her mind was beginning to grow little wings.

In the mindfulness of body, you are simply trying to remain as an ordinary human being. When you sit, you actually sit. Even your floating thoughts begin to sit on their own bottoms. At that point, there is no problem: you have a base, solidness, and a sense of being, all at the same time. That quality of solidity seems to be the starting point of the mindfulness of body. Without this particular foundation, the practice of meditation could be very airy-fairy, back and forth, trying this and trying that. Constantly tiptoeing on the surface of the universe, not actually getting a foothold anywhere, you become an eternal hitchhiker. So the technique of the first foundation of mindfulness is based on solidity and on finding home ground.

40

Mindfulness of Life

Well-being of body is like a majestically solid mountain with no mist and no rain. Well-being of speech is like a stringed instrument disengaged from the strings so that it no longer has any desire to communicate with the musician. Well-being of mind is like a great lake with no ripples, no waves, and no wind. Well-being is simple, majestic, and uninterrupted.

I N T H E second foundation of mindfulness, mindfulness of life, you begin to appreciate the details of what goes on in your own body, speech, and mind, but you are not yet venturing into the world outside. The study of things outside comes at a later stage of meditation. The application of mindfulness has to be precise. However, if we cling to the practice, that creates stagnation. It is often thought that the meditative state of mind has to be captured, then cherished and nursed, but that seems to be a misunderstanding. The result of domesticating one's mind in that manner is regression on the path, being unable to maintain the freshness of the awareness. Awareness practice becomes a domestic hassle, like painfully going about house chores with resentment and bad feelings. Practice becomes confusing, and one begins to develop a love-hate relationship to it. The concept of practice seems to be good, but the demands it makes on you become painful, and you do not like it.

In the samsaric world, things are done without mindfulness, and we thrive on that. Consequently, everything that we do, without exception, is somewhat disjointed. Things don't click; they don't fit. Although you might be a very reasonable, good person, everything you do is still somewhat off, somewhat illogical. The problem is that fundamental neurosis takes place all the time, which creates pain for others and pain for yourself. People get hurt as a consequence of bouncing back and forth. In that neurotic world, nobody is actually having a good time. Even if you are having a good time, it is somewhat forced; and being pushed into having a good time is a form of indulgence.

The mindfulness of life is a different approach, in that life is treated preciously and mindfully, so everything is jointed rather than disjointed. There is a coherent process happening constantly within your state of mind, so there is workability. There is a general map or outline as to how to conduct your life, how to exist. You begin to become literate in terms of reading the style and pattern of the world. By no means is this the final product of mindfulness, however; it is just becoming literate in how to properly read the world.

SIMULTANEOUS TOUCH AND GO

In the mindfulness of life, the meditative state is tangible, but at the same time there is a letting go. You are there, then you let yourself go. Touch and go always come together. Whenever there is a one, there is always a zero. So in mindfulness practice—both meditation and postmeditation—touch and go happen simultaneously and constantly, rather than "touch" being one thing and "go" being another. In day-to-day living, whenever there is a need for heedfulness, that also contains touch and go. In other words, touch, or being fully mindful, cannot be maintained by itself without go; and you cannot go without being fully mindful. Touch and go come together always.

With human relationships, if you have an attitude of touch and go, that creates further relationship because there is so much space and, at the same time, so much interest. The problem is that if you have too much interest, this creates claustrophobia, and the relationship turns sour; and if there's too much space, the relationship becomes stagnant or sterile. So I think the right combination is fullness and emptiness, touch and go, which is a playful kind of thing. With touch and go, you do not have to secure your practice, but you could simply tune in to it. It is a question of confidence.

SURVIVAL

In Tibetan, the second foundation of mindfulness is called *tsowa*, which means "surviving," or "to live." You are working on your survival and appreciating your survival. Survival is a constant, ongoing process. You breathe for survival, you lead your life for survival. Throughout your life, there is the attitude of trying to protect yourself from death. In the mindfulness of life, instead of regarding the notion of survival as negative, or as ego-clinging, you switch the logic around so that survival, or struggle, is brought into the practice of meditation. Whenever it arises, the survival instinct is transmuted into an awareness of being. The experience of surviving, of existence, is acknowledged—not by saying, "Thank God I survived!" but simply, "I am alive, I am here, so be it."

Whenever there is a threat, that heightens the feeling of life. When you are threatened, you take a pill, because if you don't you might die. You take the pill with the attitude that if you take it you are going to live. The feeling of sitting on a razor blade also brings warmth. Whenever there is a fear of death, a love of life comes along with it.

In the second foundation, there is a love of mindfulness, as opposed to mindlessness, which is connected with death. At this point, interestingly, the practice of meditation becomes the central focus of your life. It is more than just practice; it is part of the instinct of life. The life force, that which keeps us alive, is the practice of mindfulness. Mindfulness brings clarity, skill, and intelligence. You are brought from the level of intense confusion to the psychosomatic body, and then to the real body. So the practice of meditation is not a borrowed idea from some eccentric yogi who had a fixation to meditate all the time—it is the total experience of any living being who has the instinct to live or to survive. We are including the whole big world. So practicing meditation or developing mindfulness is not regarded as the activity of a minority—it is a wide-world approach, tuning in to life.

You are not tuning in to life in order to live further, but rather to experience the survival taking place this very moment. You are here, you are living; let it be that way. Such mindfulness has strength: your heart pulses, you breathe, everything is happening at this very moment, all at once. Let mindfulness work with all of that; let that be mindfulness. Let every beat of your heart and every breath be mindfulness. You don't have to breathe in a special way—as it is, breathing is an expression of mindfulness.

Whenever we sit and meditate, our tendency is to have an attitude of renunciation, or austerity. We feel that we are being good, and that we are getting away from the ugly world, that we are becoming pure. Meditation practice feels fitting, clean, secure. We are renouncing the world for the moment and doing, or at least imitating, the austere practice of the yogis of the past. Although we may not actually meditate or live in a cave, we regard the corner of our home reserved for meditation as a cave, as if we were in the mountains. That attitude is a problem. It is devoid of life. With that approach, we remove the practice of meditation from our actual living situation.

The mindfulness of life is the opposite of that, not in the sense of indulgence, but in its basic psychological approach. If you are meditating in a room, you are meditating in a room, rather than regarding the room as a cave; if you are breathing, you are breathing, rather than pretending to be a rock. In the mindfulness of life, no imagination is involved—you just do it. If your meditation place is in a rich setting, you are in the midst of it; if it is in a simpler setting, you are in the midst of it. You are not trying to get away from somewhere to somewhere else. Such segregation mentality does not apply. Mindfulness is the essence of being here and now.

Having such an outlook and relationship to the practice of meditation brings enormous strength, energy, and power. Such strength can only be achieved if your relationship to the present situation is accurate; otherwise, you cannot achieve strength, because you are removed from the current energy existing at this given time. So dignity, strength, and delightfulness take place when you sit and meditate, because you are doing something that is applicable this very moment, without any implications. Because there are no implications behind it, it is direct and right on the point. However, once you have that kind of experience, that sense of life, you do not hang on to it—you just touch and go. You could just be in it without further analysis or reinforcement.

Trying to reinforce yourself is the attitude of death. You would like to make sure that you are alive, not dead. However, if you know that you are alive, that's good enough. You do not have to make sure that you actually are breathing, that you actually can be seen by somebody, that you actually have your shadow. Mindfulness is not pushing and hanging on, but being there on the spot this very moment.

WELL-BEING

The basic approach of the mindfulness of life is that what goes on with your body and your state of consciousness is worthy of respect. There is a feeling of well-being. You see further subtleties, and sense perceptions are more appreciated. Mindfulness of life is rediscovering your world. You develop reverence and respect, which is more than just an attitude; it is something you actually experience in your relationship to yourself and to the world. You are able to experience magic, majesty, beauty, and well-being not only in the meditative state, but in ordinary states as well. That experience is based on being able to see the process of contact with the phenomenal world, which is divided into preparing, proceeding, and touching.

It is important to describe the idea of well-being clearly, as there are several notions of well-being. It may mean that you are secure, and because you are secure, you can afford to relax and to extend yourself. Well-being may be based on a feeling of power, meaning that you are ready to defend yourself or conquer others. It may mean you are on top of the world, that you feel extremely healthy and physically comfortable. You have had a good meal; the clothes you are wearing are elegant; your company is exciting and amiable; everything is completely secure. In this case, well-being is similar to that which is felt by somebody who is on vacation or at a ski resort. Well-being in terms of the meditative state is unlike any of those. In the case of the second foundation of mindfulness, well-being is based on appreciating your own existence, rather than being conditioned by that or this.

Well-Being of Body, Speech, and Mind

There are several analogies for well-being in the scriptures. Well-being of body is like a majestically solid mountain with no mist and no rain. Well-being of speech is like a stringed instrument disengaged from the strings so that it no longer has any desire to communicate with the musician. Well-being of mind is like a great lake with no ripples, no waves, and no wind. Well-being is simple, majestic, and uninterrupted.

The three types of well-being are referred to in the scriptures as *chok-shak namsum*. *Chok* has the feeling of perkiness or cheerfulness. *Chok* is also a synonym for a soup ladle. A soup ladle is uniquely curved, with a definite shape and its own self-expressive perkiness, and you can hold it in your hand. *Shak* means "rest," or "put down." The combination, *chokshak*, is fundamental well-being, rather than conditional well-being. It is not based on comfort or entertainment. In fact, chokshak is not based on any conditions at all. *Namsum* means "three aspects," so *chokshak namsum* means "three aspects of well-being."

Chokshak is egoless and free from dualistic notions. Nevertheless, there is a personal experience of immediateness. You are not concerned with security, but at the same time, there is consciousness and there is body. Although we talk about "letting go" or the "death of ego," that is at the philosophical level of greater vision. Obviously, in our ordinary experience, there is the world and there is you. Recognizing this does not mean that you are going against the Buddha's teaching of egolessness. There is definitely something there, which is the working basis and magic of the path. You cannot negate the fact that you taste a good cup of coffee. You cannot say that there is no coffee and there is no "you" to taste it—there *are* such things! Mindfulness of life is based on that kind of immediate appreciation. The meditation practice is to learn to appreciate the immediateness of what is happening right here and now.

Irritation as an Expression of Well-Being

In the second foundation of mindfulness, you are not getting into the world and beginning to dance with it—you are purely paying attention to what is happening. In that sense, it is a distant approach. Because it is distant, and because that discovery is so precise, so good, and so obvious, looking for further entertainment becomes irrelevant. You are thrown back to your boredom. But that boredom does not become irritating. You simply realize that instigating further possibilities does not work. In other words, the boredom is based on realizing you cannot trick yourself anymore. It is a very light touch.

In the second foundation of mindfulness, you relate with irritation as an expression of well-being. With physical sensations, such as an itch on your shoulder while you are meditating, the automatic reaction is to scratch and get it over with. But there is another approach. Instead of trying to get away from that particular itch, if you related with it, that itch could become an expression of well-being. In other words, if you feel irritated and tense, then feeding that irritation and tenseness by doing something to get rid of it does not help—not at all! Instead, you could relate with that irritation as an expression of survival.

There is no point in suppressing the sense of survival or security that comes up in the mind during sitting meditation practice. The very fact that you are capable of experiencing irritation means that your psychological state is refined, sensitive, and intelligent. That is why you can tell that certain irritations are arising in your body or your state of mind. You can relate with those physical sensations and psychological tensions as expressions of well-being. This is by no means a myth or hypothetical ideology. It is true.

In mindfulness practice, working with the breathing is based on a subtle level of effort. The concentration or focus on the breathing has to be maintained and kept alive. That subtle effort is also an expression of well-being, or survival. The analogy that Buddha gave the musician was that he shouldn't tighten his strings too much and he shouldn't loosen his strings too much. So it is necessary to develop effort that is not too tight or too loose. If you have no effort and you are completely spaced-out, you do not have a chance to experience well-being, nor do you have a chance to develop good meditation practice. At the same time, trying to achieve an ideal or perfect meditative state is also a problem. Perfectionism is a hang-up. In the second foundation of mindfulness, any awkwardness that occurs in the state of meditation practice is regarded as a further expression of well-being.

BREATHING TECHNIQUE: REDISCOVERING THE SENSE PERCEPTIONS

Mindfulness of life is an essential experience. When your mind is made relatively tranquil and quiet by means of the breathing technique, you begin to discover the subtleties of sight, smell, feeling, and hearing, and touch. Everything that arises sharpens your consciousness. So it is a question of being able to relate with all that thoroughly and completely.

In meditation, you do not deliberately try to arouse your sense perceptions by stroking your body, extending your arm, grasping a stone, listening to a brook, or playing sensual music. You may be sitting in a quiet, uninspiring room. You may be sitting and meditating with no source of entertainment, none whatsoever—but when your mind is completely clear and simplified purely into the technique of breathing meditation, you begin to discover an entirely new world. That world is extraordinarily beautiful and colorful, bright and loud. You find that you are completely bombarded with all sorts of sense perceptions. Your sense consciousnesses become highly sharpened. Those experiences happen in the midst of nowhere!

People can develop similar experiences by artificial means, such as taking LSD, mescaline, peyote, and so forth. They get experiences such as seeing bright colors and visions that they haven't seen before. The problem is that they know this is the product of a particular drug, and they are so intrigued that they become inspired to explore further and further, until their conscious perceptions become numb. They begin to lose track. In contrast, a meditation practice of this kind does not have such a frivolous and numbing quality, because physically and psychologically you are completely well-balanced. You are not influenced by drugs or dogma or bliss. You are at the level of being extraordinarily bored and extremely intelligent. Boredom and intelligence together act as real clarity. The boredom is the cool, fresh mountain air, and the intelligence is what notes the particular events that take place in your sensory world.

The awareness of sense perceptions happens at the same time as your awareness of breathing. As you are sitting there and breathing, there is an awareness of the totality of experience. The lighter the touch of awareness on the breathing, the more other areas of awareness will begin to arise. If you try to put too much emphasis on the breathing and make that too heavy-duty, then you will kill the whole thing. You find yourself breathing deliberately, very heavily, and you become very tight and tense. Your practice becomes mechanical. So the idea is that mindfulness of breathing is a very light touch. It is almost as if the breathing does not exist. You go out with the breathing, and the breathing dissolves. If your effort is a mere suggestion, twenty-five-percent effort, then a lot of possibilities arise around you. Out-breathing is a way of communicating to the sense perceptions; it's like extending your tentacles. In-breathing is allowing room or space to be. If your approach is not too heavy-handed, there is no conflict between the two.

LIGHT TOUCH

As you become one with the breathing, your mind is not completely, one-pointedly involved with the breathing alone. You begin to feel the effect of clarity. The breathing becomes a working base. It is as if you do not have any bodily defects or malfunctions, so you can walk easily, move your arms easily, wink easily, and breathe easily. You can do other things as well, and in the meantime you can think. The whole thing could coordinate together in that way. It is a question of having just a light touch on the breathing, which allows other areas to be explored. Meditation then becomes total experience.

Meditation is not regarded as a project. The breath is just there, and you allow the awareness to be whatever it is going to be. There is no problem with that because the unifying factor of well-being is always there. You may feel you have to involve yourself in things one hundred percent, if not two hundred percent. However, a very interesting point about meditation is that you begin to discover that you don't have to be involved in things one hundred percent. You do not need to be heavy-handed. You can radiate your consciousness in all directions and be able to detect every area with light but precise observation.

In mindfulness of breathing, you will have problems if you try to remold or reshape yourself like dough. That only reinforces the difficulties, and your breathing becomes too complicated. If your approach is lighter at the beginning, if your attention to the breathing and to the sense perceptions is equally light, that makes your practice complete and total. Otherwise, it will be lopsided. You might think you are sitting perfectly, but when you get up at the end of the meditation you find that you have pins and needles, which you never noticed before. If you are too serious, meditation becomes an imprisonment for you, rather than an expression of freedom. Too much seriousness becomes an obstacle.

If you are not working too hard, your meditation becomes less demanding. You can get into it after a few seconds, and you can practice without any difficulties. In our society we never sit doing nothing, nothing whatsoever, for more than half an hour; and if we do one thing, we feel guilty that we should be doing something else. Even when we drive, we work very hard trying to stay on the road. We are physically sitting down, but it is still work. In the beginning, practice might be physically difficult because we are not used to it. But apart from that, there are no hang-ups; instead, any irritations could be used to regenerate our meditation.

Any problems that come up will be self-liberated by practice, as long as your approach is light and right there. That kind of meditative state is actually happening at this very moment. You have a sense of the room you are in and the people around you; at the same time, there is expansiveness. That is a real and very ordinary thing that happens to all of us. When you decide to sit and meditate, if you try to become somebody else, that seems to be a problem. That is why the term *peace,* or *shamatha,* and the term *liberation* are used a great deal. Meditation is already there—you just have to tune in to that state of being. Formal sitting periods make it more definite. They draw the line so that meditation practice could be made into a part of the path, or discipline, and so that you can invoke the magic involved.

In the second foundation, the focal point is still on the breathing. If you try to cultivate a particular sense perception, suddenly that sense perception drops you, and you have to find another one to latch onto. If you try to fight a sense perception, that particular consciousness fights back, trying to make you pay more attention to it. So the idea is to pay attention to the breathing as the ongoing focus, and let the rest come and go.

Mindfulness of life is an extremely important part of the four foundations of mindfulness. Having established your discipline and developed an ongoing relationship with the eight types of consciousness, you begin to explore the subtleties of those consciousnesses. You are rediscovering a brand new world—the old-new world. At this level, there is a hint of prajna. However, this kind of experience is by no means extraordinary. It is very ordinary.

In the mindfulness of life, appreciation is spacious, not hungry. There is a quality of subtlety. Not only are you appreciating your survival in the conventional sense, but you feel that you have things at your disposal, at your command. You appreciate the details of life. For instance, you appreciate that it is a good day today. The whole environment is absolutely nonparanoid. There is lots of room for everything—including your own appreciation.

41

Mindfulness of Effort

With mindfulness of effort you are clearly on the path. Effort is like the wheel of a chariot, which connects the chariot and the road. It's like the oar in a boat, which connects the boat to the water. Effort is the connection that makes things move forward and proceed. So mindfulness of effort—the sudden reminder or sudden jerk of mind-fulness—is extremely important for the practice of meditation.

T HE THIRD foundation of mindfulness is mindfulness of effort. You might feel that mindfulness of effort is a contradiction to the well-being of the second foundation, to the organic familiarity with meditation and the appreciation of sitting practice. However, although it might seem contradictory to develop effort and well-being at the same time, the effort of the third foundation of mindfulness is extraordinary.

DISCIPLINE, PATIENCE, AND EXERTION

Effort is a question of discipline, patience, and exertion. It seems that there is a conflict between the ethical aspect of life, or what one should be doing, and the instinctive aspect, or what one would like to do. Our instinct is not properly matched with our ethics. That conflict brings tiredness, struggle, and loss of heart in the practice. Mindfulness of effort is about the meet-ing point of instinct and ethics, and how they can be put together.

Effort is often talked about in the pejorative sense, in terms of going against the natural flow and trying to behave yourself. In that sense, it is a source of alienation. You are alienating yourself from reality, which brings a great deal of nonmindfulness. The question is whether there is a natural instinct that is right and appropriate. If so, there is no problem. However, it is not so simple to realize that natural instinct. We prefer the casual instinct of indulgence, viewing it as a good gift and going along with it haphazardly.

First Flash: Duality

In the practice of mindfulness of effort, we are developing clear-seeing vision in order to be able to relate with the natural instinct of exertion and patience. By instinct, we mean the instinct of self-consciousness, almost an unconditional self-consciousness. This instinct is quite similar to the notion of survival in the second foundation of mindfulness; however, in this case we go beyond survival to self-consciousness. When you relate with things, or to the world, one of the first flashes that takes place is a feeling of duality or separateness. From that first flash, you then begin to evaluate, to pick and choose, to involve yourself in decision making. You begin executing desire and will.

In the mindfulness of effort, you are not particularly trying to be good or absolutely perfect, but you are going back to that first flash. If the meditation practice presented to you has nothing to do with you, but is a way of transforming you into a better personality, you have already been alienated by the very idea of practice. You feel that you are not good enough, that you could be better if you practiced more. In contrast, mindfulness of effort is not a way of reforming yourself—it is starting with what you are. It is being what you are with exertion and discipline. You don't have to start by trying to be the best—you just do it.

In mindfulness of effort, you start with the experience of duality. That duality is there already. You don't particularly have to make a study of it. You are simply utilizing tendencies that exist in your psychological system, the first one being that sense of duality or separateness. The instinct to practice arises because there is somebody to practice. It is like eating food: having the idea that such a thing as food exists makes you more interested in eating. If you had no concept of food, you would be constantly hungry, but you wouldn't want to eat. There would be nothing to do. So the existence of self-consciousness is the basis of practice.

At the level of simple cognition, cognitive mind is somewhat unconditional, because you have not yet made up your mind—you have just projected. Then, because of your projection, you get feedback that you are projecting, that you exist. You are here, and that is there, and that's more or less it. At this level there is no hope and fear, nothing further is involved: it is just simple recollection, simple memory. That seems to be a basic pattern. Without realizing or recognizing that quality of self-consciousness, it would be difficult to develop effort.

If you regard practice as a way to get away from the problem of duality, you are re-creating that reference point and solidifying the problem. But if your attitude suggests a fresh, direct experience of duality, you can utilize it. Rather than deliberately trying to sabotage that self-consciousness, you could work with it so that everything is included. Having developed that somewhat unconditional reference point, it is possible to extend that and to utilize it in living situations. Through such awareness, it is possible to develop effort that is not based on a particular plan or aim, but on the simple, unconditional effort to be.

The Game of Resistance

In the mindfulness of effort, at the beginning you are usually just breaking the ice, so to speak. It seems that an unknown force is imposing its power on you: you don't want to get into the practice of meditation. There is almost a childish mentality, like not wanting to go to school. That problem could be easily broken down, however, by being aware of the resistance. In doing so, you have already started. Your resistance has been used as a doorstep to walk over. Beyond that, there are no further problems, except for little practice hassles such as irritating thoughts and bodily discomfort.

Some form of resistance is ongoing, otherwise there wouldn't be any journey. By relating with the resister and the resistance, you have already begun the journey. If you try to eliminate resistance, you are feeding it, whereas if you just acknowledge that such a thing as resistance exists, there is no problem. As the idea of practice occurs in your mind, that much resistance occurs in your mind at the same time. If you make a big deal of the resistance or try to eliminate it altogether, that makes the resistance greater. Looking for smooth practice, for practice with no resistance, only increases the resistance.

The breath and resistance are similar, in that the breath is an alternating experience that comes and goes, and resistance is also a sort of pulsation. The impulse to resist comes in spells. In following the breath, sometimes the breathing acts as a way of distracting your attention from mindfulness or awareness, and sometimes the breathing becomes a help. So the same technique can have two uses. That's why any one technique is not regarded as one-hundred-percent good. Any technique we introduce could take you away from the integrity of the practice, although at the same time it could help. That is part of the game of resistance. If you include the whole thing as just one big sweep that continues throughout your life, there is no problem. You do not have to try to discriminate fish from fowl.

When you have resistance, if you have awareness of it, then that in itself is mindfulness. You are already sitting, so in any case you've been caught. Formal sitting practice is not a big deal; it is just one of the expressions of mindfulness that may happen in your life. Even if you are a particularly good sitter, only one-eighth of your life may consist of sitting. So mindfulness does not only refer to sitting cross-legged on a cushion. You develop the attitude that mindfulness happens to you anyway. You think you can get away from sitting practice by resisting, but you find that you are still doing it. Once the idea is introduced into your head, it's very haunting.

Mistaken Effort

There are many kinds of effort. One kind of effort is the effort to achieve something by struggling. You try to push your way through, and once this struggle has picked up momentum, you speed along in the fashion of a roadrunner. Your only problem is slowing down, or how to put on the brakes.

Another kind of effort is based on dragging yourself along with an attitude of tremendous meaningfulness and seriousness. There is no upliftedness or inspiration in your work; you are simply being dutiful. In this form of effort, you just crawl along, slowly and surely, and eat up your life like a worm in a tree. Such effort may seem to have a similarity to right effort, in that examples of right effort, such as a tortoise's walk or the walk of an elephant, also seem to be about being slow and unexcitable, just plodding along. But those examples have a quality of surveying the area, which makes them different from a worm eating a hole through wood. A worm has no way to take a panoramic view. It just bites whatever comes in front of its mouth and chews it, and however much it chews through, that is how much space it has for its body and its belly. In fact, that is its entire space! In contrast, although the walk of an elephant or a tortoise is likewise slow and seemingly serious, it also has the quality of being cunning or playful.

Bringing Yourself Back to Mindfulness

The effort of the third mindfulness practice has not quite matured to the level of dancing with the situation, or being so completely inspired by the sitting practice of meditation that you don't even have to sit, but sitting just comes to you. If you keep looking for an inspiration that will lead you to forget your pain and keep bringing you back to your practice naturally and effortlessly, then it ceases to be right effort. Instead, it becomes entertainment.

In right effort, the main technique that has developed is to constantly bring yourself back to mindfulness of the breathing. When your mind begins to wander, you realize it and bring it back. As far as the sitting practice of meditation is concerned, this technique is an extremely effective and useful trick. The interesting point about the technique of bringing your mind back is that you do not have to prepare. You do not have to hold your mind and drag it back, as if you were trying to prevent a naughty child from doing something terrible. Trying by deliberate effort to bring your mind back to the body, to the consciousness, to the here and now, seems to go against the general rhythm of expanding and going out with the breath. It seems to be directly contradictory. In right effort, you are not bringing your mind back in such a deliberate way. Instead, you are simply bringing your mind back from the dream world into reality. You are breathing and you are sitting—that is what you are doing—and you should be doing that completely, fully, and wholeheartedly.

Sudden Flash: The Abstract Watcher

There is a way to bring your mind back, which we might call the "abstract watcher." The abstract watcher does not have an aim or goal; it is just mind being aware of itself. In mindfulness of effort, there is a sudden flash of the watcher's being there. At that point, you don't think in terms of getting back to the breath or trying to get away from thoughts. You do not need to have a concrete and logical mind that repeats to itself the purpose of sitting practice. You don't need any of that. Instead, there is a general sense that something is happening here—and you are suddenly brought back. Without even a name or an idea why, how, or where, there is a quick glimpse or change of tone. That is the core of mindfulness of effort.

Mindfulness of effort cannot be manufactured. It comes along when there is discipline, which sets the general pattern of the sitting practice. Once you have the attitude or idea of discipline, then there's something that reminds you: *that! that! that!* "That what?" and "What is that?" no longer apply. Just *that!* So the mindfulness of effort triggers an entirely new realm of thinking, a new state of consciousness that brings you back automatically to sitting practice. It brings you back to the mindfulness of breathing and the general awareness of well-being.

Right effort is instant effort. You could call this sudden kind of effort "leap," "jerk," or "sudden reminder." You could call it "amazement," or "sudden, abrupt amazement." It could also be referred to as "panic," or "panic without conditions." It is unconditioned panic because it comes to you and changes your whole course. The idea is not to try to maintain that sudden instant of mindfulness, to hold on to it or to cultivate it, but to get back to the meditation. Rather than nursing the reminder or entertaining the messenger, you should relate to what the messenger has to say. That sudden flash of effort, or instantaneous reminding trick, is universal to all practices of meditation, from hinayana practices up to the highest level of tantra. Therefore, effort is the most important point in the practice of meditation.

The trick of bringing your mind back does not only apply at the time of sitting meditation; it also applies to postmeditation experiences, or meditation in action. It applies to day-to-day living. In the case of eating, for instance, you don't meditate on the breathing while you are eating—you just eat. When that flash comes up, you relate with the food. In daily life, that sudden jerk happens constantly.

Mindfulness of body creates the general setting, bringing meditation into the geography of your life. Mindfulness of life is about making a personal relationship with the meditation practice. Mindfulness of effort makes both the mindfulness of body and the mindfulness of life more valid and workable. With mindfulness of effort you are clearly on the path. Effort is like the wheel of a chariot, which connects the chariot and the road. It's like the oar in a boat, which connects the boat to the water. Effort is the connection that makes things move forward and proceed. So mindfulness of effort—the sudden reminder or sudden jerk of mindfulness—is extremely important for the practice of meditation.

The sudden jerk of effort is not about improving your meditation, but about bringing it back to the ground, sitting on a cushion and breathing. With that sudden jerk, you are meditating properly; without it, you could be sitting for five hours a day and find that you had actually gotten back to your breathing practice only fifteen minutes during the whole period. Instead, you were reading your own autobiography and doing all kinds of other things.

You cannot bring about mindfulness of effort just by hoping a flash will come to you and you will be reminded. You cannot leave it up to that flash of effort to just happen to you. You have to set up some kind of general alarm system, so to speak, or general atmosphere of effort. That atmosphere of effort is important. You need to be diligent and not have the faintest notion of looking for any form of entertainment, none whatsoever. You have to give something up. Unless you give up reservations, it will be virtually impossible to develop instantaneous effort or to have it dawn on you. So it is extremely important to have respect, appreciation, and the willingness to work hard.

You need to understand the virtue and importance of effort. Diligence is an extremely powerful thing. If you are willing to give birth to such an inspiration, or if you have that conviction already, then that spontaneous, abstract flash of effort occurs more easily. In terms of the flash, you have to develop the sense that you are completely possessed and haunted, that you can't get rid of it, rather than that you have to cultivate it—which is an entirely different approach.

In the mindfulness of effort, appreciation is said to be similar to falling in love. When you are in love with a person or care for a person, your whole attitude is open toward that person. You get a very sudden abstract flash of your lover as being *that! That* is what first comes into your mind. Later you might ponder it, enjoy your daydreams, or entertain yourself by thinking about that person in detail, but those are afterthoughts. The idea is that first there is this jerk. You don't have to figure out where it came from; it just happens to you. You don't have to figure out, "Because I love this person, this thought occurred to me." You don't have to say that—it is in your *being*. You are in the state of love, rather than being in love with somebody. It is almost as if you were in love with yourself. There is always such a result with openness: something flashes. It is like a bubble rising in the water. In the mindfulness of effort, sudden flashes of *that* and *me* happen.

In the Buddhist tradition, the two main analogies for right effort are that of a person in a love and a hunter. A hunter hunting for animals doesn't have to think of a stag or a mountain goat or a bear or any particular animal—he is looking for *that*. As the hunter is walking, if he hears a sound and senses the subtle possibility of finding an animal to shoot, he doesn't think of which animal he is going to find—just the feeling of *that* comes up. Anybody in any kind of complete involvement—at the hunter's level, the lover's level, or the meditator's level—has that same kind of openness. Such openness brings about sudden flashes, an almost magical sensation of *thatness*—without name, without concept, without idea.

That openness is the most important aspect of effort—awareness happens afterward. Within openness there is an instant flash of effort, concentrated effort, and awareness follows. Having disowned that sudden experience, awareness occurs very slowly and brings things back to level. If you are able to relate with this sudden mindfulness of effort, then you have no problem as to where you are coming from—you came from somewhere. That is what I mean by disowning the experience. You do not entertain the messenger and you do not have to find out where you came from. Instead you could be like a snowflake released from the clouds, just about to come down onto the ground. You have no choice: you are going to land on the ground in any case. It feels very real.

Ordinary Effort versus Mindfulness of Effort

One of the problems with ordinary effort is that it becomes so dreary and stagnant. Ordinarily, any effort we apply to ourselves has to rely on subconscious verbalizations, such as "I must go and help somebody because it is half-past one" or "I must watch such and such in case anything happens." Ordinary effort is based on thinking, "It is a good thing for me to perform this duty." Duty is always verbalized. Though the speed of our conceptual mind is so fast that we do not even see the verbalization, the content is clearly felt, so the effort is still conditioned by thought. That makes things very boring and extremely unsuccessful in the long run.

In the case of a temporary job or waiting for your retirement, it might be okay to apply such verbalized conditioned effort. You might win a gold medal. But meditation is a life's work. You cease to sit and meditate in this life when the last breath runs out of your body on your deathbed. If meditation is your life's work, you have to apply mindfulness of effort constantly, not taking any vacations. If you rely on ordinary effort, your meditation practice becomes so stupid and confused that you wonder why you are doing such a thing. You wonder why on earth you started this in the first place. All kinds of confusions begin to pop up when you use the wrong type of effort. It confuses you and makes you extraordinarily resentful, and your practice becomes aggravating and uninteresting.

Don't misunderstand this. I don't mean that right effort will make your meditation interesting or entertaining. I mean that mindfulness of effort will keep things completely balanced. You begin to appreciate your practice, rather than enjoy it in terms of pleasure. Abstract effort takes place in a fraction of a second, without any name or idea attached to it. It is a jerk, a sudden change of course. The rest of one's effort is like a tortoise's walk: going slowly, step-by-step, and observing the situation around you.

At this point, the notion of patience comes in. Patience does not mean putting up with problems or bearing pain; it is the effort to maintain non-aggression. That is the definition of patience: maintaining nonaggression. Aggressiveness brings up the attempt to develop productivity through sitting practice. It brings evaluation, the attempt to gain something that will act as an encouragement, landmark, or achievement. The purpose of patience is to overcome such achievement orientation, or aggression. However, you can't be completely without goal orientation. You can't even open your mouth without it; it is an ongoing energy. With mindfulness practice, if you add in a spiritual implication, you create a greater goal, which is a greater problem. So you should be simply mindful, purely mindful, with nothing further being implied.

CONTINUITY OF EFFORT

The Sanskrit term for working hard is *virya*. In Tibetan it is *tsöndrü,* which is commonly translated as "energy." However, tsöndrü is not energy alone; it is applying energy, being hardworking. As has been said in the shastras, or commentaries on the Buddhist teachings, being hardworking is based on developing the prajna of virya; it is based on developing appreciation or joy in the practice. If there is less effort to *create* effort, then effort becomes self-existing. Such effort stands on its own two feet rather than needing another effort to trigger it. If you need to trigger it, then the whole thing is manufactured.

Exertion, or virya, is the unceasing interest in sitting practice and in awareness practice in general. In mindfulness practice, problems such as sloppiness come from always looking for the right way to do the whole thing. You think that such problems are there because you are doing it the wrong way, and that if you find the right way, everything is going to be okay. You think you will have smooth meditation, smooth awareness, and a smooth life. However, looking for alternatives is itself the problem. Exertion is nondiscriminating. You just push everything into that area and you go along with it. It is like driving on a wet highway: you disregard all the signposts, all the road marks, all the different transports you might pass by—you just keep driving.

That nondiscriminatory approach of exertion does not mean that a person has to be somewhat dull or dumb, or transform into a tank. It is a question of continuity: steadiness is very much necessary. The point is that mindfulness practice requires a lot of work, a lot of energy, effort, and surrendering. It is based on the recognition that a working base does exist, and one doesn't have to look for another, better alternative. You regard the whole thing as an ongoing journey, which has already begun. In that context, a little progress toward the goal is by no means a big deal. So exertion has to be a constantly ongoing process. Effort is not pushing out, nor holding on to, bare attention to what is happening—you just keep going.

Not Looking for Entertainment

Effort means that you are not looking for entertainment, but you can entertain yourself through the very non-entertainment-inspiring quality of sitting meditation. You appreciate not having lavish, resourceful entertainment; therefore, you feel completely secure and grounded with your own boredom. This is particularly workable if you have developed a regular daily, weekly, or monthly practice schedule, because then you begin to find it easy to relate with strenuous effort. That approach may be subtly entertaining, but it isn't entertaining as far as sowing further karmic seeds of wandering mind, frivolousness, and confusion. The whole thing is interconnected. By developing a regular physical routine, you can bring about a psychological change. You experience a glimpse of awareness coming to you.

The problem with entertainment is not only that you are entertained, but that you become weakened, softened, unable to handle situations. One entertainment makes you addicted to the next entertainment, so you become unable to face whatever pain or suffering comes up. That is what is traditionally known as bad karmic creation. It is regarded as bad karma because it sows further karmic seeds, and it encourages further involvement with the samsaric world. You are not able to cut the root of samsara. Any practice without effort, any practice based on impatience, leads to the creation of further karmic imprisonment. So effort, particularly the effort of the third foundation of mindfulness, is extremely important.

Meditation does not have to be painful or pleasurable; it could be either. Any struggles involved—with your breathing, your awareness, your body, or with keeping track of thoughts, excluding thoughts, or including them—are part of the whole show. One cannot say that problems such as mental chatter are valuable or not valuable—they are part of sitting. So there's no problem.

I think there is a need for humor about practice. If you take everything too seriously, then it becomes something entirely other than the path. Rather than eliminating karma, you are producing karma. The path is supposed to eliminate karmic causality, so there is a need for softness. On the whole, what we are trying to do is to be straightforward with ourselves. You cannot cut off whatever you experience, like a finger. You can't reject yourself like that. If there is a feeling of well-being, a big scope, then such struggles are just landmarks. So hinayana practice automatically includes larger thinking.

Meditation is a discipline. You do not have to be subtle or delicate about it. You could just do it in a very peasantlike way. You sit and breathe. Gentility does not apply. That's why it is so workable right at the beginning. Breathing is a very integral part of you. As long as you are working with the breathing, there will be a quality of alternation, rather than fixing your mind on one thing. It is quite different from visualizing a pink lotus with diamonds on it. Because neither the diamond nor the lotus breathes, there is no energy in that relationship.

Effort is all-pervasive throughout the four foundations of mindfulness. Although the four foundations indicate levels of practice, in terms of the technique there is no change at all, none whatsoever. Working with the four foundations is like making introductions: you introduce the person first; then you introduce the family of the person; then you introduce the town the person is living in; then you introduce the country the person is living in. The mindfulness of body introduces you to what actually happens in your experience of body and breathing. The foundations of life, effort, and mind introduce more and more large thinking. So studying the four foundations is a way to create a total picture of mindfulness.

42

Mindfulness of Mind

The transcendental watcher purely looks at the present situation. It does not speculate about the past or future, but purely looks at what is happening in this moment. That sort of heedfulness of what is happening at this very moment is the purpose of the fourth foundation of mindfulness.

T HE FOURTH foundation of mindfulness, mindfulness of mind, is the self-conscious awareness of what is happening to us as we sit and meditate. This awareness brings up all kinds of choices and directions. Mindfulness is often referred to as watchfulness, watching what is happening, but that is a misunderstanding. Mindfulness is being watchful, rather than watching. Mindfulness of mind has a quality of intelligence, rather than being a purely mechanical process. It has both light-handedness and balance. It is like opening the windows and doors a little bit to allow in the freshness from outside.

Without mind, you cannot meditate or develop balance; without conflicts of mind, you cannot develop anything at all. So the conflicts that arise from the mind are regarded as part of the process. At the same time, however, those conflicts are being controlled, to the degree that you come back to the technique of mindfulness of the breath. Everything could be worked with in that way. The point is to maintain your discipline so that you are not constantly lost in daydreams, but at the same time you keep a quality of freshness and wakeful mindfulness.

Different temperaments bring different approaches to the practice of meditation. People's approaches to meditation may also vary due to their

changing moods. Some people are extremely orthodox and in fact dictato-
rial with themselves; some are extremely loose, just hanging out in the
meditation posture and letting everything go through; some people are
fighting back and forth between those two problems, not knowing exactly
what to do. But no matter what the approach, it is necessary to maintain
a sense of freedom.

The definition of mindfulness of mind is being with the mind. When
you sit, you are there—you are being with your mind. You are being with
your mindfulness of body; you are being with your mindfulness of life;
you are being with your mindfulness of effort; and you are being with your
mindfulness of mind—all at the same time. You are being there. You have
mindfulness of presence, accuracy of presence. If you are not there, you
might miss yourself; but that could be a double take, in that realizing you
are *not* there means you *are* there, so you are brought back to square one.

One Dot at a Time

Mindfulness is a very simple process, but unfortunately, explaining that
simplicity requires a lot of vocabulary, a lot of grammar, and yards and
yards of audiotapes. However, it is a very simple matter. Meditation concerns you and your world—nothing else. It doesn't particularly concern
enlightenment, and it doesn't concern metaphysical comprehension. In
fact, it doesn't particularly concern the next minute or the minute before;
it only concerns that very small area where you are. Usually we operate on
a very small basis. We may think we are great. We may think that we cover
a large area, make history, and have a future—and here we are in the "big
deal" present. However, if we reduce ourselves into grains of sand and
look at ourselves this very moment, we see that we are just little people
concerned with this dot of existence called *nowness*. We operate one dot
at a time, and mindfulness of mind approaches things from that angle.
You are being there and approaching yourself on the very simple basis
of *this*, which doesn't have many dimensions or too much perspective. It
is one simple thing. That is what is called austerity. If you work on that
basis, it is possible that you will begin to see the truth of the matter—what
mindfulness really means.

People may think of meditation as getting into a state of trance, and
being so completely high and so absorbed in such a state that you are
uncertain whether you are coming or going, existing here or somewhere

in outer space. It is actually knowing what is happening that makes the difference between that idea of meditation and this very realistic one. That is why the fourth foundation of mindfulness of mind plays an extremely important role. With mindfulness of mind, you keep track that you are sitting on the meditation cushion, working on the breathing and on the upheavals of the emotions and energies. All sorts of things happen: they come and go; they pass by; they have their own energies evolving. So knowing what is happening is regarded as extremely good and necessary. It is an integral part of mindfulness practice. You could relate to mindfulness of mind straightforwardly and easily as uncomplicated consciousness, which takes care of what is happening at this very moment—just simple, ordinary thinking. That consciousness has its root in the primordial mind, but it is not interpreted that way in the hinayana literature. It is simply described as that which is able to take notice of what is happening.

Mindfulness of mind is a very personal experience and is very revealing. Such experience is your experience alone. You might be tempted to share it with somebody else, but then it would become that person's experience. And you cannot make it your experience and their experience jumbled together, because people have different experiences of reality. Dictators have tried to jumble people's experiences together to make one big concoction that could be controlled by one person. But they have failed in their attempts to make such a pizza.

In sitting practice or awareness practice, you are not trying to solve the problems of all kinds of dimensions, but you are looking at one situation, which is very limited. It is so limited that there is no room to be claustrophobic. It is precise. It is there. If it's not there, you missed it, you didn't get it—and if it's there, it's there. That seems to be the pinpoint of mindfulness of mind: simplicity, up-to-dateness, and directness.

Perception is immediate, and we perceive only one thing at a time. By constantly applying mindfulness to that one-shot mental perception, you get a complete picture: that is happening, that is happening, that is happening. There is no escape. Even if you try to escape, this is also a one-shot deal that it would be easy to focus on: you could be mindful of your escape; you could be mindful of your sexual fantasy or your aggression fantasy.

One thing at a time always happens. "I think. I think I hear a sound. That's it—I hear. I think I smell scents. I think I feel hot. I think I feel cold"—things always happen at that level. Therefore, mindfulness of mind is recommended, as it approaches things very precisely and directly. We tend to think that we are so clever that we could approach everything from the back door or from the loft, and prove ourselves to be intelligent, resourceful, cunning, and shifty. But somehow that doesn't work. When you think you are approaching things from the back door, it is rather that you are already at the back door, so there is nothing to approach. If you think you are approaching things from the loft downward, you are already in the loft. All of you is up there, so there's nothing to go down to, nothing to invade and control—nothing at all. It's a one-shot deal, which is always taking place. Things happen once, at one level; therefore, mindfulness of mind is applicable. Otherwise, if mind had eight personalities or ten personalities and was all over the place, it would be difficult to control and difficult to work with.

We are approaching practice in a very simple and basic way, which seems to be the only way that it can apply to our experience of what we actually are. We don't have the illusion that we can do a hundred things at one time, or concern ourselves with "While I'm doing this, something else is happening. What should I do?" You could have the illusion that you are conquering the universe by multiplying yourself into a hundred personalities, but that's like a dream state. You have actually fallen asleep. It doesn't happen that way. While you are doing this, you are doing this. If something else happens, you are somewhere else. Two things cannot happen at once. Your journey back and forth may be very speedy, but even then you are doing one thing at a time. You are jumping back and forth rather than being two places at once, which is impossible. Mindfulness of mind slows down that fickleness.

ENDURANCE

Mindfulness of mind is not exactly a discipline; instead, it is the end result of mindfulness practice. Mindfulness of effort could be said to be the gardening that brings it about. So mindfulness of mind is the result of strict discipline. It is the result of forbearance, endurance, and continual practice, the result of not quitting because of irritation or physical and psychological discomfort. Mindfulness of mind is a result of constantly keeping up your practice. You continue to practice whether it is raining or snowing, hot or cold, whether you are depressed or excited, satisfied or frustrated, hungry or full. The meditator should be like a rock in the mountains: a rock is never tired of being a rock. It lives through the snows, the rains, and the four seasons. Unless you have that same kind of endurance, you cannot put into practice the techniques of mindfulness or develop ideal mindfulness. Such techniques are not trickery; they grow out of the practice itself. From forbearance, patience, and constant sitting come suggestions on how to improvise your sitting practice in the direction of mindfulness of body, mindfulness of life, and mindfulness of effort.

When we hear descriptions of all the meditative experiences that might occur to us, but nevertheless did not, we might begin to wonder whether we have been cheated or did not receive the complete methods. But it could be that we did not get into the practice rather than that we were cheated. It is total commitment that brings about an understanding of the real meaning of the four foundations of mindfulness. You may want to surrender your ego, your hang-ups, your problems, and commit yourself to the discipline with exertion. But often when you give in to a discipline, you begin to pick up something else. That is not quite surrendering. In the case of mindfulness of mind, surrendering means being on the dot. You are even surrendering any notion of surrendering. There is nothing but just this—this existence. Such surrendering is completely unfabricated and genuine.

Transcendental Watcher

Mindfulness of mind is based on a somewhat glorified watcher—a transcendental or divine watcher, as opposed to an ordinary watcher. The term *divine* does not mean that a foreign agent is coming to help us, but that a superordinary watcher supersedes the ordinary watcher. The ordinary watcher is simply the state of consciousness that watches what is happening within us, takes note of it, evaluates it, and tries to compare whether it is good or bad, should happen or shouldn't happen. The ordinary watcher has feelings of fear, aggression, impatience, and all kinds of things mixed up with its ordinary watching. In contrast, the transcendental watcher is simple self-consciousness. It is not clumsy self-consciousness that feels me-ness, bigheadedness, and a faint element of embarrassment. It is simply being aware and conscious of what is happening, completely and totally. The superordinary watcher is able to see what is happening while the application of awareness of breathing is taking place. Knowing intelligently what is happening is still not complete freedom from the point of view of mahayana or vajrayana; nevertheless, it is the only way to develop the potential of prajna, or discriminating-awareness wisdom.

The best way you can begin to practice this is to be aware of what you are doing. There's no other way than that. From there, you begin to develop more space. Being aware of what you are doing does not have to become heavy-handed. You can just do it. Just be aware of what you are doing. Just *be* there and then disown: touch and go. You don't have to utilize that experience for something spiritual or metaphysical. For example, you might see that you are washing your dish. You see it. That's it. Disown it. Don't cling to it. Just continue. Don't break your bowls and plates; do it properly. Then look at yourself doing it properly. Go ahead and see yourself rinse them and put them into the cabinet. Just look at yourself. Look! That is all the mind can accommodate at that time. If you try to add something else, you will probably lose your grip or miss a speck of dirt. We are not secularizing mindfulness by doing this; instead, we are creating sacredness out of the secular. Whatever you are doing, such as driving, using the computer, or buying postage stamps, does not have to be a religious act—but whatever you do is dignified.

Effort comes into practice at the beginning and at the end—and during, occasionally. It is not that you have to strain to hang on to your effort and push yourself. A journey back and forth is taking place, rather than effort constantly being maintained. Otherwise there is no practice, and the whole thing becomes a big deal of effort all the time. There's no experience, no meditation, just effort. You are being effortful rather than actually meditating. So in meditating, something other than effort is happening: an alternating, shifting situation is taking place.

If you are one-hundred-percent effortful, you blow the whole thing. There's nothing left but a lump of tense muscle sitting in the middle of a field. If you are kneading dough and you knead too hard, you no longer have dough in your hand, you are just pushing on the board. So in working with the dough, you have to make some compromises. Otherwise, your effort ruins the whole thing. It doesn't work.

At the beginning, pushing yourself to the practice takes effort. During the practice you occasionally check that you are still keeping up with it. You may try to make effort continuous and solid, like a pipe running through the ground, but it is not solid, it is pulsating. In the end, you decide to deliberately let go of that particular project. So effort in the

Buddhist tradition of meditation is based on an enormous trust in imper-manence. Nothing is continuous, but just let it be that way. Death and birth are taking place moment to moment. Let us work with that rather than work toward eternity.

This particular technique of Buddhist meditation allows a certain amount of subconscious gossip. Such gossip is not at the level of repeating or replaying events of the past or expectations of the future; it is simply taking note of what is happening at this very moment. It is keeping track of the nowness. That much gossip seems to be necessary at this point. We cannot expect complete perfection without any thought process or thought movement at all. If we try to do so, we are inviting the further confusion of real subconscious-gossip. We are engaging in fistfights with ourselves while we are sitting. In mindfulness of mind, mind is that which knows, that which takes note of what is happening. While still being fully mindful and steady, ongoing and patient, it is keeping track of the sitting practice of meditation and the techniques that have developed.

Temporary Meditative Experiences: Nyam

In Jamgön Kongtrül's writings, there is a very useful description of the various experiences that happen in one's state of mind in mindfulness practice. He describes these as experiences, rather than realizations, because they are temporary. A realization is something that stays with you as a result of having practiced meditation, whereas experiences are temporary. Real, solid realization is like a mountain, whereas experience is like a mist over the mountains. Such temporary experiences could either be regarded as interruptions or as adornments. However, if you reject them, you are feeding them and turning them into demons. The Tibetan word for this type of experience is *nyam*, which means "a temporary flash of experience."

Temporary experiences, or nyam, can be experienced not only in sit-ting practice, but during everyday life as well. So in eating, sleeping, work-ing, reading, or whatever you are doing, there should be bare attention to what is happening. The way to do that is not by making yourself stiff, or holding on to awareness and mindfulness while you cook or while you work, but by a sudden flash of awareness. That sudden flash of awareness could be repeated, but whatever happens after that, you disown. In that way, you don't find everything becoming rigid. There is a reminder of now, a flash of awareness of now, and then you let things flow. That practice plays a very important part in everyday life. In fact, awareness practice is more useful and workable in everyday life than in formal sitting practice, because sitting practice is an artificial situation. In sitting practice, there's nothing to struggle with because everything is already set up, whereas in everyday life, there is struggle. There is a light touch of that and this—a dichotomy—which constantly reminds us to recollect a sense of being.

Five Basic Nyam

There are five basic nyam. In addition to these five, there are three further, more fundamental categories of nyam, making eight altogether. All eight of these nyam are temporary as opposed to permanent. The first five nyam are experiences of temporary physical or psychophysical sensations, rather than more fundamental states of being, or states of mind.

BROOK ON A STEEP HILL. Within the first set of nyam, the first nyam is the speed and movement in your mind, which is like a brook on a very steep hill. The first nyam is very busy, like water rushing down from the hills with no turbulence, none whatsoever, just like a pipe running from a gravity feed.

TURBULENT RIVER. In the second nyam, your relationship with your mind is like a turbulent river in a gorge between two rocky valleys. This river has lots of rocks with waves hitting all kinds of big stones. The second nyam has an appreciation of its existence. The turbulent river hitting those rocks reemphasizes the waterness of it, whereas the rushing brook is very speedy, very fast, but also quite nonchalant.

SLOWLY FLOWING RIVER. In the third nyam your mind is like a slowly flowing river. The thought processes that go on in your mind have become familiar and easy to live with. You are familiar with what's happening with your practice, so there are no particular problems and no particular speediness. It is smooth, like a big river slowly flowing.

OCEAN WITHOUT WAVES. The fourth nyam is the experience of absolute stillness. It is an experience of meditative absorption, which is like an ocean without waves.

CANDLE UNDISTURBED BY THE WIND. The fifth nyam is somewhat extra. It is a reconfirmation of the accomplishment of the fourth. That is, the fifth nyam confirms that what you have experienced as stillness is real stillness, like a burning candle undisturbed by wind.

If you look at these experiences from the ordinary point of view, you might think the fourth nyam is nicest, the third is nice, and the others are undesirable. But in actual fact, they are all temporary experiences, so all of them are the same. They are just experiences that occur in your state of mind, rather than one state of mind being higher or more spiritual than another. So there are no differences, none whatsoever, absolutely not! They are all just temporary experiences.

Three Fundamental Nyam

The second set of nyam is more fundamental, in a sense. These three nyam denote the progress you are making, although the experiences themselves are by no means permanent. You are still not arriving at, or achieving, a permanent state of realization. These temporary experiences are the landmarks, somewhat, of one's growth, one's spiritual path, and one's meditation. However, it is very tricky if you try to re-create them. They are temporary, so you can't hang on to them. That would be like seeing a signpost on the highway saying "New York City," and thinking you had gotten to New York City already, getting out of the car and settling down at the bottom of the signpost.

BLISS OR JOY. The first of the three fundamental nyam is bliss, or joy. In Tibetan it is dewa. You are completely refreshed, like after a long day of skiing when you have had a hot bath, a good dinner and good wine, and you are settling down to bed. It is completely refreshing, and there is a feeling of absolute well-being. Physically, tingling sensations and pulsations may happen in the body. Psychologically, there are little twinkling flashes of light and joy, and feelings of being good, extremely cheerful, and highly inspired. In everyday life, you might feel that you can do anything you want, and do it beautifully. Whatever work you are doing, whatever handicraft you are doing, all of it is inspired.

In comparison, in the second foundation of mindfulness, mindfulness of life, the quality of well-being is not all that dramatic. It is just a sensation of being, of having a body and some kind of ground. You experience a much more solid sense of well-being and security based on the inspiration of the teachings.

In the first fundamental nyam, the experience of bliss is romantic and flimsy. It has a flowing quality. The only solidity would be if you were self-perpetuating it and you began to feel that it was ongoing. In sitting practice, your experience is a tremendously pleasant one of radiating love and kindness to everyone. It feels extraordinarily rewarding to sit and practice, and you feel that you are worthy to be here. The first fundamental nyam includes all those extraordinarily good and absolutely splendid feelings. However, the experience of bliss could be an obstacle if you regard it as permanent. If you feel that everything comes along very easily, thoroughly, and smoothly, there is no room for effort. It is like moving from the mountains to an apartment, where everything is automatic and easy. It begins to make you very impatient and soft. Therefore, you have to come back to the fourth foundation of mindfulness practice, the mindfulness of mind.

LUMINOSITY. The second fundamental nyam is luminosity. The Tibetan term *selwa* means "luminosity," "brilliant light," or "clarity." However, luminosity does not mean that you literally see a brilliant light; it means that you are able to work with a tremendous amount of energy. You are able to create a link between your body and mind, a link between the psyche and your physical existence. It is as if you were the mechanism to run the universe. You create the link between that and this. You feel very able, extraordinarily able, in the sense that you could order the universe. It is not as abstract and joyful as the first fundamental nyam, but it is more industrious. It is pragmatic in that you are able to handle anything that comes along, without disjointing the experience. You are able to make things workable. There is tremendous confidence and light, a farseeing quality, panoramic vision.

NONTHOUGHT. The third fundamental nyam is called mitokpa, which means "nonthinking," or "without thought." This does not refer to a complete state of being without thoughts, but rather to a quality of stillness. There is a quality of solidity and stillness that does not want to move. Any experience that occurs in your state of mind is very still and solid. Nothing happens.

This nyam could bring tremendous depression. You may feel that you are almost going backward, that you are stuck somewhere, with nothing happening. Everything is getting very monotonous and repetitious. It is difficult to summon energy. Even a suggestion of moving outward is too tiring to think about. You just want to stay in one spot. You may feel drowsy and faintly aggressive. At the same time, this nyam could lead to a state without thoughts. As you sit, everything is so smooth and ordinary. In this case, you are not excited or depressed. There are no thoughts, no irritations. When the end of meditation occurs, you find it very easy to stop. You are not getting into a trancelike state of meditative absorption, but there is a quality of stillness and solidity.

Like the first five basic nyam, these three fundamental nyam are also temporary experiences. They can be perceived as temporary by mindfulness of mind, that self-conscious awareness. The idea is not to dispel these experiences nor to cultivate them, but just to acknowledge them: "This is happening. This is happening. This is happening." You do not have to try to pigeonhole or categorize. Instead, whenever any extraordinary experience occurs, you could relate with it simply as a temporary experience, or nyam. That seems to be the point.

Further Thoughts on Nyam

There is a story about the great Kagyü meditation master Gampopa experiencing such nyam when he was studying with the yogi-poet Milarepa. He kept running back and forth between his cave and his teacher Milarepa's cave, reporting all the experiences and visions that he had. And Gampopa was very tricky: when Milarepa said, "Now perhaps you should go back to your cave," Gampopa interpreted that as "Milarepa said that *now* I should go back. Every other time I went back he said, 'Go back,' but this time he said, '*Now* you should go back.' Maybe that means that the *next* time whatever occurs to me might be valuable and real, because he said *now*, which he didn't say before." But even for someone like Gampopa, such experiences were only temporary and could not be sustained.

Nyam are not quite like hallucinations or illusions. A hallucination is a misunderstanding that has become wild, which happens in three steps. First you see something and you are confused by it; then you try to redefine it; then you misunderstand it fully, get more confused, and begin hallucinating—or maybe somebody hits you on the head and you begin to see stars. Hallucinations are ungrounded. In contrast, although nyam are somewhat trippy, they are very grounded. You simply experience things in those ways. A person could feel extraordinarily sane and solid and meditative, and still experience nyam. Nyam are very direct, very immediate. You find yourself speeding; or you find yourself settled down, but with a lot of stuff still going through your mind; or you find yourself very smooth and quiet; or you find yourself completely solid, still, and vast like the ocean. A nyam is a direct experience rather than a hallucination.

The difference between the first five basic nyam and the three fundamental nyam is that the first five nyam are more temperamental. They are still involved with speed, all of them. The ordinary experiences people feel—their depressions and excitements and everything—are more or less on the level of the first five. In the last three nyam, something more is happening than purely pulsations in your state of mind. They are not permanent, but they are somewhat more solid than the first five; they are semipermanent. Experiencing these three is a mark of some effort on the path.

A lot of people are deceived by these three fundamental nyam, thinking they are permanent. Such experiences may occur to people as they go through popular intensive-training programs. At the end of such programs, everybody definitely gets something. People may regard what they experience as enlightenment, but that experience only lasts for a few days after they leave. In any kind of intensive practice, people could get to the level of these three nyam—rather than fundamentally getting somewhere.

The fourth foundation of mindfulness is the measure of intelligence that covers all our meditative experiences, and keeps track so that we will not be led astray by such extraordinary experiences. Instead, all experiences could be regarded as ordinary and workable. There is nothing sensational, nothing exciting, nothing far-out anymore. That seems to be the purpose of developing the fourth foundation of mindfulness, or the transcendental watcher. The transcendental watcher purely looks at the present situation. It does not speculate about the past or future, but purely looks at what is happening at this moment. That sort of heedfulness of what is happening at this very moment is the purpose of the fourth foundation of mindfulness.

From that perspective, memory is also a present experience. We are not literally going back to the past when we think about how our mothers used to change our diapers. That is not literally happening right now.

Instead, the present state of mind is reflecting that back; therefore, it is happening here this very moment. Memories are not recalling the past, because practically speaking, you cannot literally recall the past, otherwise you would still have your great-grandparents hanging around. Memory means that you are looking at a past version of the present mind. Western psychological traditions talk about your case history: you had a bad mother, therefore you feel wretched; you had a bad father, therefore you are too aggressive. As you struggle with your life, you build up your case history more and more, thicker and thicker. But in terms of the mindfulness of mind, that approach is questionable, because mind cannot actually have a case history. If it could, there could not be enlightenment, because that case history would be so thick. After millions and millions of billions of years of confusion, now somebody obtains enlightenment on the spot—how could it be possible? In mindfulness of mind, the point is that the present situation is a clear situation, a free situation. The present situation is freedom, as well as the potentiality of freedom. So it is very direct and simple. That is why Buddhism is sometimes said to be a humanistic approach: it is very personal.

VIPASHYANA:
THE PRACTICE OF AWARENESS

43

The Freshness of Unconditional Mind

First there is shamatha to tighten up your practice, to make it defi-
nite and ordinary. Beyond that, you try to let go of any notion of
inhibition . . . while still retaining the heart of the practice. The
precision is carried over, but a sense of freedom is added on.

VIPASHYANA REFERS to the sense of precision that could arise from
the sitting practice of meditation and slowly infiltrate our everyday
life. There are two different schools of vipashyana: the analytical contemplative way, and the nonanalytical experiential way. The analytical school
talks about the possibility of becoming more aware if you ask more questions and examine the nature of reality and your own state of mind. In our
tradition, in accordance with Jamgön Kongtrül, we talk mainly in terms
of the nonanalytical, or experiential, approach. Because of that emphasis,
the Kagyü tradition is known as the practice lineage.

Shamatha provides the ground, but too much emphasis on shamatha
practice could be a problem. It is said that one should not be attached to
the pond of shamatha, but let the flower of vipashyana bloom, like a pond
beautified by a lotus flower. Taking shelter in shamatha is a perversion of
shamatha discipline, so it is very important to convert the relaxation of
shamatha meditation into the postmeditation activity of vipashyana. Traditionally, it is said that you should try to achieve a fifty-fifty balance

between shamatha and vipashyana. Having properly regrouped your state of mind and linked it with sanity, the postmeditation experience could be a tremendous expansion toward awareness.

Vipashyana is entirely different from shamatha. Shamatha practice could be regarded as a way of quieting and pacifying the mind. It is a paring-down process that leaves us very little reference point and very little to work on except the technique itself. Shamatha is a way to quiet oneself. It is the development of peace. Having already become quiet, having practiced and achieved that basic ground of shamatha, we could expand out and extend ourselves. With vipashyana, rather than cutting down our mental perceptions, we sharpen our awareness.

Vipashyana is referred to as insight, or the seed of prajna, in that we are preparing ourselves to become worthy of listening to the teachings. Through vipashyana we can hear the teachings properly. We are able to perceive the subtlety and the depth of the teachings. That is precisely why vipashyana is an important practice: it begins to open the gate of wisdom. Vipashyana practice includes the contemplative approach of pondering the dharma intellectually, as well as the meditative practice of the development of awareness.

In the contemplative practice of vipashyana, speculative mind is used as a way of looking beyond oneself. You have certain ideas and conclusions, and through philosophical speculation you try to create further ideas and conclusions in order to transcend yourself. In Buddhist philosophy, you are venturing out into different ground than the ground that you find secure. When you find it very confusing to understand things, then rather than formulating new ideas to make sure you have some ground to stand on, the Buddhist approach is to take a further leap and create your own nest in space. That is the philosophical approach in Buddhism. It is precisely the approach of vipashyana, if not prajna.

Vipashyana awareness arises from several different conditions, but fundamentally it comes from being without aggression. The definition of dharma altogether is the absence of aggression. It is a way of dealing with aggression, and shamatha is the starting point. Shamatha brings clear thinking and slows you down, because the only thing you have to work on is your breathing. Because aggression or anger is based on speed and confusion, shamatha leads to the absence of aggression. So shamatha is the development of peace.

In order to perceive or to understand the dharma, you have to develop a state of mind without aggression, a mind based on non-ego and non-speed. Dharma being without aggression means the materials of our experience are workable and could be woven into the pattern of the path. It may seem like a tall order to be without aggression, and it may seem impossible for beginners to develop such perfection. However, even for beginners, momentary states of mind occur that have elements of nonaggression and non-ego.

EGO, GAP, AND SUDDEN GLIMPSES OF AWARENESS

The eight types of consciousness and the five skandhas are all momentary events. We develop our first skandha after a gap, and from there onward we develop the other skandhas, up to the fifth skandha, then the whole thing goes back to the gap and starts all over again. So ego is not a constantly smooth-running, highly secured situation at all—there are psychological gaps of all kinds. Those gaps allow disorder for the ego, and at the same time, allow the possibility of ego reasserting its position. In fact, a gap of non-ego goes on constantly, and within that we rebuild the ego again and again, from the first skandha up to the fifth skandha. So ego, or the five skandhas, is regarded more as fickleness than as continuity. Because of that, the application of vipashyana is possible.

Through vipashyana, we can relate with those momentary open gaps. Such gaps are unconditioned psychologically, unconditioned by dualism, unconditioned by passion, aggression, and ignorance. A gap is very sudden: it happens in a fraction of a second, about one-hundredth of a moment. However, although it is very fast, within us there is still the possibility of one-hundred-percent gap. The reason we can arouse potential prajna by means of vipashyana is because there are such gaps. Because of those gaps, it is possible to insert vipashyana, to relate with unconditional mind.

VIPASHYANA TECHNIQUE

The technique or means of developing vipashyana practice is exactly the same as in the third foundation of mindfulness, mindfulness of effort: it is sudden effort, a sudden glimpse of awareness that brings us back to the practice. The basic technique is to see the shadow, or echo, of the awareness and then disown it. When a sudden glimpse of awareness comes to you, you *be* with it—but at the same time, you disown it. That same approach is used for all practices. We should not hang on to any meditative technique or trick we might use; rather, we should take advantage of it and then throw it away. However, although you throw it away, you never lose it. It comes back to you—that's the biggest trick about it!

In vipashyana there is a new attitude toward that sudden abstract flash. In shamatha, you have a flash and then you faithfully go back to shamatha practice. In vipashyana, when you have that sense of shadow, or echo, you do not quite go all the way back, but halfway. You are making use of that flash, not trying to go right back. You don't come back completely to being absolutely one with the breathing, and you don't *bring* yourself back—however, you do come back. You are approaching it from the outer realm rather than the inner realm, although as far as the flash itself is concerned, there is no difference.

Vipashyana-type flashes of awareness have to grow out of the shamatha-type at the beginning, so early vipashyana practice will still be shamatha-like. Much later, you begin to realize that there is a different approach, which creates another type of flash—a vipashyana-type flash that is associated with the unconscious mind.

In meditation practice, you definitely need a technique to work on, such as breathing or walking. Having an ongoing technique or discipline is the basic core of the whole journey. The technique of awareness of the breathing is the epitome of being down-to-earth. You are on the earth and breathing. As long as that is going on, your attitude doesn't make all that much difference. You will be aware or mindful naturally.

AWARENESS OF BREATHING

One of the subtleties of vipashyana practice is that we can still apply exactly the same methods of meditation that we used at the beginning, in shamatha. With vipashyana, mindfulness of breathing becomes awareness of breathing. With awareness of breathing, there is a sense of precision and accuracy, but there is also accommodation, in that one doesn't have to constantly nurse the experience of being mindful. In the case of mindfulness, we still tend to trust a great deal in the messenger. The messenger brings back the message of what's happening and checks if we are being mindful on the spot; the messenger also checks on the sense of totality and of well-being. So a sense of *thisness* is still happening, rather than *otherness*. That seems to be the difference between shamatha and vipashyana. In the case of shamatha, importance is still placed on thisness. In spite of going out with the out-breath and dissolving oneself into the atmosphere, shamatha practice still belongs to the area of this, rather than to the area of other, or that.

A Sense of Atmosphere

In the case of vipashyana, there is less emphasis on *this*. There is a very subtle and very faint emphasis on some kind of security—but then the emphasis is on letting go, letting be. In vipashyana, the *other* is more important. We can afford to let go more with the breathing. In shamatha practice, we are purely relating with the verge of breathing, the outline of breathing, using a light touch. In vipashyana it is slightly more than that. It is not more in the sense of letting go of our mindfulness of breathing, or making it looser and more casual, but in the sense that our attitude to the breathing has otherness involved with it. The breathing happens not only on its own accord, but in the realm of the atmosphere around it. When we talk about otherness, we are talking about atmosphere or totality—something completely outside of our body, completely outside of our antennae's radiation.

It could be very difficult to understand exactly what we are getting into with vipashyana, but if a person has a really good understanding of shamatha practice and its own sense of space, the vipashyana practice becomes much easier to work with. In some sense, the difference between the two meditation practices is that in spite of its vision, its feeling, its inspiration, and its discipline, shamatha is very literal, whereas vipashyana is more romantic or idealistic. In vipashyana there is room for ventilation or fresh air. Quite possibly a person at the early stage of vipashyana practice who is used to shamatha practice might feel extremely guilty for doing something unkosher, but that is just a form of hesitation. It is like not wanting to undress at a public swimming pool: although there are swimming suits available and you can put one on, it is still regarded as a big deal.

LETTING GO

First there is shamatha to tighten up your practice, to make it definite and ordinary. Beyond that, you try to let go of any notion of inhibition or product of that meditation practice, while still retaining the heart of the practice. The precision is carried over, but a sense of freedom is added on. After you have practiced shamatha meditation, from then onward up to tantric practices, most of the techniques you practice are letting-go techniques of all kinds. At each stage, you think you have been letting go completely, but because of the dogma that you are involved in, you find that you have been keeping something private and personal. So as you go along, you find something to let go of constantly. With each new practice, you are learning to let go. Actually, the path is deliberately designed in that way.

Sometimes it might be necessary for the meditation master to change a student's style of practice. For instance, a student might find herself or himself in vipashyana, but feel guilty that what she or he is doing may not be orthodox enough. Students might mislead themselves. So the role of the teacher is to present a more and more loose and free style of practice. In going through the yanas, as one style of practice becomes orthodox, the teacher presents a new approach connected with the next yana, which in turn also becomes orthodox, and so on.

THE ECHO:
LIGHTNESS AND SENSE OF HUMOR

In vipashyana, as in shamatha, sitting practice relates with the breathing. As breathing is felt, you go out with the breath; as the breath dissolves, you dissolve. But there is also an echo—not exactly a moderator, but an echo. You have developed your mindfulness practice so that as you breathe out, you know you are breathing out. You are mindful of that. At the same time, you are aware of your mindfulness, so there is a kind of delayed action of going out and going out; dissolving and dissolving; space and space. There is a kind of echo, a self-existing awareness. That echo is not regarded as harmful or dangerous; in fact, there is a strong possibility that such awareness may be the seed of discriminating wisdom.

Going out and going out is a kind of shadow created by vipashyana practice. It is almost on the level of verbalization, or of feeling, "It's happening, it's happening." But it is not a confirmation; it is just a remark, a careless remark. It is simply seeing things. In other words, mindfulness is very serious—but if you have awareness with that mindfulness, you begin to see the seriousness of the mindfulness, and your mindfulness is lightened. So with awareness, your mindfulness becomes much lighter and less heavy. However, it doesn't become completely free and careless, because you are still continuing your practice, your basic training. You do not develop a completely free style of practice outside the technique. In fact, the whole process is still somewhat boring and technical. But that secondary spokesperson, or secondary awareness, allows the possibility of extending yourself to greater awareness practice.

The echo cuts the seriousness of your practice. If your basic mindfulness practice has gotten very clear and strong, and the whole thing has become too serious, it becomes self-destructive. Your honesty and seriousness get in your way. With the echo, there is a little humor. It is as if you were saying something very meaningful, and somebody kept repeating it back to you. Because somebody is making a joke out of it, your statement has less impact and is not as heavy. It is as literal as that. The seriousness of shamatha's one-shot deal is lightened by the echo.

Mindfulness followed by awareness is like settling down and having the dust come up. From a purely shamatha perspective, the element of vipashyana results in your actions not being as honest and as good as in the past. But in trying to make your practice definite, in solidifying the whole thing, you have a problem: you do not know your territory or what you are doing. However, if you have the awareness or mindfulness coming toward you, rather than you being aware of something, there is no problem. Awareness happens, and it also dies. You do not have to be aware of the breathing as *your* breathing, particularly. Even at the level of shamatha practice, you don't have to do that. The point is that breathing is happening properly. It doesn't really matter who is who or what is what, as long as there is flow taking place.

At this point, we are not discussing anything all that advanced. What we are discussing is just a light little shadow that goes along with your mindfulness, which is known as awareness practice. Meditation practice can become very awkward. The function of early vipashyana practice is to make one less awkward. As far as the meditation technique of vipashyana is concerned, it continues to be based on the coming and going of the breath. However, with awareness, we learn how to handle ourselves, to work with ourselves. Since there is a one-shot deal as well as a soft landing, vipashyana allows us to be less awkward.

44

Beyond Picking and Choosing

Whatever you do is sacred action. By sacred action we do not mean magical or God-ridden, but shamatha-vipashyana-ridden. There is always room for precision and there are always vipashyana possibilities in whatever you do. Nothing is regarded as unsuitable. That approach is very helpful. So please pay attention to everything!

V IPASHYANA IS that which enables you to see the potential for egolessness. The Tibetan term for vipashyana is *lhakthong*. *Lhak* means "superior," or "special," *thong* means "seeing"; so *lhakthong* means "seeing in a special or superior way." That is, vipashyana is seeing without personally localized ambition or ego-centered projects of any kind. Such seeing is necessary because we tend to fixate on sense objects such as sights or sounds, and put them into categories such as liking or disliking. The vipashyana experience of awareness replaces such categorizing altogether. At the same time, it keeps the precision of seeing the sights or hearing the sounds as they are. So in vipashyana, categorization is replaced by awareness.

DEVELOPING EQUILIBRIUM

In vipashyana, you are trying to develop a higher level of awareness, but in doing so you don't play deaf and dumb; you are still able to see and hear, and your reactions are still sharp and precise. In terms of sight, you see blue as blue, yellow as yellow, and red as red; in terms of sound, you hear higher tones as higher tones, lower tones as lower tones; in terms of taste, sweet is still sweet, and sour is still sour; and in terms of feeling, cold is still cold, hot is still hot. But beyond that, accepting and rejecting are not exactly removed, but nullified or neutralized. Cutting accepting and rejecting does not make you into a zombie; it makes you more capable of handling your existence. Your capabilities are heightened because you don't have any emotional carryover, and you are not upset by what you experience. Usually if you see a dreadful red, you want to see a lovely yellow; if you taste a terrible sweet, you look for something nice and sour to eat. But in this case, you are not picking and choosing in that way.

In vipashyana, the sense perceptions continue to function. A sense is picked up because you have a brain and you have a heartbeat. Your sense organs are alive, so they automatically relate with sense objects. But along with the six sense organs and their corresponding sense objects, there are also six sense consciousnesses. A sense consciousness does much more than simply relate with sense objects. It has an editorial function, almost on the level of accepting and rejecting, but not quite as extreme. It is more like an adviser to the accepting and rejecting, or the vanguard. With seeing, for example, the visual sense consciousness goes out and researches what it has seen; then it comes back and tells headquarters whether it should accept red or reject blue. You cannot just shut off the sense perceptions. Without them, you would not have any physical functions. However, the sense perceptions can be controlled, or moderated, by awareness; and the subtle consciousness associated with selecting, with liking and disliking, can be removed by means of meditation practice. As a result, you have more equilibrium.

Catching Thoughts as They Arise

This process begins with shamatha practice, with the technique of labeling thoughts "thinking." By giving thoughts a name, a reference point that doesn't go beyond the thoughts themselves, they have less fundamental value to you. You simply see thoughts as thoughts. You may think such labeling is just a psychological technique, but it has a karmic effect as well. By mentally labeling thoughts, you do not become personally involved with the thoughts, and you do not say that a thought is a bad thought or a good thought—you simply say "thinking," which nullifies good or bad, liking or disliking. In labeling, you cannot cut what has already happened;

but while a flicker of thought is happening, you can cut it, and you can make sure that the next one does not come up.

When you begin to catch thoughts as they arise, they do not have a chance to get to the level of liking or disliking, or to fall into the categories of love and hate, so they don't plant further karmic seeds or debts. Therefore, you are free. Labeling thoughts "thinking" begins to nullify karma. It is the vanguard of trying to overcome karma altogether. So labeling is a very valuable practice. In order not to sow karmic seeds, it is important to develop mindfulness. Vipashyana could be said to be the postmeditation experience that develops out of shamatha. However, cutting actions through awareness is too late. Except for sitting meditation, any action is a result of the past. Sitting practice is not a result of previous actions—it is a fresh start. So vipashyana definitely has to be combined with shamatha.

VIPASHYANA AWARENESS

With awareness in your system, you begin to attain what is known as "vipashyana heedfulness," or "vipashyana awareness." And out of that, you begin to develop continual samadhi, or the stillness that comes from being able to communicate with the fundamental goodness of the world. You see that the world is neither for you nor against you. The world is workable: it is no longer problematic, nor is it extraordinarily helpful.

Some people feel that reacting to situations is always worthwhile. Modern psychology in particular talks about building our egos. In Buddhist psychology, when we talk about egolessness, one of the big problems we run into is that modern psychologists think we are advocating some kind of zombie-ism or jellyfish-ism. Some psychologists think that when we encourage people to sit and meditate, we are encouraging them to experience complete dullness, to the extent that if somebody pinched their arms, real Buddhists wouldn't even say, "Ouch!" But Buddhist practice is not going to turn people into zombies. Far from it; it may turn you into buddhas!

Vipashyana awareness develops during postmeditation. It is offset by mindfulness practice, or sitting meditation. Your sitting practice could be concentrated into half an hour or an hour; the rest of the time, you could develop vipashyana. Whether you live in the country or the city, in order to integrate shamatha and vipashyana into your daily life, you need to properly organize your time. Vipashyana is all over the place. A city is living vipashyana. In the city, you could tune in to vipashyana very easily. You don't have to feel deprived if you live in the city, and you don't have to feel privileged if you live in the countryside. Such a dichotomy does not exist. It is all in the mind.

Developing vipashyana does not mean that you are graduating from shamatha. It is not that shamatha is only the sixth-grade level, while vipashyana is the fifteenth-grade level. Shamatha is the basic discipline of how you handle yourself in sitting practice, while vipashyana is how you handle yourself in postmeditation experiences. You could also have good vipashyana during your sitting practice. Shamatha experience builds up to one-pointedness, a pinpointed focus. Vipashyana, while still maintaining that pinpointedness, diffuses it into larger-scale experience.

Shamatha coordination comes from good vipashyana, from the vipashyana experience of synchronizing hearing, seeing, tasting, and so on. From that experience, you might be relieved to come back to your gomden and sit as a simple meditator. Some people say that it is easier to practice on the cushion, and some people say it is the other way around. I suppose more ambitious people would say that it is not workable on the gomden, and people who are more contemplative would say that it is. Milarepa would definitely say it is more workable on a gomden.

Shamatha and vipashyana work together. The Kagyü lineage often speaks of the indivisibility of shamatha and vipashyana. Likewise, the Japanese tradition talks about shikantaza, which means shamatha and vipashyana put together. You do not graduate from shamatha to vipashyana. You do not get better or worse. You do not go from anywhere to anywhere! Shamatha and vipashyana are two different situations, and each is helpful to the other.

ENJOYING THE GAP

It is important to spend time doing strict shamatha practice. However, in vipashyana the emphasis should be more on the gaps than on the sitting practice alone. But then once you have had a gap, you no longer have a gap, because by then you have analyzed your gap. You have closed your gap by realizing that you had a gap. So you have to be careful. You have to leave your gap alone. Just have a gap and relax! You can relax when you realize that you are not all that bad and not all that trapped. You are on the right path; therefore, you could relax a little bit. You could protect your gaps by not emphasizing them and by not jumping on them. If you begin to jump on your gaps, you begin to close them. Just enjoy your gap!

Usually we regard all the little things we do as incidental. As Buddhists, however, we regard everything that we do as very important—not a big deal, but important. You should practice vipashyana discipline when you walk out of the shrine hall. You should practice vipashyana when you pick up your laundry, fold your clothes, make your bed, or talk to your friends; when you write a letter to your friend, lick your postage stamp, place it on your envelope, and mail it; when you cut a slice of bread, chip off a piece of butter and smooth it on your slice of bread, break your bread, and lift it to your mouth; when you begin to open your mouth and chew it up; when you use your tongue to circulate the food in your mouth; when you swallow it and have a conversation at the same time.

SACRED ACTION AND NATURAL ORDER

Whatever you do is sacred action. By sacred action we do not mean magical or God-ridden, but shamatha-vipashyana-ridden. There is always room for precision, and there are always vipashyana possibilities in whatever you do. Nothing is regarded as unsuitable. That approach is very helpful. So please pay attention to everything!

Doing things properly has an intrinsic logic of its own, which is already established. Beyond that, we have the idea that something is good or bad; we have our personal likes and dislikes. That is what we are trying to overcome. The way things should be done, the way things work, is simply in accordance with the natural order. For instance, you don't wash your hands with coal, which makes them more black, but you wash your hands with soap, which makes them clean. In the winter there should be snow and ice; in the spring there should be rain; in the summertime the flowers should blossom. Things take place properly. It is very basic and very simple. Beyond that, there are one's likes and dislikes, and one's ideas of how things should be or how one wants things to be. We tend to jumble together doing things properly and our personal likes and dislikes. However, liking and disliking are purely the result of our passion and aggression. There is no intrinsic logic to liking and disliking beyond that.

Through vipashyana, you can experience the vastness of the world. It does not help to be self-centered in your own world; you won't be able to expand very much. You have to experience the vastness of the world you are expanding into, the world that you are about to deal with. If you were dumped in the middle of the black hole of Calcutta, for instance, how would you handle yourself? You would probably feel sorry for yourself once you were there. Curiosity would be quite good, although it might not last all that long—but having a glimpse of vipashyana provides another reference point altogether.

The merit of vipashyana discipline is that we begin to work with the neutral areas. We have the perfect opportunity for realizing awareness when we don't let hope or fear, liking or disliking, come into the picture— when we actually taste the bread and butter in our mouth without letting passion and aggression enter into it. Then eating a good piece of bread with nice butter on it does not produce any karmic seeds or debts. That is how, even as beginners, we can actually reduce samsaric possibilities and free ourselves from future karma.

We have to be very methodical. It is not all that easy to cut through karmic debts and the possibility of being born in the lower realms. We could end up in one of those realms. However, if we are able to work with situations properly and effectively, we can block the possibility of being born in the lower realms. Having done so, we can begin to prevent the possibility of being born in the higher realms as well. Finally, we can be born in Sukhavati, the pure land of Amitabha, the buddha of boundless light. We might even attain enlightenment; that's always possible.

But we have to start at the beginning, at the bread-and-butter level. We really have to earn it. We have to accomplish it. We *ourselves* have to do it. That is what is meant by nontheism: nobody is going to save you. If you are in trouble, you can't pay twenty-five pesos to somebody and say, "Father, please save me." In this tradition, nobody will say, "Yes." Instead, the Father probably will say, "Have you saved *yourself* yet?" If you can do that, then you are saved already.

45

The Art of Everyday Living

*In vipashyana, a kind of intimacy is happening with our daily hab-
its so that as we go through the day, our life is a work of art. That
is why I call vipashyana "art in everyday life." In vipashyana, we
are able to see the uniqueness of everyday experience every moment.*

VIPASHYANA PRACTICE brings an appreciation of art, in the sense
of artfulness, or how to handle ourselves in body, speech, and mind.
The practice of vipashyana includes the study of movements and interactions. As a result of shamatha practice, we develop a sense of being;
and as a result of vipashyana practice, we develop confidence in *how* to
be. Awareness practice is highly psychological: the appreciation of mind
brings an appreciation of everyday life. Vipashyana brings new material
into our life and provides a way of relating with the material that we
already have. In awareness practice, all of that could be used and worked
with, and we find that we are surrounded by all sorts of possibilities of
expressing and experiencing our artistic talent.

There is a difference between the shamatha and the vipashyana
approach to the art of living. In the case of shamatha, we are developing an acute and precise mindfulness. Although we are just touching the
verge of the breathing and there is a quality of freedom, there is still a
feeling of duty and restriction. The tension of being mindful may be very
light; nevertheless, we are still placing a demand on ourselves. In contrast,
vipashyana is based on appreciation. Nothing is hassling us or putting
demands on us; instead, we simply tune in to the phenomenal world, both

inwardly and outwardly. So in vipashyana, the idea of the artist is very important and necessary.

Through vipashyana, we begin to appreciate our surroundings in life, whatever they may be; they do not have to be good, beautiful, or pleasurable. In vipashyana, we are able to see the uniqueness of every-day experience every moment. We might be doing the same thing every day—we brush our teeth every day, comb our hair every day, cook our dinner every day—but that seeming repetitiveness becomes unique every day. In vipashyana, a kind of intimacy is happening with our daily habits so that as we go through the day, our life is a work of art. That is why I call vipashyana "art in everyday life."

You may have attended one of the many special programs that attempt to develop awareness of the body and awareness of one's surroundings. However, if you are unable to relate with and appreciate the insignificant details of your everyday life, there is a problem. Doing special awareness-practices might seem extraordinarily fruitful and liberating; neverthe-less, due to the quality of importance or seriousness you place on such experiences, there is still a dichotomy between such experiences and your everyday life. In fact, the more you feel that an experience is important and serious, the more your attention to the development of vipashyana is going to be destroyed. Real vipashyana cannot develop if you chop your experience into categories or put it into pigeonholes.

In cultivating an appreciation of everyday life, some deliberateness or watchfulness seems to be necessary. That is, you need to try to tune in to your day-to-day behavior. However, although you need effort, that effort does not have to be meaningful effort. When you try to do something very meaningful, you usually just become numb. In vipashyana, whenever you are practicing or studying, you just do it: you just sit or just study. And when you sit, you do not just sit there like a jellyfish; you exert yourself into the energy of meditation and take part in it.

AGGRESSION IS ANTI-ART

The refinement of vipashyana is related with artistic expression. To create a work of art, you need some kind of watcher; you need the awkward-ness of seeing yourself being awkward. You have no other choice. You also need a sense of humor, which makes that watcher less serious. Such humor creates the possibility of improvisation. The opposite of humor

THE ART OF EVERYDAY LIVING

is aggression. Looking at the humor of aggression could become art, but aggression by itself has no room for artistic creation.

The attitude of aggression is that everything is the same: "What's the difference? So what?" Aggression is the attitude of a street fighter. It is the outlook on life that the whole world is involved in a plot against you, and there's no point even attempting to make it workable or being involved in the details. Aggression is the seed of crudeness, as opposed to artistry. Crudeness is extremely dumb and blind, and misses the subtleties of life and its interesting points. If we begin to see an aspect of that subtlety, aggression deliberately shuts us down from being able to see further.

Aggression brings with it the idea of the needlessness of being meticulous. If you are not able to see a particular situation clearly the first time, you might need to go back a second time, third time, fourth time, and so forth. But with aggression, you are unwilling to engage in repetitious effort. Aggression kills that potential of going back; it prevents you from developing the patience to actually experience something. So we could quite safely categorize aggression as anti-art. The genuine artist overcomes aggression and impatience.

Artistic training and meditation practice both require patience and discipline. Until you realize that your discipline and training are your possessions and you could do what you like with them, you will be regarded as halfhearted. When your training and discipline are inherent and you possess them completely and thoroughly, it is then up to you how you present them. It is the same with the wisdom of the lineage: that wisdom is handed down to a particular lineage holder, but that lineage holder exercises his or her own authority as to how to present it to a particular generation.

The artistic and meditative traditions of the East have always been very orthodox and conservative, involving a long and painful training process. In the West, particularly in the twentieth century, people do not always want to go through such thorough training. But that approach is very chancy. The problem with the quick-training approach is that it is marked by impatience and aggression. Although you might start the process with a clear head about patience and aggression, you begin to be swept up by the speed. Such an approach to art does not work. Similarly, if you are a meditator, you may think that you don't have to sit for three years in retreat, but you can sit for four months or six weeks and then you are done! You think you could outsmart those great yogis who used to sit for such a long time. However, in actual fact the joke is on you, rather than

345

on the great yogis of the past. That attitude of speed and aggression, your desire to be faster and quicker than others, goes against the natural pace of the cosmos. You are so uptight, upset, and angry at the world that you want to see summer in the middle of winter. Unreasonably, you want to feel warm and see greenery and flowers. That kind of childish unreasonableness could be eliminated.

Aggression has all kinds of manifestations. There is aggression that would like to move outward, and there is aggression that would like to move inward. When you are not in an aggressive state of mind, you feel rich, resourceful, and infinitely inspired. However, when you are angry and uptight, it cuts all possibilities of spontaneity.

Your approach to meditation practice may also be based on speed and aggression. In some meditation programs, you feel you are getting into an exclusive course of some kind. The advertisement says that you are going to become a better person, happier, more creative, and so forth. The whole thing is built up and built up. That approach to meditation practice is so speedy that we could almost go so far as to say that the situation is hopeless. With genuine practice, you push yourself and follow a definite discipline, but there are no promises. When you sit, whether you get it at that moment or not is up to you—and if you don't get it, bad luck; just go and sit more. That is a very clear message.

Vipashyana Artistry

In vipashyana, there is tremendous appreciation of life and how to conduct one's life. Vipashyana practice is not only sitting meditation or meditation in action; it is a unique training in how to behave as an inspired human being. That is what is meant by being an artist from the vipashyana point of view. In vipashyana, you do not want to get hold of just one chunk of mindfulness and stick with it, but you experience the mindfulness along with its shadow and the environment around you. That vipashyana experience of being able to see the shadow of one's watcher is based on being patient.

In vipashyana, your abilities or potentials are completely opened, so art comes naturally. You don't need much inspiration, much vocabulary, or any tricks in order to create good poetry, painting, music, or other art forms. You simply express the experience you have experienced: you just say it, just play it, just paint it. When the psychological aggression is transmuted into the energy of artistic talent, you begin to realize that you can do all kinds of things—to your amazement! And once you have begun to break through that kind of backwater, there are gushes of all kinds of energies. Then since the first attempt was free, clear, and resourceful, the second, third, and fourth creations of art are no problem at all.

The vipashyana experience of art also includes relationships. It has to do with how to communicate, how to speak, how to cook, how to choose your clothes in a shop, how to select food at the supermarket—all those little details. Some people get extremely paranoid because they weren't brought up in a cultured society, so to speak, and had no opportunity to learn how to behave. Such people may get very aggressive and hufty-pufty, and come down on gentility as just being another trip. They may say they are quite happy with their crudeness, but the problem is not the need to tune in to a tradition or a particular style of eating or dressing; the problem, again, is the aggression. Gentility has nothing to do with a particular culture; rather, it has to do with your instincts being open and having the room to bring your potentialities into action.

The art of learning how to make a perfect cup of tea or the art of learning how to entertain friends is not connected simply with becoming a genteel member of society. If you link such training with vipashyana practice, it is much more than that. It has to do with becoming a bod-hisattva, the most supreme, highest-society person you could ever imag-ine. The bodhisattva is known as the great host, the ship, the bridge, the highway, the mountain, the earth—all those images deal with interactions with people. You do not have to start on such a big scale—your energy, money, space, and experience may be limited—but at least you can start on the practical level of developing your awareness of that potential or possibility. That element of gentility can be applied on the hinayana level of vipashyana practice as well.

Within vipashyana experience is the awareness that everyday life is a work of art, if you see it from the point of view of nonaggression. That point is extremely important in order to overcome not just ordinary clumsiness and crudeness, but fundamental, phenomenological clumsi-ness and crudeness. Art is not about creating charm and beauty alone—it is anything that is workable or rich. In terms of art in everyday life, or vipashyana experience, transcending aggression is the root of all the artis-tic talent one could ever imagine. Like the sword of the wisdom bodhisat-tva Manjushri, genuine art cuts the speed and the aggression of the ego.

46

Glimpses of Emptiness

Vipashyana experience and practice is absolutely necessary for a person who follows the Buddhist path and really wants to understand the dharma. Both intellectually and intuitively, vipashyana practice is necessary. You have to make an acquaintance with yourself. You have to meet yourself, to know who you are and what you are. Without vipashyana experience, you do not have any idea of who you are, what you are, how you are, or why you are, at all!

To UNDERSTAND buddhadharma, a person must meditate under the guidance of a teacher and be properly trained in vipashyana. Without an understanding of vipashyana, such discoveries as the four noble truths or egolessness cannot be completely comprehended or experienced.

Vipashyana practice is divided into various categories. In one system, vipashyana is divided into lower vipashyana and higher vipashyana. Lower vipashyana is a shamatha-type of vipashyana, based purely on concentration; higher vipashyana is more inspirational, based on such insights as discovering the four noble truths.

In another system, vipashyana is divided into two aspects: discriminating awareness and immovability. Discriminating awareness is the ability to see clearly, and through that clarity to develop definite mindfulness practice. Immovability is a kind of absorption in which awareness is constantly present and stable, and cannot move or shift. Different degrees of immovability happen in the various stages of vipashyana. Immovability is a powerful experience, based on the confidence that you have found the correct path, and therefore you cannot forget it. You finally realize that there is no other practice than this. You have been converted to vipashyana, and you have faith and trust in it.

THREE STAGES OF VIPASHYANA

Traditional texts describe three stages that are very important to understand in connection with vipashyana: *chipa nyerchö*, or "acting like an infant"; *ro-nyam* or "equal taste"; and *teshin mikpa*, or "seeing things as they are."

Acting like an Infant

The first stage is called chipa nyerchö. *Chipa* means "infant," *chö* means "acting," and *nyer* means "being closer to it"; so *chipa nyerchö* means the "acting like an infant" level of meditation experience. Chipa nyerchö is the first glimpse of vipashyana. It is like teaching an infant to walk. Chipa nyerchö develops from very intense shamatha practice, which brings up what are called "visions of emptiness."

When you suddenly stop speeding and you become absolutely still, you get a kind of backfire of speed within the stillness. Because you are so confused between stillness and speed, you create visions, or hallucinations, which do not have any substance. The Japanese Zen people call such hallucinations *makyo*. Such nonexistent hallucinations have no root or background. Things shift in front of your eyes, or you begin to see smoke passing by. You might begin to have a sense that your toes are gigantic and your body is tiny, or you have a gigantic head and a small body. You might think the ceiling is sinking above your head, or your zafu is shifting around. Your vision changes and all kinds of sounds are heard. Some people hear a complete orchestra, with singing and chanting. Different tingling sensations occur in the body. Sometimes there is terror that you don't exist.* Such experiences may seem profound, but as long as there is humor or play, I don't think they are a problem.

---

* When a student asked at this point what that experience of terror was like, Trungpa Rinpoche replied, "I suppose more or less like this," and continued to sit normally.

Equal Taste

The second stage is called ro-nyam. *Ro* is "taste," and *nyam* means "equal"; so *ro-nyam* means "equal taste." Ro-nyam is a slightly higher stage, a little bit more on the adult level. You begin to experience the four noble truths and you also begin to experience the simplicity of awareness, so although the sensorial hallucinations might continue, they don't mean anything to you. There is a quality of one flavor, or one taste. Your shamatha practice continues in a very solid way. You have developed mental stability and you are able to stay with the practice. Because you are already completely involved with shamatha, you also begin to see the simplicity and straightforwardness of vipashyana. So at the second stage, or ro-nyam, shamatha and vipashyana are combined. That combination is the goal of the Burmese meditation schools in particular. They highly recommend the second category of vipashyana as a most important experience.

Seeing Things as They Are

The third stage is called teshin mikpa. *Te* means "that," *shin* means "like"; so *teshin* means "like that." *Mikpa* is "perception," "understanding," or "knowledge"; so *teshin mikpa* means "seeing things as they are," which is known as the mahavipashyana experience. The mahavipashyana experience creates a link between hinayana and mahayana practice, in that you begin to experience emptiness, or shunyata. *Shunya* means "empty," and *ta* makes it a noun; so *shunyata* means "emptiness." You sense that you are basically shunya, or empty. Your psychological makeup, the embellishments you indulge in, and your thought process are all nonexistent. Because awareness is very direct, precise, and simple, it brings spaciousness and a glimpse of shunyata. You begin to see not only simplicity, but emptiness, or intangibility. In mahavipashyana, a quality of conviction begins to take place, a primitive shunyata experience. So mahavipashyana is a step further than ro-nyam, because with mahavipashyana you have a glimpse that you are inherently nothing—not as a meditation experience alone, but as a kind of fundamental devastation.

In mahavipashyana, there's an enormous feeling of being helped "out" rather than helped "in." You are pulled out of whatever realm you are in, into a realm, or psychological state, that is completely empty. You begin to realize that you do not have an origin, and you don't belong anywhere.

You are treading on a path that is a path in terms of experience but is no longer a concrete path, so there is a lot of fear. It is as if you are riding and you lose your grip on the reins, or as if your car begins to go by itself and the steering wheel doesn't work. Something slowly begins to take over so that the path comes to you; you don't go to the path. Practice becomes constantly apparent. It is in your mind all the time, so there is a lot of fear and a lot of concern.

But mahavipashyana experience can also lead to celebration. It depends on your attitude. If your attitude is that the world is playing a trick on you, you will complain to everybody, or at least try to find a source of complaint, so that your ground will be solid and your ideas will be appreciated. However, if you don't have that attitude of competitiveness, then realizing that there is no ground becomes a source of celebration and joy.

At this stage, the experience that you have nothing to hold on to is continual. And that experience will go on, until at a certain level of vajrayana it takes a different form, with further sophistication. However, in this case it is just the simple experience that you exist, but at the same time you do not have any ground. You have no ground because awareness is constant, and the characteristic of awareness is emptiness. Awareness does not have a portrait, a reflection, or identification. So a positive feeling of nothingness becomes very real at the stage of teshin mikpa, or mahavipashyana experience.

In mahavipashyana, it is as though you have been released. It is like catching a fly and throwing it out the window so that the fly flies away rather than being squashed on the table. The idea of release or liberation in mahavipashyana discipline is to have a glimpse of groundlessness. The basic idea is that the closer you are to enlightened mind, the more your development takes you in that direction, the more groundless you are.

In terms of the idea of egolessness, the closer you are to enlightenment, the less ego there is. Egolessness is the root of vipashyana. Since the ego provides an ongoing ground and reference point, you are losing your foundation; therefore, you are helped "out." You lose your reference point and you become thinner and thinner, so to speak. Vipashyana experience cannot be given birth to, developed, or taught unless there is some understanding of egolessness. At the mahavipashyana level, you have been introduced to the egolessness of self, and you are just about to be introduced to the egolessness of phenomena. But you haven't actually been completely introduced yet—you just have a "flu" of it.

In ordinary language, shamatha is simply the experience of concentration. It has been said in the texts that even hunters develop shamatha. By one-pointedness with the target, hunters develop their mindfulness or concentration. So you could develop a form of shamatha independent of vipashyana, but to shift from that to a Buddhist-type of concentration, or shamatha, you have to have some experience of, or feeling for, egolessness. You have a sense that there is that possibility, that it is just about to present itself to you, and you practice in that way.

Mahavipashyana is influenced by the mahayana. When you become highly trained in the hinayana and thoroughly absorbed in shamatha practice, your outlook and your experience naturally become mahayana-like. No matter which hinayana school you may be in, the various doctrinal or philosophical labels and distinctions are irrelevant as far as you are concerned.

Unless you develop vipashyana and realize the importance of wakefulness, you will have only a very distant view of vajrayana or even the higher levels of mahayana. It is necessary to have that kind of basic training and growth. So vipashyana experience and practice is absolutely necessary for a person who follows the Buddhist path and really wants to understand the dharma. Both intellectually and intuitively, vipashyana practice is necessary. You have to make an acquaintance with yourself. You have to meet yourself, to know who you are and what you are. Without vipashyana experience, you don't have any idea of who you are, what you are, how you are, or why you are, at all! So it is very important and absolutely necessary to respect the need for vipashyana experience and practice.

47

Investigating the Subtleties of Experience

Our teachers have taught us that it is necessary to conquer both
undisciplined mind and individualistic mind. Undisciplined mind
is conquered by shamatha practice; individualistic mind is con-
quered by vipashyana.

A REALIZATION AND understanding of shamatha will help you to
hear the teachings properly. When you receive instructions for practice, if you do not hear the whole thing, it is going to be very difficult for
you. It is like asking somebody for directions: if you only hear part of
the answer, you will never get anywhere. Therefore, shamatha discipline
is important in studying the experiences and practices of the nine-yana
tradition.

Vipashyana is the insight that brings you to realize things very clearly
and fully. The greater reference point of vipashyana includes both the
meditation and the postmeditation experience. With vipashyana, there
is no gap of any kind between sitting and nonsitting. Your entire life,
twenty-four hours a day, is pure awareness.

When you are completely captivated, captured on your cushion by
intensive shamatha discipline, you wonder, "What's going to happen next?
How am I going to study the dharma? How am I going to make this work
for me?" That kind of inquisitive mind and awareness is the beginning
of becoming not only a good sitter, but also a good student of dharma.
That is why prajna is important. It is the ability to separate dharmas and
to comprehend the teachings. Prajna is connected with awareness, and
awareness is a result of being perked up by shamatha.

With shamatha you develop delight and joy, as if you have just had a very good appetizer; and with vipashyana, you wonder what the actual meal will be. However, I would like to make it clear that in this case the appetizer is not regarded as a subsidiary of the main course—the appetizer is a meal in itself. So you have to pay close attention and eat your appetizer properly. In fact, the appetizer continues throughout the whole meal, in the same way that shamatha practice continues throughout the whole of Buddhist practice.

Four Categories of Vipashyana

There are four categories of vipashyana: discriminating dharmas, fully discriminating dharmas, completely comprehending dharmas, and completely investigating dharmas.

Discriminating Dharmas

The first category is being able to discriminate dharmas, which in Tibetan is *chö nampar jepa*. *Chö* means *dharma,* but in this case *dharma* does not mean teachings; it means any "entity," any "knowledge," any "knowable situation." *Nampar* means "varieties," and *jepa* means "separating"; so *chö nampar jepa* means "separating dharmas." There is so much to learn, so much to know, but you are not overwhelmed by that. You are willing to jump into the giant ocean of dharmas, the ocean of information and experiences. When you develop awareness, you are aware of all the things that are happening in your life and in your world, but you are not overwhelmed. You can handle each situation according to its own particular merit, style, or virtue. Some kind of intelligence is working in you, both during your sitting practice and when you walk out of the shrine room. You see everything clearly.

When you first begin to experience vipashyana awareness, you might be completely shocked. It is like putting on your first pair of glasses: you realize how many things you have missed. However, when you begin to see clearly, you also realize how many things are irritating, so you might prefer to take your glasses off or throw them in the wastepaper basket. You may not really want to perceive that much phenomenal reality; you feel so naked. You don't want to go all the way; you prefer to walk away from that nakedness rather than face reality. That turning away is due to a lack of awareness and a lack of mindfulness, the "ignorance is bliss" approach. In contrast, vipashyana is a natural process of brightening yourself up and seeing things clearly. And you are able to do so because you have already developed mindfulness, so mindfulness and awareness work together. Vipashyana and shamatha are fundamentally inseparable.

Fully Discriminating Dharmas

The second category of vipashyana is *raptu jepa*, which means "fully able to separate." *Raptu* means "very much," and *jepa*, again, means "separating," so *raptu jepa* means "fully separating." At this stage, having caught a glimpse of phenomenal objects, not only are you not startled by how detailed they are, but you actually want to investigate them. You become more daring in relating with your world. For instance, if you are having some fantastic private pornographic subconscious gossip in your mind, at first you are completely shocked, but then you want to find out where that visualization is coming from. So you don't just close the door; once you have seen what's in your mind, you investigate. You feel out what's happening; you experience it. You do this, not in order to fulfill your lust, but purely in order to find out where in the name of heaven and earth it is coming from. You want to find out how things occur and what they are like. You want to know what texture they have, whether solid or transitory or flighty or flickering or mushy or flowing.

Whatever occurs, the idea of this second category is that you investigate that particular phenomenon. If somebody in the street says, "Fuck you!" you investigate. What does that mean? What kind of reaction do you have? Who said it? Why did it happen? Why you? What is the environment? Is it a rainy day or a snowy day or a sunny day? You happen to hear those particular words from that particular person, and you begin to react to them, to have afterthoughts—and you look with awareness into how such situations happen. But be careful—this does not mean analyzing everything from the point of view of Freudian psychology, or trying to find out whether your fantasies represent this or that. For example, if you have an itch on your cheek, you may not know whether it's a bedbug bite or a mosquito bite or whether you haven't washed your face, but it doesn't really matter—you have an itch. With vipashyana, you are looking at dharmas directly and finding out how they arise, dwell, and disappear in your life and in your mind. That is why vipashyana is referred to simply as insight, or clear thinking. It is very clear thinking.

Completely Comprehending Dharmas

The third category is *yongsu tokpa,* which means "completely comprehending." *Yongsu* means "completely," "thoroughly," and *tokpa* means "comprehending," so *yongsu tokpa* means "completely comprehending." With yongsu tokpa, you are experiencing thoughts of a very crude nature. You experience the big ups and downs, which are very aggressive, very passionate, or very ignorant. Whether such thoughts occur during sitting practice or during the postmeditation experience, you could study them and look at them. You could exert your awareness on them.

This is not the same as being mindful of thoughts. In mindfulness practice, you are just seeing thoughts and labeling them "thinking." Here, there is a more general awareness of the presence of crude thoughts. With an awareness of the atmosphere created by your crude thought process—your passion, aggression, or ignorance—you are able to see such thoughts one by one, rather than suddenly being hit by some big thought and being completely overwhelmed. When you are surprised in that way, you may want to call for help or take an aspirin, but when you practice insight, you are not overwhelmed because you are able to dissect your emotions, to separate one from another.

For instance, when a thought of tremendous aggression suddenly occurs, you may feel overwhelmed and start to sweat, but then you apply your awareness. You look at your thoughts and you dissect them. You notice how they arise, how they dwell, and how they disappear. Even if they do not disappear, the first flash disappears, and you have the chance to see the second flash coming into your state of mind. So even if a gigantic pterodactyl runs into you, you don't just scream. First you look at it and see whether you are in a prehistoric situation or not. Realizing that you are still in the twentieth century, you say, "This couldn't happen. Where did this pterodactyl come from? How did it land in front of me? How did this happen?" You don't panic; you just examine what has happened to you.

There is a sense of decency about this. When crude emotions land on your lap and they are glaring at you, you don't just say, "Aagh!" Instead, you see them and dissect them with your vipashyana. This is possible because you have practiced enough shamatha to begin with; therefore, your mind is able to handle anything that happens. Once you have worked with shamatha thoroughly, your mind is like Play-Doh, so you have no problem working with anything that comes up—you cannot be shocked.

Completely Investigating Dharmas

The fourth category is *yongsu chöpa,* which means "completely investigating." *Yongsu* means "completely," and *chöpa* means "investigating," or sometimes "theorizing," or "studying," so *yongsu chöpa* means "completely investigating." Yongsu chöpa is a much more refined investigating than number three, yongsu tokpa, because the thoughts being seen are so minute. Completely investigating does not refer to obvious thoughts that are very easy to comprehend, but to the small, meaningless, and insignificant flickers of thought that occur. With yongsu chöpa, you also apply vipashyana to those types of thoughts.

Sometimes you will find that small thoughts are being investigated by small awareness, so it looks as if one subconscious gossip is chasing another subconscious gossip. When you find a little idea in your life being looked at by a little effort, you may think you are perpetuating the whole thing, but that's not the case. In this fourth category of vipashyana, the chaser, so to speak, has awareness. What's being chased—that little thought, or that little, little thought—could be insignificant, meaningless, and almost harmless, but we are trying to make sure that nothing gets away. We have to cover the whole ground completely, as much as we can. We have to investigate whatever goes on in our ego-mind.

The idea of looking into that level of thought process may seem small, but the practice of vipashyana is very tidy and precise. You investigate where those small thoughts come from. You might simply have a memory of your grandfather eating his sandwich twenty years ago, and you might remember how he used to slur his words while he ate his sandwich. You might remember seeing a tree on your way to somewhere or other. Meaningless thoughts like that also have to be conquered, otherwise you cannot develop discriminating-awareness wisdom. You have to apply a blanket approach to awareness.

When you practice shamatha, you are still involved with effort, hard work. Vipashyana is somewhat effortless, but it is more watchful, so in a sense you could say that it takes *more* effort. You are not allowing any gaps in your awareness—none whatsoever! When you practice mindfulness, you concentrate on one particular area, and when you stop concentrating on that one area, you relax. However, that relaxation is looked at by awareness, so the pinpoint as well as the sense of general radiation is covered completely.

Our teachers have taught us that it is necessary to conquer both undisciplined mind and individualistic mind. Undisciplined mind is conquered by shamatha practice; individualistic mind is conquered by vipashyana. Vipashyana is based on dealing with the ego—with the distant territory of ego as well as its more immediate territory. We are trying to attack our ego, mock it, conquer it, invade it, subjugate it. Individualism, or ego, means that which is not seen as a working basis for the general atmosphere of awareness. Wandering mind, confusion, and the inability to discipline oneself—all of those factors derive from the fundamental principle of ego.

What is the root of all this? Why do we practice vipashyana at all? We understand that it will be helpful to us, but why is that so? If we approach practice in the style of mental gymnastics, it is like expecting that if we do lots of exercises, our body will get in shape. But what are we getting in shape for? Why are we doing this at all, in the name of heaven and earth? It has to do with ego! So as you continue sitting and working with your basic shamatha discipline, you could add in a little bit of vipashyana, or awareness. In fact, you could practice vipashyana during all your waking hours. While you're taking a shower, while you're brushing your hair, while you're pressing your clothes, or while you're preparing your cup of tea, it would be helpful to practice vipashyana.

48

Sharpening One's Perception

Vipashyana is the heart of the buddhadharma. It sets the general tone of the psychology of Buddhism. A Buddhist has clear thinking and an objective view of the world. He or she is able to recognize and use relative logic. There is no chance that such a person will be swayed by fascinations or extremes. With vipashyana, everything becomes very precise and very direct.

W HATEVER IS knowable in the world, of either relative or transcendent nature, can be understood and experienced by means of vipashyana meditation. Vipashyana leads to a complete understanding of the knowable. This does not mean that you will become a great scholar by practicing vipashyana, but that the attitude and approach of vipashyana opens your way of thinking, so that obstacles to learning are no longer prominent.

THE SIX DISCOVERIES

There are several attributes of vipashyana experience, based largely on the intellectual sharpness developed, rather than simply on the meditative experience. These attributes develop out of the four categories of vipashyana: discriminating dharmas, fully discriminating dharmas, completely comprehending dharmas, and completely investigating dharmas. The Tibetan term for attribute, *tsölwa*, means "searching," but in this context, I thought "discovery" would be a better translation. The point is that through vipashyana, by means of hearing and seeing the dharma, you make six discoveries, or six types of tsölwa.

Meaning: Discovering the Meaning of Words

The first discovery is discovering the meaning of words, or *tön tsölwa*. *Tön* is "meaning," and *tsölwa* is "discovery," so *tön tsölwa* is the "discovery of meaning." In this discovery, you are relying more on the sense of the teachings than on the words. You develop trust in yourself as you begin to realize that you have the potential of knowledge and wisdom within you. You realize that dharma is a question of waking up, rather than painfully cultivating knowledge.

Tön tsölwa means that you have an understanding of how language works, how expressions work, and what happens when you talk dharmically. The basic point in regard to language is to have tremendous precision. You know the meanings of words; you understand the subtleties. You understand how an idea is first initiated, then described, and then understood. Interestingly, English grammar is slightly lopsided in terms of our perceptions. Suppose, for instance, you see a white horse. As far as the thought process goes, when you see a white horse, first you see the horse and then you realize the horse is white. You actually see horse-white. Likewise, you see man-good or man-bad. That is how the thought process works. However, you don't have to strain yourself to speak pidgin English. The idea is to articulate and synchronize language with your state of mind.

Tön tsölwa is connected with an interest in language and the expressions of language. It is an understanding of the grammar used to express dharmic language. Fundamentally, this means that you have an understanding of threefold logic. For instance, when you say "individual salvation," you don't just jumble the sounds together; you understand the meaning of the word *individual*, and the meaning of the word *salvation*. In this example, the ground is the individual; the path is salvation; and the fruition is that the individual is freed—therefore it is "individual salvation." If you are trying to describe the dharma, you could say "good dharma" or "The dharma is good." If you say "good dharma," that can be taken as ground or as fruition. If you say "The dharma is good," that is path. Dharma is being *qualified* by good. First we reflect on dharma, and then we realize that dharma is— What? Good or bad? Good! Vipashyana discipline allows us to ponder our thinking process and how we relate with words.

Form: Discovering the Objects of Inside and Outside

The next discovery is *ngöpo tsölwa*. *Ngöpo* means "object," or "gross thing." It is "thingness," "tangibleness." *Tsölwa* is "discovery," so *ngöpo tsölwa* is the "discovery of objects." In this discovery we learn to discriminate between our individual world and the world around us. We are discovering the objects of outside and inside. "Inside" means personal situations and emotions; "outside" means the external setup. Outside includes such things as good weather or bad weather, or the favorable or unfavorable rate of exchange from Canadian to American dollars.

This discovery is also called the "search for reality." All experiences in life, every word and every situation, involve subtleties, and those subtleties are clearly seen. Such discernment has nothing to do with paranoia; it is very relaxed. Once you have had an experience of vipashyana, of going out or expanding yourself, neurotic discrimination or paranoia no longer applies. It becomes irrelevant or useless.

Discovering the objects of inside and outside means discriminating between this situation and that situation, between introversion and extroversion. In terms of relationship and communication, you see the greater importance of going out and giving, rather than holding back. You might think this is quite a bizarre way of categorizing things, but when you work with the subtleties of the awareness process, you are able to see whether here and there are working together, whether they are synchronized or not. Then the discovery of this and that, inside and outside, becomes very powerful and important.

Characteristic: Discovering the Nature of Perception

The third discovery is the "discovery of the nature of perception," or *tsen-nyi tsölwa*. *Tsen* means "mark," "sign," or "characteristic"; it is analogous to the mark of being female or male. *Nyi* means "itself"; so *tsen-nyi* refers to how things are categorized according to their own individual existence. *Tsölwa*, again, means "discovery," so *tsen-nyi tsölwa* is the "discovery of individual characteristics." It refers to how things could be shared or not shared between yourself and others, or how things could be the first thought or second thought. For example, when you give birth to a thought—"Ha! Cup of coffee"—that is first thought. The second thought is, "How and where can a cup of coffee be purchased or manifested?" There is the thought process of journeying from here to there.

This discovery refers to the nature of your perception, how you operate your prajna. For instance, when you want to turn on a light, you first think of the switch, then you can turn the light on or off. So it goes "switch," then "light." It is the same with listening and hearing, or looking and seeing. You discover how you first perceive your world by first thought, and how that is then translated into second thought.

Traditionally, this category has to do with both private and public, almost like the previous category of inside and outside. You are not confused about basic logic, and you can figure out the origin of thought patterns in communication. As a practitioner of vipashyana, you are not completely insulted, because although at face value someone is rude or aggressive to you, you are able to look beyond that to the causal characteristics of that person's reactions.

Direction: Discovering Sides

The fourth discovery is discovering sides. The Tibetan term *chok* means "direction," or "side"; *tsölwa* means "discovery," so *chok tsölwa* is "discovering sides." Discriminating the good side from the bad side is quite ordinary: you see whether you are on the side of the dark or the light. Being on the side of the dark means that you are causing harm to yourself or others; being on the side of the light means that you are being a positive influence on yourself and others. This category is about knowing what to do and what not to do. It is about discrimination and common sense. You are able to detect that which is not suitable or a hindrance to the path, whether it is a negative or a positive experience.

Discovering sides is not based on picking and choosing, or on making yourself comfortable. It has broad vision and an unyielding quality. You are able to seek wisdom, to seek good attributes. That is, you have an allegiance, or natural instinct, as to what is right for you and what is not. You are able to tune yourself instinctively in to the appropriate situations. It is very simple. In this discovery, you are relating with the common norms of good and bad, but with tremendous wisdom and clarity.

Time: Discovering Past, Present, and Future

The fifth discovery is discovering time. *Tü* means "time"; *tsölwa* means "discovery," so *tü tsölwa* means the "discovery of time," or "not being confused by time." This is not as simple as realizing whether it is daytime or nighttime. Tu tsölwa means that time should be considered, so that what you have experienced in the past, what you are experiencing now, and what you might experience in the future are not confused. Past is past, present is present, and future is future.

You need to develop clear thinking, both intellectually and intuitively, so you are not confused by time or the duration of things. People have tremendous paranoia due to their confusion about time. For instance, you might regard what you think you will experience in the future as a present threat or problem, or because you have experienced something in the past, you might think that in the future it will happen again. There are all kinds of analogies for such paranoia. For instance, you might think that because the Second World War happened, another Hitler is waiting to do the same thing in the future. However, you could develop a clear sense of time so that what you have experienced is what you have experienced; what you are experiencing is what you are experiencing; and what you might experience is what you might experience. You could develop clarity in your experience of past, present, and future.

The instruction in a nutshell is that you could take advantage of your present situation. You have power over the present. Your future situation can be attained and achieved because you have the information and resources of the past: the past has gotten you this far, to the present; and at present, you have what you have. You understand that your future is somewhat predetermined by the present situation, and you realize what you are doing. You have inherited information, credentials, and knowledge from the past; therefore, you know how to act now, in the present, and you can attain what you might attain in the future. So the future is entirely dependent on you, whether or not you would like to put it into effect.

Because of this realization, you do not feel trapped in any way. You have confidence and dignity. You are no longer subject to the whirlpool. You no longer fear that once you jump into the rushing river, you are bound to be swept down Niagara Falls. By practicing vipashyana discipline, you are trying to get out of karmic encirclement. You are trying to cut through karmic cause and effect, so that you can realize your dignity and elegance. You can be arrogant in the positive sense because you can cut through the vicious circle of karma by applying the techniques that have been presented to you. That is the realization or discovery of time.

Insight: Discovering Knowledge

The sixth discovery is discovering knowledge, or insight. In Tibetan it is *rikpa tsölwa*. *Rikpa* is "insight," and *tsölwa* is "discovery," so *rikpa tsölwa* is the "discovery of insight." In this context, *insight* refers to scientific insight, insight into cause and effect. It refers to relative reference, the ultimate logical mind. The Tibetan term for insight is *rikpa,* and the Sanskrit term is *vidya,* which means "knowledge," and in particular "scientific knowledge." That is what we are discovering: knowledge. We are beginning to know the nature of cause and effect. In other words, we have an understanding of karma. In the simple example of planting a seed, we know that when we care for the plant, it is going to grow and develop to fruition. Insight involves faith and the appreciation of scientific discoveries. Albert Einstein could be an example of this kind of discovery. I heard that Einstein was more interested in knowledge than in cash, so he used to use his checks as bookmarks.

Vidya, like science, is based on understanding and trusting the norm of truth that exists in the phenomenal world. It is said in the texts that the knowledge that comes from vipashyana is based on understanding that fire is hot, water is liquid, and so forth. Understanding the elements of earth, water, fire, and air—that earth is solid, water is wet, fire burns, and so on—is basic science. Anything that scientists have discovered is included in the teachings, even simple things, like if you bang your head on the wall, it hurts. You might think this is the kind of lesson you get in sixth grade, and that you are above it. Nonetheless, you have to consider how much you have taken for granted, how much you have ignored, how little trust you have had in the cause and effect of circumstances.

The workings of the elements are very important. If you realize the workings of the elements, you begin to realize the workings of the cause and effect of karma as well, because they are basically the same. According to Buddhism, if you kill, you get killed. You might not have to go through the courts and receive capital punishment, but if you kill somebody, sometime in the future it will happen to you. Through insight, or vidya, we discover the truth about karma. This allows the kleshas, or confused emotions, to dry up by themselves.

APPLYING THE SIX DISCOVERIES

You could apply these six discoveries to anything in your life. As an example, in dealing with pain, the first discovery, meaning, is connected with one's psychological attitude toward the experience of pain or pleasure. Form has to do with not being deluded by your imagination, but beginning to make a connection with the reality of the pain. That is, pain is pain; the meaning of pain is pain; and the feeling of pain is pain. The characteristic, or nature, of pain is that it is threatening to one's existence. Pain may involve the fear of death, or the fear of continuing to live. All kinds of fears are involved, which provide various reference points toward the pain. With direction, you are discovering how much space pain occupies and how much space pleasure occupies. And within that space, you discover how important your body and this particular existence is to you. As for time, in relating with pain you apply time, whether it is the duration of a situation that you created yourself, or an experience that is presenting its case to you. With insight, you have an overview. You are viewing all of life, or in this example all your pain, in terms of its meaning, form, characteristic, direction, time, and insight.

The six discoveries are the result of the clear thinking of vipashyana, the result of the process of seeing very precisely. They are not something to look for; instead, they are behaviors or patterns that develop. Vipashyana is the heart of the buddhadharma. It sets the general tone of the psychology of Buddhism. A Buddhist has clear thinking and an objective view of the world. He or she is able to recognize and use relative logic. There is no chance that such a person will be swayed by fascinations or extremes. With vipashyana, everything becomes very precise and very direct.

Throughout the teachings, and in all the practices you are given, nothing is held back. All the aspects and the attributes of the practices, all the definitions of terms and their contexts, are given to you right at the beginning. Nothing is a mystery. You know everything back to front, which exhausts your expectation of anything extraordinary. There is no reason to be excited about vipashyana. If you are in the state of vipashyana, so what?

On the whole, we are studying dharma so that we know how to handle our life properly. We do not just naively go along with everything, nor for that matter do we become overly paranoid. Instead, as Buddhists we have an understanding of balance. We know how to handle life, and we understand cause and effect. We do not regard our life as though we are constantly being cheated. Whether we are being cheated or not, if we extend ourselves too far or indulge ourselves, we will be cut short. If we are overly sensitive, some accommodation will be provided. That is how the world works according to the vipashyana vision of discriminating-awareness wisdom, which comes from relaxing your mind. So in Buddhism, we are doing more than purely relating to our meditation practice in the shrine hall—we are training in how to live our life.

49

Self-Perpetuating Awareness

Vipashyana exists within us, and although we may not yet have experienced it, there is such a thing as complete awareness beyond the technique of simple breathing meditation and walking meditation. We might not expect that there could be a state that is completely clear and empty, spacious, without any problems. However, it is possible and we could experience it.

I N VIPASHYANA you develop a sense of the world containing its own intelligence. Since the world automatically has its own intelligence, you do not need to add a new perspective to it; instead, you could just tune in to that intelligence. You are not trying to discover Martians; you are simply relating to color, form, and experience. The very fact of reality, so-called reality, begins with the reality that you have a body. You have sense perceptions; therefore, you can function. You can see, you can hear, you can taste, you can feel, you can smell, you can exist. That is why we are known as human beings.

The purpose of vipashyana is to fully experience and communicate those sense perceptions. You can experience the reality of sight, sound, taste, touch, and smell thoroughly and properly. You are not lost in complexities. When you eat, you eat; when you hear, you hear; when you smell, you smell. You experience what is there. You never miss an inch. The point is that you experience reality as real.

BURNING CONCEPTUAL MIND

In his synopsis of vipashyana experience, Jamgön Kongtrül writes about seeing the phenomenal world as empty space. He says that the phenomenal world is empty—it does not have any form, any qualities, any perceptions, any anything at all. Out of that nonexistence, and because of it, we are able to shape forms, objects, colors, and conceptualizations of all kinds. Fixed concepts, shapes, and colors arise, but they are like firewood. That firewood is an aspect of one's intelligence, or discriminating awareness; and the fire is the discipline that burns the fabric of discriminating mind. That is, through the experience of vipashyana, apparent phenomena are seen as fuel. Such firewood should be burned so that there is no difference between the phenomenal world and its occupants—they are one. When the fuel of fixed concepts is burned up by the fire of discipline, we have nothing to hang on to. And having discovered nothing to hold on to, we find that the whole thing dissipates. That is the total experience of vipashyana.

RIKPA AND REFINED DISCRIMINATION

Although solid discrimination is burned up like wood burned by fire, ashes of refined discrimination, or rikpa, remain. In the larger vision of vipashyana, beautiful flower petals and dog shit on the pavement are the same; at the same time, dog shit is still seen as dog shit, and a flower is still seen as a flower, because discriminating awareness remains. It is very simple and very ordinary. For instance, when Jamgön Kongtrül was writing texts, he had three pens—one thick, writing in big letters; one medium; and one small—and he never confused the three of them. They were each put in their particular place on his desk.

To realize vipashyana, you must study and use your intellect, or rikpa. It is like getting a PhD. Rikpa is the instigator of vipashyana. Vipashyana exists within us, and although we may not yet have experienced it, there is such a thing as complete awareness beyond the techniques of simple breathing-meditation and walking meditation. We might not expect that there could be a state that is completely clear and empty, spacious, without any problems. However, it is possible and we could experience it. The space we live in is filled with perceptions and nonperceptions. It is like breathing pollution and fresh air simultaneously. With vipashyana, we are trying to relate more with the fresh air so that the pollution can be transformed at the same time.

TOTAL EXPERIENCE

Vipashyana experience is total experience that goes beyond techniques and beyond mindfulness. Vipashyana awareness expands and opens constantly. We could call it active space, self-perpetuating space, or self-perpetuating awareness. Through vipashyana, you have a different way of being, in that you are more open to life both psychologically and physically. Everything should be included in the process of awareness. Such self-perpetuating awareness is possible. It is not so much that you can *do* it, but there is the possibility that you can *see* it. When the firewood has burned up, the original fire and wood no longer exist. They have dissolved into open space, which is very real to us and very personal.

Vipashyana practice is a growing-up process. You are transcending infancy. As you grow up, you discover that there are lots of things that your parents haven't told you, but you pick up yourself. As you come across experiences in your world, you discover a lot of details and learn a great deal about the world. Vipashyana is that kind of personal experience. A very key point of vipashyana practice is that it is directed toward growing and developing.

Through vipashyana, you begin to realize how much of the world you have missed, and you begin to pay attention to it. With the help of shamatha tranquillity and its concentration—by joining shamatha and vipashyana—you begin to experience the world as if the sun and moon were put together, or for that matter, as if your right and left eyes were put together, or your right and left ears. Through shamatha-vipashyana, you could have a cheerful, celebratory life. You do not need to take your life too seriously, but you should not be too frivolous either. You could maintain both your discipline and your cheerfulness. Shamatha and vipashyana work together: they are like sky and earth, ocean and land, sun and moon, the four seasons.

Part Four

THE FOUR NOBLE TRUTHS

50

The Snowballing of Deception

Instead of just having our own anxiety, we produce a further state
of anxiety in others. We generate their anxiety, and they also gener-
ate it themselves; and we end up with what is known as the "vicious
cycle of samsara." Everybody is constantly making everybody else
feel bad. We have been participating in this tremendous project, this
constant mishap, this terribly bad mistake, for a long time—and we
are still doing it.

W E ARE BORN as human beings, as we are quite aware, and we have to maintain ourselves and keep up our humanness. We do this by breathing, so that our body has the proper circulation and pulsations it needs to survive. We do it by eating food as fuel, and by wearing clothes to protect ourselves from the weather. (Originally, people started wearing clothes because of the cold, but later on human beings became more complicated. They became shy, and started wearing clothes throughout the year.) But we can't maintain ourselves in those ways alone, just by eating, wearing clothes, and sleeping so that we can wake up with the daylight and collect more food to eat. There is something else happening beyond that level: emotionally, we feel that we need to accept and reject.

Sometimes we feel very lonely, and sometimes we feel claustrophobic. When we feel lonely, we seek out partners, friends, and lovers. But when we have too many, we become claustrophobic, and we reject some of them. Sometimes we feel good. Everything has developed ideally for us.

We have companionship; we have clothing to keep ourselves warm; we have food in our stomach; we have enough liquid to drink to keep from being thirsty. We feel satisfied. But any one of those satisfactions can subside. We might have companionship, but not a good meal; we might have a good meal, but no companionship. Sometimes we have good food, but we are thirsty. Sometimes we are happy about one thing, but unhappy about other things. It is very hard to keep together the myriad things that go on and on, up and down. It is very hard. It turns out to be quite a handful, quite a project, for us to keep everything at the ideal level. It is almost impossible to maintain an even sense of happiness.

Even though some of our requirements might be achieved, we still feel anxiety. We think, "At this point my stomach is full of food, but where am I going to get my next meal when my stomach is empty and I'm hungry? At this point, I'm all right, but the next time I become thirsty, where am I going to get a drop of water? Right now, I'm fully clothed and I feel comfortable, but just in case it gets hot or cold, what will I do? I'm completely well-equipped with companions now, but in case they don't keep me company, where will I find more companionship? What if the person who is presently keeping company with me decides to leave me?"

There are all sorts of jigsaw puzzles in life, and the pieces do not perfectly meet. Even if they did meet—which is highly improbable, one chance in a million or less—you would still be anxious, thinking, "Supposing something goes wrong, then what?" So when you are at your best and you feel good about things, you are even more anxious, because you may not have continuity. And often, you feel cheated by your life, because you do not have the facility to synchronize thousands of things at once. So there is natural, automatic pain and suffering. It is not like the pain of a headache, or the pain you feel when somebody hits you in the ribs—it is anxiousness, which is a very haunting situation. People might say, "I have everything sorted out, and I'm quite happy the way I am. I don't have to look for something to make myself more comfortable." Nonetheless, people are always anxiety-ridden. Apart from simply functioning, the way we gaze at the wall or the mountains or the sky, the way we scratch, the way we timidly smile, the way we twitch our faces, the way we move unnecessarily—the way we do everything—is a sign of anxiousness. The conclusion is that everybody is neurotic, that neurosis creates discomfort and anxiety, and that basic anxiety is happening all the time.

In order to rectify that basic anxiousness, we create heavy-handed situations. We come up with intense aggression; we come up with intense passion; we come up with intense pride. We come up with what are known as the kleshas, the conflicting or confused emotions, which entertain our basic anxiety and exaggerate it altogether. We do all sorts of things because of that basic anxiety, and because of that we begin to find ourselves in more trouble and more pain. As the afterthought of expressing our aggression and lust, we find ourselves feeling bad; and not only do we feel bad, but we feel more anxious. That pattern happens all the time. We are in a state of anxiety, and each time we try to make ourselves feel better, we feel worse. We might feel better at the time, if we strike out with our particular flair or style; but then there is a tremendous letdown and tremendous pain. We feel funny about it—in fact, we feel wretched. Not only that, but we make other people feel wretched as well. We can't just practice passion, aggression, and ignorance on ourselves alone; we do it to somebody else as well, and someone always gets hurt. So instead of just having our own anxiety, we produce a further state of anxiety in others. We generate their anxiety, and they also generate it themselves; and we end up with what is known as the "vicious cycle of samsara." Everybody is constantly making everybody else feel bad.

We have been participating in this tremendous project, this constant mishap, this terribly bad mistake, for a long time—and we are still doing it. In spite of the consequences, in spite of the messages that come back to us, we still do it. Sometimes we do it with a straight face, as if nothing had happened. With tremendous deception, we create samsara—pain and misery for the whole world, including ourselves—but we still come off as if we were innocent. We call ourselves ladies and gentlemen, and we say, "I never commit any sins or create any problems. I'm just a regular old person, blah blah blah." That snowballing of deception and the type of existence our deception creates are shocking.

You might ask, "If everybody is involved with that particular scheme or project, then who sees the problem at all? Couldn't everybody just join in so that we don't have to see each other that way? Then we could just appreciate ourselves and our snowballing neuroses, and there would be no reference point whatsoever outside of that." Fortunately—or maybe, unfortunately—we have one person who saw that there was a problem. That person was known as Buddha. He saw that there was a problem, he worked on it, and he got beyond it. He saw that the problem could be reduced—and not just reduced, but completely annihilated. He discovered how to prevent the problem right at the source. Right at the beginning, cessation is possible.

Cessation is possible not only for the Buddha, but for us as well. We are trying to follow his path, his approach. In the twenty-six hundred years since the time of the Buddha, millions of people have followed his example, and they have been quite successful at what they were doing: they managed to become like him. The Buddha's teachings have been handed down from generation to generation, so that right now, right here, we have that information and experience. We can practice the path of meditation in the same way and style as the Buddha and our lineage ancestors. We have the transmission of the way to practice in order to overcome anxiety, deception, and neurosis. We have it and we can do it.

51

Recognizing the Reality of Suffering

*Seeing our pain as it is, is a tremendous help. Ordinarily, we are
so wrapped up in it that we don't even see it. We are swimming
in oceans of ice water of anxiety, and we don't even see that we
are suffering. That is the most fundamental stupidity. Buddhists
have realized that we are suffering, that anxiety is taking place. . . .
Because of that, we also begin to realize the possibility of salvation
or deliverance from that particular pain and anxiety.*

T HE REALITY of pain, or suffering, is one of the basic principles of
the hinayana teachings. There is suffering and pain—someone actually has to say that. It is not polite conversation, it is serious conversation:
there is pain. However, unless we have an understanding and acceptance
of pain, we will have no way to transcend that pain. The Sanskrit term
for "suffering" is *duhkha,* which also has the sense of "anxiety." We realize that throughout our life we are struggling. We struggle because, in
our being, we feel we are what we are and we cannot change. We are
constantly anxious. Why? Goodness knows! Only because we have basic
goodness in us, or innate wholesomeness, can we feel the counterpart of
basic goodness, which is discomfort, anxiety, and confusion. In order to
take a photograph, not only light, but shadow is necessary.

Pain comes from anxiety, and anxiety comes from neurosis. The Sanskrit word for "neurosis" is *klesha,* and in Tibetan it is *nyönmong,* which
means "conflicting emotions" or "defilements" Neurosis is a kind of
stuffiness. Lots of stuffiness leads us to neurosis—*is* neurosis, in fact. In
whatever we do, we experience nyönmong: when we scratch ourselves,

it is nyönmong; when we eat our food, it is nyönmong; when we sit on the toilet seat, it is nyönmong; and when we smile at each other, it is nyönmong. Since we experience freakiness and unwholesomeness continuously in our ordinary life, we may begin to feel that we are being cheated. If we are theists, we get angry at God, thinking that God has cheated us; if we are nontheists, we blame karma. In either case, we feel we have been cheated by somebody, somewhere. So we begin to be resentful and doubtful, and we find that sitting on our meditation cushion is painful.

There is no relief or relaxation when we are in the samsaric world; there is always some kind of struggle going on. Even when we are supposedly enjoying our life, there is still struggle and all kinds of discomfort. We may try to solve that problem by going out to restaurants, or the cinema, or by enjoying our friends; nonetheless, nothing really helps. That is what is called the first noble truth, the truth of suffering. Seemingly we are trapped without hope or any way out. And once we are in that situation, we are *always* in that situation: we are in pain all the time. The Buddha's teachings do not tell us how to skip out of that pain or how to abandon it; they only say that we have to understand our state of being. The more we understand our state of being, the more we will understand why we are in pain. What we find is that the more into ourselves we are, the more we suffer, and the less into ourselves we are, the less we suffer.

Since we yearn to cure our anxiety, we are always looking for potential pleasure, but that search in itself is painful. Whenever we look for pleasure, it is always painful pleasure. Without fail, the end result is completely painful. That search for pleasure is the illogic, or bad logic, of samsaric existence. Suppose you become rich, a millionaire; along with that you collect the anxiety of losing your money, so now that you are a millionaire, you are even more anxious. Situations like that happen all the time.

Regarding pleasure from the point of view of pain is a kind of animal instinct. It is the instinct of the lower realms existing within the human situation. If you do not have the reference point of pain, you cannot seem to enjoy anything. For instance, you might have bought a bottle of wine for three thousand dollars. Very painfully, you spent your three thousand dollars on this bottle of wine. So you say, "This is such fine aged wine. I paid all this money for it. Now let us have a good occasion!" But instead, it becomes a painful occasion. You worry, "What if somebody doesn't appreciate their sip of wine?" We call this "nouveau riche samsara."

Samsara is nouveau riche—it is crazy and stupid, without any dignity, and it goes on all the time.

Unless we realize the facts of life, we cannot begin to practice dharma. Being in the heat is what allows us to enjoy swimming; being in the cold is what allows us to wear nice woolen clothes. Those contradictions are natural; there is nothing extraordinary about them. Basically, we are in pain, we are suffering. Sometimes we become accustomed to our suffering, and sometimes we miss our suffering, so we deliberately invite more suffering. That is the samsaric way to exist.

The Buddhist three-yana path begins with the hinayana, the immediate vehicle. The hinayana is very practical, very pragmatic. It begins with the truth of suffering. We all suffer, and we rediscover that suffering or anxiety again and again. During sitting practice, that anxiety might take the form of wanting to slip into a higher level of practice, using meditation as a kind of transcendental chewing gum. During daily life, you might find that samsaric misery in your neighborhood and in your immediate surroundings; it may be connected with your relatives, your best friends, your job, or your world. Wherever you look, anxiety is always there. Your personal anxiety is what stops you from cleaning your dishes; it is what stops you from folding your shirts properly or combing your hair. Anxiety prevents you from having a decent life altogether: you are distracted by it and constantly hassled. Whether those hassles are sociological, scientific, domestic, or economic, such anxiety is very painful and always present.

Every day seems to be different; nonetheless, every day seems to be exactly the same in terms of anxiety. Basic anxiety is taking place in your everyday life all the time. When you wake up and look around, you might think of coffee, or food, or taking a shower; but the minute you have had your coffee or your breakfast, you realize that the anxiety is still there. In fact, anxiety is always there, hovering and haunting you throughout your life. Even though you might be extremely successful, or so-called successful, at whatever your endeavors might be, you are always anxious about something or other. You can't actually put your finger on it, but it is always there.

Seeing our pain as it is, is a tremendous help. Ordinarily, we are so wrapped up in it that we don't even see it. We are swimming in oceans of ice water of anxiety, and we don't even see that we are suffering. That is the most fundamental stupidity. Buddhists have realized that we are suffering, that anxiety is taking place. We have understood that anxiety does exist; and because of that, we also begin to realize the possibility of salvation or deliverance from that particular pain and anxiety.

According to the hinayana teachings, you have to be very practical: you are going to do something about suffering. It is a very personal approach. To begin with, you could give up your scheme of what you ideally want in your life. Pleasure, enjoyment, happiness—you could give up those possibilities altogether. In turn, you could try to be kind to others, or at least stop inconveniencing others. Your existence might cause pain to somebody—you could try to stop causing that pain. As for yourself, if you find your anxiety and your desire comfortable, you could make sure that you question that perspective. In doing so, there is room for humor. As you begin to see the kind of communication that goes on between pain and pleasure, you begin to laugh. If you have too much pleasure, you can't laugh; if you have too much pain, you can't laugh; but when you are on the threshold of both pain and pleasure, you laugh. It is like striking a match.

The main point of the first noble truth is to realize that you do have such anxiousness in your being. You might be a great scholar and know the Buddhist path from top to bottom, including all the terminology, but you yourself are still suffering. You still experience basic anxiety. Look into that! At this point, we are not talking about an antidote or how to overcome that anxiety—the first thing is just to see that you are anxious. On one hand, this is like teaching your grandmother to suck eggs, as the British say, or like teaching a bird how to fly; on the other hand, you really have to understand samsara. You are in samsara and you actually have to *realize* that.

Before you have been taught about samsara, you have no idea where you are; you are so absorbed in it that there is no reference point. Now that we are providing a reference point, look at what you are doing. Look at where you are and what you are in the midst of. That is a very important message. It is the beginning of the best enlightened message that could ever come about. At the level of vajrayana, we might talk about the nonduality of samsara and nirvana, or fundamental wakefulness, or the flash of instantaneous liberation—but whatever we might talk about is concentrated in this very, very ordinary message: you have to review where you are. It might be a somewhat depressing prospect to realize that you are so thoroughly soaked in this greasy, heavy, dark, and unpleasant thing called samsara, but that realization is tremendously helpful. That understanding alone is the source of realizing what we call "buddha in the palm of your hand"—the basic wakefulness already in your possession. Such vajrayana possibilities begin at this point, right here, in realizing your samsaric anxiousness. Understanding that anxiety, which is very frustrating and not so good, is the key to realizing where you are.

The only way to work with this anxiety is by means of the sitting practice of meditation: it is by taming your mind, or shamatha practice. That is the basic idea of pratimoksha, or individual liberation: taming yourself. The way to tame yourself, or to talk yourself out of this particular anxiety, is through the concentrated practice of shamatha discipline. The beginning of the beginning of the path of buddhadharma is about how you can actually save yourself from samsaric neurosis. You have to be very careful; you are not yet up to saving others.

In practicing buddhadharma, you cannot bypass anything. You have to begin with the hinayana and the first noble truth. Having done so, mahayana and vajrayana will come along naturally. We have to be genuine parents: instead of adopting a child who is sixty years old because we want to be the mother or father of somebody who is already accomplished, we prefer to conceive our child within our marriage. We would like to watch the birth of our child and its growth, so that finally we will have a child who is competent and good because of our training.

The progression of hinayana, mahayana, and vajrayana is well taught by the Buddha and by the lineage. If you don't have a basic foundation of hinayana, you will not understand the mahayana teachings of benevolence and loving-kindness. You won't know who is being benevolent to what. You first have to experience reality, things as they are. It is like painting: first, you have to have a canvas; then, once you have the canvas properly prepared, you can paint on it—but it takes a while. The vajrayana is regarded as the final product of the best beginning; therefore, understanding the hinayana and practicing shamatha discipline are very important and powerful. You have to stick with what you have—the fact that your body, speech, and mind are in pain. The reality is that we are all trapped in samsaric neurosis, everybody, without exception. It is best that you work with reality, rather than with ideals. That is a good place to begin.

52

Dissecting the Experience of Suffering

The first noble truth, the truth of suffering, is the first real insight of the hinayana practitioner. It is quite delightful that such a practitioner has the guts, bravery, and clarity to see pain in such a precise and subtle way. We can actually divide pain into sections and dissect it. We can see it as it is, which is quite victorious.

T HE PATH of dharma consists of both qualities and consequences. In the Buddhist nontheistic discipline, we always work with what is there. We look into our own experience: how we feel, who we are, what we are. In doing so, we find that our basic existence is fundamentally awake and possible; but at the same time, there are a lot of obstacles. The primary obstacles are ego and its habitual patterns, which manifest in all sorts of ways, most vividly and visibly in our experience of ourselves. However, before we look further into who we are or what we are, we first need to examine our fundamental notion of "self." This is known as studying the four noble truths: the truth of suffering, the truth of the origin of suffering, the truth of the cessation of suffering, and the truth of the path.

The four noble truths are divided into two sections. The first two truths—the truth of suffering and the truth of the origin of suffering—are studies of the samsaric version of ourselves and the reasons we arrived in certain situations or came to particular conclusions about ourselves. The second two truths—the truth of the cessation of suffering and the truth of the path—are studies of how we could go beyond that or overcome it. They are related with the journey and with the potentiality of nirvana, freedom, and emancipation. Suffering is regarded as the result of samsara, and the origin of suffering is regarded as the cause of samsara. The path is regarded as the cause of nirvana, and cessation of suffering is regarded as the result of nirvana. In this regard, samsara means ongoing agony, and nirvana means transcending agony and such problems as bewilderment, dissatisfaction, and anxiety.

The first noble truth is the truth of suffering. The Sanskrit word for "suffering" is *duhkha. Duhkha* could also be translated as "misery," "restlessness," or "uneasiness." It is "frustration." The Tibetan word for "suffering" is *dug-ngal. Dug* means "reduced into a lower level"—"wretchedness" may be the closest English word—and *ngal* means "perpetuating"; so *dug-ngal* has the sense of perpetuating that wretchedness. The quality of dug-ngal is that you have done a bad job already, and you are thriving on it and perpetuating it. It is like sticking your finger in your wound. We don't particularly *have* to suffer, but that is the way we go about our business. We start at the wrong end of the stick, and we get suffering—and it's terrible! That is not a very intelligent thing to do.

You might ask, "Who has the authority to say such a thing?" We find that the only authority who has a perspective on the whole thing is the Buddha. He discovered this; therefore, it is called the first noble truth. It is very noble and very true. He actually realized why we go about our bad job and he pointed that out to us, which is the second noble truth. We begin to understand that and to agree with him, because we experience that there is an alternative. There is a possibility of taking another approach altogether. There is a possibility of saving ourselves from such misery and pain. It is not only possible, but it has been experienced and realized by lots of other people.

The first noble truth, the truth of suffering, is a necessary and quite delightful topic. The truth of suffering is very true and very frank, quite painfully so—and surprisingly, it is quite humorous. In order for us to understand who we are and what we are doing with ourselves, it is absolutely necessary for us to realize how we torture ourselves. The torturing process we impose on ourselves is a habitual pattern, or ape instinct. It is somewhat dependent on, or produced by, our previous lives; and at the same time, we both sustain that process and sow further karmic seeds. It is as if we were in an airplane, already flying, but while we were onboard, we began to plan ahead. We would like to book our next ticket so that when we reach our destination, we can immediately take off and go somewhere else. By organizing ourselves in that way, we do not actually have to stop anywhere. We are constantly booking tickets all over the place, and as a consequence, we are traveling all the time. We have nowhere to stop and we don't particularly want to stop. Even if we do stop at an airport hotel, our immediate tendency is to get restless and want to fly again. So we call down to the desk and ask them to book another reservation to go somewhere else. We do that constantly, and that traveling begins to produce a lot of pain and tremendous suffering.

In terms of the notion of self, we are not actually one individual entity per se, but just a collection of what are known as the five skandhas. Within this collection, each mental event that takes place is caused by a previous one; so if we have a thought, it was produced by a previous thought. Likewise, if we are in a particular location, we were forced to be there by a previous experience; and while we are there, we produce further mental events, which perpetuate our trip into the future. We try to produce continuity. That is what is known as karma, or volitional action; and from volitional action arises suffering.

The first noble truth, the truth of suffering, is the first real insight of the hinayana practitioner. It is quite delightful that such a practitioner has the guts, bravery, and clarity to see pain in such a precise and subtle way. We can actually divide pain into sections and dissect it. We can see it as it is, which is quite victorious. If we were stuck in our pain, we would have no way to talk about it. However, by telling the story of pain, we are not perpetuating pain. Instead, we have a chance to know what suffering is all about. That is quite good.

The Eight Types of Suffering

Altogether we have eight kinds of suffering: birth, old age, sickness, and death, coming across what is not desirable, not being able to hold on to what is desirable, not getting what we want, and general misery. Whether subtle or crude, all pain fits into those eight categories. The first four— birth, old age, sickness, and death—are based on the results of previous karma; therefore, they are called "inherited suffering." These four types of suffering are simply the hassles that are involved in being alive. The next three—coming across what is not desirable, not being able to hold on to what is desirable, and not getting what we want—are referred to as the "suffering of the period between birth and death"; and the last is simply called "general misery," or "all-pervasive suffering."

Inherited Suffering

Inherited suffering includes birth, old age, sickness, and death.

1. BIRTH. First, there is the pain of birth. When a child is born, we celebrate its coming into our world; but at the same time, that child has gone through a lot of hassles. It is painful being born—being pushed around and pulled out. Calling "birth" the first experience of suffering may not seem valid, since nobody remembers his or her birth. It may seem purely a concept that once you were in your mother's womb feeling very comfortable, swimming in warm milk and honey, sucking your thumb, or whatever you might have been doing in there. You may have conveniently forgotten your birth. But the idea is that there was a feeling of satisfaction, and then you were thrust out, and had to take some kind of leap, which must have been painful.

Although you may have forgotten your birth, if you do remember it, or if you have watched a child experiencing the pain of birth, you see that it is very literal, ordinary, and quite frightening. As you are born, you are experiencing your first exposure to the world, which consists of hot and cold and all kinds of inconveniences. The world is beginning to try to wake you up, attempting to make you a grown-up person, but your feeling as an infant is not like that: it is a tremendous struggle. The only thing you can do is cry and rave in resentment at the discomfort. Because you can't talk, you can't explain yourself. You feel ignorant and inadequate.

More generally, the pain of birth is based on your resistance to relating with the new demands that come at you from the world. Although it applies, first of all, to your physical birth, or the literal pain of being born, the pain of birth could also apply to your ordinary life as a grown-up. That is, you are always trying to settle down in a situation in which you think that at last you've got it made. You have planned everything down to the last minute, and you don't want to change your scheme. Just like an infant settling down in its mother's womb, you don't think you ever have to come out: you do not want to deal with the hassle of being born.

This type of birth takes place all the time. Financially, you have achieved confirmation; in your relationships, you have decided how to deal with your friends and your lovers; economically, you feel that you have reached a comfortable level: you are able to buy a comfortable home, complete with dishwasher, refrigerator, telephone, air-conditioning, and what have you. You feel that you could stay in this womb for a long time; but then somebody comes along somewhere, and through no fault of your own—or maybe it is your fault—pulls the rug out from under your feet. All that careful planning you have gone through to try to remain in the womb has been interrupted. At that point, you begin to freak out right and left, talking to your friends, your lawyer, your spiritual adviser, and your financier. You wiggle around all over the place, as if you had grown ten arms and twenty legs.

You don't want to be born into the next world, but unfortunately the situation is such that you *are* born into the next world. You might be able to save yourself a little piece, a tiny corner, but that little piece causes you so much hassle that it doesn't satisfy you all that much. Being unable to settle down in a situation is painful. You think you can settle down, but the minute you begin, you are exposed and given another birth. It is just like a baby being pushed out of its mother's womb and exposed to another world. We are not able to settle down. That is the truth.

2. OLD AGE. The second form of inherited suffering is the pain of old age. It is very inconvenient to be old. Suddenly you are incapable of doing all kinds of things, goodness knows what. Also, when you are old, you feel that you no longer have time. You no longer look forward to future situations. When you were young, you could see the whole world evolving, but now you do not have the fun and games of watching the upcoming sixty years.

Old age does not purely refer to being old; it refers to aging, to a person progressing from infanthood to old age. It is the process of things in your life slowly being changed. Over time, there is less kick taking place, less discovery or rediscovery of the world. You keep trying, but things become familiar, they have already been experienced. You may think you should try something outrageous just once, so you try that too; but nothing really happens. It is not so much that something is wrong with your mind or with yourself, but something is wrong with your having a human body that is getting old.

An old body is physically unable to relate with things properly. As a child, you explored how to manipulate your fingers, your legs, your feet, your head, your eyes, your nose, your mouth, your ears, your hands. But at this point, everything in your system has already been explored, whatever you can use to entertain yourself on the bodily level. You haven't anything left to explore. You already know what kind of taste you are going to experience if you taste a certain thing. If you smell something, you already know exactly what it is going to smell like. You know what you are going to see, what you are going to hear, and what you are going to feel.

As we get older, we are not getting the entertainment we used to get out of things. We have already experienced practically everything that exists in our world. An old person who just came out of Tibet might experience phenomena like taking a sauna, or watching movies, or watching television as interesting, but the novelty quickly wears off. New entertainment presented to older people lasts only for a few days, whereas for growing-up people, it might last a few years. On the day we first fell in love with somebody, it was very beautiful, but we do not get that feeling back. The day you first had ice cream was amazing, and the first day you experienced maple syrup was fantastic and great—but you have done all those things already.

Aging is very unpleasant. We realize that we have collected so much that we have become like old chimneys: all kinds of things have gone through us and we have collected an immense thickness of soot. We are hassled and we do not want to go any further. I do not mean to insult anybody, but that is old age. And although some old people actually hold together very well, they are trying too hard.

The suffering of aging could apply to the psychological experience of aging as well as to physical aging. Initially, there is the feeling that you can do anything you want. You are appreciating your youth, dexterity, glamour, and fitness, but then you begin to find that your usual tricks no longer apply. You begin to decay, to crumble. You can't see, you can't hear, you can't walk, and you can't appreciate the things you used to enjoy. Once upon a time there was that good feeling. You could enjoy things, and certain things used to feel great. But if you try to repeat them now, in old age, your tongue is numb, your eyes are dull, your hearing is weak—your sense perceptions do not work. The pain of old age refers to that general experience of decay.

3. SICKNESS. The third form of inherited suffering is the pain of sickness. Sickness is common to both old and young. There are all kinds of physical and semiphysical, or psychological, sicknesses. Sickness is largely based on the occasional panic that something might be terribly wrong with you or that you might die. It depends on how much of a hypochondriac you are. There are also occasional little polite sicknesses. You may say, "I have a cold, but I'm sure I'll get over it. I'm well, thank you, otherwise." But it is not so lighthearted as you express in your social conversation. Something more is taking place.

Sickness is an inconvenience: when you are really sick, your body has gotten so much in the way that you wish you could give up the whole thing. In particular, when you check in to the hospital, you feel that you have been pushed into a world full of broken glass and sharp metal points. The atmosphere of hospitality in hospitals is very irritating. It is not an experience of comfort and lightness. You feel helpless. One of the big themes in the Western world is to be active and helpful to yourself and not to depend on anything or anyone else, including tying your own shoelaces. So there is a lot of resentment toward that condition of helplessness.

We may experience sickness as discomfort. If we do not get good toast for breakfast, it is so irritating. The suffering of sickness includes all kinds of habitual expectations that no longer get met. Once upon a time, we used to get the things we wanted, and now they are discontinued. We would like to check with our doctor so that we can get our habitual patterns back. We want our own particular habits to keep happening, and we do not want to give anything up, viewing that as a sign of weakness. We are even threatened by not getting good toast with butter on it. We feel that the rug has been pulled out from under our feet, and a sudden panic takes place. That is a problem that the Occidental world is particularly prone to, because we are so pleasure oriented.

Sickness, while it is largely based on pain and unfamiliarity, is also based on resentment. You resent not being entertained; and if you are thrown into unreasonable situations, such as jail, you resent the authorities. The first signs of death also tend to occur to you in sickness. When you are sick, you feel physically dejected by life, with all sorts of complaints, aches, and pains. When you get attacked by sickness, you begin to feel the loss of the beautiful wings and the nice feathers you used to have. Everything is disheveled. You can't even smile or laugh at your own jokes. You are completely demoralized and under attack.

4. DEATH. Last, but not least, is the pain of death. Death is the sense of not having any opportunity to continue further in your life or your endeavor—the sense of total threat. You cannot even complain: there is no authority to complain to about death. When you die, you suffer because you cannot continue with what you want to do, or finish the unfinished work you feel you have to accomplish. There is the potential of fundamental desolation.

Death requires you to completely leave everything that you love, including your one and only beloved ballpoint pen. You leave all of those things. You cannot do your little habitual patterns; you cannot meet your friends anymore. You lose everything—every single item that you possess and everything you like, including the clothes you bought and your little tube of toothpaste, and the soap you like to use to wash your hands or face. All the things you personally like, all the things you appreciate for the sake of keeping yourself company, everything you enjoy in this life—every one of them completely goes. You are gone, and you cannot have them anymore. So death includes the pain of separation.

There is a further sense of pain associated with death, in that you have identified yourself so completely with your body. You can imagine losing the people you associate yourself with—your wife or husband or your closest friend—and you can imagine that when you lose your best friend or your wife or husband, you will feel completely freaked out. You can imagine such possibilities taking place in your life, but can you imagine losing your own body? When you die, you not only lose your wife or husband or friend, but you lose your body. It's terrible, absolutely ghastly. Nobody imposes that on you; you impose it on yourself. You could say, "I didn't take care of my body. I didn't eat the right food and I drank too much. I had too many cigarettes." But that does not solve the problem.

Eternally saying good-bye to our own body is very difficult. We would like to keep our body intact. If we have a cavity in our tooth or a cut in our body, we can go to our doctor and get fixed. However, when we die, that body will no longer exist. It is going to be buried, or burnt and reduced to ashes. The whole thing is going to disappear, and you will have no way to identify yourself: you won't have any credit cards, and you won't have your calling cards, or your driver's license. You will have no way to identify yourself if you bump into somebody who might know you.

Death is a question of leaving everything that you want, everything you so preciously possessed and hung on to—including the dharma, quite possibly. It is questionable whether you will have enough memories and imprints in your mind to return to a new situation where the Buddhist teachings are flourishing. The level of your confusion is so high that you will probably end up being a donkey. I don't want to freak you out particularly, but that is the truth. It is the first noble truth, the straight truth, which is why we can afford to discuss these subtleties. But death is not so subtle—it is terrible to die, absolutely terrible.

You think you can fight against death. You call the doctors, priests, and philosophers, and ask them for help. You look for a philosopher who has the philosophy that death doesn't exist. You look for a very competent doctor, one who has fought death millions of times, hoping you could be a candidate to be one of those who never has to go through with death. You go to a priest, who gives you Communion, and tells you that you will gain everlasting life. This may sound humorous, but I am afraid it is really terrifying when we come to think of it. It is terrible.

In your ordinary, everyday life you experience situations similar to death all the time. Death is an exaggeration of the previous three types of suffering. You start with birth, and having been born, you begin to settle down. You tend to put up with old age as an understandable and ongoing process, and you can relate with sickness as a natural situation. But, finally, you find that the whole scheme is going to end. You realize that nothing lasts very long. You are going to be dropped very abruptly, and you're going to be suddenly without breath. That is quite shocking!

Suffering of the Period between Birth and Death

Having discussed the inherited suffering of birth, old age, sickness, and death, we come to the second level of suffering. This level of suffering is related to our psychological situation and is connected with the period between birth and death. It has three categories: coming across what is not desirable; not being able to hold on to what is desirable; and not getting what we want. We are never satisfied. We are constantly speeding around and always trying very, very hard. We never give up. We always try to get the few leftover peanuts out of the corner of the can.

5. COMING ACROSS WHAT IS NOT DESIRABLE. The first category is the pain of coming across what is not desirable. Our attitude to life is usually quite naive: we think that we can avoid meeting ugly or undesirable situations. Usually we are quite tricky and quite successful at avoiding such things.

Some people have tremendous problems and experience one disaster after another, but they still try to avoid them. Other people have led their lives quite successfully, but even they sometimes find that their tricks don't work. They are suddenly confronted with a situation that is completely the opposite of what they want. They say, "Terrible! Good heavens! I didn't expect that! What happened?" Then, quite conveniently, they blame somebody else, if they have a scheming-enough style of thinking; and if they don't, they just freak out with their mouths open.

6. NOT BEING ABLE TO HOLD ON TO WHAT IS DESIRABLE. The second category is the opposite of that. It is the pain of trying to hold on to what is desirable, fantastic, lovely, splendid, terrific. It is as if you are trying to hold on to a good situation, and suddenly there is a leak. What you are holding in your arms and cherishing so much begins to sizzle out like a balloon. When that occurs, you begin to be very resentful, or try to see it as somebody else's problem.

7. NOT GETTING WHAT YOU WANT. Underlying the previous two categories is the third, which is that, on the whole, we can't get what we want. That is the case. You might say, "One day I'm going to become a great movie star, a millionaire, a great scholar, or at least a decent person. I would like to lead my life happily ever after. I have this plan. I'm going to be either a saint or a sinner, but I'm going to be happy." However, none of those situations happen. And even if you do become a great movie star or a millionaire, something else crops up, so that being such a person doesn't help. You begin to realize that there are further problems with your life and that, on the whole, your life is very grim. Nothing will satisfy you. Nothing will be wish-fulfilling at all, absolutely not. Something is not quite working. Whether you are smart or dumb, it doesn't make much difference: things don't quite work. That creates tremendous anxiety, chaos, and dissatisfaction.

General Misery

8. GENERAL MISERY OR ALL-PERVASIVE SUFFERING. The last category, general misery or all-pervasive suffering, is quite a different form of suffering altogether. The previous seven were understandable situations of pain and suffering. Number eight is not worse, but more subtle. It is the

subtle sense of general misery and dissatisfaction that goes on all the time—completely all the time. This general misery that exists in us is not recognized. We just feel that we are in our own way. We feel that we are an obstacle to ourselves and to our own success. There is a quality of ongoing heaviness, hollowness, and wretchedness. If you are having the greatest time in your life, a moment of fantastic enjoyment, there's still an edge to it. Things are not one-hundred-percent fulfilled. You can't fully relax without referring to the past or the future. A big sigh has been taking place all the time, ever since you were born.

General misery, or all-pervasive suffering, is based on the inheritance of neurosis. Even when we experience joy or pleasure in our lifetime, if we do at all, that pleasure has a tinge of sour in it. In other words, sourness is part of the definition of pleasure. We cannot experience just one thing, without having some contrast to it. That is the highest experience of spirituality: there is a little bit of sweet and sour always. All-pervasive suffering is connected with constant movement: flickering thoughts, latching onto one situation after another, or constantly changing subjects. It is like getting out of a car and walking into a building, and getting out of the building and walking into a car, and being hungry and settling down in a restaurant and eating food, and going back. It is connected with what you are doing right now.

Our life consists of a lot of shifts. After boredom, such shifts may seem pleasurable and entertaining. For instance, if we have had a long ride, getting out of the car is good; getting out of the car and walking into a restaurant is better; ordering food is better still; and ordering some liquor or dessert is best of all, great. At such times, things seem good, and you are experiencing nothing wrong in your life. Everything is ideal, fine. There is nothing to complain about and everything is solid and fantastic. But even in that kind of feeling, an element of pain still exists. That sense of satisfaction is largely based on no longer feeling the pain that you experienced before.

It is questionable how much we are dealing with previous experiences and how much we are ready to deal with life in terms of oncoming new experiences. Quite possibly, we will find that we fit even new experiences into our old categories. In doing so, we do not experience satisfaction, but pain. In Buddhism, satisfaction is minute. When we are satisfied, we may have a sense of accomplishment and self-snugness; but at the same time, we see that as being questionable. So we are never fully satisfied.

This last form of suffering, general misery, is supposedly so subtle that it can only be perceived by realized ones. Only they have experienced a contrast to that anxiety, the absence of anxiety. However, although it has been said that this form of suffering is very difficult for people to understand, it is not really all that sophisticated. It is actually very simple. The point is that ordinarily you are immune to your own suffering. You have been suffering for such a long time that you don't notice it unless you are attacked by very vivid or very big problems. In that way, you are like somebody who is very heavy. A three-hundred-pound person may be quite jolly and happy because he feels that all that weight is part of his body. He doesn't feel that carrying this big heavy weight is particularly painful, until he begins to have shortened breath or thoughts of heart problems. Likewise, you are immune to your own suffering. Since you carry your burden of suffering with you all the time, you have grown accustomed to it. You have learned to live with it. On the whole, even though you carry this burden of fixation, which constantly perpetuates your mental events of disaster, you do not recognize it. You are immune to the disaster of the kleshas—the negative, unwholesome mental confusions of aggression, passion, and ignorance that make you stupid and keep you wandering around. You are immune to the general sense of suffering that takes place all the time.

THREE PATTERNS OF SUFFERING

The eight types of suffering were previously divided into inherited suffering, the suffering of the period between birth and death, and general misery. However, suffering can also be described in terms of three patterns: the suffering of suffering, the suffering of change, and all-pervasive suffering.

The Suffering of Suffering

The suffering of suffering includes the categories of birth, old age, sickness, death, and coming across what is not desirable. It is known as the suffering of suffering because first you have birth, which is terribly painful, and on top of that you have old age, sickness, and death. Having been born, you get all of that lumped upon you; and on top of that, you come across things that are not desirable. Since all of those sufferings are piled up in that way, this is called the suffering of suffering. An analogy is that you have cancer, and on top of that you go bankrupt, and your house collapses on you.

The Suffering of Change

The suffering of change includes two categories: trying to hold on to what is desirable; and not getting—or not knowing—what you want.* In the first case, you discover something desirable and then it is gone. In the second, you are unable to discover what you want, which causes you tremendous anxiety. Either you fail to find out what you really want, or it keeps changing. An analogy for the suffering of change is being at your wedding reception and having a bomb explode in the middle of the dining room table. A milder analogy is having a great dinner and finding that the dessert is a disaster. The suffering of changeability includes anything that has a good beginning and a sour ending.

All-Pervasive Suffering

All-pervasive suffering is the equivalent of the eighth type of suffering, or general misery. Our condition is basically wretched because of the burden of the five skandhas, which perpetuate our neuroses and our habitual thought-patterns. Because of that, we begin to find that, on the whole, we have never experienced any real happiness. There is one particular point that I would like to make: there is no such thing as real happiness. It's a myth. In the way we go about it, there is no such thing as real happiness at all. We've been striving so hard for it, trying all the time to cultivate so much goodness, so many pleasures—but we started at the wrong end of the stick from the very beginning. Something went wrong as we began ourselves. We are trying to entertain ourselves in the wrong way—by having an ego, by having fixation. But we can't get any pleasure out of fixation; and after that, the whole thing goes down the drain. However, we could

---

* The traditional Buddhist understanding of this form of suffering is not getting what you want; Trungpa Rinpoche expands it to include not knowing what you want.

start at the right end of the stick, without fixation, without clinging—that is always possible. That is what is called the second half of the four noble truths: the truth of the cessation of suffering and the truth of the path.

By the way, the first noble truth is not quite the same as the theistic concept of original sin. You have not failed, and you are not being punished or thrown in jail. You just started at the wrong end of the stick. Therefore, what you experience is a general sense of pain, the source of which you cannot find. If you could find out where it came from, you could probably solve it, but you haven't been able to do so. In contrast, the right end of the stick is to start properly, with lots of discipline. By becoming more sensitive to all-pervasive suffering, you have a chance to overcome it.

OVERCOMING NEUROTIC PAIN

Altogether, lots of hassles take place. Having been born is very painful, and having a body is also extraordinarily painful. On top of that, we are sick until we die. We die because we are sick. Since we were born, we have never been cured; otherwise, we could not die. In whatever we do, even at the highest level of pleasure, there is always a tinge of pain. This pain is overall pain rather than a little pain. It is almost the entire consistency of our life, the water we make our soup out of, our life in detail.

In regard to suffering, to pain and pleasure, whenever an element of sanity begins to take place, the neurotic pain is lessened and becomes somewhat less dramatic and personal. At the same time, because of the clarity of mind, the pain itself becomes more pronounced—not because the pain is more, but because the confusion is less. Therefore, with greater clarity, pain is experienced more harshly, more precisely and directly. According to the abhidharma, the unwise feel pain as the stroke of a hair on the hand, but the wise feel pain as the stroke of a hair on the eye. So the wise feel much more pain, because they are freer from neurosis. They feel *real* pain and the real precision of pain. Jamgön Kongtrül says that the ultimate understanding of pain is that you cannot get rid of your pain, but you can have a higher understanding of pain. That seems to be how things go.

At this point, we are dealing with the brass-tacks level. At the beginning, at the hinayana level, Buddhism is somewhat crude, but it is presentable to people. There is the notion of pain and misery, and the notion that we can actually save ourselves from that misery if we practice the teachings. That may be crude, but it is true, and it makes sense to people. It is very real and honest. You can't psychologize the whole thing by saying, "You have pain, but regard it as nonexistence," and then just go about your philosophical discussion. That approach doesn't help very much, so you have to stick to the level of primitive truth. And if you look into it subtly, you realize that it is not all that primitive, but it is very, very sophisticated. You have to present dharma as a workable situation; otherwise, it is not actually communicable to anybody, and it becomes a fairy tale. You could say, "Sit and practice. Then you will be out of your misery." It is not exactly a promise, or something you have up your sleeve, but it is true. Very simple.

In discussing the first noble truth, we are not saying that somebody should not be born, should never get old, should never get sick, and should never die. However, in regard to the *suffering* of those things, a person can experience birth without pain, old age without pain, sickness without pain, and death without pain. We are not concerned with going against the laws and norms of the phenomenal world. We would never have any Buddhists if they were not born. So I'm afraid that you are stuck with birth, old age, sickness, and death. You can overcome the pain aspect of it, but you cannot overcome the totality.

The hinayanists said that about the Buddha himself: that he was born and he died, so he was still subject to the samsaric norm, to some extent. The Buddha had a human body, and he lived on the earth; he was not a superman. He was a good person, but he still had to stick with the worldly norms: he had to eat his food and he had to die. And we have the same situation. We're not trying to go beyond that. We're not trying to refute any scientific laws.

We can actually declare that, as nontheistic Buddhists, we can free the whole world from pain. That's the greatest news. And we are doing it properly, rather than by worshiping somebody or going into a trance. We are doing it methodically, scientifically, psychologically. Starting with ourselves, we are expanding that news to others in turn. It is very definite and ordinary—and at the same time, it is quite remarkable.

53

The Power of Flickering Thoughts

Everything starts on a minute scale at the beginning and then expands. Things begin to swell and expand until they become very large—immeasurably large, in a lot of cases. We can experience that ourselves. Such minute shifts of attention are what create the emotions of aggression, passion, ignorance, and all the rest. Although those emotions are seemingly very heavy-handed, large-scale, and crude, they have their origin in the subtle twists that take place in our mind constantly.

S UFFERING, THE first of the four noble truths, comes from absent-mindedness; it comes from stupidity or ignorance. We are not fundamentally incapable of being mindful, but we are unable to develop exertion or striving on the path. Absentmindedness, not being aware, brings a sense of "lost and split." That kind of basic confusion naturally brings pain. Because of that sense of dissatisfaction, of not finding your right place, you try to attack the world outside or to complain—but, actually, the complaint should be on yourself. The original problem began because you lost your awareness. You cannot lay that on someone else.

The basic quality of suffering is that you cannot behave in the proper manner. The first glimpse of suffering is a sense of clumsiness: you are unable to coordinate your body, speech, and mind. That sense of complete clumsiness can be referred to as "ape instinct." From suffering comes the notion of irritation. Because you are not quite in accordance with your environment, the world begins to attack you. You may sit in a very uncomfortable chair, which simply doesn't fit you, so you feel painfully cramped. You may step in some dog shit on the pavement, and suddenly you have no idea whom to blame: the dog who shat, yourself, or the uncleanness of the city. There is an ongoing bewilderment or grudge against the world. You are supposed to say something to somebody who attacks you—but you have created the inconvenience yourself, so you do not know what to do. Basically, any movement you make by not being aware creates suffering and pain. Losing track, losing context, losing a reference point of openness brings pain.

Understanding suffering is very important. The practice of meditation is not designed to develop pleasure, but to understand the truth of suffering; and in order to understand the truth of suffering, one also has to understand the truth of awareness. When true awareness takes place, suffering does not exist. Through awareness, suffering is somewhat changed in its perspective. It is not necessarily that you do not suffer, but the haunting quality that fundamentally you are in trouble is removed. It is like removing a splinter: it might hurt, and you might still feel pain, but the basic cause of that pain, the ego, has been removed.

The second noble truth is about the origin of suffering: how suffering and dissatisfaction arise. Suffering begins with very simple and ordinary flickers of thought, which derive from basic bewilderment. Before intention begins, there is a state of utter uncertainty, in the sense of a generally dull and stupefied state of mind. That uncertainty or bewilderment occurs every fraction of a second in our state of being. It goes on all the time. We don't know whether we are coming or going, perceiving or not perceiving. Due to that uncertainty, we prefer to spin in circles rather than to look around and extend outward. Our actions are colored or flavored by a kind of fundamental ape-instinct; our only guidance is our own very fermented body odor or mind odor. It is like the blind leading the blind. We are just sniffing around. In this stupefied state, you are willing to step into a corral or den, like an animal, not knowing that the consequences will be painful. In that way, you are drawn toward pain rather than toward pleasure.

That tendency toward pain comes not from either pain or pleasure, but from wanting to bury your head in yourself and smell your own wickedness. You would rather stick with your family than go out and meet strangers. You prefer to relate with your own nest, which happens to be a bad choice, and the result is pain. So you start with ignorance, which is very self-snug, like living in a cocoon. Due to ignorance, you prefer to let a gigantic growth develop in you rather than be operated on and feel better, because the operation is too painful, and it is too big a deal to do anything about it. You even take pride in that approach. However, although you are looking for pleasure, it turns out to be pain. For you, basic goodness has not yet come up. Basic goodness is like getting up and taking a shower, which wakes you up; but you would rather not do that, even though you have a bathroom. You prefer to doze in your bed. It's less of a hassle and you don't have to sacrifice or give anything up. It is much easier just to swim around in your dirt. You don't take a shower, you don't wash, you don't go to the barber and cut your hair, you just grow a long beard and long hair and kick around with your own little pleasure. This is as close as we can get to the notion of samsara.

Within that stupidity you begin to find something, and that something is passion or lust. You don't even know what you are lusting for, but you are willing to indulge yourself. Desire or lust is that which ignites. It is based on wanting to build yourself up. But you do not need desire. You could take a walk with the desire of building yourself up, but you could also take a walk without trying to build yourself up. You could just take a walk, very simply and straightforwardly. Doing so would be very opening. There doesn't have to be a second meaning all the time, and you don't have to philosophize everything. There could be pure motivation.

The natural, instinctive yearning toward pain is known as *künjung* in Tibetan, and in Sanskrit it is *samudaya*. *Kün* means "all" or "every," and *jung* means "arising"; so *künjung* means the "origin of all." Künjung is an abbreviation for *nyönmong künjung*, which means the "origin of all the defilements (kleshas)." It is where all the defilements and pain are created. Künjung gives birth to the twelve nidanas—the links in the chain of causation (ignorance, formation, consciousness, name and form, the six senses, contact, feeling, craving, clinging, becoming, birth, and death). It is the origin of the five skandhas, which are permeated with the kleshas.

According to the abhidharma, künjung can arise as flickering thoughts, and it is connected with the notion of *semjung*, the fifty-one mental events arising from the mind. Künjung is also associated with two forms of *drippa*, or obscuration: *pakchak kyi drippa*, the "obscuration of habitual tendencies," and *nyönmong kyi drippa*, the "obscuration of negative emotions." The flickering is pakchak kyi drippa, which sets off the emotions, or nyönmong kyi drippa. The flickering acts like the pilot light on your stove, which is always on and sets off all the rest of the burners. Likewise, there is always some pakchak kyi drippa waiting to light any of the skandhas or kleshas, which are ready and waiting to be lit up.

The idea of künjung, the origin of suffering, is that it progresses. When we project ourselves into a situation or into a particular world, we begin with a very small and minute shift of attention; and from that, things become enlarged and exaggerated. According to the abhidharma, the connection between small ideas and large ideas is very important. For instance, sudden dramas, such as murdering somebody or creating immense chaos, begin on the level of minute concepts and tiny shifts of attention. Something large is being triggered by something quite small. The first little hint of dislike or attraction for somebody eventually escalates and brings on a much more immense scale of emotional drama or psychodrama. So everything starts on a minute scale at the beginning and then expands. Things begin to swell and expand until they become very large—immeasurably large, in a lot of cases. We can experience that ourselves. Such minute shifts of attention are what create the emotions of aggression, passion, ignorance, and all the rest. Although those emotions are seemingly very heavy-handed, large-scale, and crude, they have their origin in the subtle twists that take place in our mind constantly.

Because of that sudden shiftiness of attention, and because our mind is basically so untrained, we begin to have a sense of casualness about the whole thing. We are constantly looking for possibilities of either possessing someone, destroying someone, or conning somebody into our world. That struggle is taking place all the time. The problem is that we have not properly related with the shiftiness. We experience the arising of such thoughts right now, all the time; otherwise the second noble truth wouldn't be truth—it would just be theory.

It is possible for people who have been practicing meditation and studying the teachings, who are opened up and intrigued, to see this pattern. If you have been practicing, you are somewhat raw and unskinned, which is good; although if you are too ripe, you might want to run away or try to grow thicker skin. Being able to relate with the subtleties of mental shifts is connected with the hinayana principle of paying attention to every activity that we do in smaller doses. There is no such thing as sudden psychodrama without any cause and effect. Every psychodrama that takes place in our mind or in our actions has its origin in little flickering thoughts and little flickerings of attention.

54

The Development of Set Patterns

One way to deal with suffering is to understand its mechanics, how it develops and functions. However, we are not just presenting successive lists of problems and letting it go at that, without going on to discuss the cure for such problems. At the same time, if we began by immediately discussing the cure, it would not particularly help. First, you have to slow down and take the time to understand how suffering originates. There is no other cure for suffering at this point, except to understand its makeup and psychology.

T HE ORIGIN of suffering, strangely, can come either from trying to be highly disciplined and aware or from completely losing one's awareness. Generally, if you are not mindful and aware, suffering begins to arise; whereas if you are mindful and aware, suffering does not arise. However, suffering can also come from using your awareness discipline as a means of securing yourself by developing set patterns in life.

SEVEN EGO-ORIENTED PATTERNS THAT LEAD TO SUFFERING

There are seven ego-oriented patterns that arise from both attitudes and actions, and lead to suffering: regarding the five skandhas as belonging to oneself; protecting oneself from impermanence; believing that one's view is best; believing in the extremes of nihilism and eternalism; passion; aggression; and ignorance.

Regarding the Five Skandhas as Belonging to Oneself

The first set pattern is regarding the five skandhas (form, feeling, perception / impulse, concept / formation, and consciousness) as belonging to oneself. This is known as the "bad view," or the "view that is not so good."

Protecting Oneself from Impermanence

The second set pattern, held by a lot of people, is protecting oneself from impermanence and trying to develop eternal life. Believing that you are or could be eternal, the first thing you do is to seek the wrong kind of master, someone who promises, "If you practice my way, I will give you eternal life. You will live forever!" It's the old Shangri-la approach. Although you know that your body cannot last forever, you hope to at least make your spirit last forever by seeking a spiritual master and asking to be saved.

Believing That One's View Is the Best

The third set pattern is believing that one's view is the best. It is based on a spiritually materialistic approach to holiness. You think, "This place is sacred, this body is sacred, and this practice is sacred," but that feeling of holiness is founded on the very confused ground of spiritual materialism. It is based on the belief that some magical power is going to save you.

Believing in the Extremes of Nihilism or Eternalism

The fourth set pattern is believing in the extremes of nihilism or eternalism. In the extreme of nihilism, everything is regarded as completely empty, nothing. Nothing in your life matters. Whatever happens—whether you are on the beach or in the mountains, watching the sunset or the sunrise, seeing birds fly or flowers grow, hearing bees hum—nothing really matters.

The extreme of nihilism comes from the philosophical belief that if you don't believe in anything at all, you are free from everything. It is connected with the shunyata experience of no form, no speech, no emotions, and so forth. Every experience is completely philosophized. That nihilistic philosophy is reinforced by saying that you should appreciate everything as an expression of emptiness. For example, you listen to the sound of the ash falling from the incense stick as the sound of emptiness, as shunyata. By appreciating things as an expression of emptiness, you think everything is going to be okay.

In the extreme of eternalism, you think that everything is everlasting and secure. However, instead of just thinking everything is going to be okay, you feel that you have to make a connection with what is happening around you. You feel that you have to be one with the earth and the trees, one with nature, which is eternal. Purely enjoying something, appreciating it, and saying nothing is a problem, doesn't help—you have to get into the details and make it more personal. You have to eat the right food, do the right kind of exercises, wear the right kind of clothes. You have to get into the right kind of yin-and-yang rhythm. You believe in a norm or law that governs our life, and the idea is that you should connect with that, be on the right side of the cosmos, so that you do not have any problems or hassles.

Once you begin to believe in one of those two extremes, you feel that you do not need to sit and meditate; instead, meditation comes to you. Unfortunately, that is not quite true. Something *else* comes to you: the belief in nihilism or eternalism. Although that may be a pleasant experience, temporarily speaking, you cannot solve the nihilist or the eternalist extremes or transcend the origin of suffering without a definite practice and discipline taught by a lineage holder in an authentic tradition. Practice brings a sense of presence and simple awareness, so that experience is very real, rather than having either a nihilistic or eternalistic shadow behind it to make everything feel solid. In terms of nihilism, instead of saying, "Yes, the sun rose. Sure. So what?" you simply say, "The sun rose!" And in terms of eternalism, rather than saying, "I had a macrobiotic meal for my dinner," you simply say, "So what? I had food!" The hinayana level of consciousness is very profound.

This is a very simplified version of nihilism and eternalism. The philosophers and theologians of Hinduism talk about these two extremes in a very sophisticated way; however, at this point, we are presenting these two views in terms of contemporary eternalists and nihilists who live in California or New York City. Basically, both eternalism and nihilism are ways of trying to nourish one's existence and one's ego. They are extreme views in the sense that either you couldn't care less and nothing is a problem, or there *is* a problem, so you have to be on the right side of it. In relating to these two extremes, the point is neither to abandon both extremes nor to believe in both. Instead, you have to develop an entirely different system of thinking in which there is no security and no ego. Only awareness brings a real sense of that nondual approach.

Passion, Aggression, and Ignorance

The last three set patterns are a very familiar group: passion, aggression, and ignorance. Passion, or lust, strangely enough, has a very interesting psychological back-and-forth play with aggression. That is, the problem of passion comes from its not being pure and complete passion, which would be straightforward and true. The passion or lust we experience in the realm of ego is quite the opposite. There is a touch of hatred in it, which brings wantingness, grasping, and possessiveness. You feel that you don't have something, so you want to grasp it. You think, "Because I feel that I am not really here, I feel this pain. How can I maintain myself properly?" And the instruction you get from yourself is that in order to be passionate, you have to be slightly aggressive. Similarly, in aggression, there is a faint sense of desire and lust, which makes the aggression more powerful. So having an aggressive attitude to somebody is equal to having a love affair with somebody. As far as ignorance is concerned, it has elements of both passion and aggression: the desire to learn is mixed with a faint touch of hatred. You think your state of mind may not be intelligent enough to know; therefore, you begin to ignore what you might know and develop hatred toward knowledge and learning.

These set views, or set patterns, are the basic constituents of the origin of suffering. If we approach the second noble truth with the flavor of contemplative practice, we find that these basic constituents are obvious and personal. We realize that once we have fallen into any one of them, or all of them, we experience constant struggle, competition, pain, and confusion.

As a practitioner, you realize that these patterns don't particularly go away, but at least you know what they are all about, and as you go along, you will probably know what you should do about them. You may think that once the dharma or the truth has been spoken, it should solve those problems automatically, but that is not the case. First, you have to get into the dharma, then you can think about what you can do. Unless you are a businessperson, you can't discuss bankruptcy.

One way to deal with suffering is to understand its mechanics, how it develops and functions. However, we are not just presenting successive lists of problems and letting it go at that, without going on to discuss the cure for such problems. At the same time, if we began by immediately discussing the cure, it would not particularly help. First, you have to slow down and take the time to understand or realize the second noble truth, the origin of suffering. There is no other cure for suffering at this point, except to understand its makeup and psychology.

It is like making a telephone call. If you want to make a phone call, to begin with, you need to know that there is such a thing as a telephone company. You learn that each time you dial a number, it is transmitted through electricity, which connects you to the other person's telephone. Once you have understood the mystery of talking over a machine and having somebody at the other end hear you, you have confidence. Because you know the logic of the telephone, if your telephone breaks down, you can complain to the telephone company. Before you get into the details of how to solve the problem, however, you need to know the basic logic. Likewise, in discussing the second noble truth, we begin by understanding how these set patterns work. The telephone runs on electricity, and human emotions and samsaric problems run on the mind.

55

Perpetually Re-Creating Suffering

Our habitual pattern is that whenever we encounter anything
undesirable and unappealing, we try little ways within ourselves
to avoid it. We could watch ourselves doing that. The little things
we do, the little areas in which we try to entertain ourselves—that
process which takes place all the time—is both the product of suf-
fering and the producer of suffering. It is the origin that perpetually
re-creates suffering, as well as what we are constantly going through
as the result of suffering.

T HE ORIGIN of suffering, künjung, is based on the belief in eternity.
That belief in eternity marks the difference between theism and
nontheism. Out of the belief in eternity comes the hope of maintaining
oneself, of continuing to be, and the search for longevity of the self, or
ego. Along with that comes a fear of death. We look for all sorts of alternatives, for some way to occupy ourselves. We keep groping around in
order to survive. That groping process is connected with the development
of the kleshas. We begin to look outward from ourselves to others, out
into the world, and grasp at the world as a way of maintaining ourselves.
We use the world as a crutch. That process leads to suffering as a result,
because the various ways we try to maintain ourselves do not actually
help to maintain us—in fact, they hinder us—so our scheme begins to
break down. The more it breaks down, the more we have to rebuild; and
as that rebuilding takes place, the suffering returns, so again and again we
go back to rebuilding. It is a vicious cycle. The process of samsara goes
on and on. We have to understand its workings, for once we know how

samsara operates, we will know how to work with it. We will know what to overcome and what to cultivate.

The path or journey becomes important because it breaks down fixation—holding on to oneself and holding on to others—which could be said to be the origin of suffering. There are two types of künjung: the künjung of kleshas and the künjung of karma. The kleshas are one's state of being, one's state of mind. Kleshas such as passion, aggression, arrogance, and ignorance are all internal situations; they are purely mental events. The künjung of karma is acting upon others as a result of such kleshas. Both types of künjung could be considered karmic; however, the second type of künjung is much more karmic because it involves making decisions, dealing with others, and actually doing something with the phenomenal world. The künjung of kleshas could be said to be an embryonic expression of the künjung of karma. As an example, if something pops into your mind as you are meditating and you recognize it immediately, it does not have the same karmic weight as if you had acted upon it. Once you see through it, it is just a game rather than a serious plan that you have; whereas if you write it down in your little notebook so you can remember to call your friend and tell her about it, you have already planted a karmic seed. Simply perceiving it through your mind and seeing the futility of it, realizing it is just a game, is the saving grace. That seems to be the point of the practice of meditation.

THE SIX ROOT KLESHAS: CONFLICTING EMOTIONS THAT LEAD TO SUFFERING

Kleshas are defilements or conflicting emotions. There are six root kleshas and twenty secondary kleshas.* Kleshas are minute at the beginning, but their consequences are large and disastrous. The origin of conflicting emotions is that you are jumpy and always looking for entertainment. Kleshas seem magically to manifest out of the blue and come to your attention,

---

* According to Yeshe Gyaltsen's *Mind in Buddhist Psychology*, trans. Herbert Guenther and Leslie Kawamura (Emeryville, Calif.: Dharma Publishing, 1975), the twenty secondary kleshas are indignation, resentment, slyness-concealment, spite, jealousy, avarice, deceit, dishonesty, mental inflation, malice, shamelessness, lack of sense of propriety, gloominess, ebullience, lack of trust, laziness, unconcern, forgetfulness, inattentiveness, and desultoriness.

but they do so because you are ready for them. Having already created an object and directed your attention to it, you develop further confusion, in which desirable things are seen as undesirable, and undesirable things are seen as desirable. That little perversion takes place; the process is slightly twisted. You do not know who you are or what are your actual desires. There are all kinds of possibilities, but with all of them, there is a slight twist, which could be described as mistaken perception. Out of this basic mental setup, passion, aggression, ignorance, and all kinds of subsidiary emotions begin to arise.

Traditional texts describe the nature of emotions as disturbance and chaos. Conflicting emotions are the ups and downs and irregularities that take place in your mind. There are supposedly six root-emotions: desire, anger, pride, ignorance, doubt, and opinion.* Those six kleshas are known as "that which disturbs tranquillity," as if there were any tranquillity at all when you are bogged down in the samsaric world. Generally, we have a very hard time finding any little space in which to have the experience of tranquillity, or peace. Tranquillity is simply a temporary relief from indulging in one of those six states of being. The six root kleshas arise in succession out of basic stupidity or bewilderment. That is, from the bewilderment of not knowing what to do comes a sudden flickering of thoughts. That begins to make you very passionate and lustful.

Desire

So the first klesha is desire. Actually, it is more like lust than desire. You become horny about yourself and your state of bewilderment.

Anger

Then, since you are unable to experience the proper fulfillment of that horniness, you experience anger.

Pride

Out of that anger and inability to fulfill yourself comes pride or arrogance, as a kind of self-preservation, or self-maintenance.

---

* See the footnote on page 260.

Ignorance

After that comes carelessness, uncertainty, or ignorance. This ignorance is a different sort of ignorance than the initial triggering process. It is not basic bewilderment, but rather simply boycotting situations, ignoring things, refusing to see things in an intelligent way. So passion leads to aggression, which leads to pride, which leads to a stupidified sort of noncaring. Those are the first four kleshas.

Doubt

Ignoring then develops into the fifth klesha, which is known as doubt. You do not trust any possible alternatives and you do not want advice or any way out. You doubt the teachings, the teacher, and the buddhadharma. You even doubt the simple, sensible norms of everyday existence.

View

From that comes the sixth klesha, which is known as view, or opinion. You form a certain opinion, which you use to solidify your trip. You say, "This is it. I've got it. I know it, and I refuse to believe anything else. This is my view; this is my idea; this is what I have come to believe is the right thing to do."

In terms of the künjung of kleshas, it has been said that ignorance is the source of suffering; it has also been said that passion is the origin of suffering, but there is no particular conflict between those two views. Passion refers to the confusion of always wanting to grasp the next possible situation. By continuously clinging to situations, we perpetually give birth to desire. So passion is a driving, impulsive force; but underlying that is uncertainty, bewilderment, and ignorance. So the origin of suffering could also be said to be fundamental ignorance. The term *fundamental* refers to the ground in which we find ourselves suffering. Basic bewilderment and suffering are existence. They *are.* They don't have any partnership, they just *are.* You are your own suffering, your own ignorance. The klesha of ignorance (Skt.: moha; Tib.: timuk) is just superficial bewilderment. In contrast, fundamental ignorance (Skt.: avidya; Tib.: marikpa) is the refusal to relate at all with the totality of suffering. You want to boycott the whole situation.

KARMIC PATTERNS THAT LEAD TO SUFFERING

The origin of suffering as karma is quite simple and definite. It begins with ignorance; ignorance is, therefore, the origin. Ignorance, in turn, causes volitional action. From volitional action, the entire chain reaction of karma, one nidana after another, can take place. So we have the concept of a karmic chain reaction—not only the concept, but the fact of karma begins to be born in our world and in our life.

Both psychological states or attitudes and the physical environment bring about karmic consequences. The karmic force that exists in our ordinary everyday life is unavoidable. If we are poor, it is unlikely that suddenly we will become rich—although if we are rich, we may find it easy to suddenly become poor! If we are young, we cannot suddenly be old; if we are old, we cannot suddenly become young. Those self-existing situations that we are stuck with are expressions of the origin of suffering. We are stuck with them and we have no choice. Not only have we no choice, but we have to deal with them, which is a hassle. That is a karmic problem.

Beyond that, depending on how we handle ourselves, we can continue to create further debts, or we can try not to create further debts. How we handle that depends on our state of existence and on our ordinary, everyday life. We are stuck in our particular world because of such karmic patterns, and we find ourselves involved in trying to perpetuate pleasure and avoid pain, even down to the most remote little details. If we feel discomfort, we might pick up a Life Saver and put it in our mouth and try to live on that for a few seconds, or we might take a cigarette and light it, or we might decide to stand up and stretch our legs and turn around and look out the window. All those little gestures are expressions that we are subject to some kind of problem. But we are only perpetuating that problem by indulging in more unnecessary activity. However, that does not mean that one should not eat Life Savers or stand up and look out the window—that would be too simple. But our habitual pattern is that whenever we encounter anything undesirable and unappealing, we try little ways within ourselves to avoid it.

We could watch ourselves doing that. The little things we do, the little areas in which we try to entertain ourselves—this process that takes place all the time—is both the product of suffering and the producer of suffering. It is the origin that perpetually re-creates suffering, as well as what we are constantly going through as the result of suffering. From that point of view, everything is extraordinarily hopeless. However, it is better to take that attitude of hopelessness than to view the whole thing as a big joke. Regarding everything as a big joke is an adharmic, or anti-Buddhist, approach. It is freestyle Buddhism. So we should stick to facts and figures, to what we are going through in our life. We are all subject to these problems, and we ought to realize that and try to understand it. Later on, we may be able to relate to the third noble truth, the truth of cessation, and look into how we can be inspired. But for now it is better to be very realistic. That is absolutely important.

Unmeritorious Karma

The künjung of karma can be divided into unmeritorious karma and meritorious karma. Unmeritorious karma comes from a seed of fundamental aggression. It is not based on a polite form of aggression, but comes from a deeper level of resentment and anger. Even before you start to act or begin to create suffering, you have all sorts of wicked desires to plant bad karmic seeds. The unmeritorious karma arising from fundamental aggression is composed of what are known as the ten evil acts, which are divided into three sections: body, speech, and mind.

Unmeritorious Karma Connected with the Body

The first three acts, which are related to body, are taking life, stealing, and sexual misconduct. They are a mixture of passion and aggression. The first two, taking life and stealing, are connected with aggression. The third one, sexual misconduct, is connected with passion—or possibly with aggression, depending upon one's outlook on the world. All three are attempts to bring the outer world into your own wicked world. You are trying to build some kind of empire, based on your own version of things. Taking life, stealing, and sexual misconduct are conditioned by ulterior motives of all kinds. If you can't work with somebody, you reject him: you try to kill him or you try to steal from him. And if you accept somebody, if you include him in your territory, you try to have sex with him. It's a very immediate way of dealing with situations.

Sometimes we put animals in cages and study them—how they eat, how they mate, how they produce babies, how they bring up their young. But in fact, we don't need to put animals in a cage; we can watch ourselves do all those things. We are already in a samsaric cage, and we are a perfect zoological study. Life in samsara is very crude. If we had some other perspective, it might be seen as quite embarrassing; but since we have no other perspective, the whole thing is accepted. Taking life, stealing, and sexual misconduct are regulated by social norms. Some forms of these actions are approved by law because they go along with the basic scheme of society; others are not approved by law because they interfere with that scheme. But all of them, whether lawful or unlawful, are connected with the scheme of rejecting and accepting. It all boils down to that.

Unmeritorious Karma Connected with Speech

The next four of the ten evil acts are connected with speech. Number four is telling lies. You want to defend your particular cause, so you try to deceive. Telling lies is connected with a mixture of passion and aggression: you are trying to reject somebody and to include them in your world, both at the same time. Lying, in this context, means telling elaborate, obvious lies, with the intention to promote your own prosperity or your own security.

Number five is intrigue, which is based on trying to divide. When you find that the world is too solid, that it has developed a united front against you, you try to break it down by intrigue. You make somebody your friend and somebody else your enemy. You try to win by drawing some people to yourself and putting off others.

Number six is negative words. You feel that you can proclaim tremendous wisdom by speaking critically of somebody or some particular topic. You speak harsh words. You hope that if you speak your harsh words loudly and clearly, they will be a kind of weapon or bomb that you can throw into the midst of society, into the midst of your friends, or into the midst of your enemies. You hope that your words will give you power over others. As the creator of harsh, destructive words, you hope that you can destroy society, concepts, ideas, feelings, and theories of all kinds.

Number seven is gossip, or, for that matter, anything other than functional talk. You gossip in order to pervert others, in order to destroy those who have developed great exertion and discipline. You would like to break their discipline and bring them down to your level by talking about crocodiles and the weather and your idea of their idea. Such chatter has a tremendously evil effect on others because it is so effective. It does not provide sharp points; it just lures others into further discursive thought. It lures others into chattering. We know that there are a lot of people who are experts at that.

Unmeritorious Karma Connected with the Mind

The last three of the ten evil acts are connected with mind. Number eight is envy, which is connected with wishful thinking and poverty mentality. You have so much desire to grasp what you don't have, yet you feel inadequate to do so. You envy other people's situations. You feel basically inferior, that you have less wisdom, less clarity of mind, less skillful means, less concentration, less whatever it might be. When you look at somebody who has slightly more than you, you feel greedy, completely hurt. You feel bad if somebody else has a good idea or if somebody has tremendous vision, so you invent all sorts of logics and reasons in order to prove them wrong. You indulge in one-upmanship, trying to bring them down, or to put down their concept or theory. As an example, when you hear about the possibility of indestructible wakefulness and fearlessness, you get freaked-out. You feel jealous and envious. Because you feel so rugged and primitive, you are afraid that you might be excluded from that vision, so you stick to your particular logic, your jumbled-up confusion, your poverty mentality.

Number nine is deliberately hoping to create harm, or having bad feelings about somebody. You don't feel good about someone, and you wish that something will go wrong for him or her. Because of the tremendous influence of theism, particularly of Christian morality, you might say that you would never think ill of anyone or wish anyone harm, that you don't even have any enemies. You could deceive other people quite easily in this regard. However, if you look at yourself very closely, you will begin to find that, in fact, you do have some kind of ill will. It might be just the slightest tinge, but you do have aggression, resentment, or hatred toward somebody.

The last of the ten evil acts is disbelieving in truth, or disbelieving in sacredness. You refuse to work with the sense of reverence. This might make you feel like sitting on the shrine, tearing down sacred objects, or stepping on sutras, the words of the dharma. But there is something more than that. You feel totally, utterly disgusted with anything that might add new meaning to life—a sense of holiness, richness, or sacredness. You relate with meditation practice as a way of just hanging out, and chanting as just chatter. In fact, anything that you do deliberately, anything that constitutes mindfulness, is regarded as a hassle. It all boils down to an excessive casualness, not relating with yourself as having dignity or confidence. The only thing that matters to you is to stay alive—to have a roof over your head and food to eat. You simply don't believe in fundamental dignity. You believe in the wretchedness of the world rather than the sacredness of the world.

MERITORIOUS KARMA

Next we have the ten meritorious deeds of karma. Although they are meritorious, nevertheless you should still regard all of them as producing further suffering, further karma. Whether you act virtuously or whether you act in a degraded manner, you are still producing pain and suffering. This continues until you realize the alternative, until you grab the other end of the stick.* The ten meritorious deeds are very simple: they are the reverse of the ten evil acts. Instead of taking life, for instance, you develop respect for life. Instead of stealing, you practice generosity. In your sexual conduct, you practice sexual wholesomeness and friendship. Instead of telling lies, you practice truthfulness and develop wholesome speech. Instead of intrigue, you practice straightforwardness. Instead of harsh words, you practice good wisdom. Instead of useless speech, or gossip, you develop simplicity: you speak very simply, and what you say is meaningful. Instead of wishful thinking and greediness, you have a sense of openness. Instead of destructive thoughts and bad feelings, you practice gentleness. Instead of disbelieving in sacredness, you commit yourself to understanding sacredness. Those are the ten wholesome deeds.

THE SIX TYPES OF KARMIC CONSEQUENCE

The general notion of karma is that uncertainty, delusion, or ignorance begins to trigger the mechanisms of lust, or passion, and aggression, which then produce karmic consequences. These consequences are divided into

---

* In discussing karma, Trungpa Rinpoche places the teaching of transforming bad karmic circumstances into good ones in the context of the possibility of transcending karmic cause and effect altogether.

six sections, which represent six ways of organizing our world very badly: (1) the power of volitional action, (2) experiencing what you have planted, (3) white karmic consequences, (4) changing the karmic flow by forceful action, (5) shared karmic situations, and (6) interaction of intention and action. It is quite predictable: since our world is created from passion, aggression, and ignorance, we get back from it what we have put in. Things are happening constantly in that way. It is very steady and very predictable.

1. The Power of Volitional Action

The first type of karmic consequence, known as the power of volitional action in karmic situations, has four subcategories.

GOOD BEGINNING, BAD ENDING. The first subcategory is good beginning, bad ending. Although the overall karmic situation you enter into might be virtuous, the result is bad. The traditional analogy is that you are born as a human being endowed with intelligence and wakefulness, or potential wakefulness; but you are born into bad circumstances. For instance, you may be poor, so although you have great intelligence, there is no freedom to practice and study because you have to keep struggling with your life. Being poor is not regarded as wicked, but it creates unreasonable obstacles for you and all sorts of extra demands, hassles, and pains—and if you are not resourceful, you remain stuck in your own poverty.

BAD BEGINNING, GOOD ENDING. In this second category, although your karmic circumstances might be bad, you receive a good ending. This is likened to being born in a rich family of *nagas* (serpentlike deities), which we could retranslate as being born in a Mafia family. It is a bad karmic situation to be born into a Mafia family. However, although your life may be leading you toward destruction, within such a family you have richness and resourcefulness, and the possibility of doing all sorts of good things. So this subcategory is quite the opposite of the previous subcategory.

BAD BEGINNING, BAD ENDING. In the third subcategory, your volitional action and what you receive from your volitional action are both bad. This is like being born into hellish circumstances, and being forced to remain in that bad situation.

GOOD BEGINNING, GOOD ENDING. In the fourth category, your volitional action is good, and what you receive is also good. This is like being born as a *chakravartin*, or "universal monarch." You have the opportunity to do all sorts of things because the situation is very congenial to you.

2. Experiencing What You Have Planted

The second type of karmic consequence, experiencing what you have planted in your karmic situation, is divided into three subcategories. The first is experiencing your karmic results immediately. When you begin to act aggressively with anger, passion, and ignorance, then automatically, on the spot, you get your results. It is like having a fight with someone, then driving off and ending up in a car crash. It is very immediate.

In the second subcategory, the karmic consequences are experienced later; they do not hit you until your next birth. In the third subcategory, you experience the karmic consequences ripening from a previous birth. As an example, you are born in the world with an opportune situation, but somebody else comes along and disrupts that for you. You could say that this is like being born in Tibet, then getting chased out by the communists, and ending up working in a gas station in America.

3. White Karmic Consequences

The third major type of karmic consequence, white karmic consequences, refers to good karmic situations that are perpetually growing. It has three subcategories.

The first is emulating the three jewels—the Buddha, dharma, and sangha. You continuously get good karmic results out of that, naturally and perpetually.

The second subcategory is emulating and appreciating somebody else's virtue. That also leads to good karmic results and a well-favored situation. When you are inspired by somebody's wakefulness, you become wakeful as well. That is the virtue of influence.

The third subcategory is practicing the dharma. Even though your mind might be wandering, you are still practicing the dharma. Due to the fact that you are sitting on your cushion and practicing, you are not committing any sins. So you have a good karmic situation in spite of the wandering of your mind.

4. Changing the Karmic Flow by Forceful Action

The fourth karmic consequence is that although currently you have ended up with a very bad situation, you can suddenly change the karmic flow with a tremendous, quite sudden and forceful effort. You may have ended up in a tremendous depression, but you are able to make a jump in your life and overcome that. You are able to change the flow of your particular lifestyle. You might be used to being very lazy and sloppy, but sitting practice could tighten up your lifestyle so that suddenly you become a tidy, vigorous, and uplifting person.

There are second thoughts happening each time you act. There is hesitation, and from that hesitation, or gap, you can go backward or forward. Changing the flow of karma happens in that gap. So the gap is very useful. It is in the gap that you give a birth to a new life.

5. Shared Karmic Situations

The fifth karmic consequence, shared karmic situations, falls into two subcategories: national and individual karma within national karma.

NATIONAL KARMA. The first subcategory is national karma. For instance, you may be born in a particular country where you always have to relate with 7-Elevens, take-out pizza, and badly made cars. You end up in certain environments or worlds, but you cannot totally blame that on yourself. The whole country is made up that way.

INDIVIDUAL KARMA WITHIN NATIONAL KARMA. The second subcategory is individual karma within national karma. For example, if the sewage system in your neighborhood is not good, that karma is particularly and personally yours, in a sense, because the pipes keep breaking and costing you a lot of money and effort. Another example is winding up with a bad teacher who gets very grumpy because he is poorly paid by the school system. On one hand, that situation is not your fault; but on the other hand, you did end up in that particular school. You have a television network, but you have your own personal TV with which to tune in, and you also choose your own particular station. It's very simple. Environmental and individual karma complement each other; they feed each other.

6. Interaction of Intention and Action

The sixth and final karmic consequence is the interaction of intention and action. It is divided into four subcategories.

WHITE INTENTION, WHITE ACTION. The first subcategory is called completely white. An example of completely white karma is respecting your teacher and having devotion. Because that whole approach is related with healthiness rather than revolutionary thinking, ill will, and resentment, a lot of goodness comes out of it. So perpetual whiteness is created.

BLACK INTENTION, BLACK ACTION. The next subcategory is completely black. This is like taking somebody's life without any particular excuse or motivation. You have murdered somebody or destroyed something. That is completely black.

WHITE INTENTION, BLACK ACTION. The third and fourth subcategories are mixtures of black and white. The third category is basically positive: with the good intention of protecting the whole, you perform a black action. For instance, with the good intention of protecting the lives of hundreds of people, you kill one person. That seems to be a good karmic situation. If somebody is going to press the button of the atomic bomb, you shoot that person. Here the intention is white, but the action itself is black, although it has a positive effect.

BLACK INTENTION, WHITE ACTION. In the fourth subcategory, the intention is black and the action is white. This is like being very generous to your enemy while you are trying to poison him; it is a mixture of black and white.

Although people are not generally one-hundred-percent sane, they are worthy of our respect for their partial goodness. It's the same as saying that we can't expect perfect weather. Instead we have to expect the occasional sunshine of goodness, in spite of the snow. All six types of karmic consequence are arrived at partly due to your being in a wrong environment and partly due to your own neurosis. It is our intention to avoid such karmic consequences. However, once those two conditions come together, it is very hard to push against them. The only way to do so is by rousing the personal inspiration to try to change one's national and domestic karma.

UNPLUGGING SAMSARA

To review, the origin of suffering is divided into two main sections: the künjung of kleshas and the künjung of karma. It seems to be quite simple: The künjung of kleshas consists of the six root kleshas, followed by the twenty secondary kleshas. The künjung of karma includes unmeritorious karma and meritorious karma (which are each subdivided into body, speech, and mind), plus karmic consequences.

In hinayana, in order to cut the root of samsara, the strategy is to unplug or disconnect everything. We could actually unplug the refrigerator of samsara. It might take several hours to defrost; nevertheless, as long as we have unplugged that particular refrigerator, defrosting is going to happen. So we shouldn't feel that we are stuck with those karmic situations. We should feel that we always have the opportunity to interrupt the flow of karma. First, we have to interrupt our ignorance, and secondly, we also have to interrupt our passion. By interrupting both our ignorance and our passion, we have nothing happening in terms of the samsaric world. We have already unplugged the refrigerator.

THE CESSATION OF SUFFERING

56

Awakening and Blossoming

*It is possible to experience a moment of nirvana, a glimpse of ces-
sation. That is what Buddha taught in his first sermon in Sarnath,
when he delivered the teaching of the four noble truths, which he
repeated four times. The Buddha said that . . . suffering should be
known; the origin of suffering should be renounced; the cessation
of suffering should be realized; and the path should be regarded as
the truth to resolution.*

THE THIRD noble truth is the truth of cessation. The truth of
cessation (*gokpa* in Tibetan) is related to the concept of tharpa, or
liberation. In discussing the possibility of cessation, we should get rid
of fictitious stories about how great it is to get there and become somebody at last. Such ideas may be obstacles. In relating to tharpa, the question is whether we have to use our imagination or whether we actually
can experience a sense of relief or freedom. The truth of the matter is that
in regard to cessation, imagination does not play a very important role. It
does not help at all in getting results.

The experience of cessation is very personal and very real, like the
practice of meditation. Generally, however, our experiences of freedom
or liberation are quite sparse and minute—and when we do have an occasional glimpse of freedom, we try to catch it, so we lose it. But it is possible to extend such glimpses. For example, if somebody is waking for the
first time from a deep sleep, she might see the midnight stars. But if she

waits long enough without going back to sleep, she will begin to see not only stars, but the dawn, then the sunrise, and then the whole landscape being lit by a brilliant light coming from the sky. She will begin to see her hands, her palms, her toes, and she will also begin to see her tables, her chairs, and the world around her. And if she is clever enough to look at a mirror, she will see herself as well. The truth of cessation is a personal discovery. It is not mystical and it does not have any connotations of religion or psychology; it is simply your experience. If you spill boiling water on your hand, it is a personal experience: you get hurt. For that matter, if you have an orgasm, it is your personal experience: nobody else experiences it. Likewise, cessation is not just a theoretical discovery, but an experience that is very real to you—a sudden gain. It is like experiencing instantaneous good health: you have no cold, no flu, no aches, and no pains in your body. You feel perfectly well, absolutely refreshed and wakeful! Such an experience is possible. Based on the fact that somebody in the past has already experienced it, you too will experience it sooner or later—although there is no guarantee, of course. The person who has already experienced the cessation of suffering is the Buddha. The Sanskrit word *buddha* is translated into Tibetan as *sang-gye*. *Sang* means "awake," and *gye* means "expansion," or "blossoming." The word *sang* is related with awakening from the sleep of pain; and within the pain, suffering, and unawareness, *gye* is like a blossoming flower, so *sang-gye* is "awakening and blossoming." Since you are awake, you collect bundles of knowledge. The knowable has become known to you through awareness and mindfulness.

From the viewpoint of the four noble truths, what we are trying to do is to become sang-gye. We are trying to blossom. We're trying to be wakeful. That is precisely what we are doing. Quite possibly we have a glimpse of sang-gye happening endlessly. Although we may think that we are fooling ourselves—and sometimes we *are* fooling ourselves—that element takes place constantly. According to the third noble truth, cessation is possible. On the path of the four noble truths we are trying to become buddhas, real buddhas, real sang-gyes.

THE THREE CATEGORIES OF SAMSARA

The main obstacle to becoming buddha is samsara. The Tibetan word for samsara is *khorwa: khor* means "spinning," or "circulating," and *wa* is "-ness"; so *khorwa* means "to spin," or "those who are spinning around."

Khorwa, or samsara, is equated with the ocean, because the ocean continually circulates around the world: it comes in, goes back out, comes back in, and so on. Similarly, samsara is endless circulation. The samsaric ocean is based on three categories: the essence, the cause, and the result.

1. The Essence of Samsara: Bewilderment

The essence of samsara is the complete opposite of buddha, or awakening from suffering: it is ignorance, stupidity, basic bewilderment. Bewilderment is a psychological state that we all experience; it includes the dream state and the sleep state. Due to bewilderment, we are constantly drifting around, not knowing exactly what is happening—which is the opposite of awareness. Not seeing, not knowing, not experiencing what is happening, constantly drifting—that is the essence of samsara.

2. The Cause of Samsara: Fixation

The second category of samsara is the cause. The cause is holding on to vague concepts. That is what is called "fixation," or in Tibetan, *dzinpa*. *Dzin* means "to hold," and *pa* makes it a noun; so *dzinpa* means "fixation," or "grasping." Since we do not have clear perception, we must hang on to vagueness and uncertainty. In doing so, we begin to behave like a Ping-Pong ball, which does not possess any intelligence but only follows the directions of the paddle. We are bounced back and forth like a Ping-Pong ball by our fixation.

We would like to express ourselves if we feel we are undermined or if we are not acknowledged—we would like to stick our neck out—but again we are Ping-Ponged. Sometimes we feel we have so much responsibility that we would like to retire and fade away, but again we become a Ping-Pong ball. Whatever we do, our actions are not perfectly right because, based on this neurotic game, we keep being Ping-Ponged. Although it may appear that the Ping-Pong ball is commanding the players, although it seems amazing that such a little ball has so much power to direct the players' actions and even draw spectators to watch it going back and forth—actually, that is not true. The Ping-Pong ball is just a ball. It does not have any intelligence; it's just operating on reflex.

3. The Result of Samsara: Suffering

Finally, we come to the result. The essence of samsara is bewilderment; the cause of samsara is fixation; the result is suffering. Since you have been constantly bounced back and forth, you begin to experience dizziness. As the Ping-Pong ball, you feel very dizzy and you ache all over your body because you've been bounced back and forth so much. The sense of pain is enormous. That is the definition of samsara.

CESSATION IS POSSIBLE

According to the third noble truth, what we are doing is preventing samsara, or causing its cessation, by behaving like sang-gye, or a buddha. It seems that the only way we could identify ourselves with even a pinch of the experience of buddhahood is through the experience of awareness and mindfulness practice. That is the message. At this point, cessation is not regarded as pure cessation or the complete answer—it is the message that it is possible. It is possible to develop understanding. It is possible to undo the mythical, fictional aspect of cessation and experience a glimpse of cessation as a reality, although it may be only a very short, small glimpse. The first step is to realize you are in the samsaric mess. Although many people have heard this for years, they still do not actually recognize that they are being Ping-Pong-balled. That is precisely why you are in samsara—because you know what you are doing, but you still keep doing it. However, in being a Ping-Pong ball there are still gaps of not being one. There are gaps in which something else is experienced. In fact, during that Ping-Pong-balling, another experience takes place constantly: the experience of awareness. You begin to realize what you are, who you are, and what you are doing. But that realization could lead to spiritual materialism, which is another form of fixation—you are being Ping-Pong-balled by spirituality. However, you also realize that if there is no speed, then there is no fixation; therefore, you can transcend spiritual materialism.

A person experiences a glimpse of cessation as a kind of appetizer. If the appetizer is good, you have an idea of how the main course will be. The basic point is to *experience* cessation rather than to have a theory or a dream about it. As several contemplative gurus in the lineage have warned, too much description of the outcome is an obstacle to the path. Teachings should be based purely on the level of workability and direct personal experience. So we are following that recommendation. However, in the context of practice, as long as the approach is free from samsara, hearing descriptions of the details of the path is not particularly problematic. We could develop a very detailed and precise understanding of the nature of the path based on the process of coming back to mindfulness and awareness.

The contrast to samsara is nirvana, or peace. At this point, however, we don't have anything but samsara and little points of light that rise from the midst of darkness. Our first alternative to samsara is the practice of awareness or mindfulness, which brings us through the journey of the four noble truths. That seems to be the only way. We have to come back to becoming like Buddha. The third noble truth is very simple: nirvana is possible. Before you have complete cessation, you have to have the message that it is *possible* to have complete cessation. That message is like seeing a star in the middle of the sky on a new-moon night. Eventually, you are inspired by the crescent moon, the full moon, and then by the dawn—and finally you are inspired by the whole thing.

It is possible to experience a moment of nirvana, a glimpse of cessation. That is what Buddha taught in his first sermon in Sarnath, when he delivered the teaching of the four noble truths, which he repeated four times. The Buddha said that cessation could be experienced. He said that suffering should be known; the origin of suffering should be renounced; the cessation of suffering should be realized; and the path should be regarded as the truth to resolution. That's almost word for word.

57

Meditation as the Path to Buddhahood

The path of meditation also leads to shinjang, being thoroughly processed or trained, which is the result or achievement of sha-matha-vipashyana meditation. Although you haven't experienced the final development yet, it is no big secret that there is a final development. You can't pretend that the Buddha didn't exist and still talk about his teachings, because he actually did it—he achieved enlightenment.

T HE THIRD noble truth is based on recognizing the contrast between samsara and nirvana. In the technique of meditating on the breathing, there is automatically and naturally such a contrast. You realize that something is alternating in you, that your sanity and your insanity are alternating. You experience a gap. Relating to that gap is relating to the contrast between samsara and nirvana.

The traditional analogy for the cessation of suffering is the blowing out of a candle. This refers to the final stage of cessation, when you have become buddha. But effort and energy is required even to get to the idea of blowing out the candle. You first need to realize that the candle is not all that powerful, that it is feeble, so you could actually blow it out. Once you realize you can blow out the candle, even at a distance, you have gotten the message. And when that message is a reality, blowing out the candle becomes simply a matter of effort.

The cessation of samsara happens when you act like Buddha. The Buddha was just one person, however. The liberated state of mind could be different, or have a different style, for each individual. What we are concerned with now, however, is training. Once you have been trained, you might exercise that training in your own particular way. For example, after you pass the driver's test, which is the same for everyone, you might drive differently than other people who passed the test. In the vajrayana, or tantra, the different levels and styles that people operate with are categorized. But as far as hinayana is concerned, it is simply a question of experiencing basic liberation.

Attaining liberation takes work. It is like making jewelry. When you go to a jeweler, he has solid gold, solid silver, or solid brass lumps hanging around that are ugly and don't look particularly ornamental. But when you ask him to make a ring or a necklace or some earrings, he gets out a lump and begins to make something out of it, and it becomes a beautiful thing. Likewise, when you buy a car, you could remember that your newly bought automobile is not born out of a lotus, but it's made in a factory. It may seem as if it's born out of a lotus, but that's not quite true. It is the same thing with buddhahood, which is supposed to be spotless and fantastic. To become buddha is a final inspiration; to become buddha—wow! But the Buddha did not come out of a lotus—he came out of a factory.

The cessation of suffering is connected with the fourth noble truth, which is the path, or *lam* in Tibetan. Cessation and the path work together: when there is a path, cessation automatically dawns; and when there is cessation, that allows you to follow the path. The path consists of following the example of the Buddha through the practice of meditation, through mindfulness and awareness. That practice is one of the merits of the hinayana discipline.

The reason the hinayana is known as the "lesser vehicle" is because it is straight and narrow. There isn't much room to improvise. Since there is no improvisation, we can develop what is known as individual salvation. Individual salvation is not a selfish goal; it is self-discipline, straight and simple. It is simple in the sense that there is not much to do other than just fully being there. The path of meditation also leads to shinjang, being thoroughly processed or trained, which is the result or achievement of shamatha-vipashyana meditation. Although you haven't experienced the final development yet, it is no big secret that there is a final development. You can't pretend that the Buddha didn't exist and still talk about his teachings, because he actually did it—he achieved enlightenment. We can't keep that a secret.

In the meantime, however, you could regard any sense of promise that comes into your mind, any hope that comes up, as another thought. If there is a strong desire to achieve a result, that will push you back. You could relate to hope as respect for the dharma, or the truth, rather than a promise. It is like a schoolchild seeing a professor: one day she too might become a professor, but she still has to do her homework. Similarly, particularly in the hinayana, there is a journey going on all the time.

Shinjang happens in stages. It begins with the achievement of clarity. This level is like seeing one glimpse of what it would be like if you had that glimpse constantly. In order to achieve permanent cessation, you have to continue with the practice. So first you have a glimpse, which is like the appetizer; then that appetizer makes you hungrier. You want to have a big meal; therefore, you are willing to wait, maybe hours and hours, for the big meal to come.

When you develop shinjang, the sense of turmoil and misery subsides. Therefore, both physically and mentally, there is a feeling of comfort. Comfort does not mean euphoria, but the sense that things are soothing because you have simplified your life. Simplicity brings tremendous relief. Nonetheless, you don't look for final results and you do not become goal oriented; you just keep on practicing. Having practiced enough, achievement comes naturally. If you are constantly trying to achieve cessation, it is a problem—you will not achieve it in that way. Whenever you take an ego-oriented approach, you become allergic to yourself. There is no other way but to step out of that. So attaining individual salvation does not come from seeking salvation—salvation simply dawns. Cessation and salvation come to you as you become a reasonable person. You become reasonable and meticulous because you cease to be sloppy and careless. Therefore, there is a sense of relief. Meticulousness is exemplified by *oryoki* practice, a formal style of serving and eating food that has its origins in Zen Buddhism. In this practice you are aware of everything that is being done, every move. At the same time, you are not uptight, for once you become self-conscious, you begin to forget the oryoki procedures. This logic also applies to keeping your room tidy, taking care of your clothing, taking care of your lifestyle altogether. Being meticulous is not based on fear, it is based on natural mindfulness.

As a final achievement, if you lose your mindfulness, a reminder comes back to you directly in the process of acting sloppy. Such reminders are a result of first having tremendous discipline. Because you have been with your practice constantly, reminders come up. If you have spent time with a friend, someone whom you love very much, and that friend goes away, each time you think of your friend, you develop more affection for him or her. In the same way, if you are at the more advanced level of shinjang, whenever sloppiness happens, that sloppiness itself automatically reminds you and brings you back. So a natural system of checks and balances begins to take place. In that way, you become like the Buddha. Every little detail of your life has meaning. There is a natural and dignified way to eat food, and a natural and dignified way to relate with anything else that occurs in your life. Instead of your life being a situation of suffering, it becomes soothing. That is why shamatha is known as the development of peace. Peace does not mean pleasure seeking, but harmony. You don't create chaos for yourself or for others, and you start by first working with yourself.

Traditionally, there are four ways of taking care of your body and developing wholesomeness. The first way is relating properly to food. As in oryoki practice, you don't consume large amounts of food, nor do you eat too little. Rather, you eat enough to leave some room in your stomach. The second way is relating properly to sleep, or rest. You don't push yourself constantly, but you learn how to rest. Resting in this way is different from resting in the ordinary sense, where you are sometimes still working hard.

The third way is taking care of details, which means physically taking care of yourself: taking care of your body, taking care of your clothing, taking care of your environment. How you move physically, how you handle things, is more important than simply how you appear. Beyond mere appearance, there is a quality of meticulousness. The fourth way is meditation: without that reference point, there would be no real relief or wholesomeness. So food, sleep, taking care of the details of your well-being, and meditation are the four ways to develop wholesomeness, and such wholesomeness leads you to develop the state of individual salvation. That is why it is said that the dharma is good in the beginning, good in the middle, and good in the end.

In working with yourself, you start with the outer form; then that outer form brings an inner feeling; and finally that inner feeling brings a deeper sense of freedom. So it is a threefold process. This same process could apply to anything you do. In the beginning, it is mostly a big hassle; in the middle, it is sometimes a hassle and sometimes it is natural; then finally it becomes natural. With sitting practice as well: first it is a struggle; at some stage it is both a struggle and a relief; and finally it is very easy. It's like putting on a new ring: for the first few days, it feels like it is in the way, but eventually it becomes a part of your hand. It is that kind of logic.

As for myself, since the age of five, I was raised in an environment of constant discipline. If I lost my awareness, I would be reminded by my tutor or by my disciplinarian, not just by myself, so by now it seems to have become natural. It's not that I myself have achieved a great thing, particularly; but it is thanks to my disciplinarian and my teacher.

58

Transcending Samsara and Nirvana

Cessation means transcending the turmoil and problems of life and the neurosis that goes along with them. However, we try so hard to transcend all that, that we are unable to do so, because the very fact of trying so hard is the way we got into trouble in the beginning. So in regard to cessation, definitely the most important point is that it transcends both samsara and nirvana. By transcending both samsaric and nirvanic possibilities of confusion, we are transcending cessation itself, so there is no ground. . . . But that groundlessness itself could become a very powerful expression of cessation.

F ROM THE hinayana point of view, cessation means being able to prevent problems or use them up. The Sanskrit word for "cessation" is *nirodha,* and in Tibetan it is *gokpa,* which in verb form means "to stop," or "to prevent." The idea of cessation is not so much being calmed down, but as suddenly being stopped. Sometimes gokpa refers to the final goal, the state of enlightenment, or freedom. However, in this case, gokpa is not regarded as the final goal; instead, it simply means that temporarily problems have been prevented. We have been able to cut through them, to cut them down. Having cut unnecessary garbage, we are able to develop real living sanity and to let that shine through. Cessation refers to the prevention of unnecessary hassle; however, a level of hassle still remains. It is like having nice food and being satisfied with your particular dish, but still having the hassle that you have to pay for it.

Gokpa has the quality of a vaccination: once problems are prevented, it is for good. Cessation means that we are actually able to prevent karmic chain reactions as well as karmic consequences on the spot. That possibility comes from our own realization and experience of the journey. We begin to feel that we could prevent such problems by being highly disciplined and by having a genuine connection with our own mind-and-thought patterns, which could be good or bad, virtuous or otherwise.

The question is how to unplug, how to switch off the electricity without getting a shock. As far as shamatha practice is concerned, the way to do so is by nonparticipation in the samsaric world. You become a monk or a nun. You become a good practitioner who sits a lot, for during sitting practice you are preventing karma, or at least you are not committing any wrongdoings. That logic might seem simpleminded, but it is not simply that if you don't do anything, that is good, and if you do lots of things, that is bad. The logic is that when you are meditating, you are actually boycotting the process of furthering anything at all. There are various degrees of cessation. There could be a lesser, medium, or greater degree of cessation. Because we understand how cessation evolves, we begin to feel that we are actually making progress. We develop a sense of friendliness, ease, and self-respect. We have fewer complaints and less resentment. We can look at ourselves in the mirror and see how much we have changed from when we first started to practice. We see that we have developed a sense of confidence and genuineness. Basically, we see that we used to eat garbage and now we are beginning to change our diet; and we realize that we would never do that again. Those very simple things are signs of nirodha.

Although you begin to recognize those signs of cessation, at the same time you don't need to hang on to such signs. You don't need confirmation or reassurance, you just keep going. Looking for reassurance would be returning to künjung, the origin of suffering, and you don't want to do that. One experience of pain is good enough. The fascination that drives you back to pain no longer applies. Would you put your finger on an electric burner when it is burning hot, if you had done that once already? Obviously not. Likewise, once you have realized the truth of suffering and the origin of suffering fully and properly, you never make the same mistake again. This happens by instinct, as well as by studying and practicing. The mahayanists would say that everyone possesses the nature of wakefulness, called *tathagatagarbha,* or buddha nature, which forces you to see through your pain and make sure that it is not repeated.

Experientially, cessation means that thoughts become transparent. Thoughts are no longer a big hassle in sitting practice. With cessation, such thoughts become too absurd to occur. Experiencing the transparency of thoughts seems to depend on the long-range discipline of the student. During sitting practice, very powerful thoughts take place. We get angry with this and that—my this and my that, other people's this's and that's. There are occasional punctuations of wondering what kind of food we are going to eat, whether we have to take a shower and buy some shampoo. All sorts of thoughts, both little thoughts and powerful thoughts, occasionally take place, but all of those thoughts are seen to be transparent rather than solid. Cessation occurs when there is no implication behind such thoughts—they are just ripples in the pond.

THE TWELVE ASPECTS OF CESSATION

Traditionally, the discussion of cessation is divided into twelve topics. In *The Treasury of Knowledge,* Jamgön Kongtrül also listed these twelve topics.

1. Nature

The first topic is the nature of cessation, which has three categories: the origin, what should be given up, and what should be cultivated.

THE ORIGIN: MEDITATIVE ABSORPTION. The origin of cessation is meditative absorption, a pure state of mind beyond ignorance. You begin to understand the nature of reality by developing meditative absorption through the practice of shamatha discipline, which reduces kleshas.

WHAT SHOULD BE GIVEN UP: NEUROSIS. What should be given up, overlooked, or transcended is neurosis. Through mindfulness and awareness, you experience the possibility of not committing yourself to the kleshas. You are beginning to develop a sense of goodness and toughness, which automatically prevents you from being sloppy.

WHAT SHOULD BE CULTIVATED: SIMPLICITY. What should be cultivated is simplicity. Simplicity means that you keep everything to a minimum. You keep your life very simple: you could get up, practice, eat breakfast, go to work, come back, have dinner, practice again, and go to sleep. Ideally, good practitioners are supposed to sandwich their lives between morning and evening meditation practice. This simplifies things and cuts through unnecessary entertainment. In terms of sitting, you don't create any conditions at all, such as asking, "Should I sit in the morning? Should I sit in the evening?" There is no question about it. You are totally and completely influenced by your shamatha practice and by the simplicity of your involvement with the buddhadharma.

Fundamentally, the nature of cessation is based on a pure state of mind. Having overcome or seen through the temporary obstacles or veils that prevent us from seeing things as they are—seeing properly with clear vision—there are no further difficulties. Having overcome our inability to relate with our basic nature, nothing needs to be prevented and nothing needs to be cultivated. The obstacles covering our basic sanity are not regarded as hardened, as fastened on with powerful glue or difficult to remove, but as detachable. It is like removing clouds in order to see the sun. Nonetheless, it can be hard to see things that way.

2. Profundity

The second topic is profundity. Profundity means developing subtleness in your attitude toward cessation, understanding that cessation is nobody's property. Cessation does not come from elsewhere, it is part of you; and at the same time, seemingly, it is not particularly a part of you. Basically, what is part of you and what is not part of you are always questionable. Cessation cannot be regarded as the product of either your personal effort or someone else's suggestion. So as a practitioner, you should not take pride in your effort or feel arrogant, thinking that you have brought about the cessation of the samsaric world. It is not *your* cessation—at the same time, cessation does not belong to others.

You practice due to your own inspiration. Nobody can make you do it if you don't want to. You do not have to depend on local deities or national deities or religious sectarian deities. Such inspiration seems to be a natural part of you; but in fact, the path is not part of your basic system, because it is foreign to your usual style of thinking, which is neurosis. There is a problem when your inspiration develops into a sense that knowledge and you are completely one, for if there is complete oneness, there is no urge to follow any discipline, such as the hinayana discipline of creating no harm. That kind of discipline seems to lose the quality of naturalness.

Somebody presenting the language of sanity to you is using a different kind of logic than the habitual logic of neurosis, however philosophical and natural or religious it may seem. At the same time, you cannot ignore the fact that basic sanity exists naturally in your state of being, and that through discipline you are able to understand both the origin and the cessation of suffering. So if you ask whether the path is part of your basic system or not, the answer is that it is both. Dharma is based on a sense of separation, in that foreign information is coming to you. However, when that information cannot be properly and fully absorbed or digested, and you continue to regard it as separate, you have a problem. It is also problematic if you try to maintain your particular territory by picking and choosing what has been given to you.

On one hand, there is no difference between dharma, discipline, and yourself: dharma is an expression of yourself. On the other hand, if you think there is no difference between you and the dharma, so you can make up your own dharma as you go along, that is not quite the case. You have inherited examples of the dharma through a lineage, and you have to follow such examples. You can't be that freestyle. The dharma is not absolutely everything and it is not absolutely nothing—it is both. It is not even both, and it is absolutely not neither. Dharma is not yours and it is not others'. Dharma is both yours and others'. At the same time, dharma is not made out of both you and others jumbled together, like a sweet-and-sour dish. Therefore, you and the dharma are not one, nor are you and the dharma completely separate. So what do we finally have? Very little, or quite a lot. The only possibility is that at one and the same time, the simplicity of the practice can be developed with respect to the tradition and discipline, and your intuition can be developed according to your own basic understanding of life. That is the point of profundity.

3. Sign

The third topic is sign. The sign that you have achieved cessation, or gokpa, is that the kleshas have begun to subside. Little by little, you find that they gradually cease to exist. You begin to become somewhat bland, ordinary, and boring. Because of your practice, you cease to play games and you become a decent person. You are cleaned up, so to speak, and you become a more reasonable person—on the spot, or gradually. The ultimate sign is realizing that there are no more hang-ups of any kind. At that point, you have achieved nirodha and begun to experience nirvana.

Sign, or token, means that you are giving up worldly commitments in the sense of pure, unreasonable indulgence. Even sensible worldly people would not regard such indulgence as good. Beyond that, you are becoming highly disciplined. You are realistic, proper, and industrious; you have self-discipline, and you project dignity. Such ordinary decency is recognized as a token of cessation. There is virtue in such everyday logic as driving carefully and not bouncing your checks. Although those virtues may seem superficial, little things like that are still considered to be related with the possibility of gokpa. That is, the logic of ordinary household life is directed toward cessation: there is an element of sanity and of transcending samsara. Although that may seem like a vague possibility, such logic has juice in it, and truth.

4. Ultimate

The fourth topic is ultimate. It is based on applying the understanding and discipline of prajna, or knowledge, in our approach to life. Through prajna we begin to realize the origin of our problems and our mistakes, which occur from ignorance. We develop a real understanding of where the confusion and chaos take place. Having understood that, there is no possibility of regressing. From this point of view, our journey could be considered a one-shot deal. It is never regarded as purely a rehearsal.

Through the practice of shamatha, you begin to develop "noble prajna"—supreme prajna that transcends the ordinary world.* You realize on an intellectual level how and why suffering and the origin of suffering can be overcome. You develop a genuine understanding of how things work. In other words, you don't panic. When you panic, you lose sight of noble prajna. You just beat around the bush, asking, "How should I be doing this? Why should I be doing this?" You become a beggar of

---

* "Noble prajna" is a translation of the Sanskrit term *arya-prajna*. The word *arya*, "noble," was applied in ancient times to honorable people. Modern Western scholars adopted the term to designate the Indo-European ethnic group as "Aryan," and the Nazis subsequently promoted the fiction of a morally superior "Aryan race." Trungpa Rinpoche thus encouraged his translators to avoid *arya* and use the phrase "noble prajna" out of sensitivity to this troubling connotation.

incompetency. But with noble prajna, you become confident. You begin to see the value of the intellect, which in this case means sharpened clarity rather than theory. Instead of resorting to the Jungian or Freudian styles of psychologizing everything, you are simply experiencing your life and understanding how it works. In the experience of prajna, you know what to do and how to do it properly and fully. Through intellect, you are able to overcome what should be avoided: the seed, or origin, of suffering.

5. Incompletion

The fifth topic is incompletion. When you reach a certain level of spiritual achievement, or cessation, you begin to understand that although you have been able to reach that level, things are not properly completed. You understand that although you have overcome problems and obstacles, you have not yet blossomed.

The student of hinayana who first enters the discipline is known as a "stream-winner." Having entered into the system of discipline, you have overcome the hang-up against clear seeing. But once you join the path of clear seeing, or seeing things as they are, you find that along with that, there are further hang-ups.

There are also students who have reached the level known as "once-returner," meaning that you only return to the world for one more lifetime; you do not keep returning due to karmic debts. Although you have not completely overcome the world of pleasure and passion, or completely clarified the world of desire, and therefore still have problems, you are still regarded as a person who has achieved a kind of liberation or salvation.

Even for those who in their next life do not return to the world of samsara, people called "nonreturners," the attainment of gokpa is still incomplete or temporary. All such students are partially delivered and partially confused; nonetheless, their incomplete cessation could still be called a form of salvation.

6. Signs of Completion

The sixth topic is signs of completion. At this point you have become an arhat, somebody who has completely overcome or controlled any obstacles to the path. Arhats have already restrained what should be restrained and developed what should be developed. Your learning is completely accomplished and you have reached a state of nonlearning. However, this state of no more learning refers purely to the arhats on the hinayana level, rather than to the bodhisattva or the buddha level. It refers to arhats who have reached the state of no more learning as far as their own particular arhatship-world is concerned. It has nothing to do with the five paths in vajrayana, in which the path of no more learning would be buddhahood.

To review, in the hinayana there are stream-winners, once-returners, nonreturners, and arhats. When students first enter the path, they are called stream-winners. Since stream-winners and once-returners emphasize meditative absorptions, or *dhyanas* (or jhanas), they remain within the realm of passion. Nonreturners are able to conquer the realm of passion, but they are still working with samsaric mind and with the Hindu notion of attaining divine achievement. They continue to work with that until they become complete arhats, when finally they cut the whole thing. Nonreturners are incomplete because they are still in the process of not returning. (I think Nagarjuna would like that particular wit.*)

Arhats progress through the four jhana states, or meditative absorptions, and beyond. Nobody knows exactly what happens at that point; there is a lot of philosophical disagreement about that. In my school,† we take the position that when somebody is able to completely overcome the four jhana states, as well as the formless jhanas, he or she becomes a real Buddhist, rather than wandering in samsara. In other words, because the jhana states are still involved in samsaric possibilities, such meditative absorptions should be transcended.

7. Without Ornament

The seventh aspect of gokpa is without ornament, without embellishment. At this stage, although you have developed prajna, which has led you to fully overcome conflicting emotions, you are not adorned with any

---

* The great logician Nagarjuna (second to third century) developed a dialectical approach of systematically undercutting any attempt to establish a solid logical position. This became the basis of the "middle way," or Madhyamaka school.

† Trungpa Rinpoche trained in both the Kagyü and Nyingma schools of Tibetan Buddhism.

signs of holiness or dignity. You have accomplished much on a personal level, but you do not manifest that to the rest of the world. Some texts would call this being unable to perform miracles, which is a somewhat questionable subject. We could refer to miracles more as a real command over the world. Basically, "without ornament" means that you are not ready to be a teacher, although you have developed yourself thoroughly and fully. You may have transcended neurotic hang-ups, but you are still unable to manifest to students, to yourself, and to the world as a highly accomplished person. So you are unadorned as a teacher.

8. Adorned

The eighth topic is adorned; it is gokpa with embellishment or ornamentation. At this point, you have become a teacher. You have developed confidence and flair, and your individual discipline has also developed. Having already overcome the veil of neurosis and the veil of karmic obligations, you have achieved power over the world.

9. With Omission

Number nine is with omission. Although you have transcended the passions and neurosis of the human realm, you are still unable to accomplish real sanity completely and properly. You have attained freedom, in knowing how to avoid being born in the world of desire, which includes the hell realm, the hungry ghost realm, the animal realm, the human realm, the jealous god realm, and part of the god realm. You have also transcended the world of form, the realm of the form gods. But you have not transcended the formless world, the realm of the formless gods. That portion of the realm of the gods is the holiest of holy, the highest samsaric realm. This is exemplified in the Hindu religion by the striving to attain brahmahood and then to transcend it. In Hinduism, there are levels beyond brahmahood, where Brahma (the Godhead) becomes the universality of Brahman (the Absolute). In terms of Christianity, we could say that you have completed your training, but you haven't quite connected with the Godhead. Since the neurosis of an abstract notion of the ultimate has not been completely conquered, there is an omission. Even would-be arhats, would-be bodhisattvas, or would-be buddhas practicing the path of buddhadharma still have such subtle theistic hang-ups.

10. Without Omission

The tenth topic is without omission. Without omission means that you have transcended even the majestic and mystical concept of Godhead or brahmahood. You have finally conquered the whole theistic world. Here, all the neuroses and habitual patterns are transcended. However, that does not mean you are becoming a bodhisattva or a buddha. We are talking about somebody who is on the hinayana level. At this level, you have just barely managed to cope with things as they are. You have seen that the hassles of samsara are fantastically vivid and obvious, but that the hassles of nirvana are much more so. So when the hassles of nirvana are overcome, and you are actually able to become a reasonably respectable nirvanic person, it is quite a big deal. That is the definition of *gokpa,* or "cessation," from the true hinayana point of view. You become a good citizen of hinayana, somebody who has truly attained the state of cessation.

11. Especially Supreme

The eleventh topic is known as especially supreme, or extraordinary. At this level, you have transcended both samsara and nirvana. You do not mingle in samsaric neurosis, but you have also transcended the potential of nirvanic neurosis. This topic seems to have been inserted by the mahayanists; however, since it is a part of the list accepted by Jamgön Kongtrül in his *Treasury of Knowledge* text, we better go along with that. Nirvana means dwelling in peace and openness, and samsara means dwelling in one's neurosis. In achieving ultimate gokpa, especially supreme cessation, you finally have the ability to refrain from dwelling in either samsara or nirvana. This topic is tinged with mahayana; the pure hinayana version does not mention not dwelling in nirvana, since that is their goal.

12. Beyond Calculation

The twelfth topic is beyond calculation. When we actually experience cessation properly, we realize that whatever needed to be overcome has been overcome. We attain an ultimate state of peace, relaxation, and openness, in which we are no longer hassled by the samsaric world. The topic of beyond calculation includes within it several further aspects of gokpa. These definitions of gokpa are not particularly categorized, but random.

RENUNCIATION. The first definition is renunciation. Having already renounced, you have reached a state in which you do not have to try to renounce anything—you are already there. This is like somebody who has given up smoking and who has no desire at all to smoke more cigarettes, or an alcoholic who has become a teetotaler with no desire to drink. You have renounced your whatever and reached the state of gokpa.

COMPLETE PURIFICATION. The next definition is complete purification. There are no hang-ups involved in the journey of reaching the state of gokpa—everything is purified.

WORN OUT. Gokpa has also been called "worn out," or the "wearing-out process." It is the wearing out of subtle neurosis and obvious neurosis, both at the same time. Everything is well worn-out: it is a sort of bankruptcy of all levels of neurosis.

PASSIONLESSNESS. Gokpa is passionlessness, which is the basic definition of dharma.

CESSATION. Once we have reached the state of gokpa, since there is no desire or aggression, there is cessation. More closely, there is no desire to initiate further involvement in the samsaric world.

COMPLETE PEACE. Gokpa is complete peace, which is connected with the idea of energy. It is not that somebody is dead and we write on the dead person's tombstone that this person has gone to his final rest, as in "Rest in Peace." Buddhists have a different concept of peace than the theistic world might have. Peace is energetic; it has immense power and energy. Actually, that is the source of a sense of humor, which is also a definition of cessation.

SUBSIDING. The last definition is what is known as subsiding or setting, like the sunset. Subsiding is giving up hope, not hanging on to the possibility of sunrise. You are giving up altogether all the neuroses and problems of the previous eleven possibilities.

In looking at the view of cessation and the various definitions of gokpa, we need to know how we could use these concepts and ideas. Altogether, cessation means transcending the turmoil and problems of life and the neurosis that goes along with them. However, we try so hard to transcend all that, that we are unable to do so, because the very fact of trying so hard is the way we got into trouble in the beginning. So in regard to cessation, definitely the most important point is number eleven, "especially supreme": the transcendence of both samsara and nirvana. By transcending both samsaric and nirvanic possibilities of confusion, we are transcending cessation itself, so there is no ground. At the same time, that groundlessness itself could become a very powerful expression of cessation. We can actually achieve cessation if we have no personal involvement in it. However, when we want to watch our own cessation, we are simply cranking up the wheel of samsara all over again, in the name of freedom. We are returning to the first and second nidanas: to ignorance and formation. But when we have abandoned any personal ego input, any personal bank account, we begin to achieve proper cessation. In the long run this would be our best investment, but it appears to be a very bad business deal because we don't have any legal contract to protect ourselves—we are no longer existing!

59

The Doubtless Path

The nature of the path is more like an expedition or exploration than following a road that already has been built. When people hear that they should follow the path, they might think that a ready-made system exists and that individual expressions are not required. They may think that one does not actually have to surrender, or give, or open. But when you actually begin to tread on the path, you realize that you have to clear out the jungle and all the trees, underbrush, and obstacles growing in front of you. You have to bypass tigers and elephants and poisonous snakes.

T HE FOURTH noble truth is the truth of the path. The nature of the path is up to you: it is your doing, in a sense, but there are guidelines. A do-it-yourself kit is presented to you by your teacher. You are given all the necessary equipment and all the necessary attitudes; then you are sent off to the jungle and you have to live by means of your survival kit. In the midst of this samsaric jungle, you have to learn to survive and come out the other side.

THE SEQUENCE OF THE PATH

As you begin your path, you encounter impermanence, suffering, emptiness, and egolessness as a sequential process. These could be viewed as

443

problems or promises, but basically, when traveling on the path, you need to know what to expect and what to overcome.

Encountering Impermanence and Overcoming the Notion of Eternity

The first thing to overcome is the notion of eternity. In the case of the nontheistic path of buddhadharma, looking for eternity could become problematic; so in order to transcend the concept of eternity, we have the wisdom of impermanence. The wisdom of impermanence applies to whatever is subject to becoming, to happening, or to being gathered together. It is all very transitory.

Encountering Suffering and Overcoming the Search for Pleasure

The second thing to be overcome is our constant search for pleasure. Our searching for pleasure, whether simple or complicated, is prominent and continuous. It is connected with the problem of spiritual materialism. In order to overcome that obstacle to the path, we have the slogan: "Because everything is impermanent, everything is always painful and subject to suffering."

Realizing the Possibility of Emptiness

Once there is suffering, a sense of desolation takes place as you begin to realize that both the things that exist outside you and the things that exist inside you are subject to impermanence and suffering. You realize the possibility of emptiness, a gap of nothingness—pure, plain emptiness. Things are empty-hearted and nonexistent.

Encountering Egolessness

Having realized emptiness, you also begin to realize that there is no one to hang on to that realization or to celebrate that experience. You encounter egolessness. Ego refers to the notion of self that we always feel, the sense of center. "Centering" has become a popular concept in the jargon of spirituality, but there is no mention of giving up or surrendering—it is more like having a little doggie bag inside you to hold your leftovers. The problem with centering is that you are coming back to your individual being, as opposed to a selfless center. A center that is very full, definite, solid, and concretized in that way is called ego.

Having such a solid sense of isness, you no longer have a path. But at the same time, having such a problem means that you have something to work on. However, what Buddhism is trying to tell you is that you could do your fieldwork without having any central headquarters, and you do not need to have a bureaucracy of meditative techniques. Dignity is not based on self and other, but comes from heaven down to earth—and the more you let go, the more dignity takes place.

FOUR QUALITIES OF THE PATH

The path has been described as having four qualities: path, insight, practice, and fruition. Altogether, the nature of the path is more like an expedition or exploration than following a road that already has been built. When people hear that they should follow the path, they might think that a ready-made system exists and that individual expressions are not required. They may think that one does not actually have to surrender, or give, or open. But when you actually begin to tread on the path, you realize that you have to clear out the jungle and all the trees, underbrush, and obstacles growing in front of you. You have to bypass tigers and elephants and poisonous snakes.

The realization that you actually have to make your own way through this jungle of samsaric chaos may be a shock, but such a shock might be appropriate and good. If you do not have any understanding of that quality of the path, and instead feel that blessings are going to descend on you just like that, there is no point in having a path. The path would no longer be a journey. Instead, it would be like simply buying your ticket, checking yourself in, depositing your baggage, and getting your seat; then sitting and getting bored; and finally someone announcing that you are at the end of the journey already so you can get off the transport. In that approach, there is a feeling of being cheated. There is no development taking place. The path is designed both to clear out obstacles and to develop particular patterns or qualities. It is very hard work.

1. Path: Searching for the Real Meaning of Suchness

The first quality of the path is that it is, in fact, a path: it is a search for the real meaning of dharma, the real meaning of isness or suchness. However, you do not try to pinpoint the isness—and if you try *not* to pinpoint it, you are doing it already. But this is getting beyond the hinayana, becoming more Zenny. In the Buddhist-English terminology that has developed, suchness or isness refers to something that is fully and truly there. It is connected with rediscovering buddha nature.

2. Insight: Through Clarity, Transcending Neurosis

The second quality of the path is that it is a path of insight. The journey that you are going along, and the discipline that you are going through, is based on sitting meditation practice, as well the experience of day-to-day living. Both are supposed to be aids for transcending neurosis, but it seems to be necessary to put your mind and effort into it. This may seem like a somewhat goal-oriented approach, but at the hinayana level, there is no other choice. The sitting practice of meditation is based on shamatha discipline, which provides immense clarity and the ability to relate with situations very fully, precisely, and completely. Any neurosis that comes up becomes extremely visible and clear—and each time a certain neurosis arises, appropriate to the time, that neurosis itself becomes a spokesperson to develop further clarity. So a neurosis serves two purposes: showing the path and showing its own suicidal quality. That is what is known as insight, knowing the nature of dharmas as they are.

3. Practice: Associating with Basic Sanity

The third quality of the path is known as practice. Practice enables us to relate with misconceptions of the dharma, such as eternalism and nihilism. Once you are able to relate with sitting meditation, and you are familiar with that particular experience, you find that sitting practice is not an endurance contest or a way of proving who is the best boy or girl. Instead, meditation practice is about how you can become a rock or an ocean—a living rock or a living ocean.

By sitting, we can absorb a lot of things and we can reject a lot of things; nevertheless, things do not particularly change. It is a larger-scale approach to life. In ordinary situations we may think that we are so sophisticated and that we know what we are doing. In terms of our domestic life, we may feel we have everything under control. We know how to book tickets on airplanes or to hitchhike across the country, and we have all the maps figured out. However, although we may feel we have everything under control—or we may not feel that way, and wish we could—there are still a lot of loose ends. Such loose ends cannot be covered by simply running down a list. Our list becomes so large that finally we cannot handle it without more and more energy.

In contrast, in the sitting practice of meditation, you are becoming like a rock, like an ocean. You do not have to go through any list; you just *are* that way, you are just *being*. You percolate or freeze in your own way. You just *be* that way. It is not particularly rewarding, but there is satisfaction, clarity, and immense dignity. Through meditation practice, you are associating yourself with basic sanity, which takes place continuously. So practice plays a very important part.

4. Fruition: Permanent Nirvana

The fourth quality of the path is fruition. In the hinayana approach to life, fruition is the idea of a permanent nirvana. Permanent nirvana means that we have learned the lesson of neurosis and its tricks, which are played on us all the time and take advantage of our weakness. Once we have learned this lesson, it is quite likely that we will not do the same thing again. That is also the case with our habitual patterns, unless we are complete maniacs.

At this point, although we have learned our lesson, ordinary little habitual patterns are still going to pull us back over and over. Those little habits, although similar to larger-scale mistakes, are not that problematic. The idea of fruition is that we are not going to keep making large-scale mistakes—like wanting to be saved, or wanting to be blissed-out, or wanting to indulge. We have learned from our mistakes, so we are not going to make the same mistake twice.

If there is a complete understanding of the nature of the path, it seems to be a doubtless path. But this does not mean that you do not question anything. Questioning is in accordance with the doubtless path; within that path, doubt is part of the methodology, and questioning is necessary. One should not be too gullible. Constant suspicion is very good—it is a highlight, like a Star of David—but at the same time, the path transcends all doubts. Fruition is knowing that we finally have a direction, in spite of all the little freak-outs taking place all the time. We no longer say things like, "Well, this path is better than others, but something else might be better still and more pleasurable," because we have cut through the idea of pleasure, and we have also cut through the idea of eternity and the self-snugness of the ego. Everything has been cut through.

60

The Five Paths

The path does not really exist unless you are available. It is as if you are the road worker, the surveyor, and the traveler, all at once. As you go along, the road gets built, the survey's done, and you become a traveler.

F ROM THE practitioner's point of view, there's an interesting link between the first noble truth and the last noble truth: the first noble truth could be described as the ground on which the fourth noble truth is founded. That is, the realization of suffering brings an understanding and discovery of the path. The problem with the word *path* is that we automatically think that the road has been built and the highway is open, so we can drive nonstop. There's a possibility of taking too much comfort in having a path, thinking that since the path has already been laid down, you do not have to choose which path to take—there's simply *the* path. That attitude seems to be the product of misunderstanding or cowardliness on the part of the student. In fact, the path does not really exist unless you are available. It is as if you are the road worker, the surveyor, and the traveler, all at once. As you go along, the road gets built, the survey's done, and you become a traveler.

There is another kind of path that *has* already been built for you, which you should know about, called the "general path," or the "common path." In the general path, value judgments and morals have already been developed, such as the virtues of democracy, the idea of a good man or good woman, or the purity of the social worker—you just enlist, become a member, and go to work. The common-sense path tells you that it's nice to be polite, that good manners always work, and that kindhearted people are constantly loved. It might also include Buddhist teachings such as "Control your senses, control your mind, get to know yourself." On the common spiritual path, there is an emphasis on getting psychologically high, becoming an accomplished meditator. By concentrating on a burning candle, you could develop your concentration, attain a state of samadhi, and experience the One, the realm of the gods.

The common path is not as accurate or profound as the Buddhist path, but it is not by any means the object of mockery. As Buddhists, we too follow common rules and regulations. For instance, we don't shoplift, but we pay for the things we buy. However, in terms of dharma, such norms are just sidelines, not what we concentrate on. Many scriptures, and even sutras, talk about the common path as the starting point for students who are beginning at the beginning. For students who see the world in a very naive way and have naive attitudes toward spirituality, goodness is the issue, peace is the issue, euphoric states of samadhi are the issue; therefore, they try to cultivate those things. However, from the Buddhist point of view, that is dwelling in the *devaloka*, the god realm. In cultivating meditative absorptions, or jhana states, you are appreciating the advertisement, rather than wholeheartedly getting into the path itself. The extraordinary thing about the Buddhist approach is that such conventionality is regarded as unnecessary. On the Buddhist path, instead of trying to cultivate the jhana states, you come directly to the mind—a mind that is developing its awareness, openness, painfulness, or whatever it may be.

The path has many stages. At first, it is a series of steps, then it becomes a county road, and finally a highway. At the beginning, the path is just a footpath, a trail. We have to cut down and tame ourselves much more at the beginning than at the end. We have to develop renunciation. If we simply stepped out of our house into a luxurious limousine and drove along the road, there would be no sense of journey, no sense of giving. Therefore, renunciation is extremely important. We have to renounce our home—our snug, comfortable samsaric world. There are two types of renunciation: genuine becoming and contentment. The first type of renunciation in Tibetan is *ngejung: nge* means "real," or "genuine," and *jung* means "becoming," or "happening"; so *ngejung* is "real becoming." Renunciation is true, real, definite. We are disgusted and put off by the samsaric world we have been living in. The second type of renunciation is contentment, or *chok-she* in Tibetan. *Chok* means "contentment," "satisfaction," or "enough," and *she* means "knowledge," so *chok-she* means "contentment-knowledge." We know that things are enough as they are. We do not make further demands and we don't insist on having all the local conveniences, but we are satisfied to live in poverty. This does not refer to psychological poverty, however, for practitioners are supposed to have a quality of generosity and richness.

Traditionally there are said to be five paths: the path of accumulation, the path of unification,* the path of seeing, the path of meditation, and the path of no more learning.†

1. THE PATH OF ACCUMULATION

The path of accumulation is based on getting acquainted with the teachings and the teacher. You are putting in a lot of hard work in order to learn the teachings. It is the layperson's or beginner's level. You are new to the teachings and not yet an accomplished meditator, so you start the whole path right from the beginning—but it is a good way of beginning at the beginning. You do not have to go back to the common path, but this does not mean that you act against common law or that you become a criminal, or anything of that nature. Instead, your attitude is very direct and simple. Although you are a beginner, your approach to the path is not based on the conventional law of goodness and badness. On the path of dharma, behaving well or becoming a good person is not the point. The issue of goodness or wickedness does not particularly belong to the realm of dharma. Dharma has to do with sanity, with issues of clarity and confusion. Dharma is more psychologically oriented than behavior-pattern-oriented.

---

* This path is commonly referred to as the path of application.

† This ancient division of the path into five stages is discussed by Atisha Dipankara (990–1055) in his work *Lamp on the Way to Enlightenment* (Skt.: *Bodhipathapradipa*), Geshe Sonam Rinchen, trans. Ruth Sonam (Ithaca, N.Y.: Snow Lion, 1997). It is also discussed in *The Jewel Ornament of Liberation*, Gampopa (1079–1153), ed. Ani K. Trinlay Chuodron, trans. Khenpo Konchog Gyaltsen Rinpoche (Ithaca, N.Y.: Snow Lion, 1998). For more on the path of accumulation, see chapter 63, "The Lesser Path of Accumulation"; chapter 64, "The Middle Path of Accumulation"; and chapter 65, "The Greater Path of Accumulation."

The first path, the path of accumulation, is finding your foothold in the teachings as a layperson. Having found that foothold in the teachings, you begin to make the journey upward. In Tibetan, the path of accumulation is *tsoglam*. *Tsog* means "group," "collection," or "gathering"; *lam* means "path," so *tsoglam* means "path of accumulation." On the path of accumulation, we are working with ourselves and we are inspired to make sacrifices. We accumulate good merit by developing a good attitude and performing good deeds. We cultivate simplicity and sacrifice.

On the path of accumulation we also learn to sacrifice our mind; that is, we don't indulge in our thought process or our subconscious gossip. We give that up by means of the very basic and ordinary discipline of shamatha practice. Usually, whenever we have a bright idea of how to go about something, whenever we have any kind of desire, we automatically try to follow it up. We would like to raid the refrigerator, so to speak. We would like apple juice, orange juice, cottage cheese, ice water—anything to avoid boredom. Through shamatha, we discover that we do not need to jump to conclusions or act purely out of impulse. All those impulses are canceled out by the process of mental discipline.

When we practice shamatha discipline, we begin to see that our mind is full of stuff. But when we examine our passion, our attachments, and our desires for all sorts of things, we see that they are basically a bad job—purely thought patterns, sand castles, paper tigers. We see that if we wallow in our own lethargy and stupidity, there is no shelter or comfort in that either. By not buying our own habitual thought-patterns, we begin to develop discipline and mindfulness.

Joining Relative and Ultimate Truth

On the path of accumulation, our experience of mental processes is becoming very real. Passion, aggression, ignorance, and all the subconscious mental activities that take place in our mind become very ordinary and understandable. This leads to a realization of *kündzop*, or relative truth. When we relate with relative truth, we are no longer shocked by our mind. We begin to see the simplicity and the reality of things. When we sit on our cushions and practice, we come across all sorts of thought patterns and desires. Whether we are rereading our autobiography, so to speak, discovering all sorts of choices, thinking we should leave, and or thinking we should stay—all of that is included in the relative truth of our thought patterns.

When we sit and practice, we begin to realize what is known as the transparency and impermanence of time and space. We realize how much we are dwelling on our little things and that we cannot catch any of it and build a house on it. We cannot even lay the foundation. The whole thing keeps shifting under our feet and under our seat. The rug is being pulled out from under us completely, simply from that experience of working with ourselves. Nobody is pulling it, but we find that the rug constantly moves. We begin to feel that we ourselves are moving.

When we realize that we cannot catch hold of phenomena at all, that is what is known as *töndam,* or "absolute truth." There is an absolute quality to the fact that we cannot fool ourselves. We can try to fool our teacher, who tells us to sit; and we might think that we can fool the dharma, which says, "Go sit. That is the only way." But we cannot fool ourselves. We cannot fool our essence. The ground we are sitting on cannot be fooled. That is the twofold truth of kündzop and töndam.

When you put kündzop and töndam together and they become one unit, it becomes possible to make things workable. You are not too much on the side of töndam, or you would become too theoretical; you are not too much on the side of kündzop, or you would become too precise. When you put them together, you begin to realize that there is no problem. The combination of kündzop and töndam works because it is simple and dynamic. You have hot and cold water together, so you can take a really good shower. So kündzop and töndam are both very important; you can't stick with either one separately. Ultimately, through the experience of combining kündzop and töndam on the path of accumulation, you develop renunciation, simplicity, satisfaction, and contentment in the practice. That is the first of the five paths, the path of accumulation.

2. THE PATH OF UNIFICATION

The second path is the path of unification, in which your actions and your psychological state are beginning to work together. When you sit in meditation, you begin to develop a glimpse of sanity, a glimpse of the bodhisattva path. The second path is called the path of unification (*jorlam* in Tibetan) because we join our mind and body and all our efforts together.

It has five categories: faith, exertion, recollection, one-pointedness, and intellect.

Faith

The first category is tepa, which means "faith." We feel very steady and confident in what we have done so far. We appreciate what we have done. We realize what should be avoided and what should be cultivated. That is, subconscious gossip and grasping should be avoided; steadiness of mind should be cultivated. Tepa also involves delightfulness. We realize that we are not in the dark as far as our practice is concerned. We know our directions, roughly speaking, where we are and where we are going.

Exertion

The second category is tsöndrü, or "exertion." When we have realized what we are doing, we develop confidence. We realize the isness or the suchness of the truth that we have been told. We experience upliftedness as a result of shamatha discipline, and from that we develop further exertion. If we are served a dish that we like, and if we like the cook and the restaurant, we don't mind eating that dish a second, third, or fourth time because we know that it is going to be good. There is delight in going back again and again to the same restaurant. Similarly, exertion does not mean taking pains; it means appreciation. Appreciation makes things more and more enjoyable; and when we enjoy something, we do it over and over, even though there is tremendous effort involved. On the path of unification, our shamatha practice is becoming enjoyable, so we do it again and again, eternally.

Recollection

The third category of the path of unification is trenpa, which literally means "recollection." Recollection means that what you have done and what you have experienced are not forgotten, but remain as part of your awareness and mindfulness. There is a sense of respect and genuine appreciation for what you have received and what you are doing. Recollection means experiencing what you have done, which is your practice; and what you are, which is your state of mind. Recollection is very awake and precise. If somebody tells you that you have a chore in the kitchen at five o'clock, it is very simple: you just do it. There are no hang-ups involved.

Memory, in contrast, could be based on nostalgia for samsara. For instance, you might have had a bad fight, and by remembering it, in some perverted way you are able to maintain your whole being. You also might indulge in nostalgia for goodness, as a sort of psychological orgy. Such memories begin to have no gap, so you have no chance to be precise and clear.

One-Pointedness

The fourth category, tingdzin, meaning "meditation," or "samadhi," in this case refers to one-pointedness. You never lose track of anything; you develop tremendous awareness. Your mind becomes very focused, very accurate. You appreciate sense perceptions, but you are not trapped by them, and they do not create samsaric, karmic problems. Because you are able to perceive, to appreciate, and to focus your mind one-pointedly, you develop composure.

Intellect

The fifth category is sherap, or prajna in Sanskrit, which in this context means "intellect." You understand how to see things, how to separate various experiences. There might still be occasional upheavals—both experiences of satisfaction or achievement, and experiences of obstacles and doubts—but you can clearly separate what should be avoided from what should be cultivated. There is both clarity and discrimination.

Through those five categories of the path of unification, we are able to hold things together, as though we were holding the fort. We do not experience any chaos; instead, we begin to feel that everything hangs together. That is why this path is known as the path of unification.

3. THE PATH OF SEEING

In this path you develop further clarity in distinguishing or discriminating the different approaches to reality according to the buddhadharma.

The path of seeing is *thonglam* in Tibetan. *Thong* means "seeing," and *lam*, again, is "path," so *thonglam* means the "path of seeing." The path of seeing is at a much more advanced level than the path of unification. You begin to see how the path operates and how it could be applicable to yourself.

The Seven Limbs of Enlightenment

There are seven categories in the path of seeing, known as the seven limbs of enlightenment, or *bodhi:* recollection, separating dharmas, exertion, joy, being thoroughly trained, samadhi, and equilibrium. In Tibetan this is called *changchup yenlak dün. Changchup* is "enlightenment," *yenlak* is "limb," and *dün* is "seven," so *changchup yenlak dün* means the "seven limbs of enlightenment."

RECOLLECTION. The first of the seven limbs is trenpa, or recollection (which came up previously as the third category of the path of unification). Recollection means not forgetting the path of seeing, the sense of forward vision. You do not stay in one place, trying to be a faithful old person. Instead, you develop further ambition, not in the negative sense, but in the sense of going forward. That ambition is triggered by memory, or recollection.

SEPARATING DHARMAS. The second limb is connected with sherap, or intellect. As in the previous path, there is a quality of discrimination, of separating dharmas and realizing the isness of things. There is no uncertainty about experience. In each of the paths you need sherap, which is connected with actually being able to open up. On the path of unification, prajna was partial, somewhat embryonic, but on the path of seeing it is closer to complete prajna.*

---

* In the *1973 Seminary Transcripts: Hinayana / Mahayana* (Halifax: Vajradhatu Publications, 1974), in reference to prajna and the five paths, Trungpa Rinpoche places the complete expression of prajnaparamita on the fourth path, the path of meditation, which includes levels two to ten of the traditional stages, or bhumis, of the bodhisattva path. An ordinary student begins with the path of accumulation; catches a glimpse of mahayana possibilities on the path of unification; enters the first bhumi on the path of seeing; practices bhumis two to ten on the path of meditation; and attains complete enlightenment on the path of no more learning.

EXERTION. The third limb is tsöndrü, exertion, which in this case has a slightly different meaning than previously. In cultivating a constant furthering of vision on the path of seeing, you never give up, you never settle down to the situation at hand. You have the positive ambition of forward vision.

JOY. The fourth limb is *gawa*, which means "joy." You are able to take care of both body and mind. This is not a situation where your mind is highly developed but your body is rotting, or your body is well-cared-for but your mind is rotting. Instead, your body and mind are synchronized, well connected. The samsaric hassles of dealing with your mind and body begin to subside. You are able to handle your body and mind completely, so you develop good health. You know how to avoid unnecessary hassles: you don't collect further garbage in the interest of either mind or body. The joy of simplicity begins to develop, along with a sense of precision, genuineness, and obviousness.

BEING THOROUGHLY TRAINED. The fifth limb, shinjang, means being thoroughly soothed or trained. Your body and mind are totally relaxed. As a result of shamatha practice, your mind and body are tamed, trained, developed. There is a tremendous sense of humor and relaxation, and openness, gentleness, and goodness. You are beginning to feel the effect of your practice. It is beginning to work, and you feel positive. It is like coming out of a steam bath: your muscles have relaxed; you feel so healthy.

SAMADHI. The sixth limb is tingdzin, which means samadhi, or "one-pointedness." You are focused, one-pointed, and at the same time, you are humble. In spite of your achievements, you never get puffed up.

EQUILIBRIUM. The seventh and final limb is tang-nyom, which means "equilibrium." You are not subject to sluggishness or laziness, and you are also free from wandering and excitable mind. A quality of evenness is taking place all the time. You are neither disturbed nor completely asleep. It should be quite clear that equilibrium does not mean becoming a jellyfish or an even-tempered ape. In this case, you have command of the whole world. You have tremendous confidence in dealing with your world; therefore, you don't have to push anything either positively or negatively. You don't have to dwell on anything or exaggerate anything.

That concludes the seven limbs of enlightenment, or bodhi, the seven categories of the path of seeing.

4. THE PATH OF MEDITATION

The fourth path is called the path of meditation, or *gomlam*. Traditionally, *gom* means "to think about"; in Buddhist terms, it means "to meditate." In the nontheistic tradition, meditation means just meditation, rather than meditation on anything, and *lam*, again, means "path," so *gomlam* means the "path of meditation." On the path of meditation, your sense of style begins to be closer to an enlightened style rather than a neurotic style.

On the path of meditation, you begin to cut karma. Karma is based on fundamental ignorance. Whenever there are two, you and other, that is already the beginning of a karmic situation. When you not only have "you" and "other," but you begin to elaborate on that, you are at the level of the second nidana, or samskara (formation or concept). You have begun to roll the wheel of karma.

Fundamental ignorance is pre-dual. In the phrase "I am," pre-dual ignorance is pre-"am"—it is the "I" stage. Duality does not yet exist, so calling it "nondual" would be jumping the gun. Although there is no duality, however, there is still a false sense of suchness, or isness. There is a kind of anti-shunyata sense of existence or fullness, which has to be cut.

Although fundamental ignorance begins to be cut on the path of meditation, it is not thoroughly cut at this point. You have cut the consequences of karma, but not the causes. When you cut both the consequences and the causes—the karmic situation altogether—that is the path of no more learning, which is enlightenment.

The Noble Eightfold Path

There are eight categories of the path of meditation, which are collectively known as the noble eightfold path.* The eight limbs of the noble path are perfect view, perfect understanding, perfect speech, perfect end of karma, perfect livelihood, perfect effort, perfect recollection, and perfect meditation. At the level of the path of seeing, you began to see, and now you

---

* Trungpa Rinpoche also discusses the eightfold path in *The Myth of Freedom and the Way of Meditation* (Boston: Shambhala, 1988).

are able to make something of it. Your whole being has been thoroughly trained physically, psychologically, and in terms of working with others.

PERFECT VIEW. The first limb of the noble path is yang-dak-pe tawa, or "perfect view." Perfect view means that you are able to cut through the absorptions and fixed views of your previous experiences, which may have made you somewhat sleepy and theoretical. At the level of the path of seeing, you might have been able to gaze at the ultimate truth, but yang-dak-pe tawa enables you actually to see through.

"View" does not mean good view or bad view, but simply understanding things as they are. You are able to cut through and you are able to analyze and to theorize in the positive sense. This does not mean that you are scholastic or that you psychologize, but you are able to see the differences between the first, second, and third paths. You are able to see how things work geographically and chronologically. Because you can see through things at this point, you are becoming less dependent on your teacher, or elder. Your elder is wise and scholarly, brilliant and compassionate, but you don't have to depend on him or her. You are able to see through by yourself; therefore, you are becoming somewhat independent.

PERFECT UNDERSTANDING. The second limb is *yang-dak-pe tokpa*, "perfect understanding," or "perfect realization." You have learned how to relax. Based on what you have experienced, there is no questioning and no doubt. You have understood, and you appreciate what you have understood; therefore, you learn how to relax and let yourself go.

PERFECT SPEECH. The third limb is *yang-dak-pe ngak*, "perfect speech." You have found a way of declaring yourself fully and thoroughly—how you are, why you are, what you are—without being arrogant, aggressive, or too humble. You have learned how to be moderate in presenting yourself. Ngak, "speech," does not refer simply to how you speak, but also to how you reflect yourself to the world—your general demeanor, or decorum. You can become reasonable, decent, and enlightened.

PERFECT END OF KARMA. The fourth limb is *yang-dak-pe lekyi tha*, which means, the "perfect end of karma." You begin to understand how to prevent karmic cause and effects suddenly, precisely, and thoroughly. The end of karma means that you might return once or twice to the world because your immediate karmic situation has not yet been cut through; however, your previous karma has been cut through already by means of perfect view, perfect understanding, and perfect speech. Your habitual patterns and your whole behavior begin to be more accurate, more enlightened. By behaving naturally, you are able to cut through karma and karmic consequences.

In cutting through karma, you are constantly dealing with ignorance, the first nidana. Since volitional action is driven by ignorance, if you are able to cut through that ignorance, you stop the course of volitional action. You can do so, because at the level of the path of meditation, your style of relating with the dharma becomes very natural and instinctive. In contrast, the style of volitional action is that you are always looking forward to the next carrot. You see the carrot as somewhat distant from you, and you work yourself up to run from here to there, from yourself to the carrot. In doing so, you crank up more karma; and when you get there, you end up with the next karmic cause. So you end up with a lot more karma—and you have created the carrot, as well! We never say that in the samsaric world, but in the enlightened world we can say it.

In cutting karma, disgust and renunciation are regarded as important. Although it is a neat, ugly trick for you to put the carrot in front of yourself, you know you shouldn't be doing that. By renouncing that, you are able to cut the second nidana, which is formation, or impulsive accumulation. At this point, you are becoming so accomplished in this that even if you plant a karmic promise in other people, you are able to cut through their karmic cause and effect as well.

PERFECT LIVELIHOOD. Number five is *yang-dak-pe tsowa,* which means "perfect livelihood." Because you are able to handle karmic cause and effect, you can also relate with your own life and livelihood. You do not have to depend on others. You have enough skill to be able to handle your livelihood thoroughly and fully.

PERFECT EFFORT. The sixth limb is *yang-dak-pe tsölwa,* which means "perfect effort." This has the sense of not holding back, but exerting yourself. You have tremendous energy. You cultivate genuine energy in both working with yourself and working with others. As you go from path to path, you develop more and more effort, more and more industry. You begin to become a decent person, no longer a nuisance.

PERFECT RECOLLECTION. The seventh limb is *yang-dak-pe trenpa,* "perfect recollection." As before, trenpa refers to mindfulness, or one-pointed mind, and to the recollection of your previous experiences.

PERFECT MEDITATION. The eighth and last limb of the noble path is *yang-dak-pe tingdzin,* or "perfect meditation." In this context, tingdzin means that you are able to enter into certain samadhis. You begin to look ahead toward the notion of enlightenment. At this point, you might be able to completely cut through twofold ego fixation (ego of self and ego of dharmas).*

5. The Path of No More Learning

The final path is the path of no more learning, which is the attainment of enlightenment. In Tibetan it is *mi-lob-lam. Mi* is a negation, *lob* is "learning," and *lam* is "path," so *mi-lob-lam* is the "path of no more learning." Since at the hinayana level, you have only a very rough idea about how enlightenment takes place, the fifth path includes the remainder of the mahayana path and the attainment of enlightenment.

Progressing on the Path

The five paths, which are very complicated and complex, have been briefly described to give you an idea of a student's psychological development through the practice of meditation. In that way, you can have guidelines on the path, not only from your teacher, or your friends, or neighbors, but from yourself. There is a journey taking place, and if you ask who is the judge, I think that you yourself are the best judge of the level of pain and confusion you are experiencing.

When we discuss the path, or Buddhism in general, we have to face the fact that there is something corny taking place. We say that we are not striving for the result of enlightenment, that we are not interested in that, that we don't have an ego, so we are free of all that. But at the same time, we *do* talk about enlightenment. We say we are going to attain enlightenment, that we are going to become better people. We have to

---

* The belief in an "I" and the belief in an "other" are both cut through. Neither the self nor external phenomena are seen to be independently existing.

face that obvious fact. There is no point trying to make ourselves more sophisticated than everybody else on earth who has followed a spiritual path. It may be disturbing to realize that you have fallen back into the common logic, to realize that everybody is searching for pleasure and so are you. However, that is the fact. In Buddhism, we talk about decreasing neurosis, which automatically means decreasing ego-oriented pain. We talk about attaining enlightenment—a state in which there is no need for security, but ultimate security develops. Without such logic, the Buddha could not truly teach human beings at all.

The teaching exists in order for you to get better, in order for you to develop; that's a known fact. You could say that you're not interested in any such thing, thinking that's the best thing to say, but if you're not interested in anything like that, you've caught yourself already. You think you're very smart, but you are fooling yourself. You have to become stupid, dumb, and simpleminded, in a sense, in order to commit yourself to the teachings and the path. And whether you like it or not, Buddhism is a doctrine of some kind. Even though it may be a transcendental doctrine, it is still a doctrine. So let us not try to be too sophisticated. There is no such thing as "cool dharma" or "hip truth." If it's the truth, it's the truth.

On the Buddhist path you are expected to develop certain states of mind; you are expected to show certain signs. You are also expected to share these things with the rest of your brothers and sisters on earth and to work with them as well. But none of this is regarded as a good thing to do—it's just ordinary flow, like a river. If a river flowed backward or a waterfall went upstream, we would think either that we were hallucinating or that something was wrong with the landscape. Similarly, the logic of the path has to flow, just like water is always expected to flow down and slowly make its journey to the ocean. Such norms are obvious. The sun is expected to rise in the east and set in the west—we can't be very hip and unconventional; we can't change the direction of the sun.

In terms of signs on the path, you are not particularly waiting for something to happen, but when it happens, it happens—and it is sure to happen sooner or later. However, there is not the expectation that once you get to the next level, you are going to be okay. In fact, it is quite possible that at each new level you discover more problems. For instance, attaining arhatship sounds good, but once you get there, you might find more problems and troubles. As you progress along the path, you are in a constant process of becoming more and more intelligent. The more intelligent you become and the more aware you are of all the details of the overall vision, the more things you find wrong with yourself.

You don't particularly expect happiness out of the path. However, you do expect sophistication and the relief or confidence that something is actually happening. You don't have to know where you are on the path, but you need to know that you are moving and that you are going to get to your destination. However, if you are too concerned with getting from here to there as fast as possible, you find yourself in a lot of pain. It is not how fast you can get there but the movement that matters. On the path, you are not stuck, but you are constantly moving. As soon as you switch on the stove, the food is cooking.

The whole path may seem to be at the folk level, but the teachings are not particularly folksy—nor, for that matter, are they for scholars, magicians, royalty, or monks and nuns. The teachings are not *designed* for anything. The dharma is straightforward teaching. It contains certain common, basic truths; otherwise, you could not communicate it and you could not appreciate it. No matter how many restaurants you might eat in, or how fancy they may be, you still eat by putting food in your mouth; there's no other way to eat. No restaurant offers food to consume in any other way.

In working with the five paths, you begin with the first path and the practice of shamatha. As you go on, you begin to evolve, and there is some sort of progress report. The five paths might seem hard to relate to, but they are real and you could aspire to them. There is nothing unreasonable about them: they are both reasonable and possible. If you aspire to joy, you can attain it, because you have joy in you. Similarly, you also have exertion, concentration, and prajna. Those things are all household terms, nothing exotic or primitive. So the message is very simple: it is possible and you can do it. You can work with the four noble truths.

Because suffering is fundamental, there is a fundamental cure for it as well. That cure is saddharma: real dharma. Real dharma can actually cure fundamental pain; that is why it is known as *sad*, or "truth." It is genuine dharma. Fundamental suffering is based on a basic karmic mishap, arising from ignorance. However, when you begin to work with your state of mind, you realize the consequences of your ignorance, and you see how you can correct it. Your fundamental ignorance is the cause of all karmic coincidence, but instead of stupidly going along with that, you begin to wake up by means of meditation practice. You are aware of trying to cut through twofold ego fixation—the ego of dharmas and the ego of self—and you are beginning to knock the guts out of the whole thing. You are putting lots of effort and energy into that. It is very straightforward.

Practice is fundamental. It is a genuine cure. You have a genuine ego and genuine suffering, with cures to match. It has been said that dharma is medicine, the teacher is a physician, and you are the patient. If you have a sickness that medicine can cure, the teacher can diagnose you and treat it. And as you go on through the yanas, from the hinayana to the vajrayana, that cure becomes much tougher and more accurate. That is the notion of saddharma. Saddharma is the ultimate cure because it deals not only with the symptoms, but with the sickness itself.

Part Five

THE HINAYANA JOURNEY

61

Shravakayana:
The Yana of Hearing and Proclaiming

Loneliness is the essence of shravakayana discipline. It is like sud-
denly being pushed from a centrally heated house onto the top of
Mount Everest. There is a sudden chill. Not only is there a sudden
chill, but it is also very sharp and penetrating. In fact, it takes your
breath away, it is so refreshing.

THE NYINGMA school of Tibetan Buddhism divides the path into
nine yanas, or vehicles, of which the first two—shravakayana and
pratyekabuddhayana—are in the hinayana category. Within the hinayana,
the first yana, the shravakayana, is basic Buddhism. It provides the background for understanding the foundations of Buddhism—its expressions,
wisdom, and discipline. Western writers on Buddhism, particularly those
writers who get their information from old encyclopedias of world religion, base their descriptions of Buddhism largely on a kind of distorted
notion of this particular yana, so it is necessary to understand the first
yana quite clearly.

The shravakayana is simple and understandable. Its approach is somewhat analytical: you are analyzing samsara and the need for nirvana.
When you first come to the teachings, what you should first hear are
the four noble truths and the teachings of hinayana. That seems to be
important.

The Tibetan term for "shravaka" is *nyenthö. Nyen* means "listening," and *thö* means "hearing"; so *nyenthö* means "listening and hearing." In a further elaboration, it means not only listening, but also proclaiming or propagating. So in the shravakayana, first you hear from a teacher, and then you proclaim what you have heard to others. Your proclamation could be an internalized version as well, proclaiming it to yourself in your own mirror mind, so to speak. However, although the shravakayana is the yana of listening and proclaiming, shravakas have not yet developed authority of their own. They are just passing on what was said by the Buddha. So it is like saying, "Buddha said so," rather than really proclaiming.

SAVING YOURSELF FIRST

The shravakayana begins with the notion of freedom, and the question of how you can relate with that freedom. Should you try to save others first, or should you first try to save yourself? Is it possible to save yourself and others together? And the shravakayana response is that you should save yourself first. Their attitude toward salvation is that of somebody who is just concerned about himself or herself—period. This is known as individual salvation, or soso tharpa. The idea of soso tharpa is that you do not, in the middle of your confusion, run out right away and join the Red Cross or the Peace Corps. You do not try to help others when you yourself are going through immense transformations and confusion. The danger of just blindly rushing off to help is that you will not particularly help anyone, but instead contribute further garbage to the people you are trying to help.

The notion of skillful help is a very strong point in Buddhism, and continues throughout the nine yanas. It could be said that you waste a lot of time by going to college, that you spend almost half of your life doing nothing but studying. But you need to prepare yourself before you do any charitable work, otherwise the charitable work you do for others could be questionable. Due to your own lack of composure, your approach might be wrong and you might be helping the wrong people altogether. It is necessary to know who actually needs help and who is just asking for help, to know that some people get more benefit by not being helped and other people really need help and should get it.

Individual salvation simply means that you should save yourself and evolve on the path. The problem in trying to save somebody else first is that it might interrupt your attempt to save yourself. If you try to save others, quite possibly you may not personally be up to it, and you both may be destroyed. The larger world is already confused enough. If you just jump in and contribute your own little confusion, and if hundreds of other people are doing the same thing, it is going to create enormous chaos. So instead of creating further confusion, you keep to your own discipline. Saving yourself first seems to be good and necessary.

RENUNCIATION AND LONELINESS

In the shravakayana, ethics are based on renunciation. By means of renunciation, we cease causing harm to others. We refrain from harm and from its original foundation. The idea of renunciation is to develop a sense of aloneness, or loneliness. In the modern world, constant entertainment is provided for us. We are attracted to all kinds of possibilities—cinemas, theater, dance, music, handicrafts, body-awareness tricks, spirituality—all kinds of things. We have so much company. Even if we do not want it, the newspaper is pushed into our mailbox, and somebody is advertising some great thing we might do. If we are bored and lonely, we might join in and have a good time. We are constantly being seduced by all kinds of things in all kinds of ways, so it is not possible to just renounce and be done with it.

The basic teaching of the shravakayana is to contain yourself within your own loneliness so that it does not pollute the world. It may be extraordinarily painful, but that is part of the teachings. You begin to realize the truth of suffering. Loneliness provides an immense sense of openness and romanticism. The simplicity of wanting to deal with your life without anybody fussing over you, without anyone to console, without anyone to get mad at or to make love to—simply existing by yourself—is very powerful. Very few people experience that or appreciate it. In the shravakayana, you renounce entertainment at all levels—spiritual, material, and psychological. You are renouncing that and trying to be contained within yourself. You begin to do just what is actually necessary in order to provide yourself with a reasonably comfortable living situation. The rest of life is a spiritual search and spiritual practice.

Although shravakas practice renunciation, at the same time the Buddha talked about the importance of feeding yourself. On one occasion, Buddha said to Ananda, "If you don't take good care of your body, there will be no body. If there is no body, there is no dharma. And if there is no dharma, there is no liberation." He did not want students to fast for the sake of liberation, or do anything terrible to themselves. He did not want people to wear completely ragged clothes or to eat bad food. In fact, when tantric teachers in Tibet talk about wearing ragged clothes and eating bad food, they consider that to be a sign of insanity rather than of ascetic discipline or passionlessness. So you should relate reasonably with yourself and your body, and take care of your needs.

The constant-entertainment approach is based on arrogance and self-indulgence. Renouncing that combination of neurotic arrogance and indulgence is important. With renunciation, we begin to see everything inside out. We see through all the holes that exist, all the deceptions we go through, all the garbage, and we begin to renounce all that. Renunciation does not mean leaving our mommy and daddy behind or rejecting our culture; it is more fundamental. Renunciation means that we do not cause further harm to others and ourselves, and we do not continue to create the origins of harm. That is what real and proper renunciation is.

One of our problems is that we are unable to bear the thought of being alone. If a little chill goes down our spine, that is an expression of our loneliness, and if some heat rises to our head, that is also an expression of our loneliness. And we cannot really speak about it or communicate it to anybody. When we really feel lonely, it is unspeakable, ineffable.

You could be alone. You could be lonely. Aloneness is a bit too euphemistic; it is what people say when they do not want to talk about loneliness. But loneliness is very definite; you have no expectations. All your tricks have worn out, and you are on your own—listening to the whistling wind in the pine trees, your percolating coffeepot, or the occasional humming of your refrigerator. You are yourself, just by yourself. Finally, you do not have to pretend anything or be anything other than yourself. Being yourself is very lonesome. People do not like it. You would like to visit your friend and say how fine you are doing or how terrible you feel. But in doing so, you are still looking for entertainment.

Loneliness is the essence of shravakayana discipline. It is like suddenly being pushed from a centrally heated house onto the top of Mount Everest. There is a sudden chill. Not only is there a sudden chill, but it is also very sharp and penetrating. In fact, it takes your breath away, it is so refreshing. Excessively refreshing. Very romantic, actually. Loneliness is very touching. It makes people write poetry, compose music, and become highly artistic and creative.

The View of Shravakayana

The view of shravakayanists is that of the four noble truths. The first noble truth, the truth of suffering, is the first real insight of the shravaka-yana. The approach of this particular yana is that samsaric hang-ups are a very severe disease, like cancer, which will never leave you until you are killed. In order to cure your particular sickness, you study the cause of the sickness, the second noble truth. Realizing that the cause of sickness can be eliminated is the third noble truth. Having heard of the possibility of being cured, then how you actually are cured is by following the doctor's prescription, which is the path, the fourth noble truth.

The attitude of the shravakayana is that you personally want to get out of this particular disease called samsara. There is a sense of alarm. You are freaked-out about the prospect of samsaric hell and misery, and you are delighted to hear that individual salvation exists and is possible. The shravakayana is very immediate, very simpleminded, and not at all that sophisticated. Nevertheless, it is very true and real, and quite genuine on the whole.

The Shravaka Understanding of Reality

As far as the shravakayana understanding of so-called reality—or unre-ality—is concerned, it is that by means of prajna, or discriminating awareness, a person begins to realize the nonexistence of individual ego. Although you fixate on life situations such as pain and pleasure, they are not really such a serious matter. You realize that the individuality itself is the confusion, and you begin to experience the nonexistence of "I." It is very simple and direct. The "I" who wants to attain individual sal-vation is the problem. That problem of individuality has to be solved, gone beyond. In doing so, you attain the first category of non-ego—you overcome the ego of self.

According to the shravakayana, the real fixation, or stronghold, is the most obvious one: "me," "myself," and "I." This thing, this "I," is the problem. This "I" is based on rejecting any possibility of realizing anything beyond itself. You think, "This 'I' has been with me for a long time, and this 'I' is what I would like to overcome. This 'I' has led me to this pain, and this 'I' won't allow me to attain individual salvation fully and completely." That this "I" has become problematic is very easy to see. First, you experience pain, then the existence of the "I" who experiences pain is realized. Therefore, in order to get rid of pain, you have to get rid of the one who is experiencing the pain. But that does not mean that you should commit hara-kiri, or destroy yourself, for that too would be based on belief in the existence of "I." The approach of shravakayana is much more sophisticated than that.

Overcoming the ego of self is a very sophisticated way of going beyond obstacles, hang-ups, and blockages. You realize that such blockages are not so profound, not so powerful. At this point, however, you have not yet transcended the second aspect of ego, the ego of dharmas (the belief in external reality). You have already overcome "I," but you still have "am" left hanging around. This makes things very complicated: it means that you still have to have some form of "I"; otherwise, you would not know what was out there ("am"). So shravakas have not completely attained enlightenment.

The ego of dharmas is related with the idea that there are further subtleties of ego beyond the ego of self.* Actually, the ego of dharmas helps you to realize the egolessness of self. It is like being on a boat and using a rope to pull yourself in: you hang on to the ego of dharmas to eliminate the ego of self. It is not a bad approach. You can't be totally independent. To give up one aspect, you have to take on another aspect; to get rid of this thing, you latch onto that thing. Doing so gives you some kind of break, or relief. It takes the edge off, as they say.

At the shravakayana level, by using one aspect of ego, a subtler form of ego, you try to eliminate crude ego completely. So at this point you still believe in some kind of continuity. You believe that the continuity of time is a reality, the continuity of atoms is a reality, and the continuity of subtle consciousness is a reality. Based on that view, two Buddhist philosophical traditions began to evolve.

---

* Trungpa Rinpoche also referred to the ego of self as the "ego of individuality" and as the "ego of individual existence." He referred to the ego of dharmas as the "ego of phenomena."

Atoms and Instants

Shravakas realize that solid things are not all that solid. Their approach to egolessness is to break things into smaller and smaller parts, and reduce them into individually existing atoms or particles. So while they question the solidity of existence, they still believe that atoms exist as the finest level of things, and that infinitesimal moments exist as the finest level of time. So at that finest, finest level, some reference point still exists, and there is continuity of some kind. For that reason, shravakas are sometimes accused of being eternalists.

But they are right. Everything *is* made out of other things. Nothing is monolithic. There's some gooeyness to everything that exists: your own body, your own intellect, your own time concept, your own concept of security, death, eternity, and all kinds of things. Imagine drinking a glass of water, and thinking that it is not one solid thing quenching your thirst but little atoms that make you think, in your equally spotty mind, that your thirst will be quenched. Everything, the whole of life, begins to change at that point.

In the shravakayana, you apply mindfulness to everything that you do. You are always practicing mindfulness. When you walk, you see that neither the place you walk nor the walking itself is solid. When you breathe, you see that it is not really one breath, but questionable breath. You see everything with microscopic vision. If you actually can experience that this tree or this rock is not monolithic, but is made out of little atoms, it is a beautiful discovery. You are learning to sort things out. Time is made out of little moments strung together, and space is sort of bouncy. If you push it, it bounces back, as though the whole world were made out of rubber. Everything is made out of particles. Nothing is solid. Can you imagine experiencing that?

Some shravakas experience reality as if they were using a microscope: they see that atoms are filled with and surrounded by little spaces. They say that even though we might think of ourselves as having existence, time, and consciousness, each moment of consciousness is surrounded by space, just as physical atoms and bits of time are. There is space, and within that are birth and death.

As ordinary people experiencing things in the ordinary way, and as people who have never heard of such a thing as shunyata, the approach of breaking things down into atoms is something that we can actually learn.

It can be taught to the person in the street. You can be told to feel that the chair you are sitting on is made out of little atoms and that it's not solid, and the mind you are thinking with is made out of little atoms and that you are not really thinking with it. Breaking things down in that way is a very powerful thing to do.

Shravakayanists continue to believe that everything is very much existent at the level of atoms. They believe that at that level, everything does exist very solidly and profoundly. Because things are so visible and real to them, shravakas believe very highly in the practice of trying to avoid wrongdoing and cultivating good deeds. Although they no longer believe in the existence of the ego of self and they are able to cut through concepts, they only manage to cut through up to a certain point. They still believe that the cutting itself is real. That causes them to put a lot of emphasis on discipline, both monastic and lay discipline. They talk about virtue as being real, and they view sin or wrongdoing as real also, as something one should get rid of.

Four Levels of Students

In general, individual salvationists, or soso-tharpists, are categorized according to the particular hinayana vows they have taken, and the discipline they have committed themselves to. There are four orders of soso-tharpists. The Tibetan term for each type of practitioner has both a masculine and a feminine form, so there are eight categories altogether.

Nyen-ne / Nyen-nema

The first type of soso-tharpist, nyen-ne (f: nyen-nema), or in Sanskrit upavasa (f: upavasi) is the pioneer, someone who is about to become a student of Buddhism, about to take a vow. A pioneer is still rehearsing their vows, so to speak.

Genyen / Genyenma

The second type of soso-tharpist is genyen (f: genyenma), or upasaka (f: upasika) in Sanskrit. An upasaka is somebody who has taken refuge in the Buddha, dharma, and sangha—that's the basic refuge vow—and might have taken some or all of the Buddhist precepts as well. There are levels of upasaka, according to the specific vows taken: somebody may have taken just the basic refuge vow; somebody may have taken the refuge vow and the five precepts as well; somebody may have taken just two or three precepts.

The first precept is not to destroy life; the second is not to tell a lie; the third is not to steal; the fourth is the vow of perfect *brahmacharya,* or celibacy; and the fifth is not to drink alcohol. Students can progress through those five precepts. For some reason, the first and second must come together—there is no such thing as somebody who has taken just the first vow alone. Beyond that, a student can take one or more of the remaining precepts.

Getsül / Getsülma

The next category of soso-tharpist is getsül (f: getsülma), or in Sanskrit *shramanera* (f: *shramanerika*). A shramanera is a novice monk or nun who has taken the ten basic vows of a would-be bhikshu. The ten shramanera vows are in addition to the basic five precepts of the full genyen, or upasaka.*

Gelong / Gelongma

The last category is *gelong* (f: gelongma), which in Sanskrit is bhikshu (f: bhikshuni). *Ge* means "virtue," *long* means "begging"; so *gelong* or *bhikshu* means "virtue-begging."† A bhikshu has 253 rules to keep.‡ These rules cover things like how to deal with sexuality, how to behave in public and privately, and how to take care of daily living. They are not exactly rules; it is more that your whole life has been planned.

As the early sangha—a group of very smart, revolutionary people— began to do a little experimentation in their lives, there began to be rules.

---

* In connection with this category, Trungpa Rinpoche also mentions a rank of ordination for women that falls between getsülma and *gelongma* called *gelobma* (Skt.: *shikshamana*).

† Trungpa Rinpoche is citing a secondary meaning of *long;* more generally it means "give rise to." In that sense, *gelong (dge slong)* would mean those who are giving rise to virtue.

‡ Bhikshunis, in most lineages, keep 364 rules.

A lot of these rules are very basic. For instance, one of the lesser rules says that one must not pee on the green grass. As another example, once one of the monks was washing his bowl in the rushing water of a stream, and he dropped his begging bowl, which broke into pieces. Consequently he didn't have a bowl for a day or so. So the Buddha said, "Let us make a rule that in the future no monks should wash their begging bowls in rushing water."

On the whole, the idea of such rules is not to complicate your life, but to enrich your life. For instance, not eating a meal in the evening but just having one meal at midday, which is another of the rules, keeps you very awake, and also makes you fresh when you wake up in the morning. You simplify your whole life. As a monk, you are allowed to possess only thirteen articles, including a razor and a square white cloth to put your hair in when you shave, your top robe and bottom robe, skirt and shawl—just basic household articles. So the idea is to keep your life extremely simple. You do your own laundry. Nobody irons your robes. You just wash your clothes in a mountain stream.

The Meditation Practice of Shravakayana

Meditation in the shravakayana is primarily pure shamatha practice, which allows individuals to realize the egolessness of individuality. Because you keep concentrating on something, such as the breath, you begin to develop a kind of hollowness in your own individual message, what you project out from your ego. In other words, there is a general loss of reference point. Because the discipline makes you somewhat dizzy, you begin to experience a feeling of no anchor, the possibility of no peg. There is nothing holding you; you are just projected out. When you are mindful, you are exposing the egolessness of individuality. When you are mindful, if you are opening a Japanese fan, your mind is very completely occupied with how you are going to open your fan, so the ego of individuality has been taken away from you. That is precisely what mindfulness means—taking yourself out. That is why we work on the out-breath alone, to take your mind out. The egolessness of individuality could develop by working "there" rather than "here." So working with the out-breath provides a lot of going out, emptying out, and making the whole thing "there" rather than "here."

The Activities of Shravakayana

The activities of shravakas are those of purely working for oneself. We mustn't look down upon that. It is very important, and we must not think that's a terribly selfish thing to do. Rather, it is that you begin by dealing with the closest person you have in your world. Who is the closest person to you? It is yourself, obviously. Working with that is very important and necessary; otherwise, nothing would happen. If you try to deal with somebody over there and you forget to deal with yourself, you find yourself destroying both you and that other person together.

The Achievement of the Shravakayana

The achievement of the shravakayana has two categories: the wearing-out process and nonbirth. The wearing-out process means that, when the shravakayana has been practiced fully and properly with proper shamatha discipline, you no longer have the occurrence of conflicting emotions. Nonbirth means that such emotions not only do not occur, but they do not plant seeds for the future. They will never be born again. The ultimate attainment of the practice of wearing out and nonbirth is called arhatship.

The hinayana is real dharma. It is not lesser, but it is the first step of how to teach the common, ordinary person how to experience the "real truth," or saddharma. How the hinayanists view the world is profound and workable. You can teach it to your children and develop them in that way. Later you can teach them the mahayana and the vajrayana. That is a natural process, which applies to a lot of things. The hinayana makes sense if you tune your mind in to it.

62

Pratyekabuddhayana:
The Yana of Individual Salvation

When you become a pratyekabuddha person, you become fully soso-tharpa-ized, completely individually liberated. That may sound mean-spirited, but without that approach you would not have any notion of how to develop maitri toward yourself, which is a problem, and could lead to difficulty on the mahayana level. The very notion of compassion begins with feeling kindness toward yourself.

THE PRATYEKABUDDHAYANA, like the shravakayana, is based on individual salvation. The idea of the pratyekabuddhayana is that the awakened state of mind could be achieved by oneself alone, without working with anybody else. According to this yana, a person can attain realization without working with an instructor or teacher. The distinction between the shravakayana and the pratyekabuddhayana is largely based on the personality types of the practitioners, rather than a progression from one yana to the other. We would not say that those who enter the shravakayana go on to the pratyekabuddhayana as the next leg of their journey, although the remaining yanas do have that sense of progression or journey. It is more a question of individual behavioral characteristics and one's relationship to the teachings.

CHARACTERISTICS OF PRATYEKABUDDHAS

Pratyekabuddhas are classified as either parrots or rhinoceroses. Parrots are very sociable and rhinoceroses are very individualistic: there is no happy medium. As a general tendency, only a few pratyekabuddhas are sociable; most of them seem to be antisocial, and therefore fall into the rhinoceros category. Even today, some people would like to just retreat back to their own environment. They do not want to relate at all with the energy level of the world or the society that exists around them.

Pratyekabuddhas are arrogant in that they prefer not to seek a personal teacher or an individual guide. Having developed an understanding of truth and discipline, they hide themselves within solitary situations where teachers are not needed. They have very little desire, so for the most part, except for the parrots, they are not particularly keen on socializing. Because they are highly intelligent and intellectual, they are able to accomplish a degree of liberation. Their general assumption and approach to life is that they have their own resources already and they can do better without anybody's help. Pratyekabuddhas are very self-reliant and knowledgeable, from knowing how to tie a shoelace efficiently up to how to survive in the wilderness.

Pratyekabuddhas are very individualistic. They do not want to relate with anybody above, nor to be under anybody's directions. Instead, they would like to search for themselves. They do not want to relate with any hierarchy, organization, or institutionalized setup. It is the self-made-person approach. Quite possibly such people would appreciate nature and poetry as well as hardship and industrious work. They do not like any kind of religion, preferring to search in their own way by their own means.

Pratyekabuddhas have less tendency for neurosis, except for the neurosis of their own arrogance. So it is hard to put them on the spot. They have very little need for entertainment and little confusion. Usually we talk to other people to try to untangle our confusion or because we need some kind of companionship, but in this case there is none of that. Rhinoceroses are antisocial. They are unwilling to give up their arrogance and become friends with others. They don't want to submit to anyone who is seemingly more highly developed or deepened in the spiritual journey. There is a rejection of the notion of lineage. Another factor is that pratyekabuddhas have very little compassion. They do not want to bother to relate with anybody else. They do not want to help anyone or teach anyone. They would simply like to be left alone.

Although parrots like to socialize, they do not socialize from the point of view of sharing with others. It is not like real parrots who actually chit-chat with each other and warn each other of enemy attack. In this case, if there is danger, every parrot has a different alarm system. In that sense, parrots and rhinoceroses are not actually that different.

I am not particularly trying to paint a black picture of pratyekabuddhas—they could be very admirable people, nice, wonderful. One of their best virtues is that quite certainly and definitely they are not nuisances to society. But they do not contribute anything to society either. They do not take part in anything.

The View of the Pratyekabuddhayana

Pratyekabuddhas hear the message of the four noble truths, and the message that possibly one has to give up one's existence. Then they go off to analyze and think by themselves, trying to add to the understanding of the four noble truths already developed in the shravakayana.

Pratyekabuddhas relate with life in terms of relative reference points. That is how they make sense of things. Everything is completely interrelated and interdependent. Black is black because there is white. There is a need for reference points of some kind, so you can actually experience and begin to see. If you walk out in the winter, you feel cold, and if you don't eat food, you get hungry. The reference point of "If this happens, therefore that happens" always seems to be necessary. It is the reference point of simple causality, or the nidana principle.

The pratyekabuddha view is that incidental situations are meaningful. We could quite safely say that the wisdom of discovering reference points of that nature goes a long way, all the way to the vajrayana. The pratyeka-buddha approach is an analytical one, in which you perceive yourself and the rest of the world at the same time. The whole thing is extremely intelligent. You are able to see how things happen from many different angles, but all those angles are completely governed by the basic principle of the twelve nidanas.

According to the pratyekabuddhayana, nirvana and samsara are related reference points, which are ultimately true. Pratyekabuddhas define salvation as the nonexistence of ignorance. Crude reference points colored by passion, aggression, and ignorance, by hope and fear, are obviously not true—but the relative reference points of transcending such neuroses are necessary and valid. You actually experience such reference points anyway. Basically, pratyekabuddhas still hang on to the reference point of the nonexistence of ignorance as salvation.

THE DISCIPLINE OF THE PRATYEKABUDDHAYANA

As far as the discipline of the pratyekabuddhayana is concerned, it is the same as that of the shravakayana. For both the shravakayana and pratyekabuddhayana, there is an emphasis on monasticism and monastic discipline.

Pratyekabuddhas base their discipline on an understanding of cause and effect, as is expressed in the traditional Sanskrit chant: "Om ye dharma hetu-prabhava hetum tesham tathagata hyavadat tesham cha yo nirodha evam vadi mahashramana svaha" (Regarding dharmas that arise from a cause, the tathagata taught their cause and also their cessation. Thus the Great Mendicant taught). You realize a subtle, fundamental pattern of cause and effect, as well as the cause and effect of good and bad actions. The idea of cause and effect is based on the continuity between two separate events. If you plant a seed, it will grow into a plant, providing you nurse that plant properly. Because of separation, there is continuity. It is very simple, like sitting next to your neighbor. That is precisely the idea of the nidanas: events being separate, events having continuity. It is a jigsaw, an interlocking situation, a mosaic approach. You cannot breathe out the rest of your life, but you have to breathe in, in order to breathe out. So there is an evolving process taking place all the time.

THE PRACTICE OF PRATYEKABUDDHAYANA

The focus of practice or contemplation in the pratyekabuddhayana is on study, on an intellectual and speculative approach to the world. A student of this nature traditionally wanders around in charnel grounds. He sees a skeleton or a piece of bone and begins to question, "Where did this come from?" "This came from death." "Where does death come from?" "Death comes from birth, and birth comes from pregnancy, and pregnancy comes from the meeting of two people, and the meeting of two people comes from passion or desire, and so on." An understanding of the twelve nidanas begins to develop in that way. It is a contemplative and, at the same time, an intellectual way of working things out.

The same process could occur with contemporary topics. We could start with the question, "Where does pollution come from?" "Pollution comes from having too much industry and too many cars." Then we could ask, "Where do those things come from?" and so forth. We could go back that way with all kinds of things, as a form of ecological study. Such studies are based on the discovery of chaos and the result of the chaos, which is immense decay, confusion, and unpleasantness. The attitude of pratyekabuddhayana students is that of wanting to clean up the world. They experience revulsion against problems of that nature. They would like to find out about the world primarily in order to save themselves from that particular mess. The information and knowledge they gain might be useful to people of the next generation, but that is uncertain.

In their practice of shamatha-vipashyana meditation, pratyekabuddhas are caught up in their own formal sitting practice rather than working with postmeditation. The postmeditation experience, the practice of meditation in action, is not properly emphasized, which is problematic.

The pratyekabuddhayana style of teaching is to attain arhatship and then manifest various miracles. In the pratyekabuddhayana, an accomplished person demonstrates the teachings instead of talking about them. Some teachers refuse to talk, preferring to teach by pantomime. Such teachers manifest in such a manner that an open-minded person can experience the subtleties, profundity, and power of the teachings. Pratyekabuddhas realize that if somebody is trying to teach you cause and effect, talking doesn't help. Somebody has to demonstrate it in reality, in very simple situations. This approach differs from the previous yana. Shravaka people proclaim and propagate, but in the pratyekabuddhayana, there is no talking. One simply manifests one's state of existence.

THE ACHIEVEMENT OF
THE PRATYEKABUDDHAYANA

Students of the pratyekabuddhayana have achieved what is known as the one-and-a-half-fold egolessnesses. They have achieved the first egolessness, the egolessness of individuality, by working back through the twelve nidanas to ignorance, and they have begun to develop the second egolessness, the egolessness of dharmas. They understand the nonexistence of substantiality. Because things are composed of atoms or particles, they are like beads on a string, or hairs on a yak. Then in order to make beads into a *mala* (Skt.: prayer beads), you must string a lot of beads together.* Pratyekabuddhas realize that there are gaps between one bead and another, and they realize that the beads themselves are also nonexistent, let alone the gaps.

Pratyekabuddhas see that things are composed of individual parts put together. At the same time, those individual parts themselves have no substance—they are empty, egoless. However, although pratyekabuddhas have achieved the egolessness of dharmas, their understanding is only partial, because they try to hang on to the egolessness of dharmas itself as a solid thing. So there is a subtle state of mind that is still hanging on to the egolessness of dharmas, and because of that, onto the egolessness of individuality as well.

The ego of dharmas has two aspects: grasping and fixation. Grasping is the grosser level of the ego of dharmas, and fixation is more subtle. With grasping, when you perceive the phenomenal world, you begin to possess it or to latch onto it. After that, you develop a fixation on it, and the whole thing begins to sort of soak into your sense of existence. So first you grasp, then you possess. By overcoming grasping, but not fixation, the pratyekabuddha has achieved a one-and-a-half-fold realization of egolessness.†

A person who has realized the egolessness of self has achieved some understanding, but at the same time he is somewhat at a loss. He has learned to say, "I don't exist," but when he sees a chocolate bar or some ice cream, he still wants to eat it. The dharma of ice cream is still there. He finds again and again the problem of laying his hands on things and beginning to possess them completely.

Another way to think of it is to imagine you had just picked up an object in the shop and brought it to the counter and said, "I would like

---

* A *mala* is a string of beads, which in the Tibetan tradition is usually comprised of 108 beads. Malas are used to count recitations of mantras or prayers and, as such, they are similar to Catholic rosaries or Muslim prayer beads.

† According to Elizabeth M. Callahan, pratyekabuddhas realize the absence of self-entity of the perceived object (*gzung ba*, "grasping"), but not of the perceiver (*dzin pa*, "possessiveness," "fixation"). Jamgön Kongtrül, *The Treasury of Knowledge: Frameworks of Buddhist Philosophy*, trans. Elizabeth M. Callahan (Ithaca, N.Y.: Snow Lion, 2007), page 343, endnote 453.

to buy this." Although you have not yet paid money for it and it has not yet become your possession, there is still a quality of grasping. In the case of the pratyekabuddha, grasping is no longer there. He doesn't buy anything, and if he did buy, he wouldn't grasp, he would simply pay for it. The ownership is still there, but the fascination is not. However, although he has given up grasping, the other half of the egolessness of dharmas, giving up the fixation of possessiveness, has not quite been achieved. The pratyekabuddhayana person has not quite dealt with the level of purchasing the object and taking pride in the ownership.

That kind of ego fixation remains, in spite of "I don't exist" or "Nobody home." In fact, you have to be home in some sense, because if nobody is home, you cannot have any ideas of any kind. The ego of self and the ego of dharmas interact with each other completely, so you cannot talk about one without the other. At this point, you have received the basic clue that you do not really exist. You are just an assortment of skandhas, rather than an individual holding it all together and being a really definite person. But the attraction of other experiences still has not been completely conquered, and that tends to make this ego much more solid. So the pratyekabuddha does not actually experience the egolessness of self in the fullest sense. He denies the existence of "this" and "that," but he still believes in the denial. That is the problem. The truth that you can experience or witness may be good, but it's not good enough.

At this point, the understanding of the egolessness of self is on a somewhat intellectual, experiential level. You have not quite fully felt it. If you had complete freedom from the ego of self, then how could the product of that ego still be operating? And the fixation, the second portion of the ego of dharmas, has not been tapped at all, which is why that kind of problem exists. That is what is meant by one-and-a-half-fold egolessness. So the whole idea of egolessness has to become much more mature.

There have been differences in the various schools of thought on this subject. Some say that the pratyekabuddha's final attainment should be a realization of both egolessnesses. But other scholars claim that pratyekabuddhas have not realized the second part of the egolessness of dharmas, because of their fixation on self.

As a pratyekabuddha, you have made a discovery that actually works for you, and you do not want to mingle in further problems. Figuring out your own problems is a big enough project already, and it is hard to inspire compassion when you have so much to work on. So there is little notion of charity, apart from not bringing harm to others. For pratyekabuddhas, everything is very cut-and-dried, very individualistic. You regard your discoveries as your own property, and although you may be nice, you do not believe in letting people be involved in your life. Compassion means inviting people into your territory, which is very hard to do.

Pratyekabuddha Mentality

Pratyekabuddha mentality is that if you recycle and recycle and recycle, then after recycling, things are going to be purified. You can actually work your things out—and the final and last recycling process is inspirational. It is the arhat level, so you have no problems. The pratyekabuddha journey is more a circling journey rather than a straight journey, which from a mahayana or vajrayana point of view seems quite alien.

It may seem as if we are simply paying lip service to the pratyekabuddhayana because it is included in the nine-yana setup. However, although it may seem outdated, I don't think we can ignore pratyekabuddhas, because they still play an important part in the Western psychological or spiritual journey, both Buddhist and non-Buddhist. It is an interesting approach to the spiritual journey, so we do not want to bypass it.

There has always been this type of approach, in which you really do not care about helping anybody else, but you are only concerned about your own little things. People like that come to see me all the time with their own variations on that. There is no concern or respect for the lineage. They have already done their research, so there is no need for information. When I have interviews with such people, I am sometimes speechless, not knowing what to say to them. They want to check with me to make sure that they are doing okay, but if I tell them they are doing okay, they don't buy it because they do not want to listen to anyone. They are too arrogant. I end up offering them cigarettes or a glass of sake, and we begin to talk about the weather or their family history, which makes them much softer. I have a very hard time relating with such people. My personal feeling is that if you really want to work with them, you have to try to present passion, because it is connected with compassion. You invite them to dinner or for a drink; something like that is more important than just talking about philosophy, which makes them more and more distant. The neurosis of pratyekabuddha people is helpless and hopeless and horrifying. They are on a circular tightrope, so they go around and around all the time in midair.

SHRAVAKAS AND PRATYEKABUDDHAS

In the shravakayana, the basic emphasis is on the realization that samsara is duhkha, an abundance of pain. Realizing that, we begin to practice the four noble truths. We learn how to develop and understand our mind, and we begin to tame our mind by way of vinaya and shamatha discipline in order to bring about the cessation of suffering. Thus we attain the principles of the shravakayana by means of taming ourselves properly with the technique of shamatha discipline at its best.

Going beyond that, we begin to develop superior discipline. We develop awareness on top of the mindfulness that we developed through shamatha. We develop vipashyana, along with prajna, or intellect. Intellect in this case does not mean intellectualization, but stimulating wisdom. By means of prajna, we understand and experience the twelve-nidana chain reaction of karmic cause and effect, starting from ignorance and continuing through to death. Awareness begins to include our eating habits, sleeping habits, talking habits, walking habits, sitting habits, and all of our other daily activities. All of these things are appreciated and understood within the framework of the twelve-nidana principle, and we begin to gain pratyekabuddha-hood.

Beyond that, we develop humbleness with regard to any learning or achievements we have accumulated through hinayana discipline. Arrogance arises when we don't experience the fact that everything is suffering and everything is discipline. In the shravakayana, we realize that everything is suffering, which brings us down and simplifies things. In the pratyekabuddhayana, we realize that everything is discipline. Once we begin to realize those two points, everything is workable. We don't have room for arrogance anymore because everything is streamlined. We do not store up our realization to manifest it when we feel like it. Whatever arrogance we may have manifested, whatever sense we may have of not being in touch with reality, is reflected back to us, so we develop further humbleness. We realize that humbleness is the dwelling place of the ancestors, and we begin to emulate and appreciate our teacher. We sense that our teacher is the living dharma altogether. Therefore, we experience a tremendous sense of appreciation and gratitude toward the teacher. By emulating the teacher, we begin to attain individual salvation. That seems to be the hinayana path in a nutshell.

When you become a pratyekabuddha person, you become fully soso-tharpa-ized, completely individually liberated. That may sound mean-spirited, but without that approach you would not have any notion of how to develop maitri toward yourself, which is a problem, and could lead to difficulty on the mahayana level. The very notion of compassion begins with feeling kindness toward yourself. That is very difficult to do if you have not worked on individual salvation properly and you do not have a proper sense of the twelve nidanas—which is completely the domain of the pratyekabuddhayana.

On the shravakayana level, you are simply entering into the four noble truths. It is the level of dharmic gossip. On the pratyekabuddhayana level, you are actually doing it. Who are you doing it to? You are doing it to yourself. That is why we call it *individual* salvation. You practice Buddhism in yourself, by yourself, and for yourself. In doing so, you become a pra-tyekabuddha, a self-made person. That is not so bad. If you learn how to take care of yourself properly, if you learn how to be tender to yourself, you develop bodhisattva possibilities as well. But to begin with, you have to learn how to be tender and kind to yourself. This is the seed of your ability to expand tenderness and kindness to others.

Wakefulness and Openness

Because of vipashyana you do not get stuck at the level of individual salvation. Vipashyana is the source of prajna, or discriminating-awareness wisdom, which is extremely inquisitive and keeps looking further. And as you develop awareness, you develop further mindfulness as well. With mindfulness-awareness, everything is looked at, and everything is very much cared for. Whenever there is a speck of dust in your cereal bowl, you see it. You begin to expand your world in that way, so your world is not stuck. Your intelligence is so sharpened and quivering that your aware-ness is almost bursting with energy. You can't really clamp down on that and make it into a regular domesticated thing.

Prajna scans all over the world with your seeing, hearing, feeling, smelling, and tasting. That is why doing your postmeditation practice is even more important than sitting meditation at this point. In postmedita-tion, you want to be on the dot all the time, each time. It is not that you are particularly nervous or hyperactive about it, but a general sense of wakefulness and openness is taking place always. As Buddhists, you should always be open and awake in whatever you do. You are doing your awareness practice in order to allow yourself to be inquisitive. With awareness, you do not get stuck, but you are on your way somewhere—you are on your way to full awakening.

63

The Lesser Path of Accumulation

As a student who has no idea of dharma and no mind training, you decide to commit to the path and to train yourself. As you train your mind, you begin to see all kinds of things. What you see is not so much the inspiration of a glimpse of enlightenment, or buddha nature. Instead, the first thing you see is what is wrong with samsara.

T HE SPIRITUAL journey could be looked at in terms of yanas or in terms of the five paths. In terms of the yanas, the journey begins with the hinayana, and in terms of the five paths, it begins with the path of accumulation. The path of accumulation is divided into three levels: lesser, middle, and greater. It is designed for ordinary people. For that reason, it is worth looking at in some detail. The path of accumulation is referred to as "accumulation" because you are gathering knowledge that is congenial to the path. You are accumulating dharmas of all kinds, and by doing so, you are also heightening the sophistication of the community.

On the lesser path of accumulation, you are predominantly working with the four foundations of mindfulness and with shamatha-vipashyana practice. Meditation practice at this level is a way of developing greater mental and psychological sharpness, so that dharmas could be perceived properly. You are becoming aware of your psychological hang-ups and confusions, and discovering all kinds of insights into the teachings. The analogy for a person who has developed such psychological sophistication is that of a well-polished mirror: the more dirt you remove from the mirror, the greater its capacity to reflect objects. So as you polish your mirror mind, you are learning to see the subtlest of the subtlest of dharmas.

The path of accumulation is about accumulating dharmas, as well as educating the accumulator. As a student who has no idea of dharmas and no mind training, you decide to commit to the path and to train yourself. As you train your mind, you begin to see all kinds of things. What you see is not so much the inspiration of a glimpse of enlightenment, or buddha nature. Instead, the first thing you see is what is wrong with samsara. With vipashyana, you begin to see the dharmas of samsara very clearly and precisely. This experience is by no means samadhi or higher prajna. It is simply that you are becoming more and more educated; therefore, you have more facility to handle the information coming into your mind. As a product of your training, you also begin to develop artistic talent and sensitivity. You begin to appreciate beauty and the subtleties of the sensorial world. But in particular, you discover the nature of samsara. You discover the secrets and functions of the samsaric manifestation.

In making the journey slowly along the noble path of the arhat, there is a need for faith or devotion to begin with. Such faith is partly blind and partly intelligent. It is blind because you are uncertain as to what you are going to get into, and it is intelligent because you know what you are getting out of. Faith and renunciation go together, for although you want to get out of samsaric imprisonment, you have no idea of the world outside. You feel so nauseated that you try to get out, but what is outside of that prison is uncertain, and your experience and information about it are both vague and incomplete. You realize that samsaric imprisonment is the worst of the worst, so if there is anything other than that, it must be better. But insomuch as the alternative is unknown to you, you are taking a chance. Therefore, faith becomes extremely important.

Faith in the Buddha, dharma, and sangha inspires you to take refuge. You have to turn to somebody who has much greater scope and wisdom, and the only outsider you know is the lineage holder. So you take refuge in the lineage holder as the manifestation of the Buddha, dharma, and sangha. Devotion to the lineage of the past gives you a feeling of the richness of that particular lineage, and devotion to the present teacher gives you the feeling that those riches you have read about are not mythical, but reality.

THE THREE WAYS OF LEARNING

A person on the level of the path of accumulation has to develop simultaneously the three ways of learning: hearing, contemplating, and meditating.* "Hearing" is *thöpa*. *Thö* means "to hear," as in to hear intellectual studies, to hear the dharma. "Contemplating" is *sampa*. *Sam* means "to think or contemplate." You are pondering a subject you have learned, such as the nature of impermanence—and since such information is received from a teacher in the beginning, you are also working with thöpa. "Meditation" is gompa. *Gom* means "meditation." In all three terms, the suffix *pa* makes the term into a noun. On the path of accumulation, you have to go through thöpa, sampa, and gompa—all of them simultaneously. You hear a message from your teacher, you contemplate that message, and you meditate all at the same time. That prepares you for further thöpa. Because your mind is more readied, you are able to hear more teachings. So it is a constant, ongoing process. That is how it works on the path of accumulation.

UNDERSTANDING THE THREE
MARKS OF EXISTENCE

One outstanding discovery at the first level of the path of accumulation is the understanding of the three marks of existence.† This is by no means the result of ordinary speculative mind—it is definitely a product of the sitting practice of meditation, which is the highest way of learning about the dharma. By means of sitting practice, the student on the path of accumulation develops a greater vision and knowledge of the three marks than someone purely learning from books without such mental and psychological preparation. Therefore, the path of accumulation

---

* These three ways of learning are also discussed in chapter 69, "Taking the Teachings to Heart."

† For the third time, and in a new context, Trungpa Rinpoche returns to a discussion of the characteristics of samsaric existence uncovered through meditative practice. In previous chapters, these three marks—impermanence, suffering, and egolessness—were joined by a fourth, that of nirvana or peace. See chapter 1, "Beginning at the Beginning," and chapter 6, "Achieving Sanity Here on Earth." In this instance, Trungpa Rinpoche focuses on the first three marks, examining how the recognition of impermanence leads to the experience of egolessness, and how that combination produces suffering.

is considered to be the first stage of the ordinary person's conversion into the dharma. It is the first time you apply ordinary patience and ordinary discipline. There is nothing *paramita,* or "transcendental," about it—you just practice bare attention to breathing, and bare attention to mental activities. You develop a patient attitude to pain as you sit and practice, whether alone in retreat, in daily life, or in group practice.

Impermanence

Understanding the nature of impermanence and egolessness and how that combination leads to suffering is a central part of the contemplative practice of the path of accumulation. The realization of impermanence usually begins with a sense of appreciation. In order to realize the impermanence of something, you first need to see its value and to appreciate it. When you begin to appreciate the teachings, the opportunity to practice, the teacher, and the unique circumstances that brought you to the teachings, you also realize you might lose these precious things, and you begin to get paranoid. So the psychological pattern of appreciating the greatness of the practice, the teaching, and the teacher brings the first notion of impermanence. You realize that all kinds of obstacles could occur, that your learning could be interrupted by physical sickness, death, commitments, and the demands of relatives and friends. Basically, you see that you might not be able to hold on to this opportunity. Once you have realized the unique situation that you are in, rather than either competing with the teacher or having an inferiority complex, you simply experience the rare occasion that you have.

Such an approach to impermanence may be simple, even crude, but it is extremely important. It is a simplistic approach, but it is effective. This approach is called the style of *kusulu,* or "simpleton." The Sanskrit term *kusulu* refers to a simple yogi who does only three necessary things: eating, shitting, and sleeping. It does not refer to a person so wealthy that he or she doesn't have to work, but a person quite satisfied with a simple existence. Kusulu-type practice is called *joggom.* In Tibetan, *jokpa* means "rest," *gompa* means "meditation." *Jog* and *gom* are combined to form *joggom,* which means "resting meditation." You are simply following your instinct, so to speak. Another approach is more subtle, more metaphysical. It is called the style of the pundit. The pundit approach is called *chegom: chepa* means "to analyze," and *gom* means "meditation"; therefore, *chegom* is analytical meditative practice.

Once you are able to relate with the impermanence of the crude world, seeing that time flies so there is no time to relax, you begin to realize a more subtle form of impermanence. You realize that you cannot hold on to anything psychologically or experientially. Whenever you try to hold on to solid ground, the ground itself shifts. It is like holding a pot by the handle, and having the handle break off and the pot fall on the floor and break. You cannot hold on to anything because things are constantly and fundamentally changing. There is no place for real rest or security. In order to develop security, you sit down and try to figure out some scheme, but there is not even a place to sit down. The rug moves under your feet before you can sit down. The shiftiness or slipperiness of psychological existence is a more fundamental level of impermanence. In order to realize this more subtle form of impermanence, some traditions have a formula about impermanence that you repeat again and again, in an attempt to let it seep into your subconscious mind that you cannot cling or hold on to anything.*

Once you begin to realize that psychologically you cannot hold on to anything, seemingly solid phenomenal objects also cease to be solid, because these objects have to be confirmed by conscious analysis. In order to solidify an object, one's thoughts have to be solidified, one's being has to be solidified, but you cannot solidify your basic existence in any way at all. It is like a rushing river; you have nothing to hold on to. We could call this experience "developing an empty heart." The whole thing is hor-rifically, frighteningly empty—and trying to hold on to any of it breeds further empty heart. It is as if you are a person who is highly susceptible to heart attacks who must be very attentive to whatever you do. Even lifting a cup of tea and sipping is uncertain. You do not know whether you will last long enough to finish the cup of tea. So there is a tremendous sense of groundlessness. You are fully and utterly haunted. In that state, even fear could be said to be security, for if you could develop real fear, real panic, you would have something to hold on to. But you are not even

---

* One example of such a contemplation is the practice called the four reminders. In this practice you contemplate over and over again (1) the preciousness of a human birth, (2) the reality of impermanence and death, (3) the inescapability of karma, and (4) the ocean of suffering.

capable of experiencing fear, because you have nothing to be fearful of, and because everything is moving so fast that nothing sticks and there is nothing to hold on to. At this level, the experience of impermanence is so fundamental that it is almost mystical.

Egolessness

An understanding of impermanence is preparation for the experience of egolessness. As a practitioner, you have to develop a feeling for egolessness, as you did for impermanence. In the contemplative tradition, we do not talk about ego as consisting of the five skandhas or eight types of consciousness. We do not approach ego philosophically—it is our immediate experience.

Basically, ego is a psychological bank, or pool, in which we store memories and ideas so that whenever we are running out of external entertainment, we could churn them out and entertain ourselves. It's like an animal with no food to eat who burps out the food from its stomach and begins to chew it all over again. Predominantly, the purpose of ego is to entertain us, to create the simple pleasure of occupying ourselves when we are bored, frightened, or unhappy. It gives us something we could stick to, something we could work with, which makes us relatively happy. We have someone else to keep us company. As the proverb says, "Misery loves company." That somebody who keeps company with your misery is the ego.

However, having realized impermanence, the experience of no ground, you see that the idea of having somebody to keep company with your misery, someone to cheer you up or entertain you, is a gigantic hoax. You think you are being entertained, but actually you are creating your own illusion. There is really no such thing. Psychologically, when you experience ego, you experience it as other than yourself. Philosophers say this is your ego, that is your ego; but in experiential terms, in your immediate experience, you begin to realize that there is no one to keep you company, and you have no hold on anything. This may be a very simpleminded approach to egolessness, but that kind of simplemindedness is absolutely necessary at this point.

Egolessness, from a contemplative point of view, is the alarm created by the experience of empty heart, the double take created from the realization of impermanence. You see that everything is impermanent, and you become empty-hearted. Then you say, "Wait a minute, what about this?" And then: "Nothing! It's all about nothing!" The whole thing is completely gone. At this point, you may get angry. You may feel deprived or cheated, and you might try to blame your parents for bringing you into this world, or blame your minister, guru, or schoolteacher.

When you discover egolessness, there is a faint sense of anger. It is so alarming, so bad, like a distasteful joke that one is playing on oneself. You lose your temper in the same way as when you realize someone has been playing a practical joke on you. The discovery of egolessness is a further sense of "lost." You are utterly lost; there's no ground to hold on to; there is a total sense of poverty. And the slight aggression or anger you experience perpetuates that notion of the nonexistence of oneself. It worsens the experience.

The experience of egolessness is very real. We could say that the experience of impermanence is one of discontinuity, and with the experience of egolessness, there is nothing to continue the discontinuity since the moderator is also nonexistent. This is an actual emotional experience very close to the heart and very desperate. You are constantly looking for confirmation, for a moderator to qualify your existence, but you discover none. That is the notion of egolessness.

Suffering

The experience of impermanence and egolessness leads to suffering. Although nothing is permanent and nothing is functioning in the realm of ego, if you really look at yourself fully, you see that there is still anger. You might think that if the whole thing is nonexistent, you should feel relief, or that you should not have to experience any more pain. You might think that if everything is gone, it could be a kind of honorable suicide. But the fact that those expectations are not met, that things don't happen in that way, creates even more pain. The logic that says, "Because ego does not exist, therefore you should not suffer," does not work. In fact, the reason suffering is so acute, so oppressive, and so painful is because suffering has no root. If there were a root, if there were a case history, you could follow it back. Suffering would become vulnerable. But suffering is, in fact, indestructible and self-existent. Therefore, it happens to be real, unlike the nonexistence of ego. Suffering is the most real thing in one's realm of experience.

Suffering is the only solid thing there is; otherwise we would not suffer. The idea of the path is that you don't fight back at the suffering, but you learn to make yourself at home with the suffering. Reality is suffering. Even at the tantric level, we talk about *maha* duhkha, or *great* suffering. Suffering is what made the Buddha turn the wheel of the dharma. And when he opened his mouth, the first word he spoke was *duhkha*. In the sutras, it is said that we survive in suffering; we work in suffering; we dwell in suffering, in a state of woe. The realization of suffering is the starting point. It is the seed of awakening. That is why it is called the *first* noble truth: it is for ordinary folks, people on the path of accumulation, people from the street, so to speak.

There are different kinds of suffering. There is physical suffering that is not psychosomatic pain, and there is physical suffering that is psychosomatic by nature. There is psychological suffering and pain. There is restlessness, discomfort, and uneasiness. As practitioners begin to discover that there is no permanent experience and no ego, they realize that the whole world is made only out of suffering. They enjoy in the suffering; they suffer in the suffering; they function in the suffering. This is the definition of samsara, going around and around in the ocean of pain. Even seemingly pleasurable things are actually pain. Not only do they bring pain later, but they are actually painful by nature. The reason the nature of pleasure is suffering is because pleasure is so claustrophobic; as a result, pleasure has an element of imprisonment in it. Maybe your bars are ornamented with flowers; nevertheless, it is a prison.

There is a bodhisattva called Tag-ngu who is eternally crying. *Tag* means "eternally," *ngu* means "cry"; so *Tag-ngu* is "He who cries eternally." Tag-ngu is the example of a bodhisattva who sees the truth of suffering in the samsaric world. So the realization of suffering is real. It should be very real and most outstanding. The only reality in the samsaric world is pain and suffering—and suffering becomes more real if there is no ego, no permanence, and no eternity. Transitoriness and egolessness bring more suffering, crystallizing the liveliness of the suffering and the energies around it.

Suffering is so full, and egolessness is so desolate. Whenever you find suffering to be too oppressive and claustrophobic, you go to the other extreme, egolessness, which is too spacious. So you can't really enjoy the spaciousness—and if you do try to hold on to it, the impermanence begins to wipe you out completely. But you cannot step out of that. As far as the real dharma, the root dharma, the foundation of the dharma is concerned, there is no other alternative than the three marks of existence. You don't need inspiration or entertainment. You have no choice other than to experience pain. But then, somehow or other, you begin to become involved in the *realness* of the pain. That is how you begin to go on to the four noble truths. The reality of egolessness becomes apparent, and because of that, the experience of pain is immediate, like putting your hand on burning metal without wearing gloves. It is too immediate. That is how the practitioner sees the world at the first stage of the path of accumulation. It is the vipashyana experience of seeing impermanence, egolessness, and suffering in the fullest sense.

As far as Buddhism is concerned, that is the total picture of the samsaric world, which is why it is called the three marks of existence. The three marks are a synopsis of the nature of the world. It is important to remember that the world we are referring to here is the phenomenological world. It is the world we perceive, according to our phenomenal experience. If we were not here, there would not be a world, as far as we are concerned. However, that doesn't mean that when we die, the world will disappear. However, our version of the world will not be there anymore, so as far as we are concerned, we create our own world. That is our experience, and at this point it is important to stick with experience and not become too philosophical.

The practitioner's view of the world should derive from the experience of meditation. Without the practice of meditation—both sitting practice and meditation in everyday life—one is not moving at all on the path. Purely learning on the intellectual level alone is like revving the engine but not shifting it into gear: your truck only begins to move when meditation is engaged in everyday life. The whole point of the path of accumulation is that the knowable, or dharmas, cannot be known unless there is a knower who is fully trained by means of the practice of meditation. That is the point of shamatha and vipashyana. Vipashyana, in particular, becomes very prominent. It brings you into a full human being, so to speak, a complete human being who is worthy of following the path. It sharpens the intellect and heightens the awareness.

The experiential approach to the three marks of existence comes from the tradition of contemplative practice rather than the tradition of scholars. As far as mahayana Buddhism is concerned, there are two schools of thought: the school of intellect and the school of contemplative practice. Asanga (the founder of the Yogachara school) is said to have introduced the contemplative practice of mahayana, and Nagarjuna (the founder of the Madhyamaka school) is said to have introduced the intellectual aspect. Those are the two means and methods that developed for training students. Nevertheless, it seems that the intellectual aspect also should have a contemplative aspect, and vice versa. If you begin with the contemplative approach, the student's insight will slowly be turned toward intellectual understanding; and if you begin with metaphysical understanding, that slowly turns back into contemplative practice.

The Kagyü and Nyingma traditions of Tibetan Buddhism are within the contemplative tradition, which first introduced the simpleminded approach to understanding things like impermanence and egolessness. They take a simple approach to life, meditation, and the path, almost on the level of being stupid. They use the layperson's, rather than the scholar's, approach to reality. From that simple layperson's approach to reality, you can build a good foundation. And from that, you begin to be more and more sophisticated and subtle. It is like the story of how the tradition of roast pork began in China. There was a piggery that caught fire and all the pigs were roasted. When the fire died down, people decided to taste the pigs, and when they did so, they found them to be extremely delicious. Later on, an exquisite cuisine developed from that experience.

Having developed a true understanding of the four noble truths and the three marks of existence, a student may be inspired to renounce the samsaric world. You have no comparison to samsara, no world other than the samsaric world—yet the samsaric world you live in is nauseating and unpleasant. At this point, we could say that the whole approach becomes somewhat goal oriented. On the path of accumulation, a goal exists and a journey exists. There is a direction. You are choosing nirvana as opposed to samsara. Such a choice is based on becoming disillusioned with samsaric fascinations and somewhat revolted. Samsara not only feels bad, but it hits the basic core of your existence and makes you throw up. However, although the samsaric world is not very attractive, and renunciation seems to be necessary, you should not take renunciation too literally. If you try to run away from samsara, the very act of running away becomes in itself a samsaric act. Renunciation has to be unconditional renunciation.

64

The Middle Path of Accumulation

[On the middle level of the path of accumulation,] you begin to realize the virtues and faults of your behavior. Your neurosis and sanity are clearly seen. . . . [But] you first need inspiration. You need to identify with the teaching and feel that you are a part of the lineage—that it is your family wealth, your heirloom. . . . From that conviction, and with tremendous faith and directness, you then automatically behave in an ethical way.

B EGINNING WITH the first of the five paths, the path of accumulation, we are directing our journey toward the mahayana. So an ordinary hinayana practitioner on the path of accumulation is already on a journey toward the mahayana. The second, or middle, path of accumulation is inspired by the lesser path of accumulation. As an ordinary practitioner, you enter the second stage of the path of accumulation when you have managed to cut the cause of being born in the lower realms—the hell realm, the hungry ghost realm, and the animal realm. In Tibetan what you are cutting is called *ne-ngen len-gyi gyu*. *Ne* means "dwelling place," *ngen* means "lower," *len* means "entering into a life," *gyi* means "of," and *gyu* means the "seed"; so *ne-ngen len-gyi gyu* means the "seed of entering into a life in a lower dwelling-place."

On the middle level of the path of accumulation, you are slowly and surely moving away from ordinary religious or spiritual practices of purely saving yourself and reaching a higher level of spirituality. You are slowly moving away from the theistic approach with its notion of a savior. The lesser level of the path of accumulation is the common yana, one which theistic traditions that believe in an external deity could also follow. In theistic religions, you also see the foolishness of egohood and the foolishness of looking for security, but there is no notion of egolessness. The idea of renunciation is also not at all unfamiliar. In fact, renunciation is one of the highlights of the theistic approach. So the change from the lesser to the middle path of accumulation is that you cease to have the idea of a savior. You are actually moving away from theism. The second level of the path of accumulation marks that point extremely clearly, whereas in the first level of the path of accumulation, it is still questionable.

At this point, you are finally becoming independent from theistic dogma. However, there is still the possibility that you could end up in the god realm by means of meditation. The saving grace is prajna. Vipashyana allows you to develop the insight and intelligence to be able to sort fish from fowl, that which is ego-centered from that which is not. That is one of the outstanding qualities of Buddhism—it sows the seed of intelligence in students' minds so that they know how to separate those two approaches to the spiritual path.

The Mantra of Experience

In the middle path of accumulation, you practice what is called the "sixteen incantations," or the "mantra of experience." In reciting this incantation, you are shifting your conceptualization much closer to the truth. By doing so, you begin to get a glimpse of clarity and sanity so that your conceptualizations become much more sophisticated. One of the beauties of the hinayana teaching is that you are not looking for a higher goal, but you are simply manipulating your confusion in a wiser way. In that way, you begin to find yourself closer to freedom. So the hinayana is a very ground-level approach.

The mantra of experience is not particularly spectacular. In fact, it seems to be quite ordinary. It is the repeating of the four noble truths in four different ways. This formula is said to cut the root of being born in the lower realms, and as such it is very important and profound. Reciting the mantra of experience has nothing to do with magic or with calming the mind; it is simply that you are more convinced the more you ponder it. It is a form of brainwashing, but the brain that you wash out is the ego. You begin to have second thoughts about your previous commitment to your confusion, and you develop a lot of doubts, which begins to shatter the foundation of ego. You shatter ego's foundation by mocking it with the notion that it is not valid or secure. But you do not try to destroy the whole thing completely, for the hinayana path is a gradual process.

In reciting the mantra, you begin to become more aware of the totality, as an organic thing, and you no longer look for one particular highlight. You actually begin to see an alternative to samsara. By reciting the four noble truths in this way, the whole of existence becomes a manifestation of truth or liberation, and you could identify with it as a totality.

The Sixteen Incantations

The first set of incantations is:

Suffering should be seen.
The origin of the suffering should be avoided.
The goal should be attained.
The path should be actualized.

The second set of incantations is:

Suffering should be realized as impermanent.
The origin of suffering should be realized as impermanent.
The goal should be realized as impermanent.
The path should be realized as impermanent.

The third set of incantations is:

Suffering should be seen clearly.
The origin of suffering should be seen clearly.
The goal should be seen clearly.
The path should be seen clearly.

The fourth set of incantations is:

No suffering.
No origin of suffering.
No goal.
No path.

The first set familiarizes you with the basic logic of the four noble truths. With the second set, you discover that the four noble truths do not provide security because they are all just transitory experiences. With the third set, having seen the transitory nature of those experiences, you should develop some personal identification with these truths. They should be seen clearly and properly. The fourth set of incantations points out that, in actual fact, the only requirement is to cut the karmic root of suffering, the origin of suffering, the goal, and the path. Therefore, there is no suffering, no origin, no goal, and no path. That is the final statement of vipashyana experience—that we should cut the root of confusion altogether.

The Importance of Conviction

How is it possible that by knowing those four ways of seeing the four noble truths, you can cut the cause and effect of being born in the lower samsaric realms? It is because you have become completely and thoroughly identified with the teaching, so the teaching is no longer a myth. The reason we should repeat these four noble truths four times is to increase the sense of identification with the practice and the teaching that we have learned. It is to build "real conviction," *ngepar shepa*. Ngepar shepa is not just ordinary conviction, but real conviction, knowing completely and thoroughly.

If you do not have enough pride in the teachings, you will be unable to cut the karmic umbilical cord. In the mahayana, you are proud of yourself because you have buddha nature. At the hinayana level of the path of accumulation, you are proud because for the first time you are able to relate to the teachings. You have heard the four noble truths in their absolute meaning. You develop tremendous excitement because you have taken refuge in the dharma and you can identify with the dharma. That is why you are proud. But although there is pride, it is still underdeveloped. So the idea of reciting sixteen incantations is to build up your identification with the real teaching.

Ethical Guidelines

The middle level of the path of accumulation is very ethically oriented, with an emphasis on behaving properly, in accordance with the practice. You exclude what is undesirable and include what is desirable in terms of the path, and you develop dompa, or binding. Identifying with the teachings is the factor that binds you together with the practice. That is the definition of shila, or morality: that which binds you to the practice and the teachings. But you cannot develop a very powerful binding force unless there is some kind of pride.

One of the problems with the ethical approach is that there is a tendency to feel guilty or fearful of punishment. You become afraid of the consequences, feeling that you might get punished in purgatory or hell unless you keep your rules. In this case, it is quite the opposite: the reason you keep your discipline is that you are inspired by your understanding of the sixteen incantations of the four noble truths. That realization brings you much closer to the teachings. You have something to live for, rather than just living a myth.

Having identified with the teaching and been inspired by its implications, you begin to realize the virtues and faults of your behavior. Your neurosis and sanity are clearly seen. That is the ethical guideline. Cutting the karmic root of entering the lower realms is not dependent on behaving in a moralistic, ethical way, or being good. You first need inspiration. You need to identify with the teaching and feel that you are a part of the lineage—that it is your family wealth, your heirloom. So first you have that conviction, and from that conviction, and with tremendous faith and directness, you then automatically behave in an ethical way. Such conviction rouses you to relate with the teaching and pull yourself together.

We could say that the middle path of accumulation is a way to make yourself more intelligent. The first level, or lesser path of accumulation, is a training process. At that level, we are uncertain whether we are intelligent or not. We are simply following certain rules and regulations and recommendations from a person we trust, teachings we trust, and a tradition we trust—but it is still based on devotion and guesswork. That is the only way to convert ordinary people to the path: to first give a set of disciplines, rules, and regulations that are seemingly workable and roughly logical. At the same time, the teachings are also experientially logical, in that you have experienced the reality of death, impermanence, egolessness, pain, and so forth. On the lesser path of accumulation, you have understood the teaching somewhat roughly. But it doesn't quite click in the fundamental sense until you identify with the real teaching of the four noble truths by repeating these sixteen incantations.

A basic point of the middle path of accumulation is to rouse yourself to the drum of the dharma, the trumpet of the teachings. The proclamation of the four noble truths is heard four times, and each time it is clearer and clearer. The ability to identify yourself with that teaching is a kind of heroism. It is how you bring yourself into the path. If you join the army, first you have security. Your house, your uniform, and your food have been prepared for you. Then you have the heroism of being in the army—the flags, bugles, horses, and whatnot—and you make yourself very loud, convincing, and colorful. That seems to be the quality of the middle path of accumulation.

65

The Greater Path of Accumulation

We need both devotional virya and ongoing virya. Those two viryas seem to be important. They are the basic core of the shamatha-vipashyana marriage—and shamatha-vipashyana is recommended as the vanguard of the mahayana practice of shunyata.

A T THE level of the greater path of accumulation, a person begins to develop not only isolated awareness or mindfulness practice, but the practice of being aware and mindful at the same time, or shamatha-vipashyana. Having started with shamatha, you may have begun to place more emphasis on vipashyana—but you then begin to realize the limitation of dwelling on vipashyana alone, so you go a step further, and you happen to rediscover shamatha.

TWO TYPES OF EFFORT

In joining together shamatha and vipashyana, the scriptures talk about two types of effort: the practice of surrendering and the practice of conti-nuity. The Sanskrit word *virya* (Tib.: tsöndrü) means "effort," "diligence," or "working hard." The practice of surrendering, or devotional virya, is called *küjor—kü* meaning "respect," or "devotion," and *jorwa* meaning "application" or "practice," so *küjor* means the "practice of devotion." The practice of continuity, or ongoing virya, is *tagjor. Tag* means "continu-ity," and *jorwa* again means "practice," so *tagjor* means "the practice of continuity." With tagjor, your practice is ongoing. You have engaged with the practice, and your practice is diligent and devoted—and you are willing to go along with that for the rest of your life.

The two viryas balance one another. Devotional virya could become impulsive, and ongoing virya could be without devotion or inspiration, just dragging along. So we need both devotional virya and ongoing virya. The two viryas seem to be important. They are the basic core of the shamatha-vipashyana marriage—and shamatha-vipashyana is recommended as the vanguard of the mahayana practice of shunyata. Shamatha-vipashyana is the way you step out of the path of accumulation onto the path of unification, the second of the five paths. The combination of shamatha with vipashyana is the leverage.

In shamatha-vipashyana practice, when you sit you have an awareness of your surroundings. Your sense perceptions have been taken into account in developing vipashyana awareness, and you also have the shamatha practice of deliberateness, of getting into things directly. Bringing together those two types of practice is said by the Kagyü lineage father Gampopa to be one of the most enlightening and promising techniques ever developed in the dharma.

In the Burmese Theravada tradition, the late Burmese meditation master Mahasi Sayadaw was a great revolutionary in the meditation field. He reintroduced meditation practice into the Theravada world with a particular emphasis on the combination of shamatha-vipashyana. It is an important point that having already accomplished shamatha and vipashyana independent of each other, we can combine them together by application of the two types of virya. This approach is highly recommended by all kinds of great teachers.

When we combine shamatha and vipashyana, we feel the verge of the breath, or the touch of the breath going out, rather than being heavy-handedly involved in it. At the same time, there is a feeling of completeness around us everywhere, in all directions, an environmental feeling. We sense that when the breathing dissolves, it is an expanding process—dissolving at this point, dissolving at that point, and further points, and further, further points. That dissolving is taking place in the whole universe, and you are, in a sense, nowhere. Finally, you lose the reference point as to who is breathing and where the breathing is dissolving. But that sense of complete desolation cannot take place unless the precision and accuracy of the breathing is happening at the same time. The accuracy of shamatha happens to be independent of the particular department that perpetuates the sense of reference point. But even if there is no point of reference with shamatha, as the breathing goes out, it is real and complete breathing going out.

The sense of reference point is connected to the psychosomatic body, which is the source of security. If you lose that reference point, you may feel that you have at last freed yourself from the world of desire, and your psychosomatic sickness has no control over you anymore. But you still have a long way to go. You have not yet touched shunyata. Although it may be subtle, there is still a sense of self. Although the heaviest part of the neurosis has been removed, there is still a feeling of duality. For the practitioner, the sense of self abides in the teachings and the practice itself. That is the only security there is: trusting in the truth of the teachings. With practice, there is definitely a change, because you experience the desolation of things being not all that solid and definite. Your belief in physical existence is being pulled apart, but you still believe in the discontinuity. There is the abstract belief that what pulls you apart is a form of security. There is still some kind of trust that you are going to continue, and you have a practice to work with. So although you lose your body, you can still practice.

In shamatha-vipashyana, mind and space mix together. That mixing of mind and space comes from the two types of virya. The virya of devotion, küjor, leans toward the practice of precision, of bending one's fantasies to the simple breath. It is the shamatha aspect. The virya of continuity, or tagjor, is related with vipashyana. In shamatha-vipashyana, you need küjor and tagjor happening together simultaneously.

The Four Legs of Miracle

On the third or greater level of the path of accumulation, we approach shamatha-vipashyana in terms of what are called the "four legs of miracle": strong interest, effort, recollection, and investigation.

Strong Interest

The first leg is called *dünpa*, or "strong interest." It is the attitude that you are going to apply yourself to shamatha-vipashyana practice. There is a quality of conviction connected with the fact that developing shamatha-vipashyana is the way to cut not only the three lowest realms, but the world of passion altogether. Before, at the lesser and middle levels of the path of accumulation, you were just cutting the animal, hungry ghost, and hell realms; but at the greater level of the path of accumulation, the root of the world of desire is cut.

It is important to know which particular world we are conquering in the various stages of meditative development. There are three world-realms: the formless realm, the world of form, and the world of passion or desire. The world of desire includes the jealous god realm, the human realm, the animal realm, the hungry ghost realm, and the hell realm, plus a portion of the god realm. So a portion of the god realm is considered to be within the realm of desire, and the remainder of the god realm is considered to be within the form and formless world realms—heavenly realms of progressively more subtle states of meditative absorption. In the realm of desire, you have not only the existence of form, but you experience a heavy demand on your body, speech, and mind. Mind is related with the formless world, speech with the world of form, and body with the world of desire. Very refined desire is related with the formless god realm, subtle desire with the world of form, and crude desire with the world of desire. From the world of desire to the world of form to the formless world, the quality of desire is progressively more refined and subtle.

Meditative development is one of first conquering crude desire, then subtle desire, and finally very refined desire. Shamatha-vipashyana practice is extraordinarily important because it is the only way you can cut the realm of desire. Of the three world-realms, the desire realm is the heaviest realm, and at this point the root of this realm has been cut.

Effort

The second leg of miracle is effort, or tsöndrü. It is strenuousness. Much stronger obstacles occur when you involve yourself in shamatha-vipashyana practice. Quite possibly you are putting many eggs in one basket, because you are trying to collect your span of attention into one-pointedness, and at the same time you are increasing your span of awareness. Putting those two into one basket at the same time is highly demanding. You cannot practice shamatha-vipashyana unless you have gone through shamatha first and vipashyana afterward. You need to have training in both practices separately before coming to shamatha-vipashyana practice, because combining the two takes a lot of effort.

Recollection

The third leg is *trenpa**, or recollection (Skt.: *smriti*). Recollection is used greatly by the contemplative traditions of the West, particularly by the Catholic tradition of monasticism and the mystical schools. The *satipatthana* practice of the Theravadins and the *smrityupasthana* practice of Sarvastivadins are also practices of recollection. Recollection doesn't mean capturing experiences, but being awake in a different way. You are totally awake and free from any unnecessary commitments. Recollection has nothing to do with memory—it is entirely different. Trenpa could refer to "recalling the past," but *tren* also means "to think."

Trenpa does not mean recalling past details, like digging up old things from the attic; but it is based on habitual mind, which automatically has reference points. The indoctrination of reference points is implanted in your mind. For instance, you could not suddenly say, "There is a car" without any reference to the past. You could not say, "There is a car" if you had not remembered that it was a car before you experienced it. So trenpa ceases to be a reference point, in that we do not have to dig up all our memories and love and hate from the past; and at the same time, it *is* a reference point. Even a simple statement such as "There is a car" is not quite free from the past.

Even our awareness practice is a product of the past. You have been told that it is good to develop awareness, to sit and do it, so you do it because you have been told to. However, when you are doing it, you do not have to go back and check on it. You just flash it. If someone is going to hit you, you cover your head with your hand. In part, that is the result of indoctrination—but it is a spontaneous act, nevertheless. So immediate experience, or seemingly immediate experience, has its root in the habitual thinking of the past. Nevertheless, such habitual patterns also have subconscious, clear, resourceful, and present intelligence.

Reacting to confusion and hassles takes place in the present. You have no time to go back. With the five skandhas, for example, you have no chance to go back step-by-step. You may be on the brink of the fifth skandha, but you have all five of them simultaneously. All hands on deck at one moment! There is a taste of looseness, stillness, and desolation. You have no chance to relate with your case history anymore—you are right there.

---

* Most sources associate the third leg with "mind" (Tib.: sem; Skt.: chitta).

Animals instinctively react to any attack. They decide to make a move, whether it is logical or illogical. When a cat sees cars coming, it might decide to cross the road or try to go back. There is no logic, particularly; it is an expression of freedom.

Trenpa is the sense of perspective. You are aware of your meditative practice being an entirely different approach than your ordinary way of relating with your life. You are aware that you are just about to give up your lovable world, the world of desire. You begin to have all kinds of panic and fear, feeling that the good old days were beautiful but now there is a threat. You realize that practice is very threatening.

Investigation

The last leg of miracle is called *chöpa,* or "investigation." When you are in a state of shamatha-vipashyana practice, you have to examine yourself constantly. A lot of investigation needs to be done. Unless there is a continual reexamining of yourself, quite likely the hassles involved with the practice would put you off. Because it is so strenuous, you would not want to get into it. Unless you are able to get inspired by strenuous investigation, you will no longer be able to identify yourself with the teachings.

This third stage of the path of accumulation is extremely important. It is the last possibility for an ordinary person to be able to transform himself or herself into a higher person, a noble person. That is why it is called the *greater* path of accumulation. It is the only way that you—as an ordinary layperson, who is neither an arhat nor a bodhisattva nor a buddha—could become one of the noble ones.

The beginning of the hinayana path, the shravakayana, is the level of an ordinary student. The specialities of shravakayana are following monastic rules, listening, and talking. It is the level of the four foundations of mindfulness and the four noble truths. In the third stage of the path of accumulation, you are approaching the pratyekabuddhayana. You have a sense of freedom, liberation, and emancipation. You discover that you are about to cut the realm of desire and enter the desireless realms. Shamatha-vipashyana practice is the only one that could bring you to that supernormal, superhuman level—there is no other way.

66

The Path of Unification

The path of unification is complete preparation for the mahayana, but it is not the mahayana as such. On the path of unification, you have sensed the possibility of treading on the path of the bodhisattva and becoming a mahayanist who is fully dedicated to working with sentient beings, so tremendous conviction comes up. You are excited by the possibility that you might enter into the mahayana at some point.

W HEN A person has developed shamatha-vipashyana practice not only in the meditative state alone, but on the meditation-in-action level as well, that person has begun to approach the second of the five paths, which is the path of unification. The path of unification, or jorlam, connects or unites the ordinary samsaric person with the level of higher beings who are able to turn the wheel of dharma dispassionately. You begin to get a sense of accomplishment as you go from the greater level of the path of accumulation into the first level of the path of unification. You realize that the idea of shunyata and the idea of losing one's concept of self, or ego, is no longer fearful. In other words, you begin to realize that you have nothing to lose and nothing to gain. That is the first hint of shunyata experience.

MEDITATIVE EXPERIENCE

The meditation experience of the path of unification is *nampar mitokpa*. *Mitokpa* is "nonconceptualization," and *nampar* means "completely," or "properly"; so *nampar mitokpa* is a "completely, properly nonconceptual-ized state." It is the final realization of the desolateness of the meditative state. You begin to have very solid and tangible feelings of the three marks of existence. Suffering, impermanence, and egolessness are completely understood and actualized in your own practice. So shamatha-vipashyana plays a very important part. It is the only way you could enter into shun-yata practice and realization. It is the only way that you could transform yourself from a subhuman or subsentient being to a supersentient being—an arhat or bodhisattva.

DEVELOPING DISCRIMINATION

On the path of unification you develop what are known as the four stages of discrimination: heat, peak, patience, and higher dharma.

1. Heat / Trö

The first stage of discrimination is referred to as *trö,* which means "heat." Trö is like rubbing sticks together to produce fire: before you produce fire, you feel heat. Trö has nothing to do with yogic practices. It is more like heat in the sense of an animal going into heat in the mating season. There is a possibility of mating with somebody; you have a whiff of that. Likewise, you get a hint of the shunyata possibilities because you no longer are afraid of your possible involvement with the non-ego realm, non-ego doctrine, and non-ego livelihood. You have given up all your desires—they have already gone away—so you no longer feel the deso-lateness, loneliness, and pain of the three marks of existence. They are no longer a problem, but a reality. You are benefiting, again and again, by the three marks of existence. That is the particular hint of heat you begin to catch. Since you have begun to get a glimpse of the mahayana, you have a feeling of delightedness.

2. Peak / Tsemo

The second stage of discrimination is referred to as *tsemo,* which means "peak," or "crest," as in the tip of a tree or plant. In this case, it has the sense of once in a lifetime. It is like the tip of a tree, because you are just beginning to touch a sensitive point of your development. It is once in a lifetime because it cannot be achieved unless you are able to relate with that particular insight as potentially explosive, and you are willing to live with it. It is potentially explosive because there is the possibility for the first time of becoming superhuman. You feel you have swallowed an atom bomb and at any minute it's going to burst. With tsemo, there is a sense of penetratingness as well as heat. You feel a sharpness happening inside you, as if you had swallowed a razor blade and it's just about to cut you from inside out. There is a sense of a magnificent and somewhat terrifying sharpness taking place within your being—an enormous conviction.

3. Patience / Söpa

Having developed conviction, and having gone through heat and peak, trö and tsemo, the third type of discrimination is *söpa,* or patience. You develop patience, for nothing has been censored in the teachings. This type of patience is an entirely different kind of patience—it is not just forbearance of pain, it is that you are willing to wait to receive the teachings. The teachings are a part of your system, and you are not impatiently looking forward to the next excitement. The result of such patience is that you develop enormous mental power to memorize the words you heard from the teacher and read in the teachings. Part of the egoless approach toward sentient beings is that it brings unforgetfulness. The mental hangup of forgetfulness occurs because you would like to preserve things for yourself. You would like to treat yourself well and never let anybody else see what you have. Such selfishness brings forgetfulness. When there is no selfishness, that brings a tremendously sharp memory and powerful recollection. That is the element of patience.

4. Higher Dharma / Tamchö

The fourth type of discrimination is called the higher dharma (Tib.: *tamchö,* damchos; Skt.: *saddharma*). Having developed conviction and powerful mental recollection, you begin to have the idea that you are a holder of the dharma. Although you have not yet become a teacher, you have a sense that you are becoming part of the lineage. There is a hint of that, a sense of identifying with the higher dharma.

The four stages of discrimination—heat, peak, patience, and higher dharma—are the last development in the path of unification, the second path.

FIVE PERCEPTIONS

The combination of heat and peak, trö and tsemo, leads into a further process: a development of energies of perceptions known in Tibetan as *wangpo nga*. *Wangpo* means "sense organs," and *nga* means "five," so *wangpo nga* means "five sense organs." These five are the meditative equivalent of the sense organs. These psychological sense-organs are developed through the practice of shamatha and vipashyana and the realization of the three marks of existence. Having developed such senses, you have reached the level of direct application. You know how to bring together the teachings, the teacher, the student, and the practitioner's means and methods into one unity. Without these five organs, you will have no way to bring those together as personal experience. You will still view the teachings as a foreign element, something that you cannot actually relate with.

The reason you may find it very difficult to practice and to put into effect whatever you have learned and studied is not because you are stupid and unable to comprehend. It is not that you are lazy, slow, or pleasure oriented. None of those reasons apply. The only reason you are not able to relate with the teachings is that you are unable to identify with them as personal experience. If you are able to identify with the teachings as personal experience, your intellect naturally flows out, and your meditation experience and awareness flow out as well. Energy and joy in practicing flow out because there is devotion to the path, which has become an integral part of your existence. In order to create an effective marriage, a couple has to develop love for one another. Similarly, you need to personalize the teachings in order to unite with them and bring them into your system, into your whole being. The teachings are based on personal experience, personally applied to individuals, rather than on theoretical speculation or metaphysics. When you identify with the teachings as personal experience, there is well-being and ultimate security. The teachings are alive, and they apply to your day-to-day living.

The first perception is *faith* in your discovery (Tib.: tepa). The second perception is *exertion* (Tib.: tsöndrü). It is diligence, perseverance, working hard. The good news that there is an alternative to samsaric existence brings both discipline and delight. You are not tired of what you are trying to do, but highly energized. It takes energy to renounce the samsaric world, so diligence is absolutely necessary.

The third perception is *recollection,* or awareness (Tib.: trenpa). The practice of meditation and other techniques is kept very vigorous by the combination of awareness and diligence. You are relating with the teachings, with vipashyana as the basis of both meditation in action and sitting meditation. Awareness is twenty-four-hour work. You are completely at the mercy of the dharma. Trenpa also brings an experience of egolessness. Your only interest is in awakening your mind of enlightenment, or *bodhichitta.* You have no personal interest in anything else.

The fourth perception is *one-pointedness,* or meditation (Tib.: *ting-nge-dzin*). It is almost at the level of obsession. Even ordinary thoughts, such as fantasies of aggression or fantasies of sex, become part of the inspiration of the path. Ordinary thoughts become workable as part of the complete conviction of absorption. Since you have a personal understanding and relationship with practice, there is a feeling of well-being. That plays an extremely important part, for without that, the simplicity of shamatha and the clarity of vipashyana—the very idea of meditation—become pure myth.

The fifth perception is *intellect,* knowledge, or prajna (Tib.: sherap). Prajna is the complete experience of vipashyana. You begin to discover all kinds of subtleties in the world, subtleties of colors and shapes and implications of energy exchange. Whatever happens in your life becomes tremendously sharp and fantastically revealing by its own condition, rather than according to your own preconceived ideas, or ego's version of things. There is a tremendous selflessness, and the notion that you are actually advancing on the path. At this level, prajna is an intellectual understanding and appreciation of the subtleties of the dharma. You are not bound by emotions or intuition alone, but you have an intellectual understanding of the whole path.

FIVE POWERS

Along with the five perceptions, five powers or strengths develop at this point. The five powers are as follows: faith never needs to be sought; exertion never needs to be sought; recollection never needs to be sought;

one-pointedness never needs to be sought; and intellect never needs to be sought. With the five powers, you have complete command. So first you develop the five perceptions or abilities. Then, as a further development, you become confident about those abilities.

The path of unification is complete preparation for the mahayana, but it is not the mahayana as such. On the path of unification, you have sensed the possibility of treading on the path of the bodhisattva and becoming a mahayanist who is fully dedicated to working with sentient beings, so tremendous conviction comes up. You are excited by the possibility that you might enter into the mahayana at some point.

Part Six

KNOWLEDGE / PRAJNA

67

Ego:
The Thought That We Exist

The approach of nontheism is to realize fully and learn to acknowledge egolessness. In fact, one definition of the Buddhist path is egolessness. If you don't understand egolessness, there is no Buddhist path. When you understand egolessness, when there is no ego, when you have cut through ego—that is the cessation of suffering, it is the definition of nirvana.

W E C O U L D say that theism and egoism are part of our being. Until we come to the true dharma fully, we can't shake them off. Egoism is not regarded as theory, but as our ongoing practice. It is the root of samsara; and to overcome it, we have to develop some antidote. Egoism begins with one thing: the thought that we actually exist, that we actually are here. We may have our doubts about ourselves, but we don't have any doubts about the notion of being.

By perpetually overlapping one level of consciousness with the next, we try to make ourselves solid, but the result is just patchwork. It may seem as if there is one big sheet, called "myself," "my own existence," but we are not one big sheet. However, since we have not actually realized that, we constantly try to overlap ourselves. From a distance, we may appear to be one big sheet, one solid block, but if you look closely, you see that we are made out of fragments, which survive only momentarily.

That momentary survival itself is not really solid, for if you look closely at each particular fraction of it, you see that each fraction is also very patchy.

That patchwork is what is known as "mind," or sem in Tibetan. Mind is not one continuous thing. Mind seems to be ongoing, but that is precisely because it is *not* one solid mind. Every fraction of a second, mind needs to nurture and sustain itself. It is analogous to the situation of a dying man who is on life support with machines pumping blood into his heart and food into his veins: the constant fickleness of the machines is what is keeping him alive. Likewise, we do not actually exist per se, but we are fed constantly, step-by-step, portion by little portion. We hear a dog bark, we hear radiators creak, we hear our own breathing, we feel our own pulse, we check our own breath. We constantly confirm ourselves through the sense perceptions. We look at things, listen to things, smell things, taste things, feel things, think things. All six sense perceptions (the five sense perceptions and the perception of mental contents) are constantly trying to sustain us—and all of them are just short moments of fickleness trying to overlap each other. Seeing is being overlapped by hearing, and hearing is being overlapped by tasting and smelling, and so on.

This process goes on all the time, so that on the whole we think we are just one big thing existing here—but if we look at the details, we see that passing the buck is what is taking place. Your mind is actually not one mind at all. It is minds, lots of them, jumping around constantly, trying to take shape, trying to maintain themselves. It is as if you had a stutter, and you were trying to speak, and your speech was covered over by background music. Although it would seem as if you were speaking in full sentences, if you examined your speech more closely, you would realize that you were actually stuttering. That is the gross level of egolessness: not being one big thing. And that "not one big thing" is known as mind.

Mind is constantly trying to transfer its identity and existence from moment to moment, with a tremendous amount of failure and constant forgetfulness. The transfer of one thought, one theme, is very short-lived. Traditionally, it is said to last only one-sixtieth of a second. And even that so-called existence is divided into three sections: about to happen, actually happening, and fading away. We don't have very much of an existence at that level at all. So although the mind is regarded as a big deal, it is just patchwork. That very poor existence, which you can hardly call an existence, is mind.

Mind projects to various situations. Within the short period of a fraction of a second, we project out and we draw in—we sustain ourselves very quickly. From that process of projection, we develop an extremely short memory, based on feeling certain pinpoints. It is like having lots of pins and needles in our legs, all pricking us at the same time. So our memory is transferred in very small portions into what are known as habit-forming thoughts—and those habit-forming thoughts are usually much more wooly and misty than the original mind.

Finally, all these small sneezes of your mind are put together, and they begin to be deflected into the echo chamber of your world. It becomes like a song made out of lots of sneezes, each lasting only a fraction of a second. It is like the hum of bees: if you listen from a distance, it sounds like one big orchestra; but if you listen to each bee individually, you realize that the sound is made up of little beings who are trying to orchestrate their own very minute things.

All sorts of patterns develop out of that. We begin to have a memory bank consisting of all sorts of things: the pleasantness of the past or the dreadfulness of the past; the goodness of the future or the terribleness of the future. We begin to develop kleshas, such as anger and lust, with which we make ourselves completely stupid and bewildered. We lose our temper, which is painful. The first explosion of temper makes us look, for a second, like a zombie. Then we recover from that and begin to proclaim our anger in order to justify ourselves or to create territory. That same pattern takes place with lust. At the beginning, our lust also makes us like zombies, but then we begin to interpret and to analyze. We not only analyze, but we go along with the feel of it. We would like to grasp the object of our desire. Out of such kleshas we create the chain reactions of karma. We create good karma and bad karma, less bewildering situations and more bewildering ones.

You might be able to present yourself as dignified and seemingly together. Incredibly, you may actually try to presume that nothing is happening. Nevertheless, if you look into the details of what is going on in you, altogether it is somewhat terrible, deplorable, absurd—and so embarrassing. All those things go on in your mind constantly, whether you are wise or stupid, rich or poor—and when you begin to look at yourself, you feel that the whole thing is somewhat ridiculous. But you can't get away from that kind of problem right at the beginning. There is a need to become somewhat religious and to develop a sense of sacredness. You need to feel that there is room for sacredness, for further evolution, in spite of your little ego.

The only way to deal with that terrible situation is by the practice of meditation. In meditation you are actually dealing with all that is going on in yourself. Through meditation, you begin to accentuate the notion of the nonexistence of your whole being, your whole ego, your whole mind. You take a pinch of your mind and look at it. Who's looking at what? You are looking at yourself! In doing so, you find yourself perpetually disrupted by the fickleness of the whole thing, but you also find ground in which that fickleness can be workable. Rather than jumping away from the territoriality, the sense of survival, you sit down with yourself and look at yourself very thoroughly and fully. That is what is called mindfulness, shamatha, the development of peace.

Peace, in terms of shamatha practice, does not mean bliss or a euphoric state. It means that at last there is some rest. Simply by looking at the fickleness of thoughts and of your own mind—the jumpiness of your whole being—that shaky quality is somewhat grounded. That is a relief. You say to yourself, "Everything's going to be okay. There's no need to jump around. Sit down and look at your mind. Look at yourself. Just do it." Then the other part of you says, "I don't want to do it. It makes me so embarrassed and uncomfortable." And the first one comes along and says, "Nevertheless, everything's okay. We know that, don't we? So let's do it. Just do it."

By practicing shamatha, you develop sympathy for yourself, and a friendly and healthy attitude. Your jumpiness and not wanting to stay on any one point comes from aggression, from disliking yourself. In spite of the jumpiness, there is a feeling of gentleness and goodness, reasonability and decency. You actually have learned to be with yourself. That may be somewhat terrible, or at least difficult, but you also begin to feel that it is quite good, quite terrific. You can actually go so far as to be with yourself. You are simply learning to be.

For the first time, you are trying to breathe out and in and simply exist. In doing so, you might discover a kind of hollowness in yourself, a vacuum, a kind of foolishness, as you begin to realize the bad news that you may not actually exist. It is not even hollowness, for when we say "hollow," it implies there is some kind of shell that is solid. It is intangible. One's basic substance is not there. You don't wear solid clothes, but clothes made out of feathers—and everything falls apart when you begin to ruffle.

In shamatha, there is a general sense of being unable to hold or grasp on to anything. That seems to be okay, as long as you feel that such intangibility includes your nonexistence. That is to say, you can't grasp anything while you are sitting, but that is not regarded as a problem. Instead, you include that difficulty as part of a total experience that does not have any substance to it. Experience does not have to be substantial, particularly—you could have nonsubstantial experience. It would still be some kind of feedback—or nonfeedback. It is an ongoing process in spite of the nonexistence of the ongoingness, if you'd like to put it that way.

Sitting removes psychological pain. By looking into your existence, survival mentality is cut out altogether. You begin to feel extremely raw and rugged, right at the beginning. That is how a beginner's sitting practice should be: raw and rugged, with no excuses and no promises. When you begin the path as a good Buddhist and a good practitioner, the first thing that should happen is an insult to ego, whether it is fully effective or just ten-percent effective. According to the first dharma of Gampopa, you are becoming identified with the dharma, mixing your mind with the dharma. When you begin to realize what dharma is all about, you see that it allows no concessions, no compromises, and not much future planning. Just simply—that's it. When you go to the barber and get a haircut, you can't ask him to grow it back on your head.

There is a world that does not exist in your mind, could not exist in your mind, which is revealed by exertion, by trying very hard. Continuous exertion gives you the first glimpse of the nontheistic journey. Realizing that you can't make any profit, you still continue. At the beginning, the journey may give you some feedback, or seeming profit—but you don't have any bag to put your profit into, and you have no bank account. That is the open ground of shamatha. There is no substance being deposited for your benefit, for your desire for eternity, and you begin to accept that. You realize that this is the only way.

As we practice, all sorts of things are churned up—attempts to solidify our trips, various thought-patterns, subconscious gossip, and concepts—but we regard them as waves in the ocean, ripples in the pond. Step-by-step, as we go through all that, we begin to cut back the tremendous investment of ego and karma. We are cutting short our fixations by not giving in to them or participating in any further seed-sowing. It is like clearing a field: First, we cut down the crops and take them out, by not relating with subconscious gossip. Then we begin to remove the seeds.

We have a great drought, so the ground is once more empty. That is our first attempt to stop samsara. It sounds like a dreadful idea from the point of view of wanting to perpetuate samsara; but from another point of view, it is quite delightful. It is tremendous good news that we can actually short-circuit samsara by sitting practice.

Cutting the crops and removing the seeds evolves naturally. When you relate with your breath, you both cut the crops and take out the seeds. If you have a McDonald's hamburger in your mind, and you cut that crop down, that's fine. But then you have a more startling experience. You think, "What is becoming of me? What am I doing here?" At that point, you have reached the level of seeds. You are about to cut something more basic, so there will be occasional fears. You need to step on them, to go beyond them; that much aggression is necessary. A doctor has to puncture the skin in order to give an injection.

In the abhidharma, or Buddhist psychology, we study what needs to be cleared out, and we clear out everything from top to bottom, starting with the six realms of hell, hungry ghosts, animals, human beings, jealous gods, and gods. We are clearing out any possibility of rebirth. The idea is that we actually cut the root of samsara. That is the particular role of nontheistic discipline. In the theistic approach, certain desires have been cut out, but the leftovers are used to further one's ego. The approach of nontheism is to realize fully and learn to acknowledge egolessness. In fact, one definition of the Buddhist path is egolessness. If you don't understand egolessness, there is no Buddhist path. When you understand egolessness, when there is no ego, when you have cut through ego—that is the cessation of suffering, it is the definition of nirvana.

On the nontheistic path we are trying to cut ego-mind back by means of the sitting practice of meditation. We are working with ourselves in terms of individual salvation. We are not concerned with dogma; we are simply trying to work with what is there. We are working with that which creates our pain and makes us crazy. That is our first concern. At this point, theism does not come into the picture. It is not a problem. It could be present in your subconscious gossip or in your memory bank, due to your Sunday school, your Communion, your temple, or church. But those memories are just flickers of the mind, just thought patterns, the same as yesterday's cup of coffee. What we are really concerned with is what we are now, and how we could start as soon as possible to cut the samsaric root at this very moment. That seems to be our concern—and the sooner the better. That is the function of the practice of meditation. Mindfulness is simply looking at ourselves and cutting the roots of bewilderment and jumpiness. It is fully being there.

Basically, at its core, shamatha discipline is cutting the samsaric root. It is like cutting hair: Usually, when you go to the barber and have your hair cut, it begins to grow back. But it is possible that your hair had such a big shock when it was cut for the first time that it is afraid to grow back. So that first impression is very important. Likewise, when you first practice meditation, the whole impetus of growing back and becoming further well-equipped with your armor is lessened somewhat, because you have hit a nerve center. After that, even if you have not meditated for a great length of time, your ego shell has been softened. The sitting has definitely begun to take effect. If you reject that and take a defensive attitude, trying to rebuild your whole ego-oriented approach, it is questionable whether you could come back and re-soften again. So in regard to sitting practice, the idea is constancy, because each time you sit, you get softened more and more.

68

Cutting Through the Numbness of Ego

When you develop awareness, there is no one who is aware. It is like a movie screen without an audience. It is like a television in an empty room. The clarity of awareness is like plastique, or dynamite, which takes down the walls of ego. Such clarity does not allow any obstacles to get through or to project out. Clarity is like a light shining out.

WHEN YOU are meditating, as you are trying to tune yourself in to the breath or to mindfulness, you may find that suddenly there's a problem and you can't do it. The reason you can't do it is because there is this sense of "me-ness," this "I-ness." The obstacle comes from holding on to yourself. That sense of "my existence" is the cause of discursive thoughts and the displays of the sense perceptions. You become numb, playing around in your private, imaginary, hallucinatory show. As a result, you begin to project things out of your numbness. Your sense of "thisness" begins to produce all sorts of counterreactions that get in the way of mindfulness, such as visual distortions, auditory distortions, and intellectual distortions. Numbness, or ignorance, is the root of samsara altogether. That numbness is not so easy to get rid of, but at the same time it is workable. Shamatha discipline is the first step in freeing yourself from such samsaric problems. Cutting through discursive thoughts and bringing your attention back to mindfulness cuts the numbness of ego.

The fundamental characteristic or essence of ego consists of ignoring your existence. If you look at your existence, you see that it is full of tremendous pain. Even if you have a good marriage, even if you have pleasurable surroundings, even if everything is going right for you and all your external situations are excellent, there is still this "me-ness," this "I-ness," which if you reflect on it, is ultimate pain. When you begin to realize that you do not exist, however, one hundred percent of the pain is gone. When you realize that you don't exist, and you have developed your mindfulness and awareness, you are made out of practitioner rather than out of down-home Mr. or Mrs. Whoever.

The quality of ego-pain may manifest as boredom with yourself. You have been hanging out with yourself for twenty or thirty or more years, and you have become tired of yourself. That is only the apparent problem, however. Beyond that, there is the pain of carrying yourself around altogether. It is as if you have this *thing* inside of you. You feel it is a part of you, your accessory garbage, but you love it and you can't get rid of it. Sometimes you wish you could throw it away, but at the same time you would like to keep it, because you regard it as a family heirloom. There is this *thingy*—yourself—which is not *in* you as a separate entity, but *is* you. It is your "me-ness," your "I-ness."

That fundamental, heavy, and painful state of existence is pervasive. It may manifest in the form of boredom or frustration or inadequacy or longing; but its essence is that quality of heaviness, or me-ness. That sense of me-ness is expressed very vividly in the English language. Take, for example, having a cup of tea. When we try to convey to someone else, "I would like to have a cup of tea," the first thing we say is "I." In doing so, we are expressing some kind of burden to the person who is going to serve us tea. "Tea" doesn't come first; "I" comes first. "Tea" qualifies "I," as in "I . . . would like to have . . . a cup of tea." So the whole thing gets completely weighted down. You can experience the tone you use when you say "I." It is as if that "me" and "myself" were hanging out together and had become so inbred that "*I* would like to" almost means "*We* would like to." It is as if "I," and the thing "I" has been fighting with all along, are speaking jointly to a foreign agent who is going to serve tea from over there. "I would like to have a cup of tea"—"I," a little thingy.

There is a subtle sense of shakiness when you say "I." No matter how you say "I," there is a little tinge of frustration and unfriendliness. All your bad dreams are boiled down to one word, one syllable: "I." There is also another aspect of ignorance, a further aspect of "I," which is not so tentative. When you simply say "I," you are tentative because you are embarrassed by your own ignorance. But then you say "I *want*"—"I want a cup of tea." You express "I want" in the form of kleshas such as aggression, passion, jealousy, or arrogance. "I want" does not allow you any space to reflect on your surroundings. Your mind is completely filled with "I wants."

The basic ignorance of "I" can be cut through by practicing the shamatha discipline of mindfulness. By paying attention, by looking at things very clearly, you begin to experience clarity and freshness. After that, the wantingness can be cut through by vipashyana awareness. Awareness enables you to experience the totality around you and within you, so you are not so caught up in "want" this and "want" that. That sense of totality is connected with letting the atmosphere be there without "you." The idea of discriminating awareness, which develops out of vipashyana, is that this awareness becomes a natural state of being, rather than a person developing awareness. It is not important for *you* to develop awareness— what you are aware of is more important. That is how you can step out of egohood. When you develop awareness, there is no one who is aware. It is like a movie screen without an audience. It is like a television in an empty room. The clarity of awareness is like *plastique,* or dynamite, which takes down the walls of ego. Such clarity does not allow any obstacles to get through or to project out. Clarity is like a light shining out.

When you have "me-ness," you cannot develop the subtleties of awareness, because you are in the way. Ordinarily, self-consciousness means feeling embarrassed, but there is a more fundamental self-consciousness, which is simply that *you* are there. Because of that, you become deaf and dumb: you don't see anything and you don't hear anything. That is the definition of ignorance: you are so concerned with *this* that you are not aware of anything else.

With awareness, relaxation arises. Your mind has been processed by shamatha practice, so discriminating awareness, or prajna, begins to occur. At least there is not any more stupidity—and there may even be a sense of brilliance, which begins to light things up. You are not afraid to relate with your own environment. Awareness brings prajna, so you are no longer blindfolded or stupefied—you are no longer involved with yourself all the time. You are beginning to develop a greater sense of head and shoulders, a good posture, a good walk, a good way of eating, and a good way of talking. You are beginning to branch out in terms of your awareness. That is why vipashyana is known as insight. With vipashyana, possibilities of cheerfulness happen. Such cheerfulness is not only a state of mind—it is a tool to cut through your "I-want-ness."

When you begin to project further into mindfulness, and beyond that into awareness, you can relate with the simplicity of your lifestyle: you eat when you eat, you sit when you sit, you walk when you walk. So your life becomes much simpler. Of course, there could be complications, but I don't think they are worth mentioning. Simplicity is the point.

Simplicity brings with it a kind of purity. You are fundamentally clean, and you don't hold a grudge against anybody. When you eat, you eat mindfully and with awareness. When you sit on your meditation cushion, you sit properly. When you walk, you walk simply. You live in a total atmosphere of awareness. Your world becomes so simple that you don't need to reflect and you don't need feedback. When there is no need for feedback, this "I" has become invalid, out of order. It has been dismissed. You have sacked yourself. Therefore, "want" is no longer workable—it too is obsolete. So "this" and "that" become obsolete. That is a basic understanding of egolessness. Rather than discuss it philosophically, I think the best way to understand egolessness is from the point of view of practice, for then you can see that it is possible.

In letting go of "this" and "that," you are not just reducing yourself into nothing. By means of great discipline, you have a way of letting go, and because of that, strength and energy arise—but not from "me," not from "want." In fact, because it is not from "me" and not from "want," there is tremendous room and the possibility of tremendous freedom. You could be a really free person—completely, fundamentally free. You could feel tremendous fresh air and freedom as a result of the mindfulness and the awareness you have developed through shamatha and vipashyana practice. So prajna is closely connected with freedom and with the practice of awareness and watchfulness.

In order to make yourself a person of the world, you have had to fight for every inch. Whenever you write your name on the dotted line, you are proclaiming your warfare to somebody. You are trying to prove yourself and your existence. "I do exist. I am writing this letter to somebody to complain, to say hello to my relatives, to be nice to my girlfriend or boyfriend." All the time, you are trying to occupy territory. Even when you are pressing your dress, or busy organizing a cocktail party or a Christmas dinner, there is always an undercurrent of trying to prove something, to achieve something. Whatever you are doing involves some kind of macho-ness or chauvinism. In fact, chauvinism could be one definition of ego. However, individual chauvinism can be overcome by individual salvation. The achievement of mindfulness and awareness gives you tremendous freedom: that is the idea of individual salvation. And having achieved individual salvation, you realize that there is no need to fight, no need to wage warfare.

The development of awareness and discipline leads to tremendous relaxation, gentleness, and peace. We realize that those qualities are not out of character, but that we have such possibilities and potentialities in us already. We are capable of freeing ourselves from ourselves; we are capable of not holding on to any little tricks we might have—and we have lots of them. We realize that we have had a bad opinion of ourselves, but that we are capable of being decent and gentle. We realize that we don't have to push so hard to maintain ourselves, which only makes us deaf, dumb, and blind. We could open our eyes and listen with our ears. We could feel the universe around us. We could actually relate to the world fully, in the sense of final freedom. That is a tremendous awakening for most of us—it has been and will be and presently is so.

We feel so much relief that at last somebody has opened the window and there is ventilation. Before that, we had been stuck in this stuffy room for such a long time. That sense of relief is a glimpse of awakening. It does not come from outside of you; it is your own discovery from having practiced. Having gone through the processes of shamatha and vipashyana, you have developed prajna. For the first time, you feel friendly to yourself. At that point, when you say, "I would like to have a cup of tea," it is no strain on you. You can say it quite freshly, quite simply, quite beautifully: "I would like a cup of tea." Your voice doesn't shake and you don't stutter. You just say, "I would like a cup of tea." You have developed your own discipline, your own sense of dignity, and your own gentleness. You yourself have taken the first step in actually making a connection with the phenomenal world—but the other "yourself" is gone. So you don't have "I am," you just have "This wants a cup of tea." That is your introduction to mahayana.

But first, in order to enter the mahayana and awaken bodhichitta in yourself, it is extremely important to do the fundamental practices of shamatha and vipashyana. The practice of mahayana is not just based on how to handle others. It is based on how to handle yourself to begin with, and working with others will come along. That is the basic clue, so to speak. Everything follows that same logic.

Once you have attained a state of mind in which you can relax and actually trust something, you come up with two problems: "I" and "am," *what* and *what-what-what*. *What* is "who I am," "what I am," "where I am"; *what-what-what* is "what's going on." Traditionally, these two are described as the ego of individual existence and the ego of dharmas. So there are two basic types of ego: your existence as a full-fledged individual and your existence as a full-fledged individual reacting to various situations.

In Tibetan, the ego of self-existence is *kangsak ki dak*. *Dak* means "ego," *kangsak* means "individual," and *gi* means "of," so *kangsak ki dak* is the "ego of self." The ego of dharmas is *chökyi dak*. *Chö* is "dharma," *kyi* is "of," and *dak* is "ego," as before, so *chökyi dak* is the "ego of dharmas." Chökyi dak refers to ordinary dharmas, or phenomena, such as the dharma of cooking food or brewing tea. It is an extension or expansion of your existence, whereas kangsak ki dak is the experience of your existence without any other reference point. Together, they are "me" and "mine": kangsak ki dak is "me," chökyi dak is "mine." What you *have* is chö, and what you *are* is kangsak. "Me" and "mine"—that's our basic pattern. Sometimes there are problems of "me," and sometimes there are problems of "mine."

These two situations—"me" and "mine"—are nonpeace, they are turbulence. Your experience of yourself is very hassled and confused, and even further hassles take place because there are also things that belong to you. The ego of individual existence is like a bachelor, who has hassles already, and the ego of dharmas is like being married, which creates further hassles. If you add the extra syllable *me*, meaning "not," to *kangsak ki dak* and *chökyi dak*, you have *kangsak ki dag-me* and *chökyi dag-me*: the nonexistence of individual ego, and the nonexistence of projected ego. This is known as peace, or twofold egolessness. "Peace," or shiwa, transcends both forms of ego. It does not mean euphoria, but relaxation, presence, and nonhassle.

"I" is the individual ego, and "am" is the ego of reference point. "I" is me, and "am" is my existence—and "am" is then qualified by somebody who says "You are." "I" and "am" together make "I am." It is a very basic A-B-C-D process. Because the ego process is so simple, an understanding of egolessness is possible. "I" not; "am" not; "I" no; "am" no. Why? It is because "I" is made out of impermanence, suffering, and emptiness.

When you say "I," it is a very lonely statement, whereas "am" would like to have a cup of tea. The whole thing begins to build up, so that finally you have our example of "I would like to have a cup of tea," which is a very solid situation. In the grammatics of the skandhas, the language of the first skandha, or form, is "me"; the second skandha, or feeling, is "have"; and so forth.

"I" is made out of emptiness. It is empty because there's nothing you can find out about "my existence." In fact, the phrase "my existence" is not quite right; it should be "me-existence." The point is that there is nothing you can find that is "I" at all. It is empty, impermanent. If it is empty, there is nothing; otherwise, you can't say it is empty. My father died a long time ago; therefore, I am empty of my father. He's gone. Just empty. Gap. But something comes along with that gap—the *experience* of gap. Gap cannot actually be experienced without an understanding of "am"—so you have the "I am" question again.

The world says that you do not exist. You do not have a chair to sit on; therefore, you can't sit. You do not have food; therefore, you can't eat. So you are hungry and seatless. The world does not let you know who you are; therefore, you are without title, without name. The world may react to you by saying that you are a son of a bitch or asking, "Who are you, anyway?" However, behind the whole thing is the voice of emptiness, which says everything is full of shit—empty of shit. Fundamentally, no reactions exist. All those reactions going back and forth are simply phantoms of your imagination, and, quite possibly, of their imagination as well. There is simply nothing real taking place, no absolutely one-hundred-percent real things are taking place at all. They are not happening, absolutely not.

The loss of ego is a real loss. It is very depressing. You have lost your ego, your strength. But you have gained some gentleness, and through practice you can mingle the two, as if you were milk poured into water. Relaxation and relief take place as you realize, "After all, I don't need to play this game." You'd be surprised. You can experience self without a reference point. You could burn your fingers on the stove without having fingers.

According to hinayana abhidharma, dharmas are not quite real. They are as real as if you had a cup of tea in your hand, as real as what you have in your reality, but that is a temporary reality. It is impermanent. Ultimately, nothing is real; there is nothing to hold on to, and nothing is holding on to anything. That is why egolessness is possible. You feel every-thing as surface, as waves floating back and forth continuously, but none of it is true or real. Such ripples go on all the time. If you are empty of your father, it is like a ripple in your imagination. It is like a ripple in your pond, another sunset or sunrise in your life. Things come and go. Nothing is real but the awakening, the touch that wakes you up.

"Am" does not exist; therefore, "I" does not exist at the same time. So you cannot say, "I have achieved egolessness." And if you don't experience "I," then "am" is also questionable. But "am" *may* exist, so "am" may be a problem. You can't have that. You have to do a complete job. The logic goes: "I am blind, so the sun does not exist for me. Therefore, the sun does not exist, and I do not exist, because the sun has not been seen."

Due to emptiness and impermanence, you cannot actually pinpoint anything at all. You can't pin down the universe, pin down truth and lies, or pin down facts and figures with one-hundred-percent certainty. Trying to pin things down is a mathematical problem, so in a sense the biggest threat of egotism in the Buddhist world is mathematics. Mathematicians say that since zero exists, there should be one, and since there's one, there are two, three, and four. But what the mathematicians are doing is build-ing a ring around the emptiness rather than attacking the nonexistence itself. As one ring echoes, the next ring begins to happen, but mathemati-cians cannot reach across the whole universe to make a complete circle. It would be like trying to bend a crescent moon into a circle. There is a space, or gap, between the horns of the crescent moon, which is not a mathematical problem but an experiential problem. You can't squeeze it closed by force, and you can't relax too much either. There is still a gap. So although mathematicians may think they have built a whole ring, actually it is just an arc, not a complete circle. There is a gap. So the zero returns as an important point. When you begin to realize the egolessness of dhar-mas and the egolessness of self, zero comes back in. It is not a matter of counting, but of catching up with your present moment, right where you are, which is perfect zero. Then you can expand if you like, if you want to count.

When you realize the egolessness of dharmas and the egolessness of individuality, you see that both "that" and "this" are problematic. They do not have any substance at all. The higher level of prajna is like a sword that says, "Cut both edges. Cut the sword itself. Cut both." Simply cutting "this" and "that" is still superficial, however, because when you do cut both, you realize who is doing the cutting. You think, "I am cutting both." So at that level of prajna swordsmanship, you need to commit hara-kiri. Seppuku. Ouch!

The notion of egolessness is empty, but at the same time it is utterly and completely full. Egolessness is not understood to be a loss. People may have the idea that egolessness is the Buddhist version of transcendental deprivation. They may think that you are being deprived of your existence by force and by faith. But that's not true. I've experienced it, and it's not true. It is not deprivation at all—it is like giving birth. When a mother gives birth, her womb is emptied out completely, including the placenta and umbilical cord, but the mother ends up with a child. From the point of view of wanting to hold on to something, the mother has lost the child—but the mother has also gained a child. So giving birth is an expression of both loss and gain together. It is full and empty at the same time.

That is precisely the experience of egolessness. It is a very moving experience. You feel you could cry and laugh at the same time. You could cry because you are lost, and you could laugh because you have gained something—and you do that over and over again. You cry, laugh, cry, laugh. But nothing actually is new: everything happens all over again; it is the same old world.

The experience of prajna and egolessness takes place due to the relaxation of ordinary confused mind. But first you have to learn how to stop and be bored, how to sit, how to renounce. If that isn't taking place, there is no prajna. It would be like somebody composing poetry without learning the alphabet. So without meditation experience, there is no prajna. You cannot just jump into prajna so easily. You need gut-level experience.

69

Taking the Teachings to Heart

Prajna is both sharp and gentle. . . . When your knife is sharp, it is very easy to cut meat. It is gentle, but dramatic. . . . So the sharper, the gentler. Shamatha-vipashyana discipline brings out tremendous power in you. It sharpens prajna and brings out your respect for learning. You should not be afraid of being sharp, but take pride in the sharpness. That is your practice manual, . . . the practitioner's way of experiencing the hinayana path properly and fully.

A T THE hinayana level, it is fairly easy and straightforward to step onto the path of dharma. You do not have to change your attitude or state of mind; you can simply slide into it. You are not really practicing a religion or joining a cult. Rather, it is simply a matter of being in touch with your natural faculties, and doing that in a somewhat Buddhistic style. It is not even Buddhism, but just the way of the Buddha. In this context, the development of prajna involves the transformation of your state of mind into further cognitive comprehension of things as they are.

We have a tendency to indulge in our stupidity, which makes us feel homey and comfortable. Indulging is easy to do, and we tend to get into that state too often. But at some point, sooner or later, we find that such indulgence is quite a hassle. We find that we have trapped ourselves, and nobody else can clear that up for us. But we do not need to indulge ourselves in the comfort of stupidity. We can afford to open the window and experience the world outside. That is the first step toward developing prajna.

Training in prajna is one method of entering into a greater world and expanding your vision into greater depth and possibilities. The reason such expansion is necessary is because, in developing prajna, you are beginning to work with the alaya consciousness—a nonreferential, clear consciousness that is neither religious nor nonreligious. Through the practice of meditation, you could slide into alaya consciousness, cognitive mind at the highest level. Alaya consciousness is the ground we work from—and on that ground, the state of mind of prajna is available to you. It is quite simple, like yawning and then falling asleep. Training in prajna is not a matter of developing a religious consciousness. It is simply being fully present and knowing how to comprehend the realities of life.

The general intelligence in your basic state of being creates a feeling of workability and allows you to develop discrimination. Discriminating awareness, or prajna, is not discriminating between what is good for you and what is bad for you, and it is not discrimination in the sense of racial prejudice. It is more like having enough openness to choose the right thing at the right time. Prajna actually helps you to take unworkable situations and make them workable. So whatever happens in your state of being becomes unquestionably soothing and smooth. At that point, your attitude begins to open up. You lighten up, so to speak, recognizing that the world around you is not a brick wall, but there is some form of openness or aperture everywhere.

That openness helps you to maintain your attention. You begin to experience enjoyment, soothingness, and a sense that you are doing the right thing. You are traveling on this open path without any drastic unexpected ambushes in your way due to concepts and preconceptions. When you do not have any preconceptions whatsoever, seventy-five percent of those ambushes are controlled. Prajna wakes you up and makes you more open and more fascinated in the right sense. Rather than being based upon intrigue, greed, or the desire to make yourself comfortable, fascination in the right sense is based on first thought, best thought. If you are intrigued by something, you don't feed your fascination; you just go ahead and do the job on the spot. You don't let that fascination brew and ripen into preconceptions or wishful thinking. Then fascination becomes more workable, because it is much simpler. It's like doing a business deal right away, rather than first taking someone out for lunch and then dinner and then drinks.

With prajna, your vision begins to expand, not through struggling or feeling that you ought to expand your vision, but through a natural sense of connection to the world around you. With prajna, or sherap, the teachings of the Buddha no longer seem monolithic or overwhelming. They become as natural a part of you as if the Buddha were talking in your brain.

HIGHER AND LOWER PRAJNA

Prajna can be divided into higher prajna and lower prajna. Higher prajna is called superior, the highest or best recollection, because it is not foreign to us. It is part of us. It has always been part of us, although we may have lost it for a long time. We reconnect ourselves by hearing the name of the Buddha, by meeting our teacher, and by coming to a dharmic environment. In doing so, the dharma is no longer a foreign entity; it is real, and we can hear it, learn it, and cherish it. It is important to understand that prajna is not just something out of Indian philosophy, and it is not a psychological description of an ideal state. Prajna is a faculty that exists within you—it is your intelligence.

Lower prajna is just basic training, basic craftsmanship. It is connected with the idea of literacy. Lower prajna is like going to school and learning how to read and write; it is like being educated in the ordinary sense. You can spell because you possess human intelligence, not because spelling is imposed on you. Because you are a human being, you can always reawaken your intelligence. It is the combination of the crude prajna of your basic education and the refined prajna of your karmic link with the teaching and a teacher that brings you together with a teacher so that you can study the dharma and hear it properly.

THE THREE ASPECTS OF PRAJNA

Prajna has three aspects: hearing, contemplating, and meditating.

Hearing

The first prajna principle is the prajna of hearing the dharma. Hearing the dharma refers not only to listening to a tape, reading a newspaper clipping, hearing a radio broadcast, or seeing something on television.

Hearing also includes observing examples of the teaching, examples of how human beings could behave or maintain themselves within a certain atmosphere.

Prajna is an extremely sharp, powerful, and moving experience. It is like meeting your parents from whom you have been separated for a long time. For over twenty years you have remembered your father, who was strong and kind, who raised you to adulthood. You remember his words very clearly, and sometimes they even come to you in your dreams. You remember how he used to tell you to sit up properly at the dining room table and taught you table manners. You remember how he used to take you for walks or for hunting expeditions or to go swimming or hiking. He knew how to handle all kinds of situations. If you got stuck with him in the mountains with no provisions, he would always find some way to feed you. He even used to cook your soup and mend your shoes. You knew that you would always be okay, as long as he was with you. You remember your mother, who was very gentle and kind. She was very strong, but also very emotional. Whenever you made a mistake, she would panic, and she would tell you how to correct yourself. She was very concerned with whether your belly was full, whether you had a roof over your head, whether your clothes were clean. In general, she exuded care for your welfare.

After many years, suddenly you meet your parents again. They may be slightly older than you remember, but they still smile and rejoice at seeing you again. They still have the kind of strength they used to have. You realize that they have never given up on you. They have never regarded you as completely lost to them. When you first meet them, you are not very emotional—you are too shocked for that—but you spend time with them and you eat with them. And as they watch you, they begin to be delighted that you have grown up. They begin to appreciate you. Then you break down and cry because their strength is still there, and it was their strength that brought you up.

The first level of prajna is something like that experience of recognition and reconnection. You are reconnecting with something from a long time ago. It has been a long, long time—you have no idea how long, maybe millions of *kalpas* (an endlessly long period of time)—since you lost your connection with something or other. But now you have reconnected yourself by means of the teachings of buddhadharma. The teachings are the only thing that brought you back to meeting your proud parents again. You are very moved, and you feel that you can now hear properly and fully.

One could say that vipashyana is the practice inspired by prajna. Vipashyana is the development of awareness, and prajna is the product of awareness. Once you have practiced and achieved vipashyana, prajna is already there. With vipashyana, you can work both on awakening and developing your intrinsic prajna. Awareness gives birth to prajna, but once you have achieved prajna, you continue to work with it. You don't stop there.

The first prajna principle is connected with learning. The Tibetan word for learning, or thöpa, means "hearing." However, hearing does not mean just using your ears; it means using all your senses. For instance, when you hear a dharma talk, you may smell the incense burning on the shrine, which inspires reverence for the lineage. After that, whenever you burn incense, you have a memory of that, and a connection with the teachings you heard in that setting. You could say that you are smelling the dharma.

You also feel the dharma. That is, you receive teachings in a certain environment. You are dressed in a certain fashion and you have the physical feeling of sitting on your meditation cushion, which is a different feeling from sitting on a chair or lying in the dirt. So feeling and smelling are both part of hearing the dharma. Obviously, you also hear the dharma, whether you are listening to a recording or you are listening to a live person.

You also use sight. You look at the person who is talking to you, and in traditional shrine rooms you also have visual aids. For instance, there may be banners showing dharmic symbols or representing the idea of a dharmic kingdom. There may be pictures and shrines to look at. You can watch the teacher talking and making gestures such as opening a fan and closing a fan, or looking back at you.

It is possible to create a dharmic world in which every aspect of your sense perceptions is used. In such an atmosphere, you can smell the dharma, you can feel the dharma, you can hear the dharma, you can see the dharma, you can touch the dharma. Everything in such an atmosphere is real and direct and simple. In such an atmosphere in which there is no time off, you can learn so well. The dharma is a part of your daily existence. When you go to your room and lie down, or flush your toilet, or take a shower, you are still within that dharmic environment. You are flushing the toilet of dharma, taking a shower of dharma. Such an atmosphere is highly concentrated and powerful. When you enter, there is a feeling of coming into a dharmic world, a new world altogether. It is a completely dharmic situation. So the first prajna, or hearing, is experiencing with your whole body, with all your sense perceptions, that everything you do in your life is connected with dharma. Learning involves your whole being.

Dharma consists of what has been told by the scriptures and what has been experienced by practitioners. With the first prajna principle, you can study and you can learn. It is important for you to understand basic Buddhist logic and to become familiar with the terminology, so study is extremely important. If you study and if you are a good practitioner, you could take a further step: you could transmit what you have learned to others. You are not expected to work on yourself alone. You need to expand to the world outside; you need to articulate the teachings.

The buddhadharma is limitless. It shows you, from beginning to end, why the world is formed the way it is. It tells you who you are, what you are, and why you are. It tells you why the world is and how the world is. That is why the learning process is important. The buddhadharma also gives you the confidence and wisdom you need to be able to answer everyone's questions—from your three-year-old daughter's to a Jesuit theologian's. Once you have learned the dharma properly and fully, once everything has been spelled out, you have no difficulty in expounding it to others. But learning is not just important because you have all the answers—it is because you begin to feel that there is no mystery. You cannot say, "I have no idea how that happened." You could explain everything, from why somebody cut his finger while chopping potatoes in the kitchen to why somebody has died or why somebody has committed suicide. You can understand how things happen and why they work a certain way because the teachings are so thorough and so full and so real. If you put enough energy into the learning process, you find that the teachings are limitless.

It has been difficult to find people to translate all the dharmic literature that is available. Unfortunately, thanks to the communist destruction of Tibet and the degeneration of the rest of the Buddhist world, we have probably lost at least seventy-five percent of the literature and commentaries that we might otherwise have had. But from what remains of the texts, as well as from the oral tradition passed on from teacher to teacher, the dharma has been planted in the minds of many people. Therefore, we can actually regenerate the whole thing completely and fully.

The vastness of dharmic learning is delightful. It sharpens and reawakens your prajna. Learning dharma is quite different from studying science or mathematics. In the case of dharma, when the students have studied and learned most of the information, the rest is awakened intrinsically. This is so because the teachings begin to connect with students' basic existence and their karmic connection with a dharmic person. So when teacher and students work together closely and properly, we have a one-hundred-percent dharmic situation, and we do not regret or suffer from the loss and destruction of texts by our friend Mao Tse-tung.

Learning propagates prajna. You should not feel that you are inadequate; you should perk yourself up. You should realize that you are a great vessel of dharma, that you are ready for the dharma, and that you will be able to understand it. Although it might be difficult for you at the beginning, soon you will understand it. Then you will experience the joyousness that comes from training your mind in the shamatha discipline of mindfulness and the vipashyana discipline of awareness. You will make a connection with the dharma as your family heirloom.

The dharma makes you feel so genuine and real. Whether you are Tahitian or American or Norwegian, the dharma is your family heirloom, which you will discover. You possess buddha nature, you have a connection with dharma and an interest in dharma, and you will reawaken your family heirloom, which is quite rightfully yours. The teacher's role is to make sure you understand that, and to make sure that you don't feel belittled or begin to shrink from hearing so many terms and ideas. You could overcome that by thöpa, the learning process—by propagating intrinsic prajna.

Contemplating

The second prajna principle is contemplating what you have heard. In Tibetan it is sampa. *Sampa* means "thinking about," or "having thought of it." You contemplate what you have heard and what you have been taught. With sampa, or contemplation, you are sharpening the sword of prajna. Contemplation comes from awareness and the understanding that there are teachings in every situation. The mindfulness of your shamatha discipline has prepared the basic ground, during postmeditation experience as well as during sitting practice. Beyond that, you have vipashyana awareness. In contemplating the dharma and relating it with yourself, you experience a feeling of disgust with samsara, and at the same time you appreciate that you are a dharmic person.

With sampa you are picking up a sense of the atmosphere. You begin to feel that there is something to what you have heard, but you can't quite click into it or understand it. You feel as though you are about to understand, but you have no idea why and how. It is like picking up the very distant smell of onions cooking: you have caught wind of something, but you are not quite certain whether it is onions or garlic or scallions.

That experience comes after you have heard and studied the teachings and they have already been spelled out for you. You have a sense that you are about to get it, but you can't quite understand fully. At that point, the best approach is to raise your confidence in yourself and your connection with dharma, and in the reason you came to the dharmic world altogether. You just contemplate what you have heard in a very simple, ordinary way, following very ordinary, simple, straightforward logic.

As an example, you may recall that one of the definitions of dharma is passionlessness. Then you think of another definition of dharma, that it is the development of peace. You might be puzzled by the word *passionless,* and how it connects with peace. Ordinarily, the first thing you might do would be to dig up your notes, or buy a book and read about it, or put it through the research mill, like traditional scholars. You might call up some professor. But with contemplation, instead of doing that, you think back to when you heard those teachings. You remember the particular environment where those teachings were presented to you. When you heard the dharma, all your senses were involved. So years later, you can reflect on that environment and that particular presentation of the teachings. You can think of the smell that was in the room when you heard the words, "The dharma is passionlessness; it is peace." You can remember the sounds and you can remember how things looked. You can reflect back. What day was it? What time and what circumstances? What was the atmosphere like when you heard those words spoken? Through that process, you begin to come to an understanding that passionlessness also means peace. You understand that when there is no passion or grasping, you are contented; therefore, your mind will settle itself. So finally you are able to put passionlessness and peace together.

Dharma is never taught outside of the right circumstances. Dharma can only be uttered—and it only makes sense—in the right circumstances. When dharma is taught by a confident teacher, it makes sense to you at that very moment. Teachers who are not fully realized might teach the dharma in completely disconnected circumstances. When that happens, the dharma becomes self-secret. Improperly taught dharma will only confuse students. It is as if a teacher were to present the dharma by saying, "Let's open the window and look outside. Do you see the trees and greenery?" But when the students look outside, they find no trees and no greenery—only snow. That kind of teaching doesn't click. It only confuses people.

Contemplation means tracking back. It means coming to a personal understanding. So it is important to reflect on the occasion and circumstances in which you heard the dharma. If you have lost your memory and you get hung up on terms, just reflect back to the particular occasion on which you heard a particular word, expression, or teaching. Through contemplation, you understand that the basic logic of dharma applies to you, yourself—always.

Meditating

The third prajna principle is gompa, which means "meditating on." The term *meditation* in this context means taking something into your heart completely. Meditation is thorough involvement, whereas contemplation is convincing yourself or committing yourself to the situation. Contemplation is like sharpening your sword as opposed to putting the sword in your sheath. Once you put your sword in its sheath, you know that it is sharp already.

What you have heard and what you have contemplated should be taken into your heart properly and thoroughly. For instance, you might reflect on the nausea, pain, ugliness, and savageness of samsara. You begin by contemplating that, but then you take it into your heart completely. Beyond sitting practice alone, you are bringing those teachings into your heart. This approach might bring you overwhelming experiences of all kinds. When you begin to look at the wretchedness of samsara, you might actually feel wretched yourself; you might feel trapped. However, that kind of temporary experience or discovery is supposed to be extremely necessary and good. We are not particularly recommending that you freak out, but that's the way it is.

In presenting the dharma, we are talking about a black-and-white world. You should realize that. It is not that everything is all right—in fact, there is darkness and there is light. Sometimes people have the idea that Buddhist wisdom tells you to keep everything quiet and peaceful. They think that if you ignore everything, meditate, and wander in the mountains, everything will be all right. But that approach is slightly naive. So it is important to emphasize prajna. With prajna, or discriminating awareness, you see that samsara is black and quite terrible; and freedom from samsara, or nirvana, is extremely white and immaculate. You have to face that fundamental hinayana truth. You have to realize that. We are not trying to become soupy and throw everything into the pot to see what will come out of it.

As accurate students of Buddhism at the hinayana level, you are working on a process by which you could actually overcome your kleshas—your stupidity and ignorance. You are working on sharpening the best of your wisdom, your prajna, which you possess intrinsically, as a family heirloom. You are trying to build that up. You are trying to do a thorough and complete job. That is the idea of meditation, or gompa.

In overcoming the kleshas, you could fall into a very subtle attitude of rejecting negative or crazy states of mind. But you do not have to regard your negative mind-states with hatred. You could use that negativity as a means of wearing itself out. If you have a pair of shoes you don't like, instead of throwing them away, you could walk around in them. You could wear them out completely, use them up, exhaust them. Then you can put on new shoes. So the idea is not to reject evil and encourage goodness in the crude sense, but to make use of your neuroses as a way to climb to the castle of liberation. Instead of throwing away your old staircase, you can chop it into pieces and burn it in your fireplace to keep your house warm. If you are a farmer, instead of casting away your shit, you can make use of it as manure to grow excellent crops. This approach is somewhat mahayana, but it still applies very much to the hinayana. The third prajna principle, or meditation, presents a somewhat black-and-white picture, but that black-and-white picture is a pragmatic one.

With the first prajna, hearing, you are studying and learning; with the second prajna, contemplating, you are sharpening your knowledge; and with the third prajna, meditation, your knowledge becomes workable.

Those are the three prajna-principles. But none of those disciplines can arise unless you become a refugee and practice shamatha and vipashyana.

Prajna is both sharp and gentle. If I may use an ordinary analogy, when your knife is sharp, it is very easy to cut meat. It is gentle, but still dramatic. You don't have to put much pressure on the meat, you just go over it lightly and the meat is separated. So the sharper, the gentler. Shamatha-vipashyana discipline brings out tremendous power in you. It sharpens prajna and brings out your respect for learning. You should not be afraid of being sharp, but take pride in the sharpness. That is your practice manual, so to speak; it is the practitioner's way of experiencing the hinayana path properly and fully.

APPENDIX 1:
A HINAYANA
MORNING LITURGY

This traditional hinayana morning liturgy includes an homage to the Buddha, the refuge vow, and the five precepts. It is recited in Sanskrit, as are most international Buddhist liturgies, with the hands in the position of *anjali* (as when you bow and say "namaste"), which is a gesture of greeting, supplication, and respect.

HOMAGE TO THE BUDDHA

Namas tasmai bhagavate 'rhate samyak sambuddhaya.

I prostrate to him who has conquered the enemy, who possesses virtue, who has transcended, who is worthy of respect, the completely and fully enlightened one.

THE REFUGE VOW

Buddham sharanam gacchami; dharmam sharanam gacchami; sangham sharanam gacchami.

I go for refuge to the Buddha; I go for refuge to the dharma; I go for refuge to the sangha.

THE FIVE PRECEPTS

Pranatipata-viratih shikshapadam samadiyami.

I take on the precept of abstaining from the destruction of life.

Adattadana-viratih shikshapadam samadiyami.

I take on the precept of abstaining from stealing.

Mrishavada-viratih shikshapadam samadiyami.

I take on the precept of abstaining from lying.

Abrahmacarya-viratih shikshapadam samadiyami.

I take on the precept of abstaining from sex.

Sura-maireya-madyapana-viratih shikshapadam
    samadiyami.

*I take on the precept of abstaining from drinking intoxicating
liquor.*

—*Translated by the Nalanda Translation Committee*

APPENDIX 2:
WORKING WITH
THREEFOLD LOGIC

Judith L. Lief

INTRODUCTION

Working with threefold logic is a way to study the teachings with clear-headedness and an understanding of how things evolve. In studying the dharma, you are relating with your own mind rather than simply learning a philosophy or psychology. Therefore, your approach should be simple and direct. It should be gut level, with no compromises.

Threefold logic is based on respect for language and an awareness of how language can create a state of mind. It is based on the idea that speaking dharma, or truth, is sacred. Trungpa Rinpoche said that his own talks always followed threefold logic, so an understanding of that approach is helpful for studying his teachings. But threefold logic cannot be forced or applied mechanically. If you try to force it, it becomes a way of complicating rather than simplifying. It begins to promote conceptual mind rather than directness and clarity of thought and expression.

The basic approach of threefold logic is to take a theme, elaborate on that, and make it solid. One way of doing so is in terms of ground, path, and fruition, with ground as the basic perspective, path as how you practice that, and fruition as realization. However, there are other possibilities. You could use the logic of definition, nature, and function. Here you begin by defining what you are talking about, then you discuss its nature, and how it functions. If you are discussing water, for instance, you might say that it is defined as a mixture of hydrogen and oxygen, that its essence is wetness, and that its function is to quench thirst. Another variation is to think in terms of essence, cause, and effect. For instance, you could say that the essence of a vegetable is its nutrients, its cause is that it was planted and nurtured to maturity, and its effect is to satisfy hunger.

In thinking about a topic in terms of threefold logic, there are two basic paradigms. In the first, you examine what is happening now and see how it arose, starting with step three and working backward. In the other, you examine what is happening now and see where it leads, starting with step one and working forward. In the first paradigm, for example, you might begin by observing that you are feeling sad (fruition). You then look back to find that the ground was a bad dream, and the path was responding to that dream as if it were real. In the second paradigm, you again begin by noticing that you feel sad, but this time it is the ground. You go on to see that the path perpetuating this feeling is self-pity, and the fruition is depression.

EXAMPLES

The following chart contains additional examples of threefold logic, which may help you get a feel for the process.

Ground	Path	Fruition
See	Examine	Pigeonhole
This is the case.	What shall I do?	How do I do that?
Vagueness	Action	Clarity
How did this happen?	What is the process?	Where is it going?
Because this has happened	This is the cause	So this will happen
Sun	Sun shines out	Dispels darkness
Something is burning.	It radiates heat.	Therefore it is fire.
Having passion	Seeing possibilities of release	Peace
Mindfulness	Expanding awareness	Insight
Seeing one thing at a time precisely and accurately	Awareness of totality	Insight

APPENDIX 3:
OUTLINE OF TEACHINGS

The numbered lists of teachings in this book have been organized into outline-style here as a study aid. The lists are in order of appearance in the text.

PART ONE. ENTERING THE PATH

Encountering the Dharma

Chapter 1. Beginning at the Beginning

Chapter 2. The Frozen Space of Ego
The Five Skandhas / Heaps
1. Form
Three Stages of Ignorance
a. Birth of ignorance
b. Ignorance born within
c. Self-observing ignorance
2. Feeling
3. Perception / impulse
4. Concept / formation
5. Consciousness

Chapter 3. The Path of Individual Salvation
Three Key Principles of Hinayana Understanding
1. Shila / discipline
2. Samadhi / meditation
3. Prajna / knowledge

Four Marks of View
1. Impermanence
2. Suffering
3. Egolessness
4. Peace

Chapter 4. Opening to the True Dharma
Two Levels of Dharma
1. Ordinary dharma
2. Higher dharma (saddharma)

Contents of All Saddharma
1. Discipline / Shila
2. Meditation / Samadhi
3. Knowledge / Prajna

Twofold Egolessness
1. Egolessness of self / individual existence
2. Egolessness of dharmas / phenomena

Three Qualities of Dharma
1. Good at the beginning
2. Good in the middle
3. Good at the end

Two Aspects of Dharma
1. Profundity
2. Vastness

Threefold Logic of Hearing the Dharma
1. Personal experience
2. Theory
3. Confirmation

Ten Definitions of Dharma
1. What is knowable
2. The path
3. Freedom from pain
4. Perception of mind
5. Sense of reward
6. Sense of time

7. Doctrine
8. Complete true message
9. Prediction or prophesying
10. Particular religious beliefs

Two Types of Dharmic Literature
1. Sutras
2. Shastras

Three Baskets / Tripitaka
1. Vinaya / monastic discipline
2. Sutras / dialogues of the Buddha
3. Abhidharma / Buddhist psychology

Five Aspects of How Dharma Is Presented
1. Properly, fully, and completely
2. For the benefit of sentient beings
3. Teachers say it always
4. Nothing is hidden or kept secret
5. Always workable

Information and Understanding
1. Information / lung
   a. Subject is meaningful
   b. Language is clear
   c. Transcends confusion
   d. Leads to gentleness
2. Understanding / tokpa

Five Songs of Dharma
1. Like thunder
2. Like a flute
3. Soothing
4. Clarifying
5. Never contradictory

Chapter 5. Joining Study and Practice
Categories of Buddha's Teaching (Tripitaka)
1. Vinaya / monastic vows and discipline
2. Sutras / discourses and dialogues
3. Abhidharma / philosophy and psychology

Threefold Logic
  1. Ground
  2. Path
  3. Fruition

Chapter 6. Achieving Sanity Here on Earth
  Two Levels of Prajna
    1. Lower prajna
    2. Higher prajna

  Two Approaches to Spirituality
    1. Theism / spirituality as ego confirmation
    2. Nontheism / spirituality transcending ego-fixation

  Four Dharmas of Gampopa
    1. Grant your blessing so that my mind may be one with the dharma
    2. Grant your blessing so that dharma may progress along the path
    3. Grant your blessing so that the path may clarify confusion
    4. Grant your blessing so that confusion may dawn as wisdom

  Four Aspects of Nontheistic Dharma
    1. View: the four norms of dharma
        a. Impermanence
        b. Suffering
        c. Egolessness
        d. Peace
    2. Practice: meditation transcending spirituality
    3. Action: beyond the extremes of austerity or indulgence
    4. Result: having nothing to give up

Chapter 7. The Path, the Vehicle, and the Traveler
  The Nine Yanas
    Hinayana
        1. Shravakayana
        2. Pratyekabuddhayana
    Mahayana
        3. Mahayana
    Vajrayana / Tantra
        4. Kriyayogayana
        5. Upayogayana

Taking Refuge

Chapter 10. Buddhadharma Fever
   The Refuge Vow
      1. I take refuge in Buddha
      2. I take refuge in dharma
      3. I take refuge in the sangha

Chapter 11. Taking Refuge in the Three Jewels
   The Three Jewels
      1. Buddha / awakened mind
      2. Dharma / teachings or truth
      3. Sangha / community

Reflecting on the Three Jewels

Chapter 12. The Sutra of the Recollection of the Noble Three Jewels

Chapter 13. The Buddha
   Epithets of the Buddha
      1. Buddha / Awakened One / Sang-gye
      2. Bhagavat / Having Conquered the Four Maras / Chom-den-de
         The Four Maras
            a. Devaputra-mara / personal gratification
            b. Klesha-mara / negative thought-patterns
            c. Skandha-mara / solidified sense of self
            d. Yama-mara / fear of death
      3. Tathagata / Gone Beyond Just like the Previous Buddhas / Teshin Shekpa
      4. Arhat / One Who Is Worthy / Drachompa
      5. Samyaksambuddha / Complete Buddha / Dzok-pe sang-gye
      6. The Learned and Virtuous One
         Eight Superior Ways of Seeing
            a. Learned / rikpa denpa
               i. View
            b. Virtuous / shapsu denpa
               ii. Understanding
               iii. Speech
               iv. End of karma
               v. Livelihood
               vi. Effort

vii. Recollection

viii. Meditation

7. Sugata / Gone Beyond with Joy / Dewar

Qualities of the Buddha

1. In accord with all merit
2. Does not waste the roots of virtue
3. Ornamented with all patience
4. Incomparable form
5. Unstained by desire, form, or formless realms
6. Liberated from suffering
7. Liberated from the skandhas
8. Liberated from the dhatus and ayatanas
9. Free from bondage
10. Free from torment
11. Liberated from craving
12. Does not abide in nirvana
13. Abides in ultimate perfection
14. Dwells on bhumi where he sees all sentient beings

Chapter 14. The Dharma

Qualities of the Dharma

1. Good in the beginning, good in the middle, good at the end
2. Excellent meaning and words
3. Uncorrupted
4. Completely perfect, completely pure, completely purifies
5. Well-taught by the bhagavat
6. Brings complete vision
7. Free from sickness
8. Always timely
9. Directs one further
10. Fulfills one's purpose
11. Brings discriminating insight for the wise
12. Thoroughly teaches training
13. Shows the path of renunciation
14. Causes one to arrive at perfect enlightenment
15. Without contradiction and pithy
16. Trustworthy
17. Puts an end to the journey

Chapter 15. The Sangha
Ten Conditions for Shaping a Noble Sangha
1. Entering properly
a. Entering completely
b. Entering insightfully
c. Entering straightforwardly
d. Entering harmoniously
2. Being worthy of veneration
e. Worthy of veneration with joined palms
f. Worthy of receiving prostration
3. Receiving generosity
g. A field of glorious merit
h. Completely capable of receiving all gifts
i. An object of generosity
j. A great object of generosity

PART TWO. DISCIPLINE / SHILA
Taming Neurosis

Chapter 16. The Loneliness and Joy of Discipline
Ground of Discipline
1. Taming / dülwa
2. Decorum / pagyö

Six Categories of Aloneness
1. Less desire
2. Contentment
3. Avoiding unnecessary activities
4. Morality
5. Not wandering in the world of desire
6. Working with discursive thoughts

Chapter 17. Taming the Neurotic Mind
The Four Mental Obstacles
1. Stupidity
2. Mindlessness
3. Emotional upheavals
4. Lack of faith

Chapter 18. Cutting the Root of Samsara

Chapter 19. Continually Gnawing Rock
Three Categories of Tsültrim / Discipline
 1. Good
 2. Action
 3. Binding factor

Three Gates of Discipline
 1. Body
 2. Speech
 3. Mind

Cultivating Virtue

Chapter 20. Becoming a Dharmic Person
Seven Characteristics of a Dharmic Person
 General guidelines: Creating a Proper Physical Environment
 1. Passionlessness
 2. Contentment
 3. Fewer activities
 4. Good conduct
 5. Awareness of the teacher
 6. Propagating prajna
 7. Attitude of goodness
 extra step: Remembering to be dharmic

Chapter 21. Refraining from Harm
The Five Precepts
 1. Refraining from killing
 2. Refraining from stealing
 3. Refraining from lying
 4. Refraining from sexual misconduct
 5. Refraining from intoxicants

PART THREE. MEDITATION / SAMADHI
Shamatha: The Practice of Mindfulness

Chapter 22. Simplicity
Threefold Mindfulness
 1. Mindfulness of body / hell realm / anger
 2. Mindfulness of speech / hungry ghost realm / desire
 3. Mindfulness of mind / animal realm / discursive thoughts

Chapter 34. Cutting Thoughts and Short-Circuiting the Kleshas
Results of Shamatha Practice
1. Pagyö / a residue of mindfulness
2. Tren-she / recollection-knowing
a. Trenpa / recollection
b. Sheshin / knowing
3. Overcoming the six root kleshas
a. Ignorance
b. Aggression
c. Passion
d. Pride
e. Jealousy
f. Avarice

Chapter 35. An Element of Magic

Working with the Mind

Chapter 36. Transcending Dualistic Mind
Three Aspects of Mind
1. Sem / act of minding
2. Rikpa / brightness
3. Yi / mental sensitivity / the sixth sense consciousness

Chapter 37. Rediscovering Your Own Mind
The Eight Consciousnesses
1. Eye consciousness
2. Ear consciousness
3. Nose consciousness
4. Tongue consciousness
5. Body consciousness
6. Yi / mind consciousness
7. Nyön-yi / instigator of the kleshas
8. Alaya vijnana / storehouse

Two Types of Alaya
1. Alaya vijnana / the eighth consciousness /
2. Fundamental alaya / higher form / dharmadhatu-level

Sense Faculties
1. Twelve ayatanas / Six sense organs plus six sense objects
2. Eighteen dhatus / Six sense organs plus six sense objects plus six
sense consciousnesses (See chart on p. 278.)

Chapter 52. Dissecting the Experience of Suffering
The Eight Types of Suffering
Inherited Suffering
1. Birth
2. Old age
3. Sickness
4. Death
Suffering of the Period between Birth and Death
5. Coming across what is not desirable
6. Not being able to hold on to what is desirable
7. Not getting what you want
General Misery
8. General misery or all-pervasive suffering

Three Patterns of Suffering
1. The suffering of suffering
a. Birth
b. Old age
c. Sickness
d. Death
e. Coming across what is not desirable
2. The suffering of change
a. Trying to hold on to what is desirable
b. Not getting, or not knowing, what you want
3. All-pervasive suffering
a. General misery or all-pervasive suffering

The Origin of Suffering

Chapter 53. The Power of Flickering Thoughts

Chapter 54. The Development of Set Patterns
Seven Ego-Oriented Patterns That Lead to Suffering
1. Regarding the five skandhas as belonging to oneself
2. Protecting oneself from impermanence
3. Belief that one's view is best
4. Believing in the extremes of nihilism and eternalism
5. Passion
6. Aggression
7. Ignorance

Chapter 55. Perpetually Re-Creating Suffering
The Six Root Kleshas / Conflicting Emotions
1. Desire
2. Anger
3. Pride
4. Ignorance
5. Doubt
6. View

Karmic Patterns That Lead to Suffering
Unmeritorious Karma
Body
1. Taking life
2. Stealing
3. Sexual misconduct
Speech
4. Telling lies
5. Intrigue
6. Negative words
7. Gossip
Mind
8. Envy
9. Hoping to create harm
10. Disbelieving in sacredness

Meritorious Karma
1. Respect for life
2. Generosity
3. Sexual wholesomeness
4. Truthfulness
5. Straightforwardness
6. Good wisdom
7. Simplicity
8. Openness
9. Gentleness
10. Understanding sacredness

The Six Types of Karmic Consequence
1. The power of volitional action
   a. Good beginning, bad ending
   b. Bad beginning, good ending

3. Sign
4. Ultimate
5. Incompletion
6. Signs of completion
7. Without ornament
8. Adorned
9. With omission
10. Without omission
11. Especially supreme
12. Beyond calculation
   a. Renunciation
   b. Complete purification
   c. Worn out
   d. Passionlessness
   e. Cessation
   f. Complete peace
   g. Subsiding

The Truth of the Path

Chapter 59. The Doubtless Path
  The Sequence of the Path
    1. Overcoming the notion of eternity
    2. Overcoming the search for pleasure
    3. Realizing the possibility of emptiness
    4. Encountering egolessness

  Four Qualities of the Path
    1. Path: searching for the real meaning of suchness
    2. Insight: through clarity, transcending neurosis
    3. Practice: associating with basic sanity
    4. Fruition: permanent nirvana

Chapter 60. The Five Paths
    1. The Path of Accumulation (Tsoglam)
    Twofold Truth
      a. Relative truth / kündzop
      b. Absolute truth / töndam
    2. The Path of Unification (Jorlam)
    Five Categories
      a. Faith

b. Exertion

c. Recollection

d. One-pointedness

e. Intellect

3. The Path of Seeing (Thonglam)
The Seven Limbs of Enlightenment

a. Recollection

b. Separating dharmas

c. Exertion

d. Joy

e. Being thoroughly trained

f. Samadhi

g. Equilibrium

4. The Path of Meditation (Gomlam)
The Noble Eightfold Path

a. Perfect view

b. Perfect understanding

c. Perfect speech

d. Perfect end of karma

e. Perfect livelihood

f. Perfect effort

g. Perfect recollection

h. Perfect meditation

5. The Path of No More Learning (Mi-lob-lam)

PART FIVE. THE HINAYANA JOURNEY

The Journey in Terms of Yanas

Chapter 61. Shravakayana: The Yana of Hearing and Proclaiming
Four Levels of Students

1. Pioneer: Nyen-ne / nyen-nema / upavasa / upavasi

2. Refuge taker: Genyen / genyenma / upasaka / upasika

3. Novice monk or nun: Getsül / getsülma / shramanera / shramanerika

4. Full monk or nun: Gelong / gelongma / bhikshu / bhikshuni

Chapter 62. Pratyekabuddhayana: The Yana of Individual Salvation
Two Types of Pratyekabuddhas

1. Parrots

2. Rhinoceroses

The Journey in Terms of Paths

Chapter 63. The Lesser Path of Accumulation
The Three Ways of Learning
1. Hearing / thöpa
2. Contemplating / sampa
3. Meditating / gompa

The Three Marks of Existence
1. Impermanence
Two Approaches to Impermanence
a. Joggom / resting in meditation / approach of the kusulu
b. Chegom / analytical meditation / approach of the pandit
2. Egolessness
3. Suffering

Two Schools of Thought in Mahayana Buddhism
1. Contemplative practice of Asanga
2. Intellectual practice of Nagarjuna

Chapter 64. The Middle Path of Accumulation
Sixteen Incantations of the Four Noble Truths
First Set
1. Suffering should be seen
2. The origin of suffering should be avoided
3. The goal should be attained
4. The path should be actualized
Second Set
5. Suffering should be realized as impermanent
6. The origin of suffering should be realized as impermanent
7. The goal should be realized as impermanent
8. The path should be realized as impermanent
Third Set
9. Suffering should be seen clearly
10. The origin of suffering should be seen clearly
11. The goal should be seen clearly
12. The path should be seen clearly
Fourth Set
13. No suffering
14. No origin of suffering
15. No goal
16. No path

Chapter 65. The Greater Path of Accumulation
Two Types of Effort
1. Küjor / the application of surrender or devotion
2. Tagjor / the application of continuity

Four Legs of Miracle
1. Strong interest / dünpa
2. Effort / tsöndrü
3. Recollection / trenpa
4. Investigation / chöpa

The Three Worlds and Six Realms
1. World of desire / crude desire / body
   a. Hell realm
   b. Hungry ghost realm
   c. Animal realm
   d. Human realm
   e. Jealous god realm
   f. Portion of god realm (6 classes of gods)
2. World of form / subtle desire / speech
   Portion of god realm (36 classes of gods)
3. Formless world / very refined desire / mind
   Portion of god realm (4 classes of gods)

Chapter 66. The Path of Unification
Four Types of Discrimination
1. Heat / trö
2. Peak / tsemo
3. Patience / söpa
4. Higher dharma / tamchö

Five Perceptions
1. Faith
2. Exertion / energy
3. Recollection / awareness
4. One-pointedness / meditation
5. Intellect / knowledge / prajna

Five Powers
1. Faith never needs to be sought
2. Exertion never needs to be sought

3. Recollection never needs to be sought
4. One-pointedness never needs to be sought
5. Intellect never needs to be sought

PART SIX. KNOWLEDGE / PRAJNA

Unraveling the Myth of Ego

Chapter 67. Ego: The Thought That We Exist

Chapter 68. Cutting Through the Numbness of Ego

Chapter 69. Taking the Teachings to Heart
Three Aspects of Prajna
1. Hearing
2. Contemplating
3. Meditating

GLOSSARY

This glossary includes terms in English, Tibetan (Tib.), Sanskrit (Skt.), Pali, and Japanese (Jpn.). Tibetan terms are spelled phonetically, followed by the transliteration in parentheses. Tibetan equivalents of Sanskrit words are first written phonetically, then transliterated.

abhidharma (Skt.). Superior or higher dharma. The Buddhist teachings can be divided into three parts, called the "three baskets," or Tripitaka: the sutras (general teachings of the Buddha), the vinaya (teachings on conduct), and the abhidharma (teachings on philosophy and psychology).

abrahmacharya-viratih shikshapadam samadiyami (Skt.). The vow to refrain from sexual misconduct; the fourth of the five precepts. *See also* appendix 3, under *The Five Precepts* (chapter 21).

acharya (Skt.; Tib.: loppön; slob dpon). A learned spiritual teacher.

adattadana-viratih shikshapadam samadiyami (Skt.). The vow to refrain from stealing; the second of the five precepts. *See also* appendix 3, under *The Five Precepts* (chapter 21).

adharma (Skt.). That which is not in accord with the teachings of buddha-dharma.

alaya (Skt.; Tib.: künshi; kun gzhi). The fundamental ground that gives rise to both samsara and nirvana, or the basic split. Not to be confused with alayavijnana, or alaya consciousness, the eighth consciousness.

alayavijnana (Skt.; Tib.: künshi nampar shepa; kun gzhi rnam par shes pa). The base, or storehouse consciousness; the basis of duality and of all mental activities, also referred to as the eighth consciousness.

Amaterasu Omi Kami (Jpn.). Shinto goddess of the sun.

arhat (Skt.; Tib.: drachompa; dgra bcom pa). In Sanskrit, "worthy one"; in Tibetan, "one who has conquered the enemy" of conflicting emotions and grasping at a self-entity. A fully accomplished practitioner of the hinayana path who has achieved liberation from the sufferings of samsara. The realization of emptiness is not perfect at this stage, however, because the arhat has yet to enter the mahayana path.

aryasangha (Skt.). Noble sangha.

Asanga (300–370). Fourth-century Buddhist teacher and one of the founders of the yogachara, or mind-only, school.

asura (Skt.). Jealous god. *See also* appendix 3, under *The Three Worlds and the Six Realms* (chapter 65).

Atisha Dipankara (980 or 990–1055). A Buddhist scholar at the great monastic university of Vikramashila, who is known for his teachings on mind training and the cultivation of bodhichitta.

avidya (Skt.). Fundamental ignorance. First of the twelve nidanas, represented by the blind grandmother. *See also* appendix 3, under *The Twelve Nidanas* (chapter 9).

ayatana (Skt.; Tib.: kye-che; skye mched). Sense field. The twelve ayatanas are comprised of the six sense organs of eyes, ears, nose, tongue, body, and mind; and the six sense objects of sights, sounds, smells, tastes, touchable objects, and mental objects. The Tibetan translation, *kye-che,* literally means "arising and spreading."

basic split. The simultaneous arising of both samsara and nirvana, the birth of duality.

bhagavat (Skt.; Tib.: chom-den-de; bcom ldan 'das). Lord; an epithet of the Buddha. The Tibetan translation means one who conquers the maras, possesses the six excellent qualities (lordship, form, glory, fame, wisdom, and exertion) and has transcended samsara and nirvana.

bhava (Skt.). Becoming; the tenth of the twelve nidanas, represented by copulation. *See also* appendix 3, under *The Twelve Nidanas* (chapter 9).

bhavachakra (Skt.). The wheel of life, Tibetan iconographic portrayal of the activities of samsara in the form of a wheel held in the jaws of Yama, the personification of death.

bhikshu / bhikshuni (f) (Skt.). Fully ordained monk or nun. *See also* gelong.

bhumi (Skt.). Stage, level; the progressive stages on the path of the bodhisattva that lead to enlightenment.

bodhi (Skt.; Tib.: changchup; byang chub). Awake. Full illumination or enlightenment.

bodhi tree. The tree in Bodhgaya, India, under which the Buddha was meditating when he attained enlightenment. A descendent of the original tree still exists in Bodhgaya and is a powerful pilgrimage site.

Bodhicharyavatara (*The Way of the Bodhisattva;* 700 CE). Mahayana text by Shantideva in ten chapters dedicated to the development of bodhichitta through the practice of the six paramitas.

bodhichitta (Skt.; Tib.: changchup kyi sem; byang chub kyi sems). Enlightened heart / mind. Ultimate, or absolute, bodhichitta is the union of emptiness and compassion, the essential nature of awakened mind. Relative bodhichitta is the tenderness arising from a glimpse of ultimate bodhichitta, which inspires the practitioner to train in working for the benefit of others. The discovery of bodhichitta is a mark of one's transition from the hinayana to the mahayana stage of the path.

bodhisattva (Skt.; Tib.: changchup sempa; byang chub sems 'dpa). Awake being. In Tibetan, literally "hero of the enlightened mind." A person who has largely overcome confusion and who is committed to cultivating compassion and wisdom through the practice of the six paramitas (transcendent actions or perfections) in order to free all beings from suffering. *See also* paramitas.

bodhisattva vow. The vow to attain enlightenment for the benefit of all beings, marking one's aspiration to enter into the mahayana path of wisdom and compassion and one's intention to practice the bodhisattva discipline of the six paramitas.

brahmacharya (Skt.). Celibacy. One of the vows of the hinayana monastic.

Brahman (Skt.; Tib.: tsangpa; tshangs pa). In the Hindu tradition, the eternal, imperishable absolute; the state of pure transcendence that cannot be grasped by thought or speech.

brahmayana (Skt.; Tib.: tsang-pe thekpa; tshangs pa'i theg pa). Complete or pure vehicle, by which one binds oneself to hinayana discipline.

buddha / Buddha (Skt.; Tib.: sang-gye; sangs rgyas). Awakened one. In a general sense, "buddha" may refer to the principle of enlightenment or to any enlightened being. In particular, "the Buddha" refers to the historical Buddha Shakyamuni, or Gautama Buddha. "Buddha" is also the first of the three jewels of refuge. *See also* appendix 3, under *The Three Jewels* (chapter 11).

buddha in the palm of your hand. An expression in Buddhism used to describe the perfect wakefulness that every human being intrinsically possesses.

buddha nature (Skt.: tathagatagarbha). The intrinsic state of wakefulness inherent in all sentient beings.

buddhadharma (Skt.). The teachings of the Buddha.

chak cha-we ösu kyurpa (Tib.: phyag bya ba'i 'os su gyur pa). Worthy of receiving prostration; a quality of sangha.

chakpa (Tib.: chags pa). To be attached; desire, passion, lust.

chakravartin (Skt.). One who turns the wheel. A universal monarch; in ancient Buddhist and Vedic literature, a king who rules the entire world by his wisdom and virtue.

changchup yenlak dün (Tib.: byang chub yan lag bdun). The seven limbs of enlightenment, or bodhi.

chegom (Tib.: dpyad sgom). Analytical meditative practice.

chepa (Tib.: dpyad pa). To analyze.

chipa nyerchö (Tib.: byis pa nyer spyod). "Acting like an infant." First of the three stages of vipashyana. *See also* appendix 3, under *Three Stages of Vipashyana* (chapter 46).

chitta (Skt.). Mind or heart.

chö (Tib.: chos). Dharma. *See also* dharma.

chö nampar jepa (Tib.: chos rnam par 'byed pa). Fully separating dharmas. First category of vipashyana. *See also* appendix 3, under *Four Categories of Vipashyana* (chaper 47).

chö raptu nampar jepa sherap (Tib.: chos rab tu rnam par 'byed pa shes rab). Knowing how to fully separate one dharma from another. Discriminating-awareness wisdom.

chö tham-che dagmepa (Tib.: chos thams cad bdag med pa). All dharmas are marked by emptiness; third of the four marks of existence.

chok tsölwa (Tib.: phyogs 'tshol ba). Discovering sides (fourth of the six discoveries of vipashyana). *See also* appendix 3, under *The Six Discoveries* (chapter 48).

chokshak namsum (Tib.: chog bzhag rnam gsum). Well-being of body, speech, and mind.

chok-she (Tib.: chog shes). Contentment. Satisfaction-knowledge.

chökyi dag-me (Tib.: chos kyi bdag med). Egolessness of dharmas, the nonexistence of projected ego.

chom-den-de (Tib.: bcom ldan 'das). Bhagavat; an epithet of the Buddha. *See also* bhagavat.

chöpa (Tib.: dpyod pa). Investigation, analysis. Also, fourth of the four legs of miracle. *See also* appendix 3, under *The Four Legs of Miracle* (chapter 65).

chung ne dro sum (Tib.: byung gnas 'gro gsum). The arising, dwelling, and disappearing of thoughts. Literally, "arising, dwelling, going, the three."

cool boredom. An expression of well-being in which the thinking process becomes less entertaining and thoughts become transparent. According to Trungpa Rinpoche, cool boredom is like what mountains experience. It is hopelessness at its most absolute level.

dakini (Skt.; Tib.: khandro; mkha' 'gro). One who walks in the sky. A wrathful or semiwrathful female deity, or yidam, signifying compassion, emptiness, and prajna.

devaloka (Skt.). The god realm.

devaputra-mara (Skt.). One of the four maras. Indulging in personal self-gratification. *See also* appendix 3, under *The Four Maras* (chapter 13).

dewa (Tib.: bde ba) Pleasure or bliss. One of the three fundamental nyams (temporary experiences). *See also* appendix 3, under *Three Fundamental Nyams* (chapter 42).

dharma (Skt.; Pali: dhamma; Tib.: chö; chos). Truth, law, phenomena. The second of the three jewels of refuge. Specifically, the buddhadharma, or teaching of the Buddha. Lower dharma is how things work on the mundane level; for example, how water boils. Higher dharma is the subtle understanding of the world: how mind works, how samsara perpetuates itself, how it is transcended, and so on. The term *dharmas* can also simply refer to phenomena.

dharmadhatu (Skt.; Tib.: chökyi ying; chos kyi dbyings). Sphere of dharma, or sphere of reality. All-encompassing space in which all phenomena arise, dwell, and dissolve. Unconditional totality, unoriginating and unchanging.

dharmakaya (Skt.; Tib.: chöku; chos sku). Dharma body. *See also* kayas, three.

dharmapala (Skt.; Tib.: chökyong; chos skyong). An enlightened emanation or a being bound by oath to protect practitioners and the integrity of the dharma. Aid to practitioners in taming of inner and outer obstacles.

dhatu (Skt.; Tib.: kham; khams). Sense faculty. The eighteen dhatus or sense faculties are comprised of the six sense organs of eyes, ears, nose, tongue, body, and mind; the six sense objects of sights, sounds, smells, tastes, touchable objects, and mental contents; and the six corresponding sense consciousnesses of seeing consciousness, hearing consciousness, smelling consciousness, tasting consciousness, touching consciousness, and mind consciousness. A description of the process of perception.

dhyana (Skt.; Tib.: samten; bsam gtan). Meditation, stabilization, concentration.

döchak (Tib.: 'dod chags). Desire, passion; a klesha. *See also* appendix 3, under *The Six Root Kleshas* (chapter 55).

dompa (Tib.: sdom pa; Skt.: samvara). Vow; binding factor. One of the three categories of tsültrim. *See also* appendix 3, under *Three Categories of Tsültrim* (chapter 19).

dug-ngal (Tib.: sdug bsngal; Skt.: duhkha). Suffering, dissatisfaction. *See also* duhkha.

duhkha (Skt.; Tib.: dug-ngal; sdug bsngal). Suffering. The first of the four noble truths. Physical and psychological suffering of all kinds, including the subtle but all-pervading frustration experienced with regard to the impermanence and insubstantiality of all things.

dülwa (Tib.: 'dul ba). Taming; discipline; the vinaya.

dülwar chepa (Tib.: 'dul bar byed pa). Taming. The fifth of the nine stages of shamatha. *See also* appendix 3, under *The Nine Techniques of Shamatha Practice* (chapter 31).

dünpa (Tib.: 'dun pa). Aspiration, strong interest. Also, first of the four legs of miracle. *See also* appendix 3, under *Four Legs of Miracle* (chapter 65).

dzinpa (Tib.: 'dzin pa). Grasping, fixation, holding on to.

dzokchen (Tib.: rdzogs chen; Skt.: maha ati). Great completion or great perfection; considered in the Nyingma tradition the highest teachings of the Tibetan Buddhist path. *See also* maha ati.

dzok-pe sang-gye (Tib.: rdzogs pa'i sangs rgyas; Skt.: sambuddha). Perfect buddha; an epithet for the Buddha.

eightfold path, noble. Fundamental components of the Buddhist path as expounded by Gautama Buddha. The path that leads to the cessation of suffering. *See also* appendix 3, under *The Noble Eightfold Path* (chapter 60).

five precepts. Vows taken by a hinayana practitioner, which are refraining from killing, stealing, lying, sexual misconduct, and intoxicants. *See also* appendix 3, under *The Five Precepts* (chapter 21).

five skandhas. The collection of phenomena we take to be the self or ego: form, feeling, perception/impulse, concept/formation, and consciousness. *See also* skandha.

Four Dharmas of Gampopa. A traditional four-line chant attributed to Gampopa:

Grant your blessing so that my mind may be one with the dharma.

Grant your blessing so that dharma may progress along the path.

Grant your blessing so that the path may clarify confusion.

Grant your blessing so that confusion may dawn as wisdom.

See also Gampopa.

four foundations of mindfulness. In Trungpa Rinpoche's presentation: mindfulness of body, mindfulness of life, mindfulness of effort, and mindfulness of mind. In traditional texts usually presented as: mindfulness of body, mindfulness of feelings, mindfulness of mind, and mindfulness of mental contents.

four marks (Tib.: chaggya shi; phyag rgya bzhi). The four marks of impermanence, suffering, egolessness, and peace. How to view the world from the point of view of the path or doctrine. This list comes up in different contexts as the "four marks of existence," the "four marks of view," and the "four norms of dharma." A related list, called the "three marks of existence," includes impermanence, suffering, and egolessness, but not peace.

four norms of dharma (Tib.: chökyi domshi; chos kyi sdom bzhi). The first aspect of nontheistic view: impermanence, suffering, egolessness, and peace. *See also* four marks and appendix 3, under *View: The Four Norms of Dharma* (chapter 6).

Gampopa (1079–1153 CE). One of the main lineage holders of the Kagyü lineage. A student of Milarepa and a great scholar, he established the first Kagyü monastery.

gawa (Tib.: dga' ba). Joy.

gelong / gelongma (f) (Tib.: dge slong / dge slong ma; Skt.: bhikshu / bhikshuni). "Asking, or begging for virtue." A fully ordained monk or nun. The fourth category of "soso-tharpist." *See also* appendix 3, under *Four Levels of Students* (chapter 61).

Geluk (Tib.: dge lugs). One of the four major school of Tibetan Buddhism, characterized by an emphasis on scholarship and intellectual analysis.

genyen / genyenma (f) (Tib.: dge bsnyen / dge bsnyen ma; Skt.: upasaka / upasika). The second category of "soso-tharpist," which describes a male or female practitioner who has taken the refuge vow. Specifically, householders who keep the five precepts. *See also* appendix 3, under *Four Levels of Students* (chapter 61).

getsül / getsülma (f) (Tib.: dge tshul / dge tshul ma; Skt.: shramanera / shramanerika). The third category of "soso-tharpist" describing a novice monk or nun. *See also* appendix 3, under *Four Levels of Students* (chapter 61).

gokpa (Tib.: 'gog pa; Skt.: nirodha). Cessation.

gomden (Tib.: sgom gdan). A block-shaped, rectangular meditation cushion designed by Chögyam Trungpa.

gomlam (Tib.: sgom lam). Path of meditation. *See also* appendix 3, under *The Five Paths* (chapter 60).

gompa (Tib.: sgom pa). Meditation. *See also* appendix 3, under *The Three Ways of Learning* (chapter 63).

gyündu jokpa (Tib.: rgyun du 'jog pa). Continuously resting. Second of the nine stages of shamatha. *See also* appendix 3, under *The Nine Techniques of Shamatha Practice* (chapter 31).

head and shoulders. Holding oneself upright with a quality of presence, positive arrogance, and decorum.

Heart Sutra (Skt.: *Prajnaparamita Hridaya Sutra*). One of the most important sutras of mahayana Buddhism, studied and recited by many schools of Buddhism. A concise encapsulation of the prajnaparamita teachings and an essential discourse on emptiness.

heruka (Skt.; Tib.: thraktung; khrag 'thung). The masculine principle in tantric symbolism representing skillful means, the action aspect of wisdom. A semiwrathful or wrathful male yidam.

hinayana (Skt.; Tib.: thekpa chung; theg pa chung). Lesser or narrow vehicle. The spiritual path of individual salvation, based on meditation practice and an understanding of basic Buddhist doctrines such as the four noble truths. Also known as the foundational vehicle, it provides the essential instruction and training that serves as a basis for both the mahayana and the vajrayana.

Jamgön Kongtrül (1813–1899). Important Tibetan scholar and proponent of nonsectarianism and religious tolerance, known as *ri-me* (Tib.). Author of the important and extensive compilation of teachings known as *The Five Treasures*. Jamgön Kongtrül's *The Treasury of Knowledge* was one of the primary resources Trungpa Rinpoche consulted in preparing his Seminary teachings.

jara-marana (Skt.). Old age and death; twelfth of the twelve nidanas, represented by a funeral procession. *See also* appendix 3, under *The Twelve Nidanas* (chapter 9).

jati (Skt.). Birth; the eleventh of the twelve nidanas, represented by a woman in childbirth. *See also* appendix 3, under *The Twelve Nidanas* (chapter 9).

jethop (Tib.: rjes thob). Postmeditation.

jhana (Pali; Skt.: dhyana). State of meditative absorption. According to Chögyam Trungpa, attachment to such states is an obstacle that can lead to becoming trapped in the god realm, and therefore, it is better not to seek them out.

jin-pe nesu kyurpa (Tib.: sbyin pa'i gnas su gyur pa). An object of generosity; a quality of sangha.

joggom (Tib.: 'jog sgom). Resting meditation; meditation in which the mind rests, or is placed, on a focal object without wandering.

jorlam (Tib.: sbyor lam). Path of unification. *See also* appendix 3, under *The Five Paths* (chapter 60).

jorwa (Tib.: sbyor ba). Application or practice; effort.

Kagyü. One of the four major lineages of Tibetan Buddhism, known as the practice lineage for its emphasis on meditative training. Chögyam Trungpa was a lineage holder in this tradition.

kalpa (Skt.). An aeon, or a long period of time.

kangsak ki dag-me (Tib.: gang zag gi bdag med). Nonexistence of individual ego.

karma (Skt.; Tib.: le; las). Action. The chain-reaction process of action and result, or cause and effect, arising from the habit of ego fixation. According to this doctrine, one's present experience is a product of previous actions and volitions, and future conditions depend on what is done in the present. Virtuous actions lead to positive results, and nonvirtuous actions to negative results. Ultimately, the goal is to break the karmic chain by means of wisdom and skillful means, and free oneself from the destructive habit of ego.

Karmapas. The Karmapa lineage is the oldest continuous lineage in Tibetan Buddhism, and since the time of the first Karmapa Tüsum Khyenpa (1110–

1193) the Karmapas have served as the spiritual leaders of the Kagyü tradition. The sixteenth Karmapa Rikpe Dorje (1924–1981) was the Kagyü lineage holder during Trungpa Rinpoche's lifetime. The current or seventeenth Karmapa is Ogyen Trinley Dorje (b. 1985).

karmic seed (from Skt.: karma). Every action, whether of thought, word, or deed, sows seeds that will eventually bear fruit in terms of experience, whether in this or future lives. *See also* karma.

kayas, three (Skt.). Body. The three bodies of a buddha: the nirmanakaya, sambhogakaya, and dharmakaya. Nirmanakaya means "emanation body," or "body of manifestation." It is the communication of awakened mind through form—specifically, through embodiment as a human being (guru). Sambhogakaya, "enjoyment body," is the energy of compassion and communication linking the dharmakaya and the nirmanakaya. The dharmakaya is the "body of dharma"—the aspect of realization beyond form or limit, time or space.

kham cho-gye (Tib.: khams bco brgyad). Tibetan for the eighteen dhatus. *See also* dhatu.

khenpo (Tib.: mkhan po). Master scholar, a title of academic accomplishment; khenchen, or "great teacher," is an even more honorific title.

khorwa (Tib.: 'khor ba). To spin. Cyclic existence; the vicious cycle of transmigratory existence. *See also* samsara.

klesha (Skt.; Tib.: nyönmong; nyon mongs). Defilements; conflicting emotion; poison. Kleshas are properties that dull the mind and lead to unwholesome actions. The three main kleshas are passion, aggression, and ignorance or delusion.

klesha-mara (Skt.). The state of mind that entertains passion, aggression, arrogance, jealousy, ignorance, and other poisonous emotions. *See also* appendix 3, under *The Four Maras* (chapter 13).

küjor (Tib.: gus sbyor). Devotional exertion. Exertion that strives for virtue with an attitude of respect, devotion, and delight.

kündzop (Tib.: kun rdzob). Relative or conventional truth; contrasted to töndam, or "absolute truth," in the teaching of the two truths.

künjung (Tib.: kun 'byung; Skt.: samudaya). Origin of suffering. Künjung is based both on kleshas, or conflicting emotions, and karma, the habitual entanglement of cause and effect. This process is supported by the misperception of the self as a solid, independently existing entity. The five skandhas, or five components making up the self, are permeated with künjung.

künjung of karma. Bringing about suffering for oneself and others by acting upon others as a result of the arising of the kleshas.

künjung of kleshas. Bringing about suffering for oneself through the arising of the kleshas.

künlong (Tib.: kun slong). Motivation.

küntu yang jin-pe nesu kyurpa chenpo (Tib.: kun tu yang sbyin pa'i gnas su gyur pa chen po). A great object of generosity; a quality of sangha.

kusulu (Skt.). A simple yogin who does only three necessary things: eat, sleep, and shit.

lam (Tib.: lam). Path.

lama (Tib.: bla ma; Skt.: guru). Teacher.

Lankavatara Sutra (Skt.; *The Descent into Lanka Sutra*). One of the principle texts of mahayana Buddhism.

lappa (Tib.: bslab pa). Training.

le (Tib.: las). Karma or action. *See also* karma.

lek-che (Tib.: legs spyad). Good; regarded as the best; well thought of. One of the three categories of tsültrim. *See also* appendix 3, under *Three Categories of Tsültrim* (chapter 19).

lekpar shukpa (Tib.: legs par zhugs pa). Entering completely; a quality of the sangha.

len-te jokpa (Tib.: bslan te 'jog pa). Repeated placement, or literally resting. Third of the nine stages of shamatha. *See also* appendix 3, under *The Nine Techniques of Shamatha Practice* (chapter 31).

lesu rungwa (Tib.: las su rung ba). Workable or suitable. A quality of mental activity and functioning.

lhakthong (Tib.: lhag mthong; Skt.: vipashyana). Superior seeing; insight; higher view. Awareness practice. *See also* vipashyana.

lhakthong yenlak gye (Tib.: lhag mthong yan lag brgyad). The eight superior ways of seeing the world for the learned and virtuous Buddha (the same eight categories as the noble eightfold path).

loppön (Tib.: slob dpon). Master of learning. *See also* acharya.

lung (Tib.: rlung). Reading transmission; information.

lung sem sewa (Tib.: rlung sems sre ba). Mixing mind and breath.

madhyamaka. The middle-way school, a philosophical school based on the dialectical approach of undercutting any attempt to establish a solid logical position, developed by the great logician Nagarjuna (second to third century CE).

maha (Skt.). Great.

maha-ati (Skt.; Tib.: dzokchen; rdzogs chen). Great perfection or great completion. The primary teaching of the Nyingma school, which considers this teaching to be the final statement of the fruition path of vajrayana. It is called "great" because there is nothing higher; it is called "perfection" because no further means are necessary. According to the experience of maha ati practitioners, purity of mind is always present and needs only to be recognized.

mahaduhkha (Skt.). Great suffering.

mahasangha (Skt.). Great sangha (community of practitioners). In hinayana Buddhism, sangha usually refers only to the monastic community; in the mahayana, a more expanded notion of sangha, or mahasangha, refers not just to the monastic community but includes lay practitioners, as well. *See also* sangha.

mahavipashyana (Skt.). Seeing things as they are, the third stage of vipashyana, which brings spaciousness and a glimpse of shunyata.

mahayana (Skt.; Tib.: thekpa chenpo; theg pa chen po). Great vehicle, the second of the three yanas (hinayana, mahayana, and vajrayana) emphasizing the union of emptiness and compassion, the practice of the paramitas, and the ideal of the bodhisattva.

Maitreya asana (Skt.). A posture of meditation used while sitting in a chair. Maitreya, the bodhisattva of loving-kindness, is often depicted sitting with his legs hanging down, as if in a chair. *Asana* means "posture," or "position."

maitri (Skt.). Loving-kindness.

makyo (Jpn.). Illusions or fantasies.

Manjushri (Skt.). The bodhisattva of wisdom, whose two-edged sword is said to cut in one stroke through aggression and twofold ego. *See also* twofold ego.

mara (Skt.). Evil, seductive forces. Mara is the demon who tempted the Buddha with seductive visions. *See also* appendix 3, under *The Four Maras* (chapter 13).

Marpa (1012–1097). Renowned Tibetan Kagyü yogi and translator; principle teacher of Tibet's poet-saint Milarepa.

Milarepa (1040–1123). One of the forefathers of the Kagyü lineage. A student of Marpa who attained enlightenment in one lifetime, he is the most famous of Tibetan saints and is known for his spontaneous spiritual songs (*dohas*).

mi-lob-lam (Tib.: mi slob lam). Path of no more learning. *See also* appendix 3, under *The Five Paths* (chapter 60).

mitakpa (Tib.: mi rtag pa). Not permanent; subject to dissolution. The first of the four marks of existence.

mitokpa (Tib.: mi rtog pa). Without thought. One of the three fundamental nyam (temporary experiences). *See also* appendix 3, under *Three Fundamental Nyams* (chapter 42).

moksha (Skt.). Freedom. *See also* pratimoksha.

momo (Tib.: mog mog). Tibetan dumpling.

mrishavada-viratih shikshapadam samadiyami (Skt.). The vow to refrain from lying; the third of the five precepts. *See also* appendix 3, under *The Five Precepts* (chapter 21).

mudra (Skt.). Symbol; ritual hand gesture.

nagas (Skt.). Snakelike beings associated with jewel treasures and knowledge, considered to be guardians of the prajnaparamita teachings.

Nagarjuna (second to third century CE). A great Indian teacher of Buddhism, the founder of the madhyamaka school of Buddhist philosophy. He contributed greatly to the logical development of the doctrine of shunyata and was the author of many key texts. According to tradition, he was also the guru of various important Buddhist teachers.

nama-rupa (Skt.). Name and form; fourth of the twelve nidanas, represented by the person in a boat. *See also* appendix 3, under *The Twelve Nidanas* (chapter 9).

nampar mitokpa (Tib.: rnam par mi rtog pa). Complete nonconceptualization.

nampar shiwar chepa (Tib.: rnam par zhi bar byed pa). Thoroughly pacifying. The seventh of the nine stages of shamatha. *See also* appendix 3, under *The Nine Techniques of Shamatha Practice* (chapter 31).

Naropa (1016–1100). An important scholar at Nalanda University in India, a powerful Buddhist saint, or *mahasiddha,* and one of the founding teachers of the Kagyü lineage. The teacher of Marpa, who brought many of Naropa's teachings and practices to Tibet.

ne-ngen len-gyi gyu (Tib.: gnas ngan len gyi rgyu). The seed of entering into the lower realms. Cutting this seed marks one's entry into the middle path of accumulation.

neten (Tib.: gnas brtan). Elder, or learned one.

nga-gyal (Tib.: nga rgyal). Pride. *See also* appendix 3, under *The Six Root Kleshas* (chapter 55).

ngak (Tib.: ngag). Speech.

ngejung (Tib.: nges 'byung). Renunciation.

ngelek (Tib.: nges legs). Final good; experience beyond samsara.

ngepar shepa (Tib.: nges par shes pa). True or complete conviction.

ngöpo tsölwa (Tib.: dngos po 'tshol ba). Discovery of objects of inside and outside. Second of the six discoveries of vipashyana. *See also* appendix 3, under *The Six Discoveries* (chapter 48).

nidanas, twelve (Skt.). Chain of causation. The twelve links of interdependent origination: ignorance, formation, consciousness, name and form, six sense faculties, contact, feeling, craving, grasping, becoming, birth, and old age and death. The twelve links of mutually conditioned psychological and physical phenomena that constitute individual existence, and entangle sentient beings in samsara.

nirmanakaya (Skt.; Tib.: tülku; sprul sku). Emanation body. *See also* kayas, three.

nirodha (Skt.; Tib.: gokpa; 'gog pa). Cessation.

nirvana (Skt.; Tib.: nya-ngen ledepa; mya ngan las 'das pa). Extinguished. The Tibetan translation of this word means "gone beyond suffering," a state of no more suffering achieved when one is enlightened; used in contrast to samsara.

nonreturners. Those who in their next life do not return to the world of samsara.

nyam (Tib.: nyams). Temporary experiences. *See also* appendix 3, under *Three Fundamental Nyams* and *Five Basic Nyams* (chapter 42).

nyampar jokpa (Tib.: mnyam par 'jog pa). Resting evenly. Ninth of the nine stages of shamatha. *See also* appendix 3, under *The Nine Techniques of Shamatha Practice* (chapter 31).

nya-ngen ledepa shiwa (Tib.: mya ngan las 'das pa zhi ba). Going beyond suffering, or nirvana, is peace; the fourth of the four marks of existence.

nyen-ne (Tib.: bsnyen gnas; Skt.: upavasa / upavasi). A male or female householder who takes vows for one day at a time; a discipline generally connected with fasting practice. The first category of "soso-tharpist." *See also* appendix 3, under *Four Levels of Students* (chapter 61).

nyenthö (Tib.: nyan thos). Listening and hearing; a shravaka.

nyewar jokpa (Tib.: nye bar 'jog pa). Closely or thoroughly resting. The fourth of the nine stages of shamatha. *See also* appendix 3, under *The Nine Techniques of Shamatha Practice* (chapter 31).

Nyingma (Tib.: rnying ma). The ancient ones. The oldest of the four principal schools of Tibetan Buddhism, focusing on the early transmission of Buddhist teachings brought from India to Tibet by Padmasambhava and monks and scholars such as Vimalamitra and Vairochana in the eighth century.

nyönmong (Tib.: nyon mongs; Skt.: klesha). Defilement or conflicting emotions. *See also* klesha.

nyönmong künjung (Tib.: nyon mongs kun 'byung). Origin of suffering in terms of conflicting emotions or kleshas.

nyönmong kyi drippa (Tib.: nyon mongs kyi sgrib pa). The obscuration of defilements, or conflicting emotions, brought about from pakchak kyi drippa, or habitual tendencies.

nyön-yi (Tib.: nyon yid). Seventh consciousness; klesha mind, or afflicted mind. The mental consciousness that possesses the kleshas.

once-returners. Those who return to the world of samsara for just one more lifetime.

oryoki (Jpn.). A Zen Buddhist practice of mindful eating. The ritual of eating meals in a shrine room.

Padma Sambhava (eighth century). "The lotus born." Also known as Guru Rinpoche. One of the founders of the Tibetan Buddhist tradition revered by the Nyingma school as the "second Buddha."

pagyö (Tib.: bag yod). Heedfulness, conscientiousness, attentiveness.

pakchak kyi drippa (Tib.: bag chags kyi sgrib pa). Obscuration of habitual tendencies; flickering thoughts.

pakpheppa (Tib.: bag pheb pa). Relaxation.

pancha-shila (Skt.). Five precepts.

paramitas (Skt.; Tib.: pharchen; phar phyin). Perfection; in Tibetan, "gone to the far shore." The six paramitas are the transcendent virtues of generosity, discipline, patience, exertion, meditation, and prajna (knowledge).

Patrül Rinpoche (1808–1887). A leading teacher in the Nyingma tradition. Author of *The Words of My Perfect Teacher,* one of the best-loved introductions to the foundations of Tibetan Buddhism.

postmeditation. Follow-up to formal sitting practice. Bringing the practice of mindfulness and awareness into all the activities of one's daily life.

prajna (Skt.; Tib.: sherap; shes rab). Perfect knowledge, meaning wisdom, understanding, or discrimination. Higher prajna is dharmic insight. Ordinary prajna is understanding the world and how things work on a mundane level; in the beginning of the path, higher prajna encompasses direct experience of the mind and its processes; in later stages, it encompasses penetrating insight that discovers both the world and the self to be illusory. Along with shila and samadhi, one of three key principles for the hinayana path. *See also* appendix 3, under *Contents of All Saddharma* (chapter 4).

prana (Skt.; Tib.: lung; rlung). Wind, air, or breath.

pranatipata-viratih shikshapadam samadiyami (Skt.). The vow to refrain from killing; first of the five precepts. *See also* appendix 3, under *The Five Precepts* (chapter 21).

pratimoksha (Tib.: soso tharpa; so so thar pa). Buddhist disciplinary vows for monastics found in the vinaya. *See also* vinaya; Tripitaka.

pratyekabuddha (Skt.). Solitary realizer. A term for a person who has realized one-and-a-half-fold egolessness (egolessness of self and a partial realization of the egolessness of phenomena) due to insight into dependent arising, without relying on a teacher. *See also* appendix 3, under *The Nine Yanas* (chapter 7) and *Two Types of Pratyekabuddhas* (chapter 62).

pratyekabuddhayana (Skt.). The path of the "solitary realizer" of the hinayana. *See also* appendix 3, under *The Nine Yanas* (chapter 7).

pure land of Amitabha (Skt.: Sukhavati). "The blissful." The western buddha field reigned over by Amitabha, the buddha of boundless light. One can be reborn there and lead a blissful life. A state of mind in which teachings flourish; a place where the practice of buddhadharma comes naturally and easily.

raptu jepa (Tib.: rab tu 'byed pa). Fully able to separate. Second category of vipashyana. *See also* appendix 3, under *Four Categories of Vipashyana* (chapter 47).

refuge vow. The vow marking one's formal entry into the Buddhist path, and one's commitment to the Buddha, the dharma, and the sangha.

rikpa (Tib.: rig pa). Insight; awareness; intelligence.

rikpa denpa (Tib.: rig pa ldan pa). Learned one; an epithet for the Buddha.

rikpa trungpo (Tib.: rig pa grung po). One who has a clever mind.

rikpa tsölwa.(Tib.: rig pa 'tshol ba). The discovery of insight, the sixth discovery of vipasyhana. *See also* appendix 3, under *The Six Discoveries* (chapter 48).

rikpar shukpa (Tib.: rig pa zhugs pa). Entering with wakefulness; a quality of the sangha.

rinpoche (Tib.: rin po che). Precious one; synonym for jewel. An honorific title for a teacher, particularly an incarnate lama, or tülku.

ritröpa (Tib.: ri khrod pa). Among mountains; a term for hermit.

ro-nyam (Tib.: ro mnyam). Equal taste. Second of the three stages of vipashyana. *See also* appendix 3, under *Three Stages of Vipashyana* (chapter 46).

roshi (Jpn.). Elder / teacher.

saddharma (Tib.: tam-pe chö; dam pa'i chos). True dharma; truth or suchness.

sak-che tham-che dug-ngalwa (Tib.: zag bcas thams cad sdug bsngal ba). The continuing wretchedness of all experience contaminated by the kleshas. As the second of the four marks of existence, the ongoing suffering resulting from the futility of creating anything permanent.

samadhi (Skt.; Tib.: tingdzin; ting 'dzin). One-pointed meditative concentration; absorption.

sambhogakaya (Skt.; Tib.: longku; longs sku). Enjoyment body. *See also* kayas, three.

sambuddha (Skt.). Completely pure, perfect Buddha.

sampa (Tib.: bsam pa). Contemplation. *See also* appendix 3, under *The Three Ways of Learning* (chapter 63).

samsara (Skt.). Cyclic existence; the continual repetitive cycle of birth and death that arises from ordinary beings' grasping and fixating on a self and experiences. All states of consciousness in the six realms, including the god realms, are bound by this process. Samsara arises out of ignorance and is characterized by suffering. *See also* appendix 3, under *Three Categories of Samsara* (chapter 56).

samskara (Skt.; Tib.: du-je; 'du byed). Formation; concept. The fourth of the five skandhas; also, the second of the twelve nidanas, represented by a potter's wheel. Fifty-one samskaras, or mental events, are included within the fourth skandha.

samten (Tib.: bsam gtan; Skt.: dhyana). Meditative stabilization, concentration.

samudaya (Skt.). Giving birth to suffering, the natural instinctive yearning toward pain. *See also* künjung.

samvara (Skt.; Tib.: dompa; sdom pa). "Binding." Bound to the discipline and to practice. *See also* dompa.

samyaksambuddha (Skt.; Tib.: yangdakpar dzok-pe sang-gye; yang dag par rdzogs pa'i sangs rgyas). Fully and completely awakened; an epithet of the Buddha.

sang-gye (Tib.: sangs rgyas). *See* buddha.

sangha (Skt.). Community. The third of the three jewels of refuge. In the hinayana, sangha refers specifically to Buddhist monks and nuns. In the mahayana, the sangha also includes lay practitioners. As an object of refuge, "noble sangha" may refer to the assembly of bodhisattvas and arhats, those who have attained realization.

Satipatthana Sutra (Pali). *Discourse on the Foundations of Mindfulness.* Originally in the Pali canon, this sutra is found in various forms in most major Buddhist schools.

selwa (Tib.: gsal ba). Clear; clarity. One of the three fundamental nyams (temporary experiences). *See also* appendix 3, under *Three Fundamental Nyams* (chapter 42).

sem (Tib.: sems). Mind.

sem jokpa (Tib.: sems 'jog pa). Placement; resting the mind. First of the nine stages of shamatha. *See also* appendix 3, under *The Nine Techniques of Shamatha Practice* (chapter 31).

semjung (Tib.: sems byung). The fifty-one mental events. *See also* samskara.

serna (Tib.: ser sna). Miserliness; avarice. *See also* appendix 3, under *The Six Root Kleshas* (chapter 55).

setting sun. An expression coined by Chögyam Trungpa and used in the Shambhala teachings. It is any attitude, thought, or action that leads one to degraded behavior.

shadayatana (Skt.). The six sense faculties; fifth of the twelve nidanas, represented by the six-windowed house. *See also* appendix 3, under *The Twelve Nidanas* (chapter 9).

shamatha (Skt.; Tib.: shi-ne; zhi gnas). Peaceful abiding. Mindfulness practice. The practice of taming and stabilizing the mind. The central practice of the hinayana path and a key component of the practice tradition throughout all three yanas.

shamatha-vipashyana (Skt.). The union of mindfulness and awareness, in which the concentration, stillness, and precision of shamatha is in harmonious balance with the expansiveness, inquisitiveness, and clarity of awareness practice.

Shambhala vision. A reference to Trungpa Rinpoche's teachings on the sacred path of the warrior and the creation of enlightened society. Shambhala teachings are closely connected with the Buddhist meditative tradition, but have a more secular and societal focus. For more on this tradition, see

Shambhala: The Sacred Path of the Warrior, by Chögyam Trungpa (Boston: Shambhala Publications, 2007).

shapsu denpa (Tib.: zhabs su ldan pa). One who is able to walk on the path; an epithet of the Buddha.

shastra (Skt.). Commentary on the Buddha's teachings written by students of the Buddha and by scholars and practitioners of Buddhism.

shedang (Tib.: zhe sdang). Aggression / anger; a klesha. *See also* appendix 3, under *The Six Root Kleshas* (chapter 55).

shepa (Tib.: shes pa). Consciousness.

sherap (Tib.: shes rap; Skt.: prajna). Knowledge.

sheshin (Tib.: shes bzhin). Presently knowing; awareness; literally, "knowing just as it is."

shikantaza (Jpn.). Formless Zen meditation practice with no technique, just sitting. A state of alert attention free from thoughts that is considered to be the purest form of practice.

shila (Skt.; Tib.: tsültrim; tshul khrims). Discipline; noble character, morality or good conduct. *See also* appendix 3, under *Contents of All Saddharma* (chapter 4); *Three Key Principles of Hinayana Understanding* (chapter 3).

shi-ne (Tib.: zhi gnas; Skt.: shamatha). Peaceful abiding. Mindfulness practice. The practice of taming and stabilizing the mind.

shinjang (Tib.: shin sbyang). Thoroughly processed or trained through meditation practice. Refers to the flexibility and serviceability of the mind to focus on whatever object of meditation is chosen. It is an overall state of well-being and ease, and is the result of shamatha practice.

shiwa (Tib.: zhi ba). Peace.

shiwar chepa (Tib.: zhi bar byed pa). Pacifying. Sixth of the nine stages of shamatha. *See also* appendix 3, under *The Nine Techniques of Shamatha Practice* (chapter 31).

shramanera / shramanerika (f) (Skt.; Tib.: getsül / getsülma; dge tshul / dge tshul ma). Novice monk / nun who has taken the ten basic monastic vows.

shravaka. One who hears, a practitioner of the shravakayana.

shravakayana (Skt.; Tib.: nyenthö; nyan thos). The path of the "hearer" of the hinayana. *See also* appendix 3, under *The Nine Yanas* (chapter 7).

shunya (Skt.). Empty. *See also* shunyata.

shunyata (Skt.). Emptiness. A completely open and unbounded clarity of mind characterized by groundlessness and freedom from all conceptual frameworks. Emptiness does not mean voidness or blankness, but an openness that is inseparable from compassion and all other awakened qualities.

six realms. Realms of samsaric existence. The three lower realms of hell beings, hungry ghosts, and animals; and the three higher realms of humans, jealous gods, and gods. *See also* appendix 3, under *The Inner Ring: The Six Realms* (chapter 9).

skandha (Skt.; Tib.: phungpo; phung po). Heap or basket; aggregate. The five skandhas describe the aggregates or collection of phenomena that we take to be a self. The five aggregates are form, feeling, perception / impulse, concept / formation, and consciousness. *See also* in appendix 3, under *The Development of Set Patterns* (chapter 54); *The Five Skandhas* (chapter 2); *The Four Maras* (chapter 13); and *Two Types of Alaya* (chapter 37).

skandha-mara (Skt.). Solidifying the belief in the five skandhas, or components of ego. The third of the four maras. *See also* appendix 3, under *The Four Maras* (chapter 13).

sönam kyi palgyi shing (Tib.: bsod nams kyi dpal gyi zhing). Glorious field of merit; a quality of sangha.

soso tharpa (Tib.: so so thar pa; Skt.: pratimoksha). Individual liberation. A practitioner of this path is called a "soso-tharpist."

sparsha (Skt.). Contact; sixth of the twelve nidanas, represented by the married couple. *See also* appendix 3, under *The Twelve Nidanas* (chapter 9).

sthavira (Skt.; Pali: thera). Elder.

stream winner. One who has entered the realm of discipline that leads to awakening.

sugata (Skt.; Tib.: dewar shekpa; bde bar gsheg pa). One who has gone beyond with joy; a buddha.

Sukhavati. *See* pure land of Amitabha.

sura-maireya-madyapana-viratih-shikshapadam samadiyami (Skt.). The vow to refrain from taking intoxicants; fifth of the five precepts. *See also* appendix 3, under *The Five Precepts* (chapter 21).

sutra (Skt.; Tib.: do; mdo). Thread, string, cord. Sutras are hinayana and mahayana texts in the Buddhist canon that are attributed to the Buddha. *Sutra* means a meeting point or junction, referring to the meeting of the Buddha's enlightenment and the student's understanding. A sutra is usually a dialogue between the Buddha and one or more of his disciples, thus elaborating a particular topic of dharma.

Sutra of the Recollection of the Noble Three Jewels (Skt.: *Arya-ratnatraya-anusmriti sutra*). A sutra on the qualities of the Buddha, dharma, and sangha studied in many schools of Tibetan Buddhism.

tagjor (Tib.: rtag sbyor). Continuity of practice.

Tag-ngu (Tib.: rtag ngu; Skt.: Sadaprarudita). The bodhisattva who cries continually.

tang-nyom (Tib.: btang snyoms). Equanimity, equilibrium. Evenness and a lack of bias toward any and all phenomena.

tantrayana (Skt.). Also referred to as tantra. A term often used as a synonym for vajrayana, the third of the three yanas or vehicles. *Tantra* means continuity, and refers both to the root texts of the vajrayana and to the systems of meditation they describe.

tathagata (Skt.; Tib.: teshin shekpa; de bzhin gshegs pa). Thus come or thus gone; an epithet for the Buddha.

tathagatagarbha (Skt.; Tib.: teshek nyingpo; de gshegs snying po). Buddha nature; the intrinsic state of wakefulness inherent in all human beings.

ten evil acts. Acts of unmeritorious karma arising from aggression. *See also* appendix 3, under *Unmeritorious Karma* (chapter 55).

ten meritorious deeds. Acts that are meritorious, but still perpetuate karma. The reverse of the ten evil acts. *See also* appendix 3, under *Meritorious Karma* (chapter 55).

tepa (Tib.: dad pa). Faith, conviction; feeling steady and confident in the path, and knowing what to cultivate and what to avoid.

teshin mikpa (Tib.: de bzhin dmigs pa). Seeing things as they are; mahavipashyana experience. Third of the three stages of vipashyana. *See also* appendix 3, under *Three Stages of Vipashyana* (chapter 46).

teshin shekpa (Tib.: de bzhin gshegs pa; Skt.: tathagata). Thus come or thus gone; an epithet for the Buddha.

thalmo jar-we ösu kyurpa (Tib.: thal mo sbyar ba'i 'os su gyur pa). Worthy of veneration with joined palms.

tharpa (Tib.: thar pa; Skt.: moksha). Liberation or salvation.

thekchung (Tib.: theg chung; Skt.: hinayana). Lesser or smaller vehicle. A more standard Tibetan term for the hinayana is *thegman* (theg dman).

thonglam (Tib.: mthong lam). Path of seeing. Third of the five paths. *See also* appendix 3, under *The Five Paths* (chapter 60).

thöpa (Tib.: thos pa). Hearing. *See also* appendix 3, under *The Three Ways of Learning* (chapter 63).

three gates. Gates that make it possible to enter into discipline: body, speech, and mind.

three jewels. The Buddha, the dharma, and the sangha. Also called the "triple gem."

three marks. Three qualities of samsaric existence: suffering, impermanence, and egolessness.

three worlds. The world of desire, the world of form, and the formless world. The world of desire includes all six realms, with the exception of a portion of the god realm. The form and formless worlds are progressively more subtle forms of god realm. *See also* six realms.

threefold logic. A way of studying the teachings by analyzing material in terms of ground, path, and fruition. *See also* appendix 2.

thünpar shukpa (Tib.: mthun par zhugs pa). Entering harmoniously; a quality of the sangha.

timuk (Tib.: gti mug; Skt.: moha). Bewilderment; emotional dullness; ignorance. One of six root kleshas. Not to be confused with fundamental ignorance, or avidya. *See also* appendix 3, under *The Six Root Kleshas* (chapter 55).

tingdzin (Tib.: ting 'dzin; Skt.: samadhi). One-pointed meditation; a state of consciousness where mental activity ceases; total absorption in the object of meditation. *See also* samadhi.

tokpa (Tib.: rtog pa). Understanding. *See also* eightfold path.

tön tsölwa (Tib.: don 'tshol ba). Discovering the meaning of the words. First of the six discoveries of vipashyana. *See also* appendix 3, under *The Six Discoveries* (chapter 48).

töndam (Tib.: don dam). Absolute truth; ultimate nature; superior understanding. Contrasted with relative truth, or kündzop, in the teaching of the "two truths." *See also* kündzop.

torma (Tib.: gtor ma). Ritual barley cake used in vajrayana feast practice.

tragdok (Tib.: phrag dog). Envy, jealousy. *See also* appendix 3, under *The Six Root Kleshas* (chapter 55).

trangpor shukpa (Tib.: drang por zhugs pa). Entering straightforwardly; a quality of the sangha.

trenpa (Tib.: dran pa; Skt.: smriti). Mindfulness, recollection. The third of the four legs of miracle. *See also* appendix 3, under *The Four Legs of Miracle* (chapter 65).

tren-she (Tib.: dran shes). Recollection and knowing; mindfulness and awareness. The union of trenpa and sheshin. *See also* sheshin; trenpa.

Tripitaka (Skt.). "Three Baskets." The canon of Buddhist scriptures, consisting of three parts: the Vinaya-pitaka, the Sutra-pitaka, and the Abhidharma-pitaka. The first "basket" (Vinaya-pitaka) contains accounts of the origins of the Buddhist sangha as well as the rules of discipline regulating the lives of monks and nuns. The second (Sutra-pitaka) is composed of Buddha's general discourses and in particular those that focus on meditation. The third (Abhidharma-pitaka) is a compendium of Buddhist psychology and philosophy.

triratna (Skt.). Three jewels: Buddha, dharma, sangha.

trishna (Skt.). Craving; the eighth of the twelve nidanas, represented by milk and honey. *See also* appendix 3, under *The Twelve Nidanas* (chapter 9).

trö (Tib.: drod; Skt.: ushman). Heat; an increasing degree of realization. One of the four types of discrimination. *See also* appendix 3, page 571, under *Four Types of Discrimination*

tsang-pe thekpa (Tib.: tshangs pa'i theg pa; Skt.: brahmayana). Complete or pure vehicle; binding with discipline.

tsechik tu chepa (Tib.: rtse gcig tu byed pa). One-pointedness. Eighth of the nine stages of shamatha. *See also* appendix 3, under *The Nine Techniques of Shamatha Practice* (chapter 31).

tsemo (Tib.: rtse mo). Peak. One of the four types of discrimination. *See also* appendix 3, under *Four Types of Discrimination* (chapter 66).

tsen-nyi tsölwa (Tib.: mtshan nyid 'tshol ba). Discovery of nature: refers to how things are categorized according to their own individual existence. Third of the six discoveries of vipashyana. *See also* appendix 3, under *The Six Discoveries* (chapter 48).

tsoglam (Tib.: tshogs lam). Path of accumulation. *See also* appendix 3, under *The Five Paths* (chapter 60).

tsölwa (Tib.: rtsol wa). Effort.

tsöndrü (Tib.: brtson 'grus; Skt.: virya). Exertion. The second of the four legs of miracle. *See also* appendix 3, under *The Four Legs of Miracle* (chapter 65).

tsowa (Tib.: 'tsho ba). Survival, sustenance, livelihood. *See also* appendix 3, under *The Four Foundations of Mindfulness* (chapter 39) and *The Noble Eightfold Path* (chapter 60).

tsültrim (Tib.: tshul khrims; Skt.: shila). Discipline; proper conduct.

tü tsölwa (Tib.: dus 'tshol ba). Discovering time; not being confused by time. Fifth of the six discoveries of vipashyana. *See also* appendix 3, under *The Six Discoveries* (chapter 48).

tüdro (Tib.: dud 'gro). Animal; literally, "to walk bent over."

tülshuk (Tib.: brtul zhugs). Yogic discipline.

twofold ego. The ego of self, or individuality, and the ego of phenomena, or dharmas.

upadana (Skt.). Grasping; the ninth of the twelve nidanas, represented by gathering fruit. *See also* appendix 3, under *The Twelve Nidanas* (chapter 9).

upadhyaya (Skt.; Tib.: khenpo; mkhan po). Preceptor or elder.

upasaka / upasika (f) (Skt.). Those who have taken the refuge vow; those who practice virtue. *See also* genyen.

upaya (Skt.; Tib.: thap; thabs). Method or skillful means.

uttara (Skt.; Tib.: lama; bla ma). What is above, upper; superior.

vajra (Skt.; Tib.: dorje; rdo rje). Ritual scepter, used in tantric practice. The term *vajra* means "indestructible," or "adamantine." According to Indian mythology, the vajra was the scepter of Indra, the king of the gods. It was such a powerful weapon that it could destroy anything, and having once destroyed, it would return to his hand. This weapon was indestructible because it could not in any way be cracked, bent, or destroyed.

vajracharya (Skt.). Holder of the vajra. An empowered teacher.

vajrayana (Skt.; Tib.: dorje thekpa; rdo rje theg pa). The indestructible or adamantine vehicle. Also referred to as tantra or tantrayana. The third of the three stages of the path (hinayana, mahayana, and vajrayana).

vedana (Skt.). Feeling; seventh of the twelve nidanas, represented by the arrow through the eye. *See also* appendix 3, under *The Twelve Nidanas* (chapter 9).

vidya (Tib.: rikpa; rig pa). Knowledge.

vidyadhara. Knowledge holder. An honorific title for Chögyam Trungpa, who in the latter years of his teaching was referred to as "the Vidyadhara." In earlier years, he was referred to as "the Vajracharya."

vijnana (Skt.; Tib.: nam-she; rnam shes). Consciousness; the fifth skandha. Also, the third of the twelve nidanas, represented by the monkey.

vinaya (Skt.; Tib.: dülwa; 'dul ba). Monastic vows, discipline.

vipashyana (Skt.; Tib.: lhakthong; lhag mthong). Awareness. In Tibetan, it is "higher" or "superior" seeing. Insight arising from direct meditative experience or contemplative analysis. An open expansive quality of meditative practice complementary to the stability and groundedness of shamatha.

virya (Skt.; Tib.: tsöndrü; brston 'grus). Exertion.

Visuddhimagga (Pali). *The Path of Purification*. An important exposition of the core teachings of the Theravada school composed by the scholar-monk Buddhaghosa in the fifth century.

Yama (Skt.). The Lord of Death, depicted as holding the wheel of life.

yama-mara (Skt.). Fear of death and the possibility of death. One of the four maras; also referred to as mrityu-mara. *See also* appendix 3, under *The Four Maras* (chapter 13).

yana (Skt.). Path or vehicle that carries the practitioner to liberation.

yang-dak-pe lekyi tha (Tib.: yang dag pa'i las kyi mtha'). Perfect end of karma. *See also* appendix 3, under *The Noble Eightfold Path* (chapter 60).

yang-dak-pe ngak (Tib.: yang dag pa'i ngag). Perfect speech. *See also* appendix 3, under *The Noble Eightfold Path* (chapter 60).

yang-dak-pe tawa (Tib.: yang dag pa'i lta ba). Perfect view. *See also* appendix 3, under *The Noble Eightfold Path* (chapter 60).

yang-dak-pe tingdzin (Tib.: yang dag pa'i ting 'dzin). Perfect meditation. *See also* appendix 3, under *The Noble Eightfold Path* (chapter 60).

yang-dak-pe tokpa (Tib.: yang dag pa'i rtog pa). Perfect understanding. *See also* appendix 3, under *The Noble Eightfold Path* (chapter 60).

yang-dak-pe trenpa (Tib.: yang dag pa'i dran pa). Perfect recollection. *See also* appendix 3, under *The Noble Eightfold Path* (chapter 60).

yang-dak-pe tsölwa (Tib.: yang dag pa'i rtsol wa). Perfect effort. *See also* appendix 3, under *The Noble Eightfold Path* (chapter 60).

yang-dak-pe tsowa (Tib.: yang dag pa'i 'tsho ba). Perfect livelihood. *See also* appendix 3, under *The Noble Eightfold Path* (chapter 60).

yi (Tib.: yid). An aspect of mind traditionally known as the sixth or mental consciousness, shortened from *yikyi nampar shepa* (Tib.: *yid kyi nam par shes pa*). Yi also can refer to the seventh consciousness, or nyön-yi.

yi la shak (Tib.: yid la bzhag). Literally, "rest in the mind." Ability to rest the mind on whatever the subject matter may be.

yidam (Tib.: yi dam). Deity. That which binds the mind to wisdom.

ying rik sewa (Tib.: dbyings rig bsre ba). Mixing mind with space.

yön yongsu jongwa chenpo (Tib.: yon yongs su sbyong ba chen po). Completely capable of receiving all gifts; a quality of the sangha.

yongsu chöpa (Tib.: yongs su dpyod pa). Completely investigating. Fourth category of vipashyana. *See also* appendix 3, under *Four Categories of Vipashyana* (chapter 47).

yongsu tokpa (Tib.: yongs su rtog pa). Completely comprehending. Third category of vipashyana. *See also* appendix 3, under under *Four Categories of Vipashyana* (chapter 47).

yul la sem pena sem (Tib.: yul la sems pas na sems). A definition of mind: "mind is that which thinks of an object."

zafu (Jpn.). A round meditation cushion.

SOURCES

THE MATERIAL in this volume is primarily taken from a series of programs taught by Chögyam Trungpa Rinpoche called Vajradhatu Seminaries. (See the Editor's Introduction for further information.) Thirteen Seminaries were held between 1973 and 1986, at the following locations:

1. 1973: Jackson Hole, Wyoming. September–November.
2. 1974: Snowmass Village, Colorado. September–November.
3. 1975: Snowmass Village, Colorado. September–November.
4. 1976: Land-O' Lakes, Wisconsin. September–November.
5. 1978: Dixville Notch, New Hampshire. March–May.
6. 1979: Lake Louise, Alberta, Canada. March–May.
7. 1980: Lake Louise, Alberta, Canada. January–March.
8. 1981: Lake Louise, Alberta, Canada. January–March.
9. 1982: Bedford Springs, Pennsylvania. January–April.
10. 1983: Bedford Springs, Pennsylvania. January–March.
11. 1984: Bedford Springs, Pennsylvania. January–March.
12. 1985: Shambhala Mountain Center, Colorado. June–August.
13. 1986: Shambhala Mountain Center, Colorado. June–August.

More details on the primary sources for each chapter are given below. When the source is a Vajradhatu Seminary, the talk name is given, followed by the year and the talk number.

PART ONE. ENTERING THE PATH
Encountering the Dharma

Chapter 1. Beginning at the Beginning
Summary of Hinayana 1976: 9

Tibetan Buddhism Class. University of Colorado, Boulder, Colorado. March 1973. *Karma and Rebirth: The Twelve Nidanas.*

Karma Seminar. Karmê Chöling, Barnet, Vermont. September 1972. *The Wheel of Life: Illusion's Game.*

Taking Refuge

Chapter 10. Buddhadharma Fever

Taking Refuge 1979: 7

Taking Refuge as Nontheistic Discipline 1980: 6

Individual Salvation and the Triratna 1980: 7

Humbleness Is the Dwelling Place of the Forefathers 1981: 6

Taking Refuge with an Attitude of Humbleness 1981: 7

Chapter 11. Taking Refuge in the Three Jewels

Taking Refuge: Buddha, Dharma 1976: 5

Taking Refuge: Sangha 1976: 6

Taking Refuge as Nontheistic Discipline 1980: 6

Individual Salvation and the Triratna 1980: 7

Reflecting on the Three Jewels

Chapter 12. The Sutra of the Recollection of the Noble Three Jewels
    Traditional text translated by the Nalanda Translation Committee

Chapter 13. The Buddha

The Meaning of Buddha: Sang-Gye 1982: 4

The Epithets of Buddha 1982: 5

The Learned and Virtuous One 1982: 6

The Qualities of Buddha 1982: 7

Chapter 14. The Dharma

The Qualities of Dharma 1982: 8

Chapter 15. The Sangha

The Qualities of Sangha 1982: 9

PART TWO. DISCIPLINE / SHILA

Taming Neurosis

Cultivating Virtue

PART THREE. MEDITATION / SAMADHI

Shamatha: The Practice of Mindfulness

Note: chapters in the Shamatha section that are followed by an asterisk are fusions of material from the following talks: (a) *Introduction to Practice Talks: 1975: 1, 1975: 10, 1976: 1, 1979: 1, 1980: 1, 1984: 1, 1985: 1;* (b) *Meditation Talks: 1973: 1, 1978: 1, 1980: 4, 1981: 1, 1983: 1, 1985: 4;* (c) *Shamatha Talks: 1974: 1, 1974: 2, 1974: 3, 1979: 2, 1981: 4, 1983: 2, 1983: 3, 1983: 7.*

Refining Your Shamatha Practice

Working with the Mind

Chapter 38. Mixing Mind with Space

First Foundation: Mindfulness of Body 1973: 4

Techniques of Mindfulness Seminar. Karmê Chöling, Barnet, Vermont. August 1974. *Talk 2.*

The Four Foundations of Mindfulness

Chapter 39. Mindfulness of Body

First Foundation: Mindfulness of Body 1973: 4

Chapter 40. Mindfulness of Life

Second Foundation: Mindfulness of Livelihood 1973: 5

Techniques of Mindfulness Seminar. Karmê Chöling, Barnet, Vermont. August 1974. *Talk 3.*

Chapter 41. Mindfulness of Effort

Third Foundation: Liveliness of Effort 1973: 6

Techniques of Mindfulness Seminar. Karmê Chöling, Barnet, Vermont. August 1974. *Talk 4.*

Chapter 42. Mindfulness of Mind

Fourth Foundation: Mindfulness of Mind 1973: 7

Techniques of Mindfulness Seminar. Karmê Chöling, Barnet, Vermont. August 1974. *Talk 5.*

Vipashyana: The Practice of Awareness

Chapter 43. The Freshness of Unconditional Mind

Comparison of Vipashyana with Shamatha 1973: 9

Chapter 44. Beyond Picking and Choosing

Vipashyana Awareness: Allowing the Gap 1981: 5

Chapter 45. The Art of Everyday Living

Art in Everyday Life 1973: 10

Chapter 46. Glimpses of Emptiness

Categories of Vipashyana 1974: 13

Chapter 47. Investigating the Subtleties of Experience

Four Categories of Vipashyana 1979: 6

PART FOUR. THE FOUR NOBLE TRUTHS

Suffering

The Origin of Suffering

The Cessation of Suffering

The Truth of the Path

PART FIVE. THE HINAYANA JOURNEY

The Journey in Terms of Yanas

The Journey in Terms of Paths

PART SIX. KNOWLEDGE / PRAJNA
Unraveling the Myth of Ego

RESOURCES

PRACTICE CENTERS

For information about meditation instruction or to find a Shambhala-affiliated practice center near you, please contact one of the following:

Shambhala International
1084 Tower Road
Halifax, Nova Scotia
Canada B3H 2Y5
phone: (902) 425-4275, ext. 10
website: www.shambhala.org

Karmê Chöling
369 Patneaude Lane
Barnet, Vermont 05821
phone: (802) 633-2384
website: www.karmecholing.org

Shambhala Mountain Center
4921 Country Road 68C
Red Feather Lakes, Colorado
80545
phone: (970) 881-2184
website: www.shambhala
mountain.org

Gampo Abbey
Pleasant Bay, Nova Scotia
Canada B0E 2P0
phone: (902) 224-2752
website: www.gampoabbey.org

Dechen Choling
Mas Marvent
87700 St. Yrieix sous Aixe
France
phone: +33 5-55-03-55-52
website: www.dechencholing.org

Dorje Denma Ling
2280 Balmoral Road
Tatamagouche, Nova Scoti
Canada B0K 1V0
phone: (902) 657-9085
website: http://dorjedenmaling.org
e-mail: info@dorjedenmaling.com

NAROPA UNIVERSITY

Naropa University is the only accredited, Buddhist-inspired university in North America. For more information, contact:

Naropa University
2130 Arapahoe Avenue
Boulder, Colorado 80302
phone: (303) 444-0202
website: www.naropa.edu

OCEAN OF DHARMA QUOTES OF THE WEEK

Ocean of Dharma Quotes of the Week brings you the teachings of Chögyam Trungpa Rinpoche. An e-mail is sent out several times each week containing a quote from Chögyam Trungpa's extensive teachings. Quotations of material may be from unpublished material, forthcoming publications, or previously published sources. Ocean of Dharma Quotes of the Week are selected by Carolyn Rose Gimian. To enroll go to OceanofDharma.com.

THE CHÖGYAM TRUNGPA LEGACY PROJECT

The Chögyam Trungpa Legacy Project was established to help preserve, disseminate, and expand Chögyam Trungpa's legacy. The Legacy Project supports the preservation, propagation, and publication of Trungpa Rinpoche's dharma teachings. This includes plans for the creation of a comprehensive virtual archive and learning community. For information, go to ChogyamTrungpa.com.

SHAMBHALA MEDIA

For publications from Vajradhatu Publications and Kalapa Recordings, including both books and audiovisual materials, go to www.shambhalamedia.org.

SHAMBHALA ARCHIVES

For information about the archive of the author's work, please contact the Shambhala Archives: archives@shambhala.org.

ABOUT THE AUTHOR

THE VENERABLE Chögyam Trungpa Rinpoche was born in the province of Kham in eastern Tibet in 1940. When he was just thirteen months old, Chögyam Trungpa was recognized as a major tulku, or incarnate teacher. According to Tibetan tradition, an enlightened teacher is capable, based on his or her vow of compassion, of reincarnating in human form over a succession of generations. Before dying, such a teacher may leave a letter or other clues to the whereabouts of the next incarnation. Later, students and other realized teachers look through these clues and, based on those, plus a careful examination of dreams and visions, conduct searches to discover and recognize the successor. Thus, particular lines of teaching are formed, in some cases extending over many centuries. Chögyam Trungpa was the eleventh in the teaching lineage known as the Trungpa Tulkus.

Once young tulkus are recognized, they enter a period of intensive training in the theory and practice of the Buddhist teachings. Trungpa Rinpoche, after being enthroned as supreme abbot of Surmang Dütsi Tel Monastery and governor of Surmang District, began a period of training that would last eighteen years, until his departure from Tibet in 1959. As a Kagyü tulku, his training was based on the systematic practice of meditation and on refined theoretical understanding of Buddhist philosophy. One of the four great lineages of Tibet, the Kagyü is known as the Practicing (or Practice) Lineage.

At the age of eight, Trungpa Rinpoche received ordination as a novice monk. Following this, he engaged in intensive study and practice of the traditional monastic disciplines, including traditional Tibetan poetry and monastic dance. His primary teachers were Jamgön Kongtrül of Shechen and Khenpo Gangshar—leading teachers in the Nyingma and Kagyü lineages. In 1958, at the age of eighteen, Trungpa Rinpoche completed his studies, receiving the degrees of kyorpön (doctor of divinity) and khenpo (master of studies). He also received full monastic ordination.

The late fifties was a time of great upheaval in Tibet. As it became clear that the Chinese Communists intended to take over the country by force, many people, both monastic and lay, fled the country. Trungpa Rinpoche spent many harrowing months trekking over the Himalayas (described later in his book *Born in Tibet*). After narrowly escaping capture by the Chinese, he at last reached India in 1959. While in India, Trungpa Rinpoche was appointed to serve as spiritual adviser to the Young Lamas Home School in Delhi, India. He served in this capacity from 1959 to 1963.

Trungpa Rinpoche's opportunity to emigrate to the West came when he received a Spalding sponsorship to attend Oxford University. At Oxford he studied comparative religion, philosophy, history, and fine arts. He also studied Japanese flower arranging, receiving a degree from the Sogetsu School. While in England, Trungpa Rinpoche began to instruct Western students in the dharma, and in 1967 he founded the Samye Ling Meditation Center in Dumfriesshire, Scotland. During this period, he also published his first two books, both in English: *Born in Tibet* (1966) and *Meditation in Action* (1969).

In 1968 Trungpa Rinpoche traveled to Bhutan, where he entered into a solitary meditation retreat. While on retreat, Rinpoche received a pivotal terma text for all of his teaching in the West, "The Sadhana of Mahamudra," a text that documents the spiritual degeneration of modern times and its antidote, genuine spirituality that leads to the experience of naked and luminous mind. This retreat marked a pivotal change in his approach to teaching. Soon after returning to England, he became a layperson, putting aside his monastic robes and dressing in ordinary Western attire. In 1970 he married a young Englishwoman, Diana Pybus, and together they left Scotland and moved to North America. Many of his early students and his Tibetan colleagues found these changes shocking and upsetting. However, he expressed a conviction that in order for the dharma to take root in the West, it needed to be taught free from cultural trappings and religious fascination.

During the seventies, America was in a period of political and cultural ferment. It was a time of fascination with the East. Nevertheless, almost from the moment he arrived in America, Trungpa Rinpoche drew many students to him who were seriously interested in the Buddhist teachings and the practice of meditation. However, he severely criticized the materialistic approach to spirituality that was also quite prevalent, describing it as a "spiritual supermarket." In his lectures, and in his books *Cutting Through Spiritual Materialism* (1973) and *The Myth of Freedom* (1976), he pointed to the simplicity and directness of the practice of sitting meditation as the way to cut through such distortions of the spiritual journey.

During his seventeen years of teaching in North America, Trungpa Rinpoche developed a reputation as a dynamic and controversial teacher. He was a pioneer, one of the first Tibetan Buddhist teachers in North America, preceding by some years and indeed facilitating the later visits by His Holiness the Karmapa, His Holiness Khyentse Rinpoche, His Holiness the Dalai Lama, and many others. In the United States, he found a spiritual kinship with many Zen masters, who were already presenting Buddhist meditation. In the very early days, he particularly connected with Suzuki Roshi, the founder of Zen Center in San Francisco. In later years he was close with Kobun Chino Roshi and Bill Kwong Roshi in Northern California; with Maezumi Roshi, the founder of the Los Angeles Zen Center; and with Eido Roshi, abbot of the New York Zendo Shobo-ji.

Fluent in the English language, Chögyam Trungpa was one of the first Tibetan Buddhist teachers who could speak to Western students directly, without the aid of a translator. Traveling extensively throughout North America and Europe, he gave thousands of talks and hundreds of seminars. He established major centers in Vermont, Colorado, and Nova Scotia, as well as many smaller meditation and study centers in cities throughout North America and Europe. Vajradhatu was formed in 1973 as the central administrative body of this network.

In 1974 Trungpa Rinpoche founded the Naropa Institute (now Naropa University), which became the first and only accredited Buddhist-inspired university in North America. He lectured extensively at the institute, and his book *Journey without Goal* (1981) is based on a course he taught there. In 1976 he established the Shambhala Training program, a series of seminars that present a nonsectarian path of spiritual warriorship grounded in the practice of sitting meditation. His book *Shambhala: The Sacred Path of the Warrior* (1984) gives an overview of the Shambhala teachings.

In 1976 Trungpa Rinpoche appointed Ösel Tendzin (Thomas F. Rich) as his Vajra Regent, or dharma heir. Ösel Tendzin worked closely with Trungpa Rinpoche in the administration of Vajradhatu and Shambhala Training. He taught extensively from 1976 until his death in 1990 and is the author of *Buddha in the Palm of Your Hand*.

Trungpa Rinpoche was also active in the field of translation. Working with Francesca Fremantle, he rendered a new translation of *The Tibetan Book of the Dead*, which was published in 1975. Later he formed the Nalanda Translation Committee in order to translate texts and liturgies for his own students as well as to make important texts available publicly.

In 1979 Trungpa Rinpoche conducted a ceremony empowering his eldest son, Ösel Rangdröl Mukpo, as his successor in the Shambhala lineage. At that time he gave him the title of Sawang ("Earth Lord").

Trungpa Rinpoche was also known for his interest in the arts and particularly for his insights into the relationship between contemplative discipline and the artistic process. Two books published since his death—*The Art of Calligraphy* (1994) and *Dharma Art* (1996) [a new edition appeared in 2008 under the title *True Perception: The Path of Dharma Art*]—present this aspect of his work. His own artwork included calligraphy, painting, flower arranging, poetry, playwriting, and environmental installations. In addition, at the Naropa Institute he created an educational atmosphere that attracted many leading artists and poets. The exploration of the creative process in light of contemplative training continues there as a provocative dialogue. Trungpa Rinpoche also published two books of poetry: *Mudra* (1972) and *First Thought Best Thought* (1983). In 1998 a retrospective compilation of his poetry, *Timely Rain*, was published.

Shortly before his death, in a meeting with Samuel Bercholz, the publisher of Shambhala Publications, Chögyam Trungpa expressed his interest in publishing 108 volumes of his teachings, to be called the Dharma Ocean Series. "Dharma Ocean" is the translation of Chögyam Trungpa's Tibetan teaching name, Chökyi Gyatso. The Dharma Ocean Series was to consist primarily of material edited to allow readers to encounter this rich array of teachings simply and directly rather than in an overly systematized or condensed form. In 1991 the first posthumous volume in the series, *Crazy Wisdom*, was published, and another seven volumes followed in the ensuing years. Carolyn Gimian gathered many of these published materials, along with a great number of preiously unpublished articles, into the eight-volume set *The Collected Works of Chögyam Trungpa*. Plans continue for many future volumes of his teachings to be published.

Trungpa Rinpoche's published books represent only a fraction of the rich legacy of his teachings. During his seventeen years of teaching in North America, he crafted the structures necessary to provide his students with thorough, systematic training in the dharma. From introductory talks and courses to advanced group retreat practices, these programs emphasized a balance of study and practice, of intellect and intuition. *Chögyam Trungpa* by Fabrice Midal, a biography, details the many forms of training that Chögyam Trungpa developed. *Dragon Thunder: My Life with Chögyam Trungpa*, is the story of Rinpoche's life as told by Diana Mukpo. This also provides insight into the many forms that he crafted for Buddhism in North America.

In addition to his extensive teachings in the Buddhist tradition, Trungpa Rinpoche also placed great emphasis on the Shambhala teachings, which stress the importance of meditation in action, synchronizing mind and body, and training oneself to approach obstacles or challenges in everyday life with the courageous attitude of a warrior, without anger. The goal of creating an enlightened society is fundamental to the Shambhala teachings. According to the Shambhala approach, the realization of an enlightened society comes not purely through outer activity, such as community or political involvement, but from appreciation of the senses and the sacred dimension of day-to-day life. A second volume of these teachings, entitled *Great Eastern Sun,* was published in 1999. The final volume of these teachings, *Smile at Fear,* appeared in 2009.

Chögyam Trungpa died in 1987, at the age of forty-seven. By the time of his death, he was known not only as Rinpoche ("Precious Jewel") but also as Vajracharya ("Vajra Holder") and as Vidyadhara ("Wisdom Holder") for his role as a master of the vajrayana, or tantric teachings of Buddhism. As a holder of the Shambhala teachings, he had also received the titles of Dorje Dradül ("Indestructible Warrior") and Sakyong ("Earth Protector"). He is survived by his wife, Diana Judith Mukpo, and five sons. His eldest son, the Sawang Ösel Rangdröl Mukpo, succeeds him as the spiritual head of Vajradhatu. Acknowledging the importance of the Shambhala teachings to his father's work, the Sawang changed the name of the umbrella organization to Shambhala, with Vajradhatu remaining one of its major divisions. In 1995 the Sawang received the Shambhala title of Sakyong like his father before him and was also confirmed as an incarnation of the great ecumenical teacher Mipham Rinpoche.

Trungpa Rinpoche is widely acknowledged as a pivotal figure in introducing the buddhadharma to the Western world. He joined his great appreciation for Western culture with his deep understanding of his own tradition. This led to a revolutionary approach to teaching the dharma, in which the most ancient and profound teachings were presented in a thoroughly contemporary way. Trungpa Rinpoche was known for his fearless proclamation of the dharma: free from hesitation, true to the purity of the tradition, and utterly fresh. May these teachings take root and flourish for the benefit of all sentient beings.

CREDITS

Some glossary entries in the three volumes of the *Profound Treasury* are reprinted from other sources. The editors gratefully acknowledge the use of the following:

Illusion's Game by Chögyam Trungpa. Boston: Shambhala, 1994.

The Chariot of Liberation by Ösel Tendzin and Dorje Löppon Lodrö Dorje. Halifax: Vajradhatu Publications, 2002. Used by permission of Lodrö Dorje.

The Three Vehicles of Buddhist Practice by Khenchen Thrangu, Rinpoche. Translated by Ken Holmes. Edited by Clark Johnson. Namo Buddha Seminar: Boulder, Colorado, 1998. Used by permission.

The Rain of Wisdom, translated by the Nalanda Translation Committee under the direction of Chögyam Trungpa. Boston: Shambhala, 1989. Used by permission of the Nalanda Translation Committee.

Glimpses of Mahayana by Chögyam Trungpa. Halifax: Vajradhatu Publications, 2001.

INDEX

Page numbers for illustrations are in italics.

BOOKS BY CHÖGYAM TRUNGPA

The Art of Calligraphy
Born in Tibet
The Collected Works of Chögyam Trungpa, Volumes One through Eight
Crazy Wisdom
Cutting Through Spiritual Materialism
The Dawn of Tantra
The Essential Chögyam Trungpa
First Thought, Best Thought: 108 Poems
Glimpses of Abhidharma
Great Eastern Sun: The Wisdom of Shambhala
The Heart of the Buddha
Illusion's Game: The Life and Teaching of Naropa
Journey without Goal: The Tantric Wisdom of the Buddha
The Life of Marpa the Translator
The Lion's Roar: An Introduction to Tantra
Meditation in Action
The Mishap Lineage: Transforming Confusion into Wisdom
Mudra
The Myth of Freedom and the Way of Meditation
Ocean of Dharma: The Everyday Wisdom of Chögyam Trungpa
Orderly Chaos: The Mandala Principle
The Path Is the Goal: A Basic Handbook of Buddhist Meditation
The Pocket Chögyam Trungpa
The Rain of Wisdom: The Essence of the Ocean of True Meaning (translator)
The Sanity We Are Born With: A Buddhist Approach to Psychology
Shambhala: The Sacred Path of the Warrior
Shambhala: The Sacred Path of the Warrior, Book and Card Set
Smile at Fear: Awakening the True Heart of Bravery
The Tibetan Book of the Dead: The Great Liberation through Hearing in
    the Bardo (translator)
Timely Rain: Selected Poetry of Chögyam Trungpa
Training the Mind and Cultivating Loving-Kindness
Transcending Madness: The Experience of the Six Bardos
True Perception: The Path of Dharma Art
The Truth of Suffering and the Path of Liberation